Praise for netbooks™

"Thanks to Wolff and friends, the cyber-swamp may just have become a little less murky."—*Entertainment Weekly*

"*NetGuide* is the computer world's online *TV Guide*™."—*Good Morning America*

"*NetGuide* will keep you from wandering around aimlessly on the Internet, and is full of good ideas for where to pull over."—*Forbes FYI*

"*NetGuide* is the liveliest, most readable online guide yet."—*USA Today*

"What you need to connect."—*Worth Magazine*

"*NetGuide* is the *TV Guide*™ to Cyberspace!" —Louis Rossetto, publisher/editor, *Wired*

"One of the more complete, well-organized guides to online topics. From photography to the Church of Elvis, you'll find it here."—*PC Magazine*

"The best attempt yet at categorizing and organizing all the great stuff you can find out there. It's the book people keep stealing off my desk." —Joshua Quittner, *New York Newsday*

"It's changed my online life. Get this book!" —Mike Madson, "Computer Bits," Business Radio Network

"My favorite for finding the cool stuff." —*The Louisville Courier-Journal*

"*NetGuide* focuses on the most important aspect of online information—its content. You name it, it's there—from erotica to religion to politics." —Lawrence J. Magid, *San Jose Mercury News*

"Not only did all the existing Net books ignore Cyberspace's entertaining aspects, but they were process-oriented, not content-oriented. Why hadn't someone made a *TV Guide*™ for the Net? Wolff recognized an opportunity for a new book, and his group wrote *NetGuide*."—Mark Frauenfelder, *Wired*

"Couch potatoes have *TV Guide*™. Now Net surfers have *NetGuide*."—*Orange County Register*

"*NetGuide* is one of the best efforts to provide a hot-spot guide to going online."—*Knoxville News-Sentinel*

"Assolutamente indispensabile!"—*L'Espresso*, Italy

"A valuable guide for anyone interested in the recreational uses of personal computers and modems."—Peter H. Lewis, *The New York Times*

"*NetGames* is a good map of the playing fields of Netdom."—*Newsweek*

"This guide to games people play in the ever-expanding Cyberspace shows you exactly where to go."—*Entertainment Weekly*

"The second book in a very good series from Wolff and Random House."—Bob Schwabach, syndicated columnist

"Hot addresses!"—*USA Weekend*

"Move over Parker Brothers and Nintendo—games are now available online. There's something in *NetGames* for everyone from crossword-puzzle addicts to *Dungeons & Dragons* fans."—*Reference Books Bulletin*

"Whether you're a hardened game player or a mere newbie, *NetGames* is the definitive directory for gaming on the Internet." —*.net*

"A wide and devoted following." —*The Wall Street Journal*

"*NetMoney* is a superb guide to online business and finance!"—*Hoover's Handbook of American Business*

"[*NetChat*] is…the best surfer's guide out there." —*Entertainment Weekly*

"A product line of guidebooks for explorers of the Internet."—*Inside Media*

In bookstores now!

NetGames

NetGames is a guide to playing games online, finding opponents, learning strategies, and discovering tips and cheats. *NetGames* covers thousands of hot games, including AirWarrior, Cyberstrike, Doom, and Bolo.

ISBN 0-679-75592-6
US: 19.00/Canada:$25.50/UK: £17.49 Net

NetChat

NetChat describes more than a thousand places in Cyberspace where people meet to pursue romances, have netsex, or just chat the night away. *NetChat* covers sex spots, fan clubs, political talk, identity forums, gay life discussions, support groups, and ethnic bulletin boards.

ISBN 0-679-75814-3
US: $19.00/Canada: $25.50/UK: £17.49 Net

NetMoney

NetMoney takes you into the world of cyberinvestments, taxes, banking, and budgeting. It is the first personal finance guide to the vast financial resources now available online, from buying a car to paying for college to getting the most out of Quicken.

ISBN 0-679-75808-9
US: $19.00/Canada: $25.50/UK: £17.49 Net

NetGuide—2nd Edition

NetGuide—The Second Edition is the only guide that covers the Internet, America Online, Prodigy, and CompuServe, plus Usenet, the Web, gophers, FTP sites, mailing lists, and chat channels. At more than 800 pages, *NetGuide II* is the most comprehensive guide to Cyberspace.

ISBN 0-679-76456-9
US: $27.95/Canada: $39.00/UK: £25.99 Net

NetTrek

NetTrek charts the amazing world of *Star Trek* in Cyberspace. *NetTrek* includes more than 400 pages detailing Trek-related online forums, chat areas, newsgroups, mailing lists, Websites, sound and picture archives, plus episode guides for all the series.

ISBN 0-679-76186-1
US: $19.00/Canada: $25.50/UK: £17.49 Net

NetSports

NetSports is a guide to sports news, game and player stats, sports talk, team sites, and fan clubs in Cyberspace. *NetSports* covers more than 60 sports, from football, baseball, and basketball to rugby, frisbee, and paintball.

ISBN 0-679-76187-X
US: $19.00/Canada: $25.50/UK: £17.49 Net

NetTech

NetTech is your guide to the tech speak, tech info, and tech support on the information highway. It also includes information on products, user groups, and software resources. *NetTech* is geared to all platforms, product brands, and user levels.

ISBN 0-679-76054-7
US: $19.00/Canada: $25.50/UK: £17.49 Net

NetMusic

NetMusic describes the new world of online music, from rock to techno to jazz to opera. Find chat groups, discographies, and photos of your favorite artists, plus concert information, fan clubs, and hundreds of sound clips. *NetMusic* is your guide to the sound of music in Cyberspace.

ISBN 0-679-76385-6
US: $19.00/Canada: $25.50/UK: £17.49 Net

Fodor's NetTravel

Fodor's NetTravel—from Fodor's and the creators of *NetGuide* and the Net Books Series—tells you how to find the best online travel sites. Find your way to brilliant travelogues and wonderful travel secrets—plus subway maps, restaurant and hotel guides, movie listings, and train schedules.

ISBN 0-679-77033-X
US: $19.00/Canada: $25.50/UK: £17.49 Net

NetTaxes '96

NetTaxes '96 tells you how to file your tax returns electronically and get an instant refund! Find out where to get forms online (for offline filing), where to get tax questions answered online, where to get tax-savings tips online, and where to file online.

ISBN 0-679-77035-6
US: $12.95/Canada: $17.50

Coming soon!

NetGames 2

NetGames 2 is the all-new, updated addition of the original bestseller. It contains more than 4,000 games, including Doom, Marathon, Heretic, and Myst, a special guide to MUDs, MUSHes, and MOOs, plus demos, tips, and free upgrades!

ISBN 0-679-77034-8
US: $22.00/Canada: $30.00/UK: £20.49 Net

NetMarketing

NetMarketing is the first book that spells out strategies for how corporate marketers and mom-and-pop businesses can use the Net to powerful advantage. It includes hundreds of successful Websites, a primer for getting started, and a directory of more than 1,000 marketing sites.

ISBN 0-679-77031-3
US: $22.00/Canada: $30.00/UK: £20.49 Net

NetJobs

NetJobs tells you how to take advantage of the Iway to land the job you've always wanted. It includes the email addresses of over 1,000 companies, special tips for '96 college grads, and a complete directory of online classifieds, help wanted, and job notice boards.

ISBN 0-697-77032-1
US: $12.95/Canada: $17. 95/UK: £11.99 Net

Now NetBooks Pocket Guides!

NetVote

NetVote is a handbook for following the '96 Presidential Campaign online. *NetVote* takes the user to all the places where the political pros and the media elite hangout. It gives the user access to the same news sources that the media uses. In fact, with *NetVote* you can be your own political reporter, lobbyist, consultant, and voice of reason (or nut case). Which party does the NetGeneration align itself with? We'll let you know which cover sells best.

ISBN 0-679-77028-3
US: $12.95/Canada: $17.50/UK: £11.99 Net

To order call 1-800-793-2665

Updates.

http://www.ypn.com/

Fodor's net travel™

Your Map to Travel Resources on the Internet and Online Services

A Michael Wolff Book

Mary Goodwin, Kristin Miller,
and Shaun Witten

For free updates visit our Website at http://www.ypn.com/

MICHAEL WOLFF & COMPANY PUBLISHING
New York

MICHAEL WOLFF & COMPANY PUBLISHING

The NetBooks Series is published by Michael Wolff & Company, Inc., 1633 Broadway, 27th Floor, New York, NY 10019, and distributed by Random House, Inc., 201 East 50th Street, New York, NY 10022, as agent for Michael Wolff & Company, Inc.

NetTravel has been wholly created and produced by Michael Wolff & Company, Inc. *NetTravel*, *NetTaxes*, *NetGames*, *NetChat*, *NetMoney*, *NetTech*, *NetTrek*, *NetSports*, *NetMusic*, NetHead, NetSpeak, and CyberPower are trademarks of Michael Wolff & Company, Inc. All design and production has been done by means of desktop-publishing technology. The text is set in the typefaces Garamond, customized Futura, Zapf Dingbats, Franklin Gothic, and Pike.

Published simultaneously in the U.S. and Canada by Michael Wolff & Company, Inc.

0 9 8 7 6 5 4 3 2

ISBN 0-679-77033-X

Manufactured in the United States of America.

New York

MICHAEL WOLFF & COMPANY PUBLISHING

A Michael Wolff Book

Michael Wolff
President and Editor in Chief

Kelly Maloni
Executive Editor

Ben Greenman
Managing Editor

Jeff Hearn
Art Director

Senior Writer: Kristin Miller

Senior Editor: Mary Goodwin

Assistant Editor: Shaun Witten

Editorial Assistants: Deborah Cohn, Donna M. Spivey

Assistant Art Director: Eric Hoffsten

Contributing Editor: Alta Campbell

Copy Editors: Bradley Bamburger, Jonathan Gregg, Hilary Handelsman, Enid Harlow, David Levine, Jill Rappaport, Pam Ritzer

Contributing Writers: Jose Alvear, Aaron Greenman, Peter Moore, Evan Neufeld, Angela Rutledge

Production Assistants: Efrat Gadassi, Rob Hardin, Jay Jaffe, Matthew Name, Linda Pattie

Vice President, Marketing: Jay Sears

Online Director: Jonathan Bellack

Technical Assistant: Patrick Vanderhorst

Web Illustrator: Cynthia Dauzier

Special thanks:

Random House Electronic Publishing—Charles Levine, Tom Willshire, Terry Chisholm, Patricia Damm, Jennifer Dowling

Alison Anthoine

Peter Ginsberg at Curtis Brown Ltd.

And, as always, Aggy Aed

The editors of *NetTravel* can be reached at Michael Wolff & Company, Inc., 1633 Broadway, 27th Floor, New York, NY 10019, or by voice call at 212-841-1572, fax at 212-841-1556, or email at editors@ypn.com.

Contents

Part 1. Travel Central

Part 2. Africa & The Middle East

Part 3. Asia

Part 4. Australia & Oceania

Part 5. Europe

Part 6. Latin America & The Caribbean

Part 7. North America

Part 8. Theme Travel

Appendices

Foreword

Sixty years ago, Eugene Fodor, a Hungarian émigré, published his first guidebook, *1936 On the Continent.* Since those early days, the world of travel and travel guides has grown in both size and diversity. Today, Fodor's sells four million guides in over 100 countries. More people are traveling than ever before, going further, and doing more—and their travel needs are changing.

Fewer and fewer travelers are now content with old-fashioned, impersonal travel planning. Instead, they want advice about trips that relate directly to them, their needs, and interests. Wander into any bookstore to see just how specialized travel has become. You will find guides for ecotourists, guides for travelers with children, guides for gays and lesbians, and even guides for adventurers with pets. The list goes on and on. But there's one guide you won't find on any bookstore shelf—a guide with your name on it. That's where the Net comes in.

Only you know exactly what you want from travel. Only you know that shellfish gives you hives, that fall leaves make your heart flutter, and that skinny-dipping in tropical waters is your quiet fantasy. We are now entering the era of customized travel guides and travel planning, where you set the tone and the pace. And the Net is the place where you're going to find all the information that makes doing it your way possible. The information is already out there; it's just a matter of organizing it.

Indeed, you could spend months journeying through travel sites on the Net and never take a real vacation. So many new sites go up every week, it's impossible to keep count of them—and many of these new sites are travel related. They range from listings by giant hotel conglomerates to Bob and June's annual letter about their vacation to Mexico. If the amount of available info is the beauty of the Net, it's also one of its drawbacks. There's so much information that it's easy to get lost in a morass of travel fluff, advertising hype, and plain bad advice. That's why *Fodor's NetTravel* is so handy—it saves you the time of having to wade through this river of information. The editors have done it for you, panning the riverbed for those shining nuggets of gold—the sites that offer really cool, useful travel information.

The Net is not some dry directory of travel statistics and schedules. Far from it. The Net has actually reintroduced romance into travel. Even if you don't know where to go or what to do, the Net can kindle the flame of wanderlust and help you plan the trip of a lifetime. Whether it's whitewater rafting on the Zambezi River or biking through the hill towns of Tuscany, the Net can strike the spark that will have you counting the minutes until your trip begins. And if you can't wait until you're packed and on your way, the Net lets you preview your destination through images, sound clips, and digitized movies. The possibilities are endless, the trips innumerable.

Another great thing about the Net is that it's interactive—if you can't find what you're looking for, just ask. Many of the travel sites have forums where readers can talk to travel experts and guidebook editors.

Interactivity also allows travelers to talk to other travelers, to draw upon the experience and wisdom of a huge community. Going to New York? Sure, you can visit a site to see what a renowned dining critic has to say about Lutece, but he probably uses words like "galicien" and "arugula," words that sound like they beamed down from an episode of *Star Trek.* What you want to know is if the food is any good, and if it's good this week. Chances are someone on the Net can tell you.

The day is fast approaching when you'll plan and arrange your entire trip yourself, from choosing the perfect destination to booking a hotel, a rental car, and your flight. The information you need to start your online travel planning is already on the Net, and *Fodor's NetTravel* is your invaluable travel companion through the world of Cyberspace. *Bon voyage!*

—Kristina Peterson

Kristina Peterson is the president and publisher of Fodor's Travel Publications, Inc., the largest publisher of English-language travel information in the world. She's also one of the biggest advocates of travel information on the Net, actively pushing her vision of travel-planning in the 21st century in conferences around the country. Under her guidance, Fodor's has just launched its own site (**http://www.fodors.com**), drawing on a massive database of travel information gathered by 50 editors and more than 500 travel experts around the world.

FAQ

"Frequently Asked Questions" about the Net and Fodor's NetTravel

1. What is the Net, anyway?

The Net is the electronic medium spawned by the millions of computers networked together throughout the world. Also known as Cyberspace, the information highway, the IWay, or the Infobahn, the Net comprises four types of networks—the Internet, a global, noncommercial system with more than 30 million computers communicating through it; the commercial online services, such as America Online, Prodigy, CompuServe, and eWorld; the discussion groups known as Usenet that traverse the Internet; and the thousands of regional and local bulletin board services (BBSs). More and more, the Internet unites all the diverse locations and formats that make up the Net.

2. What can travelers do on the Net?

You can book a cozy room in a B&B in Maine or a bungalow at a couples resort in Jamaica. You can collect travel tips from someone who just got back from where you're going, or get in on up-to-the minute cruise and airline discount information. You can publish your own travelogues online. You can check in on the current exchange rate for any country you might want to visit, and then decide whether to pack sunglasses or an umbrella by reading a weather forecast for your destination city. If your budget mandates that you stay at home during your next vacation, you can still travel—virtually—by taking online tours of cities from New Orleans to Jerusalem.

3. I'm game. What do I need to get started?

A computer and a modem, and a few tricks to find your way around.

4. Can you help me decide what computer and modem I'll need?

If you've bought a computer fairly recently, it's likely that it came with everything you need. But let's assume you have only a bare-bones PC. In that case you'll also need to get a modem, which will allow your computer to communicate over the phone. So-called 14.4 modems, which transfer data at speeds up to 14,400 bits per second (bps), are standard. You should be able to get one for less than $100. But 28,800 bps modems are fast replacing them. Next, you need a communications program to control the modem. This software will probably come free with your modem, your PC, or—if you're going to sign up somewhere—your online service. Otherwise, you can buy it off the shelf for under $25 or get a friend to download it from the Net. Finally, you'll want a telephone line (or maybe even two if you plan on tying up the line a couple of hours per day). And if

ONLINE SERVICES

America Online:
- 800-827-6364 (voice)
- Monthly fee: $9.95
- Free monthly hours: 5
- Hourly fee: $2.95

CompuServe:
- 800-848-8199 (voice)
- Basic Plan: $9.95/month includes 5 hours of access; $2.95 each additional hour
- Super Value Plan: $24.95/month includes 20 hours of access; $1.95 each additional hour
- Email: 70006.101@compuserve.com

eWORLD:
- 800-775-4556 (voice)
- Monthly fee: $8.95
- Free monthly hours: 4
- Hourly rates: $2.95
- Email: askeac@eworld.com

Prodigy:
- 800-PRODIGY (voice)
- Basic Plan: $9.95/month includes 5 hours of access; $2.95 each additional hour
- Value Plan: $14.95/month includes unlimited core time plus 5 hours of access to plus services (Internet and chat); $2.95 each additional hour
- 30/30 Plan: $29.95/month includes 30 hours of access; $2.95 each additional hour

that's still not good enough, you can contact your local telephone utility to arrange for installation of an ISDN line, which allows data to be transmitted at even higher speeds. It's not as expensive as you'd think.

5. What kind of account should I get?

You'll definitely want to be able to get email; certainly want wide access to the Internet; and probably want membership on at least one online service.

Here are some of your access choices:

Email Gateway

This is the most basic access you can get. It lets you send and receive messages to and from anyone, anywhere, anytime on the Net. Email is quickly becoming a standard way to communicate with friends and colleagues. (Yesterday: "What's your phone number?" Today: "What's your email address?") Email gateways are often available via work, school, or the online services listed here.

Online Services

Priciest but often easiest, these services have a wealth of options for the cyber-traveler. Commercial services are cyber city-states. The large ones have more "residents" (members) than most U.S. cities—enough users, in other words, to support lively discussions among their membership, and enough resources to make a visit worthwhile. They generally require their own special start-up software, which you can buy at any local computer store or by calling the numbers listed in this book. (Hint: Look for the frequent starter-kit giveaways.) AOL, CompuServe, and Prodigy all provide access to many of Usenet's more than 10,000 newsgroups, and through email you can subscribe to any Internet mailing lists. Fairly recently, the three most popular commercial services—America Online, CompuServe, and Prodigy—took a large step toward the Internet by offering full access to the World Wide Web (WWW); America Online is even incorporating links to Websites in its own forums. The cyberwalls are tumbling and the easy-to-use online services are making the Internet accessible to millions of technophobes.

Internet Providers

There are a growing number of full-service Internet providers (which means they offer email, Usenet, FTP, IRC, telnet, gopher, and WWW access). In practical terms, the Internet lets you shop for and purchase a new Fodor's Gold Guide title, read the current issue of *The Business Traveler Online*, search a restaurant database for the name of a Mexican restaurant in Seattle, Washington, subscribe to a mailing list that posts the current news in Hungary, and ask an Irishman what's the best pub in Dublin on the soc.culture.irish newsgroup. A dial-up SLIP (serial line Internet protocol) or PPP (point-to-point protocol) account is the most fun you can have through a modem. It is a special service offered by most Internet providers that gets you significantly faster access and the ability to use point-and-click programs for Windows, Macintosh, and other platforms.

BBSs

BBSs range from mom-and-pop, hobbyist computer bulletin boards to large professional services. What the small ones lack in size they often make up for in affordability and homeyness. In fact, many users prefer these scenic roads over the info highway. Many of the large BBSs are as rich and diverse as the commercial services. BBSs are easy to get started with, and if you find one with Internet access or an email gateway, you'll get the best of local color and global reach. You can locate local BBSs through the Usenet discussion groups alt.bbs.lists and comp.bbs.misc, the BBS forums of the commercial services, and regional and national BBS lists kept in the file libraries of many BBSs. See the BBS list in the back of the book for more information. Once you've found a local BBS, contact the sysop (system operator) to inquire about the echoes (or conferences) you want. These are the BBS world's equivalent of Usenet newsgroups. With echoes, you're talking not only to the people on your particular BBS, but also to everyone else on a BBS that carries the echo (in other words, a universe of millions). Even if the discussion of your choice is not on their board yet, many sysops are glad to add an echo that a paying customer has requested. Many, if not most, local BBSs now offer Internet email, as well as live chat, file libraries, and some quirky database, program, or directory unique to their little corner of Cyberspace.

Direct Network Connection

Look, Ma Bell: no phone lines! The direct network connection is the fast track of college students, computer scientists, and a growing number of employees of high-tech businesses. It puts the user right on the Net, bypassing the phone connections. In other words, it's a damned sight faster.

6. By the way, exactly how do I send email?

With email, you can write to anyone on a commercial service, Internet site, or Internet-linked BBS, as well as to those people connected to the Net via email gateways, SLIPs, and direct-network connections.

Email addresses have a universal syntax called an Internet address. An Internet address is broken down into four parts: the user's name (e.g., Shaun), the @ symbol, the computer and/or company name, and what kind of Internet address it is: **net** for network, **com** for a commercial enterprise—as with Your Personal Network (ypn.com) and America Online (aol.com)—**edu** for educational institutions, **gov** for government sites, **mil** for military facilities, and **org** for nonprofit and other private organizations. For instance, the assistant editor of this company, who knows the name of every cruise ship currently afloat on the high seas, would be shaun@ypn.com.

7. What about the Web?

The World Wide Web is a hypertext-based information structure that now dominates Internet navigation. The Web is like a house where every room has doors to every other room—or, perhaps more accurately, like the interconnections in the human brain. Words, icons, and pictures on a page link to other pages that reside on the same machine or on a computer anywhere in the world. You have only to click on the appropriate word or phrase or image—the Web does the rest. With invisible navigation, you can jump from a live chat session with the editors of *National Geographic Traveler* to an archive of the Hawaiian Islands photos to a list of youth hostels in the new Russia. All the while you've FTPed, telnetted, gophered, and linked without a thought to case-sensitive Unix commands or addresses.

Your dial-up Internet provider undoubtedly offers programs to access the Web. Lynx and WWW are pretty much the standard offerings for text-only Web browsing. Usually you choose them by typing **lynx** and **www** and then **<return>**. What you'll get is a "page" with some of the text highlighted. These are the links. Choose a link, hit the return key, and you're off.

If you know exactly where you want to go on the Net and don't want to wade through Net directories and indexes, you can type a Web page's address, known as a URL (uniform resource locator), many of which you'll find in this book. The URL for Fodor's Website, for example, is **http://www.fodors.com**. On some Web browsers, such as the current version of Netscape, "http://" is not required. In our example, you could type **www.fodors.com**.

8. What about graphical Web browsers? What are these things?

With the emergence of new and sophisticated software like Netscape (**http://www.netscape.com**), the Web is starting to look the way it was envisioned to—pictures, icons, and appetizing layouts. Some commercial services, most notably America Online and Prodigy, have even developed customized Web browsers for their subscribers; if you subscribe to one of these services, head to the Internet forum for instructions on how to get this software and how to get on the Web. Web browsers are more than just presentation tools. Most of them allow Netsurfers to see all kinds of Net sites through a single interface. Want to read newsgroups? Need to send email? Interested in participating in real-time chat? You can do it all with your browser. And many Internet providers, including Prodigy, allow subscribers to build their own Web pages.

9. And these newsgroups?

The most widely read bulletin boards are a group of some 10,000-plus "newsgroups" on the Internet, collectively known as Usenet. Usenet newsgroups travel the Internet, collecting thousands of messages a day from whoever wants to "post" to them. More than anything, the newsgroups are the collective, if sometimes Babel-like, voice of the Net—everything is discussed here. And we mean *everything*. On the **soc.culture.thai** newsgroup, travelers are asking for the names of hot nightclubs in Banghok, while on the **alt.fishing** newsgroup, anglers meet to discuss good watering holes. While delivered over the Internet, Usenet newsgroups are not technically part of the Internet. In order to read a newsgroup, you need to go where it is stored. Smaller BBSs that have news feeds sometimes store only a couple dozen newsgroups, while most Internet providers and online services offer thousands. (If there's a group missing that you really want, ask your Internet provider to add the newsgroup back to the subscription list.)

The messages in a newsgroup, called "posts," are listed and numbered chronologically—in other words, in the order in which they were posted. Usenet is not distributed from one central location, which means that a posted message does not appear everywhere instantly. The speed of distribution partly depends on how often providers pick up and post Usenet messages. For a message to appear in every corner of the Net, you'll generally have to wait overnight.

You can scan a list of messages before deciding to read a particular message. If someone posts a message that prompts responses, the original and all follow-up messages are called a thread. The subject line of subsequent posts in the thread refers to the subject of the original. For example, if you were to post a message with the subject "The best beer in the world" in **rec.travel.europe**, all responses would read "Re: The best beer in the world." In practice, however, topics wander off in many directions.

Popular newsgroups generate hundreds of messages daily. To cut back on repetitive questions, newsgroup members often compile extensive lists of answers to frequently asked questions (FAQs). Many FAQs have grown so large and so comprehensive that they are valuable resources in their own right, informal encyclopedias (complete with hypertext links) dedicated to the newsgroup's topic. For example, many of the **soc.culture** newsgroup FAQs not only list background information on the country, but also frequently give tips on traveling there as well.

10. Mailing lists?

Mailing lists are like newsgroups, except that they are distributed by Internet email. The fact that messages show up in your mailbox tends to make the discussion group more intimate, as does the proactive act of subscribing. Mailing lists are often more focused, and they're less vulnerable to irreverent and irrelevant contributions. For instance, parents can subscribe to the Natalie Sanders Family Travel mailing list for kiddie travel tips.

To subscribe to a mailing list, send an email to the mailing list's subscription address. Often you will need to include very specific information, which you will find in this book. To unsubscribe, send another message to that same address. If the mailing list is of the listserv, listproc, or majordomo variety, you can usually unsubscribe by sending the command **unsubscribe <listname>** or **signoff <listname>** in the message body. If the mailing list instructs you to write a request to subscribe ("Dear list owner, please subscribe me to..."), you will probably need to write a request to unsubscribe.

Once you have subscribed, messages are almost always sent to a different address than the subscription address. Most lists will send you the address when you subscribe. If not, send another message to the subscription address and ask the owner.

11. And telnet, FTP, gopher? Can you spell it out?

Telnet:

When you telnet, you're logging on to another computer somewhere else on the Internet. You then have access to the programs running on the remote computer. If the site is running a library catalog, you can search the catalog. If it's running a BBS, you can chat with others logged on. Telnet addresses are listed as URLs, in the form **telnet://domain.name:port number.** A port number is not always required, but when listed it must be used.

FTP:

FTP (file transfer protocol) is a method of copying a file from another Internet-connected computer to your own. Hundreds of computers on the Internet allow "anonymous FTP." In other words, you don't need a unique password to access them. Just type "anonymous" at the user prompt and type your email address at the password prompt. The range of material available is extraordinary—from travelogues of journeys through Djakarta to photographs of Paris taken from Sacré-Coeur. Since the advent of Web browsers, Netsurfers can transfer files without using a separate FTP program. In this book, FTP addresses are listed as URLs, in the form **ftp://domain.name/directory/filename.txt**. And logins and passwords aren't required with Web browsers.

Gopher:

A gopher is a program that turns Internet addresses into menu options. Gophers can perform many Internet functions, including telnetting and downloading files. Gopher addresses throughout this book are listed as URLs, with all necessary steps chained together as pieces of a URL.

12. So, how does the book work?

If you're an experienced cyber-traveler and you already know the name of the travel site you'd like to read about, or if your search for travel info is limited to a specific topic, then just turn to the *Fodor's NetTravel* index, where every site and subject covered in the book is listed alphabetically. Or, if you prefer a more leisurely approach, you can simply browse through *Fodor's NetTravel*, which is divided into eight parts:

- **Travel Central**
- **Africa & the Middle East**
- **Asia**
- **Australia & Oceania**
- **Europe**
- **Latin America & The Caribbean**
- **North America**
- **Theme Travel**

In **Travel Central**, you'll get addresses and descriptions of sites that hold travel literature, hotel listings, airline departure schedules, and budget travel advice. **Africa & the Middle East**, **Asia**, **Australia & Oceania**, **Europe**, **Latin America & The Caribbean**, and **North America** collect Web resources devoted to tourism and culture in each of the respective destinations. This is where you'll find information on languages spoken in Morocco, entrance fees for clubs in Kyoto, and lists of the best hotels in Los Angeles. Peruse these destination-related parts of the book for practical travel info, for in-depth information on a country's history and people, or for the sheer fantasy value of looking at pictures of far-away locales. **Theme Travel** focuses on Web resources for the single-minded—if you'd rather be fishing, if you want a honeymoon in Las Vegas, or if your lifelong fantasy has been to take a tour of amusement parks worldwide, you'll find the information you need to make it happen in this part of the book.

All entries in *Fodor's NetTravel* have a name, description, and address. The site name appears first in boldface. If the entry is a mailing list, "(ml)" immediately follows; if a newsgroup, "(ng)."

After the description, complete address information is provided. A red check mark (✓) identifies the name of the network—Internet, Usenet, or a commercial service provider. When you see an arrow (→), this means that you have another step ahead of you, such as typing a command, searching for a file, subscribing to a mailing list, typing a Web address (also known as a URL, or Uniform Resource Locator). Additional check marks indicate that the site is accessible through other networks; an ellipsis indicates another address on the same network; and more arrows mean more steps.

If the item is a Website, FTP site, telnet, or gopher, it will be displayed in the form of a URL to type on the command line of your Web browser. If the item is a mailing list, the address will be an email address followed by instructions on how to subscribe (remember—the address given is usually the subscription address; in order to post to the mailing list, you will use another address that will be emailed to you upon subscribing). An entry that includes an FTP, telnet, or gopher address will provide a log-in sequence.

In a commercial service address, the name of the commercial service is followed by the site's keyword (also called "go word" or "jump word"). Additional steps are listed where necessary.

IRC addresses indicate what you must type to get to the channel you want once you've connected to the IRC program.

Entries about newsgroups are always followed by the names of the newsgroups.

In addition, there are a few special terms used in addresses. **Info** indicates a supplementary informational address. **Archives** is used to mark collections of past postings for newsgroups and mailings lists. And **FAQ** designates the location of a "frequently asked questions" file for a newsgroup.

Fodor's Choice

Throughout the book, you'll enjoy highlights from the Fodor's Gold Guide series. *Fodor's NetTravel*'s Fodor's Choices showcase offline pleasures—must-see views and sightseeing attractions. *Fodor's NetTravel* introduces you to a new era of travel resources which will help you select a destination and book a trip; Fodor's Choices offer the wisdom and expertise of the Fodor's organization, reminding you of the best places to see once you're there.

13. I love travel, but what if I want to branch out and investigate other topics?

Try *NetGames, NetChat, NetMoney, NetTrek, NetSports, NetTech, NetMusic,* and the second edition of the best-selling *NetGuide*. And keep your eye out for our pocket guides *NetTaxes* and the forthcoming *NetJobs* and *NetMarketing*.

Part 1

Travel Central

Travel links

You've worked hard, got those two weeks off for vacation and a few dollars in the bank, but where to go? Sure, you could follow the crowd to Dollywood or visit Grandma and Grandpa in Akron, but why not take a trip through Cyberspace first to see what else you can turn up. Strap yourself in for an exciting cybertrip which takes you **Around the World in 80 Seconds** from Albania to Zaire. Got a location in mind? Be it Latvia or Los Angeles, **City.Net** is bound to have loads of links on your desired destination. Now that you're comfortable in the 21st century, head over to AOL's **ExpressNet** so you can book yourself on a flight to Auckland or a berth on the *Queen Elizabeth II* right from home. Still looking for something off the beaten path? Try **Genki is My Cat** or **Thierry's Travel Links** for a slightly idiosyncratic selection of travel and adventure links.

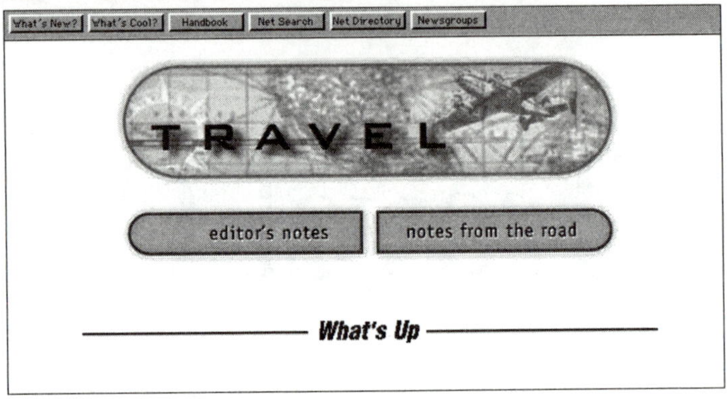

GNN's opening travel page—http://nearnet.gnn.com/gnn/meta/travel/index.html

On the Net

Across the board

Around the World in 80 Seconds It will take longer than 80 seconds to explore this collection of links—you'll hardly have time to catch your breath as you link to information on over 80 destinations worldwide. The site begins with a link to Hampton Roads, a page featuring hotel and restaurant descriptions and an events calendar for tourist towns in the Chesapeake Bay area. After contemplating vacation resources in southeastern Virginia, you can head to the Windows-to-Russia Home Page, which serves up a full helping of reports on Russian arts, culture, and businesses, and virtual tours of the Kremlin and the Soviet Archive. This comprehensive collection of travel links ends with a stop at the All Languages of the World page—you'll find dictionaries and glossaries there to help you decipher hundreds of languages. Along your way down this list of links, there are plenty of fun detours—like Yahoo Travel Sites and the Virtual Tourist, as well as sites dedicated to Northern Spain and Caribbean Culture. ✓**INTERNET**→*url* http://www.infi.net/~cwt/travel.html

City.Net This site combines tourism and cultural information on cities worldwide and is a mandatory stop for armchair travelers and vacationers. You can explore the world by region or by site name (they are listed alphabetically). A jaunt to Paris rewards you with street and subway maps, an insider's guide to the city, subway navigators, and hotel and restaurant recommendations. For a less urban trek, visit the Grampian Highlands of Scotland through online pictures and narrative, including a visit to a twelfth-century cathedral and a trip down the Malt Whiskey Trail. ✓**INTERNET**→*url* http://www.city.net/

ExpressNet American Express sponsors this full-service travel Website. The Global Guide here offers detailed guides to major cities (replete with shopping and night club suggestions), travel articles from *Travel & Leisure* magazine and major newspapers, and lists of American Express services and offices nationwide. If you have specific questions about a particular destination, post your request on ExpressNet's active message boards; you might get answers from fellow travelers who go there to exchange advice and tips. At ExpressNet you can also participate in regular online conferences which feature topics including tricks to hosteling, the rebirth of Shanghai, and live chat with travel luminaries like Arthur Frommer. ExpressNet also has links to Frommer's City Guides and Fodor's Worldview, adding the resources of two more excellent travel guides to those of the Global Guide. Don't miss the savvy Travelers Weekly Hot Tips section for bargains on airfares, cruises, and hotels. If all that weren't enough to build the perfect travel site, American Express is available to put plans into action with online booking. Don't leave home—or stay home—without it. ✓**AMERICA ONLINE**→*keyword* expressnet→Travel Info & Reservations

---

Genki Is My Cat Genki is the name of MIT doctoral candidate Maki Kajimura's adorable tabby cat. Genki is My Cat is the name of Maki's brainchild, a list of travel-oriented links that help take his mind off a chemical-engineering thesis. Latter-day trail blazers would do well to check out the Lonely Planet Guides or The Wilderness Society's maps and advice here. The Virtual Tourist transports virtual travelers to hundreds of spots worldwide at the speed of Cyberspace. And the link to HotelNet caters to those who travel in the old-fashioned, non-virtual manner. For trekkers that don't like surprises, Maki has assembled links to visa information sites, State Department travel warnings, and the essential Electricity Abroad guide. ✓**INTERNET**→*url* http://web.mit.edu/afs/athena.mit.edu/user/r/o/royk/www/GENKI.html#TRAVEL

GNN Travel Center Region/Country/City/State Guides Traveler's advisory: Begin your research here. GNN's collection of world travel guides comprises the travel site to end all travel sites. Need travel info on Alaska? Antarctica? Aruba? Austria? Austin, Texas? No problem for GNN. (And that's just a sample of the A-list.) From the France home page, you can link to the Louvre, learn about the history of Paris, and spend some cybertime on the shores of the Riviera. Peru's Web page features an interactive map and tourist-related information on all major Peruvian cities. The Kuwait Home Page even includes Kuwaiti recipes for a preview of Middle-Eastern cuisine. If you're thinking about taking a trip to somewhere on planet Earth, this site is absolutely mandatory for brainstorming your travel plans. ✓**INTERNET**→*url* http://nearnet.gnn.com/gnn/meta/travel/res/countries.html

---

Interactive Travel Guides An attractive and easy-to-follow presentation of Web links awaits you at Interactive Travel Guides. You can hop from here to the beaches of Cancun Online to the banks of the Vistula on Warsaw's home page. At every stop cybertravelers can collect helpful info on local lodgings and restaurants as well as view enticingly beautiful .GIFs of exotic locations. If you're looking for hotel, resort, or cruise recommendations, Interactive Travel Guides offers an Our Favorites section which reviews tourist stops it finds exceptional—the Royal Horseguard Thistle Hotel in London received the highest possible rating (four stars) for its balconies overlooking the Thames. ✓**INTERNET**→*url* http://www.travelpage.com/

Internet Travel Directory Flying from Cairo to Stockholm? Check here for quotes on wholesale air tickets or to order tickets online (the Directory's price beats TWA's). Ticket discounts are always appreciated, but the real premium at this site is the Special Internet Travel Directory, which provides the names and numbers of tour operators specializing in theme vacations from antiquing to whitewater rafting. If you want to spend your next vacation tending llamas on the plains of Argentina, then check here first. ✓**INTERNET**→*url* http://oim.com/

Internet Travel Mall (ITM) ITM is still in its infancy, but the concept of an electronic travel-brochure service is a promising one. Let's say you want to go to Fredericksburg, Texas. With online navigation tools, you can explore various accommodations in the Lone Star State and learn about the region from the publicity materials provided by each hotel or lodge. The Web page for the Inn on the Creek Bed & Breakfast, for instance, includes room rates and breakfast schedules and describes the history of the area. If it's Utah and not Texas that you're traveling to, you might be interested in the link here to information on a paragliding school just outside of Salt Lake City. For the time being, the pickings are a little slim, but more attractions will certainly be added. The Mall also contains dozens of useful 800 numbers, including listings for airlines, car-rental companies, motorcoach lines, international rail lines, cruise lines, and hotel / motel / resort chains. And finally, there is a link to a miscellaneous travel library that houses lists of rental-car companies' age requirements and glossaries of airline terminology. ✓**INTERNET**→*url* http://io.com:8001/

Subway Navigator Traveling underground might bewilder you whether you're in Amsterdam, Athens, or Atlanta. Demystify the experience with subway maps and a database which plots your route (including transfer points) and gives you an estimated travel time for cities around the world. ✓**INTERNET**→*url* http://metro.jussieu.fr:10001/bin/cities/english

The Travel Lane A grab bag of resources for travelers. Access several home pages, including a site for the Caribbean islands, the Prince Edward Island Visitor's Guide, and the Las Vegas Show Listing (Oooh, let's hit the Debbie Reynolds Hotel!). If you are heading to New England, check out bed-and-breakfast listings and a comprehensive Boston dining guide. ✓**INTERNET**→*url* http://www.shore.net/olm/

Thierry's Travelogue Thierry appears to be an outdoorsy kind of fellow, or so it seems from his personal collection of travel links to the Adventurous Traveler Bookstore, Fly-drive Tours in Australia, and the excellent Great Outdoor Recreation Pages (GORP), among others. Thierry also provides some links for travelers who prefer the indoors including links to the European Parliament in Brussels and cabaret schedules for Las Vegas casinos. By no means a comprehensive collection, Thierry's links are still informative and entertaining. ✓**INTERNET**→*url* http://www.belgasoft.com/travel.html

Tourism Info Internet Annotated in both German and English, this series of pages links travelers to airline home pages, subway and railway information, and accommodations worldwide—from American B&Bs to resorts in southern Spain. There are also travel reports here gathered from the wisdom of Usenet newsgroups (including rec.travel.misc) and links to destination-specific information (like a link to a virtual tour of Johannesburg). Unfortunately this Website's online newspaper, *Touristic News*, is available only in German (*sehr* unfair), and their "last-minute offers" are only applicable to certain regions in Germany. ✓**INTERNET**→*url* http://www.tkz.fh-rpl.de/tii/tii-e.html

Explore Thierry's personal travel links—http://www.belgasoft.com/travel.html

Travel, Exploration, and Sightseeing in the Real World This small selection of links to travel-related resources is worth a visit for lesser-known airline ticket discounters and pages on the charms of Prince Edward Island. New York City is well represented on this list which links to Columbia University's New York Information page, a guide to health restaurants in the Big Apple, and Explore New York. ✓**INTERNET**→*url* http://www.tagsys.com/Misc/travel.html

Travel Forum This site is a good first stop for prospective travelers. A filing cabinet of articles provides information on everything from travel insurance to Eurail pass bargains. The library is equally well stocked with articles (from Amtrak schedules to Disneyworld guides to an I-95 exit list), software, and photos. A traveler's bookstore reviews new travel-related titles and offers book-club member discounts. State Department travel advisories ensure that you don't plan any untimely trips to Libya or attempt to enter Mongolia without a visa. For the personal touch, try the travel message boards or the real-time travel café, where journeyers meet to talk about everything from fear of flying to singles cruises. ✓**AMERICA ONLINE**→*keyword* travel forum

Travel Links A collection of links for the international urban sophisticate. From here you can visit several of the world's most popular, and most interesting, cities. Looking for a pint of lager in London? Get directions online to the Friar & Firkin on Euston Road. Need the most efficient bus route from the Reichstag to Tegel airport in Berlin? You can get it here. Map links take you to several popular destinations, including some not-so-practical ones, like Mars. ✓**INTERNET**→*url* http://www.auburn.edu/~polojor/travel_links.html

Travel Online Wow, a site created by "travel professionals, dynamic marketing specialists, and PhD technical wizards"—but what do they offer? So far there are beautifully constructed search forms that reward users with no hotel listings for Santa Fe, New Mexico, and only 10 entries for New York City accommodations. Hitting the bargain page may be the best bet. There travelers will find everything from discount three-day packages at the Park Hotel in Hong Kong to special rates at the Minneapolis Hilton Towers. Travel Online promises to supplement its site with entertainment and dining guides soon. The good news: if you do find what you're looking for, you can book online here. ✓**INTERNET**→*url* http://TravelOnLine.com/

Travel Source Fancy yourself a modern-day Dr. Livingston? Click on the toucan image and get contact info for companies that specialize in bringing people nose to nose with African rhinos. Prefer a quieter time? Glance at the Blackbird Cave Resort page (it's on the Turneffe Reef Atoll). Most links are commercial in nature—Club Med and the Marble Mountain Ranch advertise their services here—but the scope is wide, encompassing sites designed for those who like to put on plaid and shout "fore!" and for those who like to wear rubber and stare down sharks. ✓**INTERNET**→*url* http://www.travelsource.com/

TravNet International TravNet International bills itself and the worldwide home of cybertourism. The centerpiece of the service is a database itinerary planner available through a telnet link. Simply submit the names of your destinations, and TravNet draws up a customized map showing accommodations, restaurants, and attractions neatly plotted along the route. TravNet promises to eventually put 4,000 pages online; currently links lead to such diverse information as dialysis services for travelers and slide shows designed to lure the weary to lush locales. ✓**INTERNET**→*url* http://www.sky.net/~eric/comdinet.htm

---

Vacation Ideas According to this collection of travel links, a "tour" requires less effort on the travelers' part than an "expedition," which entails some physical activity. If you're really gonzo, an "outfitter" is the route to go. Besides a linguistic discussion, Vacation Ideas also provides listings for a variety of "travel providers," which are travel agents specializing in cruises, resorts, ranches, and casinos. The travel providers will craft your dream trip—like Mad-Dog Expeditions, which will take you diving in Antarctica, or the Inn of Last Resort in Honduras where hotel personnel serve guests mai-tais in hammocks. The site also maintains a page of links to seasonal cultural events—in the fall read listings for London's Film Festival; in the spring, you'll find a schedule for Wagner's Ring at Bayreuth. ✓**INTERNET**→*url* http://emporium.turnpike.net/T/theme/vac/cvp.html

---

Virtual Tourist Virtual Tourist connects to a number of national and international travel guides, most of which have cultural summaries, local weather, and travel cost estimates. Information is indexed both graphically and textually and ranges from resource guides and maps to country information. The Japanese site includes an audio file of the national anthem. ✓**INTERNET**→*url* http://wingsp.buffalo.edu/world/

Yahoo Travel Links If you have the luggage and the wanderlust, Yahoo's links can provide everything else. Book an airplane or train ticket, compare rental car rates, or check on the availability of honeymoon suites in Hawaii. Chances are good that if a travel page exists, then it's probably included in this collection. Budget travel sites, travelogues, magazines, and travel agents are all online here in astounding numbers. Still, that's not all—from here it's easy to find out what shots you need for a trip down the Amazon or what the Pfennig / Peso exchange rate is. ✓**INTERNET**→*url* http://www.yahoo.com/Recreation/Travel/

The Internet Travel Directory—from http://oim.com/

Guides

Bob and Sheila swear by the Hotel California in Paris. Steven and Roger insist that La Tertulia is the place to be when in Santa Fe. But how can you trust them, especially when Bob and Sheila have been known to cover their furniture with plastic, and Steven and Roger have a decided penchant for clog dancing? Good thing there's a great big cyberworld of guides to help you. Turn to a trusted name at AOL's and eWorld's **Fodor's Worldview** (or Fodor's excellent Website). **Dining Out on the Web** and **Zagat's Restaurant Guide** will help you locate the best restaurant in Boise for a business dinner, sushi in Glasgow, and chicken fried steak in Montreal, while **The World Guide to Vegetarianism** assures you'll get your daily dose of tofu wherever you are. Looking for a less expensive (and less yuppified) alternative to Club Med? **The Rough Guide** and **Lonely Planet** are waiting to take you surfing in Nicaragua or to the late movies in L.A. And if you still want the personal touch, try the **rec.travel Library,** where the collected travel wisdom of thousands of Bobs, Sheilas, Stevens, and Rogers are stored.

Fodor's—from http://www.fodors.com

On the Net

Across the board

Around the World in 80 Clicks The world map at this site is covered with red dots. Play connect-the-dots with your mouse, and you'll access 80 different guides to destinations worldwide. Click on that dot over Chile, and it yields the Chilean Ski Guide. Hit that red dot over Japan, and you'll get a guide to dining, shopping, and going out in Japan. Click on the dot over Alaska to learn about Alaskan politics, literature, radio stations, and tourism. More dots, and guides, are added to the map each week. ✓**INTERNET**→*url* http://www.coolsite.com/arworld .html

C.D.I. Vacation Guide Before you travel to California, Colorado, Nevada, or Mexico, check out this guide for information on hotels, resorts, home and condo rentals, and local attractions in those areas. Just click on the appropriate area code, and a wealth of information, including restaurant reviews and hotel listings, is at your fingertips. ✓**INTERNET**→*url* http://www.cdiguide.com/cdi/cdihome.html

Fodor's Need to locate a top-notch hotel in Atlanta, or a moderately priced trattoria in Rome? Want to find a toll-free number for Qantas, or the Website for Avis? Maybe you're just curious about German customs and duties laws—can lederhosen be seized at the border? If so, can the customs official wear your garment without paying the prohibitive lederhosen tariff? Fodor's has been guiding smart travelers for 60 years, and if you're smart, you'll let the venerable travel publisher continue to guide you. The Fodor's Website contains thousands of listings for restaurants, hotels, and recommended activities in cities worldwide, as well as a wealth of practical travel info that ranges from the general (senior citizens should mention their age to airlines; they may qualify for a discount) to the witheringly specific (the best auto racing in New England occurs at Lime Rock Park in Lakeville, Connecticut). Information can be searched by keyword; those travelers searching for the right Fodor's guidebook can also browse a complete online catalog of more than 200 inventively-titled publications (*Alaska* focuses on Alaska, *Norway* covers Norway). ✓**INTERNET**→*url* http://www.fodors.com

---

Fodor's Worldview These online versions of the popular Fodor's guidebooks furnish generous information on hotels, restaurants, and culture worldwide. With both full-text entries and search capabilities keyed to price range, service type, and location, this is a very comprehensive database—a sample search of restaurant listings by location and cuisine turned up the only Mexican restaurant in Edinburgh (Viva Haggis?). For a fee ($9.95 for one destination, $6.95 for an additional two), Fodor's will prepare a personalized schedule of events for you—just plug in your travel dates online, and within 48 hours, the company will mail or fax a brochure detailing local events occurring at your destination during your travel dates. Currently, the resources from Fodor's guides to Canada, the Caribbean, Europe, Latin America, the Middle East, the Pacific Rim, and the United States are online at these sites. ✓**AMERICA ONLINE**→*keyword* world view ✓**EWORLD**→*go* fodors

---

Frommer's City Guides For the urban sophisticate in all of us—city guides that let you act like a native in either Albuquerque or Paris. In addition to language primers, and lodging, dining, shopping, and sightseeing recommendations, these guides provide detailed historical and cultural background information for each locale, and even suggest books and films to give you the flavor of the city—Luigi Barzini's *The Italians* and Roberto Rossellini's *Open City* are among the many recommendations for Rome. Most major U.S. and international cities are included, but there are some surprising omissions—Berlin, Barcelona, and Mexico City have no entries here. (Perhaps they'll be added later.) Frommer's also sponsors travel chat sessions and connects to the American Express online booking center. And you can order the guides online here, too. ✓**AMERICA ONLINE**→*keyword* Frommer's

---

International Traveler's Guide Spend some armchair leisure time reading the illustrated travel essays at this site—climb snowcapped peaks in the Canadian Rockies, commune with the Conch people of Key West, or cruise the Exuma chain in the Bahamas. Dining, accommodation, and recreation information is also available for selected cities in Italy, the Caribbean, and Iceland. ✓**INTERNET**→*url* http://www.iisys.com/www/travel/world.htm

---

Internet World Travel Review A collection of essays on a number of locations worldwide, including Canada, Rio, Norway, Switzerland, Hong Kong, and Japan. This guide is a great source for a short history of the country, air travel, hotel recommendations (which include pricing info), tips on local attractions (shop the large bazaar in Dhaka for bargains on leather goods, fabrics, and jewelry), and hints on when to visit certain countries for maximum travel enjoyment. (Don't visit Bangladesh from May through October unless you like rain.) There are also a few links here to other travel sites online, including the New York Dining Resources page and Convention & Visitor Bureau Resources sites. ✓**INTERNET**→*url* http://www.stempler.com/punchin/internet.html

---

Lonely Planet The publishers of the ecologically and politically correct travel guides have gone online. (Would *Condé Nast Traveler* mention the Tupac Amaru revolt when discussing Peru?) Use the interactive map to gain excellent, illustrated descriptions of the climate, history, economy, and culture of countries worldwide. Postcards from travelers in far-flung spots (like Turkmenistan) and dispatches from guide writers on the road are included. ✓**INTERNET**→*url* http://www.lonelyplanet.com.au/lp.htm

---

Natalie Sanders Family Travel Guide Sanders, a professional travel agent, offers reports and bulletins about U.S. hotels and resorts that specialize in vacations for families with children (from infants to teens). Club Meds nationwide receive emphatic treatment. ✓**INTERNET**→*url* sandorama1@aol.com ✍ *Write a request*

Period.Com Travel Use this site to take a virtual journey to many countries worldwide. You'll read essays on the food, people, and attractions of your destination country. The essays are lavishly illustrated with photographs of the various locations, which include the Bahamas, Japan, Thailand, and the United States. ✓**INTERNET**→*url* http://www.period.com/travel/travel.htm

---

rec.travel Library This site

houses a number of interesting travel guide archives. A section of the site called Where to Go is organized by country and offers travel guides written by recent visitors to a particular place. For info on more specific interests—like clothing-optional beaches, travel bookstores, and ski resorts—visitors can check into the sections of the site devoted to these topics. Whether you're interested in browsing travel recommendations from the Centers for Disease Control or checking out the financial profiles of foreign nations in the CIA World Factbook, the rec.travel Library has something for you. ✓ **INTERNET** ...→*url* ftp://ftp.cc.umanitoba.ca/rec-travel...→*url* http://www.digimark.net/rec-travel

---

rec.travel.misc (ng) Get recommendations from other travelers at this hobo's hangout—search for an apartment share in Paris, Prague, or St. Petersburg (either one); seek advice about a travel agent who wants cash up front; or get feedback on the advantages and disadvantages of specific youth hostels. ✓ **USENET**→rec.travel.misc *FAQ:* ✓ **INTERNET**→*url* ftp://rtfm.mit.edu/pub/usenet-by-hierarchy/rec/travel/misc

---

Regional & City Guides Regional and city travel guides have been culled from Prodigy member surveys, with a bit of "expert" travel advice thrown in for good measure. Choose a destination from the menu to find out what the locals really like to do and how they like to do it. For example, you'll fit in better at Billy Bob's in Dallas if you don't wear the basic black you don for dancing in New York City—the preferred colors in the world's largest honky-tonk are bright reds, yellows, and whites. ✓ **PRODIGY**→jump→travel

---

Rough Guide *HotWired* magazine and Rough Guide (the renowned publishers of more than 70 travel guidebooks, phrase books, and music-reference titles) have paired up to offer a database of travel info for the U.S. The database features recommendations on hotels, restaurants, coffee shops, bars, nightclubs, sporting events, and festivals nationwide. Click on the map here and browse down to any state or city in the U.S. Or click on the Rough Search button and search the data by location or by subject. A search of "movies" and "San Francisco" yields a list of 66 films set in the Bay Area. WorldBeat's listings are updated every month with info provided by travelers and local readers. ✓ **INTERNET**→*url* http://www.hotwired.com/rough/

Round-the-World Travel Guide So you've got at least 80 days and a pair of comfortable shoes—this guide helps make a wild dream into a reality. Conveniently divided into sections like Major Decisions, Transportation, Money Matters, Communications, and People, this guide offers practical tips on rail travel and bargaining, suggested travel routes, and a good bibliography for further research. It also offers links to offbeat travel sights like freight ships that take passengers. Don't miss the section on packing your bags: You'll learn to pack everything you think you need and then cut the load in half. ✓ **INTERNET**→*url* http://www.digimark.net/rec-travel/rtw/html/faq.html

---

Tourism Information FAQ Contact information for tourism offices worldwide. Type in "Austria" on the search form, and the names of more than 30 Österreichischer offices in Germany, Austria, the United States, Australia, and Canada appear on the screen. Some of the offices have links to their home pages here. Warning: The database is searchable only by country, so don't get careless and type in just "Paris"! ✓ **INTERNET**→*url* http://www.mbnet.mb.ca/lucas/travel/

Travel Forum This forum acts as an informal guide book, allowing Netters to post travel questions and have them answered by fellow Cyberspacers. On the message board, Sue asks for recommendations for a good restaurant in Key West. (Ken answers that The Old Conch Inn is very good.) Bob needs to know how to get a hotel in Atlanta during the Olympics. (Karen jokes that he should look for one on Peachtree Street.) Dan is traveling to Las Vegas soon, and he comes here to ask which casinos' blackjack tables are best. (Walter recommends a trip to Stardust.) Trish has even volunteered her own personal ratings of hotel pools in New York City. Pose your questions here, and somebody in the great big CompuServe world will be your virtual guide. ✓ **COMPUSERVE**→*go* travsig

---

Travel Graphics This is a small site that focuses on travel resources in the Minneapolis and Dallas areas and in Hawaii. For each of the three locations, you'll find lists of hotels, shops, and restaurants (with telephone numbers); descriptions of events, attractions, and entertainment opportunities; and tips on local business resources (convention centers, business-oriented clubs, etc.). ✓ **INTERNET**→*url* http://www.tgimaps.com/

TravelASSIST For travel adventure stories and tantalizing travel photographs, view the full text of articles from current and past issues of TravelASSIST. Find out

World Guide to Vegetarianism—from http://catless.ncl.ac.uk/Vegetarian/Guide/

how to choose a perfect travel companion, float down the Yangtze River, or luxuriate in the Pink Palace (the Beverly Hills Hotel). ✓ **INTERNET**→*url* http://travelassist.com/mag/mag_home.html

TravelBase A guide to some very specific resources in the U.S. Click on the Miami Beach, Orlando, and Key West topics here and read TravelBase's comprehensive listings of restaurants, hotels, and events in each of those cities. If you're researching a tennis, scuba, or skiing vacation, TravelBase offers searchable databases of hotels and resorts that specialize in sports themes. Just enter the state name where you would like to ski or play tennis, and the database pulls up the addresses, phone numbers, and a short description for all appropriate facilities in that state. ✓ **INTERNET**→*url* http://www.travelbase.com/

Traveler's Edge and Traveler's Corner Off to visit a city you've never been to before? These two forums, which are hosted by Weissmann Travel Reports, will help you know what to expect upon arrival. You can access Weissmann's short descriptions of U.S. and international destinations, which are divided into North American Profiles, International Profiles, and City Profiles. These little gems will tell you all the best sights to see—from the Calgary Stampede to San Francisco's Exploratorium. In addition you'll get an extremely useful list of dos and don'ts that will keep you safe and sound during your trip: do select a favorite café in Paris, but don't feed the bears, no matter where you are. Also at the site are instructions on how to order more detailed Weissmann Travel Reports, which offer pertinent information on lodging, eating, money matters. The cost is either $5.95 or $8.95 per report, depending on its length. The brainchild of Arnie Weissmann and his wife Beth Dupuis, the Reports can mean "the difference between a good trip and a great trip."✓ **AMERICA ONLINE**→*keyword* travel→travelers corner→✓ **EWORLD**→*go* travelers

Disabled travelers

Handicap Page's Travel Guide This site is still under construction, but it promises to list handicapped-accessible hotels, restaurants, and tourist attractions worldwide. ✓ **INTERNET**→*url* http://www.metropolis.nl/~pdehaas/Travel.htm

Vacations for Travelers with Disabilities Excerpts of Fodor's new guide for disabled travelers. You'll find tips on how to ensure a hotel is really wheelchair accessible, hints on what to pack for specific destinations, and lists of travel agents who specialize in resources for disabled travelers. ✓ **INTERNET**→*url* http://www.tripod.com/travel/fodors/disable/disable.html

Miscellaneous

Road Trip USA Dreaming of seeing America from behind the wheel of a '57 Chevy? This guide lets you preview what it would be like to traverse the full length on two American highways: U.S. 50 and U.S. 93. Each of the roads is profiled, with a map (click on any of the sights along the way for a brief description of the attraction), a history, and a description of what you'll see in every state that the road passes through. ✓ **INTERNET**→*url* http://gopher.moon.com:7000/1h/rt.usa

The World Sex Guide The unofficial, but comprehensive guide to finding adult pleasure in major cities on every continent. Read the steamy details, and get directions to merchants of the world's oldest profession here. ✓ **INTERNET**→*url* http://www.paranoia.com/faq/prostitution/

Traveler's Guide to Adult Services A list of American adult services nationwide. Organized first by region (Great Lakes, Northeast, Pacific, Southern, and Central) and then by state. Find the names and telephone numbers of various establishments and phone services, including topless and couples bars. ✓ **INTERNET**→*url* http://www.travelersguide.com/welcome.htm

Restaurants

Dining Out Within the depths of America Online's Cook's Online Forum is this folder of restaurant reviews and recommendations for restaurants worldwide. Find menus, tips on house specialties, pricing info, and reservations information for hundreds of food emporiums worldwide. ✓ **AMERICA ONLINE**→*keyword* cooks→dining out

Dining Out on the Web Hungry in Hungary? Got the munchies in Muncie? This massive collection of links has something to suit every taste, no matter where you are. The sprouts crew should try the World Guide to Vegetarianism; raw fish aficionados will appreciate the World Wide Sushi Restaurant Reference; those who don't mix meat and milk should turn to the Kosher Restaurant Database; and steel stomachs can head to the Chili Heads hot restaurant guide. A wealth of regional resources will help you find the best chicken-fried steak in Little Rock or a roadside café in the Netherlands. ✓**INTERNET**→*url* http://www.ird.net/diningout.html

---

Food and Drink Network Find the restaurants with the best chateaubriand in Paris or in Los Angeles with the help of this online restaurant guide. More than 1,000 restaurants are listed in the site's DineBase. Just enter a keyword like "Italian" or "Chicago Chinese," and the database produces the name, phone number, and a short review of any restaurants that match your criteria. Visitors to the site post their own reviews and vote for their favorite restaurants. Under the Food Drink and Travel topic, you can read interesting articles and guides to food-related attractions worldwide, including essays on the first cheese museum in the U.S. (it's in New York City), Germany's Reingau, and France's Champagne region. ✓**AMERICA ONLINE**→*keyword* fdn

---

Kosher Restaurant Database Want matzoh in Memphis? Visit M.I. Gottlieb's. Search the database for kosher restaurants the world over—by name, city, metropolitan area, state, country, or category (meat, dairy, vegetarian). ✓**INTERNET**→*url* http://shamash.nysernet.org/kosher/krestquery.html

---

North American Restaurant Guide Wow! Over 404,025 places to eat in Canada and the United States. Click on the interactive map for a locale and then search by town or cuisine. Although the restaurants are not reviewed, that the locations and phone numbers of all four restaurants in Jemez Springs, New Mexico, are listed is nothing short of phenomenal. ✓**INTERNET**→*url* http://westweb.com/rest/

---

rec.food.restaurants (ng) The majority of posts here ask for recommendations for good Italian / Thai / Mexican places in Chicago, Hawaii, Little Rock, and other U.S. cities. Occasionally, lovers of a certain type of cuisine offer lists of spots that specialize in their gourmet obsession—Mike's list of his favorite Malaysian places features reviews of more than 100 Malaysian restaurants that he's visited from Berkeley, California, to Auckland, New Zealand. ✓**USENET**→rec.food .restaurants

---

Restaurant Review Database Search this database of reviews by state, type of cuisine, average meal price, food quality, and (for the persnickety) service. (A search with the keyword "excellent" in the service section yielded the names of 12 restaurants in Canada, the United States, and Spain. A search of "awful service" gave no matches.) ✓**INTERNET**→*url* gopher://isumvs.iastate.edu:70/1%7Edb.DINING

Traveling Gourmet Know what to order before you get there by preparing any one of the hundreds of recipes from India, Italy, New Orleans, and France, among other places, archived at this site. Under the India section, for example, you'll find recipes for peach salad, coconut lobster, and pepper chicken with mango. Even if you're not traveling to any of these areas, the recipes provided will allow you to close your eyes, taste the local flavor, and dream a little. ✓**INTERNET**→*url* http://www.no mius.com/personal/gourmet/archive.htm

---

World Guide to Vegetarianism Traveling in Brazil and exhausted by the endless series of four-inch-thick steaks? Never fear. If you're near Belem, you can visit Sri Krsna Prasada and treat yourself to a vegetarian feast. Use this guide wherever and whenever the urge for meatless food hits you—whether you're in El Salvador, South America, or Taiwan, this site provides the names and telephone numbers of local vegetarian eateries. ✓**INTERNET**→*url* http://catless.ncl.ac.uk/Vegetarian/Guide/

World Wide Sushi Restaurant Reference This guide, garnered from the alt.food.sushi newsgroup, provides reviews of sushi servers from Alabama to New Zealand (but not Japan). A glossary of terms is included for those who puzzle over the difference between tako and tobiko. ✓**INTERNET**→*url* http://wwwipd.ira.uka.de/%7Emaraist/Sushi/

Zagat's Restaurant Survey Concise descriptions of fine dining establishments nationwide—not only basic information, but descriptions of cuisine, quality ratings, and pricing guides. Special features such as singing waiters and private rooms are duly noted. Zagat's covers all major U.S. cities, and most guides can be searched by neighborhood, type of cuisine, and price range. ✓**COMPUSERVE**→*go* zagats ✓**PRODIGY**→*jump* zagats

Magazines

Flip through the lavishly illustrated pages of travel magazines without ever having to stop by the newstand. The biggies are here: **Condé Nast Traveler,** with its island finder for aspiring beach bums; **National Geographic Traveler,** with its educational articles; **Travel Holiday,** and **Travel & Leisure,** too. But there are lesser known gems as well—**Travelmag** caters to the adventure travel constituency, while **Vagabond Monthly** serves the needs of those seeking the apex of tacky and bizarre travel. **Travel Weekly** and **Web Travel Review** help you tour Cyberspace with their reviews of online travel resources.

Condé Nast Traveler *online—from http://www.cntraveler.com/*

On the Net

Across the board

21st Century Adventures Targeted at adventure travelers, the Website for this travel magazine carries articles on such subjects as the undiscovered Indonesia and whitewater kayaking. But the site also features an interactive travel quiz (which helps refine your vacation needs), travel advice from industry professionals, and an online traveler's forum to answer those perplexing where-to-, how-to-, and when-to-go questions. ✓**INTERNET**→*url* http://www.10e-design.com/centadv/

Abacus Travel Magazine Browse this magazine's listings and articles on destinations, restaurants, hotels, and local attractions, and if you feel like doing your own research on a locale, there's online booking available. Stories range from cruise reviews to features on adventure, gay, family, and disabled travel. Travel discounts and a travel discussion forum round out this site's services. ✓**INTERNET**→*url* http://www.actravel.com/

Condé Nast Traveler Travel tips are added daily to the online version of this famous print publication, so check often for information on cheap rooms and European rail strikes. The site also has several ways to find the ideal vacation destination. The island finder, for example, suggests the perfect getaway for seven different personality types—from Ivana Trump to Margaret Mead. Click on the beach and island atlas for the lowdown on Capri or Rio. Or just plug in a word that describes the experience you are seeking and the Website's "concierge" will suggest a destination (the keyword "magic" returned Crete, Cartagena, and the Hilton Hawaiian Village!). ✓**INTERNET**→*url* http://www.cntraveler.com/

Country Inns Experience the life of gracious homes and country cottages. Illustrated articles from each monthly issue are online here—stories cover topics ranging from fall romance in the Berkshires to the Inn of the Month feature. ✓**INTERNET**→*url* http://www.virtualcities.com/~virtual/cinn/cinn01.htm

Destinations Magazine Not available at the corner newsstand, this online magazine takes readers on a virtual vacation. All tastes are catered to here—e.g., autumn tours of New England and sleep-away camps for adults. A calendar of events covers state fairs and tennis championships, and travel news and bargains are online here, too. Check the classified ads for a chance to trade a studio in Manhattan for a villa in France. ✓**INTERNET**→*url* http://www.travelersguide.com/destinations/destcovr.htm

---

Give Yourself a Break A weekly newsletter that compiles news from across the travel industry. If security is tightened at JFK in response to terrorist threats, or if America West reduces fares to Phoenix, Mexico City, and Los Angeles, you can read about it in Give Yourself a Break. ✓**INTERNET**→*url* http://www.access.digex.net/~drmemory/giveyour.html

---

iTravel This magazine is wired—the news section provides extensive annotated links to Web travel sites for cyberexplorers. But don't get distracted from the online articles, which cover adventures like camping in the Australian outback and eating paella in Castro's Cuba. Old issues are archived in an online library. Try your global awareness with the monthly news-trivia quiz. ✓**INTERNET**→*url* http://www.magi.com/~itravel/

National Geographic Traveler For more than a century, *National Geographic* has transported readers to remote and close-to-home adventures. Now it's helping travelers experience those adventures. This online magazine combines the descriptive text of *National Geographic* with practical travel information for destinations in the U.S. and abroad. A news and tips section keeps visitors abreast of events like the opening of the Rock 'n' Roll Hall of Fame in Cleveland and auto-assistance opportunities in rural Mexico. And, yes, the photography that made *National Geographic* famous is featured prominently in the online version, too. ✓**AMERICA ONLINE**→*keyword* national geographic

---

Today's Traveler Magazine According to the editors, this magazine is for serious travelers, i.e., "people whose motivation for travel is based more on broadening their knowledge than seeking travel bargains." To that end *Today's Traveler* focuses on what it calls "cultural diversity," which translates into gourmet-food reviews, celebrity interviews, and traveling tips for locations worldwide. Excerpts from current and back issues are housed here. Bonus: Internet users get a special rate if they subscribe to the print version. ✓**INTERNET**→*url* gopher://gopher.enews.com:2100/11/travel/publications/todays_traveler

---

Travel Holiday Magazine More than just previews of the newsstand version, the *Travel Holiday* site presents the full text of current and back issues. Browse or search a wide variety of articles—a search on "mysteries" produced rhapsodies on "Gauguin's Lush Marquesas" and a piece on Morocco's hotels. The magazine and online site feature travel news, discounts, a worldwide calendar of events, and a directory of travel resources and contacts to help you realize your travel dreams. To get first crack at upcoming bargains, join the site's mailing list. *Travel Holiday* also makes the full wisdom of its editors available with accommodation, dining, and getaway suggestions. While exploring this wealth of resources, don't neglect *Travel Holiday*'s message

DETOURS

Crossing Victoria Falls:

"On the Zambian side, the best at sunset, the national park is so relaxed that chaotic might be a better description. The tone is set by trails of broken cables that once led to missing light-bulbs intended to illuminate eroded walk-ways. Nearby, in a large purpose-built barn, craft salesmen will take paper money if pushed. They tend to prefer to swap carvings and drums for training shoes, shirts, soap, or anything. The dusty path tumbles into the river down sudden slopes, and freelance tracks dive off through the undergrowth to precarious vantage points where photographers can get vertigo taking panoramic shots of the dizzying gorge. In sharp contrast to the tarmac paths that thread through the small and rather self-conscious national park on the Zimbabwe side, the Zambians have scarcely developed their views of the waterfall for the tourist trade."

—from **Abacus Travel Magazine**

board, especially the entertaining and invaluable topic Worst Vacations Ever. ✓**AMERICA ONLINE**→*keyword* travel holiday ✓**INTERNET**→*email* TravelHol@aol.com ✍ *Email with general correspondence*

Travel Industry Magazine Although *Travel Industry* is billed as a publication for travel professionals, it covers plenty of stories of interest to travel amateurs. Read travel-related stories off the UPI, AP, and Reuters newswires. ✓**INTERNET**→*url* http://www.newspage.com/NEWSPAGE/cgi-bin/walk.cgi/NEWSPAGE/info/d19/d1/d1/

Travel & Leisure Flipping through the pages of *Travel & Leisure* rewards you with both traditional travel writing and offbeat features (like a guide to European flea markets or a humorous feature on spas by playwright Wendy Wasserstein). The full text of articles from back issues can be searched by locale, and a large library here contains hundreds of maps for downloading. Get on the message board for advice on cruises and frequent-flyer perks, as well as tips for trips—how about a side trip to the walled city of Cesky Krumlov in Bohemia or a stay at the Mayan Inn in Chichicastenango, high in the Guatemalan mountains? ✓**AMERICA ONLINE**→*keyword* travel & leisure

Travel Tips (ml) Steve Ginsberg, an average citizen who just likes to travel, edits this free monthly electronic newsletter with sections named Tip Offs, Rip Offs, Deals, and Basics. Mr. Ginsberg encourages submissions, which can be sent to cs@cyberpass.com. ✓**INTERNET**→*email* traveltips@cyberpass.com ✍ *Write a request*

Travel Weekly A terrific collection of travel links, but—be warned—they're described with an attitude: Connecticut's information is a "yawn," "technologically uppity" New Jersey has nothing on the Net, and all Iceland has is a talking clock. Along with the large selection of travel destinations described here, you'll find links to travel resources from Disney and the CIA, online travel agents, and tour operators who will fly you over Hawaiian volcanoes or guide you down the Grand Canyon on a burro. *Travel Weekly* also keeps you abreast of general travel news. ✓**INTERNET**→*url* http://www.novalink.com/travel/

Opening screen for Travelmag*—from http://www.travelmag.co.uk/travelmag/*

TravelGram Published every Saturday, *TravelGram* reports the latest travel discounts, including specials offered by all the major airlines, hotels, and car-rental agencies. *TravelGram* also provides a comprehensive list of toll-free numbers for airlines from Aer Lingus to Zambia Airways. ✓**INTERNET**→*url* http://www.csn.net/~johnhart/tfb.html

Travelmag Not the usual "Best Beaches" travel magazine articles. *Travelmag*, an electronic magazine, delivers reader-contributed articles on subjects like canoeing the Amazon or a Moroccan marriage market. Other features cover travel bargains, health advisories, and bizarre news from around the world ("Toad Madness Strikes Cambodia!"). ✓**INTERNET**→*url* http://www.travelmag.co.uk/travelmag/

Vagabond Monthly This nascent Web publication is designed to touch the heart of the wandering American with a fondness for velvet Elvis paintings and barbeque on a bun. A recent issue profiled "America's Cheesiest Resort" (The Dells, Wisconsin). Contribute a feature on your own hometown, or have fun with the Ameri-Quiz. ✓**INTERNET**→*url* http://www.globaldialog.com/~tpatmaho/

Web Travel Review If this magazine came in hard copy, postal workers would be miffed—it stands now at 600 Web pages, with more than 2,000 photographs. Here the Net's own travel-writing guru, Philip Greenspun, posts his award-winning travelogues. ✓**INTERNET**→*url* http://webtravel.org/webtravel/

Literature & bookstores

You can't judge a travel book by its cover. But you can judge it by its insights, its pre-sentation, and its prose. In fact, travel literature has a long and venerable history; from Sterne to Stendhal, from Twain to Theroux, and every year more and more travelers are boning up on their destinations before they pack the first travel soap. Online, dozens of travel publishers advertise their wares, from **Adventurous Traveler Bookstore** to **The Travel Bug Bookstore** to **TravelSearch Destination Sheets**. And the Net also contains a wealth of travelogues—first-person tales posted by Netsurfers, amateur travel writers, and even seasoned professionals. Follow Net travel scribe Philip Greenspun on his **Travels With Samantha**. Visit the **Gay Travel Connection**. And then travel at the speed of light to **Travel At the Speed of Light.**

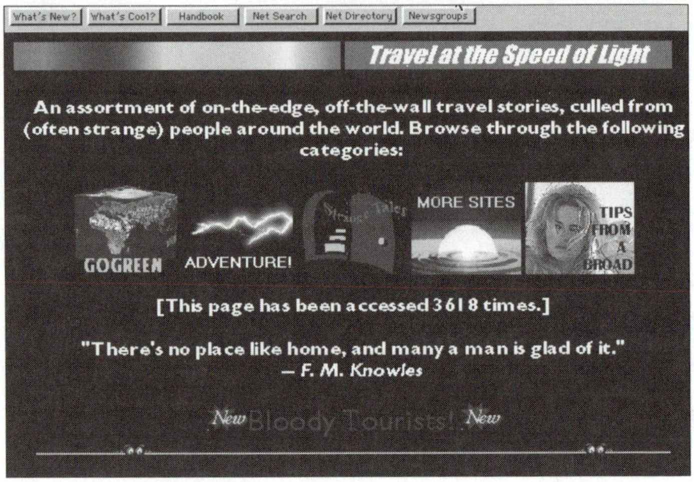

Travel, well, rather quickly—from http://www.wimsey.com/~ayoung/travel.shtml

On the Net

Bookstores

Adventurous Traveler Bookstore Don't spend hours fingering dusty volumes in cobweb-filled bookstores to find the travel title you crave! Just come to this site and take advantage of the travel literature warehouse at Adventurous Traveler. Search their catalog of over 2,200 titles by keyword (a search on "France" yields the *Western European Phrasebook*, *France by Bike*, and *Whitewater Gems of the High Alps*, among 50 other titles). Or you can click on indexes that organize titles by geographic area or by activity (e.g., hiking or scuba diving). For a hotlist of new books for the current season, just hit the New Titles and Additions links for the latest in travel guides and literature. After filling your virtual book bag, you can either order your choices online, call the telephone numbers listed here, or download an order form to snail mail your requests. ✓**INTERNET**→*url* http://www.gorp.com/atbook.htm

Blue Peter Books At Blue Peter Books, they believe that "Reading is a leisurely sport." To that end, Blue Peter offers a catalog of books about sailing in and around Canada's Bay of Fundy (which, as any oceanographer knows, has the greatest tidal variance of any body of water on earth). Short descriptions of the books, a price list, and an order form are provided here. ✓**INTERNET**→*url* http://www.discribe.ca/other/bluep.htm

Hampton's Travel Books Read a content summary and view a cover photo for each of the titles listed here, which include the *World Ecology & Cultural Travel Guide*, *Fielding's Europe 1995*, and *Insight Guides' East African Wildlife*. The selections are listed alphabetically by title. ✓**INTERNET**→*url* http://www.dynapro.com/dynamic/travel.books.summary.html

McGraw-Hill Travel Books This tiny subsection of the mammoth McGraw-Hill catalog offers titles on a variety of destinations, including *Coping with China*, *Discovering Paris Bistros*, and *Visitor's Guide to Zambia*. You can order the books online through a link to the Internet Bookshop or check a list of McGraw-Hill bookstores in your area. On CompuServe, McGraw-Hill offers a 20 percent discount on new titles, a guarantee to beat any competitor's price by 5 percent, and a clearance-sale bin full of 50-percent-off deals. Fill out an online order form to purchase. ✓**INTERNET**→*url* http://www.bookshop.co.uk/mcgraw/ ✓**COMPUSERVE**→*go* mh→Search the catalog→Travel

Moon Travel Handbooks Moon's Handbooks has been at the forefront of travel-related literature since 1973. Each handbook offers comprehensive information on a destination's historical background, outdoor recreation opportunities, restaurants, hotels, and special attractions. Moon specializes in locales in East Asia, the South Pacific, the Hawaiian Islands, Mexico, and the Western United States. At this site you can search their selection of handbooks by location or keyword. If you wish to buy one (or several) of their titles, you can order online or on the telephone. ✓**INTERNET**→*url* gopher://gopher.moon.com:7000/

Random House Search all the Random House imprints (Ballantine, Ivy Books, Fawcett, etc.) for travel titles at this site. You'll find price and publication information for books like *The Happy Island of Oceania, My Love Affair with England,* and *A Walk Across France.* To order any of these titles, link to a list of American Booksellers Association Bookstores and find a shop in your neighborhood that carries the title. If you prefer to order by phone or mail, the necessary information is provided for your convenience. ✓**INTERNET**→*url* http://www.randomhouse.com/

Random House—from http://www.randomhouse.com/

RV Adventure Library A whole cyberstore for those who roam in recreational vehicles! Titles here include *Free RV Campgrounds* and *Save-a-Buck Camping.* Read all about RV's small selection of books and order them online at this site. ✓**INTERNET**→*url* http://www.branson.net/branson/rvtravel/

Stone Bridge Books Specializing in books about travel in Japan, Stone Bridge offers a small selection which includes *Asia for Women on Business,* an interesting primer for the female business traveler. ("Take a cue from your Asian counterparts. When you feel confused, embarrassed, or upset, smile, smile, smile.") Stone Ridge provides an online order form for easy purchasing. ✓**INTERNET**→*url* http://www.stonebridge.com/~sbp/

The Travel Bug Bookstore Travel Bug wants to be your "passport to adventure." With over 6,000 travel books, guides, and maps, this site sells just about every kind of document needed for travel (except passports). Travel Bug features a number of guide book series—including the Lonely Planet, Moon, and Rough Guides—and hundreds of titles on specific geographic regions worldwide. If you get the itch to order from Travel Bug, just email them from this site. ✓**INTERNET**→*url* http://www.swifty.com/tbug/

TravelSearch Destination Sheets What's a destination sheet? It's one of TravelSearch's publications on hundreds of locales worldwide—a destination sheet tells you what's worth seeing, which shops have what you're looking for, what kind of sports activities are available, which restaurants are the best, and what kind of weather you can expect when you reach your desired location. See a sample sheet about Antigua and then order a real sheet online. ✓**INTERNET**→*url* http://www.bendnet.com/travelsearch.html

Ulysses Shop this catalog for rare

and out-of-print travel and exploration books. Ulysses offers hundreds of books, organized by geographic area (e.g., Africa, North America, and Central Asia). Each title is profiled with a brief content summary and price information in English Pounds. ✓**INTERNET**→*url* http://www.demon.co.uk/ulysses books/travel.html

WH Smith Get reviews, content summaries, cover photos, and price information (in English Pounds) for WH Smith books, including *Camping Sites in Britain 1995*, *France: The Rough Guide*, and the *Spanish Phrase Book and Dictionary*. Click on the Delivery Information topic to learn how to order the books. Worldwide delivery takes approximately 7-12 days. ✓**COMPUSERVE**→*go* whsmith→*Search by filename:* travel

Travelogues

Adventures in Travel CompuServe's resident travel writer Lee Foster pens these articles on the special spirit of places like the Galapagos or Dutch cheese country. There is practical information amidst Foster's feature articles—take a look at the cruise reviews and strategies for ecotours in Brazil or theater weekends in London. ✓**COMPUSERVE**→*go* ait-1

Gay Travel Connection Written by Ernie Alderete, these travelogues report on over 20 intimate U.S. and international destinations like the Flex Complex in Phoenix, Arizona and the Inca Spa in Peru. Some reviews contain adult subject matter and sexually explicit language. ✓**INTERNET**→*url* http://www.travelxn.com/gay /homepage.htm

Onward Travel Stories This growing collection of travelogues (available only on the Net) gathers the stories and photographs of a handful of non-professional writers and photographers. The collection includes "Big Bend," one man's tale of the biggest national park in Texas, and "No Simple Highway," a photo and text journal of a trip from Maine to Arizona during the fall and winter of 1991-1992. Aspiring beatniks will especially appreciate the homage to *On the Road* in "Remembering Jack." ✓**INTERNET**→*url* http://sun site.unc.edu/onward/

Pictures from Around the World Pack your Brownie before you head for Jamaica! Browse this collection of lavishly illustrated articles and images and then head to the library for picture-taking tips and creative inspiration. The libraries are organized by continent (Africa, Asia, Antarctica) and subject (waterfalls, buffalo, cathedrals). Head to the message boards for advice from photographic professionals. ✓**AMERICA ONLINE**→*keyword* pictures

Speakeasy Forum Travel Logs Within the depths of the Speakeasy Forum is this library, which specializes in travelogues submitted to the forum by travelers worldwide. Read an outline of practical tips for a tour of Paris—"Paris, at times, is a city hostile to walkers. The sidewalks are narrow, the drivers aggressive, and the crowds sometimes overwhelming, especially when you walk around a sidewalk cafe. But there is no better way to see the city except by walking."—or download some panoramic pictures of the Andes Mountains. ✓**COMPUSERVE**→*go* speakeasy→Libraries→Travel Logs

Travel At the Speed of Light A collection of stories by several different writers. The site includes

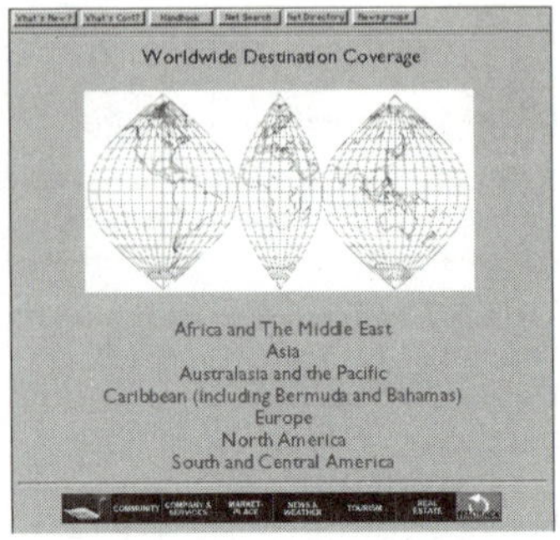

Choices from Travelsearch—http://www.bendnet.com/travelsearch.html

"Travel Tips from a Broad," by Suzy Young, which explores the complex relationship between traveler and luggage; "Raratonga," by Stuart Young, a story describing a Sunday morning church ceremony on the island of Raratonga; and "Middle Sea Diving," by Chris Jones, an essay on the secret pleasures of diving off the Cote d'Azur. A total of over 20 essays on a number of travel-related subjects are housed at this site. ✓**INTERNET**→*url* http://www.wimsey.com/~ayoung/travel.shtml

Travels with Samantha After the death of his beloved dog George, author Philip Greenspun recuperated from his loss by touring North America for the entire summer of 1993. Philip fought traffic on I-93 going through Boston, met a group of Jewish bikers in Minnesota, and almost froze to death in the Canadian Rockies. *Travels with Samantha*, which is available only online, is a touching account of a man taking to the road to work through the loss of a dear friend, and it's also a great source of practical travel info for North America. Greenspun has several other travel publications, both on- and offline, but this is a good place to start. ✓**INTERNET**→*url* http://www-swiss.ai.mit.edu/samantha/index.html

Agents & booking

With hundreds of travel agents now online, not only can you book plane tickets, hotel rooms, and rental cars all online, in many cases you can do it 24 hours a day! (Imagine the possibilities: If you wake up in the middle of the night with wanderlust, get online and shop for a destination, then head to an online agent like **Eaasy Sabre** and make the arrangements without even having to change out of your pajamas. Sinfully easy.) Wherever you wish to go, there's an online travel agent to help you get there, from **Above all Travel** to **World Class Travel**. And budget finders aren't left out—**Council Travel** and **Student Travel** cater to those with limited dollars.

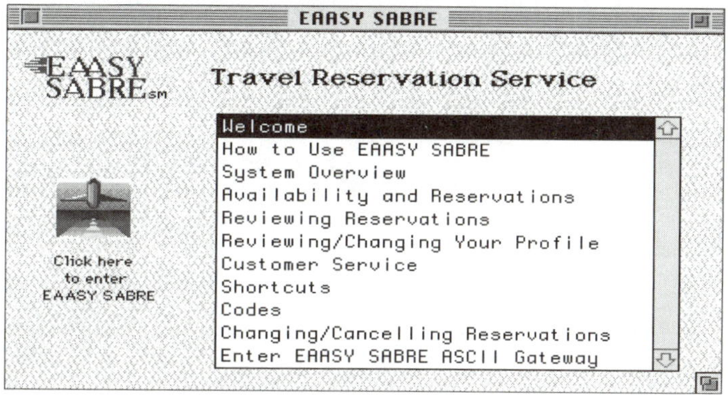

Screenshot—from America Online's Eaasy Sabre

On the Net

Across the board

Access 2 Travel An amazing index of travel agents online. To find the agency that best suits your needs, click on the section name that describes the type of travel you want to do—cruises, Europe, Caribbean, etc. You'll get a list of companies specializing in that type of travel. Each company's name, address, and telephone number is listed, and each has a direct email link with the Website. There are also links to any agencies with their own pages. ✓**INTERNET**→*url* http://www.webcom.com/~travel/

Eaasy Sabre Developed by American Airlines, Eaasy Sabre is the big dog of the online travel services, with access to 700 airlines (300 with online booking), 18,000 hotels, and 45 car-rental companies worldwide. The service is something of a task at first—new users must fill out a brief registration form, after which they are issued a user ID and instructed to choose two passwords (twice as good as one password for insuring the security of any plans you might make). From there, though, it's like a magic carpet ride. To book a flight, simply select the Flights menu, enter your destination, and then wait as Sabre retrieves all appropriate routes and airlines. The Fare command brings up a screen with round-trip and one-way prices for each flight, along with any restrictions, and if you select the Bargain Hunter option, the computer will filter for the lowest fares. Once you have settled on an itinerary and airline, just confirm the reservation online. The process of reserving rental cars and hotel rooms is just as easy. Designed originally for travel agents, Sabre has added a slightly friendlier version for the uninitiated; frequent travelers who know travel codes (quick—what's the standard abbreviation for Midway Airport in Chicago?) may want to stick with the Fasttrack option. ✓**AMERICA ONLINE**→*key word* sabre ✓**COMPUSERVE**→*go* sabre ✓**EWORLD**→*go* sabre ✓**PRODIGY**→*jump* eaasy sabre

Preview Vacations Use this online travel agent, which is sponsored by MCI, to plan and book vacations with friends and family. Read about the service's various tour packages, or catch up on travel industry news. Try the active message board for advice from real travelers on cruises, honeymoons, and the relative charms of Antigua and Anguilla. After you've decided where you want to go, head to the booking information online to seal the deal. ✓**AMERICA ONLINE**→*key word* vacations

Travel Agents Online

007Travel ✓INTERNET→*url* http://www.omnitravel.com/007 travel

1-800-FLY-ASAP ✓INTERNET→*url* http://www.indirect.com/user/ecs/

1st Choice Travel ✓INTERNET→*url* http://physc1.byu.edu/~astrosoc/first.html

5-Star Alaskan Cruise ✓INTERNET→*url* http://www.pinsight.com/~rjoksch/magic.html

Above All Travel ✓INTERNET→*url* http://www.aboveall.com/

Active Vacations ✓INTERNET→*url* http://www.castles.com/vs/vacation_station.html

Adventure Travel ✓INTERNET→*url* http://www.dtc.net/vm/adventture/adventur.html

Aer Travel, Inc. ✓INTERNET→*url* http://www.aertravel.com/browse/aer/

AESU Flights ✓INTERNET→*url* http://www.charm.net/~aesu/

Air Brokers Travel ✓INTERNET→*url* http://www.aimnet.com/~airbrokr/

Air Waves Travel ✓INTERNET→*url* http://www.xnet.com/~creacon/AWT/

Airway Travel Santorini ✓INTERNET→*url* http://www.knossos.gr/~basilis/index.html

Alkar Travel ✓INTERNET→*url* http://sashimi.wwa.com/~shopnet/alkar/index.htm

All Adventure Travel ✓INTERNET→*url* http://www.alladventure.com/

All Around Travel Network ✓INTERNET→*url* http://www.sims.net/aatn/

All Travel ✓INTERNET→*url* http://www.travind.com/alltrav/

All Ways Travel ✓INTERNET→*url* http://www.empnet.com/all_ways/

All-Inclusive Vacations ✓INTERNET...→*url* http://www.cts.com/~vacation/...→*url* http://www.webcom.com/~travel/all_inc.html

Allied Percival International ✓INTERNET→*url* http://www.miint.net/api/api.html

Allports Travel Counsellors ✓INTERNET→*url* http://pages.prodigy.com/ON/trav/trav.html

Amcan Travel ✓INTERNET→*url* http://www.halcyon.com/amcan/welcome.html

Amerispan Unlimited ✓INTERNET→*url* http://www.amerispan.com/

AMVATRAV ✓INTERNET→*url* http://www.ultranet.com/amvatrav/

Anchors Away ✓INTERNET...→*url* http://www.onestop.com/cruise/...→*url* http://www.anchorsaway.com/

AOI Travel Services ✓INTERNET→*url* http://www.xmission.com/~aoi/aoi.html

Apollo Travel ✓INTERNET→*url* http://www.uniserve.com/apollo/

Arizona Reservation Bureau ✓INTERNET→*url* http://www.widdl.com/ims/azreserv/azreserh.html

Around the World Travel ✓INTERNET→*url* http://www.highadv.com/

Asia Travel Agent Directory ✓INTERNET→*url* http://asiadir.com/Travel-leisure/index.html

Aspects of Travel with Rosenbluth Vacations ✓INTERNET→*url* http://www.rosenbluth.com

Australia/New Zealand Down Under Travel ✓INTERNET→*url* http://market.net/travel/anz/index.html

Avanti Destinations ✓INTERNET→ *url* http://www.teleport.com/~avanti/

Avanti Travel ✓INTERNET→*url* http://www.calweb.com/business/avantitravel/

Batavia Custom Travel ✓INTERNET→*url* http://www.mcs.net/~kevinkj/bct.html

Bell Travel ✓INTERNET→*url* http://www.ccnet.com/~sal/

Blaney's Travel ✓INTERNET→*url* http://www.IslandNet.com/BlaneysTravel/

Bolack Total Travel ✓INTERNET→*url* http://www.bolack.com/

Branson Gray Line Travel ✓INTERNET→*url* http://www

Travel Agents Online (cont'd)

.branson.net/branson/grayline/

Burnham Park Travel ✓INTERNET→*url* http://www.wolfgang.com/burnham/

C I Travel ✓INTERNET→*url* http://www.infi.net/citravel/

Cal-Con Travel ✓INTERNET→*url* http://www.netgate.net/~calconnb/calcon.html

Campbell Family Travel ✓INTERNET→*url* http://198.175.15.221/familytravel/index.html

Carefree Travel ✓INTERNET→*url* http://www.ernestallen.com/travel/ca/93465/CarefreeTravel.htm

Carlson Wagonlit Travel ✓INTERNET→*url* http://www.snider.net/ctravel/

Cass' Marina Sailing Adventures ✓INTERNET→*url* http://www.sonic.net/cass/

Changes in L'Attitudes ✓INTERNET→*url* http://www.changes.com/Changes/

Choice Travel ✓INTERNET→*url* http://www.aaco.com/choice/

Conlin Faber Travel ✓INTERNET→*url* http://www.branch.com/conlin/conlin.html

Continental Travel ✓INTERNET→*url* http://www.execpc.com/~bschuetz/

Cornucopia First Class Travel ✓INTERNET→*url* http://iquest.com/~marla/

Costa Travel On-line ✓INTERNET→*url* http://mmink.cts.com/costa.html

Council Travel ✓INTERNET→*url* http://www.ciee.org/cts/ctshome.htm

Dancers' Travel Network ✓INTERNET→*url* http://www.travind.com/dancers/

Destination: Catalina ✓INTERNET→*url* http://www.catalina-island.com/guide/Destination.html

Destinations Unlimited ✓INTERNET→*url* http://usa.net/destinations/unlimited.html

Devonshire Travel ✓INTERNET→*url* http://www.northcoast.com/travel/devonshire/travel.html

Diane's Travel ✓INTERNET→*url* http://www.tulsa.com/diane.html

DreamQuest International ✓INTERNET→*url* http://www.magicnet.net/cge/dq/links/air tix.html

ECB Travel ✓INTERNET→*url* http://www.ecbtravel.com/

Eco-Travel Services ✓INTERNET→*url* http://www.belgasoft.com/ets.html

El Dorado Hills Travel ✓INTERNET→*url* http://www.vpm.com/sailaway/

Endeavour Travel ✓INTERNET→*url* http://www.anzac.com/endvr/endvr.htm

Escape Artist Tours Inc. ✓INTERNET→*url* http://www.best.com/~travel/sf-escapes/

European Travel Inc. ✓INTERNET→*url* http://www.european.com/~eurofile/home.html

Ever Sun Travel Ltd ✓INTERNET→*url* http://www.intercon.net/~eversun/

FAO Travel GmbH ✓INTERNET→*url* http://www.fao.de/

Far & Away Travel Services ✓INTERNET→*url* http://www.faraway.com/default.htm

FinlandTravel ✓INTERNET→*url* http://www.fintrip.fi/

Garber Travel OnLine ✓INTERNET→*url* http://www.garber.com/garber/

Gateway Travel & Tours ✓INTERNET→*url* http://www.magna.com.au/~gatrav/

Get Outta Town Travel ✓INTERNET→*url* http://adventure-vacations.com/gott/

Global On-Line Travel ✓INTERNET→*url* http://travel.netsite.com/

Globas Vakanties ✓INTERNET→*url* http://www.globas.nl/

Go Travel ✓INTERNET→*url* http://www.gotravel.com/

Golf Getaways ✓INTERNET→*url* http://www.maui.net/~golf/getaways/

Gray Line of Niagara Falls ✓INTERNET→*url* http://www.niagara.com/grayline/

Gray Line Orlando ✓INTERNET→*url* http://www.gray-line

Travel Agents Online (cont'd)

-mco.com/

Great Australian Travel Co. ✓INTERNET→*url* http://www.magna.com.au/~hideaway/snow_ind.htm

Harbourside Travel Services ✓INTERNET→*url* http://www.tagsys.com/Ads/Harbourside/

Hawkeye World Travel ✓INTERNET→*url* http://www.exclusive.com/bizproj/hwt.html

Hideaway's Holidays ✓INTERNET→*url* http://www.magna.com.au/~hideaway/

Holiday Travel ✓INTERNET→*url* http://www.mbnet.mb.ca/~runikkel/documents/holiday.htm

Holman Travel ✓INTERNET→*url* http://www.wwwa.com/holman/

Impact Travel ✓INTERNET→*url* http://www.escape.com/travel/

In Bound Whitsunday ✓INTERNET→*url* http://peg.apc.org/~squirrel/inbound.html

Independent Holiday Shop Ltd. ✓INTERNET→*url* http://www.tcp.co.uk/~holidays/

Industrial Strength Travel ✓INTERNET→*url* http://www.slip.net/~jwithers/index1.html

Innovative Travel Services ✓INTERNET→*url* http://www.innotravel.com/

Instant Travel ✓INTERNET→*url* http://www.cgl.com/~it/

InteleTravel International ✓INTERNET→*url* http://inteletravel.com/inteletravel/

International Travel Agency ✓INTERNET→*url* http://www.comprez.com/ita/

Intra Travel ✓INTERNET→*url* http://qb.island.net/~intra/

Key West Travel Planners ✓INTERNET→*url* http://key-west.com/services/travpln.htm

LeisureTyme Travel & TravelLinks ✓INTERNET→*url* http://www.vweb.net/leisure/

Let's Travel ✓INTERNET→*url* http://www.ernestallen.com/travel/ca/93433/Let'sTravel.htm

Liberty Travel On-Line ✓INTERNET→*url* http://www.libertytravel.com/

Lifestyles Tours and Travel ✓INTERNET→*url* http://www.lainet.com/PlayCouples/

Light Blue Travel ✓INTERNET→*url* http://www.teleserv.co.uk/lbt/

Maritime Marlin Travel ✓INTERNET→*url* http://novaweb.com/sky/mmt/

Mark International Travel ✓INTERNET→*url* http://WWW.markintl.com/travel/

Megan's Friends ✓INTERNET→ *url* http://www.ernestallen.com/travel/ca/93405/Megan's Friends.htm

Meredith Travel Inc. ✓INTERNET→*url* http://meredith.cybernetics.net/

MIR Travel ✓INTERNET→*url* http://www.kiss.com/fr/ru_w/mir.html

Morris Travel ✓INTERNET→*url* http://eaglerock.if.scientech.com/morris/

New Departures Travel Inc. ✓INTERNET→*url* http://www.islandnet.com/~cvcprod/goligers.htm

Paramount Travel ✓INTERNET→*url* http://www.gate.net/paramount/index.html

PL Travel Agency Inc. ✓INTERNET→*url* http://www.bizlink.com/pl_travel/

Ponderosa Travel Club ✓INTERNET→*url* http://www.omix.com/sites/ponderosa/

Prestonwood Travel ✓INTERNET→*url* http://www.wn.com/ptravel/

Prima Travel Centre ✓INTERNET→*url* http://www.explore.com/prima.html

Ratvis Travel ✓INTERNET→*url* http://iceweb.ismennt.is/r/ratvis/

San Diego Travel ✓INTERNET→*url* http://www.geninc.com/geni/USA/CA/San_Diego/travel/index.html

Seagrave Travel ✓INTERNET→*url* http://www.keytech.com/~seagrave/index.shtml

SEATOP Reisen ✓INTERNET→*url* http://www.reise.de

See & Sea Travel Service, Inc.

Travel Agents Online (cont'd)

✓INTERNET→*url* http://www.batnet.com/shicho/see%26sea/

Sinbad Travel ✓INTERNET→*url* http://www.spb.su/ryh/sindbad.html

Splash Vacations ✓INTERNET→*url* http://www.splashvacations.com/

Sporting Life Travel ✓INTERNET→*url* http://www.edensys.com/edensys/sportlife/index.html

Star Travel ✓INTERNET→*url* http://www.bie.net/bn/biz_indx/travel-agents/startravel.html

Student Travel ✓INTERNET→*url* http://www.sta-travel.com/

SuperClubs ✓INTERNET→*url* http://www.intnet.net/SuperClubs/

Taren Systems ✓INTERNET→*url* http://taren.ns.net/

Team Elite Travel ✓INTERNET→*url* http://www.vnm.com/visual/team_elite/introtrav.html

Tee-Times Golf Vacations ✓INTERNET→*url* http://www.teetimes.com/

TeleService Resources, Inc. ✓INTERNET→*url* http://www.amrcorp.com/amr_mgmt/teleserv/resser.htm

Tickets and Travel, Inc. ✓INTERNET→*url* http://www.inetdirect.net/tnt

Tourism New Brunswick ✓INTERNET→*url* http://www.discribe.ca/tour/nb/packages.htm

Tower Travel ✓INTERNET→*url* http://www.lightlines.com/tower/

Travel Agents International ✓INTERNET→*url* http://www.tai-travel.com/

Travel Boutique ✓INTERNET→*url* http://hisurf.aloha.com/travel/hawaii.html

Travel Connection ✓INTERNET→*url* http://www.kaiwan.com/~travel/

Travel Discounts ✓INTERNET→*url* http://www.boms.com/discount/index.html

Travel Experts, Inc. ✓INTERNET→*url* http://www.prairienet.org/business/travex/homepage.html

Travel Home ✓INTERNET→*url* http://www.kern.com/travelhome.html

Travel Hound ✓INTERNET→*url* http://www.nis.net/tia/

Travel.Net ✓INTERNET→*url* http://www.nashville.com/member/travnet.html

Travel Network ✓INTERNET→*url* http://www.widdl.com/travnet/index.html

Travel Niche ✓INTERNET→*url* http://www.webcom.com/~travler/

Travel Solutions, Inc. ✓INTERNET→*url* http://www.travelsolutions.com/

Travel Store Inc. ✓INTERNET→*url* http://smartworld.com/travel/travel.html

Travel Systems International, Inc. ✓INTERNET→*url* http://www.travel-inc.com/Travel/

Travel Travel ✓INTERNET→*url* http://www.mindspring.com/~travtrav/travel.html

Travel World ✓INTERNET→*url* http://www.omnitravel.com/

Travelcraft, Inc. ✓INTERNET→*url* http://market.net/travel/tc/index.html

TraveLink ✓INTERNET→*url* http://www.travelink.com/

TravelNet Beau Travel ✓INTERNET→*url* http://www.mv.com/biz/beautravel/

Travelwise Network, Inc. ✓INTERNET→*url* http://www.shore.net/TravelWise/

TravNet! International ✓INTERNET→*url* http://www.sky.net/~eric/

TRaX Travel Software Systems ✓INTERNET→*url* http://www.trax.com/

Trek International ✓INTERNET→*url* http://www.webcom.com/~intermlt/millionaire/travel.html

Uniglobe Kalamalka Travel ✓INTERNET→*url* http://www.okanagan.com/uniglobe

Uniglobe Travel Zone ✓INTERNET→*url* http://wave.sheridan.wy.us/~z_travel/z_travel.html

Unique Travel Services ✓INTERNET→*url* http://www.magicnet.net/cge/uts/1701/pg1.html

Hotels & inns

Is there anything worse than driving all day on dusty roads and then pulling into the motel only to find that there's no room at the inn? Ensure a warm welcome with a visit to the **Hotel Reservation Center** or **Prodigy's Inn Directory** and book a room right online, or browse the massive offerings of **All the Hotels on the Web**. In Cyberspace there are hotels for all budgets and tastes—from the major chains like **Hyatt** and **Best Western** to the 8,000 small inns listed in **Go Native: Guide to B&B Inns**. Those who's idea of relaxation is being treated like a king (or queen) should head immediately to **Relais & Chateaux**, where luxury is a guiding principle. Or turn to **CompuServe's Inn and Lodging Forum** where other travelers relate their experiences with lumpy mattresses and fantastic hotel finds.

California's East Brother Light Station, Inc.—http://www.traveldata.com/biz/inns/

On the Net

Across the board

Hospitalitynet This collection of links takes you to hotel sites all over the Web, including the home pages of major hotel chains (Best Western, Holiday Inn, Hyatt, Novotel, etc.), Small Luxury Hotels of the World, and GENinc Bed and Breakfast Inns. ✓**INTERNET**→*url* http://www.hospitalitynet.nl/index/chain.htm

Index of Hotels and Travel on the Net This Website offers a collection of links to the home pages of numerous hotels and resorts worldwide, including Best Western International, Novotel, Westin Hotels and Resorts, and Hyatt. In addition to the hotel links, the site also links to many airlines (Air France, Lufthansa, and Air Canada) and cruise lines (Norwegian Line and Royal Caribbean Line). ✓**INTERNET**→*url* http://www.webscope.com/travel/homepage.html

Discounters

Hotel Discount Reservation Services Come to this site for a list of companies with discount rates for rooms in major hotels worldwide. The list includes RMC Travel, which offers discounts at over 800 hotels in Los Angeles, New York, Washington, D.C., and London; and Paradice Adventures, which operates in the Las Vegas and Reno areas. Find names, telephone numbers, and office hours for over 30 discounters. ✓**AMERICA ONLINE**→*keyword* travel forum→Hotel Discount Services

Hotel Reservation Center The Hotel Reservation Center allows you to compare rates and make reservations at thousands of hotels worldwide. Both detail-oriented—the extensive reservation form even leaves space for special requests—and economical, offering preferred rates, the site not only helps stretch your travel dollars, but it also makes planning your trip easier and more exciting. ✓**INTERNET**→*url* http://www.traveldiscounts.com/HotelResCenter/

Neptune—Travel Industry

Network Not a conventional travel agency, Neptune is a discount booking service that forwards reservations to individual hotels. The network currently works with hotels in Miami and Orlando, and plans to add links to Paris, London, Jerusalem, Atlanta, and Austin, Texas. Read descriptions and see pictures of the hotels featured by Neptune at the Website. ✓**INTERNET**→*url* http://www.neptune.com

Hotel chains

Best Western International Best Western International, Inc., the world's largest hotel chain with 3,400 properties worldwide, provides a searchable database of information on their hotels. Reservations capabilities are not yet available, so prepare yourself for an old-fashioned walk toward the phone to close the deal. ✓**INTERNET**→*url* http://www.travelweb.com/bw.html

Continental Plaza Hotels & Resorts Before planning your next trip to Mexico, be sure to peek in at the informative Website of this small Mexican hotel company with eight properties in Mexico and one in Los Angeles. Click through the map at this site to get information on Continental's hotels in Mexico City, Cancun, and Veracruz, among other locations. Besides the requisite photos of tanned, bathing beauties and the sensual, colonial curves of beachfront balconies, Continental also emphasizes the cultural and environmental aspects of travel in Mexico with essays on archaeological digs and ecotourism. ✓**INTERNET**→*url* http://www.wotw.com/wow/situr/cpl-main.html

Embassy Suites Learn about the services provided at Embassy Suites hotels worldwide and get price and contact info at this site. Online reservations services are available for interested parties. ✓**INTERNET**→*url* http://www.embassy-suites.com/

Hampton Inns "There's a new place to stay on the information superhighway," announces this humble Website. "And it has Hampton written all over it." Like its sister company Embassy Suites, efficient online reservations capabilities and snappy destination maps make this site easy to use. Read articles on late-breaking company news, and if you're not interested in corporate profiles, there are also tips for travelers here—get a recipe for Happy Highway Mix, a healthy alternative to road food. ✓**INTERNET**→*url* http://www.hampton-inn.com/

Hilton Hotels Hilton's Internet Travel Center offers a wide array of services, including current promotions, HHonors information and property locations. While not yet ready to process your reservation online, the company's agents will be happy to respond and "discuss" your request. ✓**INTERNET**→*url* http://www.hilton.com/

Holiday Inn With over 2,000 hotels worldwide (no two alike) connected directly to its graphically pleasing Net site, Holiday Inn is online in full force. Click through a list of hotels organized geographically until you reach the Inn closest to your destination, then check room availability online. If your desired room is available, you can reserve it online. ✓**INTERNET**→*url* http://www.holiday-inn.com/

Hyatt The Website offers a comprehensive list of Hyatts worldwide, but if you want to reserve a room, you'll have to call using the numbers listed here. The company's CompuServe site allows you to view a list of Hyatt hotels—from Ohio to Oswan—and then you can make reservations at the Book a Confirmed Reservations section, where there's a list of Hyatt reservations telephone numbers worldwide and a link to Eaasy Sabre. ✓**INTERNET**→*url* http://www.travelweb.com/hyatt.html ✓**COMPUSERVE**→*go* hya

Marriott Marriott believes in the personal touch—its site opens with a greeting by Bill, Jr., the head honcho himself. In addition to complete property listings (with telephone numbers for further info), there's also a full guide to the company's contract services division, which provides food service and management expertise to healthcare organizations and senior living facilities. For the Marriott investor or the curious, the Utah-based corporation also offers its recent annual financial statements. ✓**INTERNET**→*url* http://www.marriott.com/

Novotel Novotel's site prefers style over substance. With over 300 locations worldwide, the company highlights ten of its North American properties, including color photos and informative guides to both the property and its surroundings. Although the offerings are scanty, a few hotel listings are still better than no Novotels at all. ✓**INTERNET**→*url* http://www.novotel.com/welcome/

Radisson Hotels Radisson offers its online services in four languages: English, Francais, Espanol, and Deutsch. Choose from a variety of options from all the latest company press releases ("Hot Stuff") to travel tips for business travelers and vacationers, and make reservations for most Radisson properties worldwide. ✓**INTERNET**→*url* http://www2.pcy.mci.net/marketplace/radisson/

Westin Hotels and Resorts Read about the company's current special promotions and download snazzy brochures about Westin hotels around the world. ✓**INTERNET**→*url* http://www2.pcy.mci.net/marketplace/radisson/

U.S. info

Bed & Breakfast Guide Increasingly, travelers are opting for a more intimate hotel experience, especially frequent business travelers, who are turning to B&Bs for a little R&R. This guide lists more than 1,000 B&Bs in the U.S. and Canada and links to 108 B&B reservations agents with over 11,000 guest homes on file. Reasonable rates remain a priority for the compilers of this service. ✓**AMERICA ONLINE**→*keyword* b&b ✓**EWORLD**→*go* b&b

Bed & Breakfast Inns of North America Cimarron Technology has designed a home page as quaint as its advertised properties. Step off the information superhighway to the two-lane dirt roads that run by the featured guest houses, B&Bs, and country inns located throughout North America. Besides a full description and a listing of the "distinctive features" of each property, you'll be treated to color photos of each establishment. ✓**INTERNET**→http://cimarron.metronet.com/

GENinc Bed and Breakfast Inns: USA Descriptions and price information for a handful of B&Bs in California, Idaho, and Oregon. ✓**INTERNET**→*url* http://www.terminus.com/geni/b_and_b/index.html

Go Native! Guide to B&B Inns Sacramento-based Go Native! lists B&Bs throughout the 50 states and offers an entertaining traveler's journal, which posts inn-related travel stories to accompany the site's listing of over 8,000 properties. While most listings give only an address and telephone number, a "National Featured Inn of the Week" provides photo and text essays that describe the architecture and history of a spotlighted B&B. ✓**INTERNET**→*url* http://www.nbn.com/travel/

Inn and Lodging Forum Find out if that picturesque little inn in Maine really lives up to the description in its brochure or if it actually has soggy toast and even soggier mattresses. Both inveterate travelers and B&B proprietors use the message board at this forum to exchange advice on inn-related issues ranging from access for the disabled to the best B&B in Bloomsbury. The inn industry makes its presence known in the library of this forum—companies like Homewood Suites and Embassy Suites post information on their accommodations. ✓**COMPUSERVE**→*go* lodging

InnRoads Brought to you by the editors of America's Wonderful Little Hotels & Inns, InnRoads offers everything from the 15 commandments of vacation travel("#1: know yourself") to extensive national listings with personal testimonial ("Our favorite rooms come with private hot tubs.") to the inngoers' bill of rights (right #1: "the right to fair value"). And if you think you're the only one who's had a disappointing inn stay, check out the *InnRoads* newsletter's pet peeve section ("breakfast was preceded by a lengthy prayer"). ✓**INTERNET**→*url* http://www.on-the-net .com/inns/

Internet Guide to Bed & Breakfast Inns Listing thousands of properties coast to coast, this site is a definitive guide to B&Bs in America. With listings including details like number of rooms, languages spoken, nearest activities, and credit card policies, the Guide makes it easier to find the perfect B&B at your destination. Multiple search strings allow you to search for a B&B by any desired criteria. You'll get telephone numbers for all inns listed here. ✓**INTERNET**→*url* http://www

Amsterdam's Kaatje bij de Sluis—http://www.calvacom.fr/relais/accueil.html

.traveldata.com/biz/inns/

National Hotel Directory An online database available for downloading to your computer, First Look is a hotel directory with information on 1,100 properties in 25 major U.S. cities. While the listings are not as detailed as those at some other Websites, the Directory has its advantages—if you're looking to hold or arrange a business function, handy meeting-space listings will aid you in your search. ✓**INTERNET**→*url* http://www.evmedia.com/

Serenity Bed & Breakfast Inns and Country Inns Why not just skip those endless highway motels and head for something more unique? Serenity promises bed, breakfast, and a whole lot more (pillow?), at prices that are often lower than commercial hotels or destination resorts. Browse a list of elegant and romantic hideaways throughout the 50 states. However, you'll have to call the phone numbers here for brochures or to make reservations—the site is database only. ✓**INTERNET**→*url* http://www.pinon.com/serenity/index.html

The Condo and Villa Authority Specializing in condos, apartments, private homes, and villas, the CVA offers unmatched privacy in its numerous properties, often times including a maid staff, cook, and gardener. The site only whets the appetite with its few color photos and telephone numbers for each lodging. ✓**INTERNET**→*url* http://www.travelsource.com/villa/CVA.html

The Inn Traveler Just click on a state and you'll be rewarded with information on inns that belong to the Professional Association of Innkeepers International. The inclusion of innkeepers' names is a nice, homey feature. ✓**INTERNET**→*url* http://www.biddeford.com/inntravel/

The TravelASSIST Directory of Bed & Breakfasts, Inns, and Small Hotels This registry offers pictures, descriptions, and pics for hundreds of B&Bs nationwide. The listing is organized by geographical area—New England, Midwest, Rocky Mountain, etc. There are also listings for B&Bs in England, France, and Mexico. ✓**INTERNET**→*url* http://travelassist.com/reg/reg_home.html

Travel Guide Online (B&Bs) Heading for Versailles, Kentucky? There are four B&Bs that will put you up for the night. This list provides the name, address, and phone number for B&B options in your destination area. The guide covers locations nationwide, from Alabama to Wyoming, from New York City to Los Angeles. ✓**INTERNET**→*url* http://www.nbn.com/travel/

International info

AA Accommodations (UK) The British Automobile Club maintains this extensive database of hotels, guest houses, inns, farmhouse accommodations, and camping and caravan sites in Britain and Ireland. Each entry is based on an actual visit to the site and attempts to capture the flavor of the place, down to descriptions of antique fireplaces and the specials of the house kitchen. Hygienically tetchy Americans will be happy to learn that special "services" like showers and in-room baths are noted. You can search the entries by type of accommodation, city, postal code, or price range. If you wish to reserve a room at one of the locations, call the telephone numbers listed at the site. ✓**COMPUSERVE**→*go* ukaccomm

ABC Worldwide Hotel Guide If you're looking for a hotel in Ulan Bator, Mongolia, this is a good site to begin your search. This large database (7,000 listings) of accommodations worldwide can be searched by country, city, or hotel name. While no price information is included, other useful tidbits for travelers are noted in each entry, including a general description of hotel services, its neighborhood, its distance from the local airport and bus station, and "type of clientele" known to stay in the hotel. ✓**COMPUSERVE**→*go* abc

All the Hotels on the Web A mammoth network of individual pages and links that, if you're able to get past the busy home page, has its rewards. While hotel information in many countries is limited to national chains—in India, for example, only Holiday Inns and Hyatt are included—properties closer to home (England) are related in their full glory, many with online reservations capabilities. If you're thinking of traveling through Europe, you might want to make this the first stop on your itinerary. ✓**INTERNET**→*url* http://www.digimark.net/dundas/hotels/

American–International Homestays According to this site, homestays are not just for homeboys (and girls). A homestay lets you enjoy the hosts' warmth and hospitality and eat authentic, home-cooked meals. American-International Homestays represents hundreds of homestays worldwide. At the Website you can read up on the company's history and its homestay opportunities and request additional information

Old Drovers Inn, New York, USA—http://www.calvacom.fr/relais/accueil.html

through the mail. How about a little Bukhara & Breakfast? ✓**INTERNET**→*url* http://www.commerce.com/homestays/

B&B Mailing List Archive Alas, the actual mailing list is now defunct, but this archive offers the collected stories of B&B travelers, allowing them to post their experiences and to compare notes with other B&B goers. Besides accounts of various visits across the United States, there is also a section on B&Bs in Estonia, where Alvar gladly relates stories of his visits to Kandimaa-farm. ("Sauna is a 'traditional' mixture of Finnish-Estonian and can be used as well. Yeeaahh!"). ✓**INTERNET**→*url* http://www.cais.com/aevans/bandb/bandb.html

Lanier Travel Guides B&B List A listing of bed-and-breakfasts in the United States, Canada, and the Caribbean, courtesy of Lanier Travel Guides. The site offers information on over 11,000 inns, including their phone numbers and descriptions of their services, the types of meals they serve, accessibility for the handicapped, accommodation for children and pets, and price range. ✓**COMPUSERVE**→*go* inns

Leading Hotels of the World This Chicago marketing organization highlights properties in one country at a time. If $700 room rates in Courchevel are your style ("as luxurious as a palace and as warm as a chalet"), write down the phone numbers and call this service for more information or to make reservations. The site also offers a link to the Hotel Reservation Center. ✓**INTERNET**→*url* http://www.interactive.line.com/alan/lead/

Notable B&B Directories on the Web Brought to you by Internet Concepts and the Professional Association of Innkeepers International, this site is a springboard to begin your online B&B search, offering links to over ten other sites with lists of small-hotel accommodations. Most notable is the Châteaux & Hôtels de Charme, a Belgian marketing outfit that highlights over 200 leading small hotels worldwide, including the illustrious French Château de Fère ("The hotel is carved out of your dreams"). ✓**INTERNET**→*url* http://www.paii.org/paii/directories.html

Prodigy Inn Directory This convenient service allows you to find an inn by location. Selecting domestic or international inns, and then narrowing your search to your destination area, you can access a map that shows all nearby inns available in your desired area. Click on an inn name and get its map coordinates, information on rates, services, child and smoking policies, and a description of the "ambience." The information in this database comes from the innkeepers themselves, so prices should be current, but the descriptions tend toward the picturesque. ✓**PRODIGY**→*jump* inns

Relais & Chateaux *Lifestyles of the Rich and Famous* comes to the Web. This company offers rooms at over 400 luxury "chateaux and country houses" which are listed at the site by locale and theme. Pictures accompany each entry, and you can even check the availability of the queen's (or Duke's or whatever's) suite online. ✓**INTERNET**→*url* http://www.calvacom.fr/relais/accueil.html

Travel Web An online lodging network with databases of hotel chains and independent hotels. Simply plug in your desired destination—say, perhaps, Fiji, Cleveland, or Cancun. You'll then get capsule descriptions of properties, complete with price and amenities info. You can limit your search by type of lodging (B&B, resort, guest ranch, etc.). The site also offers links to other travel sites on the Net, including the Internet Guide to Bed & Breakfast Inns and Club Med. ✓**INTERNET**→*url* http://www.travelweb.com/

Women's Hospitality Exchange International Network (WHEIN) A worldwide network of women offering accommodations to other women. Get more information here. ✓**INTERNET**→*url* http://www.globalx.net/whein/

Resorts

Resorts come in many varities, as do tired tourists seeking serenity or the perfect suntan. Envision yourself drinking Mai Tais in a hammock by the sea? Then perhaps the **Ciboney** in Jamaica or **Crystal Sands** on the Gulf of Mexico is the place for you. If pondering the crashing surf on a rockbound coast or contemplating in the quiet of a silent forest is more to your liking, **BALSAMS Wilderness Grand Resort Hotel** in New Hampshire or **The Algonquin** on the Bay of Fundy in Canada are awaitng your arrival. If you are one of those tedious types that insist on vacationing in paradise, there's always **Swept Away Resort** in Negril and **Kiahuna Plantation** in Hawaii. Follow the other sheep to **Club Med**'s page or get away from the crowd at **Exotic Resorts**.

Wish you were here—from http://www.clubmed.com/cm/pages/home page

On the Net

U.S. info

BALSAMS Wilderness Grand Resort Hotel While not a romantic New England Marge and Cal escape, BALSAMS offers virtually unparalleled seclusion with its 15,000 private acres high in New Hampshire's White Mountains. Call the legendary Dixville Notch property via their toll-free phone numbers. ✓**INTERNET**→*url* http://www.shore.net/~rvbooth/balsams.html

Beachwalker Rentals, Inc Everything you need to know about planning your Kiawah Island, South Carolina, vacation is included in this visually appealing site. And feel free to bring along the kids for Kamp Kiawah at the Night Heron Park Complex. ✓**INTERNET**→*url* http://www.aesir.com/Beachwalker/Welcome.html

C.D.I. Vacation Guide, Main Directory The C.D.I. Vacation Guide lists select condominiums, homes, hotels, and lodges in California, Colorado, Nevada, and Mexico. While listings are few, a standout in any directory would be Joie de Vivre Hotels, with eight unique properties located throughout the San Francisco area. ✓**INTERNET**→*url* http://www.cdiguide.com/cdi/cdihome.html

Crystal Sands Fronting the Gulf of Mexico, Crystal Sands offers a full array of modern amenities through its combination of suites fronting the Gulf of Mexico and individual one- and two-bedroom villas flanking the attractive palm-lined drive. ✓**INTERNET**→*url* http://www.sarasota-online.com/s_crys.html

Enclave Suites at Orlando An all-suite property in Disney country offers an online brochure. ✓**INTERNET**→*url* http://www.prov.com/enclave.html

Hale Hamoa Beach House Rent the Hale Hamoa House or any one of a number of lovely Maui vacation properties. Email for details. ✓**INTERNET**→*url* http://www.best.com/~travel/h-hamoa.html

Key West Reservation Service An online travel agent service helps you find accommodations in resorts or guesthouses at the southernmost point in the continental United States, only 90 miles from Fidel and Cuba. ✓**INTERNET**→*url* http://www.travelbase.com/destinations/keywest/key-west-reservations/

Kiahuna Plantation *Ekomo mai.* Welcome to a property of plantation-style condominium units on sunny Poipu Beach. Online booking capabilities. ✓**INTERNET**→*url* http://www.sierra.net/village/poipu.html

Kona Condo on the Big Island, Hawaii Owner Jim Speier offers his one-bedroom hideaway in Kailua Kona, Hawaii, for rental. ✓**INTERNET**→*url* http://www.widdl.com/Hawaii/Kona/condo.html

Ocean Pointe Suites at Key Largo Download color images of these reasonable vacation properties located on the northernmost Florida Key. ✓**INTERNET**→*url* http://www.prov.com/op.html

Sailport Resort on Tampa Bay Experience Florida's Gulf Coast by staying at this modern vacation property offering one- and two-bedroom suites for long-term rental. ✓**INTERNET**→*url* http://www.prov.com/sailport.html

Sam's Town Casino Sam's Town Casino, the first riverboat casino in Kansas City, premieres a 28,000-square-foot casino on three decks, with over 1,000 slots and 48 table games. ✓**INTERNET**→*url* http://www.vegas.com/hotels/samstown/kansascity/

Samoset Resort Samoset is located on 230 oceanside acres in the beautiful and rugged midcoast area of Maine and has offered spectacular views of Penobscot Bay since 1889. ✓**INTERNET**→*url* http://www.sourcemaine.com/samoset/

Schlitterbahn Waterpark & Resorts There's nothing quite like satisfying your tube-chute fetish at the Schlitterbahn, Texas's largest waterpark. Whatever you do, don't skip the Dragon Blaster. ✓**INTERNET**→*url* http://www.schlitterbahn.com/

The Algonquin One of its early promoters praised its "salubrious and healthful climate." The property embraces picturesque Passamaquoddy Bay on the Atlantic Ocean's Bay of Fundy, just a short drive from Maine's U.S.-Canadian border. Visit the beautiful, historical St. Andrew's-by-the-Sea. ✓**INTERNET**→*url* http://www.cygnus.nb.ca/travel/algpg1.html

The Vacation Shoppe With more than 20 resorts from which to choose, The Vacation Shoppe primarily concentrates on Florida's southwest vacation destinations, including Sanibel Island, Captiva Island, Estero Island, and Bonita Beach. ✓**INTERNET**→*url* http://www.gate.net/~shoppe/

Vail, Colorado Oy Vail! The posh Vail Valley has an equally lavish and impressive Website featuring everything from lodging, dining, and ski conditions to area businesses and available real estate opportunities. ✓**INTERNET**→*url* http://vail.net

Villa Vosilla Tannersville, New York, never seemed such an exciting place. The mountain resort "with the Personal Touch," Villa Vosilla offers an elegant nightclub, live music, shows, dining, and dancing to complement its quality accommodations. ✓**INTERNET**→*url* http://www.interstar.com/advert/vvosila.html

Walt Disney World Resorts and Theme Parks From Disney-MGM Studios to EPCOT to the Magic Kingdom, all the different areas of Disney World are represented here with color pictures and descriptions of the various rides. ✓**INTERNET**→*url* http://www.travelweb.com/thisco/wdw/wdwhome/wdw.html

Wild Dunes Resort With photographs of this South Carolinian resort, it's easy to see why *Golf Digest* has called The Links course, one of the two courses at Wild Dunes, "the ultimate in seaside golf in America." If only you'd bought that pair of shoes and practiced more during those college days. ✓**INTERNET**→*url* http://www.persimmon.com/WildDunes/

International info

108 Resort Located just over five hours northeast of Vancouver, British Columbia, 108 Resort offers 63 rooms in a remote mountain setting close to a most-prized Canadian animal, the mighty caribou. Email for reservations inquiries. ✓**INTERNET**→*url* http://netshop.net/~100mile/108rst.html

Australian Resorts Established in 1976, Brisbane-based Australian Resorts operates five Queensland Island properties, along the length of the Great Barrier Reef. ✓**INTERNET**→*url* http://peg.apc.org/~austresorts/

Banyan Resort Ready for a good rest after an afternoon drive down from the diving glories of Pennekamp? Try out Banyan Resort, a secret Caribbean hideaway tucked away in the heart of historic Old Town Key West. While Banyan may highlight its historicity, it also accepts email reservations. ✓**INTERNET**→*url* http://www.travelbase.com/destinations/keywest/banyan/

Boscobel Beach Part of the four-property SuperClubs monolith operating throughout Jamaica, Boscobel Beach, like its sister properties, offers plenty of everything. All food, drinks, and activities at this base of bacchanalia for couples, singles, and families are included in the room rate. ✓**INTERNET**→*url* http://www.Intnet.net/SuperClubs/Boscobel.html

Ciboney Located outside Ocho Rios, Ciboney, a Radisson resort, offers everything from Green Mountain Coffee tours to horseback riding. For those looking to tie the knot, reserve a luxurious honeymoon villa—with Roman tub, private swimming pool and whirlpool, personal attendant, and, of course, a fully stocked bar. ✓**INTERNET**→*url* http://www.ciboney.com/Ciboney/

Club Med From the people who pioneered the tropical getaway, the Club Med home page now offers more than a few ways to spend those beads. With online promotional footage and up-to-date weather reports from villages throughout the world (is there ever anything but sun?), Club Med has definitely embraced high tech. ✓**INTERNET**→*url* http://www.clubmed.com/cm/pages/homepage

Couples Resort "Welcome to a place dedicated to a simple idea: romance," announces the Couples home page. Another all-inclusive destination resort, the property offers everything under the Jamaican sun to jumpstart you and your loved one's physical prowess: table tennis, volleyball, and reggae dance classes. Go on—take a couple. ✓**INTERNET**→*url* http://www.intnet.net/Couples/

Dundee Resort Take an online tour of the beautiful Dundee Resort in Breton Woods, Nova Scotia. And for a real treat, book an adventure on the *Elsie*, a 56-foot yawl built in Baddeck by Alexander Graham Bell in 1917 for his son-in-law. ✓**INTERNET**→*url* http://www.chatsubo.com/dundee/home.html

Exotic Resorts Travel Source highlights some of the world's most exclusive international resorts. Don't miss Blackbird Caye Resort, located on a secluded island off the coast of Belize. ✓**INTERNET**→*url* http://www.travelsource.com/exotic/

Golf Los Cabos, Mexico A polished Website from the folks at Koll Company, who operate this upscale golfing mecca on the Mexican peninsula. ✓**INTERNET**→*url* http://www.persimmon.com/koll/

Grand Lido Another of the glorious SuperClubs family, Grand Lido fills the Jamaican resort conglomerate's adult couples' and singles' niche. In other words, leave the kids at home. ✓**INTERNET**→*url* http://www.Intnet.net/SuperClubs/Glido.html

Hotel Plaza Iguana Vacation Club Book reservations online at this Puerto Vallarta hotel and timeshare property. ✓**INTERNET**→*url* http://www.spinners.com/resort/welcome.html

Jamaica, Jamaica The SuperClub with a Jamaican flavor offers rates on a shared basis only, as well as the requisite unlimited bar service and nightly lounge performances. ✓**INTERNET**→*url* http://www.Intnet.net/SuperClubs/Jamjam.html

Markland Coastal Resort, Cape Breton Island The Markland, set on 70 pristine acres on the northern Nova Scotia coast, offers value-oriented, five-to-ten-day rates on their charming beachside cottages. ✓**INTERNET**→*url* http://www.webcom.com/~morandan/markland.html

Nassau Marriott Hit the ball. Hit the beach. Hit the jackpot. Hit the hay. It's all here at the most colorful Marriott under the sun. Old Madame Gites de France would be rolling over in her Loire grave. ✓**INTERNET**→*url* http://www.southwind.net/IMS/nassau/

Swept Away Resort Like the other Jamaican super inclusives, Swept Away offers a lot of bang for the buck. This property, located in Negril, is designed primarily for couples. ✓**INTERNET**→*url* http://www.swept-away.com/Swept/

Whistler Resort In winter or summer, the pristine coastal mountains of British Columbia offer something of interest for the avid outdoors enthusiast. At night, check in to the Whistler Resort, rated the Number One Ski Resort in North America for the fourth consecutive year by *Snow Country* magazine. ✓**INTERNET**→*url* http://www.bendtech.com/tourism/whistlerresort/index.html

Windows on the World Showcasing primarily upscale Mexican hotels, though also the occasional San Diego property or larger chain operation (Club Med), Windows offers attractive Net marketing to smaller luxury properties. If Mexican beach seclusion is your wildest dream, do not pass go before visiting the Hotel Bel-Air Costa Careyes. ✓**INTERNET**→*url* http://www.wotw.com/wow/mexico/resort/resort.html

Air travel

Yes, they lost your suitcase, there was a baby screaming in your ear for 16 hours, and you missed your connection in Auckland, but there's really only one reasonable way to get from Boston to Bali—by air. At least these days you can plot your own route and compare prices thanks to sites like **The Air Traveler's Handbook** and **The Internet Travel Network. Eaasy Sabre** lets you shop for and book tickets right online. If you want to travel, but even proletarian class seems like a stretch, take a look at the **Cheap Tickets FAQ** for insight. **Airlines of the Web** will connect you to people who fly almost anywhere, from LOT Polish Airline to Court Helicopters in South Africa. Finally, the **Information Skyway** will tell you exactly where the bar is located at Pittsburgh International—who could ask for more?

American Airlines—from http://www.amrcorp.com/aa_home/aa_hom.htm

On the Net

Across the board

Healthy Flying A former airline hostess shares her flying tips at this site. Did you know that placing a cup full of steam over the ear will alleviate in-flight auricular pain? And the only sure way to keep a steward from waking you up to ask you if you want a blanket, dinner, air-sickness bag, or peanuts is to wear a sleeping mask with "Do not disturb" printed on it. If you use the tips at this site, the author promises that you'll "look good and feel good as you travel." ✓**INTERNET**→*url* http://www.maui.net/~diana/

Net Traveler Survey Take this air travel survey and you might win a free ticket courtesy of Net Traveler! Plus, you can complain about tiny seats, lost luggage, and the problems with opening those little bags of peanuts. ✓**INTERNET**→*url* http://www.thegroup.net/cic/survey

rec.travel.air Collecting hundreds of messages per week, this newsgroup serves as a travel classified ad board, travel advisor, and travel magazine. Regulars sell their airline tickets, ask for airline recommendations, debate smoking restrictions, and post their inter-flight adventures. ✓**USENET**→rec.travel.air *FAQ:* ✓**INTERNET**→*url* http://www.cis.ohio-state.edu/hypertext/faq/usenet-faqs/bygroup/rec/travel/air

The Air Traveler's Handbook Homepage The Air Traveler's Handbook is the collected knowledge of the folks at rec.travel.air. Eventually there will be an offline version of the Handbook, which will contain four times as much info as the Website. That's hard to imagine when you explore the vast resources available here, which include airline and travel agency contact info, airport layouts, links to online reservation systems, lists of courier agencies and ticket consolidators, hotel info, listings of travel book publishers, and much more designed for those who have terminally itchy feet. ✓**INTERNET**→*url* http://www.cs.cmu.edu/afs/cs/user/mkant/Public/Travel/airfare.html

Airports

The Information Skyway: Commercial Airports on the Internet Navigating this site is somewhat like navigating O'Hare on a snowy day—you have to know the inside track. In this case, you have to know the baggage tag code for the airport you're trying to get info on. Once you determine that KIX represents Kansai International Airport in Japan and BNA stands for Nashville's airport, you click on the appropriate tag and get flight info, airport maps, shopping opportunity info, and sometimes even photographs of the airport you're researching. Use this site to unlock the secrets of the world's biggest airports, including Sheremetyevo-2, Russia's air gateway (and the only airport at this site with a red baggage tag!). ✓**INTERNET**→*url* http://w3.one.net/~flypba/AIRLINES/av.airports.html

---

The Virtual Manchester Airport It has often been said by Brits that nothing becomes Manchester like the leaving of it—discover the escape routes with an online visit to the airport. Flight times, departure and arrival gates, and even a peek in the control tower are accessible here. A link to Virtual Manchester might just convince you to stay in Manchester after all. ✓**INTERNET**→*url* http://www.u-net.com/~swiscot/

Budget tickets

Cheap Tickets FAQ Is there such a thing as a cheap airplane ticket that doesn't involve classifying yourself as air freight? This detailed document explains how to beat price fixing by flying courier or buying through ticket consolidators. Telephone numbers for appropriate agencies are included. ✓**INTERNET**→*url* http://www.cis.ohio-state.edu/hypertext/faq/usenet/travel/air/cheaptickets/top.html

---

Discount Airline Tickets FAQ This site is definitely not about stand-by, courier, or cargo flights, but it does offer information and warnings about charter flights, bucket shops, and airline discounts. Assembled by a travel industry professional, this FAQ can save you from being burned by a fly-by-night ticket discounter. ✓**INTERNET**→*url* http://www.slip.net/~jwithers/indexa.html

Carrier info

800 Airline Numbers Airfares are high enough, so call toll-free! Search these alphabetical lists for numbers of carriers worldwide. Don't worry if you get a busy signal at the first number you try—many of the airlines list up to four numbers! ✓**INTERNET**...→*url* http://www.xmission.com/~aoi/f103.html ...→*url* http://www.princeton.edu/Main/air800.html

---

Airline Codes Ever wonder what all those codes on your ticket mean? Before you do business with travel agents, it may be useful to know that "SM" and 731 are both codes for Aberdeen Airways, or that the airline abbreviation "RV" stands for Reeve Aleutian Airways. ✓**INTERNET**→*url* http://www.xmission.com/~aoi/f100.html

---

Airlines of the Web The fruit of a graduate dissertation on the airline industry, this collection of airline information is the most comprehensive on the Web. The airlines listed here range in size from the small Mount Cook Airways serving only New Zealand to the massive, globe-circling TWA. Links are also provided to cargo carriers, aviation newsgroups, airport pages, frequent flyer information, and car-rental operations. If you're interested in a piece of the airline action, this site even provides a link to airline stock quotes. ✓**INTERNET**→*url* http://haas.berkeley.edu/~seidel/airline.html

Frequent flyers

Frequent Travel Management A promotional page for a company that tracks over 40 frequent flyer programs, which involve over 120 airlines, 50 hotels, and 10 rental-car companies. FTM combines this info in its FTM AirMax software, which allows users to plug their mileage into different programs to see which gives the best benefits per mile. FTM posts price and ordering info for its software at this site. ✓**INTERNET**→*url* http://www.ten-io.com/ftm/

InsideFLYER Magazine If you're one of the estimated 35 million people who participate in frequent flyer programs, you may want to browse the pages of InsideFLYER. It's the only online publication devoted to keeping track of frequent flyer bonus news and updates. Get subscription information and the table of contents of current issues here. ✓**INTERNET**→*url* gopher://gopher.enews.com:2100/11/travel/publications/flyer

Online booking

1-800-LOW AIRFARE A promotional page for a booking agent that promises to quote the lowest airfare and to deliver the ticket the next day anywhere in the continental U.S. This Website offers a short description of its service and an 800 number. ✓**INTERNET**→*url* http://www.interstar.com/avert/airfare.html

Airline Tickets Wholesale Find an online rates-request form here for Travel Discounters, who guarantee to deliver your tickets at 17 to 30 percent off the market price. The offer is only valid for flights within the continental U.S. ✓**INTERNET**→*url* http://www.tagsys.com/Ads/NetSale/

Eaasy Sabre Use Eaasy Sabre to reserve tickets on many different carriers. You will fill out an online questionnaire with some basic information (travel days and times, departure and return city, etc.). Then shop for your fare and choose from several different options—full coach, budget, one way, round trip. Eaasy Sabre will display all itineraries on as many airlines as fit your criteria. If you have a Sabre account, you can purchase your tickets online with a credit card. ✓**AMERICA ONLINE**→*keyword* sabre ✓**COMPUSERVE**→*go* sabre ✓**EWORLD**→*go* sabre ✓**PRODIGY**→*jump* eaasy sabre

Genie Travel Services Submit a fare-request form online for flights worldwide, and Genie will call you back with available rates. ✓**INTERNET**→*url* http://www.genietravel.com/

Internet Travel Network After you register (at no cost), you can search the Apollo reservation system for seats on airlines, and soon for hotel rooms and car rentals. Then, select an online travel agent, and they'll arrange the purchase of the tickets. ✓**INTERNET**→*url* http://www.itn.net/cgi/get?itn/index/

National Center For Educational Travel Just fill in this online questionnaire with some basic information (departure date, departure city, destination city, return date, etc.), and NCET emails you with the lowest rate it can find. Group rates are also available through this service. ✓**INTERNET**→*url* http://www2.ios.com/~ncet/

Official Airline Guide Full lists of all airline flights, schedules, and fares. The service is rather pricey, with access running $10 per hour during off-peak hours and soaring to $28 per hour in the heart of the business day. Still, the resources are impressive: for any route, OAG displays all flights and combinations of flights currently available, along with all possible fares. If your choice is available, you can book it immediately. Hotels and motels can also be reserved through OAG, and the guide offers a number of specialized databases on cruises, skiing, resorts, discount travel, frequent flyer programs, and weather. ✓**COMPUSERVE**→*go* oag

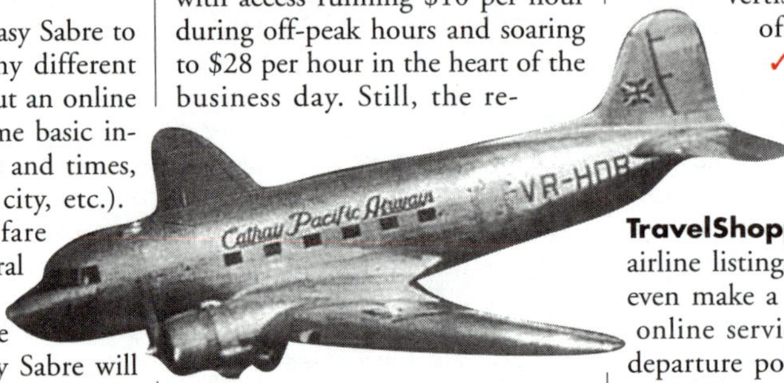

PC Travel Check airline fares and schedules, make reservations, and purchase tickets online with a major credit card (a credit card is required to search fare and schedule information although no charges are incurred unless you buy a ticket). PC Travel will deliver your ticket via overnight FedEx. ✓**INTERNET**→*url* http://www.pctravel.com

The Great Australian Travel Co. You can read about this company's discount airfares to Australia, New Zealand, and the South Pacific (from Europe, Asia, and America), but you'll have to email The Great Australian Travel Co. to confirm the rates listed at this site. ✓**INTERNET**→*url* http://www.magna.com.au/~hideaway/air_ind.html

Travel Gems This no-frills Website lists telephone and fax numbers for this ticket agency that advertises "5 to 10 percent off all airline tickets." ✓**INTERNET**→*url* http://branch.com/gems/gems.html

TravelShopper Browse through airline listings, compare prices, or even make a reservation with this online service. Simply choose a departure point, destination, and travel dates, and TravelShopper will generate a list of all available flights. Then fill out a brief personal profile to determine fare eligibility, select the cheapest flight still remaining, and book your tickets. Because the service is affiliated with TWA and Northwest, you must fly one of those carriers to have the tickets mailed to you directly. Otherwise, your tickets will be mailed to a nearby affiliated travel agent or be waiting for you at the airport. ✓**COMPUSERVE**→*go* worldcim

Other air travel

Space Available Travel on Military Aircraft A "military hop" is not a variation of the Lindy performed in uniform! It's soldier-speak for the free flights available to qualified military personnel on some U.S. Department of Defense aircraft. Also referred to as "Space-A" travel, the rules and regulations for participation are outlined here. ✓**INTERNET**→*url* http://www.ee.umd.edu/medlab/spacea/spacea.html

Carriers Online

Africa

African and Middle Eastern Airlines ✓ INTERNET→*url* http://w3 .one.net/~flypba/AIRLINES/OAL/airlines.africa.me.html

Alliance Airline ✓ INTERNET→*url* http://150.252.25.26/Uganda/Alliance.htm

Chartair ✓ INTERNET→*url* http://www.aztec.co.za/biz/africa/chartair.htm

Court Helicopters ✓ INTERNET→*url* http://os2.iafrica.com:80/travel/safrica/glblserv/court.htm

Kenya Airways ✓ INTERNET→*url* http://150.252.25.26/Uganda/Kenya.htm

South Africa Airlink ✓ INTERNET→*url* http://www.pix.za/business/travel/ztsairln.html

South African Airways ✓ INTERNET→*url* http://www.broflo.com.au/saa.html

Uganda Airlines ✓ INTERNET→*url* http://150.252.25.26/Uganda/Ugacrane.htm

Asia

Air China ✓ INTERNET→*url* http://www.bath.ac.uk/~cescz/china.html

All Nippon Airways ✓ INTERNET ...→*url* http://metrotel.co.uk/travlog/ana.html ...→*url* http://www.fujiint.co.uk/Sumo/ANA_DATA/index-e.html

Asiana Airlines ✓ INTERNET→*url* http://www.asiana.co.kr/

Cathay Pacific ✓ INTERNET→*url* http://www.cathay-usa.com/

China Airlines ✓ INTERNET→*url* http://metrotel.co.uk/travlog/ca.html

Garuda Indonesia City Check-In ✓ INTERNET→*url* http://www.inn.bppt.go.id/commercial/check-in.html

Hang Khong Vietnam ✓ INTERNET→*url* http://qqq.com/vietnam/travel/

Indonesian Airlines ✓ INTERNET→*url* http://www.emp.pdx.edu/htliono/trans.html

Japan Airlines ✓ INTERNET→*url* http://www.spin.ad.jp/jal/home-e.html

Korean Air ✓ INTERNET→*url* http://www.koreanair.com/

Malaysia Airlines ✓ INTERNET ...→*url* http://www.sino.net/asean/malaysia.html#travwtc ...→*url* http://www.cucruising.com/cu/malaysia.html

Sempati Airlines ✓ INTERNET ...→*url* http://ios.com:80/~asianet/Asia_Trade/Travel-leisure/Sin/Preair/Sempati/index.html ...→*url* http://asiadir.com/Travel-leisure/Sin/Preair/Sempati/index.html

Thai International Airways ✓ INTERNET→*url* http://metrotel.co.uk/travlog/thaiair.html

Australia & Oceania

Air New Zealand ✓ INTERNET→*url* http://www.clearfield.co.nz/hotpac/hotpac.htm

Air Pacific ✓ INTERNET→*url* http://www.singapore.com/pata/airpac.htm

Ansett Australia ✓ INTERNET→*url* http://www.ansett.com.au/

Mount Cook Airlines ✓ INTERNET→*url* http://www.clearfield.co.nz/mount_cook/

Qantas Airways ✓ INTERNET→*url* http://www.anzac.com/qantas/qantas.htm

Southern Australia Airlines ✓ INTERNET→*url* http://www.moenet.com.au/~stottd/southern_air.html

Central America

Aero Costa Rica ✓ INTERNET→*url* http://www.centralamerica.com/cr/tran/aero.htm

Travelair ✓ INTERNET→*url* http://www.centralamerica.com/cr/tran/travlair.htm

Europe

Adria ✓ INTERNET→*url* http://www.abm.si/~si21/aa/

Aer Lingus ✓ INTERNET→*url* http://www.hursley.ibm.com:80/aer/

Aeroflot ✓ INTERNET→*url* http://www.seanet.com/Bazar/Aeroflot/Aeroflot.html

Air Atlanta ✓ INTERNET→*url* http://www.centrum.is/atlanta/

AirUK ✓ INTERNET→*url* http://

Carriers Online (cont'd)

HIGHLIGHTS

Air France Bonjour! You can't book an Air France flight through this service, but you can read all about a number of services offered by the airline. Find out exactly which cities Air France services in Europe and beyond; learn which seven U.S. cities are Air France gateways (Indianapolis is one of them); dream about flying in Air France's enormous first-class seats by reading the descriptions of its service classes; choose the frequent flyer deal that's best for you from the list provided here. And of course, you can check on all of Air France's current flights. The carrier's Website is not quite as exciting; click on topics like Reservations and learn that "reservations are required for every flight." The page does offer a few practical tips, e.g., that special meals can be requested up to 24 hours before a flight. More interesting is Air France's second Web page, which offers black-and-white photographs of stars like Alfred Hitchcock and Anouk Aimee aboard Air France flights. ✓COMPUSERVE→ *go* af ✓INTERNET→*url* http://www.airfrance.fr ...→*url* http://cannes.cyber.ad.jp/~cannes/sponsors/airfrance/index2.html

www.airuk.co.uk

Alitalia ✓INTERNET→*url* http://www.zenonet.com/italiatour/fly_drive.html

Austrian Airlines ✓INTERNET→*url* http://www.aua.co.at/aua/

British Airways ✓INTERNET→*url* http://www.biztravel.com/guide/uk/airlines/britair.html

Castle Air ✓INTERNET→*url* http://www.zynet.co.uk:8001/smiles/castleair/"

EasyJet ✓INTERNET→*url* http://205.164.229.4/easyjet

Ernir Airlines ✓INTERNET→*url* http://www.snerpa.is/kynn/e/ernirair/tariff_e.html

Eurowings ✓INTERNET→*url* http://www.eurowings.de/

Finnair ✓INTERNET→*url* http://www.interactive.line.com/finland/finair.home.html

Hely Air ✓INTERNET→*url* http://sun.iccs.acad.bg/privat/23.html

Hemus Air ✓INTERNET→*url* http://sun.iccs.acad.bg/privat/23.html

Iberia Airlines ✓INTERNET→*url* http://www.civeng.carleton.ca/SiSpain/travelli/iberia/menu.html

Icelandair ✓INTERNET→*url* http://www.arctic.is/Transport/Icelandair/Icelandair.html

Interworld Airlines ✓INTERNET→*url* http://www.xs4all.nl/~kvdw/vaindex.html

JetClub ✓INTERNET→*url* http://www.eunet.ch:80/Customers/jetclub/#JetClub

KLM ✓INTERNET→*url* http://www.ib.com:8080/business/klm/klm.html

Lauda Air ✓INTERNET→*url* http://www.laudaair.com/engl/indexe.htm

LOT Polish Airline ✓INTERNET→*url* http://info.fuw.edu.pl/pl/LOT-schedule.txt

Lufthansa ✓INTERNET→*url* http://www.tkz.fh-rpl.de/tii/lh/lhflug-e.html

Malmö Aviation ✓INTERNET→*url* http://www.wineasy.se/maviation/

SwissAir ✓INTERNET ...→*url* http://www.swissair.ch ...→*url* http://www.ehi.com/travel/ehi/swiss.html

Tarom Romanian Air ✓INTERNET→*url* http://www.niyp.com/cgi/nyp_details.cgi?2;1660359;1660360;1660361

Tigerfly ✓INTERNET→*url* http://ayla.avnet.co.uk:80/tigerfly/

Transwede Airlines ✓INTERNET→*url* http://www.transwede.se

Virgin Atlantic ✓INTERNET→*url* http://www.fly.virgin.com/atlantic/

Middle East

Emirates ✓INTERNET→*url* http://www.onu.edu/~mparham/uae/emirates/emir.html

Saudia ✓INTERNET→*url* http://ee.wpi.edu/~zakharia/saudi-communications.html

U.S. & Canada

Air Canada ✓INTERNET→*url* http://www.aircanada.ca/ ✓COM-

Carriers Online (cont'd)

PUSERVE→*go* aircanada

Alaska Airlines ✓INTERNET→*url* http://www.metronet.com/~olesen/tree.html#AS

America West Airlines ✓INTERNET→*url* http://www.cucruising.com/cu/amwest.html

HIGHLIGHTS

American Airlines You might visit this site just to see its amazing opening graphic—it puts you right behind the wing of an AA jumbo jet. But there's tons of information here too, starting with a full schedule of AA flights (including in-flight movie listings!). You'll also get a list of all U.S. AA ticket offices and toll-free reservations numbers to use around the world. If you're wondering whether the steward will let you check that overstuffed suitcase, look here for baggage restrictions (sorry, no one piece can exceed 70 lbs.). In addition, you can also read about AA's Air Travel Card, which functions much like a credit card, allowing users to bill flight expenses to their card number. ✓INTERNET→*url* http://www.amrcorp.com/aa_home/aa_home.htm

American Trans Air ✓INTERNET→*url* http://www.xmission.com/~aoi/fata.html

AMR ✓INTERNET→*url* http://www.amrcorp.com/

Canada 3000 Airlines ✓INTERNET ...→*url* http://vanbc.wimsey.com/~gordona/cmm.html ...→*url* http://www.cucruising.com/cu/canada3.html

Canadian Airlines ✓INTERNET→*url* http://www.CdnAir.CA/

Canadian Airlines International ✓INTERNET→*url* http://www.cucruising.com/cu/cp.html

Carnival Airlines ✓INTERNET→*url* http://www.carnivalair.com/

Continental Airlines ✓INTERNET→*url* http://www.cucruising.com/cu/contin.html

Delta Air Lines ✓INTERNET→*url* http://www.com-stock.com/dave/delta.htm

Eastwind Airlines ✓INTERNET→*url* http://www.prodworks.com/trenton/travel.htm

Frontier Airlines ✓INTERNET ...→*url* http://www.cuug.ab.ca:8001/~busew/frontier.html ...→*url* http://www.cucruising.com/cu/frontier.html

Mexicana Airlines ✓INTERNET→*url* http://www.mexicana.com/index.html

Midwest Express ✓INTERNET→*url* http://www.cwru.edu/Cleve/hopkins/midwest.html

Northwest Airlines ✓INTERNET→*url* http://www.winternet.com/~tela/nwa-info.html

Presidential Airlines ✓INTERNET ...→*url* http://www.presair.com/ ...→*url* http://www.cucruising.com/cu/presair.html

Reno Air ✓INTERNET→*url* http://www.sierra.net/renoair.com/

Southwest Airlines ✓INTERNET→*url* http://www.iflyswa.com/

Sunjet International ✓INTERNET→*url* http://www.cucruising.com/cu/sunjet.html

Taesa ✓INTERNET→*url* http://www.wotw.com/wow/mexico/city/taesa.html

TWA ✓INTERNET→*url* http://www.inlink.com/~jack/twa.html

HIGHLIGHTS

United Connection United Airlines' site provides flight availability information and online booking—and as an added lure—online sign-up for frequent flyer miles. Research your flight either by time and date or choose the Fare Shopper Path and find the cheapest way to go. The trip planning option also offers car and hotel availability for your destination city. A personal travel profile remains on file for future travel plans. Online real-time assistance ensures that you don't book yourself to Botswana instead of Boise. ✓COMPUSERVE→*go* united

ValuJet ✓INTERNET→*url* http://www.cucruising.com/cu/valujet.html

Vanguard Airlines ✓INTERNET→*url* http://www.cucruising.com/cu/vanguard.html

Western Pacific Airlines ✓INTERNET→*url* http://www.cucruising.com/cu/wpair.html

Car rental

You booked the airline or rail tickets, and now you're finally at your destination— a seedy old station in downtown Orlando, miles and miles away from Disneyworld. What should you have done? Booked a car on the Net in advance, of course. The biggies are here—**Budget**, **Alamo**, **Hertz**, and for those on a budget, **Rent-a-Wreck**. If you're heading to Geneva, **Elite** will be happy to provide you with a Mercedes to take you to your four-star meal. And if you're in Hawaii, get a Range Rover from **Maui Car Rentals** and head for the hills.

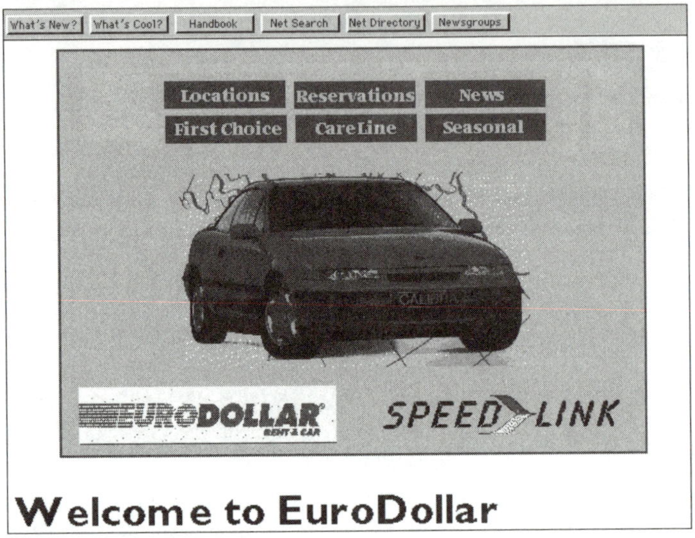

EuroDollar's home page— http: //www.eurodollar.co.uk/

On the Net

Across the board

Car Rental Guide A valuable checklist of questions to ask when renting a car (make sure to ask about blackout days for any special rates you're trying to get). The list of acronyms here will help you decipher exactly what your car agency is charging you for—PAI stands for personal accident insurance. ✓**INTERNET**→*url* http://tsw.ingress.com/tsw/talf/ftc/10.html

Eaasy Sabre Car Rental Fill out an online reservations form (have your pick-up and drop-off locations and times handy), and reserve cars worldwide from companies like Enterprise, National Sears, and Eurodollar, among others. ✓**AMERICA ONLINE**→*keyword* sabre ✓**COMPUSERVE**→*go* sabre ✓**EWORLD**→*go* sabre ✓**PRODIGY**→*jump* eaasy sabre

U.S. national

Alamo Alamo's Website offers information on everything from baby-seat rental to paying for your rental car with cash. But to actually book online, you'll have to visit the company's site on CompuServe. You'll fill out a questionnaire by entering your pick-up time and location, desired model, and other standard information, and your guaranteed reservation will be complete within minutes. After reserving your car, check into the site's Travel Tips and Car Games for Kids sections to help make your trip smoother. ✓**INTERNET**→*url* http://www.freeways.com/bookit/rules.html ✓**COMPUSERVE**→*go* al

Budget Although this site is not yet fully operational, Budget has reserved its space on the Net for booking a car online. ✓**INTERNET**→*url* http://www.infi.net/~budget/

Car Rental List This is a no-frills list compiled by a private citizen. It collects the names and phone numbers of hundreds of American car-rental agencies from Agency Rent-a-Car to Hertz to Sears Rent-a-Car. ✓**INTERNET**→*url* http://www.creativedir.com/html/106.html

Rent-a-Wreck This site features contact information for the company's 400 U.S. and 8 international locations. Also find a direct link to the online Weather Channel. ✓**INTERNET**→*url* http://www.charm.net:80/~ken/

U.S. regional

Alaska Destinations & Adventures Fill out an online form with standard info (like desired car make, price range, age of driver, etc.) and send it to this service which will locate a rental agency in Alaska. ✓**INTERNET**→*url* http://www.alaskan.com/promos/rentalcar.html

American Discount Rent a Car If you want to tour the great Northeastern United States, call American Discount to rent an automobile, truck, or cargo van. ✓**INTERNET**→*url* http://www.channel1.com/users/adrc/

Austin Car Rental Companies A helpful guide to renting a car in Austin. This site lists major car rental companies, like Avis, Alamo, and National Car Rental, with offices in the Austin area. ✓**INTERNET**→*url* http://www.tab.com/Travel/Austin/Austin.carrent.html

Florida Auto Rental Tour the Sunshine State in a convertible or sedan from this agency which operates in the Fort Lauderdale, Miami, West Palm Beach, and Orlando areas. ✓**INTERNET**→*url* http://www.introweb.com/fl/

Hawaiian Car Rentals A promotional page for car rentals on selected Hawaiian islands. ✓**INTERNET**→*url* http://hisurf.aloha.com/travel/Car.html

Maui Car Rentals This Hawaiian company advertises "special Internet rates," so don't forget to tell them you're a Netter when calling for a rates quote or reservation. ✓**INTERNET**→*url* http://www.mauiweb.com/travel/autos/

Orlando Area Car Rental Services A searchable database of car agencies in Orlando. Enter the name of the desired agency and get its local telephone number. Or scan the entire list to pick a company. ✓**INTERNET**→*url* http://www.travelbase.com/destinations/orlando/orlando_car_rental_search.html

Pinellas An advertisement for a Tampa Bay area agency. Telephone numbers and a short description of its services are available here. ✓**INTERNET**→*url* http://www.gate.net/~jbesedic/pages/pinellas.htm

Savon Car Rental A Los Angeles-based service with six offices in the L.A. area. Call them to rent full-size and luxury cars, passenger vans, 4 x 4s, and convertibles. ✓**INTERNET**→*url* http://www.ernestallen.com/TR/CA/SavonRent-A-Car/

Seattle Yellow Pages Listing A listing of Seattle car-rental companies—the online version of the Yellow Pages phone book listings. ✓**INTERNET**→*url* http://www.seattle.net/yellow/yautorent.html

Value Rent-a-Car An agency covering rentals in the Sunshine State. Make a reservation online, and then head to the land of oranges. ✓**INTERNET**→*url* http://www.neptune.com/value/value.html

Washington D.C. Budget Rental The clickable map at this site shows you the location of all Budget offices in the Washington D.C. metropolitan area and lists their phone numbers and addresses. ✓**INTERNET**→*url* http://www.globescope.com/web/budget/

International

Abel Rentals Contact information for rental companies in Queensland, Australia. ✓**INTERNET**→*url* http://peg.apc.org/~squirrel/abel.html

AutoRent AutoRent offers 10 rental offices strategically located throughout Israel. Click on the links here to learn AutoRent's terms, rates, and locations. AutoRent offers cellular phone service in its rentals. ✓**INTERNET**→*url* http://www.macom.co.il/Tourism/AutoRent/index.html

Elegante The next time you're in Costa Rica, you can rent a car from one of Elegante's nine offices nationwide. You'll find an illustrated catalog of its car fleet, rates information, and toll-free telephone numbers for Elegante here. ✓**INTERNET**→*url* http://www.infoserve.net/dynamic/elegante.home.html

Elite A Geneva-based company with five offices in Switzerland and one in Southern France. It advertises a large selection of cars and free drop-off service anywhere you need it. Email, phone, or fax a rates request or reservation. ✓**INTERNET**→*url* http://is.eunet.ch/GenevaGuide/elite/elite1.html

Eurodollar Pick up a Lincoln in Liverpool or a Mercedes in Manchester by reserving a car from this agency that serves all of England and Wales. Telephone numbers and addresses for its offices are listed here. ✓**INTERNET**→*url* http://www.eurodollar.co.uk/

Hertz Asia Email addresses, phone and fax numbers, addresses, and office hours for a number of Hertz car agencies in India, Indonesia, Korea, the Philippines, Malaysia, Singapore, and Thailand. ✓**INTERNET**→*url* http://www.singapore.com/companies/hertz/

Trains & subways

Is there anything more embarrassing than finding out that you're on the A-train going uptown when you're trying to get to Christopher Street? Or when you can't remember if that club in Berlin is near the Adenauerplatz or Attilastraße? **Subway Navigator** will save the day by providing metro info for cities worldwide. **European Rail Information** will ensure that you never get that sinking feeling that occurs when you've misread the schedule and suddenly the train is crossing the Albanian border. Try the **Amtrak's Station on the World Wide Web** to find out when, and if, trains to Mobile will be leaving Penn Station.

On the Net

Across the board

misc.transport.urban-transit There's plenty of transit talk from around the world here. Should subways be bilingual? (They are in Brussels, Montreal, and New York.) "What's the new light rail line in Denver like?" "Fast and smooth" replies Michael—"try it!" A wide range of issues are discussed, including fare increases (which everyone agrees to oppose), crime, and new rail system routes . Read the postings from New York and Chicago—they might improve your appreciation of the system in your city. ✓ **USENET**→misc .transport.urban-transit

U.S. info

Amtrak's Station on the World Wide Web Everything Amtrak is here, from routes and schedules to a company history to travel tips. Which trains have space for storing automobiles? Can you take your pet iguana on the train? Stop here for the answers. All aboard! ✓ **INTERNET**→*url* http://www.amtrak.com/

Commuter Rail Schedules in the U.S. and Canada Need to know how long it will take to get to your co-worker's suburban wedding? To the shopping mall in Jersey City when you're in Montclair? From the Alaska Railroad to Connecticut's Shore Line, you can download maps (which include connections to Amtrak and Via Rail) and view schedules and fares for commuter rail lines in over 20 major cities. ✓ **INTERNET**→*url* http://www.libertynet.org/~dvarp /other.html

Railroad Related Internet Resources Reach pages about city subways and Amtrak schedules plus rail travel newsgroups. For those planning a European trip, the link to train schedules in cities across the Atlantic is especially useful. ✓ **INTERNET**→*url* http://www cse.ucsd.edu/users/bowdidge /railroad/rail-home.html

International info

European Rail Information Traveling through Europe via rail is a more viable option than in the U.S. or Canada. An eight hour trip from London (including Channel crossing) can take you through England, France, Belgium, The Netherlands, and Germany; the same time on Amtrak would barely get you through the Virginias. Travel package information, EuroStar and Le Shuttle schedules for Channel crossings, excursions, and Eurailpass rates are available here. ✓ **INTERNET**→*url* http://www.eurorail.com/

Subway Navigator Info on subway and tram lines in cities in four continents is listed at this Website. It features a function that allows you to calculate the most direct connects between points in your destination city. Enter the name of the station you're leaving and the one you're trying to reach, and then click. Like magic, the navigator plots the route (including transfers) and gives an estimated trip time and map where available. ✓ **INTERNET**→*url* http://metro .jussieu.fr: 10001/bin/cities/english

TrainsEuropean Railway Schedules Isn't train travel romantic? In Europe, riding the rails can often save time and multiply your destination options. Deutsche Bahn AG and CompuServe have joined forces to provide this extensive booking and browsing service for European railways. Learn about all available trains, their services (sleeper car, dinettes), and prices. Consult the station appendix to find out if you can rent a car, or at the very least expect a fleet of taxis, when you arrive. At this time you can only book if your travel plans include Germany, but schedule information is transnational. ✓ **COMPUSERVE**→*go* railway

Visas & embassies

Find out what you shouldn't leave home without (other than a credit card) at Visa, Passport and Entry Requirements, or **The Electronic Embassy.** The **U.S. State Department Travel Warnings and Information Sheets** have a few terse words to say on every nation—"frequent clashes with guerrilla forces" or "we will not guarantee traveler's safety" are two pretty clear warning signs that you ought to make another vacation choice. Save yourself several hours of standing on line for "emergency" services in New York, Toledo, or Atlanta by checking first at **U.S. Passport Info** which will tell you where and when to get one with ease. If you still can't face the bureaucracy, **Visa Advisors** will take care of all the red tape, at least all the red tape Uncle Sam serves up (when in Bulgaria, you're on your own).

Department of State, Washington, D.C.—http://dosfan.lib.uic.edu/DOStour.html

On the Net

Across the board

The Electronic Embassy For travelers the E-Embassy provides official consular information on passports and visas, travel advisories, and import regulations. Visit the press offices and cultural attaché links for information on special events at your travel destination. ✓**INTERNET**→*url* http://www.embassy.org/

The Embassy Page This is the official connection for a number of consulates and embassies in the U.S. and the best place to start visa research. Visit the Australian Embassy via the Web and learn about Aussie visa and customs requirements. The Indian Embassy page gives the details on entering the country and even offers up news and travel stories to entice you to visit. ✓**INTERNET**→*url* http://www.finnemb.nw.dc.us/web/gsis/embpage.html

U.S. Passport Info Learn all about the U.S. passport—who's eligible, where to apply for one in person, how much it costs, what to do if your passport is stolen, etc. ✓**PRODIGY**→*jump* passport

U. S. State Department Travel Warnings and Information Sheets Everyone who carries a U.S. passport should check here before planning a trip to Tripoli. Find your destination on the alphabetical list of countries and click for travel advisories, entrance requirements, and a map of the region. ✓**INTERNET**→*url* http://www.stolaf.edu/network/travel-advisories.html/ ✓**COMPUSERVE**→*go* State

Visa Advisors A site sponsored by a visa and passport processing service in Washington, D.C., which helps (for a fee) travelers get their paperwork in order with haste and without hassle. For the general traveling public, the site's database provides tips on international travel requirements—for a Moldovan visa contact the embassy in D.C. or Moscow; if you're only going to stay in Macau a few days, you can get a visa upon your arrival. ✓**COMPUSERVE**→*go* visa

Visa, Passport, and Entry Requirements This collection of links serves many needs. Head to The Embassy Page for the official word on any travel advisories from your destination country. Another site details entry requirements for several countries—one, which shall remain nameless, requires U.S. citizens to be tested for the AIDS virus before an extended stay. Or link to the State Department's gopher and learn how to obtain a passport. ✓**INTERNET**→ http://gnn.com/gnn/meta/travel/res/visa.html

Maps & reference

Tired of saying "I'm terribly sorry, but I don't speak...Spanish / Estonian / Finnish?" Try an online dictionary like **Jeffrey's Japanese-English Dictionary Server**. Wonder if your laptop will work when you plug it into a socket in Brussels? Check the **World Electric Power Guide**. Uncertain of whether you should pay for dinner for your hosts in Djakarta? Head to the online sensitivity training offered by the **Web of Culture**. Is that cute little dress in a shop in Montmartre really such a bargain? Double check with the **Universal Currency Converter**. **The National Holidays** site will tell you if you should pack your finery for May 9th in Moscow, and **How Far Is It**? is all you need to forestall the most annoying of all travel questions "Are we there yet?"

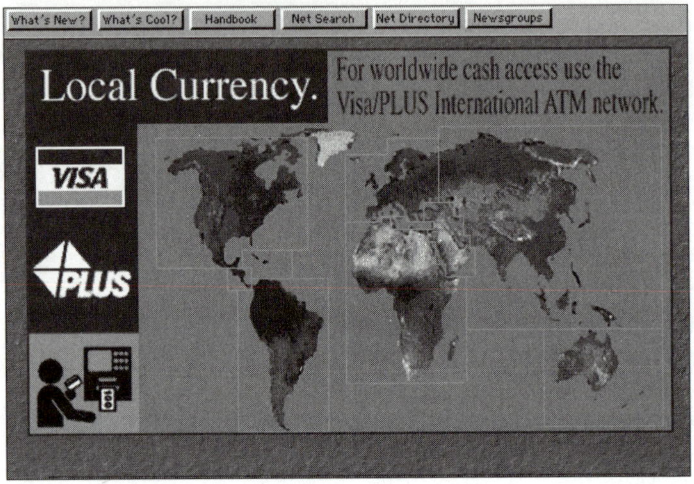

Find out where the money is—http://www.visa.com/visa/locator/atm_region.html

On the Net

Calendars

National Holidays A text listing of national holidays worldwide—days it may be difficult to exchange currency or days when your trip across Manhattan might be interrupted by a parade. February 16th is big in Lithuania, while March 20th is a special day to the people of Tunisia. ✓**INTERNET**→*url* http://www.sas.upenn.edu/African_Studies/Country_Specific/Holidays.html

Conversions

Conversion Table A site featuring measurement and temperature conversion tables. ✓**INTERNET**→*url* http://sol.acs.uwosh.edu/~wallinp/convert.html

Unit Conversions Enter a mile and convert to centimeters. Enter days and convert to seconds. Enter Celsius and convert to Kelvin. The site supports conversion programs for time, temperature, volume, density, and weight. ✓**INTERNET**→*url* http://eardc.swt.edu/cgi-bin/ucon/ucon.pl

World Electric Power Guide A text guide to the wide world of electricity that outlines current capacities in major cities worldwide. If you're on the way to Paris, make sure you get current and plug adapters, or the visit to the City of Light will be the last one for your CD player. ✓**INTERNET**→*url* http://www.cris.com/~kropla/electric.htm

Country info

The World Factbook 1994 Country profiles, compiled by the CIA, for every nation on the planet. The site includes geographical, political, economic, and social information about countries ranging from Afghanistan (its infant mortality rate for the year 1994 was 155.8 deaths per 1,000 live births) to Zimbabwe (its government is a parliamentary democracy). A map is linked to each profile, and the site also maintains information on weights and measures conversion, international organizations, the United Nations, and environmental agreements. ✓**INTERNET**→*url* http://www.odci.gov/94fact/fb94toc/fb94toc.html

Web of Culture This site aims to foster greater understanding in this increasingly small world. Choose one of the five cultural awareness quizzes at this page and test your knowledge of cultures around the world with questions like "What is the appropriate wedding gift in the Sudan," and "What is the proper form of address for Taiwanese business colleague Li Tzu-shan?" Links to country resources provide more information on each nation. ✓**INTERNET**→*url* http://www.earthlink.net/~webofculture/

Flags

National Flags Make sure the ship coming up on leeward is under Greek registry rather than Libyan with this handy full color collection of national flags. ✓**INTERNET**→*url* http://155.187.10.12/flags/nation-flags.html

Language guides

Bertelsmann Lexikon A German-language dictionary produced by Bertelsmann Electronic Publishing. Instructions are entirely in German. ✓**COMPUSERVE**→*go* beplexikon

ECHO-Eurodicautom An excellent, albeit excruciatingly slow, site for translating words from one European language to another. The site supports English, French, German, Italian, Spanish, Danish, Dutch, and Portuguese. ✓**INTERNET**→*url* http://www.uni-frankfurt.de/~kurlanda/eurodicautom.html

English-Estonian Dictionary Are you getting love letters written in Estonian by a hyper-secretive (or long distance) admirer? Search this online dictionary for an instant translation. The site also translates from English to Estonian—in case you want to respond. ✓**INTERNET**→*url* http://www.ibs.ee/dict/

English-Slovene Dictionary Search for the Slovene translation of an English word. ✓**INTERNET**→*url* http://www.fer.uni-lj.si/dictionary/a2s.html

English-to-Spanish Dictionary Translates English to Spanish. The dictionary includes translations for approximately 1,300 words. ✓**INTERNET**→*url* http://www.willamette.edu/~tjones/forms/spanish.html

Foreign Languages for Travellers How do you say "Do you accept credit cards?" in a goulash restaurant in Hungary? *Elfogadnak hitelkártyát*, of course. This site helps travelers negotiate in German, French, Italian, Russian, Hungarian, English, Spanish, Portuguese, Dutch, and Polish by offering translations of basic phrases, links to dictionaries, and even sound files. ✓**INTERNET**→*url* http://insti.physics.sunysb.edu/~mmartin/languages/languages.html

French-English Translation Dictionary This site (which includes a Macintosh digest and art galleries), carries a searchable English-French dictionary, a searchable French-English dictionary, and grammar and vocabulary tests for students of French. ✓**INTERNET**→*url* http://mlab-power3.uiah.fi/

German Dictionary Enter a word, or part of a word, and the site responds with a German translation (or an English translation of a German word). ✓**INTERNET**→*url* http://calamity.rz-berlin.mpg.de/eg.html

HyperSurfing English-French Dictionary More helpful than your average English-French dictionary, the site retrieves not only the direct translation of your word or phrase, but also a list of the terminology most commonly related to the topic. ✓**INTERNET**→*url* http://mlab-power3.uiah.fi/EnglishFrench/avenues.html

Jeffrey's Japanese-English Dictionary Server A sophisticated dictionary for English-to-Japanese translations. Although browsers supporting Japanese text are encouraged, Netscape users can view illustrated representations of Japanese characters. ✓**INTERNET**→*url* http://www.wg.omron.co.jp/cgi-bin/j-e

Molfile Place Enter a word in Finnish and get the English translation. ✓**INTERNET**→*url* http://mofile.fi/-db.htm

Nynorskordliste A simple, searchable Norwegian dictionary. ✓**INTERNET**→*url* http://www.nr.no/ordbok/nynorsk?

Russian-English and English-Russian Dictionary Besides offering Cyrillic fonts to download, this site allows users to get the Russian translation of an English keyword, and vice versa. ✓**INTERNET**→*url* http://www.elvis.ru/cgi-bin/mtrans

Spanish-English Dictionary Translates Spanish into English. The dictionary includes translations for approximately 1,300 words. ✓**INTERNET**→*url* http://www.willamette.edu/~tjones/forms/span2eng.html

Thresor de la Langue Françaíse A searchable French thesaurus with more than 18,000 entries. The thesaurus is based on the 1606 edition of Jean Nicot's

Thresor de la Langue Française. ✓**INTERNET**→*url* http://tuna.uchicago.edu/forms_unrest/TLF.html

Maps

Automap Download the program and you are your own cartographer. Plug in any two points in the U.S. and the system comes up with the most direct route between them (not necessarily the most scenic). Print out the result and you're on your way. ✓**E-WORLD**→*go* automap

Geographic Maps Online A thorough index of all the map and geography sites on the Net. ✓**INTERNET**→*url* http://ipl.sils.umich.edu/ref/RR/GEN/Atlas-rr.html

How Far Is It? Plug in two locations in the U.S. and this site calculates the distance between them. How far is it from Springfield, Massachusetts to Manhattan, New York? 116 miles. Mountain View, California to Palo Alto, California? Well, 335 miles if you're heading to the Palo Alto in San Bernadino County, but only 5.04 miles if you're visiting the one in Santa Clara County. ✓**INTERNET**→*url* http://gs213.sp.cs.cmu.edu/prog/dist

Magellan Basic Maps Put your trip into perspective with this collection of maps showing 500 different regions worldwide. A formidable license agreement needs to be read and accepted before accessing the maps, but once done, the whole world is ready to be downloaded. ✓**COMPUSERVE**→*go* Magellan

Perry-Castaneda Library Map Collection One of the largest map collections on the Net, with everything from the maps in National Park Brochures to satellite maps of the planet. The site offers an interesting style of organizing its offerings—maps are grouped together under categories like "Islands, Oceans, Poles," "Maps of Current Interest: Bosnia, Zaire, Gaza, Chechnya," and "Maps of U.S. City Halls and Monuments." ✓**INTERNET**→*url* http://www.lib.utexas.edu/Libs/PCL/Map_Collection/

TIGER Mapping Service & the US Gazetteer This incredible public resource will take the name of any town, county, city, or river in the United States, determine its longitude / latitude, and generate a high-quality, detailed map of the queried location and its surrounding terrain. The maps are downloadable, but again, be prepared to wait—the graphics files are very large. ✓**INTERNET**→*url* http://tiger.census.gov/

USA CityLink Project Detailed maps of America's cities and towns. Information about local municipal services (police stations, government offices) are noted on each. ✓**INTERNET**→*url* http://www.NeoSoft.com:80/citylink/

World Maps High-resolution world and continent maps available for downloading. ✓**INTERNET**→*url* http://www.parc.xerox.com/map/

Money

10AM EST Exchange Rates A list of current exchange rates from the Federal Reserve Bank of New York updated every day at, you guessed it, 10:00 a.m. Eastern Standard Time. ✓**INTERNET**→*url* gopher://una.hh.lib.umich.edu/00/ebb/monetary/tenfx.frb

Exchanging Money—Koblas Currency Converter Select a country (China, for instance) and convert any currency in the world into its equivalent amount in Chinese Yuan. The site can convert the currency of any country into that of any other. Exchange rates are updated weekly. ✓**INTERNET**→*url* http://bin.gnn.com/cgi-bin/gnn/currency

Foreign Exchange Rates This

VIBE's world map—http://www.pathfinder.com/vibe/vibeworld/worldmap.html

site does not allow you to convert specific amounts of cash—it posts the exchange rates and lets you do the math yourself. ✓INTERNET→*url* http://www.dna.lth.se/cgi-bin/kurt/rates/

The Money Abroad FAQ The hows and whys of spending money worldwide are explained here—from the best credit cards to carry in Egypt to the intricacies of the world's darkest black markets. ✓INTERNET→*url* http://www.inria.fr/robotvis/personnel/laveau/money-faq/money-abroad.html

Universal Currency Converter Updated weekday mornings at 10:30 a.m. (Eastern Standard Time), this site will tell you the conversion rate of any amount of currency into another—today a hundred Egyptian Pounds was worth 39.25 Canadian Dollars. ✓INTERNET→*url* http://www.xe.com/xenon/currency.htm

VISA ATM Locations Worldwide Knowing there are 19 automatic teller machines in Brunei might come in handy. Affiliated banks worldwide are represented on an interactive map. ✓INTERNET→*url* http://www.visa.com/visa/locator/atm_region.html

Phones & addresses

Area Code Look-Up Use this database to find the area code of any city in the U.S. ✓INTERNET→*url* gopher://odie.niaid.nih.gov/77/deskref/.areacode/index

Internet Country Codes Have you received an email with "se" at the end of the address and not been sure what country it came from? Refer to this A-Z list of countries and country codes used in Internet addresses. ✓INTERNET→*url* http://www.ics.uci.edu/WebSoft/wwwstat/country-codes.txt

National Address Server Type in the full address, minus the ZIP code, and the site will return a nine-digit ZIP code for any address in the United States. ✓INTERNET→*url* http://www.cedar.buffalo.edu/adserv.html

U.S. Postal Service Address Quality & ZIP Code Locator Besides delivering your snail mail, the U.S. Postal Service will help you send it to the right place with this Website that will give you the zip code of any U.S. city. ✓INTERNET→*url* http://www.usps.gov/ncsc/

Time

Date and Time Click on a country's time zone for the current date and time. ✓INTERNET→*url* http://www.bsdi.com/date?

Local Times Around the World Quick—if it's 6 a.m. in Hobart, Tasmania what time is it in Buenos Aries? (Why 4 p.m. the afternoon before, of course.) Get the current time for major cities worldwide. ✓INTERNET→*url* http://www.hilink.com.au/times/

Timezone Converter Plug in a date, time, and two locales and get the time for each—very useful for flight planning or long distance telephone calling. ✓INTERNET→*url* http://hibp.ecse.rpi.edu/cgi-bin/tzconvert

VIBE's World Map Click on the map for the local time. Connections to Web servers in the area make it easy to visit the Canary Islands or Uppsala, Sweden, even in the middle of the night. ✓INTERNET→*url* http://www.pathfinder.com/vibe/vibeworld/worldmap.html

DETOURS

"French Polynesia:

"Overview: Since 1962, when France stationed military personnel in the region, French Polynesia has changed from a subsistence economy to one in which a high proportion of the work force is either employed by the military or supports the tourist industry. Tourism accounts for about 20% of GDP and is a primary source of hard currency earnings.

National product per capita: $7,000

Inflation rate: 1.7%

Unemployment rate: 10%

Electricity capacity: 75,000 kWh
Electricity production: 275 million kWh
Electricity consumption per capita: 1,189 kWh

Agriculture: coconut and vanilla plantations; vegetables and fruit; poultry, beef

Currency: 1 CFP franc (CFPF) = 100 centimes"

—from **The World Factbook**

Health & safety

Ebola in Africa, cholera in Peru, malaria in the Philippines, Hanta virus in Arizona, Legionnaire's Disease on the high seas, bombs in the Paris subways, and open season on Germans in Florida. It's a dangerous world out there—but don't let that scare you. Just check out the medical news at the **Centers For Disease Control**, and gather healthy eating and drinking and bug spray tips from **Staying Healthy in Asia, Africa, and Latin America** and **Wilderness Health Information.** The **Traveler's Checklist** helps you deal with problems of a non-parasitic type—pickpockets, thieves, and scammers. And well, if worse comes to worse, and you decided to avoid these travel dangers altogether, **Travel World Insurance** will refund your canceled trip.

For all your global emergency medical needs—from http://www.globalmed.com/

On the Net

Across the board

Centers for Disease Control You'll find the blue sheet of cholera warnings, cruise-ship inspection ratings, and up-to-the-minute news on contagious-disease outbreaks. General travel precautions are also included—e.g., boil water in Guatemala. Find out what shots you need for a visit to Vatican City or Djakarta. ✓**INTERNET**→*url* http://www.cdc.gov/travel/travel.html

High Altitude Illness High altitude illness doesn't affect only those trekking in the Himalayas. A visit to Santa Fe, New Mexico, which is 7,000 feet above sea level, can leave some travelers feeling low. This text document clearly explains the causes of the curious illness and gives hints on how to acclimatize and thus avoid it. ✓**INTERNET**→*url* http://www.princeton.edu/~rcurtis/altitude.html

International Travel and Health Be sure to stop here for the official news from the World Health Organization—vaccination requirements, malaria bulletins, and other health hazards classified by region. ✓**INTERNET**→*url* http://www.who.ch/TravelAndHealth/TravelAndHealth_Home.html

International Travelers Clinic The site carries the Medical College of Wisconsin's guide to a healthy vacation. It recommends that travelers pack a medicine kit with antihistamines and topical steroid cream, explains the immunization requirements for different countries, and gives advice on dealing with altitude and motion sickness. True hypochondriacs can check the graphic description of the incubation periods and symptoms of infectious diseases. ✓**INTERNET**→*url* http://www.intmed.mcw.edu/travel.html

Staying Healthy in Asia, Africa, and Latin America This online guide clearly describes preventive measures to be taken before departure and after arrival at destinations in Asia, Africa, and Latin America. See also the extremely important information on how to get medical care in foreign nations. ✓**INTERNET**→*url* http://www.moon.com/staying.healthy/travel.health.html

Tips for Travellers No, don't take the salmon-pink chiffon on the biking trip in the South of France, unless, of course, you're a Grace Kelly wannabe. This handy little guide helps you pick out what to pack and even gives tips on how to get it to fit in the suitcase. ✓**INTERNET**→*url* http://www.webfoot.com/travel/tips/tips.top.html

Travel Safety Some of the information on this list borders on the paranoiac: "Always assume you're being watched," and "Find out what the favorite scams are locally." The list goes on to explain some of the more common (and more entertaining) scams: "Yuppie in distress lost wallet; pregnant woman (pillow) needs bus money; kids surrounding you using cardboard or magazines to block your view; purse snatchers on scooters; drop change or spill food on you so you will put your bags down at airport or train station; cutting open backpacks; sleeping gas in trains or buses; drugged cups and drinks (Asia and Italy); fake porters taking your bags; snare bags under seats with umbrella." ✓**INTERNET**→*url* http://www.solutions.net/rec-travel/general/safety.txt

Traveler's Checklist A list of some good tips on staying safe during your trip. A section of the site especially for women advises, "Aggressive behavior from men is not unusual in certain countries. If you want to be left alone, say so, clearly and emphatically. It also helps to know some key words in the local language." ✓**INTERNET**→*url* http://www.ag.com/Travelers/Checklist/safety

Wilderness Health Information There's more to wilderness health than how to deal with snake bites and bear attacks. Stanford's travel medicine service provides good general advice for all travelers, including what to include in a first-aid kit, how to deal with Montezuma's revenge, and what insect repellents actually repel insects rather than fellow travelers. ✓**INTERNET**→*url* http://www-leland.stanford.edu/~naked/stms.html

Insurance

AAAHawaii For those traveling to the Hawaiian Islands, there is the assurance of insurance provided through this major American car service. ✓**INTERNET**→*url* http://www.at-hawaii.com/aaa/insurance.html

Chatham Insurance Agency A site with descriptions of plans for individuals and families seeking holiday insurance, business travelers, and those planning an extended stay abroad. ✓**INTERNET**→*url* http://kentnet.co.uk/chatham_insurance/travel.htm

Innovative Insurance Travel insurance packages for Canadians traveling outside of Canada. Contact the company with the info listed here. ✓**INTERNET**→*url* http://vaxxine.com/innovative/canadian.html

London Drugs Insurance This insurance agency with the strange name is licensed to sell coverage in the Canadian provinces of Alberta and British Columbia. Learn about three types of insurance plans, including annual coverage that insures you for all trips during the year, single-trip plans, and even a plan for those on their way to Canada for a visit. ✓**INTERNET**→*url* http://www.london-drugs.com/travelin.html

STA Travel USA A low-rate service for students traveling abroad (in case you cut your lip on a beer mug at the Munich Oktoberfest). ✓**INTERNET**→*url* http://www.sta-travel.com/Insurance.html

The Sussex Financial Group A group specializing in insurance for travelers and foreign nationals. They offer a variety of plans—among them are the Patriot International Plan for U.S. citizens traveling abroad and the Patriot America Plan for foreign nationals visiting America. Phone and fax numbers for the company are listed here. ✓**INTERNET**→*url* http://www.ipworld.com/market/finance/sussex/homepage.htm

Travel World Insurance Learn about the diverse plans offered through Travel World at this site, which describes each plan (including basic rates information) and provides contact numbers. Travel World offers medical insurance, car collision insurance, and, best of all, trip-cancellation and lost-baggage coverage. ✓**INTERNET**→*url* http://www.omnitravel.com/007insurance.html

Services

Global Emergency Medical Services Info on Global Emergency Medical Services, an organization that provides medical services worldwide through a network of English-speaking doctors and clinics. ✓**INTERNET**→*url* http://www.globalmed.com/

Weather

When you travel, you think about the destinations, the attractions, and the prices, but all too often, you forget about the weather—and it's a terrible oversight. Who can forget that trip to Miami that ended in disaster when Hurricane Andrew decimated the city? How about that lovely weekend getaway to Mexico City that just happened to coincide with the worst earthquake in almost a century? And what about the Japanese tour that ran afoul of a vicious typhoon? There's an old Czech saying, "You can outrun man or god, but not the weather," and travelers who have been beaten into submission by an ugly purple sky know how true it is. Get weather reports, warnings, and tips for smarter trips at **clari.news.weather**, **WeatherNet**, and the **Interactive Weather Browser**.

It's a twister, Auntie Em!—from http://taiga.geog.niu.edu/chaser/photo.html

On the Net

U.S. info

Current USA Weather Map A National Weather Service forecast, updates on extreme weather conditions across the country, and more. ✓**INTERNET**→*url* http://www.arc.com/map.html

Interactive Weather Browser The Interactive Weather Browser lets you choose graphically, by way of a point-and-click map, what U.S. weather information you wish to view. Get the report on the weather in your destination city without any static. ✓**INTERNET**→*url* http://rs560.cl.msu.edu/weather/interactive.html

National Weather Service (NWS) Homepage Although you may have to try a few times to get through to this very popular U.S. weather site, it's definitely worth it for the detail that's available. The site offers local and regional temperature, humidity, and "comfort index" info for locations across America. You'll find the two-day, five-day, ten-day, and monthly forecasts helpful to varying degrees, depending upon how long you're staying at your vacation or business destination. ✓**INTERNET**→*url* http://www.nws.noaa.gov/

The Weather Channel A perfect site for the weather neophyte, the Weather Channel allows you to check out current conditions and the forecast for your favorite U.S. city and to view nifty weather maps for any region nationwide. ✓**INTERNET**→*url* http://www.infi.net/weather/

Weather Weather reports for hundreds of U.S. cities, along with a U.S. map. You can also find reports on ski conditions, beaches and boating, and fall foliage, where applicable. ✓**PRODIGY**→*jump* us weather

Weather News Daily weather maps, a dazzling array of interesting statistics (high-temperature records, low-temperature records), satellite maps, thunderstorm outlooks, precipitation outlooks for the continental U.S., and an index of U.S. forecasts. All of this information is displayed via slick, easily understood online graphics. Additional resources include a weather-related current events section, a foreign cities' forecast section, and a ski condition report. ✓**AMERICA ONLINE**→*keyword* weather

Weather Report Weather reports for most major cities in the United States, including national maps, radar reports, and more. ✓**COMPUSERVE**→*go* weather

Weather Underground Who needs Willard Scott? Bryant Gumbel, perhaps, and Katie Couric, certainly, and maybe the thousands of Americans who want to celebrate their hundredth birthdays with the roly-poly ambassador of meteorological goodwill. In fact, he's probably a national treasure. But that's hardly the point. This is: The Weather Underground provides extensive weather reports for the U.S. and Canada, as well as special reports for ski conditions and occasional occurrences such as hurricanes, earthquakes, and hot hail. Eat your heart out, Willard. But remember—America still loves you. ✓**INTERNET**...→*url* telnet://downwind.sprl.umich.edu:3000...→*url* telnet://measun.nrrc.ncsu.edu:3000...→*url* telnet://wind.atmos.uah.edu:3000...→*url* telnet://ucsu.colorado.edu:3000

International info

clari.news.weather (ng) Straightforward weather news and reports for regions worldwide. ✓**USENET**→clari.news.weather

INTELLiCast Home Page Offering detailed international weather information, this Website includes U.S. weather reports, national (and international) weather forecasts, weather-related images and movies, selected city forecasts from Amsterdam to Warsaw, links to local weather resources, and detailed ski condition reports. The SunCast service, which predicts daily levels of ultraviolet rays, the form of radiation most responsible for "adverse health effects," is also accessible from this site—as if you want to think about that on your vacation! ✓**INTERNET**→*url* http://www.intellicast.com/

Weather Information Superhighway A collection of links to weather report sites around the world. Find out if it's sunny in the Sudan, raining in Remagen, or snowing in Sydney. ✓**INTERNET**→*url* http://thunder.met.fsu.edu/~nws/wxhwy.html

Weather Maps and Satellite Images Satellite images of the earth, showing air flows, tidal currents, storm activity, and numerous other climate-related events. A great way to determine whether you'll need a bikini or an umbrella while you're packing for Miami Beach, Grand Cayman Island, or Nice. ✓**INTERNET**→*url* gopher://gopher.awis.auburn.edu:70/1/images

Weather Section A small part of eWorld's larger News Board, produced for eWorld by Reuters. The international weather information featured at this site is usefully sorted by geographic region, with each regional section containing a brief synopsis of local weather, as well as a short selection of major weather-related news stories. ✓**EWORLD**→*go* news→Weather Section

WeatherNet Sponsored by the slightly sinister-sounding Weather Underground at the University of Michigan, this is the Internet's premier source of weather links. With more than 250 weather sites listed and new links being added every day, WeatherNet is the most comprehensive and up-to-date on-ramp there is to the world of Web weather data. From here you can access weather reports and forecasts for just about any location worldwide that can be reached by plane, train, or automobile. ✓**INTERNET**→*url* http://cirrus.Sprl.Umich.Edu/wxnet/

Lightning strikes the same place thrice—from http://taiga.geog.niu.edu/chaser

Budget travel

Are your travel plans bigger than your bank account? That doesn't mean you have to settle for a weekend at the Motel 6 a few miles from home. Turn to **Shoestring Travel Ezine** or the **Rough Guides** for advice on places to sleep and eat that don't involve unknown meats or sharing space with Norman Bates. There's plenty of travel help for terminally-poor students at **College Travel International** and the **International Student Travel Confederation. Hostelling International** provides invaluable information on where there's hot water galore or a good party scene. Is it the airfare that's standing in your way? Don't ship yourself parcel post—try the **World Wide Courier Association** instead.

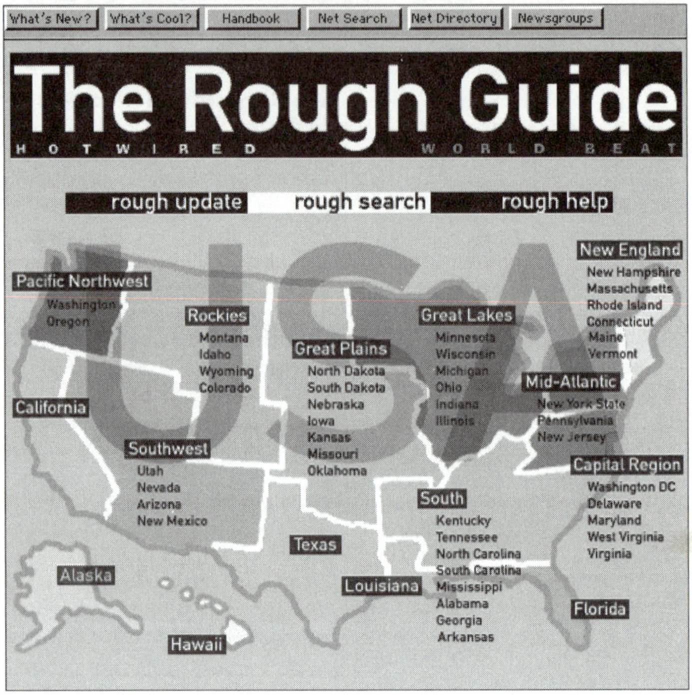

Opening screen of HotWired*'s Rough Guides—http://vip.hotwired.com/rough/*

On the Net

Across the board

Clever Ways to Travel Free or for Little Cost Check here for Eurail and cheap flight information and for budget-travel insight on everything from car rentals to hostels to hitchhiking. ✓**INTERNET**→*url* http://adam.cs.uwec.edu/~andersts/travel.html

Global Passage A work in progress, Global Passage's site encourages travelers to "take a trip on-line." Its creators hope it will become an online club of travelers sharing information and advice with other voyagers. There's a message forum where you can exchange tips and also a link to a detailed guide on the Aussie backpacking scene. ✓**INTERNET**→*url* http://www.globalpassage.com

rec.travel.marketplace (ng) You know that section in *The New York Times* devoted to good deals and advice on travel accommodations? Well, this is much better. Ask about international air fares, and travel agencies will post their best offers. Inquire about a cheap hotel in Amsterdam, and you'll get recommendations like "Stay at BOB's Youth Hostel if you don't mind a bunch of students who just like to kick back and get stoned!"). Discount fares, time shares, and apartment sublets are posted regularly. ✓**USENET**→rec.travel.marketplace

Rough Guides A comprehensive guide to eating, sleeping, and having fun on your vacation without spending too much money. The detailed listings are linked to VOX, a discussion space where you can read what others have to say about budget travel. Put together by *HotWired* magazine, the site only covers the U.S. at the moment, but it plans to grow.

✓**INTERNET**→*url* http://vip.hotwired.com/rough/

Shoestring Travel Ezine If you're sick of wading through commercial postings in travel newsgroups, this is the site for you. The site's creator does all the hard work for you, collecting tips from rec.travel newsgroups and presenting the most useful nuggets on how to eat, sleep, and travel cheaply. There are also links to other relevant travel sites and info on registering as an independent travel agent. This site makes traveling on a shoestring easy. ✓**INTERNET**→*url* http://turnpike.net/metro/eadler/index.html

---

TravelGram A site laden down with advertisements for travel discounts, villas for rent, timeshares, tours, and even some travel news. The page is updated weekly, so you get the very latest news on travel bargains. Cheap airfare seems to be a special interest at TravelGram—there are pages and pages devoted to flying you there inexpensively. ✓**INTERNET**→*url* http://www.csn.net/~johnhart/tfb.html

Clubs

Traveler's Advantage This travel club advertises up to 50 percent discounts on selected hotels and even deeper discounts on "hot ticket" promotions. Read updates on the latest special values on cruises and package vacations posted here. ✓**PRODIGY**→*jump* travelers ✓**AMERICA ONLINE**→*keyword* travelers advantage

Courier

Travel Unlimited A wealth of information about traveling as a courier, including contact numbers for U.S. airline discounters and courier services. ✓**INTERNET**→*url* http://nexus.datawave.net/travel/travel.html

---

World Wide Courier Association With airfares at only a fraction of the normal cost, who wouldn't want to be a courier? For a yearly fee, the people at World Wide Courier Association will help you realize that dream—as long as you're over 21 and have a "clean cut" appearance. ✓**INTERNET**→*url* http://www.servtech.com/walls/

Hitchhiking

A Guide to Hitching If you've thought about sticking out your thumb and seeing where it would take you, this is the site for you. A Norwegian hitchhiker offers the benefit of the experience he gained hitching from Oslo to Paris with only $2 in his pocket. Though the guide has a northern European slant, the information is pretty universal. What to pack, what to wear, even where to stand—it's all in here. You wouldn't usually pack a shiny bit of plastic to attract drivers, now would you? So what is the best way to get drivers to stop? Wash! The most essential item? Humor! ✓**INTERNET**→*url* http://www.solutions.net/rec-travel/general/packing_list_hitching.html

Homestays

American International Homestay Ever wanted to travel to a foreign country, shack up with some locals, eat all their food, and have them show you around? Well, AIH tells you how to do it. The company has contacts worldwide with people who are keen on this sort of thing. And for a small fee, AIH will introduce you to them. ✓**INTERNET**→*url* http://www.commerce.com/homestays/

The International Home Exchange Network A worldwide listing of home and hospitality exchange opportunities for people who want to swap houses and enjoy rent-free accommodations on their next vacation. This is the place to list a house or respond to a listing and then arrange the exchange via email. There's also a useful bulletin board called Miscellaneous and Student Postings, where you can find travel companions as well as cheap or free accommodations. One Netter in Melbourne, Australia offered a free place to stay to American students as long as they didn't drink, smoke, or take drugs. Sounds like fun! ✓**INTERNET**→*url* http://www.magicnet/homexchange/index.html

Hostels

Hostelling International - American Youth Hostels Catalog A non-profit organisation whose goal is to "help travelers gain a greater understanding of the world and its people through hostelling." HI lists hostels in the U.S. and around the world, including addresses, contact details, and descriptions of the facilities (there's even a note if the hostel takes credit cards). One lucky hostel is featured as the Hostel of the Month with a pic, a descriptive essay, and links to resources on local attractions and nearby cities. Note: American entries are much more detailed than their international counterparts. ✓**INTERNET**→*url* http://www.gnn.com/gnn/bus/ayh/index.html

---

Hostels Europe Inveterate hostelers rate accommodations that vary from a charming lodging in the medieval French city of

Carcasonne to a rowdy party crib in Frankfurt. ✓INTERNET→*url* http://www.tardis.ed.ac.uk/~og/hostels.html

Internet Guide to Hostelling A valuable resource for backpackers and budget travelers alike with listings for more than a 100 hostels worldwide, tips for traveling cheaply through North America, and answers to the most pressing hostel-related questions, i.e., what exactly is a sleep-sheet? ✓INTERNET→*url* http://www.digimark.net/rec-travel/hostels/index.html

Russian Youth Hostel Association Addresses and contact information for the first seven international hostels in the new Russian Republic. ✓INTERNET→*url* http://www.spb.su/ryh/ryha.html

Students

College Travel International If you're under 25 and going on a trip, check with College Travel International for information about discount airline tickets, Eurail passes, and budget travel packages. You can order an American Youth Hostel card online, retrieve information on hostels, access an archive of newsletters about college travel discounts, and get all sorts of coupons for travel discounts. ✓INTERNET ...→*url* telnet://prairienet.org→visitor ...→*email* wolvie@prairienet.org ✍ *Write for help & support*

Council Travel Students and budget travelers now have access to Council Travel's services on the Net. If you want to check airfares, find hostel listings, purchase railpasses, or find summer employment abroad, they are your source. CT has offices worldwide; get the listing here, or contact CT online. Additional services are travel insurance, language programs, car rentals, and youth tours. ✓INTERNET→*url* http://www.ciee.org/cts/ctshome.htm

Welcome to Global Passage's .netSTOP—http://www.globalpassage.com

Explorations in Travel, Inc. If you want to live a number of months in a foreign country, learn a new language, and maybe even have the whole experience credited towards your college degree, this company can help you organize an internship or job and the credits. ✓INTERNET→*url* http://www.sover.net/~explore/

International Student Travel Confederation Brought to you by the makers of those little green International Student cards that get you discounts on hotels, train tickets, and museum fees the world over. This page tells you where you can get a card, as well as the savings and benefits it can bring you. The country-by-country guide is an education in itself. Who'd have thought an ISTC card would get you 10 percent off at the Tacobell in Accra, Ghana? One question is left unanswered however—why is there a person skiing across the bottom of the page? ✓INTERNET→*url* http://www.istc.org/

L'Organisation Etudiante Internationale de Logement Two starving students in Paris (a time honored tradition to be sure) have started a housing exchange service via the Internet. Leave a message if you have a cheap place you're giving up, or if you need housing. The response has been so tremendous that the site's creator now gives priority to those who pay a small fee. Students only! ✓INTERNET→*url* http://www.sct.fr/4-rent

STA Travel A company specializing in travel for the student and the budget-minded. This site offers a comprehensive guide to the services they offer, including details on discount airfares and travel insurance. ✓INTERNET→*url* http://www.sta-travel.com/

Student and Budget Travel Guide This guide for student and low-budget travelers is packed with penny-pinching tips and links to relevant newsgroups (rec.travel.marketplace), informative Websites (STA Travel), and country home pages (from Angola to Zimbabwe). ✓INTERNET→*url* http://asa.ugl.lib.umich.edu/chdocs/travel/travel-guide.html

Business travel

So your boss is sending you off to a big meeting in Melbourne on Monday, and you don't know where to stay. Don't just walk up and down the Australian streets, hollering at the kangaroos and koalas, asking for a hotel room. Check out **Traveler's Edge Destination Guide**, **Getting Through Customs**, and **City Files** for hints and tips on business travel around the world. If your needs are more financial, consult **Banks of the World**. And businesspeople planning a convention should look at the **Venue Finder**.

Welcome to the Business Traveler Online—*http://www.biztravel.com/guide/*

On the Net

Across the board

City Files This is a comprehensive guide for business travelers visiting major U.S. and international cities. The Business Services database here details where to rent cellular phones, audio/visual equipment, and computers for meetings; how to hire translators or secretaries; and what attire is appropriate for certain cities (informal in Orlando, conservative in Los Angeles). You'll learn that punctuality is not stressed in Mexico City, and that New Yorkers aren't being rude when they do business without pleasantries. Information about banking hours, U.S. currency exchange locations (American cities have a dearth of the cambios so prevalent abroad), and late-night pharmacies is provided at the Resources topic here. There are also city overviews, and information on nightlife, and transportation. ✓**EWORLD**→*go* travel→The Travelers' Edge→City Files

Getting Through Customs There's much more at this site than advice on how not to look like a drug smuggler when leaving Istanbul. Explanations of business practices and protocol, cultural customs, negotiating strategies, and even "cognitive styles" for hundreds of countries are on file here. Don't risk losing the big deal in Malaysia by putting your feet on the desk; don't offend the Swedes by not introducing yourself to everyone in the room upon entering. This site will guide you through the customs of different countries. The libraries hold additional information on world leaders and local transportation. Get set for the global economy now. ✓**COMPUSERVE**→*go* gtc-7

Traveler's Edge Destination Guide For business and leisure travelers alike, knowing something about your destination goes a long way toward a successful trip. Learn basic statistics about transportation options in your destination city, and find out if there are currently any health advisories there. Business travelers will appreciate the Dos and Don'ts section here that offers advice on how to avoid cultural faux pas: Do drink palm wine in Sierre Leone to close a deal; don't assume that your Portuguese colleague speaks Spanish. Do remember to respect the privacy of the Amish in Indiana; don't tip taxi drivers in Suriname. And do remember that in Québec, by law, business must be conducted en Français. ✓**EWORLD**→*go* travel→The Traveler's Edge→Destination Guide

Directories

Banks of the World Whether your financial-service requirements are global cash management, offshore banking, or the use of an ATM, there are links to Websites for more than 150 banks and credit unions worldwide here. And just as the financial services of banks vary widely, so do the online services offered by banks. Services range from basic information about products to full-service banking online. ✓**INTERNET**→*url* http://www.wiso.gwdg.de/ifbg/bank_2.html

Corporate Rate Hotel Directory Find the most competitive corporate hotel rates online! Listed by state or by country, information is available about hotels and amenities, as well as special rates. Email addresses are provided for reservations and for verifying information. ✓**INTERNET**→ *url* http://www.ios.com/corp_hotels/

Federal Discount Lodging Directory A comprehensive listing of accommodations worldwide that extend discounts to U.S. government employees. Hotel contact information includes addresses, phone numbers, and email addresses. ✓**INTERNET**→*url* http://www.ios.com/hotels/hotels.html

Lanier Golf Database Business meetings aren't always held in the conference room; many deals are being closed on the green. At this site you can enter a location and retrieve a list of courses in the area. There are listings for the U.S. and U.S. territories (Puerto Rico, Guam, American Samoa, and the Virgin Islands). Need to improve your game? The database offers some helpful hints here as well. ✓**COMPUSERVE**→*go* golf

Philadelphia Convention Center When William Penn proclaimed Philadelphia "The City of Brotherly Love" he obviously hadn't planned a conference there. Without the right information, it can be a nightmare. This Website will go a long way toward easing your fears. At Philadelphia's new Convention Center—near Chinatown and adjacent to the Marriott—you will find a world-class facility. There is an overview of the Center and its amenities and services, as well as various floor plans of the meeting rooms, exhibit halls, and the ballroom. And finally, the site links to Philadelphia Visitor information, which provides accommodation, dining, transportation, and airline information. ✓**INTERNET**→*url* http://www.libertynet.org/phila-visitor/pcc

Venue Finder If you're a meeting planner seeking the perfect spot for your meeting, this Website is worth a visit. You can search a directory of business venues or hotel chains by nation or city. Each search will retrieve contact information for hotels and conference locations that meet your criteria. Often a listing will link to the Website for a specific hotel or city. You can also get calendars of upcoming events for the location you're considering. After you've made your choice, check back to see if your meeting is listed here. If not, send details to the site's Webmaster. ✓**INTERNET**→*url* http://www.webcom.com/~venues/

Magazines

CEO Traveler An online quarterly magazine with features for the sophisticated traveler. Recent issues have focused on upscale Manhattan dining and destinations such as Hong Kong, the Brandywine Valley (near Delaware, where many companies have incorporated), and villas in Italy. There are also articles about cruises, hotels catering to business travelers, and package vacations. ✓**INTERNET**→*url* http://dockmaster.phantom.com/ceo.html

The Business Traveler Online Every month *Business Traveler Online* focuses on a different country. In its issue on the United Kingdom, for instance, there is information for the businessman on where to get a furnished office, obtain a cellular phone, rent a car, and perform a large currency transaction. The site also has tips on the best in restaurants, shows, and sightseeing. ✓**INTERNET**→*url* http://www.biztravel.com/guide/

Organizations

Association of Business Travelers A club that provides business travelers with hotel, restaurant, and transportation discounts. A lost-luggage tracing service is also provided. ✓**INTERNET**→*url* http://www.hk.linkage.net/markets/abt/

Meeting Professionals International This resourceful industry association's Web page assists planners in developing successful meetings and conferences. Among its online offerings are a calendar of events, listing upcoming conventions, dates, and locations, and an online bookstore, whose titles include *Accessible Meetings and Conventions*, *Words That Sell*, and *The Convention Liaison Council Manual*. Join the association, purchase books, keep abreast of industry news, and network with other professionals from here. ✓**INTERNET**→*url* http://www.metronet.com/~mbloechl

Part 2

Africa & The Middle East

Africa

For hundreds of years, travelers visited Europe, South America, and Asia, but rarely Africa. These days, though, the Dark Continent is one of the most popular tourist destinations in the world. What are the reasons? African art. African music. African culture. African politics. And, last but not least, Africa on the Net. From **Africa** to **UPenn African Studies WWW Links**, from **soc.culture.african** to **Travelnet**, there are dozens of Web resources for the traveler interested in exploring the continent. And if you're planning your trip and aiming for Nigeria, or Zambia, or Burkina Faso, head over to **Country-Specific Pages for Africa** to collect specifics on your target nation.

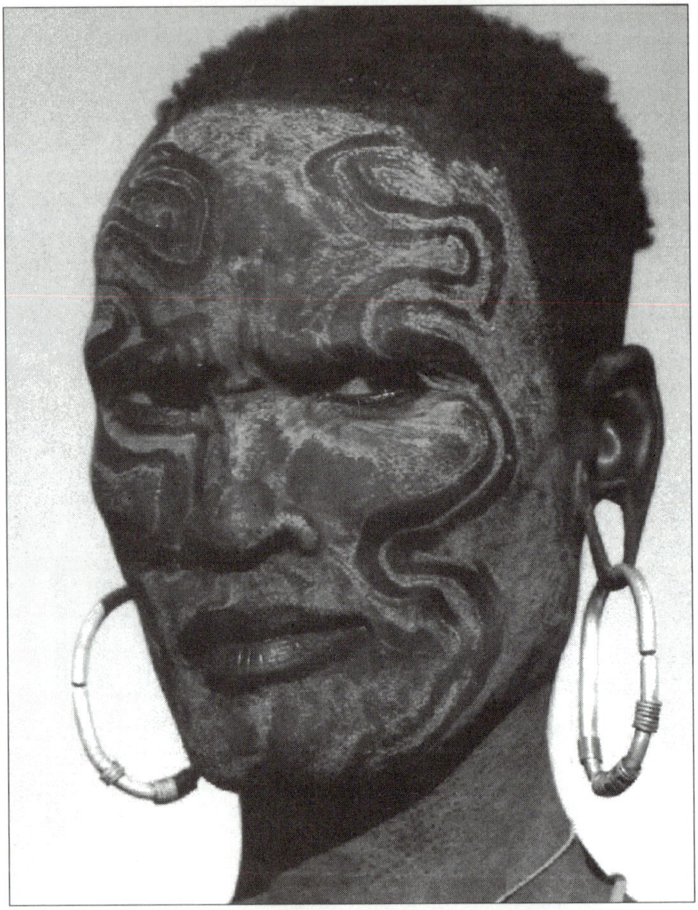

An African woman—from http://web.syr.edu:80/~decole /africa.htm

On the Net

Across the board

Africa Discover all things African here—the continent, the diaspora, and beyond. This immense collection of links leads to news digests (like the AfricaUpdate Archives), political groups at the African Rights Home Page, and to country home pages (from Ethiopia to Somalia). Learn Swahili or the art of Malipenga dance with visits to art and cultural links. Head to MELANET to chat with African-Americans or to find business and employment aid. ✓**INTERNET**→*url* http://web.syr.edu:80/~decole /africa.htm

Africa-L (ml) "You should all remember that when they first came to our lands and said 'Let's pray' they spelt the word pray with an e, i.e., 'prey.'" Africa-L is an intensely political and left-leaning mailing list, and an interesting place to get cross-cultural perspectives of Africa in the 20th century. ✓**INTERNET**→*email* listserv@ vtvm1.cc.vt.edu ✍ *Type in message body:* subscribe africa-l <your full name>

Africa-N (ml) Subscribe to this list for current news about Africa. ✓**INTERNET**→*email* listserv@vm.utcc.utoronto.ca ✍ *Type in message body:* subscribe africa-n

<your full name>

AfricaUpdate The African Studies Program of Central Connecticut State University publishes the full text of its quarterly newsletter at this site. Keep up-to-date on African political and cultural news by reading stories titled "On Women, Botswana, West Africa," "Nigeria on the Edge," and "Francophone West Africa." ✓**INTERNET**→*url* http://neal.ctstateu.edu/history/africa_update/africa_update.html

Country-Specific Pages for Africa UPenn's Africa pages are the most comprehensive in Cyberspace. The site features home pages for every African country—from Algeria to Zimbabwe. Each page offers a map, a U.S. State Department advisory, and a CIA World Factbook country profile. But most pages have unique content as well. On the Zambia page there are links to a national news service, a language database, and an article on the fertilizer industry. Wander to Marrakesh and explore Moroccan culture on the Tamazight: The Berber Culture and Language page. Look at amazing photos of animals at the Kenyan National Park site or look at photographs of the flora and fauna of Madagascar on the Madagascar Home Page. Frequent updates make these pages among the most valuable African-related resources on the Net. ✓**INTERNET**→ *url* http://www.sas.upenn.edu/African_Studies/Home_Page/Country.html

UPenn African Studies WWW Links The annotations make this collection of African and African-American links among the most useful on the Web. There are links organized by topic, to sites focusing on everything from trade to wildlife, as well as places to chat (meet with other Rastafarians at Virtual Niahbingi), places to learn (visit the University of South Africa), and places to look (see the African Mask Collection). ✓**INTERNET**→*url* http://www.sas.upenn.edu/African_Studies/Home_Page/WWW_Links.html

US News–Sub-Saharan News Current news articles covering events in Kenya, South Africa, Angola, Tunisia, and many more African countries. ✓**AMERICA ONLINE**→*keyword* us news→world→sub-saharan

Culture

African Art "African artists praise a carved figure by saying that it 'looks like a human being.'" Learn about the aesthetic elements of African art with this illustrated electronic catalog written by Benjamin C. Ray for an African art exhibition held at the University of Virginia in 1993. ✓**INTERNET**→*url* http://www.lib.virginia.edu/dic/exhib/93.ray.aa/African.html

Internet Guide to Afro-Caribbean Music Click on the Benin link at this site and you'll get a map of Africa with the tiny country (tiny by African standards) highlighted. You'll also get a list of Beninese recording artists, like Angélique Kidjo, Kiri Kanta, and Stan Tohon, plus pictures, song lists, and sound clips for their current albums. A guide to musicians of the Congo, Tanzania, Chad, Togo, and 18 other African countries. ✓**INTERNET**→*url* http://www.ina.fr/Music/index.en.html

Malipenga Dance Common throughout the formerly British-occupied countries of southern Africa, Malipenga dancing began in the 19th century when natives donned the military uniforms of their occupiers and performed mocking marches in them. To see pictures of modern Malipenga dancers and learn more about the African two-step, visit this site. ✓**INTERNET**→*url* http://cwis.usc.edu/dept/elab/oconnell/malipenga.html

MELANET On-Line African Wedding Guide Always wanted a traditional African wedding? This hypertext guide covers every detail, from the demeanor of the Warrior (best man) to choosing a

Fodor's Choice...

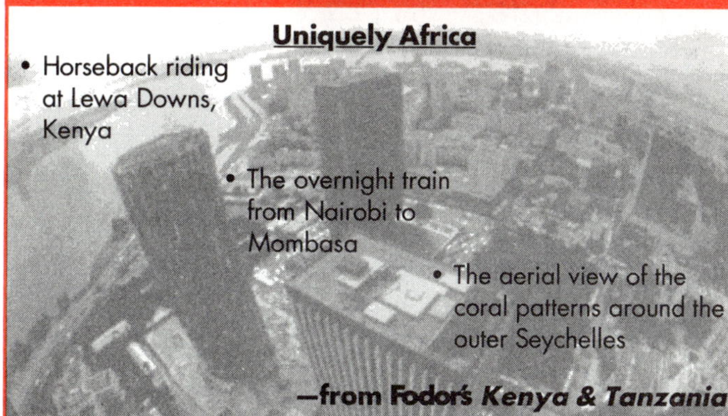

Uniquely Africa

- Horseback riding at Lewa Downs, Kenya
- The overnight train from Nairobi to Mombasa
- The aerial view of the coral patterns around the outer Seychelles

—from Fodor's *Kenya & Tanzania*

A Temple—from http://web.syr.edu:80 /~decole/africa.htm

Kente cloth pattern with both aesthetics and symbolism in mind. Don't forget the pepper to seal the covenant between the families. ✓**INTERNET**→*url* http://www.ip.net:80/melanet/wedding/

soc.culture.african (ng) The topics explored on this newsgroup are as diverse as the continent itself. At the same time that Glenda asks for African e-pals for her Canadian fourth graders, an African man describes the racism he recently experienced when entering France. Meanwhile there is a lengthy thread about the practice of infantile genital "manipulation" and its current relevancy in African society, and a post questions where someone might find a Zulu-tuned concertina in South Africa. ✓**USENET**→soc.culture.african *FAQ:* ✓**INTERNET**→*url* http://www.cs.wits.ac.za/faq/africa/africa.html

soc.culture.maghreb (ng) For discussion of issues pertinent to North Africa. The majority of the messages are in French. ✓**USENET**→soc.culture.maghreb

Guides

Travelnet South Africa and Namibia are the focus of Travelnet. For each of those two countries, the site provides a national history, seasonal weather info, and hotel and restaurant listings by city. Most of the rest of Africa is accounted for as well, with practical travel info here on Botswana, Mozambique, Zambia, and Zimbabwe, but it tends to be sketchy: e.g., "There are cottages to rent in Mozambique." ✓**INTERNET**→*url* http://os2.iaccess.za/travel/index .htm

Safaris

Allen Safaris A promotional page for a company offering photographic and sightseeing safaris throughout Eastern and Southern Africa. The company caters to small groups of people who want custom-tailored safari itineraries. Most travel is by light aircraft, and Allen Safaris treks to Kenya, Tanzania, Uganda, Rwanda, Zaire, Malawi, Zambia, Zimbabwe, Botswana, Namibia, and South Africa. The company also specializes in "visits to the gorillas and chimpanzees." ✓**INTERNET**→*url* http://michaeljones.uoregon.edu/safaris

Magari Safaris Magari lists the 11 tours it currently offers (you can choose from the Garden Route Fantasy, the Scent of the Night tour, and the Mountains of the Moon trek, among others). The company promises that its drivers specialize in all "necessary" languages, including French, English, German, and Spanish. ✓**INTERNET**→*url* http://aztec.co.za/biz/africa/magari.htm

Remote Africa Tours Visit the Mwaleshi Camp in North Luangwa National Park or the Tafika Camp in South Luangwa National Park with the help of Remote Africa Tours. Short descriptions of each of the camps are followed by contact information. ✓**INTERNET**→*url* http://www.zamnet.zm/zamnet/zntb/remote.html

Safaricenter Imagine cruising down the Nile, traipsing through the Egyptian desert, spotting a lion in Kenya, or mountaineering on Mount Kilimanjaro. Then visit this home page for a description of this California-based company offering safaris. Next step: buying a ticket. ✓**INTERNET**→*url* http://www.travelsource.com/safaris/safaricenter.html

Tamu Safaris Tamu Safaris wants to be more than your tour guide—it wants to be your teacher too. Tamu specializes in safaris in eight African countries: Kenya, Tanzania, Seychelles, Madagascar, Botswana, Zimbabwe, Namibia, and South Africa. Besides booking your hotels and restaurants, the company promises to know "the peoples and places, languages and landscapes, and the flora and fauna of each region." If you want to count elephants at the edge of the alkaline plains in Amboseli National Park, visit this home page and then call Tamu with the phone numbers listed here. ✓**INTERNET**→*url* http://www.travelsource.com/safaris/tamusafaris.html

Tours

Beachcomber Tours Mark Twain once wrote about Mauritius, an island about 2,000 km off of Eastern Africa, "You gather the idea that Mauritius was made first, and then heaven, and that heaven was copied after Mauritius." Beachcomber Tours advertises several of its tours of the island at this site. ✓**INTERNET**→*url* http://www.tcp.co.uk/~holidays/beach.html

Egypt

Most modern travelers to Egypt can only guess at the nation's history, the long sand-brown line stretching from the Bararian, Amaratian, and Gerzean, Fayum, and Merimda cultures of the Predynastic Period, through the 31 dynasties of Ancient Egypt, and on into the Greek and Roman Periods. If you're more interested in 20th-century matters than the Kushite Domination, Egypt still remains a source of fascination with leaders like Nasser, Sadat, and Mubarak guiding the nation into the present. If you're planning on visiting Giza or the Nile and want to prepare online, start at **Egypt Interactive**, the **Egypt Unofficial Home Page**, and the **Egypt-Net Home Page**.

Egypt: it's pyramidarrific!— http://www.mordor.com:80/hany/egypt/eg_pics1.html

On the Net

Across the board

A Color Tour of Egypt A series of annotated color images of the land of Cleopatra—from the majesty of the temple at Abu Simbel to the tidal fields of the Nile. ✓**INTERNET**→*url* http://www.memphis.edu/egypt/egypt.html

Abzu Egyptian Index Sponsored by the Research Archives of the Oriental Institute, Chicago, this extensive site offers a wealth of resources about ancient Egypt. Take virtual tours of computer-generated reconstructed tombs to experience the splendor of Egyptian architecture in its heyday. Read essays on Nubian wall paintings and other Egyptian artifacts for an in-depth look at the art of this fascinating culture. Pore over scholarly articles on papyrus, which include little-known facts like the following "Everybody knows the Egyptians mummified their dead: First they prepared the corpses and wrapped them in linen. Then they covered them with pieces of cartonnage covered with plaster and painted in bright colors. This cartonnage consists of several layers of papyrus. The papyri used for making cartonnage often came from recycling bins in administrative offices." There are also links to the World Factbook Egypt page and TravelWorld's Guide to the Middle East. ✓**INTERNET**→*url* http://www-oi.uchicago.edu/OI/DEPT/RA/ABZU/ABZU_NEW.HTML

Alexandria A hypertext guide to the ancient city of Alexandria, which was built by Dinocrates in 332 B.C. It offers biographies of famous residents (like Marc Antony) and links to Web pages of current residents, a picture gallery, and an audio file of a famous tune about the city. If you're tempted by the cybertour, information about Egyptian travel services is online, too. ✓**INTERNET**→*url* http://ce.ecn.purdue.edu/~ashmawy/ALEX/

Egypt Interactive With links to a virtual tour of the Manicurists' Tomb, the Egyptology Home Page, the CIA World Factbook entry on Egypt, and an Egyptian Travelogue, among other sites, this page is a good starting point to learn about every facet of Egyptian life and culture. William Potter Davis once said of the country,

"We were there long enough to see the chief objects of interest, and that was quite long enough." Decide for yourself. ✓**INTERNET**→*url* http://www.channel1.com/users/mansoorm/index.html

Egypt Unofficial Home Page Preview this collection of photos of local attractions before your tour of Egypt, or merely sight see as a virtual traveler. Whatever your reason for visiting, these pictures of Egyptian spectacles like The Temple of Philae in Aswan, Naama Bay, the Egyptian Museum, and the Citadel will get you to walk like an Egyptian. ✓**INTERNET**→*url* http://auc-amer.eun.eg/

Egypt-Net Home Page This site claims that it's still under construction, but it's hard to imagine that it could be improved by much! Besides housing the archive of the daily Egypt-oriented digest of the same name, this site offers a wealth of indigenous resources, including travelogues, Egyptian folktales, a picture gallery, articles on Net access in Egypt, country maps, and a list of home pages for all of Egypt-Net's members. And, of course, this Website also lists details on subscribing to the Egypt-Net mailing list, which delivers news and discussion of current issues in Egypt. Even Ra would be impressed by the resources at this site. ✓**INTERNET** ...→*url* ftp://ftp.cs.sunysb.edu/pub/EN/www/home.html ✓**INTERNET** ...→*email* Egypt-net@cs.sunysb.edu ✍ *Email with general correspondence*

Egyptian Photo Gallery Royce Fromme, a senior at Texas A&M University, recently toured the Land of the Pharaohs to indulge his interest in Egyptology. In the "Gallery of Assortments" at his site, he has posted pictures from his trips to the Temple of Hatshepsut (just over the mountain from the Valley of the Kings at Thebes) and to the Step Pyramid at Saqqara. Royce toured Egypt with his brother Rance; see if you can find him in the pictures. ✓**INTERNET**→*url* http://www.sci.tamucc.edu/~rwf6098/

Culture

Christian Coptic Orthodox Church of Egypt Saint Mark brought Christianity to Eygpt during the reign of the Roman emperor Nero in the first century. It has thrived there up to the present day, and Copts have contributed much to the Christian faith, including the Nicene Creed, which is recited in Christian churches worldwide ("We believe in one God, Father of the Almighty..."). This large site provides lovely photographs of Coptic churches, samples of prayers, readings, and even lesson plans for teaching non-Copts about the religion. ✓**INTERNET**→*url* http://cs-www.bu.edu/faculty/best/pub/cn/Home.html

soc.culture.egyptian (ng) "I am planning to travel to Egypt and I would like to get some information about where to go and what to do there," writes Leticia. Her request has been there for a few days, and no one has answered yet, but maybe that's because most people who visit this newsgroup are more interested in discussing current Egyptian politics and events. Debates about President Mubarak's actions in Middle Eastern politics are common; women's rights in Muslim Egypt is also a very hot topic. But cheer up, Leticia, you're not the only one being left out—no one answered Neal's inquiry about where to buy a real Ramses scarab either! ✓**USENET**→soc.culture.egyptian

The Egypt Gallery This gallery is curated by Hany, a 23-year-old Egyptian who currently lives in Jersey City, New Jersey, which has a large Egyptian community. He has assembled a .GIF of the Egyptian flag and a sound clip of the country's national anthem, pictures of tombs and artifacts from across Egypt, and collections of "cultural images," which show Egyptian Bedouins, camel riders, and boaters on the Nile. Also here are sound clips of classic and modern Egyptian songs. ✓**INTERNET**→*url* http://www.mordor.com/hany/egypt/egypt.html

Tours

Egypt on a Budget The folks at Venture Travel offer seven different budget tours of Egypt, most of which are under $1,000. Whether you want to roam from temple to temple or spend six days drifting down the Nile, Venture can arrange your trip. ✓**INTERNET**→*url* http://www.best.com/~ventures/egypt.html

Historic Tours: Egypt Choose between the 15-day Osiris tour, which takes you down the River Nile and to the House of Oberoi Pyramids, or the 10-day Isis tour. Itineraries, prices, and terms and conditions of these two tours are advertised here. ✓**INTERNET**→*url* http://www.arabbiz.com/historictours/egypt/

Megatrails Read a day-by-day description of this company's tour of Egypt's treasures. Most of the tour stays around Cairo and the surrounding areas—visiting the Citadel, Tutankhamen's tomb, the pyramids of Giza, the Sphinx, and the ruins of ancient Memphis, among other attractions. ✓**INTERNET**→*url* http://www.brainlink.com/~MEGA/egypt.html

Cairo

A visit to Cairo and vicinity certainly makes the "deluxe" offerings of the local funeral parlor look inadequate. Egyptian Pharaohs spent incredible amounts of time and slave labor building pyramids and appeasing the gods—more than the average life insurance policies allow for nowadays. Learn why in **The Egyptian Book of the Dead**. Then brush up on your mummy-making skills at the **Egyptian Museum**. Cairo still appears to be a hotspot for deities of all types—meet the Virgin Mary at **Zaitoun Church**, and the **Ultimate Angelic Mission** offers the supreme tourist experience—contact with the mystic powers of those who arrived from worlds beyond on the Chariots of the Gods (UFOs). But death and immortality aside, Cairo is a vibrant, living city where visitors will need to find a room for a single night's (rather than eternal) rest.

On the Net

Across the board

Cairo Visit the Cairo Tower, stare in awe at the Great Pyramid of Khufu, or gaze into the eyes of the Sphinx—and do it all online with the Cairo Picture Gallery at this site. You can also learn an Egyptian song (called "Om Kalthoum") and hear a sound clip of President Sadat's 1977 speech calling for peace in the Middle East. In the Cairo Visitors section, you'll find practical information on hotels, restaurants, transportation, car rental, foreign embassy locations, and even a list of places to exchange currency. If that isn't enough information to get you around Cairo, there are also several maps of the city as well as a catalog of email addresses for Cairenes and Cairo lovers. ✓**INTERNET**→*url* http://ce.ecn.purdue.edu/~ashmawy/CAIRO/

The Pyramid of King Khufu—from http://www.memphis.edu/egypt/

Attractions

Architecture of Islam Photographs of some of Cairo's star architectural attractions, including the Madrasah of Sultan Hasan and the Mosque of Ibn Tulun. You'll have to dig up background information about the sites by yourself—there are no annotations ✓**INTERNET**→*url* http://rubens.anu.edu.au/islam2/index_1.html

Monument Conservation The enormous earthquake that hit Cairo and surrounding regions in 1992 did not destroy the already-fragile monuments and ruins that make the area famous, but it did damage them considerably. This site describes efforts being undertaken to restore and fortify ancient treasures like the Mosque of Ebn Touloun. ✓**INTERNET**→*url* http://palimpsest.stanford.edu/byorg/gci/gci_news/cairo.html

The Egyptian Museum Located in the heart of downtown Cairo is the enormous Egyptian Museum, known worldwide for its definitive collection of Egyptian artifacts. Although there is little information about the museum at this site, it does offer pictures of the building's facade, of its entrance hall (a wonder in and of itself), and of one of the museum's galleries (treasure-packed exhibits and tiny walkways). ✓**INTERNET**→*url* http://auc-amer.eun.eg/museum.html

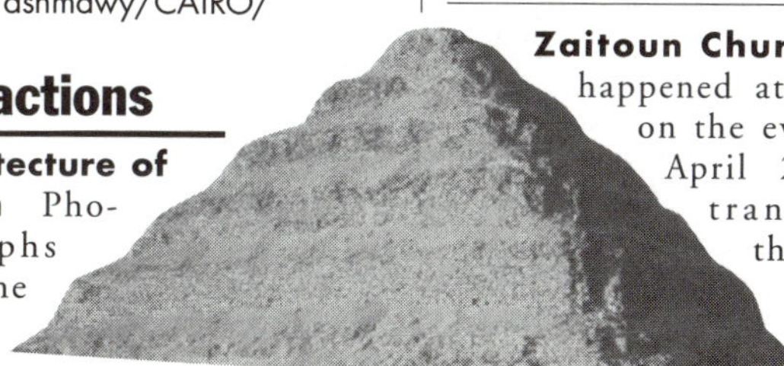

Zaitoun Church What happened at Zaitoun on the evening of April 2, 1968, transformed the church from a shabby

chapel in Cairo's suburbs into a major Christian landmark. It was on that day that the first apparition of the Virgin Mary appeared on its roof. Since then she has been reported to appear hundreds of times in different part of the church, including on window sills. The site contains a description of the church and the events that have occurred there. ✓**INTERNET** → *url* ftp://pharos.bu.edu/CN/articles/ZaitounApparitionOfSaintMary.txt

Fodor's Choice...

The Pyramids

The Great Pyramid is estimated to contain 2.5 million tons of stone, each stone weighs an average of 2.5 tons. According to Napolean, its cubic content is enough to build a wall ten feet high and a foot thick entirely around France.

—from Fodor's *Egypt*

Pyramids

Pyramid Discovered A short news article on the last pharaonic tomb to be discovered near Cairo. Unearthed May 3, 1994, this tomb is believed to have belonged to one of the daughters or wives of King Pepi I, the third king of the Sixth Dynasty. ✓**INTERNET**→ *url* http://www.newton.cam.ac.uk/egypt/newsdir/newpyr

The Egyptian Book of the Dead The walls of Cairo's pyramid tombs are famous for their haunting illustrations of the gods and goddesses of ancient Egypt. *The Eygptian Book of the Dead*, which dates from 1240 B.C., is a hymnal of praises to these deities. Read the full text of the book here. ✓**INTERNET**→ *url* http://www.lysator.liu.se/~drokk/BoD/

The Precinct of Djoser This tomb and its step pyramid are located just outside of Cairo. Glimpse its treasures with this virtual tour, which opens with a floor plan of the tomb. Click on any portion of the plan and a wonderfully detailed photograph of that part of the tomb will appear. ✓**INTERNET**→ *url* http://ccat.sas.upenn.edu/arth/zoser/zoser.html

The Ultimate Angelic Mission Some tours are too expensive. Some tours promise too much. And some tours are worth mocking for both of those reasons. This Web page pokes fun at a mystical tour of the pyramids offered by noted UFO "expert" Sean Morton. For a mere $4,000 Morton promises "high ecstasy in the Mystic Chambers of the Great Pyramid." Contact info for the tour is available. ✓**INTERNET**→ *url* http://www.infi.net/~psyspy/area51/people/morton/egypt_tour.txt

Morocco

Of all the countries in Africa, there is perhaps no nation with as exotic a reputation as Morocco. Between Casablanca (Bergman! Bogart! late-night television!) and Marrakesh (Crosby! Stills! Nash!), Morocco conjures up images of shadowy figures and bustling bazaars, Paul Bowles and Indiana Jones huddled in the corner of a dark bar while penniless undergraduates, fresh from Spain, buy drugs and write poetry. Begin your exploration of Morocco with the **Morocco FAQ**, **Solo Trip through Morocco**, and **The Moroccan Auditorium**. Brush up on your Berber at **Moroccan Languages**. And then investigate the unexpected—Moroccan golf courses—with **InterGolf's Morocco**.

Rock the Casbah—http://www.ece.scarolina.edu:80/~mouad/

On the Net

Across the board

Discover Morocco What's the national language of Morocco? French, of course, and you'll need to speak (or at least read) it in order to get much out of this collection of French-language links about the country. ✓**INTERNET**→*url* http://www.ift.ulaval.ca/~asma-net/Menu_principal.html

Moroccan Guided Tour Fez is more than just the name of a type of hat—it's also the name of an ancient city in Morocco! Explore a number of Moroccan towns through historical essays and color photographs at this site (you'll enjoy an enriched knowledge of Rabat, Marrakesh, Casablanca, and Tangier if you do). But the Guided Tour doesn't stop there—you're also treated to a list of regional and national festivals (with their dates for the current year), a gallery of pictures taken at different urban and bucolic locations around the country, a treatise on Moroccan food (it's more than just couscous and meshwee), and a quick look at sports in Morocco (they're crazy about soccer there too). This site is the next best thing to actually going there. ✓**INTERNET**→*url* http://www.dsg.ki.se:80/maroc/

Moroccan Wildside This page begins with lists of recent Moroccan news headlines, includes a guided tour of the country, and manages to confront Moroccan politics as well. The history, culture, and cuisine of Morocco captured the Western imagination long before Rick and Ilsa sang along with Sam in *Casablanca*. All information is searchable by keyword. ✓**INTERNET**→*url* http://www.ee.pdx.edu/~nadir/curious1.html

Morocco Nick Cockcroft's Morocco travelogue is more than just an interesting story. In it he recommends hotels in Fez and Casablanca and lists their prices, and he offers great tips (rent a taxi for half a day in Fez for about $9). Be sure not to miss his account of day six of his trip, when Nick visits a hamman for a bath. ✓**INTERNET**→*url* http://futures.wharton.upenn.edu/~cockcr01/morocco.html

Morocco FAQ The FAQ answers several important questions for those traveling to Morocco. "How bad is the hustling?" (It's bad, especially in the open markets.)

"What things can women do to avoid harassment?" (Tying back long hair is highly recommended.) "Where should I go?" (A list of hotels and restaurants by city is offered). There are also tips on drinking in Muslim Morocco, a brief run down of the current political situation, and a guide to what to pack (item #9: a padlock for your rucksack). ✓**INTERNET**→*url* http://www.solutions.net/rec-travel/africa/morocco/morocco.html

Culture

Marrakesh Express Use this guide to Moroccan weaving to discern traditionally woven rugs from commercial fakes. ✓**INTERNET**→*url* http://uslink.net/ddavis/

Moroccan Languages Did you know that almost a quarter of a million people in Morocco speak Spanish as their principal language? Did you know that 12 other languages are spoken in Morocco? Find out what language is spoken in the area you're planning to visit. ✓**INTERNET**→ *url* http://www.ala.doc.ic.ac.uk/~rap/Ethnologue/eth.cgi/Morocco/

Tamazight—Berber Culture and Language A French-language site that introduces visitors to Berber civilization through essays on its history, religion, art, and literature. There's even a dictionary of common Berber terms. ✓**INTERNET**→*url* http://www.ensem.u-nancy.fr/~ksahnine/Tamazight/tamazight.html

The Moroccan Auditorium Experience the sounds of Morocco at this site. Sound clips of music from a Berber wedding, the music of the Gnaua, and classical Moroccan music are all here. ✓**INTERNET**→ *url* http://www.dsg.ki.se/~v95-mel/Music/music.html

Tours

Homeric Tours For itineraries, price and reservation information, sample

A potter in the Tafilalt oasis—http://geogweb.berkeley.edu/GeoImages/Miller/

add-on airfares from major U.S. cities, tips for "doing" Morocco on you own, and great color pictures of Moroccan markets and Berber children, turn to this promotional page for Homeric Tours, a company specializing in travel to Morocco. ✓**INTERNET**→*url* http://www.traveldiscounts.com/Homeric/

InterGolf's Morocco InterGolf promises that Morocco will be the land of "kasbahs and caddyshacks." If world-class hotels and restaurants, four-star golfing, and even a few day trips to Berber villages and shops sounds good to you, then check out the info that the travel company lists at this site. ✓**INTERNET**→*url* http://www.golf.com/travel/packages/InterGolf/Morocco.Article.html

Solo Trip through Morocco Grab your touring bike and see Morocco from behind a set of handlebars. Just follow the route—which goes through Marrakesh, Ouarzazate, and Tizguy—and tips outlined in this essay, and you'll have the road trip of your life. ✓**INTERNET**→*url* http://www.math.science.unitn.it/Bike/Countries/Morocco/Tour_Reports/Trip.html

South Africa

It's perfectly acceptable to play at Sun City these days— after all, not only is Nelson Mandela finally leading the nation, but the **African National Congress Home Page** is free to all on the Web. Certainly, it was more than gold that attracted the Boers and British to South Africa—discover the nation's natural charms with a visit to the **South Africa National Parks Board** or its cosmopolitan allure at the **Johannesburg Virtual Tour**. **Travel Southern Africa** or **TravelNet! South Africa** will fill in the details. If you still want to be "politically correct," plan a tour through **Eco and Adventure Travel in Southern Africa**.

Go on a photo safari—http://www.cyberhouse.com/Safaris/Sample.html

On the Net

Across the board

Andy's Trip to South Africa Let Andy, a postdoctoral student who enjoys traveling, explain "kloofing" (jumping into ice-cold pools in the mountains), penguin colonies, and "the New South Africa" in this entertaining illustrated report of his trip. ✓**INTERNET**→*url* http://orca.astro.washington.edu/silber/africa.html

South African WWW Servers Before you head out the door to South Africa, you might want to learn more about the nation. And this site, while not primarily travel-oriented, will certainly help, with links to economic, political, and cultural resources in Grahamstown, Jo'burg, Durban, and Cape Town. ✓**INTERNET**→*url* http://www.is.co.za/www-za/www-za-map.html

Travel Southern Africa The definitive guide for travel in South Africa. Besides an exhaustive list of contact information for hotels in the region (from Cape Town to Victoria Falls), you'll also find lists of "must see" attractions (which include game parks), contact info to plan a helicopter tour or trophy hunting safari, transportation info, and even a list of national holidays organized by country. ✓**INTERNET**→*url* http://www.pix.za/business/travel/about.html

TravelNet! South Africa For anyone heading to South Africa, this is the definitive page: lists of hotels, restaurants, stores, and city and scenic tours. A history of the country and an essay on the customs and culture of South Africa provide background information for your trip. There's even a link to the South African Embassy online. ✓**INTERNET**→*url* http://www.sky.net/~eric/t/afrsou.htm

Welcome to South Africa Tourists are flocking to the jewel of the Cape. A handsome map at the Website introduces Web browsers to South Africa's attractions. Click on an ibex for a beautifully illustrated list of places to visit. Or choose a city and get the scoop on what's happening in Cape Town or Pietermaritzburg. ✓**INTERNET**→*url* http://osprey.unisa.ac.za/0/docs/south-africa.html

Attractions

Rhebokskloof Estate Begin your tour of the Cape with a tasty glass of wine from the Rhebokskloof Estate. The Estate has been around since 1692, and many of its buildings have been restored to their original Cape Dutch splendor. Use the hypertext links here to learn more about Rhebokskloof's winery (yes, there's a price list and ordering info), restaurants, and gift shop. ✓**INTERNET**→*url* http://www.os2.iaccess.za/rhebok/index.htm

Culture

African National Congress Home Page The official page of South Africa holds the findings of the African Communist Party, the Congress of South African Trade Unions, and the Human Rights Committee—all illegal not long ago. Mandela's voice is here too—from the 1955 Freedom Charter to his speeches as President. The page also provides local election information and email links to government offices. Join the Congress mailing list, ANCLST, with the subscription information at this site. ✓**INTERNET** ...→*url* http://

www.anc.org.za/ ...→*email* ancdip@wn.apc.org ✍ *Email with general correspondence*

noseWeek Billing itself as the magazine that covers "all the news you're not supposed to know," this weekly online publication reports on South Africa. A recent issue featured stories on a new national television station that is black-owned and run (a national first) and on Jani Allen, who was recently the focus of a national scandal when rumors of her affair with Eugene Terré Blanche became public. *noseWeek* will prepare you for dinner conversations with South Africans you meet on your stay there. ✓**INTERNET**→*url* http://www.aztec.co.za/users/dale/noseweek/thebe.htm

South African Soccer Page Get up-to-the-minute scores, player and team profiles, and even links to some clubs online. ✓**INTERNET**→*url* http://orff.sun.ac.za/~gerber/soccer.html

za.events (ng) A South African newsgroup for announcing local, regional, and national events of all kinds, including festivals, church fairs, and play openings. ✓**USENET**→za.events

Tours

Eco and Adventure Travel in Southern Africa African Alternatives is a company that offers every conceivable tour in South Africa. Having a hard time thinking of one? How about a white-water river tour down the Doring River, a walking tour down the Outeniqua hiking trail, a botanical-oriented jaunt through South Africa's temperate rain forests... More information and ideas are available at this Website. ✓**INTERNET**→*url* http://africa.com/~venture/index.htm

South Africa National Parks Board Experience the lush flora and fauna of South Africa's national parks, which are home to hundreds of endangered species, including the Addo elephant, mountain zebra, and bontebok. All the major parks and wildlife sanctuaries are listed along with any accommodations available in or near them. Prices are also given wherever available. ✓**INTERNET**→*url* http://africa.com/~venture/ntpks/npbhome.htm

Tourism in the Western Cape Information on hotels, guest houses, tour operators, travel agents, and the local tourism authority in the Western Cape. ✓**INTERNET**→*url* http://www.africa.com/captour/docs/wcape.htm

za.ads.lifts (ng) This newsgroup is handy for budget trekkers: the only posts are ride offers to various points in South Africa—from Middleburg to Pretoria. Check in to see if anyone is going your way! ✓**USENET**→za.ads.lifts

Cape Town

Cape Town The City Council of Cape Town sponsors this informational site, which provides national and local statistical data (57 percent of all citizens in the Western Cape are described as "coloured"), descriptions of local attractions (according to this site, Napoleon so loved the local wine of Cape Town that he languished for it while in prison), and even a listing of area businesses. The only thing missing from this site is a list of Cape Town hotels and restaurants. ✓**INTERNET**→*url* http://www.aztec.co.za/aztec/capetown.html

Cape Town Weather Watch Eliminate those nasty weather surprises the next time you travel to the Cape. Know what you should have packed before you get there! The Weather Watch features local forecasts (short-and-long term), climate readings, tidal info, and moon and sun phases for international travelers. ✓**INTERNET**→*url* http://emma.sea.uct.ac.za:80/weather/

The Cellars-Hohenhort Discover the wines of the Constantina Valley with a stay at the hotel Cellars-Hohenhort. A description of its services and price and reservation information are available at this site. ✓**INTERNET**→*url* http://www.calvacom.fr/relais/afsud/hohenort.html

Johannesburg

Johannesburg Virtual Tour The city of Johannesburg is also known as Egoli, which means "The City of Gold" in Afrikaans. It is South Africa's major point of entry and an economic and industrial hub for the entire southern African region. At this site you can learn other interesting facts about the city (18 percent of its citizens speak Swahili) and see pictures of some of its bigger attractions, such as the Botanical Gardens. Business services available in the city are also profiled here. ✓**INTERNET**→*url* http://www.pix.za/johannesburg/

Londolozi Game Reserve The word Londolozi means "protector of all living things" in Zulu, and so there is no hunting at this reserve! But advertising in Cyberspace is allowed, and price, reservation, and service information for the reserve is included. ✓**INTERNET**→*url* http://www.calvacom.fr/relais/afsud/londolozi.html

Across Africa

It might take a lifetime to explore the entire African continent. If you don't have that much time to spend on safari, you'll be happy to know that many African countries have a presence on the Web, making it possible to virtually explore Africa from Algeria to Zimbabwe (it will save you a lot of time). Visit **Eritrea** to learn about the country (and even read some poetry) or head to **Ghana—Land of Gold** to see all that glitters in Ghana. And if you can't leave Africa without seeing a lion, swing by the **Wildlife of Kenya** page.

On safari—from http://www.best.com/~travelw/africa.htm.

On the Net

Algeria

Algeria, My Country Basic information about Algeria provided by a patriotic citizen, Karim Lechilli. The site provides statistics on the Algerian population, natural resources, and economy (strangely enough, most of the economic data is under a section called Addresses). Don't leave this site without checking out the great map here—it's colorful and very detailed. ✓**INTERNET**→*url* http://www.ift.ulaval.ca/~lechilli/algeria.html

ALGNEWS (ml) A mailing list dedicated to current cultural and political events in Algeria. ✓**INTERNET**→*email* listserv@gwuvm.gwu.edu ✍ *Type in message body:* subscribe <your full name>

Angola

Angola Although the country's tourism industry has suffered greatly due to the nation's ongoing civil war, there are still plenty of reasons to visit Angola. For example, you can take a boat tour of the Cuanza River, visit the numerous national parks (including Iona, Kangandal, and Kameia e Quissama), and spot the native wildlife (like the rare palanca negra gigante). This site provides information on the economy, educational system, geography, government, hospitals, hotels, and restaurants of this complex country. ✓**INTERNET**→*url* http://www.umich.edu/~jasse/angola/angola.html

Portuguese for Travellers It would help to know a few phrases of the national language before arriving in Angola. This site offers sound clips of key words and expressions for travelers on their way to Angola—from "Where is the police station?" to "What time is it?" ✓**INTERNET**→*url* http://insti.physics.sunysb.edu/~mmartin/languages/portuguese/portuguese.html

Benin

Benin Voodoo Tour Discover the magic and danger of African voodoo! Christopher & Mayer, a German tour agency, offers to lead the way. Shrunken heads, anyone? ✓**INTERNET**→*url* http://www.roka.net/voodoo/

Cameroon

Republic of Cameroon Underneath Cameroon's brilliantly colored yellow, green, and red flag is a description of the country and its people, customs, and culture. Learn about Cameroon's geography and the fact that over 54 percent of its land is forest and woodlands. Read about the people who inhabit that land—over half of the 13 million-plus citizens practice indigenous beliefs, and 55 percent of the entire population over 15 years old is literate. And don't forget to read about Cameroon's current political situation before departing for the country; click on the government section for some basic information and follow up with the defense forces section. The tourism section here gives you some ideas on what to do when visiting the country (its 400 miles of shoreline are ideal for fishing), but you'll find no practical hotel, restaurant, or services information except a list of Cameroonian embassies in different countries. ✓**INTERNET**→*url* http://scitsc.wlv.ac.uk/~cm9032/Cameroon.html

Cape Verde

Republic of Cape Verde Home Page (Unofficial) Want a recipe for traditional Crioulous fish stew? Like to learn how to say "Good evening" in Crioul? (It's, "Boa noti.") Interested in pictures of the eruption of Mount Fogo? Then visit this site, which has a wealth of information about the history and culture of Cape Verde, and is a great place to get a list of Crioulous restaurants in the U.S. ✓**INTERNET**→*url* http://www.umassd.edu/specialprograms/caboverde/capeverdean.html

Eritrea

Eritrea (Abyssinia CyberSpace Gateway) Although Eritrea has been an independent country only since 1993, it has managed to develop a very strong Net presence. At this site you can jump to the Eritrea Information Center, Eritrea at the Model

Fodor's Choice...

Boat Trips

- The *African Queen* on the Tana River
- The new sailing shuttle from Dar es Salaam to Zanzibar
- Moonlight canoe trips from Kiwayu, Kenya

—from Fodor's *Kenya & Tanzania*

League of Arab States, the Eritrean Artists Home Page, and even to a site featuring Eritrean poetry! Besides the links, this page offers maps of the infant country, a list of Eritrean restaurants in the U.S. (most of them are in California), and several essays on the native language of Eritrea, Amharic. ✓**INTERNET**→*url* http://www.cs.indiana.edu/hyplan/dmulholl/eritrea/eritrea.html

Join Dehai Dehai is a mailing list for the discussion of Eritrean society, history, politics, economy, technology, culture, and current affairs. You have to prove Eritrean citizenship to be nominated for subscription to the list; to start the application process, fill out and submit the questionnaire found at the Website. ✓**INTERNET** …→*url* http://diglib.stanford.edu/dehaicgi/join/add.cgi?NAME …→ *email* dehai@thames.stanford.edu ✍ *Write a request*

Ethiopia

Ethiopia—A Country Study An extensive hypertext essay on the country, its history, and its people. Ethiopean ethnic groups, languages, and occupational castes are examined alongside the role of the Ethiopian military in modern society. Sections of this site range from an overview of the Ethiopian legal system to descriptions of the country's major ports. Sadly, there is no travel-specific information, meaning no hotel or restaurant info. ✓**INTERNET**→*url* http://lcweb2.loc.gov/et_00_00.html

Ethiopian News (ml) Daily reports on Ethiopian news. ✓**INTERNET**→*email* ethinfo@cleo.eng.sun.com ✍ *Write a request*

Ghana

Ghana Home Page Although this page is small, it's well worth visiting if you're planning a trip to Ghana. The site has short lists of hotels and restaurants in vital cities like Accra, Labadi, and Tetteh Quashie. The What's ON offers extensive lists of nightlife spots (with phone numbers), nature highlights, beaches, and festivals (by month and region). Some of the tips in the Dos and Dont's section are fairly commonsensical ("respect the locals"), but some are more specific to Ghana ("don't swim in lakes or rivers" and "boil your drinking water"). If you prefer to skip all this information and just look at some photographs of the country, there's an online gallery here that allows you to do just that. ✓**INTERNET**→*url* http://www.uta.fi/~csfraw/ghana.html

Ghana—Land of Gold Did you know that the largest man-made lake in the world is located in Ghana? It's Lake Volta, and you can cruise on it aboard the *Akosombo Queen.* Come to this site to discover other interesting places to visit in this golden land. ✓**INTERNET**→*url* http://acorn.educ.nottingham.ac.uk//SchEd/pages/eb/interest.html

Kenya

Kenya/Tanzania Trip Report Four friends—Chris Wee, Sandeep Michandani, and George and Shankar Narayanaswamy—all took a trip to Kenya and Tanzania together, and a copy of Lonely Planet was their only guide. They had several adventures along the way. Accounts of their adventures along with tips for budget travelers make up this Website. ✓**INTERNET**→*url* http://seclab.csucdavis.edu/~wee/east-africa .html

Wildlife of Kenya Hakuna matata! Sit back and enjoy some fantasic photos of Fred and Dot Radon's safari in Kenya. ✓**INTERNET**→*url* http://gaia.ecs.csus.edu/~reardonf/kenya.html

Madagascar

Madagascar—The Rainbow Island The site opens with a big map of this island country. Surrounding the map are hypertext links to sections on the country's history (Madagascar was a French colony from 1895 to 1960), its fauna (the island is home to half the world's varieties of chameleons), and its culture (all Malagasy adhere to the traditional vintana, a religious calendar that defines the occupations of each day of the week). A whole section of the site is devoted to tourism, which offers brief essays on the granite cliff near Ihosy and pictures of the erosion along the valley of the Irodo, but unfortunately no practical info on navigating a trip to Madagascar. ✓**INTERNET**→*url* http://lalo.inria.fr/~andry/Mada.html

Madagasikara Since Madagascar is home for most of the world's surviving lemurs, it is completely natural that this site has devoted a topic to them—click on the Lemur Sightings topic, and you'll reach links to the Lemur Home Page and Stanford University's Lemur Gallery (there's also a link to the alt.fan.lemurs newsgroup!). The site links to the CIA World Factbook entry on Madagascar, a country map, and a link to an essay called "The Languages of Madagascar." ✓**INTERNET**→*url* http://www.cable.com/madagas/madagas.htm

soc.culture.malagasy (ng) A newsgroup for discussion of the culture and people of the African island of Madagascar. The majority of the messages are in French. ✓**USENET**→soc.culture.malagasy

Nigeria

soc.culture.nigeria (ng) If you're looking for tips on where to go in Nigeria, you won't find them here. But you can turn to this newsgroup to get a feel for the political issues that might confront you while traveling in Nigeria—the phrase "Tunde Giwa for President!" comes up here frequently. ✓**USENET**→soc.culture.nigeria

Seychelles

Seychelles These beautiful islands in the Indian Ocean, with their white coral beaches and six-foot waves, were only discovered two centuries ago. At this site you'll find a list of hotels (with their addresses and phone numbers) and of houses to rent (also with phone numbers). Natalie L'Efevre, a native, also provides an es-

Rashaida women—from http://web.syr.edu:80/~decole/africa.htm

say full of practical advice for those visiting Seychelles—you can get CNN in most hotel rooms, and there hasn't been a shark attack near the islands for more than 20 years. All information at this site is also available in Dutch. ✓INTERNET→*url* http://interhealth.com/seychelles/

Somalia

soc.culture.somalia (ng) To gain insight into recent Somali political events, debate the basic merits of the Somali language versus English, or to add your vote to the "Most Valuable Somali Soccer Player of All Time" thread, you can visit this newsgroup. ✓USENET→soc.culture.somalia

Somalia A scholarly work that profiles every aspect of life in Somalia—from religion to language to health concerns to current political concerns. Although the book is not tourist-oriented, it will give readers valuable background info for their stay in Somalia. ✓INTERNET→*url* gopher://umslvma.umsl.edu/11/LIBRARY/GOVDOCS/ARMYAHBS/AAHB3

Zambia

National Parks of Zambia Zambia is well known for its excellent national parks system, which is popular with the photo safari crowd. Select the Nsumbu National Park for text descriptions, maps, and photos of Elsa the lioness running wild. ✓INTERNET→*url* http://www.cs.umn.edu/users/kumar/amin/zambia .html

Zambia Discover the glory of Zambia with the help of the Zambian National Tourist Board and Grand Travel, a travel company that cosponsors this page. A short essay on the country describes it as a land of many contrasts, with "prolific wildlife, birds in abundance, fertile valleys, spectacular waterfalls, huge lakes and winding rivers, swamps and wetlands, hot springs and vast golden plains." To find places to stay while you're there, read the descriptions of hotels and lodges, including those with thatched rondavels, wood cabins, and luxury hotels. And don't forget to check out the travel tips here before you leave—how else will you know that there are laundry facilities available in most camps, so three sets of bushwear are more than adequate! ✓INTERNET→*url* http://www.zamnet.zm/zamnet/znntb.html

A palm plantation in Zanzibar—http://challenge.tiac.net/users/dmcooper/tanzania.html

Zanzibar

Zanzibar Let the tropical East African island unfold on your computer screen through this photo essay, which takes you to several local attractions—visit the Sultan's Palace, walk through a palm plantation, and see one of Zanzibar's famous carved doors at this site. You'll also be transported to the farmer's market in Stone Town, where all sorts of tropical fruits and vegetables, fish, and meats are for sale. ✓INTERNET→*url* http://www.tiac.net/users/dmcooper/tanzania.html

Zimbabwe

Virtual Zimbabwe Become a virtual Dr. Livingston and explore Victoria Falls or the Chilojo Cliffs online. The text accompanying the stunning photos at this site describes the natural history of each region (white rhinos are once again flourishing in Matobo Hills). Links to hotels and tour operators let visitors plan their own safari. And the online presence of local arts magazines and music clubs lead to recommendations about what to do after a long day of looking at gnus. Tips for business travelers are also included. ✓INTERNET→*url* http://wn.apc.org/mediatech/VRZ10001.HTM

Zimbabwean Cricket Page Kevin Curran. Andy Flower. David Brain. These men are national cricket stars, and you might want to learn something about them before trying to make new friends in Zimbabwe. ✓INTERNET→*url* http://zikzak.net/~ddyte/

The Middle East

The Middle East is the cradle of civilization, and its long history has produced many fascinating cultures—take a virtual trip to **Middle East Studies** and **Virtual Tourist II** to see the full scope of Middle Eastern diversity. Wander through the graceful minarets and colorful mosaics at the **Islamic Architecture** site or sway gently to the sounds of the Casbah at **Arabic Music, Pictures & Film**. Be your own peace broker, stopping in at the **Virtual Tour of Israel**, and then head straight for **Damascus Old and New**. You can also visit places you'll probably never see in this lifetime by reading the **Beirut Times** or by visiting the **Iranian Cultural Information Center**.

Lebanon's MSaylHa Fortress—http://www.hiof.no/ludvigsen/webdoc/levant_servers.html

On the Net

Across the board

Arab Countries WWW Sites Though not specifically geared toward travelers, the links here will provide you with background information on Arab nations. A trip to the State of Kuwait leads to its page at the Model League of Arab States and to a profile of Kuwaiti exile Saud Alhajerí. In the Kingdom of Saudi Arabia, you'll find a virtual tour courtesy of the embassy, academic and research networks, and Sany Zakharia's touching homage to his war-torn homeland. ✓ **INTERNET**→*url* http://www.liii.com/~hajeri/arab.html

Middle East Countries, Maps, Pictures, and Culture The simple text menus on this page leave much to be desired in terms of decoration, but the information behind the links is impeccable—not only maps of the Middle East and Northern Africa, but also language databases, image archives, music, poetry, and recipes. If you have a hankering to listen to the music of Ziad Rahbani or a burning desire to prepare *khiyar wa laban* (cucumbers and yogurt), come here. ✓ **INTERNET**→*url* http://menic.utexas.edu/menic/subject/culture.htmlw

Middle East International Travelers' Health Information Sick of staying at home? Well, travel then—but don't get sick abroad. Revised monthly by the Centers for Disease Control, this report covers those diseases transmitted by insects, food and water, and contact with other people. If you're going to get the most out of your trip, learn to minimize your risk of an illness here. ✓ **INTERNET**→*url* http://www.cdc.gov/cgi-bin/includetext.pl?/Travel/regional/mideast.txt

Middle East Studies Search this academic server by keyword or browse by country page. A query on literature brought up a profile of Hanan Ashrawi, the Turkish Poetry page, Qaddafi's "Green Book," and the Khalil Gibran home page. Diplomatic types should opt for the Model League of Arab States link; debaters can jump directly to talk.politics.mideast, which is available from any country page. Architecture, cinema, music, and travel pages are also here. Stop by the Moroccan Cuisine page for a glass of mint tea and some couscous. ✓**INTERNET**→*url* http://menic.utexas.edu/mes.html

Virtual Tourist II An interactive map of the Middle East that links to information pages representing every Middle Eastern nation. What kind of information is on the pages? Population statistics, language, history, maps, and even travel and tourism info . Before you take a trip, look at Virtual Tourist. ✓**INTERNET**→*url* http://wings.buffalo.edu/imap/mideast2

Culture

Arabic Music, Pictures & Film Listen to Arabic music, or view the Isfahan mosque in Iran at this small collection of Arab cultural sites. ✓**INTERNET**→*url* http://philae.sas.upenn.edu/Arabic/arabfilm.html

International Association of Sufism Sufism is the school of Islam that focuses on the goal of spiritual truth; in addition to explaining the history and philosophy of Sufism, the IAS's home page provides information about Sufism-related events and publications. ✓**INTERNET**→*url* http://www.ias.org/

Islamic Architecture Islamic architecture ranges over Northern Africa, up as far as Spain, and over into the Middle East. Now it's on the Internet, with this collection of hundreds of thumbnails of mosques, mihrab rooms, prayer halls, and bays. ✓**INTERNET**→*url* http://rubens.anu.edu.au/islam2/index_1.html

Islamic Architecture in Isfahan—Home Page The Iranian city of Isfahan is one of ten areas designated by UNESCO as an International Heritages site, and this site includes images and essays on Islamic architecture throughout the ages, as well as maps of the city. ✓**INTERNET**→*url* http://www.anglia.ac.uk/~trochford/isfahan.html

Levant Cultural Multimedia Servers What qualifies as Levant culture? Anything that pertains to Iraq, Israel, Jordan, Kuwait, Lebanon, Palestine, Syria, and Turkey; and anything that appears at this massive archive, which collects documents and images on Levant archaeology, architecture, business, cinema, clothing, cosmetics, food, geography, health, history, humor, language, media, music, politics, religion, and travel. Travel resources include U.S. Department of State advisories and a brief first-person account of the author's summer 1995 trip to Lebanon. ✓**INTERNET**→*url* http://www.hiof.no/ludvigsen/webdoc/levant_servers.html

Middle East Resource Center Here you'll find a trilingual downloadable browser capable of reading Persian, Arabic, and English. Articles, novels, and poems in their original languages are also at this site. But it's not just linguistics here—the Center provides links to Iranian human rights sites and an online chat server. ✓**INTERNET**→*url* http://gpg.com/MERC/merc.html

soc.culture.arabic (ng) Everything is up for grabs in soc.culture.arabic, so drop by to ask your Middle Eastern travel questions or to talk about politics in the area. ✓**USENET**→soc.culture.arabic

soc.religion.islam (ng) A well-trafficked newsgroup discussing a broad range of Islamic issues, from the role of women to intermarriage to the fate of non-Muslims on Judgement Day. The FAQ, with its 15 parts, is equally far-reaching; besides an extensive discussion of Islamic beliefs, there are sections on Islamic Internet resources, human rights, and architecture. ✓**USENET**→soc.religion.islam *FAQ:* ✓**INTERNET**...→*url* http:/www.cis.ohio-state.edu/hypertext/faq/usenet-faqs/bygroup/soc/religion/islam/top.html ...→*url* ftp://rtfm.mit.edu/pub/usenet-by-hierarchy/alt/religion/islam

The Holy Quran The special feature of this English translation of the Quran is its index of specific

Fodor's Choice...

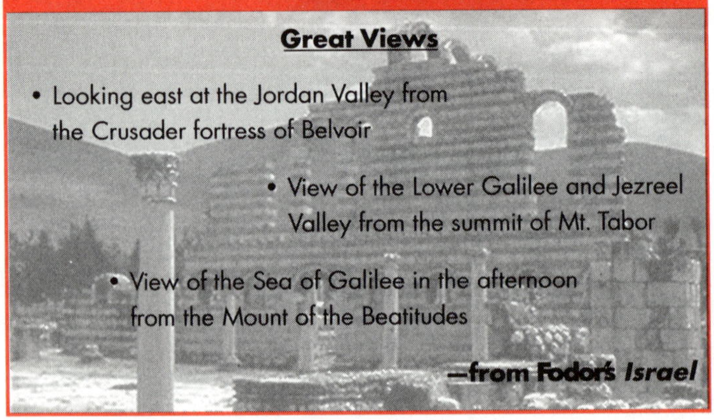

Friday Mosque, Yazd, Iran—http://phi lae.sas.upenn.edu/Arabic/arabfilm.html

references in the text. ✓INTERNET→*url* http://chestnut.enmu.edu/~st jeanp/quran.index.html

Iran

Iranian Cultural Information Center An interactive map takes cyberexplorers where most will never set foot. Listen to a Kurdish song while admiring the colorful paintings of Ostad Ali Asghar Tajvidi. Read Persian poems, recipes, and reviews of Iranian cinema. Keep time and mark holidays with any of several Iranian clock and calendar programs—today is 11 Mordad 1374. ✓INTERNET→*url* http://tehran.stanford.edu/

Iranshahr All the info on Iran that anyone could ever want, with links to literature, music, images, conferences, and lectures. A clickable map of the nation and a hotlist of other Websites with resources on the Middle East are also here. ✓INTERNET→*url* http://weber.u.washington.edu/~iranshar/

soc.culture.iranian (ng) This newsgroup clarifies cultural and political issues pertaining to Iran and grapples with the distance between ancient traditions and contemporary practices. (Many posts come from American college students.) ✓USENET→soc.culture.iranian

Israel

Dan Hotels America has its Fairmonts and its Marriotts; Israel has Dan Hotels, a "top chain with nine luxury hotels in...Jerusalem, Tel Aviv, Haifa, Herzliya, Caesarea, and Eilat." Read all about the chain and the individual properties. Even if you don't make it to Israel, you can commit some information to memory to use at a cocktail party, like the fact that the Dan Tel Aviv has both an indoor and outdoor pool. ✓INTERNET→*url* http://www.elron.net/dan hotels/

Exodus The most famous Exodus is probably still the one in the Bible, with Leon Uris's mammoth novel a close second. But in third place and closing in is this Exodus, a travelogue by Michael Bielisky, who followed the Biblical trail of Moses through the Negev Desert. While Bielisky's journey lasted only four days in June 1995, he recorded his experience for the Web, and he uses his travelogue as a starting point for exploring the relationships between man and God, technology and spirituality, and information and politics. ✓INTERNET→*url* http://exodus.bgu.ac.il/exodus/

Golan Heights Information Server While this Website is primarily political, there are several useful links for travelers, including a slide show of the region, maps, articles, and even a tourism section that highlights attractions like Mount Hermon and Katzrin. From this page Netsurfers can link to the Golan Heights FAQ and subscribe to the mailing list. ✓INTERNET→*url* http://www.golan.org.il/

Guy Tours Guy Tours specializes in private car tours, group sightseeing outings, and an "Israel Experience Tour." (All Jimi Hendrix jokes are hereby registered.) Browse itineraries, email the company, or fill out a tour request form, and Guy will respond within 24 hours. ✓INTERNET ...→*url* http://www.elron.net/guytours/ *email* ...→guytours@elronet.co.il ✍ *Email with general correspondence*

Haifa Chamber of Commerce A large listing of Haifan businesses that can be searched by keyword or browsed by category. Travelers will find info on ambulance services, film development, cosmetics, and import / export companies, which may come in handy during their trips to Israel. ✓INTERNET→*url* http://www.haifa121-coc.org.il/

Israel and Its Cities Jerusalem, Tel-Aviv, and Haifa have sites, of course, but have you ever thought of spending your days and nights in Ashkelon, Kibbutz Lavi, or Karmiel? Learn about Israel's most

O little town of Bethlehem...—http://www.cs.TU-Berlin.DE/~ishaq/pal/pics/

The Wailing Wall—http://www.hiof.no/ludvigsen/webdoc/levant/bonfils.html

famous cities and their less famous counterparts. ✓INTERNET→*url* http://gauss.technion.ac.il/~nyh/israel/cities.html

Israel Information Service Listen to an audio greeting. Browse or search the IIS WWW Document Pool, which collects a wealth of political and cultural documents about Israel. Read the full text of interim agreements between Israel and the PLO. Explore Israel's history, politics, geography, health, education, science, economics, culture, and demographics. Then decide whether a trip to visit one of the oldest and most complex societies on the planet is in order. ✓INTERNET→*url* http://www.israel.org/israelinfo/main.html

Israel Museum Israel's premier art museum is on the Web in a big way, with a virtual tour that includes everything from the Dead Sea Scrolls to the Modern Judaica Collection to the Youth Wing. This Website has brief descriptions of the museum's holdings, but no electronic uploads of actual artwork. ✓INTERNET→*url* http://www.imj.org.il/

Israel's National Parks Forget about the Grand Canyon, Yellowstone, Crater Lake, and Joshua Tree. Those are American parks, and in Israel they make about as much sense as a passport with Yasir Arafat's picture and Norman Fell's name (although, come to think of it, they do look sort of similar). In Israel natural beauty and outdoor recreation have different names, and those names are Ashkelon, Bar'am, Belvoir, Caesarea, Masada, Tel Megiddo, Nimrod's Fortress, Bet She'arim, Yehiam Fortress, and Zippori. Learn all about the parks at this site. ✓INTERNET→*url* http://www.webscope.com/inpa/

Virtual Tour of Israel You can't take all the paths of Moses, since some areas are still under construction. But a briefly annotated collection of images takes you through the Negev Desert, Western Galilee, and Jerusalem—and it will take you considerably less than 40 days and 40 nights. ✓INTERNET→ *url* http://dapsas.weizmann.ac.il/bcd/bcd_parent/tour/tour.html

Visions of Israel A two-week visit to the nation in October 1992 is the basis for this travelogue, which includes photographs and brief descriptions. Go through Caesarea, the Sinai Peninsula, Jerusalem, the Golan Heights, and the Negev. ✓INTERNET→*url* http://www.hyperion.com/~koreth/israel/

Jordan

Hashemite Kingdom of Jordan This site is a virtual tour of the Kingdom of Jordan—complete with shopping information, dining etiquette tips, and an Internet connection for Jordanians worldwide. A link to the newsgroup soc.culture.jordan gives Netsurfers access to discussions of everything from the peace negotiations with Israel to King Hussein's decision to fight alongside Muslim forces in Bosnia. ✓INTERNET→*url* http://www.mit.edu:8001/activities/jordanians/jordan/

Web Server Of The Hashemite Kingdom Of Jordan With absolutely no information on Jordan almonds, Michael Jordan, or G. Jordan Liddy—kids, if your parents tell you his name is G. Gordon Liddy, just stop up your ears with cotton—this Website is still an excellent resource for anyone thinking of traveling to the Hashemite Kingdom. Find here an archive of important Jordanian documents (the Constitution, the Na-

Kuwait City, object of Saddam's desire—http://www.ccn.cs.dal.ca/~ai474/kuwait.html

tional Charter, and the October 1994 treaty with Israel), a broadcast schedule for Radio Jordan, and a currency conversion utility that's updated weekly. Links connect to other home pages by Jordanians. ✓**INTERNET**→*url* http://iconnect.com/jordan/

Kuwait

Hotels in Kuwait A list of Kuwaiti hotels, with contact numbers and rankings is available. ✓**INTERNET**→*url* http://www.cs.cmu.edu/Web/People/anwar/kuwait-hotels.html

Kuwait A clickable map, links to other sites, a huge image of Kuwait City, and a service allowing Netsurfers to fax free of charge to Kuwait. ✓**INTERNET**→*url* http://www.ccn.cs.dal.ca/~ai474/kuwait.html

Kuwait Hotels In Safat you have a choice between the Messilah Beach Hotel and the Le Meridien Kuwait. In Farwaniya there's only the Holiday Inn Crowne Plaza. Check out this list of hotels, which is sponsored by the Association of Business Travellers and includes links to the ABT's online reservations services. ✓**INTERNET**→*url* http://www.hk.linkage.net/markets/abt/hotels/MIDDLE-E/KUWAIT.HTML

Kuwait Info Page A good introduction to Kuwait-specific resources on the Web, including a detailed map of the nation, a link to soc.culture.kuwait, a study of the Kuwaiti oil-field fires, and a useful feature that generates the current time in Kuwait. (Oddly, it's always 6:15 a.m.) ✓**INTERNET**→*url* http://www.cs.cmu.edu/Web/People/anwar/kuwait.html

Kuwait Recipes Before you visit Kuwait, acclimate your palate to the native cuisine—download postscript files of Kuwaiti dishes, such as bademjan, baghali, chelo, hashu, and sabze. ✓**INTERNET**→*url* http://www.cs.cmu.edu/afs/cs.cmu.edu/user/anwar/kuwait/recipes/

Lebanon

Beirut Times Get a description of, subscription rates for, and a free sample of the largest weekly Arab-American newspaper. ✓**INTERNET**→*url* http://www.arabbiz.com/~beirut/

SCL Lebanon Although it's affiliated with the soc.culture.lebanon home page, this Website merits a listing of its own for three reasons. First, it serves as a WWW gateway to the newsgroup's excellent FAQ. Second, it offers a large set of documents pertaining to Lebanese history and culture, including digests of the Leb-Net mailing list. Third, it contains resources that are godsends for any traveler contemplating a trip to Lebanon, including an image map of renovated downtown Beirut. ✓**INTERNET**→*url* http://eurecom27.cica.fr:8080/

soc.culture.lebanon (ng) A newsgroup for the discussion of Lebanon, its people, and their culture is here. ✓**USENET**→soc.culture.lebanon

Palestine

Palestine Information Server What's at the Palestine Information Server? A history of the dispossessed nation, historical documents (including the Declaration of Independence for the State of Palestine), Palestinian poems, books, recipes, essays on peace in the Middle East, maps, and even a link to a set of articles about Zionism (although with titles like "The Racist Nature of Zionism" and "Jewish Opposition to Zionism," they're not likely to challenge the prejudices of any hardcore Palestinian-rights activists). ✓**INTERNET**→*url* http:// www.alquds.org

soc.culture.palestine (ng) The political discussions can get pretty heated here, so if your interest in Palestine is purely from a tourist's perspective, you may want to lurk a little and take in the debates. ✓**USENET**→soc.culture.palestine

The Palestinian Home Page A collection of links about Palestine,

Propher's mosque, Medina, S. A.—http://philae.sas.upenn.edu/Arabic/

ranging from governmental resources to images to university sites is available. ✓**INTERNET**→*url* http://www.cs.TU-Berlin.DE/~ishaq/pal/palestine/pales tine.html

Saudi Arabia

Kingdom of Saudi Arabia Academic, demographic, and economic information on Saudi Arabia, including a small but useful travel section with a list of important telephone numbers, a directory of hotels and resorts, a basic Arabic-phrase book complete with phonetic pronunciations and illustrative sound clips, and a collection of photos. ✓**INTERNET**→*url* http://www.wpi.edu/~zakharia/saudi-arabia.html

Royal Embassy of Saudi Arabia The huge image map that serves as the front end for the Royal Embassy's Website takes forever to download, but the wait is well worth it for any traveler heading to Saudi Arabia. Individual pages deal with the Saudi government, current news, and U.S.-Saudi relations. Travelers setting course for the Middle Eastern kingdom should pay special attention to the Travel section of this site, which furnishes basic information along with contact numbers. Remember, all you horny, ham-loving lushes: Saudi Arabia says "no" to pornography, pork, and alcohol. ✓**INTERNET**→*url* http://imedl.saudi.net

Saudi Arabian Embassy, Washington D.C. A press release from the Kingdom of Saudi Arabia that includes pictures of its monarchs, past and present (*Murphy Brown* fans will be pleased to learn that the late King Abdul Aziz Bin Abdul Rahman Al Saud looks a bit like Robert Pastorelli). ✓**INTERNET**→*url* http://www.arabian.org

Welcome to Saudi Arabia This page proves that there are dozens of sites devoted to Saudi Arabia on the Net—student home pages created by proud Saudis, government pages, and political pages. Link to them all or browse this site's content, which includes the archives of a Saudi-specific mailing list. ✓**INTERNET**→*url* http://darkwing.uoregon.edu/~kbatarfi/saudi.html

Syria

Damascus Old and New Jesus met Saul on the road to Damascus, and while there isn't much chance that you'll meet either of them there, you can tour Old Damascus—Nizam's House, Salah Al-Dine Al-Ayoubi, Tikieh Soulimahieh—as well as New Damascus, ably represented by modern hotels like Le Meridian and the Sheraton. ✓**INTERNET**→*url* http://www.umich.edu/~kazamaza/syria.html

General Tourist Information on Syria As its title suggests, this site contains general tourist information on Syria—vague but helpful tips on finding a hotel, eating out, shopping, and taking in the sights. ✓**INTERNET**→*url* http:// 204.96.64.150:80/TRAVEL/PLACES/MIDDLEE/Syria/Country.HTM

Hotel Guide to Syria The next time you're in Damascus, stay in Marjeh Square at your own risk—according to this page, it's grimy and noisy, sort of the Times Square of Syria. Updated regularly, this guide to Syrian hotels includes address and phone information, price ranges (in Syrian pounds), Syrian Ministry of Tourism ratings, and notes on accommodations. ✓**INTERNET**→*url* ftp://ftp.access.digex.net/pub/access/alliedus/hotel-guide

soc.culture.syria (ng) Should Israel give the Golan away? What will happen to Syria after Assad's regime? While many of the posts on this newsgroup are political creeds cross-posted to other Middle Eastern soc.culture newsgroups, there are a few short threads that pertain specifically to travel in Syria. ✓**USENET**→soc.culture.syria

Syria A collection of links about Syria that covers many topics, including archaeology, architecture, maps, universities, and newsgroups. ✓**INTERNET**→*url* http://menic.utexas.edu/menic/countries/syria.html

Syrian Arab Republic This official home page of the soc.culture.syria newsgroup includes maps, demographic statistics, a brief essay on Syrian history, images, and more. ✓**INTERNET**→*url* http://www.coe.uncc.edu/~aalyoune/syria/main.html

Jerusalem

Don't forget to bring a gift when you make your trip to Jerusalem, because the city is enjoying its 3,000th birthday. (What do you get a city for its birthday anyway? A hairdryer? A mayor? A new wall?) Get the details of the celebration at **Jerusalem 3000**. **Jerusalem Mosaic** will tell you all about those 3,000 thrill-packed years that make it one of the most holy and historic cities for people worldwide. **Jerusalem One** is more firmly rooted in the present, boasting Judaic studies software and a cybermall. If you can't make the pilgrimage yourself, you can still visit the **Dome of the Rock** virtually.

The Dome of the Rock—http://www.webcom.com/~zume/GallerySight/

On the Net

Across the board

Jerusalem Mosaic This site helps you make sense of Jerusalem with maps of the city, a list of the city's attractions (including the magnificent Chagall Windows), and a history of the city, from the time of the First Temple through the Crusader and Mameluke periods and even into the current century, with the British Mandate and Israeli statehood. Read, reread, and remember, so that the next time someone tells you that Mameluke is that large but lovable cartoon dog, you can come right back with a textured and compelling account of the place of ablaq in Jerusalem's architecture. ✓**INTERNET**→*url* http://www1.huji.ac.il/jeru/jerusalem.html

Jerusalem One Billed as the most popular Jewish and Israeli information source on the Internet. Find Aliyah information, Torah and Judaic studies, a huge Jewish software and clip-art collection, a large cybermall, and a tour of Jerusalem at this site. ✓**INTERNET**→*url* http://www.jer1.co.il/index.html

Jerusalem—The Capital of Israel An exhibit mounted by the Israel Information Service, this site has illustrated capsule entries for most major attractions in the city, divided into six thematic sections (Jerusalem—The Seat of Israel's Government; The Holy City to Three Religions; The Old City—A Living History; A Collage of Neighborhoods and Streets; City of Museums, Monuments, and Culture; and Jerusalem's Parks and Promenades). Take a walk through the pedestrian mall on Ben-Yehuda Street (where "Jerusalemites can enjoy a leisurely stroll, cafes, shopping, street musicians, and more") or spend the afternoon at the Bloomfield Science Museum (which features "hands-on science exhibits with the aim of challenging and stimulating children with science and inculcating appreciation of the phenomena of the natural world"). ✓**INTERNET**→*url* http://www.israel.org/israel-info/chaim/display.cgi/chaim@jerusalem@jlemmain.htm

Culture

Dome of the Rock An octagonal building that caps the summit of Mount Moriah in Jerusalem, the Dome of the Rock is one of the most impressive buildings in the Middle East and the world. View pictures of the Dome, and get directions for visiting the real thing. ✓**INTERNET**→*url* http://www.webcom.com/~zume/GallerySight/SN.Dome/Intro.html

Jerusalem Post Search an archive of Israel's main newspaper. ✓**COMPUSERVE**→*go* jerusalem

Trimillenium

Jerusalem 3000 Throughout 1996, Jerusalem will officially celebrate its trimillenium—something that most cities will never have the opportunity to experience. (By the time New York's trimillenium rolls around, the United States is likely to be buried under miles of nuclear ash and old O. J. Simpson transcripts.) And for the big 3,000th birthday party, Israel's capital is pulling out all the stops—hosting parades, marches, fairs, concerts, readings, and more. The Web headquarters for this blessed event includes an address by the mayor of Jerusalem, a pictorial tour of the city, and a full schedule of trimillenial events. ✓**INTERNET**→*url* http://www.ladpc.gov.il/jeru/jerusalm.html

Part 3

Asia

Asia

Remember when you thought if you dug long enough in the backyard you'd reach China? Now there's an easier way—via plane or Cyberspace. **Asia Online** and **@Asia** are good places to start, filled with a mixture of history, culture, and current events for the many cultures that Westerners tend to lump together as Asian. Once your interest is piqued, try **rec.travel.asia** for suggestions on choosing Thailand or Singapore, adventure travel or luxury travel from those who've gone before. Whether you choose to delve into the deep with the **Asian Diver's Homepage** or contemplate the delicate beauty of 1,000-year-old porcelain at **Asian Arts**, **TravelASIA Hotel** will have a warm bed awaiting your return.

Welcome to Asia Online—http://www.asia-online.com/

On the Net

Across the board

AIT's Asia Info Page A clickable map of Asia with built-in links to travel information, general country information, Internet providers, and discussion groups. Below the map is a list of links to more general Asian resources, such as Asian Stock Market closings and *Asia, Inc.* magazine. ✓**INTERNET**→*url* http://emailhost.ait.ac.th/Asia/asia.html

ASEAN Information Superhighway Certainly not a comprehensive tourist site, this directory includes links to sites for each of the countries that are members of the Association of Southeast Asian Nations (ASEAN). ✓**INTERNET**→*url* http://gil.ipswichcity.qld.gov.au/~bchana/asean.html

@Asia "Come with us as we showcase the wealth and charm of twenty first century Asia." Buried deep under layers of menus, and advertisements, this Website eventually begins to fulfill its promise. A focus section on China, for instance, includes encyclopedic descriptions of the lands, people, history, economy, government, and culture of the country. The site also runs the weekly electronic version of the *Cambodian Times* (Cambodia's national newspaper) and manages to cover developments in the economies and industries of Asian countries such as Malaysia. ✓**INTERNET**→*url* http://www.jaring.my/at-asia/

Asia Online Asia has jewels, spices, and fabrics the likes of which the world has never seen. The trip is long and rigorous, but has great rewards. The trip no longer requires caravans and ships.

The temple of Angkor Wat—http://none.coolware.com/entmt/cambodia/

A computer and modem will do fine. Sponsored by SilkRoute Ventures, this Website is intended to promote Asian businesses but also does a great job meeting the needs and inspiring the dreams of travelers. You will find a regional newsfeed, a mammoth index of Asian Websites (government, university, business, etc.), a guide to corporations in Asia, and, most significant, a cyberguide to traveling in Asia. The cyberguide links to hotel listings for each Asian country (each listing includes a telephone number, fax number, address, and slightly out-of-date prices per person), country profiles, and an interesting collection of Asian Travel Resources, broken down by country. Choose Malaysia, for instance, and you are rewarded with a clickable map of Malaysia, popular Malaysian recipes, a guide to student traveling in the beautiful Penang, and a currency converter. ✓**INTERNET**→*url* http://www.asia-online.com/

Asia Travel Three months and about $2,000. You could buy a ticket to Hong Kong and spend a week, head over to Thailand for a month, visit Singapore for a few days (that's all you need), and maybe stop in Bali. Asia Travel has much of the information that you'll need to plan your trip, including hotel listings for each country organized into price categories (over $20; over $200). If a hotel is listed here, you can reserve a room by filling out a Web form. Other information available for select countries includes golf courses, car rentals, shopping, restaurants, tours, and airlines. ✓**INTERNET**→*url* http://asiatravel.com/

Bonsai's Asia Link Page A huge collection of links to Asia-related Websites, particularly sites on Japan, Singapore, Hong Kong, and Taiwan, is available. ✓**INTERNET**→*url* http://www.its.newham.utas.edu.au/bonsai/asia/asia.html

Multiworld A magazine with articles in English and Chinese on travel, art, nature, and culture. Past issues have included a diary of one writer's experiences in New York, a description of the exotic islands in the South Pacific, and an analysis of the academic experience in Taiwan. ✓**INTERNET** ...→*url* http://www.jnw.com/mw/index.html ...→*url* http://freedom.ncsa.uiuc.edu/~hye/mw/index.html

Pacific Asia Travel Association Information about the travel industry in the Asia Pacific region, including coverage of travel trends, news about travel products and services, and even links to other travel pages online. ✓**INTERNET**→*url* http://www.singapore.com/pata/

rec.travel.asia (ng) Imagine having drinks in the Peninsula Hotel in Hong Kong. A wall of glass separates you from the harbor. A gondola sails by. Huge skyscrapers tower above you. Only a few days to shop here, and then you're off to mainland China for a six-day stay. Where will you go next? Will it be a few days on the beaches of the Philippines? A trek through the north of Thailand and a couple days sightseeing in Bangkok? Or maybe a visit to another former colony—Singapore? While detours and impromptu trips may be part of some travelers' experi-

Fodor's Choice...

Special Moments

HONG KONG
Viewing the coastline from the Ocean Park cable car

MALAYSIA
Viewing Mt. Kinabalu from anywhere in Sabah

INDONESIA
Visiting the Ceremonial Houses of the Toraja, Sulawesi

—from Fodor's *Southeast Asia*

ences in Asia, the rec.travel.asia newsgroup makes it easy for travelers to ask questions, gather advice, and plan their trips well ahead of time. The hyperactive newsgroup offers an endless stream of recommendations for cheap airfare and hotels (in case you can't afford to sleep at the Peninsula), hints for trekking, advertisements for teaching English and, of course, visa information. The newsgroup is so active, and includes such detailed travel discussions—best bars in Hong Kong, traveling from Singapore to Malaysia, an art gallery in Bombay, a men's tailor shop in Bangkok, dining in Vietnam—that wannabe travelers without the time or money for the plane ride across the world can travel vicariously for a few minutes each day. Members of the newsgroup have also assembled several FAQs with travel advice and recommendations for traveling in the east. ✓**USENET**→rec.travel.asia ***Archives:*** ✓**INTERNET**→*url* http://www.digimark.net/rec-travel/asia/ ***FAQ:*** ✓**INTERNET**→*url* http://www.cis.ohio-state.edu/hypertext/faq/usenet-faqs/bygroup/rec/travel/asia/top.html

The Asia Pages It's slightly unclear who uses these pages. Although they seem to be targeted at companies and businesspeople interested in making contacts in Asia, several sets of Web pages are devoted exclusively to the traveler in Asia. Looking for hotels in Brunei? Restaurants in Malaysia? The dates of local festivals in Taiwan? The names and locations of must-see attractions in Thailand? It's here in stripped-down, no-frills text descriptions. ✓**INTERNET**→*url* http://www.iipl.com.sg/

TimeHunter's Asia Page If this site were a tour guide, you'd probably tip it well. You wouldn't leave exhausted, feeling as if you had been rushed to every tourist attraction (or, in this case, Website dedicated to Asia) so that you remembered nothing; instead, you'd probably be grateful for the effort made to keep things simple, to include only quality attractions. As far as indexes to Asia go, this one isn't the biggest, but almost all the sites listed are worth a visit. ✓**INTERNET**→*url* http://aspin.asu.edu/provider/dcgovier/asia.html

Travel & Leisure Asia Information Listings for airlines, car rental companies, nightclubs, cruises, limo services, restaurants, tour guides and escorts, and hotels. They are essentially address information and telephone numbers, but are incredibly extensive for several Asian countries, particularly Singapore and Thailand. ✓**INTERNET**→*url* http://www.asiatrade.com/Travel-leisure/index.html

Business & culture

Asia, Inc. Online The Website supplements excerpts of articles from the current and back issues of *Asia, Inc.*, with daily financial data, articles prepared exclusively for the Website, online discussion forums, links to other sites covering Asia, and a photo gallery of the magazine's covers. *Asia, Inc.*, which is a hard-core business magazine, is probably only of interest to the traveling executive. ✓**INTERNET**→*url* http://www.asia-inc.com/

Asia Now Online The online accompaniment to the weekly television program, *Asia Now*. The Website runs descriptions of stories that have aired on the program, sometimes with short movie clips and pictures. Stories range from Balinese dance to fishing in the Pacific islands to an interview with the Dalai Lama. The Website also tracks important news stories in Asia and organizes projects for student viewers. ✓**INTERNET**→*url* http://www2.hawaii.edu/hptv/

Asian Arts Bringing together highlights from Asian art exhibits worldwide, scholarly articles written about Asian art, and images of pieces from private galleries, the site offers Asian art enthusiasts a chance to see distant exhibits and travelers a chance to preview exhibits that they're planning to visit. ✓INTERNET→*url* http://www.webart.com/asianart/index.html

Asiaweek Travel to Asia may be for pleasure—it may also be for business. *Asiaweek*, a weekly newsmagazine covering business and political developments in Asia, keeps businessmen informed. Selected articles from the current issue and back issues through June of 1995 are online here. ✓INTERNET→*url* http://www.pathfinder.com/Asiaweek/

Rasa Singapura A collection of addresses and telephone numbers for restaurants serving Southeast Asian cuisine worldwide (a Malaysian restaurant in Albuquerque, New Mexico; a Balinese restaurant in Alberta, Canada). Reviews are posted when available. ✓INTERNET→*url* http://www.suspects.com/vicums/personal/footprints/makan.html

Hotels

Hotel Equatorial International Come experience hospitality the Equatorial way. The hotel chain has establishments in Singapore, Malaysia, Indonesia, China, and Vietnam. You can also email guests at the Malaysian hotels. ✓INTERNET→*url* http://www.equatorial.com/

InfoAsia An extensive directory of hotel listings for Singapore, Indonesia, Malaysia, Thailand, Philippines, Brunei, and Vietnam. ✓INTERNET→ *url* http://xenon.stanford.edu/~tantra/infoasia/country/index.html

TravelASIA Hotel A searchable guide to hotels in 18 Asian countries, with telephone, fax, address, and price information (slightly dated) for each hotel. ✓INTERNET→*url* http://www.asia-online.com/travel/tahotel/country/index.html

Miscellaneous

Asia_Adventures An advertisement for a trio of trips to Asia—Hong Kong and China, Motorcycles on the Silk Road, and Tibet-Nepal Overland Safari—that may be taken for college credit through Western Nebraska Community College. ✓INTERNET→ *url* http://shops.net/shops/Asia_Adventures/

Asian Diver's Homepage Advertisements and subscription forms for *Asian Diver* magazine and *Asian Diver Scuba Guides*, as well as profiles of popular Asian diving locations such as Bali, Kavieng, Phuket, and Sipaden. ✓INTERNET→ *url* http://www.asianconnect.com/mediapub/asian-diver/index.html

DETOURS

"Of course, life in Taiwan has its bright side, too. Good food is everywhere. One can eat at street side for $2, or in one of the fancy hotels for $30, either is good and well worth the price you pay.

"There are a lot of good books, from Jin Yong's novels to biographies of political figures. Taiwan has a large group of pop singers and the standards are very high. A lot of them can sing in Taiwan dialect, Mandarin, English, and Japanese. There is also a large selection of movies and TV programs, both Chinese and foreign. I enjoyed martial arts movies and sports programs while my wife was hooked on Chinese soap operas.

"I joined the bridge club for $2 per month. The attendance averaged ten pairs and everyone was friendly. At the end of the evening everyone got some prize. The top pair got a box of detergent each and the last usually a bar of soap."

—from **Multiworld**

China

So—you've seen *The Last Emperor*, read *The Joy Luck Club*, and can even eat without dropping grains of rice all over the carpet—what's missing from the real Chinese experience? Well, several billion neighbors for one, and a trip to the age-old empire for another. The **China Guide** is a good place to start a tour of the vast and varied land, from the junks of Shanghai to the temples of the Forbidden City. The practical aspects of touring China are explained at **China Window Traveling Home Page**, which will help you change money and book a room at the Peking Holiday Inn. Be sure you don't make a Reaganesque faux pas by calling "Taiwan" "China" or vice versa with a quick visit to **soc.culture.china.** Before you leave though, stop in at **Chinese Art and Culture** where the millennia of high culture and scientific innovation put a puny 200-year history in perspective.

The Forbidden City—from http://www.cernet.edu.cn/tour/tour.html

On the Net

Across the board

China Guide Although links at this Website to other Chinese travel sites are interesting in themselves (a library of photos of China, an explanation of the Chinese calendar, an entertaining travelogue by travel writer Paul Theroux, etc.), this guide is also one of the best tours of China offered on the Internet. Typos aside, the guide has detailed sections on Beijing, Shanxi, Xian, Suzhou, and Sichuan. Each section offers images, travel tips, and general background information. ✓**INTERNET**→ *url* http://www.atm.ch.cam.ac.uk/~oliver/chnaguide.html

China Home Page China's big. It's very, very big. This home page is as well, but despite—or perhaps because of—its size, it lacks the focus of a good travel resource. Buried between links to Chinese universities and personal home pages for Chinese citizens, the site offers an extensive tour of China (Web pages for each of the Chinese provinces with recommendations for sites to see and things to do), general information about the mammoth country, and pages on Chinese music, art, and language. ✓**INTERNET**→ *url* http://solar.rtd.utk.edu/~china/china.html

China & Hong Kong Engage in travel discussions with other AOL members about trips to Hong Kong or China. Unlike most China-related discussions online, this forum stays focused on travel issues like tour operators, hotels, airline tickets, and exchange programs. Chinese politics, economics, and culture are rarely mentioned. ✓**AMERICA ONLINE**→ *keyword* travel forum→Travel Boards→The World Traveler Board→China & Hong Kong

China—Our Beautiful Home Country An index to online pictures, maps, and resources about the art and culture of China. ✓**INTERNET**→ *url* http://www2.ncsu.edu

/ncsu/stud_orgs/cssfa/china.html

China-Window Traveling Home Page What does a traveler to China need to make his or her trip a pleasure rather than a nightmare? Information about the country's weather, geography, currency rates, hotels, and language. Where can a traveler get that information? At the Window Traveling Home Page, which also includes bonus features like a photo montage of scenes from China. ✓**INTERNET**→*url* http://china-window.com/

Chinese Art and Culture A wonderful guide to all things Chinese, from a page with images of famous pieces of Chinese art to another page with recipes for Chinese dishes (Sesame Chicken Salad, anyone?) to an explanation of the Chinese Zodiac. Travelers should definitely link to the Scenery section and take the tours of the Great Wall, the Imperial Gardens, and the Forbidden City. ✓**INTERNET**→*url* http://pasture.ecn.purdue.edu:6666/China/china.html

Tour in China Click through Web pages for each of the provinces of China. Resources include photos of popular attractions, essays on the history of regions, and descriptions of famous tourist sites. ✓**INTERNET**→*url* http://www.ihep.ac.cn/tour/china_tour.html

ZWWWZ Chinese Regional Information Although primarily an index of Internet resources for each region of China (and even areas China would like to have as regions, such as Taiwan, Tibet, and Hong Kong), the Web pages for each region offer basic information such as population, administrative history, size, etc. ✓**INTERNET**→*url* http://ftp.geog.ucl.ac.be/~patrick/zhongguo/Equyu.html

Culture

Chinese Culture and the Arts A United States government report on culture and the arts in China through the ages. The prose is quite readable and the report moves quickly from literature to drama to music to other arts. ✓**INTERNET**→*url* gopher://umslvma.umsl.edu/00/LIBRARY/STACKS/BOOKS/ARMYAHBS/AAHB9/AAH90037

Chinese History A collection of Chinese historical documents, articles about Chinese history, and sound clips (Mao speaks!). The best resources are those related to the Democracy Movement. Remember Tiananmen Square? ✓**INTERNET**→*url* http://darkwing.uoregon.edu/~felsing/cstuff/history.html

Chinese Music Page This impressive Website is a repository of sound clips for several styles of Chinese music, including traditional, folk, ceremonial, pre- and post-liberation era, cultural revolution era, and modern popular Chinese music. ✓**INTERNET**→*url* http://vizlab.rutgers.edu/~jaray/sounds/chinese_music/chinese_music.html

Finding News About China If you want to keep abreast of happenings in China, Hong Kong, Taiwan, or Tibet, check out this mammoth list of resources for Chinese news on the Internet. There are links to weekly journals of Chinese current affairs, daily Hong Kong and Taiwan Stock Exchange reports, human rights bulletins, newswires from Beijing and newswires from Hong Kong, and much more. ✓**INTERNET**→*url* http://www.hk.net/~drummond/milesj/china.html

soc.culture.china (ng) China, Hong Kong, and Taiwan aren't part of the same country. In fact, one of the most frequent topics in these three newsgroups is the distinctions and political hostilities between the "three Chinas." Soc.culture.china is dominated by PRC students doing study-abroad programs in the States, and most are taking the time to freely post anti-government messages, since they are safely out of reach of rolling tanks; Tiananmen and its aftereffects remain high-volume topics. Much conversation is conducted with embedded Pinyin phrases, so don't be surprised if you suddenly find the discussion entirely incomprehensible. ✓**USENET**→soc.culture.china *FAQ:* ✓**INTERNET**→*url* http://www.cis.ohio-state.edu/hypertext/faq/usenet-faqs/bygroup/soc/culture/china/top.html

Beijing

A Journey to Beijing Follow this tale of a modern innocent abroad by traveling with the author from London to the Forbidden City. You'll experience the trip, beginning at the Tashkent Airport and including a stay at the Mandarin Hotel Beijing, through pictures and text, tinged with Western awe. ✓**INTERNET**→*url* http://metrotel.co.uk/jvt/china.html

Destination Highlights—Beijing Each month, Worldview Systems publishes a calendar of cultural events happening in Beijing. Contact information and descriptions of the events are included. ✓**AMERICA ONLINE**→*keyword* worldview→Pacific Rim→Beijing, China ✓**INTERNET**→*url* http://nearnet.gnn

.com/gnn/bus/wview/cityhigh /ch1pek.html

TravelASSIST File—Beijing, China What to be wary of (the water), what to be mindful of (the infamous Tiananmen Square), and what to be appreciative of (spring and early autumn are the best times to visit) when touring Beijing. ✓**INTERNET**→*url* http://travelassist.com/mag/a18.html

Guangzhou

Destination Highlights—Guangzhou What's showing at the museums? Who's performing at the opera houses? Each month Worldview Systems publishes a calendar of cultural events in Guangzhou with prices, contact information, and even bus routes. ✓**AMERICA ONLINE**→*keyword* worldview→Pacific Rim→Guangzhou, China ✓**INTERNET**→*url* http://nearnet.gnn.com/gnn/bus/wview /cityhigh/ch1can.html

---

Images of Guangzhou Photos from the ancient Chinese city known to most Americans as Canton. ✓**INTERNET**→*url* http://www .slip.net/~hanrahan/China.html

Shanghai

Destination Highlights—Shanghai The Longhua Temple, Nanjing Road, the Yu Yuan Bazaar, and other popular Shanghai tourist attractions are described (contact information, admission times, and even bus routes are included). In addition, this site also includes a listing of major cultural events for the month. ✓**AMERICA ONLINE**→*keyword* worldview→Pacific Rim→Shanghai, China ✓**INTERNET**→*url* http://nearnet .gnn.com/gnn/bus/wview /cityhigh/ch1sha.html

---

Shanghai Home Page It's a city of more than 13 million people and it's one of the largest seaports in the world, but the Website devoted to Shanghai is slow and slightly barren for the moment. Nevertheless, travelers should check out the interactive Shanghai map. ✓**INTERNET**→*url* http://www.engin .swarthmore.edu/~he/shanghai/

Xi'an

The Starting Point of the Silk Road You've heard of those life-size terra-cotta figures that were found buried beneath the sand in China. Built to guard the tomb of Emperor Qin Shi Huang, under whom sections of the Great Wall were also linked together, the silent army of thousands is one of the world's major tourist attractions. The terra-cotta warriors reside just outside the city of Xi'an, and this Website provides information for visitors to this city. "Xi'an is one of the most famous ancient capitals in China. Known as Chang An in ancient times, Xi'an had been the capital for thirteen dynasties in the Chinese history. Xi'an was also the starting point of the ancient silk road." ✓**INTERNET**→*url* http://praxis .comm.cornell.edu/COMM694 /~George/xianhome.html

Other regions

Central China Home Page Although the writing suffers from poor command of English, the site offers an easy-to-navigate guide to three Chinese provinces: Henan, Hubei, and Hunan. The guide includes descriptions of the major cities and attractions in each province. ✓**INTERNET**→*url* http://www.whnet.edu.cn/'

Cruising China's Yangtze River A short article for the electronic travel magazine, TravelASSIST, describing a four-day cruise on the Yangtze River. Pictures included. ✓**INTERNET**→*url* http://travelassist .com/mag/a11.html

Fodor's Choice...

Beijing

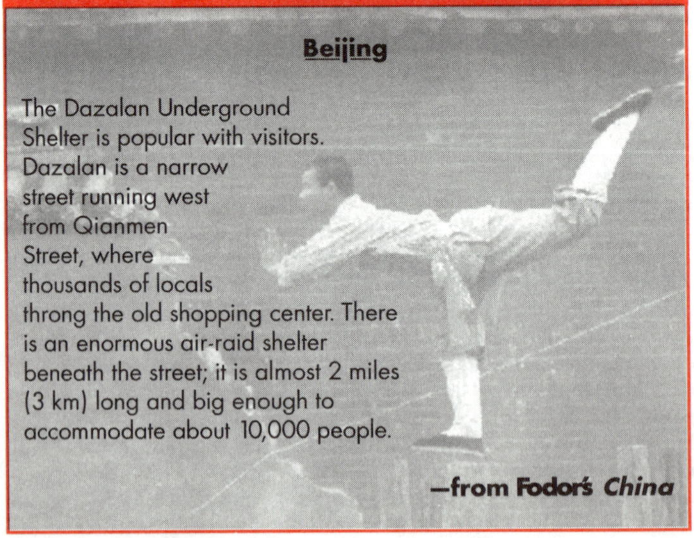

The Dazalan Underground Shelter is popular with visitors. Dazalan is a narrow street running west from Qianmen Street, where thousands of locals throng the old shopping center. There is an enormous air-raid shelter beneath the street; it is almost 2 miles (3 km) long and big enough to accommodate about 10,000 people.

—from Fodor's *China*

Hong Kong

In Hong Kong they're partying like it's 1996—an ongoing bash until the Far East's great capitalist metropolis reverts to mainland China. Find out where to dance the free market away with a visit to the local cultural nexus of the **Hong Kong Terminal**. What's made in Hong Kong these days? Other than commodities trades, action flicks, and plastic torsos for Barbie and Ken, a whole lot of culture and fun. The **Hong Kong Online Guide** and **Hong Kong Tourist Association** provide sightseeing primers on everything from local festivals to aggressive shopping strategies. CompuServe's **Hong Kong Forum** offers advice on tour operators and hotels, but **soc.culture.hong-kong** is where the real discussion of the island nation resides—among discussion of movie stars and dim sum joints lurk those sights and feelings that can turn a tourist into a traveler.

Hong Kong Wonder Net—from http://wwwhkta.org/

On the Net

Across the board

Hong Kong Forum It's a forum for travelers and a forum for Chinese Americans; it's a forum for professionals planning to move to Hong Kong and tourists looking for advice on where to shop; it's a forum where the topics of games and martial arts are as popular as the topics of dining and business. When the message boards are slow, which they often are, visit the libraries for tourist information (bargain tailors, an MTR route map, a list of museums, etc.). ✓**COMPUSERVE**→*go* hkforum

Hong Kong Online Guide The guide covers all the important aspects of visiting Hong Kong—shopping (areas, tippings, hours), doing business, finding an hotel, sightseeing, and flying to and from the island. It also offers information about Hong Kong's history, culture, and government. ✓**INTERNET**→*url* http://www.hk.super.net/~webzone/hongkong.html

Hong Kong Terminal The Terminal holds information for those living in the bustling island city and those who would like to. A restaurant database tells where to find Italian food in Hong Kong, while a culinary guide discusses the proper preparation of dim sum. Events calendars tell what's on in the clubs—a top 40 list tells you what's hip on the radio. But the highlight is a real-time chat room where visitors can chat in English or Mandarin about Hong Kong and just about anything else. ✓**INTERNET**→*url* http://zero.com.hk/z.html

Hong Kong in Pictures This site offers an astoundingly large collection of photographs of the culturally and economically rich city of Hong Kong. Get views of the cityscape from Victoria Harbour to the Bank of China. ✓**INTERNET**→*url* http://www.cuhk.hk/hk/scenery.htm

Hong Kong Tourist Association A complete online guide to the bustling city of Hong Kong. A fast-facts section reports on the cost of a local call, how much to tip, and where to find English-language television. Hotel, airport, and shopping links provide additional practical information. Don't miss the culture section for a calendar of interesting Hong Kong events (including the Monkey God Festival, in which a Buddhist medium runs barefoot over blazing charcoal). ✓**INTERNET** ...→*url* http://www.hkta.org/ ...→*url* http://zero.com.hk/hkta/hkta.html

Culture

Contemporary Architecture in Hong Kong The current building boom in Asia will yield the world's tallest buildings within the next two years in Malaysia. However, Hong Kong's not going to come up short—not if the city's architects have anything to say about it. View and download images of the city's downtown landscape at this site. There are also links here to architecture and sculpture pages and to classical and contemporary art sites. ✓**INTERNET**→*url* http://www.ncsa.uiuc.edu/SDG/Experimental/anu-art-history/hongkong.html

Destination Highlights—Hong Kong/Macau There's more to Hong Kong than shopping. Really! Worldview Systems publishes a monthly calendar of cultural events happening in Hong Kong and Macau. Check it before you get on the plane. ✓**AMERICA ONLINE**→*keyword* worldview→Pacific Rim→Hong Kong/Macau ✓**INTERNET**→ *url* http://nearnet.gnn.com/gnn/bus/wview/city high/ch1hkg.html

soc.culture.hongkong (ng) Soc.culture.hongkong is fairly evenly balanced between Chinese-Americans with Hong Kong roots and Hong Kong citizens studying in America; it also draws a certain number of non–Hong Kongers who are fans of Hong Kong film or music. Don't expect to talk about Hong Kong movies after a single viewing of *Hard-Boiled*, either—the fans here know what they're talking about, and will use the original Cantonese versions of movie and star names just to drive you mad. But just stick in there, and after a while, you'll begin to get the feel for the real Hong Kong. ✓**USENET**→soc.culture.hongkong *FAQ:* ✓**INTERNET**→*url* http://www.cis.ohio-state.edu/hypertext/faq/usenet-faqs/bygroup/soc/culture/hongkong/top.html

Hotels

Hong Kong Hotels An alphabetical listing of hotels in Hong Kong. Contact information and description of the hotels' services are included. ✓**INTERNET**→*url* http://www.hk.super.net/~rlowe/bizhk/comp/hotel.html

Tour operators

ChoYang (Hong Kong) Co. Ltd. Book passage on a container ship and travel from Hong Kong to destinations worldwide. Schedules and an online booking service are accessible through this site. Just stop by to collect all the details about the company and its services. ✓**INTERNET**→*url* http://www.dt.com.hk/choyang/kck.html

DETOURS

"Lord Buddha's birthday celebration includes religious observances in Buddhist temples, during which worshippers bathe the Buddha's statue. Many worshippers visit the Po Lin Monastery and other temples on Lantau Island for similar rituals. The rituals are the most picturesque.

"Recently, the Po Lin Monastery erected an enormous Buddha statue weighing over 200 tons and rising 24 metres above its platform on Ngong Ping plateau. It is the world's largest seated, outdoor bronze Buddha and is a major attraction to those visiting Hong Kong. A new road to the mountain-top monastery was completed in December 1993. This has made it even easier for the devout and the simply curious to see the Buddha. Interested visitors can also observe special religious ceremonies at the Ten Thousand Buddhas Monastery in Sha Tin and Miu Fat Monastery near Tuen Mun in the New Territories."

—from **Hong Kong Terminal**

Japan

Everyone knows Japan is expensive, but what else is it? That all depends where you go. In Tokyo, it's crowded and industrious, the 20th century giving way to the 21st amidst a welter of neon, compact cars, and business suits. In the countryside, it's beautiful and serene, like something out of a Hokusai print. Start your Japanese vacation at **Japan Window,** the **Japan National Tourist Organization**, and **Maps and Tourist Guides of Japan**.

The Temple of the Golden Pavillion—http://www.slip.net/~hanrahan/Japan.html

On the Net

Across the board

Japan AOL offers a friendly forum for asking questions about Japan. Discussions range from bringing laptops to Japan to things to do on Sunday nights in Tokyo, from the dos and don'ts of traveling to airfare comparisons. ✓**AMERICA ONLINE**→*keyword* travel forum→Travel Boards→The World Traveler Board→Japan

Japan Forum Gaijin and Japanese trade stories about Japanese waiters sent to Paris's finest culinary schools to learn to be surly, and debate whether the H2 rocket is an expensive flop or a prescient investment in the space market. Twenty-something tourists come here to be shocked that their favorite Tokyo nightclub, Juliana's, has closed. In the martial arts group, you can brag that your sensei is wiser, stricter, or older than anybody else's. Experts offer advice on Japanese bookstores abroad, visas and the INS, and job-hunting in Japan (add a photo and your marital status to your resume). ✓**COMPUSERVE**→*go* japan

Japan National Tourist Organization Coins are 1 yen, 5 yen, 10 yen, 50 yen, 100 yen, and 500 yen. Bank notes are 1,000 yen, 5,000 yen, and 10,000 yen. There. That's your first lesson in Japanese currency. This official online outpost of Japanese tourist information is packed with mini-lessons to help the traveler navigate his or her trip to Japan. The site describes everything from the climate of the country to the drinking etiquette, from the costs of a Japan Rail Pass to the best places to shop in Tokyo. The National Tourist Organization includes a list of recommended restaurants, suggestions of tour itineraries for budget travelers, maps, and listings for museums and galleries across the country. ✓**INTERNET**→*url* http://www.jnto.go.jp/

Japan Window The Window is a cooperative site, with information on technology, business, government, and living in Japan. Kids visiting the site are invited to learn hiragana and origami. Adults can read about the Japanese diet, find out what's on at the theater, or meet in an live chat room to talk about the lasting effects of the Kobe earthquake. ✓**INTERNET**→*url* http://jw.nttam.com:80/HOME/index.html

Japanese Information Listen to the national anthem or read some Japanese proverbs; download the constitution of Japan or get a list of mailing lists in Japan; take a tour of Kyoto or explore Japan with maps; check in for travel updates or learn the essential phrases to get around Japan. (Sound clips are included.) You can do all of these things with the links available on this site. ✓**INTERNET**→*url* http://www.ntt.jp/japan/index.htm

Maps and Tourist Guides of Japan The Japanese National Tourist Organization guides you through sightseeing and dining in Japan's major cities. Tips on budget travel include shopping advice. ✓INTERNET→*url* http://pclsp2.kuicr.kyoto-u.ac.jp/maps.html

Cities

Destination Highlights—Kyoto Detailed descriptions of monthly cultural events happening in Kyoto are provided at this site. Each description includes contact information, entrance fees, admission times, and train or subway instructions. ✓AMERICA ONLINE→*keyword* worldview→Pacific Rim→Kyoto, Japan ✓INTERNET→*url* http://nearnet.gnn.com/gnn/bus/wview/cityhigh/ch1uky.html

Destination Highlights—Yokohama Check this Website for a monthly calendar of cultural events in the city of Yokohama, as well as descriptions of some of its most popular attractions. Admission times, prices, and directions are included. ✓AMERICA ONLINE→*keyword* worldview→Pacific Rim→Yokohama, Japan ✓INTERNET→*url* http://nearnet.gnn.com/gnn/bus/wview/cityhigh/ch1yok.html

Hiroshima Information When you think of dining out in Japan, you probably think of Tokyo. When you think of Hiroshima, you probably think of the nuclear bomb. This Website challenges those preconceptions by offering a guide to the restaurant and nightlife scene in Hiroshima, as well as information on accommodations, sightseeing and tours, transportation, and the arts in the city. ✓INTERNET→*url* http://www.rerf.or.jp/Outside/ENG/Hiroshima/Contents.html

Images of Kyoto Before Tokyo was the capital of Japan, Kyoto was. This Website features a few scenes from the city. ✓INTERNET→*url* http://www.slip.net/~hanrahan/Japan.html

Kansai-Net Leisure Page You're in Japan and want to go out at night. Where do you go? Check out the guide to bars in Kyoto or the calendars of events in Kyoto, Osaka, and Nara for suggestions. ✓INTERNET→*url* http://pclsp2.kuicr.kyoto-u.ac.jp/leis.html

Osaka Like its Tokyo counterpart, this Website for the city of Osaka is an excellent resource. Need a telephone number for a business or friend? Search the online telephone directories. Not sure where you're going? Check the maps at the site. Want to know what's happening in the area? Peruse the events calendar. Also included is a guide to living in Osaka, which covers such basics as money, food, marriage registration, and earthquakes. ✓INTERNET→*url* http://kiku.stanford.edu:80/LWT/OSAKA/osaka_home.html

Culture

Japanese History A brief overview of Japan from ancient times to the present. ✓INTERNET→*url* gopher://gan.ncc.go.jp/11/JAPAN/History

Japanese/English Dictionary Gateway A searchable Japanese-to-English and English-to-Japanese dictionary. ✓INTERNET→*url* http://www.wg.omron.co.jp/cgi-bin/j-e

soc.culture.japan (ng) Out of all of the major Asian soc.culture newsgroups, soc.culture.japan is the only one seemingly largely dominated by non-Asians. Quirky discussions of cultural differences prompted by questions from returned tourists or exchange students are common. (Why are there fewer bald men in Japan than in the U.S.?) The handful of regulars posting from Japan are vested with a sort of guru status; they're asked to deliver Solomonic decisions on who's right and who's wrong about various aspects of Japanese culture. ✓USENET→soc.culture.japan

Guides

Japan Restaurant Guides This elaborate guide to dining in Japan includes restaurant reviews, directory listings of restaurants, and some recipes. Unfortunately, it's only in Japanese. ✓INTERNET→*url* http://www.twics.com/~robbs/tf-rest.html

Maps and Tourist Guides of Japan This Website has collected and created several guides for tourists heading to Japan. Planning on visiting Kyoto, Kobe, Takarazuka, or Umeda? Check the guide here for sightseeing recommendations. Need a cheap place to stay in Kyoto? Consult the list of youth hostels. Heading to Nara, the first permanent capital of Japan? Click on the tourist guide for sightseeing and transportation recommendations, along with a map and listing of upcoming events. ✓INTERNET→ *url* http://pclsp2.kuicr.kyoto-u.ac.jp99/maps.html

Tokyo

Baseball, rock 'n' roll, crowded subways, and sushi. Sounds like New York City, right? Wrong—it's Tokyo! The **Tokyo!** site will ease your culture shock by bringing you into the city on a virtual trip from Narita Airport. Continue your cybertravels with **Welcome to Tokyo!,** which even helps you change money to pay for your virtual sightseeing and dining in this fascinating city. **Tokyo Journal** offers a local view on the city's culture and tells you what the natives prefer to do in their off hours. **Tokyo Q** helps you plan your eastern evenings with a complete cultural events calendar, covering everything from a film retrospective to traditional dance performances to techno-rock concerts. And the **Tokyo Subway Page** helps you get there in time for the first inning, act, screening, or teen scream. Head to **Tokyo Disneyland** for the familiar grins of Pluto and the Little Mermaid.

Do your best to keep up with Tokyo—from http://www.iac.co.jp/tj/

On the Net

Across the board

Destination Highlights—Tokyo Whether you're in Tokyo for business or pleasure, there's always time to do something special, and there's always something special going on in this bustling city. Check this monthly calendar of cultural events in Tokyo before you go. ✓**AMERICA ONLINE**→*keyword* worldview→Pacific Rim→Tokyo, Japan ✓**INTERNET**→*url* http://nearnet.gnn.com/gnn/bus/wview/cityhigh/ch1tyo.html

Tama Zoo If you're planning a day at the zoo in Tokyo, check this site for hours, admission prices, directions, and a general description. ✓**INTERNET**→*url* http://srv.cc.hit-u.ac.jp/usr/ggem103/http/tamazoo/tamazooHome.html

The Tokyo Subway Page The map is color-coded and in Japan-

Fodor's Choice...

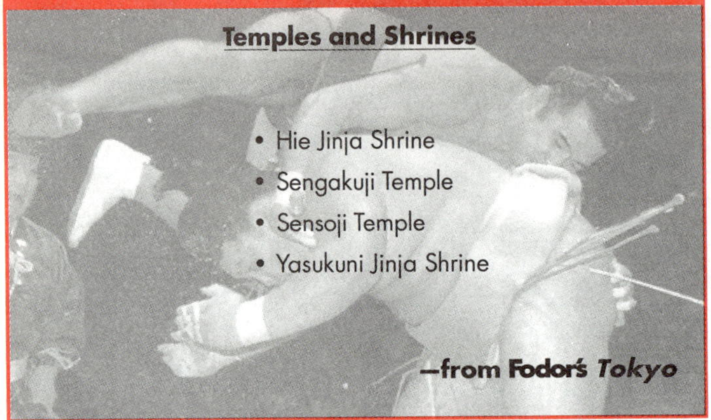

Temples and Shrines

- Hie Jinja Shrine
- Sengakuji Temple
- Sensoji Temple
- Yasukuni Jinja Shrine

—from Fodor's *Tokyo*

ese. Click on the map to magnify an area. ✓**INTERNET**→*url* http://www.eccosys.com/CHIKA/index.html

Tokyo! No need to pack for your virtual trip to Tokyo! From customs at Narita Airport, Netters can take a quick train trip to the city center (past the national sumo stadium) and then into Shinjuku. From Shinjuku they can choose where to go and what to do. Be sure to order the *onigiri* at the virtual lunch. ✓**INTERNET**→*url* http://www.twics.com/~repka/service.html

Tokyo Club and Bar Guide Lists and descriptions of Tokyo's gay bars, jazz clubs, clubs, and techno events. ✓**INTERNET**→*url* http://www.twics.com/~robbs/othclub.html

Tokyo Disneyland It's the same Magical Kingdom and the same Mickey Mouse, except everything is in Japanese. The Website, however, is in English and offers a general overview of the park and a calendar of special events. ✓**INTERNET**→*url* http://www.toyo-eng.co.jp/NewHome/Messe/Useful-Info/Play/TDL/index-e.html

Tokyo Home Page This powerhouse of a Website packs quite a punch. Not only does it link to a searchable telephone directory for Tokyo, but it also links to a monthly calendar of events, maps, and living and culture guides to the city. What's a living guide? In this case, it's information on almost everything that you'd need to know to live there—e.g., taxes, emergency numbers, driving, money, food, and travel for disabled visitors. While it's likely that knowing Japanese would be a help, this information will get you a long way. The culture guide, a great resource for the traveler, links to a monthly calendar of festivals, exhibits, and performances, and lists and describes the city's parks, gardens, libraries, amusement parks, and museums. A travel guide is in the works. ✓**INTERNET**→*url* http://kiku.stanford.edu:80/LWT/TOKYO/tokyo_home.html

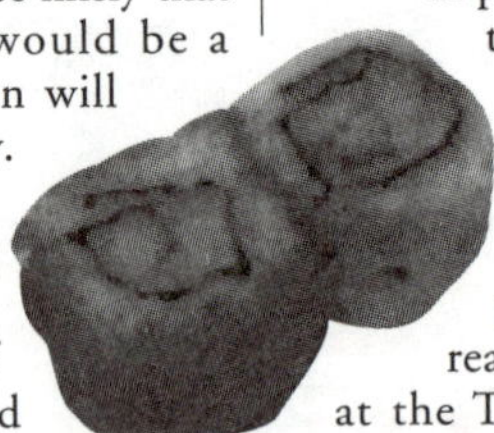

Tokyo Journal The online version of Tokyo's popular English monthly magazine, *Tokyo Journal*, is perfect for the traveler. Its Cityscope section offers regular coverage of Tokyo's nightlife, music, and art scenes, with extensive listings of places to visit in each category. The Recommendations section highlights certain events, restaurants, exhibits, music, and other cultural activities in Tokyo and features a short review. The full texts of some of the stories in the current issue are online here as well. ✓**INTERNET**→*url* http://www.iac.co.jp/tj/

Tokyo Q What's happening in Tokyo next week? The site maintains a detailed calendar of upcoming cultural events (a folk music concert at War Babies, part 17 of the Godzilla Film festival, and the Howling Loochie Brothers Band at Shibuya Crocodile). Check out the regular profiles of the hippest baths, restaurants, and nightclubs. The Little Adventures section describes Tokyo-style banana splits and underground theater. ✓**INTERNET**→*url* http://shrine.cyber.ad.jp/~rok/lastweek.html

Welcome to Tokyo! Take a virtual trip to Tokyo (arrive at the airport, head through customs, change your currency, and you're off...), which includes images, sound clips, and descriptions of places in Tokyo. Or read more about the city at the Tokyo InfoWeb, which has articles on the city's food, history, amusement parks, currency, and more. Or jump to one of several online publications with news about Japan. The site even has a page of trivia facts about Tokyo ("Tokyo means 'eastern capital.'"). ✓**INTERNET**→*url* http://shrine.cyber.ad.jp /~repka/main.html

Indonesia

Indonesia is more than a country, more than an archipelago of island paradises, more than cuisine heavy on curry and coconut milk—it's a state of mind. Yes, it's true, there is now a Club Med Bali, but that doesn't mean that the other 13,000-plus islands are populated by vacationing insurance salesmen. The **Indonesia Home Page** is a good place to try to get a handle on the thousands of islands, hundreds of languages, and innumerable sights to see. **Travelling in Indonesia** and **The Indonesia Tourist Page** step in to help organize the vacation you are undoubtedly now panting to plan. Bali is popular now, witness its own topic on AOL (**Destination Highlights—Bali**) but don't stop at the white beaches—try **Balinese Dance** too.

A view of Bali—from http://www.cntraveler.com/

On the Net

Across the board

Bimaskati: Indonesian WWW Gallery The so-called "Indonesian Yahoo" lets users search for information about Indonesia or on Indonesian sites in several categories. Travelers should click the Travel & Tourism category as well as the Art & Culture, Food, and Entertainment categories. ✓**INTERNET**→*url* http://www.cs.utexas.edu/users/adison/cgi/bimasakti

Indonesia Review your trip to Java, or ask questions about honeymooning in Bali; seek recommendations for cheap flights from Hong Kong to Djakarta, or try to find a travel partner for touring the islands. Most of the posts in this folder are about Bali, but all islands in Indonesia are open for discussion. ✓**AMERICA ONLINE**→*keyword* travel forum→Travel Boards→The World Traveler Board→Indonesia

Indonesia Tourist Pages Places to stay, attractions to see, and food to eat are all covered at this Website for tourists planning to visit Indonesia. In addition, basic information about the country, customs, and local events is offered. ✓**INTERNET**→*url* http://www.iipl.com.sg/ino/text/tourist.htm

Indonesian Homepage If you were to spend only a single day on each of Indonesia's islands, your trip would last more than 35 years—there are more than 13,000 islands. There are also more than 300 languages spoken in Indonesia. This Website devoted to Indonesia is pretty impressive as well. Click the Music topic for lyrics to traditional Indonesian songs and sound clips, the Food topic for Indonesian recipes, the General Information topic for links to the CIA World Fact Book profile on Indonesia and other Indonesian fact sheets. But that's not all. The site also links to a list of Indonesian holidays, the home page for an Indonesian daily newspaper (*Republika Online*), and even its own travel guide with recommendations on places to visit, excerpts from newsgroup posts about travel experiences in Indonesia, pictures, and travelogues. ✓**INTERNET**→*url* http://www.umanitoba.ca:80/indonesian/

Tickets and Travel to Indonesia A list of about a dozen travel agents in the United States selling tickets to Indonesia. Telephone numbers are included. ✓**INTERNET**→*url* http://www.engr.orst.edu/~muliajo/ticket.txt

TimorNet: An Information Service on East Timor For close to 20 years, East Timor has been occupied by Indonesian forces. This Website offers an introduction to the conflict, a history of the people of East Timor, and a guide to online and offline resources for the troubled nation. Although the page provides some very grave information, there is also a link to legends from Timor. Do you know the one about the crocodile that became Timor? ✓**INTERNET**→*url* http://www.uc.pt/TimorNet.html

Travelling in Indonesia A good travel guide tells you the history, legends, and stories of the region you're visiting. This virtual guide to Indonesia attempts to do the same: it shows you pictures of Indonesia (its temples, major islands, and cities) and offers interesting background information. Choose the page on Bali, for instance, and get a brief history of the island, an overview of the tourism there, and a long, annotated list of places to see in Bali. And while there are similar, detailed pages of sightseeing suggestions for Java, Sumatra, Sulawesi, Kalimantan, Nusa Tenggara, Jakarta, Surabay, and several other places in Indonesia, there is also a tour of temples across Indonesia, which links to text of several legends and myths ("Once upon a time, there was a vicious King by the name King Baka..."), and even sound clips from Indonesian folk songs. ✓**INTERNET**→*url* http://www.emp.pdx.edu/htlio no/travel.html

Culture

alt.culture.indonesia/soc.culture.indonesia (ng) The newsgroups carry as many posts in Bahasa Indonesia as in English. Members discuss religion (Christianity and Islam are big topics here), economics, and even social issues ("Indonesia is not the best country to live in because: You cannot kiss your girlfriend/ boyfriend in public."). Travelers drop by to buy and sell airline tickets to Indonesia, post questions about the country, or keep current about local news. ✓**USENET** ...→alt.culture.indonesia ...→ soc.culture.indonesia

Hotels

Hotels in Indonesia A directory of hotels in Djakarta and Bali. ✓**INTERNET**→*url* http://xenon.stanford .edu/~tantra/infoasia/hotels /indo.html

Bali

Bali Online Home Page "Welcome to Bali where the impeccable beauty of nature converges with the intricate solemnity of religious rituals and culture." If it sounds like a travel brochure and looks like a travel brochure, is it? Bali Online is the Web equivalent, which means that in addition to travel pictures and detailed descriptions of places to visit in Bali, it's also interactive—you can choose how you want to browse the information about the beautiful island. Perhaps you'd like to take a geographical tour of the Island or maybe a cultural tour (explore Hinduism in Bali, traditional Balinese paintings, wayang theaters, and more). Maybe you're more activity-focused and want to explore the shopping, golfing, snorkeling, or nightlife of the island. There are virtual mini-tours set up for these activities. The Website also includes a long list of hotels and accomodations in Bali, a guide to the restaurants of Bali with information on the types of cuisine served, a calendar of upcoming events on the island, important telephone numbers, and a travel planner that recommends guidebooks to read, travel agents, and more. Since many visitors to Bali come by way of Djakarta, there's also a page dedicated to the capital of Indonesia with hotel, restaurant, nightlife, and cultural information. And did we mention the pages on Bali's neighbors—Medan and North Sumatra? ✓**INTERNET**→*url* http://www.indo.com/

Bali: The On-line Travel Guide This site promises more of the "real Bali" than you will find in tourist brochures—and they deliver with a sound file of a Balinese Gamalan orchestra, information on low-cost accommodations and gourmet food, guides to transportation and travel, and other travel tips. ✓**INTERNET**→*url* http://werple.mira.net.au/~wreid/bali _p1a.html

Balinese Dance If you're heading to Bali for vacation, you probably know that the dominant religion of the island is Hinduism. But do you know how the Balinese worship the Hindu gods? They dance. Download clips of children perfoming the difficult dances, and use the hotel and restaurant info here to make plans to see a performance when you're there. ✓**INTERNET**→*url* http://www2.hawaii.edu/hptv/Bali/Bali .html

Destination Highlights—Bali Timely, detailed, and entertaining, this site is both a calendar of cultural events happening this month in Bali and Lombok, and a guide to some of the best sightseeing on the islands (best sunsets, best dances to catch, secret surfing spots, etc.). ✓**AMERICA ONLINE**→*keyword* worldview→Pacific Rim →Bali/Lombok, Indonesia ✓**INTERNET**→*url* http://nearnet.gnn.com /gnn/bus/wview/cityhigh/ch1dps .html

Sumatra

A Quest for Riches in Sumatra Elephants and woolly rhinos live in Sumatra—and there are pictures of them here. Tim Lee, a student at the University of California and tour guide for treks through Sumatra, has posted information about and pictures from his trips to Sumatra. ✓**INTERNET**→*url* http://www-wfcb.ucdavis.edu /www/pub/tim.html

The Philippines

There's no need to pack more than two or three pairs of shoes for your upcoming visit to Imelda's homeland. But you should do some cyber-exploring before you go—it'll be well worth it. The visual beauties of the nation, from rice terraces to volcanoes, are displayed at **Picturesque Philippines**. **Tribung Pinoy-Philippine Page of Trivia** proffers a fascinating look at Philippine history and culture; you'll learn why Spanish surnames are common and what's on at the movies in Manila. Head for the city streets at **Destination Highlights—Manila** or the jungle wilds of Mindanao at **MABUHAY at Kumusta Kayong Lahat!**. Live in luxury by booking a resort at **Philippines: Hotels and Resorts**, or head for the Crocodile Farm and the Taal Volcano courtesy of **Adventure Vacation in the Philippines**. And make friends with the linguistic prowess you gained at the **Speak Tagalog** site.

Sabang Beach at dawn—from http://www.jake.com/DIVE/sabang_f.jpg

On the Net

Across the board

Information about the Philippines Telephone codes, maps, lists of tourism offices, and links to other Websites about the Philippines, which is within four hours from Tokyo, Seoul, Hong Kong, Bangkok, Singapore, and Jakarta by plane. ✓**INTERNET**→*url* http://www.mit.edu:8001/people/mandm/rp.html

Lonely Planet—Destination: The Philippines Welcome to the Philippines! Lonely Planet has culled information from its guides and put up a Website with travel tips, historical and cultural information about the island nation, lists and descriptions of the best sightseeing attractions, photos, travelers' reports, and information about getting around. ✓**INTERNET**→*url* http://www.lonelyplanet.com.au/dest/sea/phil.htm

Philippine Tourist Pages Pick a major city in the Philippines and get a list of hotels and resorts. Read descriptions of several cultural and tourist attractions. Get a list of restaurants by cuisine. Or even browse a list of the country's malls. Basic information about this 7,100-island country is also available. ✓**INTERNET**→*url* http://www.iipl.com.sg/phi/text/tourist.htm

Philippine Travel Guide Start with the nation's national anthem, pick up a map of Manila, and then dig into the nuts and bolts of travel information at this site. What exactly are we talking about? Visa and passport requirements, lists of sightseeing attractions, descriptions of local customs, and lists of useful phrases are online here. ✓**INTERNET**→*url* http://www.sino.net/asean/philippn.html

Philippines—Essential Information For Travellers March to May is hot and dry. June to October is rainy. November to February is cool. But do you know when the banks are open? What and when you're expected to tip? What the maximum penalty for possession of drugs is? This Website covers all these essentials and more for travelers to the Philippines. ✓**INTERNET**→*url* http://silkroute.com/silkroute/travel/essen/ph.html

Picturesque Philippines Lagoons and rice terraces, cathedrals and beaches, and stilt houses and volcanoes are all part of the attractions of the Philippines. This site takes the prospective traveler on a virtual trip, introducing him or her to Manila, Filipino cuisine, shopping on the islands, the country's history and geography, and much more. Photos illustrate the Web pages, travelogues describe the attractions, and tips guide the traveler. ✓**INTERNET**→*url* http://www.europa.com/~ria/index.html

Tribung Pinoy—Philippine Page of Trivia Trivia? Yup. The site not only posts weekly trivia lists about the Philippines (What's the first word in the Philippine Constitution? Who is Evangeline de Castro?), but it also brings together a tremendous number of online resources related to the country. Take an online class in the country's history with a link to the Philippine History 101 Website, which covers topics ranging from the pre-colonial period to the Philippine Republic to a timeline of the U.S.-Philippine relationship. Explore entertainment in the Philippines with a page of links to sites devoted to Philippine comics, radio shows, movies, traditional music, and even *Miss Saigon* herself, Lea Salonga (Saigon is in Vietnam, of course, but Salonga is Filipino-American.) Get an overview of politics and government in the country, search a directory of gay and lesbian resources (bars in Manila, dyke groups in the Philippines, the Filipino Task Force on AIDS, and Filipino gay / lesbian personalities), check for daily recipes in the food guide, and much more. The site even includes a virtual tour of the Philippines. ✓**INTERNET**→*url* http://pubweb.acns.nwu.edu/~flip/ken.html

Cities & regions

Destination Highlights—Manila If you're going to be in Manila, you may want to visit the museums or attend a festival or go to a concert. This Website offers a monthly calendar of cultural events in Manila, along with a standard list of must-see sights (Coconut Palace, the Chinese Cemetery, Intramuros and San Agustin Church). Each sight is described, and relevant contact and transportation information is provided. ✓**INTERNET**→*url* http://nearnet.gnn.com/gnn/bus/wview/cityhigh/ch1mnl.html ✓**AMERICA ONLINE**→*keyword* worldview→Pacific Rim→Manila, Philippines

MABUHAY at Kumusta Kayong Lahat! A tantalizing description of Mindanao, the second-largest island in the Philippines. The article, which focuses on the Davao area, describes the attractions, accommodations, transportation, and climate of the area. ✓**INTERNET**→*url* http://gwis2.circ.gwu.edu:80/~avc123/philip.html

Culture

Mark Twain on the Philippines Travelers planning a trip to the Mississippi River bring along copies of *Huckleberry Finn*. But is Twain appropriate reading material for travel to the Philippines as well? Check out his essays on im-

DETOURS

Customs & Business:

"Eyebrows and a smile indicate a silent "hello" or a "yes" in answer to a question. Fixed eye contact between men is considered an aggressive gesture. The proper method to summon somebody is with a downward wave.

"Filipinos place great emphasis on polite language and gentle conversation. Voice tone is always soft and gentle, and direct questions should be avoided.

"Filipinos value their self-esteem, so never criticize or argue with them publicly. Most men, when so provoked, will fight for the preservation of their pride or self-esteem.

"Avoid topics such as politics, religion, corruption and foreign aid. Filipinos enjoy conversations about their families.

"Make sure you have your business cards, as Filipinos like to know who they are dealing with."

—from **Philippine Travel Guide**

Fodor's Choice...

Sights

- Intramuros, Manila
- Mt. Mayon, southern Luzon
- Magellan's Cross, Cebu
- St. Paul Underground River National Park, Palawan

—from Fodor's *Southeast Asia*

perialism and America's role in the Philippines. ✓**INTERNET**→*url* http://web.syr.edu/~fjzwick/twain_ph.html

---

soc.culture.filipino (ng) The newsgroup carries reports about events in the Philippines and some discussions of Filipino-American issues, though mostly in relation to heritage and tradition. Travelers use the group to get firsthand accounts of the best places to visit and the best way to get around. The newsgroup's Web page includes more than 200 links for Filipinos at home and abroad. Make your voice heard with a visit to the Philippine Senate Online, or head to the rec.music.filipino home page for a hot discussion of the latest release by Gil Lopez Kabayao. ✓**USENET**→soc.culture.filipino *Info:* ✓**INTERNET**→*url* http://www.mozcom.com/SCF/SCF.html

---

Speak Tagalog Learn the language of the Filipino people—Tagalog. This Website offers a tutorial with downloadable sound clips that pronounce numbers, popular greetings, and common expressions and questions. ✓**INTERNET**→*url* http://www.halcyon.com/dizon/welcome.html

Hotels

Philippines: Hotels and Resorts A short list of links to Web pages with information about accommodations in the Philippines. The site will even help you book a room. ✓**INTERNET**→*url* http://asiatravel.com/philippines.html

Miscellaneous

Adventure Vacation in the Philippines What would a vacation to the Philippines be like? Two men and a woman take you on a journey to Manila, through the local market in Puerta Princesa, to the Crocodile Farm, to the Hanging Coffins of Sangada, to the Taal Volcano. Attractions are described in great detail and illustrated with beautiful photos. The Website also links to maps of islands, general information about the Philippines, and a photo album of pictures. ✓**INTERNET**→*url* http://ionet.net/~metrovt/vacation.shtml

---

Scuba Diving in the Philippines Plunge into this stunning site and come out with all the information that a scuba diver could want about diving in the Philippines. The Website offers diving maps and information about several areas around the Philippines, including Puerto Galera, Cebu and Bohol, and the Cuyo Islands. It also carries features on underwater shipwrecks, a gallery of images, and several reference guides for diving resorts. ✓**INTERNET**→*url* http://www.jake.com/DIVE/locker.html

Rice terraces from the Banawe viewpoint—http://ionet.net/~metrovt/asia/ricet5.html

Singapore

Do not bring your can of spray paint along on your trip to Singapore, nor your pack of Juicy Fruit (gum-chewing is prohibited). If you follow these simple rules you're in for a caneless travel experience. Wander past colonial facades through Chinatown and Little India at **Singapore: The Local Scene**, then on to call upon the Komodo Dragons at the **Singapore Zoological Gardens. The Singapore Tourist Pages** explore the festivals that bring even more color to lively streets. Then start planning in earnest with the assistance of the **Singapore Online Guide**.

Downtown Singapore—http://sunsite.nus.sg/SEAlinks/Singapore-photo.html

On the Net

Across the board

Singapore Information Besides brief descriptions of Singapore's geography, people, government, economy, and communications, the site links to several large Websites about Singapore. ✓**INTERNET**→*url* http://sunsite.nus.sg/SEAlinks/singapore-info.html

Singapore: the Local Scene Flowers decorate the bridges, citizens pay for bus rides on the honor system, the crime rate is low, and colonial buildings (some constructed by the French, others by the English) reside only blocks away from the country's Chinatown and Little India. And if you're planning a visit to this urban island nation, stop by this Website for some electronic brochures. Links connect to an online guide produced by the Singapore Tourist Promotion Board, a virtual guide to Singapore art and history, the soc.culture.singapore newsgroup, pictures of Singapore, an overview of the country's arts scene, and even news highlights. The Scenes of Singapore link leads to dozens of images of the nation. ✓**INTERNET**→*url* http://www.sg/infomap/scene/scene.html

Travel Information on Singapore This site lists some common Malayan and Chinese phrases, along with brief descriptions of the many neighborhoods and attractions in Singapore (Arab Street, Chinatown, Kusu Island, Merlion Park, etc.), a list of holidays, hints on tipping and addressing people, currency conversion info, emergency numbers, and more. ✓**INTERNET**→*url* http//www.sino.net/asean/spore.html

Culture

Singapore Zoological Gardens Famous for its orangutan breeding program and its Komodo dragons (these dragons—yes, dragons—are native to Komodo Island in Indonesia and can grow up to 10 feet and live 100 years), the Singapore Zoo has descriptions of some of its animals, a short movie about the zoo, and a zoo map at this site. ✓**INTERNET**→*url* http://www.ncb.gov.sg/sog/att/abal/zoo.html

soc.culture.singapore (ng) Random and unfocused in the way that casual conversations are, this newsgroup is filled with posts from men and women who live in Singapore. Debates about articles in Sunday's newspaper, discussions about driving conditions, questions about surnames, and other miscellaneous topics are standard fare. Although travel questions are infrequent, the pool of native Singaporeans make it an excellent place to ask. ✓USENET→soc.culture.singapore

The Online Museum of Singapore Art & History Walk the cyberhalls of several art exhibits focused on Singapore. The virtual exhibits are recreations of actual local exhibits, such as "Raffles Reviewed: 175 Years Later" (a celebration of Sir Stamford Raffles, who arrived in Singapore in 1819 with the English East India Company and later signed a treaty with the Shah of Singapore to jointly rule the island nation), "19th Century Prints of Singapore" (paintings of Singapore in the nineteenth century), and "The Fall of Singapore, Dec. 8, 1941" (a hypermedia exhibit documenting the capture of Singapore at the close of World War II). ✓INTERNET→*url* http://www.ncb.gov.sg/nhb/museum.html

Guides

Destination Highlights—Singapore You've visited Sentosa, taken pictures of the Raffles Hotel, and been to the Singapore Zoo. Now what? This Website features a monthly calendar of cultural events happening in Singapore. Check in for descriptions and contact info. ✓INTERNET→*url* http://nearnet.gnn.com/gnn/bus/wview/cityhigh/ch1sin.html

Guide to Singapore Advice from a fellow traveler on what to do and where to stay when visiting Singapore. To wit: "Take a bus out to Changi Village (#1 or #2 bus) and a boat to Pulau Ubin. It is relatively undeveloped and will give you a feel for what Singapore was like before modernization." ✓INTERNET→*url* http://Alpha.Solutions.Net/rec-travel/asia/singapore/singapore-guide.html

Singapore Tourist Pages On the seventh month of the lunar calendar, the gates of purgatory open and release souls who roam the earth for 30 days. To appease the ghosts, offerings are made on certain nights throughout the month (paper money is burned, rice and fruits are left, incense papers are set ablaze, etc.). Auctions and street operas are also held. This is known as the Festival of the Hungry Ghosts, and it is just one of Singapore's festivals that are described at this site. Hungry ghosts are one thing; hungry people are another. Restaurant listings by type of cuisine are also included (although the list is far from comprehensive), as are descriptions of tourist attractions, like Sentosa, the Jurong Bird Park, and the Night Safari Park. Basic tourist information, such as bus ride costs, country customs, and taxi fees, is also available. ✓INTERNET→*url* http://www.iipl.com.sg/sin/text/tourist.htm

The Singapore Online Guide Created by the Singapore Tourist Promotion Board, this searchable guide offers extensive information about shopping, restaurants, festivals and events (a monthly calendar), the island's nightlife, and hotels (browse by price range or district). Still need more? The guide also features a downloadable movie clip about the island. And when you're ready to actually start planning your trip, you can click on the interactive tour guide, which will prompt you for answers to a few simple questions (your trip dates, your interests, and types of places that you'd like to visit) and then return a customized itinerary for each day of your stay in Singapore. Times and dates for each activity link to more detailed information, including cost and directions. ✓INTERNET→*url* http://www.travel.com.sg/sog/

Travel—Leisure on Singapore Extensive telephone and address information for airlines, car rentals, nightclubs, cruises, hotels, limo services, restaurants, tour guides, and tours operating in Singapore is provided. ✓INTERNET→*url* http://www.asiatrade.com/Travel-leisure/index.html#Sin

Hotels

Hotels in Singapore Alphabetical listings of hotels in Singapore with links to descriptions of a handful of them. ✓INTERNET ...→*url* http://www.commerceasia.com/hotel.html ...→*url* http://www.asianconnect.com.sg/tourism/sinhotel.html

Regional info

Sentosa Island It feels like a tourist attraction—an island devoted entirely to entertainment and recreation. But Sentosa, which belongs to Singapore, is beloved by Singaporeans for its museums, nature walks, and underwater attractions. Even getting to Sentosa is fun: Take the cable car or the ferry. Admission prices, general information, and a brief movie are available on the Web page dedicated to the mini-island. ✓INTERNET→*url* http://www.ncb.gov.sg/sog/att/island/sentosa.html

The Riau Islands Part advertisement for a company offering tour guides to the islands and part directions and tips for travelers willing to go it alone, this Web page covers getting to and around the thousands of small islands south of Singapore known as the Riau Islands. ✓INTERNET→*url* http://www.singnet.com.sg/~evanj/

Thailand

So now you've become addicted to Pad Thai and Singha beer—why not journey to the cuisine's homeland courtesy of Thailand Tourist Pages? The **Tourism Authority of Thailand** and **Travel Information on Thailand** will help with the practical aspects, while the **Thai Heritage Page** lets you be a virtual Anna—The King and You.

The royal barges before the Grand Palace —http://www.cs.ait.ac.th/~wutt/wutt.html

On the Net

Across the board

Country Information—Thailand This tremendous collection of links to travel and country information about Thailand includes pages devoted to the sightseeing attractions in different regions of the country, directories of hotels, lists of restaurants in Bangkok, air and bus timetables, guides to commercial activities, Thai recipes, currency rates, and much, much more. ✓**INTERNET**→*url* http://emailhost.ait.ac.th/Asia/infoth.html

Lonely Planet—Destination: Thailand Lonely Planet summarizes travel information about Thailand, highlighting the country's tourist attractions (the Grand Palace in Bangkok, the floating markets, the River Kwai, and treks in Chiang Mai), and providing general background information about Thailand. ✓**INTERNET**→*url* http://www.lonelyplanet.com.au/dest/sea/thai.htm

Thailand Tourist Pages With so much to see and do in Thailand, there's never enough time. This site lists the must-see attractions in Bangkok, North Thailand, and South Thailand, offers hotel and restaurant selections, describes local festivals and events, and supplements with basic tourist information about the only country in Southeast Asia never to have been colonized. ✓**INTERNET**→*url* http://www.iipl.com.sg/tha/text/tourist.htm

Tourism Authority of Thailand Shopping in Bangkok, treks in Chiang Mai, and beautiful beaches in the south are part of most travelers' visits to Thailand. The Tourism Authority of Thailand is online, offering assistance to travelers planning their vacations, including travel tips, dos and don'ts, descriptions of many of Thailand's most popular attractions, lists of hotels, a calendar of upcoming events in Thailand, lists of and contact information for tour operators and travel agents, and even schedules for airlines and buses. The site features a search function to help travelers quickly find the information they're looking for and clickable maps to help them browse the offerings. ✓**INTERNET**→*url* http://www.cs.ait.ac.th/tat/index.html

Travel Information on Thailand Targeted specifically at travelers, this site delivers an excellent package of travel resources, including information on local customs, currency, visas and passports, sightseeing, dining, and even the Thai language. It links to a directory of hotels, a listing of tour operators in Thailand, and tips from the Tourism Authority. The site also features Thai recipes and a sound clip of the country's national anthem. ✓**INTERNET**→*url* http://www.sino.net/asean/thailand.html

Travel-Leisure on Thailand Telephone numbers and addresses for hotels, restaurants, golf courses, nightclubs, airlines, limo services, and tourist sites for Thailand. Listings are extensive. ✓INTERNET→*url* http://www.asiatrade.com/Travelleisure/index.html#Thai

Welcome to Thailand You've heard of the prostitutes, the treks, the magnificence of the Grand Palace, the historical importance of the River Kwai, and the Golden Triangle. But what do you know about Thailand's religions, its economy, its geography, its manufacturing base, its government, and its monarchy? The site offers a basic overview of these aspects of the country and more. Links connect to a page about tourism that describe major regional sightseeing attractions. ✓INTERNET→*url* http://www.mahidol.ac.th/Thailand/Thailand-main.html

Attractions

Chiang Mai What's happening in Chiang Mai? Located in northern Thailand, this city is one of the most popular cities with travelers. Information about hotels, weather, transportation, shopping, festivals, crafts, and tourist attractions is available here. ✓INTERNET→*url* gopher://gopher.chiangmai.ac.th:70/11/./.TOURISM/.CM

Destination Highlights—Bangkok If you're heading to Thailand this month, print out this Web page. Besides offering a calendar of events in Bangkok, it's also a guide to the best sights in the magnificent city—the Grand Palace, the Wat Pho, the Floating Market at Damnoen Saduak, the Temple of Dawn. Each sight is described with contact information, admission prices and times, and bus routes included. ✓AMERICA ONLINE→*keyword* worldview→Pacific Rim→Bangkok, Thailand ✓INTERNET→*url* http://nearnet.gnn.com /gnn/bus/wview/cityhigh/ch1bkk.html

Culture

soc.culture.thai (ng) More than the other soc.culture newsgroups, the Thai newsgroup embraces questions about travel and tourism. Members ask about restaurants ("Does Thailand have the world's largest restaurant?"), visiting the beaches, finding hotels, and, of course, the sex industry. Newsgroup members have compiled information about Thailand into several FAQs—a general FAQ about the newsgroup and other sources of information about Thailand, a cultural FAQ covering topics ranging from Bangkok's full name to the traditional Thai calendar, a FAQ with information about the Thai language, a technical FAQ with networking and software information about Thailand, and an extensive travel FAQ with information ranging from credit card acceptance in Thailand to accommodations in Bangkok. ✓USENET→soc.culture.thai ***Archives:*** ✓INTERNET→*url* http://www.nectec.or.th/soc.culture.thai/archives.html ***FAQ:*** ✓INTERNET ...→*url* http://www.nectec.or.th/soc.culture.thai/master.html ...→*url* http://www.cis.ohio-state.edu/hypertext/faq/usenet-faqs/bygroup/soc/culture/thai/top.html

Thai IRC Channels Live chat channels for Thais and others with an interest in Thai culture. The most lively of the channels is usually #Siam, which also maintains a Web page with information about the participants and about Thai resources on the Net. ✓INTERNET ...→*irc* #Siam ...→*irc* #Thailand ...→*irc* #Thai ...→*irc* #Thais ***Info:*** ✓INTERNET→*url* http://www.eskimo.com/~putt/siam/

The Thai Heritage Page England has its House of Windsor, and America has its Kennedys. The Thai also have a royal family, which is beloved by most Thais, and so the number of links paying tribute to the royals on this page is no surprise. In addition to photos of Her Royal Princess Sirindhorn and images of His Majesty King Bhumibol Adulyadej of Thailand, there are features on the Royal Barges of Siam, the Temple of the Emerald Buddha, prehistory in Thailand, the Phanom Rung Sanctuary, and more. ✓INTERNET→*url* http://www.cs.ait.ac.th/~wutt/wutt.html

Hotels

Hotels in Thailand Although the highlight of the site is the directory of hotels in Thailand, you will also find general information about Thailand, tips about the country's culture and customs, a list of popular Thai food dishes, and even a long list of things to see in Bangkok. ✓INTERNET→*url* http://xenon.stanford.edu/~tantra/infoasia/hotels/thai.html

Tour operators

Diethelm Travel The largest tour operator in Thailand offers descriptions of many of its tours, including tours of Bangkok and tours to the River Kwai, Chiang Mai, and even Cambodia, Laos, Burma, and Vietnam. ✓INTERNET→*url* http://www.sino.net/diethelm/index.html

Lost Horizons: Adventure Travel in Thailand For nature lovers who prefer organized tours, this American company offers several travel packages in Thailand. ✓INTERNET→*url* http://www.gdserv.com/hps/lh/

Vietnam

Next stop is Vietnam. Check your political and historical notions about Vietnam at the door and discover a beautiful nation. **Destination Vietnam, A Travel Magazine** offers insight into Vietnamese society and culture as well as travel tips. The travelogue **Cycle Vietnam—From Hanoi to Saigon** will inspire many imitations. If Ho Chi Minh City lies in your travel plans then **Journey to Vietnam** will point you toward travel agents and airlines eager to serve your needs. The **Viet Nam Mini Travel FAQ** answers those lingering questions—where is the best pace to stay in Hanoi, and should travelers rent a bike or bring one with them? Take a walk through the **VietGate** and discover the real society beneath the tourist veneer.

Vietnamese women with baskets—http://maingate.net:80/vn/travel/cycle/page1.html

On the Net

Across the board

A Virtual Visit to Vietnam The so-called virtual visit is actually an index of Vietnam maps, images, reading lists, trip reports, tours, and even links to other sites and articles about Vietnam. ✓ **INTERNET**→*url* http://www.vietvet.org/visit.htm

Destination: Vietnam, A Travel Magazine The online version of this bimonthly print magazine with "articles on when and how to travel to Vietnam, what to do there, maps, shopping tips, and stories of local culture, art, cuisine, and history" includes the full texts of a selection of stories and images from the current and past issues of the magazine. Stories range from an interview with Vietnamese writer Bat Trang to a look at the role of rice in Vietnam to a feature on the Hanoi Marathon. But the Website's strengths are not in the excerpted articles as much as they are in the travel tips, travel resource directories, reading recommendations, and links to Vietnam tour operators online. Don't know what to pack? What voltage of electricity you should expect? Where you can make telephone calls? Check out the travel tips. Need to find a hotel, a restaurant, an embassy, or an art gallery? Browse the many directories of Vietnam establishments and resources located here. ✓ **INTERNET**→*url* http://maingate.net:80/vn/index.html

Journey to Vietnam When you think of Vietnam, do you think of Agent Orange, vets, protests, guerrilla warfare, and quagmires? Well, wake up. Vietnam is now a trading partner with the U.S. and a growing hub of tourism. This guide to business and travel opportunities in Vietnam includes small directories of travel agents, airlines, car rental companies, tour operators, travel resorts, and hotels, as well as links to other Vietnam-related travel sites on the Internet. ✓ **INTERNET**→*url* http://maingate.net:80/vn/index.html

Lonely Planet—Destination Vietnam The Web page for Lonely Planet's guide to Vietnam

Vietnamese landscape—http://maingate.net:80/vn/travel/cycle/page1.html

features a fair amount of general description of the country coupled with more specific travel information, including images of Vietnam and brief overviews of the country's environment, history, economics, holidays, geography, transportation, and attractions. The site also links to descriptions of several Lonely Planet guidebooks to Vietnam, official travel advisories for the country, a list of suggested reading about Vietnam, and other Vietnam sites online. ✓**INTERNET**→*url* http://www.lonelyplanet.com.au/dest/sea/vietnam.htm

The Internet Travel Guide to Vietnam Frequently updated, this incredible resource for information about Vietnam has sections on embassies, food, tours, airlines, Ho Chi Minh City and other places in Vietnam; there's also general information about the country, guidebooks, and Websites about Vietnam. ✓**INTERNET** ...→*url* http://sunsite.unc.edu/vietnam/vntra.html ...→*url* http://www.cis.ohio-state.edu/hypertext/faq/usenet/travel/vietnam-guide/top.html

TravNet! Vietnam Menu Although fairly empty for the moment, the site promises to collect a wide range of travel resources about Vietnam—from information about the country's culture and customs to links to home pages for restaurants, tours, attractions, hotels, and more. ✓**INTERNET**→*url* http://www.sky.net/~eric/t/seavie.htm

Viet Nam Travel Mini-FAQ Your parents aren't so happy about you going. Most parents aren't happy about their children heading off to Vietnam. But they may be less angst-filled if you can prove that you actually know something about your destination. Before breaking the news to Mom and Dad, read this FAQ, which includes general travel information about the country (climate, hotels, visa); explanations for how to get to, from, and around Vietnam (by plane, bus, car, bike, minibus, etc.); descriptions of several regions in Vietnam; and recommendations for guidebooks. ✓**INTERNET**→*url* http://maingate.net:80/vn/travel/faq.html

Culture

soc.culture.vietnamese (ng) Most of the messages in this active newsgroup are in Vietnamese on topics ranging from racism to baseball to prostitution in Vietnam. Travel discussions are rare, although soc.culture.vietnamese may be the most authoritative place online for tourists to get answers to their questions about Vietnam. ✓**USENET**→soc.culture.vietnamese

VietGate VietGate is the virtual home of the Vietnamese community worldwide. Features include links to community services, such as jobs, orphanages, and anti-gang sites, and to non-governmental organizations, such as universities, human rights organizations, and arts groups. A biweekly online magazine discusses business and political relations between the U.S. and Vietnam. Links to the Saigon.com mailing list and home page help continue the dialogue on the future of this embattled nation. ✓**INTERNET**→*url* http://www.saigon.com/

Travelogues

Cycle Vietnam—From Hanoi to Saigon Who would have imagined 20 years ago that a group of Americans would bike 1,200 miles from Hanoi to Ho Chi Minh City? Read all about their trip in this well-written, beautifully illustrated travelogue. ✓**INTERNET** ...→*url* http://192.253.114.31/Misc/Vietnam/ ...→*url* http://maingate.net:80/vn/travel/cycle/page1.html

Travel on The New York Web A scrapbook with pictures of one traveler's trip to Hanoi. Pictures are annotated with such banalities as the following: "People like to hang out at Ho Chi Minh's tomb. His philosophies aren't followed too closely these days, as many people are pursuing the almighty dollar." The photos are kind of cool, though. ✓**INTERNET**→*url* http://nyweb.com/travel/vietpart1.html

India

The Indian culture—framed by ancient traditions, a colonial past, and a democratic (albeit problematic) present—is one of the most interesting in the world, with a distinct and rich literature, cuisine, classical music, religion, and an unparalleled popular film industry. Research India's great past with the **Bhagavad-Gita**, **Indian Classical Dance Forms**, and **The Batish Institute of Indian Music and Fine Arts**. Start discovering modern India at **Discovering India**, the **Rec.travel Guide to India**, and the **India WWW Virtual Library**. And then target your exploration more specifically with the **Bangalore Homepage**, **About Calcutta**, and **Bombay, the Gateway of India**.

The Taj Mahal—from http://philae.sas.upenn.edu/Hindi/taj.jpg

On the Net

Across the board

B.G. Mahesh's India Home Page Links to everything Indian. CD-ROM software, charitable organizations, newsgroups, religious sites, educational courses, fonts, pictures, and the Indian Embassy in Washington are linked to this page. Also find out India's Corruption Ranking as calculated by the World Competitiveness Report. (Hint: India's ranking was above Sweden's but below Singapore's.) ✓**INTERNET**→*url* http://www.jagunet.com/~mahesh/india.html

Destination India Though this site bills itself as the "Tourism Page," a better name might be the "Indian Travelogue Page." Why? Well, Destination India collects stories, written in diary form, about visits to various sites in and around India. From rustic villages to tourist traps, from ancient temples to modern cities, this site covers the breadth of India, along with some specific events, such as the Great Elephant March in the Thekkinkadu Maidan. ✓**INTERNET**→*url* http://www.webcom.com/~prakash/Tourism/TOURISM.HTML

Discovering India How complex, rich, and ancient is India? Just ask your guides, historical figures Meera and Kabir, and then follow the pair to collect your answers. First, Meera and Kabir will lead you to The Speaking Tree, where you'll find the works of the contemporary poet Saleem Peeradina and JPEGs of Sikh art, along with essays about Indian culture. After you shake the tree and read the fruits, you can branch off to a number of other sections—Tapestry trumpets India's religious diversity; the India File provides statistics on Indian geography and economy and furnishes pictures of the national flag, emblem, and bird (the peacock); and Dates to Remember lists and explains important national holidays (the celebration of the Hindu Solar New Year, called Baisakhi, involves bathing in rivers and going to temple). For practical travel info, bid farewell to Meera and Kabir and visit the Discovering India message board, where Amy asks for good surfing sites in India (Jim says that Goa is the place to ride Indian waves), and Shelley wonders aloud what travel in India was like in Gandhi's time. ✓**EWORLD**→ *go* india

India Learn about many different facets of life in India at this graphics-intensive site. View travel photos of mosques and crowded bazaars, or read essays on India's religions and languages—there is plenty here to inform and educate. If you're not sated after perusing this site, check the list of links to other Indian pages, including India Online and the Gallery of Indian Film Stars. ✓**INTERNET**→*url* http://longyear.acs.nmu.edu/~bobby/india.html

India Network World Wide Web Besides publishing a newsletter on current Indian culture and politics, this site offers a wealth of travel-related info. It's a wonderful place to learn about Indian customs and Indian Customs—the full text of the Customs and Central Excise Bureau's Regulations is available here. If you're interested in previewing India's culture before your trip, you can see pictures of India's hottest cricket and film stars (most of the photos are of the actress Jayasudha, who sets new standards for subcontinental pulchritude). And there's even a link to Holiday Inn's international reservations system, which allows you to book a room online. ✓**INTERNET**→*url* http://india.bgsu.edu/

India Online Travel guides for India, Bangladesh, and Pakistan, complete with recommended restaurants, hotels, and movie theaters, and links to travel agents specializing in arrangements for the Indian subcontinent. And there are even travel tips for foreign travelers; women traveling alone in India, for example, should observe the prohibition against exposed skin: "It can be quite a hassle, although southern India is less of a problem than the north. At any rate, the best thing is to always cover your upper arms (not go sleeveless) and to cover your calves (not wear skirts). You will be hassled the least when you wear the Pakistani-style tunic-with-pants outfit." ✓**INTERNET**→*url* http://IndiaOnline.com/travel.html

India: Some Useful Information If you're looking for the number of a plumber in Bangladesh, you'll be disappointed to learn that this site's information isn't quite that useful. But if you're looking for a large collection of jokes, dialogue from movies, limericks, top-ten lists, and other Indian cultural jewels, you'll be ecstatic to stop in here. ✓**INTERNET**→*url* http://www.temple.edu/~betul/iu/index.html

India Tourist Board in the Netherlands Some crafty Dutchmen have assembled an excellent resource for anyone planning a trip to India. Find out about the Indian railway system (including price info), tourist attractions (a tour of the 30 Buddhist caves around Bombay is recommended), and areas of the country that can't be visited without a permit (don't plan on visiting Jammu or Kashmir without the necessary paperwork). Listings of hotels, beaches, local festivals, and embassy locations round out this large site. ✓**INTERNET**→*url* http://interhealth.com:80/india/

India WWW Virtual Library A large collection of articles and links about India are cataloged by subject at this Website. Hit the History topic to learn about all aspects of the country's past, especially about the role of the British in shaping the modern state. To visit the many Indian-related newsgroups and read their FAQ's, or to join a host of mailing lists on Indian culture, just turn to the Communication section. The Regions topic here provides links to resources on practically every city and region in India, including Pune, Delhi, Kandla, and Goa. ✓**INTERNET**→*url* http://metro.turnpike.net/S/spaoli/index.html

IndiaWorld Travel What locales should you include on your itinerary? If you add Mysore and Lad-

Fodor's Choice...

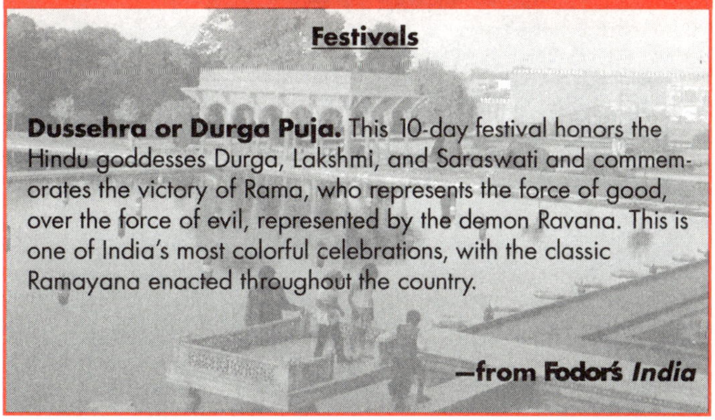

Festivals

Dussehra or Durga Puja. This 10-day festival honors the Hindu goddesses Durga, Lakshmi, and Saraswati and commemorates the victory of Rama, who represents the force of good, over the force of evil, represented by the demon Ravana. This is one of India's most colorful celebrations, with the classic Ramayana enacted throughout the country.

—from Fodor's *India*

Naee Sadak (New Road) in Chandni Chowk, Old Delhi—http://chico.rice.edu/~rakesh/delhi/

kah, then that means that Tiuchirapalli and Ootacumund are out, and there's still the matter of Jaisalmer and Khjuruaho. IndiaWorld's travel page features a wide variety of resources for the subcontinental traveler, including short essays on dozens of destinations, airline schedules, and a collection of travel tips (note this fascinating advice: "If you can, carry a Polaroid camera; Indians love to be photographed."). ✓**INTERNET**→*url* http://www.indiaworld.com/open/rec/travel/index.html

Information on India Maintained at the Indian Institute of Science, this is one of the best sites in Cyberspace for travelers wishing to explore India. With a map of the country, tips for train travel, a brief course in art history, and lavish notes on India's national parks, this site offers a great place to start, whether you're intending to spelunk in the Ellora Caves in Maharashtra state or spend a leisurely afternoon in Kashmir's Shalimar Gardens. ✓**INTERNET**→*url* http://spiderman.bu.edu/misc/india/

Prince Kohli Information Page Prince Kohli, a student at Georgia Tech, has set up a princely home page about India at his site. He must be a musical fellow—most of his page is devoted to Indian musical resources, including a link to ITRANS Song Book, an online database for Indian music. Prince Kohli also provides a list of travel agents for those wishing to travel to the subcontinent. ✓**INTERNET**→*url* http://www.cc.gatech.edu/grads/k/Prince.Kohli/Prince.Kohli.html

rec.travel Guide to India This easy-to-read guide gives some practical advice on traveling in India: When in Calcutta, "watch your pockets"; all over India "there are lots of cows"; and the main rule of the road is "the loudest person wins." Also, get tips for experiencing the "real" India. (Watch a movie in a theater to appreciate the love that Indians have for movies.) Learn about local customs and practices that will make traveling to India a safe, happy, and rewarding experience ("don't even think of renting a car and driving yourself"). ✓**INTERNET**→*url* http://www.digimark.net/rec-travel/asia/india/india-guide

The Beauty of India-Unity in Diversity With advanced hypertext technology (portions of the text serve as live links), this essay explores the past and the present of the largest democracy in the world. Click on "population," for example, and you'll be delivered to a gopher site with the latest Indian census data. Click on "religion," and you'll have the opportunity to explore India's myriad faiths, including Hinduism, Sikhism, Islam, and Christianity. And that's only the beginning. Find out more about the East India Company and the tea trade. View some ancient sculpture. Listen to sound clips from Indian movies. Learn to cook the cuisine of Tamil Nadu. It's like a long trip to India, only less time consuming. ✓**INTERNET**→*url* http://www.cs.clemson.edu/~nandu/india.html

The India Directory Flip through the directory and find statistics on Indian agriculture, commerce, culture, and religion. For lighter fare the directory also offers pictures of Indian actors to download and practical information like an essay on taking appliances to India. ✓**INTERNET**→*url* gopher://info.anu.edu.au:70/11/elibrary/country/India

The India Page A list of links to pages with information about India—on travel, culture, and religion—as well as to home pages for members of the Indian community. Travelers won't necessarily find a wealth of information connected to this page, but they can browse the links looking for the occasional tidbit. ✓**INTERNET**→*url* http://pages.prodigy.com/NJ/toshniwal/toshniwal3.html

Virtual Tour of India More than four centuries ago, the emperor Akbar built the Moghul town of Fatehpur Sikri. Tour the town—its mausoleums, its sculptures—and also visit other Indian sights, such as Jai Singh's astronomical observatory in Jaipur and the moderately famous Taj Majal. ✓**INTERNET**→*url* http://challenge.tiac.net/users/whb/India.html

Cities & regions

About Calcutta This home page is a portal to the crowded metropolis that is India's largest city. Take a virtual tour of the Marble Palace, find a place for dinner in the Restaurant Guide (stop by the Mitra Cafe for a fowl cutlet), or plan your public transportation with the help of the Calcutta Subway Guide, which calculates the shortest route between two points. ✓**INTERNET**→*url* http://www.gl.umbc.edu/~achatt1/calcutta.html

Assam—The Land Unequaled The Indian state of Assam, "the land of hills and valleys," is the focus of the page. Read about its history, listen to Assamese music, and look at pictures of the beautiful countryside and its people. Visit this page and access information on the culture, trade, tourism, and food of Assam. Where else in Cyberspace can you find out how many bison are in the Kaziranga National Forest? ✓**INTERNET**→*url* http://www.acsu.buffalo.edu/~talukdar/assam/assamhome.html

Bangalore Homepage An illustrated essay on India's Garden City, covering the Bangalore Fort and Palace, the Glass House, and Cubbon Park. The Restaurants section not only lists the names, addresses, and phone numbers of various eateries, but also throws in a list of five-star hotels in the city. ✓**INTERNET**→*url* http://spiderman.bu.edu/misc/karnataka/cities/bangalore

Bombay, The Gateway of India The largest and most cosmopolitan city in India boasts its own site, which highlights the local attractions. Use The Gateway to take a virtual tour of the Mosque of Haji Ali, the Victoria Terminus, and the Taj Mahal Hotel. ✓**INTERNET**→*url* http://www.cba.uh.edu/~manish/Bombay.html

Goa Called "the bridge between East and West" because of its many Western influences, Goa is a fascinating city to visit. Take an online tour of this transitional city through the pictures and essays provided here, which cover the history of the region from the time of Portuguese rule to the present. ✓**INTERNET**→*url* http://mrlxp2.mrl.uiuc.edu/~menezes/goa/goaweb.html

Maharashtra Home Page A page devoted to the Indian state of Maharashtra, home of Marathi, with links to essays on the history and culture of the region. ✓**INTERNET**→*url* http://wwwvms.utexas.edu/~savkar/rashtra.html

Maharashtra Tourism Point and click on a city or region on the map here, and important travel information will be yours. Hotel guides, which offer descriptions of room styles, checkout times, approximate rates, and more, are here for every location highlighted on the map. Basic city information and places to visit, as well as the major roads and bus, air, and rail transportation to and from each city, are also listed. Use the text search option to locate all resources available on a particular topic. ✓**INTERNET**→*url* gopher://soochak.ncst.ernet.in/11s/mtdc

New & Old Delhi, India Something old, something new, but all of it about the Indian city of Delhi. This collection of links takes you to a history of the city, to the newsgroup soc.culture.indian.delhi, and to a gallery of photos of the ancient town. All Delhi academic institutions with Websites have links here (in case you're traveling to India to tour universities). Don't miss the link to the awe-inspiring picture of the Qutab Minar, the ancient and majestic 288-

The Gateway to India in Bombay—http://www.bchs.uh.edu/~mdoshi/Bombay//Bombay.html

foot tower that rises above Delhi. ✓INTERNET→*url* http://chico.rice.edu/~rakesh/delhi/

Pune Before you stroll into a bar in Pune, you may wish to visit this site, which houses a dictionary of commonly used Pune slang words and a collection of the latest jokes being thrown around Pune and Marathi. ✓INTERNET→*url* http://koop.cs.uiowa.edu:6600/pune/

Shangri-La Home Page Everyone has his own idea of Shangri-La, whether it's James Hilton's 1933 novel *Lost Horizon* or a little spot on your lower back that feels like heaven when someone touches it. But the author of this Web page follows conventional wisdom in locating the legendary paradise in the Himalayan Mountains. Exclaiming the glories of these majestic mountains, which touch India, Burma, Nepal, and Tibet, the page features essays on the geography, ecology, and pollution in the range. You can experience the Himalayas at every altitude, from the high (Mount Everest, which is 8,848 meters high) to the low (the Namcha Barwa canyon, which is 5,909 meters deep). ✓INTERNET→*url* http://aleph0.clarku.edu/~rajs/Shangri_La.html

Sunil's Delhi Pictures This collection of color photographs was taken in Delhi by Sunil Kukreja. Tour the India Gate, the Parliament Building, and the Jantar Mantar (an observatory built in the 1700s) in New Delhi through this online picture gallery. ✓INTERNET→*url* http://ralph.biomed.mcgill.ca/~kukreja/travel/delhi/delhi.html

Calcutta's Victoria Memorial—http://www.gl.umbc.edu/~achatt1/calcutta.html

Culture

Bhagavad-Gita For a taste of Hindu literature, download and read the full text of *Bhagavad-Gita*, the ancient Hindu epic (written as a philosophic dialogue). ✓INTERNET→*url* gopher://gopher.vt.edu:10010/02/96/1

India Culture and Arts The highlight of this site is the collection of rather lengthy—and very informative—travelogues that give Netsurfers access to India through the eyes of other travelers. Links to other India sites are here, including a restaurant guide to Bombay. ✓INTERNET→*url* http://www.digimark.net/rec-travel/asia/india

Indian Classical Dance Forms A description of Bharata Natyam, Kutiyattam, and Manipuri, complete with pictures of such popular dance stars as Malavika Sarukkai. ✓INTERNET→*url* http://www.cis.ohio-state.edu/~sundar/noncarnatic/Dance.html

IndiaWorld's Arts and Entertainment Want to take a quiz on India? Need the lunar forecast? Eager to see a preview of a new CD-ROM on India's cultural heritage? With book reviews, contemporary Indian comic strips, short stories, and satirical columns, this site presents a rare glimpse into the hectic world of modern-day Indian entertainment. ✓INTERNET→*url* http://www.indiaworld.com/open/rec/index.html

soc.culture.indian*/rec.music.indian*/alt.culture.karnatka (ng) Hundreds of messages a week pour into these mammoth Indian newsgroups (in particular, soc.culture.indian), where Indian traditions, politics, and culture are celebrated—and are just as often attacked. Whether they're about Bengali literature, Hinduism, or vegetarianism, the discussions are usually very informed, and many would seem almost scholarly if not for their emotional undertones. The group is at its best when covering cultural topics. When a woman asked about the influence of Mozart on Indian classical music, someone else mentioned the relationship between Czech, Gypsy, and Indian music. Political debates, however, feed the strong centrifugal forces in soc.culture.indian—people are always petitioning to break away with a new newsgroup. And there are already several other Indian newsgroups: Read Indian news in misc.news.

southasia; request specific information about journal articles, visas, Internet access, and the like in soc.culture.indian.info; join the often personal discussions by Indian-Americans about preserving culture and living in the U.S. in the newsgroup alt.culture.us.asian-indian; engage in political debate in the rather quiet alt.india.progressive (most political discussions happen in soc.culture.indian); get into a flame war in the volatile alt.culture.karnataka, which also has an inordinate number of members seeking marriage partners ("alliance invited from well-educated Brahmin guys from good south Indian family for a Brahmin girl"); join the more lighthearted soc.culture.indian.telugu, where discussions often cover movies, music, and recipes, and someone occasionally seeks a travel companion, roommate, or babysitter; or turn to soc.music.indian.classical and rec.music.indian.misc for endless music conversation. ✓USENET ...→soc.culture.indian ...→rec .music.indian ...→alt.culture.karnatka

The Batish Institute of Indian Music and Fine Arts Listen to native Indian music. You can download samples of songs, then purchase cassettes, CDs, videos, and books on music and Indian fine arts. Also here are artist biographies and bibliographies on the music of India. ✓INTERNET→*url* http://hypatia.ucsc.edu:70/1 /RELATED/Batish

Food

Rasoi-The Kitchen With six general categories (drinks, appetizers, entrees, side dishes, snacks, and desserts), this page (part of MCI's Hello, India initiative) collects recipes, including any specifically stipulated dietary restrictions. ✓INTERNET→*url* http://www .helloindia.com/india/recipe /rechome.shtml

The Graduate Student's Guide to Indian Recipes Sample the flavor of India by preparing any one of the hundreds of dishes described here—curried garbanzo beans, kheer, mango ice cream, and many more. The recipes are grouped into various categories for easy searching. For those having trouble finding some of the necessary ingredients, check the Guide to Ingredients page, which lists substitute possibilities. ✓INTERNET→*url* http://s1.arc.umn .edu:80/~misra/indrec.html

News

Hindu Newspaper Updated weekly, this site provides excerpts from the national paper of India. Search stories by keyword, peruse the advertisements, and read back issues here. There's even a crossword puzzle for those who speak Hindi. ✓INTERNET→*url* http://www .webpage.com/hindu

India Today The week's cover story and selected features from *India Today*, the nation's answer to *Time* magazine (right down to the red border and the triangular spotlight in the upper right-hand corner of the cover). ✓INTERNET→*url* http://www.helloindia.com/india /it/ithome.shtml

INDOlink News All the news that's fit to print about India. For short briefs on pan-Indian topics, turn to the Headline News section, which is updated daily. You'll find libraries of feature stories on Indian business, politics, sports, and entertainment in separate sections of the Web page. ✓INTERNET→*url* http://www.genius.net /indolink/INDNews/index.html

Religion

alt.hindu (ng) Anshuman has a question about the Hindu power ladder: "It seems that most of the quotes given by those pushing Vaisnava philosophy always put the word 'Vishnu' or 'Krishna' in parentheses after the word 'Brahman' or 'prajapati' or some other supreme being appears." And Vijay has an answer: "Note that the name 'prajapati' more accurately

The display window of a sari shop—http://www.gl.umbc.edu/~achatt1/calcutta.html

Jama Masjid, a Mosque in Old Delhi —from http://chico.rice.edu/~rakesh/delhi/

describes Lord Vishnu than anyone else—although in a lesser sense, it describes Daksa and other progenitors, in another sense, it indicates Lord Brahma (the father of Daksa, etc.), but it more appropriately refers to Lord Vishnu, who is the source of Lord Brahma. We see Lord Krishna referred to as 'prapitamaha' (great-grandfather; Lord Brahma is often called 'pitamaha' or grandfather), 'sarva-lokamahesvara' (the controller of all worlds; Lord Siva is sometimes called 'mahesvara'), etc., in Bhagavad Gita, 'prajapati' [in addition to many other 'pati' titles] in Bhagavatam, etc. Similarly, 'svayambhu' ('self-born,' which often refers to Lord Brahma, but more appropriately to Lord Vishnu) appears in Vishnu Sahasranama, etc." The other participants in this moderately active newsgroup aren't always as onomastically skilled, but they have plenty to talk about from the world of Hinduism—a project to bring water to Thai villages, announcements of the public appearances of Hindu luminaries, and discussions about the nature of sin and dishonesty in the *Bhagavad-Gita*. ✓**USENET**→alt.hindu

alt.religion.vaisnava (ng) Discuss Hinduism Sanatan Dharma with other adherents of Vaisnava. ✓**USENET**→alt.religion.vaisnava

Global Hindu Electronic Network: The Hindu Universe Sponsored by the Hindu Students' Council, this site features information about Hindu festivals, Hindu organizations, and India, as well as information about a variety of other Hindu-related topics. Some previous knowledge of Hinduism might be helpful in navigating around the site. A link here connects to a sacred-text anthology. ✓**INTERNET**→*url* http://rbhatnagar.csm.uc.edu:8080/hindu_universe.html

Hinduism Today Find here the full text of current and back issues of *Hinduism Today*, an international news journal. Its features on prominent religious leaders and important temples will supply you with background information for your visits to Hindu-related sites in India. ✓**INTERNET**→*url* http://www.HinduismToday.kauai.hi.us/ashram/htoday.html

Sikhism: Religion of the Sikh People Over 20 million people worldwide practice Sikhism, but many people still don't know much about this religion that captures the faith of so many. According to this page, it is a religion that "preaches a message of devotion and remembrance of God at all times, truthful living, and equality of mankind, and denounces superstitions and blind rituals." For an excellent overview of the religion, its gurus, and their philosophies, come to this site. ✓**INTERNET**→*url* http://www.io.org/~sandeep/sikhism.htm

World Vaisnava Association Even if you're merely curious about Vaisnava, you're welcome to this site, which includes the association's newsletter and a mission statement. ✓**INTERNET**→*url* http://www.owplaza.com/wva/wvaindex.html

Travel agencies

Above the Clouds A travel agency that books trekking tours to Nepal and Bhutan and through the Himalayan Mountains. Come to this site for the company's address and phone and fax numbers. ✓**INTERNET**→*url* http://www.gorp.com/abvclds.htm

Cox & Kings A travel agency that specializes in travel to the Indian subcontinent. Peruse tour descriptions with complete itineraries and prices, and learn how to email the company for a free brochure. ✓**INTERNET**→*url* http://www.zenonet.com/cox-kings/welcome.html

Himalayan Travel Includes full address and email, phone, and fax information for Himalayan Travel. ✓**INTERNET**→*url* http://www.gorp.com/himtravel/asia.htm

Indian Subcontinent

Once you've visited the majestic cities and stunning rural locales of India, you may want to venture outside of the country, into the rest of the Indian Subcontinent. While some of the surrounding countries are risky bets for tourists (war-torn Afghanistan, for example, as **soc.culture.afghanistan** will explain), others are a sort of heaven on earth (the beautiful nation of Bangladesh, shown in stunning color at **Bangladesh: An Online Tour Guide**). And then set your sights high—Himalayan, in fact—with **The Nepal Homepage**.

Mount Everest as seen from Kala Pattar in Nepal—http://www.eunet.fi/nepal/nep_e_kh.htm

On the Net

Afghanistan

Afghan Cultural Information Center An elegant Website for a rough, rough land. The site has information on the manners and customs of Afghanis and on Afghani politics, religion, music, folklore, art and poetry, news, and more. Without dispute, the best source of information about Afghanistan online. ✓**INTERNET**→*url* http://www.gl.umbc.edu/~hqurba1/

Afghan Information Club Med isn't setting up in Afghanistan any time soon, and the war-torn country isn't an ideal spot for a family vacation, but if you're planning a visit (and you can actually get in), you'll need some information about the country. And that's just what's here—the Website includes an essay on Afghan history, descriptions of the country's "political parties," links to works of Afghan literature, and biographies of important military leaders. In addition, more light-hearted information (like lists of Afghan restaurants in the U.S.) is also available. ✓**INTERNET**→*url* http://cville-srv.wam.umd.edu/~endevour/

Afghan News Service A daily news service pulling stories about Afghanistan from Reuters, AP, Voice of America, the Itarr Tass, and the Pakistan Dawn Newswire. ✓**INTERNET**→*url* http://theyellowpages.com/viable/vtpages/afgnnews.htm

Afghans List Server (ml) Members of the mailing list discuss the possibility of peace, report news about the region, and share their thoughts on the Pashto language and culture. ✓**INTERNET**→*email* eshabon@eos.ncsu.edu *Write a request* ***Archives:*** ✓**INTERNET**→*url* http://www4.ncsu.edu/eos/users/e/eshabon/kabul/afghan.html

soc.culture.afghanistan (ng) Peter has a couple of friends who are planning on riding motorcycles from London, through Europe, the Middle East, and Afghanistan. He wants to know if they'll be safe, if there are "any restrictions for traveling through Afghanistan." Peter may have to wait a while for a response. While the traffic in the newsgroup is moderately heavy, most discussion focuses on the politics of Afghanistan, Pakistan, and the Kashmir—not on travel questions. ✓**USENET**→soc.culture.afghanistan

Bangladesh

A Short Scenic Tour Along the Country-side of Bangladesh A handful of pictures of the Bangladesh countryside, as well as links to other Bangladesh Web pages. ✓**INTERNET**→*url* http://www.tuns.ca/~abidmr/bd_tour.html

Bangladesh What time is it in Bangladesh? What are the largest cities? What's the main religion? The site carries very basic information about the pimento in the huge olive of India. ✓**INTERNET**→*url* http://www.tbc.gov.bc.ca/cwgames/country/Bangladesh/bangladesh.html

---

Bangladesh: An Online Tour Guide October to March is tourist season for The People's Republic of Bangladesh, but even out of season this Web page features information about and images of the nation's most popular resorts and tourist attractions (including Cox's Bazar, the world's longest beach), historic sites, and sightseeing tours. Currency, visa, and basic country information are also offered here. ✓**INTERNET**→*url* http://www.servtech.com/public/outcast/tour/

Bangladesh & Her Cultures Heading to Bangladesh and need an itinerary? Check out the listing for points of interest in and around the capital city of Dhaka—World War II cemeteries, sandy beaches, hilly towns, tea gardens, archaeological sites, and more. More? Well, if you're willing to travel 458 km from the capital, you can go to Sundarban, the largest mangrove forest in the world, and maybe even catch a glimpse of the exceedingly rare, powerful, and beautiful Royal Bengal Tiger. Information for the general traveler (climate, health requirements, weather forecasts, city phone codes, state department advisories, maps, and even a copy of the visa application form) is mixed in with dozens of links to sites covering Bangladesh's politics, culture, and history. ✓**INTERNET**→*url* http://path.upmc.edu/~ahmed/bdpage.html

---

Bangladesh Index An index of Websites devoted to Bangladesh. ✓**INTERNET**→*url* http://www.ccsi.com:80/bdesh/

Bangladesh—Land of the Royal Bengal Tiger For an overview of Bangladesh history, government, culture, and geography, this Website is well worth the trip. It's packed with information about and images of the country. Read estimates from the world's most respected newspapers on how many Bengalis were killed in Dhaka in 1971 or read a poem written by famous Bengali poet Jibananda Das. Get a recipe for Tikya Kebabs or read the current weather report for Bangladesh. Pick up some useful Bengali phrases or pick up a dictionary of more than 3,000 Bengali words. Take a virtual tour (pictures and history both) of capital city Dhaka or take a gander at the Bangladesh FAQ, which includes guide book recommendations and visa information. There's even a page of sound clips, and like most of the site, the clips have distinct political overtones—a poem about Bangladesh's independence war, the country's National Anthem, part of the March 7th Independence speech by Sheikh Mujibur Rahman. ✓**INTERNET**→*url* http://www.asel.udel.edu/~kazi/bangladesh/bd.html

---

Bangladesh Page Carries pictures of the Bangladesh countryside and a collection of links to other Bangladesh sites on the Internet. ✓**INTERNET**→*url* http://www2.gsu.edu/~gs02msi/bangladesh.html

---

soc.culture.bangladesh/soc.culture.bengali (ng) Most participants are not travelers, but Bengalis grappling with difficult issues facing their country. If you plan on spending all of your trip at a four-star hotel, you may not want to get embroiled in the heated discussions here. If you want more insight, these groups are musts. ✓**USENET**→soc.culture.bangladesh/soc.culture.bengali

Bhutan

Images of Bhutan Contains pictures of beautiful city scenes and landscapes of mysterious Bhutan. Some are accompanied with an audio file from the pho-

Fodor's Choice...

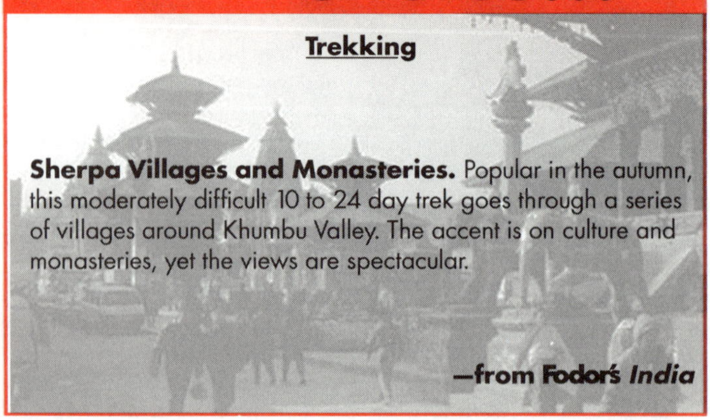

Trekking

Sherpa Villages and Monasteries. Popular in the autumn, this moderately difficult 10 to 24 day trek goes through a series of villages around Khumbu Valley. The accent is on culture and monasteries, yet the views are spectacular.

—from Fodor's *India*

tographer explaining the shot. ✓**INTERNET**→*url* http://www.webcorp.com/images/bhutan.htm

---

Traveling in Bhutan With so few resources on Bhutan, travelers can come here to find some necessary info for visiting Bhutan. Read about travel restrictions, visa information, obtaining the Bhutanese rupee, and some cities in this "beautiful and unspoiled country." ✓**INTERNET**→*url* http://www.solutions.mb.ca/rec-travel/asia/bhutan/bhutan.html

Nepal

A Visit to Nepal by Scott A. Yost Look at interactive clickable maps of Scott A. Yost's trekking trip to Nepal. Find out what equipment he used, where he went, and what he saw. Read his journal and look at some of the spectacular pictures he took on his six week journey. ✓**INTERNET**→*url* http://enigma.phys.utk.edu/~syost/nepal.html

---

Nepal Travel Log Strap on your backpack and join these hearty adventurers as you read these travelogues of trips to Nepal and the Himalayas. The site also includes other miscellaneous articles on Nepal and links to other Nepal sites. ✓**INTERNET**→*url* http://Alpha.Solutions.Net/rec-travel/asia/nepal

An Afghani plateau—from http://cville-srv.wam.umd.edu/~endevour/

A flower-picker in Bangladesh—from http://www.tuns.ca/~abidmr/bd_tour.html

---

Photos of Nepal by Sam O'Connor You say you're going to Kathmandu? Take a look here first and view beautiful Nepalese landscapes and wildlife like the Lang Tang River. See parts of Kathmandu and the Monkey Temple. Annotations accompany each picture. ✓**INTERNET**→*url* http://insane.apana.org.au/~samoc/nepal.htm

---

Royal Nepal Spectacular Nature Encounters, Ltd., is a travel company that specializes in trips to Nepal. Contact them via email, fax, or phone with the info given here. ✓**INTERNET**→*url* http://clever.net/phrantic/nature/nepal.html

---

soc.culture.nepal (ng) Discussion group for those interested in Nepal, its people, customs, politics, and culture. ✓**USENET**→soc.culture.nepal

---

The Nepal Homepage Practical information is at your fingertips here—a Nepalese phone directory, email links to other Nepalese, embassy locations, and a list of Nepalese organizations in the West. There is culture from the heights of Kathmandu here, too: recipes for momo and a collection of literature written in a Nepalese font. ✓**INTERNET**→*url* http://www.cen.uiuc.edu/~rshresth/Nepal.html

Pakistan

Karakoram Highway Travelogue A trip along the Karakoram Highway in northern Pakistan. This meticulous travelogue details the trip made by Erik Futtrup to this region in 1991—it's interesting to note the exchange rate and prices of goods and services he bought. Frequently, small details mentioned here can save travelers some headaches. ✓**INTERNET**→*url* http://Alpha.Solutions.Net/rec-travel/asia/pakistan/trip.futtrup.html

---

Pakistan Basic country profile with many links to information on the people, language, religion, and geography of this country. It even has dessert recipes! For travelers there are virtual tours of popular mosques like Mahabat Khan Mosque, Eid-gaah Mosque, and the Tomb of Bibi Jaiwindi. ✓**INTERNET**→*url* http://web.grfn.org/~falcon/

Pakistan Home Page Homesick Pakistanis stuck at school in upstate New York have created this excellent interactive map full of illustrations and information. Simply click on Lahore and say there's no place like home. ✓**INTERNET**→*url* http://www.rpi.edu/~ansars/paksa_locker/pak_mosaic/paksa_www.html

---

Pakistan & Islam Discover the religion as it is practiced in Pakistan with the collection of links provided here. ✓**INTERNET**→*url* http://www.cris.com/~hukum/ahmedi.html

---

Pakistan Music A small site that offers sound files of classical and modern Pakistani music. Sample Pakistani ear candy by Saqid Maseh & Party, Farid Khanum, Ali Haider, and others. ✓**INTERNET**→*url* http://www.mit.edu:8001/people/pheonix/home.html

---

Pakistan Profile Contains a short country profile on Pakistan: geography, exports, population, and other general information about the country. There are also links here to other Pakistani sites online. ✓**INTERNET**→*url* http://www.egr.uh.edu/~escco/Pakistan.html

---

Punjab Home Page Learn everything about the Pakistani Punjab—its geography, people and politics. Look at pictures of the mosques and tombs that make this area so robust and alive. ✓**INTERNET**→*url* http://BUCRF15.BU.EDU/~rajwi/punjab/

---

soc.culture.pakistan (ng) Discussion about Pakistani culture. Subjects like "American Cars Suck," "Bovine Joke," and "Negro Muslims" make this an interesting place. ✓**USENET**→soc.culture.pakistan

Sri Lanka

Jaffna Home Page Located in northern Sri Lanka, Jaffna is a region populated by the Tamil. At this large site you can find out more about the Tamil and their culture, the climate they live in, and their history. ✓**INTERNET**→*url* http://alfred.uib.no/People/stud1222/Jaffna.html

---

soc.culture.sri-lanka (ng) Discussion group for those interested in Sri Lanka. Get travel tips, talk cricket, or get into an argument about politics. The newsgroup's FAQ features excellent resources for those interested in traveling to Sri Lanka. Get answers to questions from "So what's so great about Sri Lanka?" to "Who's the best airline ticket agent?" to "Where can I get Sri Lankan spices in Canada?" ✓**USENET**→soc.culture.sri-lanka ***FAQ:*** ✓**INTERNET**→*url* http://www.cis.ohio-state.edu/hypertext/faq/usenet/sri-lanka-faq/faq.html

---

Sri Lanka Pictures of fishing boats on the golden beaches of this island nation welcome the cybertraveler. Jump to the Fast Facts section to read about local culture, politics, and economy. Then peruse the travelogues for practical information—beware of monkeys that collect tourists' belongings! ✓**INTERNET**→*url* http://suif.stanford.edu/~lanka/sri_lanka.html

---

Tamil Eelam An introduction to the Tamil, a group of people living in northern Sri Lanka and in the southern Indian state of Tamil Nadu. This site is a collection of links to essays on the news and history of the Tamil. ✓**INTERNET**→*url* http://uts.cc.utexas.edu/~janahan/tamil.html

---

Welcome to Sri Lanka A wealth of knowledge and information for travelers. The site contains country information, tourist tips, and suggested travel itineraries. Use the search function to find your favorite topics among the site's many information-packed pages. ✓**INTERNET**→*url* http://arachnid.cs.cf.ac.uk/Sri_Lanka/sl_home.html

A street scene in Bhutan—from http://www.webcorp.com/images/bhutan.htm

Across Asia

Moviegoers galore are probably not planning vacations to Myanmar (Burma) or Cambodia—after all, *Beyond Rangoon* is still in the theaters and *The Killing Fields* may never fade from memory. But that doesn't mean that there aren't wonders to see there—from the astounding temple complex at Angkor Wat to fabulous flora and fauna. Visit virtually at **Free Burma** or the **Internet Travel Guide—Cambodia**. Discover the relatively benign beauties of other Asian nations at **Tour in Korea**, the **Malaysia Homepage**, and **Travel in Taiwan**. But if finding inner peace rather than great souvenirs or the perfect tan is your vacation goal, head to the magical climes of the **Shangri La Home Page** or tap into the sagacity of the Dalai Lama at **Tibetan Studies**.

A public garden in Phnom Penh, Cambodia—from http://www.cambodia.org/

On the Net

Brunei

Brunei Tourist Pages Travelers to Brunei, which is run by an Islamic monarchy, should observe the local customs (see the list of do's and don'ts), should probably get a tour guide (see the descriptions of several guided tours), and, of course, should figure out where to sleep, eat, and shop. These Web pages can help the traveler with all of the above. ✓**INTERNET**→*url* http://www.iipl.com.sg/bru/text/tourist.htm

Lonely Planet—Destination: Brunei Travel information about Brunei is relatively scarce on the Web. The Lonely Planet travel guidebook series offers some comfort with this summary of travel tips, facts, and images about Brunei. Prospective visitors can read a brief history, check on health risks, get recommendations for must-see sites, and even figure out what a trip is likely to cost. ✓**INTERNET**→*url* http://www.lonelyplanet.com.au/dest/sea/brunei.htm

Burma

Burma Web The single most impressive collection of information about Burma online, this Website links to an anthology of Aung San Suu Kyi's writings; travelers' tales about visiting Burma; news from the country; photos, maps, and short movies of the country; information about Burma's languages, cultures, history, ethnic groups, and literature; and more. It's where a prospective traveler can pick up a map to turtle nesting sites off Burma and Thailand or a movie of the Burma Boat Festival. ✓**INTERNET**→*url* http://www.uio.no/~tormodl/

Free Burma If human-rights issues are important to you, you might want to stop by this Website before visiting the country that has lived under a military dictatorship since 1962. But what is the site? "Free Burma is a slogan, a hope, a certain number of web pages, and, until the people there are free and self-governing...the only one there is." It's also a collection of articles about human rights violations in the country and information about Nobel Peace Prize winner and leader of the Democracy movement in Burma, Aung San Suu Kyi. ✓**INTER-**

NET→*url* http://sunsite.unc.edu/freeburma/freeburma.html

Lonely Planet—Destination: Burma Assuming you don't mind traveling in countries with oppressive governments and that the movie *Beyond Rangoon* (plot: tourist gets stuck in Burma during a military massacre) didn't scare you too much, Burma (or Myanmar as it's now known), offers travelers the chance to visit beautiful rivers, temples and pagodas, and ancient ruins. This Website outlines the country's major tourist attractions, offers travel tips and photos of the countryside, and gives a brief overview of Burmese history and culture. The Website is maintained by the publishers of the Lonely Planet guidebook series. ✓**INTERNET**→*url* http://www.lonelyplanet.com.au/dest/sea/myan.htm

---

MYANMAR—The Land Of Pagodas When the first ATMs opened in Myanmar, the event was announced here. But while the occasional news item is announced, the site serves primarily as an index to Burmese resources online—images of pagodas in Burma, a map of the coral reefs of Southeast Asia, the Lonely Planet guide, the CIA World Fact Book profile of Burma, and movie clips from *Beyond Rangoon* and *Thagyan Moe*. ✓**INTERNET**→*url* http://triton.ori.u-tokyo.ac.jp/~moe/myanmar.html

Cambodia

Lonely Planet—Destination: Cambodia To most Americans, the name "Cambodia" evokes images of U.S. bombings of civilians or the genocide under Pol Pot's leadership of the Khmer Rouge. But Cambodia is a beautiful land which once stood at the center of a powerful empire—the Khmer Empire—that included Vietnam, Laos, and Thailand. Travelers interested in visiting the land of the temples of Angkor should stop by this Website sponsored by the Lonely Planet guidebooks for travel tips, background information about the country, and even photos (the Angkor Wat, the Killing Fields of Choenung Ek, etc.). ✓**INTERNET**→*url* http://www.lonelyplanet.com.au/dest/sea/camb.htm

---

soc.culture.cambodia (ng) What should Cambodian students do to help Cambodia? Should Cambodia reinstate the death penalty? Where can people in the United States find literature in Khmer? The newsgroup has a strong, active community of Cambodians who discuss the culture and developments in the country. ✓**USENET**→soc.culture.cambodia *Archives:* ✓**INTERNET**→*url* ftp://ftp.nectec.or.th/pub/archives/soc.culture.cambodia/

The Cambodia Times A weekly version of Cambodia's national newspaper is online with full text articles. Archives of back issues are also available. ✓**INTERNET**→*url* http://www.jaring.my/at-asia/camb_at_asia/camb_times/ct_list.html

---

The Cambodian Information Center Homepage This large Website serves as an index to Internet resources about Cambodia for travelers, scholars, and Cambodians. Resources range from an undergraduate essay on the academic view of the Khmer Rouge from 1975-1979 to archives of Cambodian news; from an advertisement for a CD-ROM entitled *Holiday in Cambodia* (even if you're not buying, the site has some fabulous photos) to photos from the countryside; from a brief history of the Khmer Kingdom of Angkor to human rights updates; and from reviews of books written about Cambodia to photos of the Angkor Wat. ✓**INTERNET**→*url* http://www.cambodia.org/

The Internet Travel Guide—Cambodia It won't replace a real travel guide, but this FAQ covers all the basics about traveling to the country formerly known as Kampuchea: geography, climate, visa requirements, money, transportation, places to visit, recommended reading, etc. ✓**INTERNET**→*url* http://www.cambodia.org/travel

Fodor's Choice...

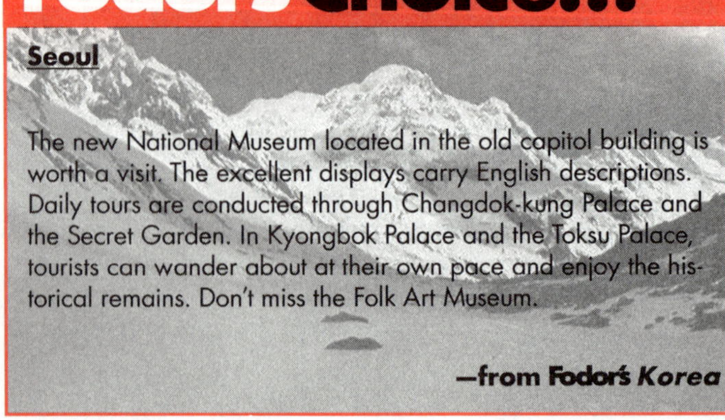

Seoul

The new National Museum located in the old capitol building is worth a visit. The excellent displays carry English descriptions. Daily tours are conducted through Changdok-kung Palace and the Secret Garden. In Kyongbok Palace and the Toksu Palace, tourists can wander about at their own pace and enjoy the historical remains. Don't miss the Folk Art Museum.

—from Fodor's *Korea*

Machhapuchhre in the Himalayas—http://aleph0.clarku.edu/rajs/Shangri_La.html

/guide.html ***FAQ:*** ✓ **INTERNET**→*url* http://www.cis.ohio-state.edu/hypertext/faq/usenet/travel/cambodia-guide/part1/faq.html

The Himalayas

Shangri La Home Page If you're searching for Shangri La, look no further than this URL. The Website offers encyclopedic information about the Himalayas, links to Web pages for countries that include Himalayan peaks, a clickable map of the mountain range with information about individual mountains, collections of photos and paintings of the Himalayas, writings about the mighty range, and more. ✓ **INTERNET**→*url* http://aleph0.clarku.edu/rajs/Shangri_La.html

Korea

Destination Highlights—Seoul You're going to Seoul. What will you see and do? For some options, visit this site which offers a monthly calendar of cultural events and descriptions of several famous attractions in the capital city. ✓ **INTERNET**→*url* http://nearnet.gnn.com/gnn/bus/wview/cityhigh/ch1sel.html

Korea Culture and Sightseeing Visit Korea prepared. Learn a little about the country's history, its people, and customs. Figure out if your trip coincides with a national holiday or if there's a local festival happening. Familiarize yourself with what there is to see in Seoul, Kyongju, the Cheju Island, and Yoido. Practice some basic Korean expressions. And do it all here. ✓ **INTERNET**→*url* http://korea.com/korea/korea.htm

Pusan Tourist Guide Home Page The city of 4 million on the southeastern tip of the Korean Peninsula is home to beautiful beaches, parks, resorts, and other tourist attractions. Visitors will have plenty to do, and this guide makes it easy to plan vacations there. Browse directories of hotels and restaurants; read descriptions of parks, beaches, and resorts; preview museums and famous cultural relics; and consult the map. ✓ **INTERNET**→*url* http://lotus.pwu.ac.kr/tour/tour.html

Republic of Korea Straight from the pages of the Korea '94 Travel Manual, the site offers fairly general information on accommodations, travel within the country, getting into the country, and sightseeing. ✓ **INTERNET**→*url* http://cair-archive.kaist.ac.kr/korea/

Seoul A simple Website focused on Korea's capital. The site has the unimpressive look of a government factsheet about the city. ✓ **INTERNET**→*url* http://www.nca.go.kr/KOREA/seoul.html

Tour in Korea Using the interactive map, visit Cheju Island, a honeymoon paradise guarded by the dragon-shaped Yonguam Rock. Or head on your cybervoyage to Pusan, Maisan, Pusoksa Temple, or Seoul—pictures and descriptions of sightseeing attractions are here. A restaurant guide and events calendar is included for each major metropolitan area. ✓ **INTERNET**→*url* http://firefox.postech.ac.kr/tour/tour_map.html

Visit Korea Little more than a glossy travel brochure about Korea. ✓ **INTERNET**→*url* http://www.nca.or.kr/VISIT/visitkor.htm

Welcome to "Land of Morning Calm" Legend says that Prince Hwanung, the son of Heaven's supreme deity, descended upon Mt. Taebaeksan along with 3,000 servants and built the "City of God," later to become Korea. From stories about the dawn of Korea to a survey of Korean history to recipes for Korean food to extensive travel information, this is one of the best online sites about Korea. ✓ **INTERNET**→*url* http://sunsite.snu.ac.kr/korea.html

Laos

Hmong WWW Homepage Read a Hmong magazine, get

Springtime in Korea—http://sunsite.snu.ac.kr/korea.html

recipes from a Hmong cookbook, download a map of Laos, and discuss the future of Laos with other Hmong students. You can link to sites to do all of these things from this Website. This mammoth index links both to resources for the Hmong community in the United States and resources about the Hmong people in Thailand and Laos. ✓INTERNET→*url* http://www.stolaf.edu/people/cdr/hmong/

Laos Articles by Author The full text of several articles from popular news magazines about Laos. ✓INTERNET→*url* http://www.umn.edu/nlhome/g450/vueb0001/BLaosArticlesAuthor.html

Laos Information A very brief description of the country with links to a few other Internet resources for Laos. ✓INTERNET→*url* http://sunsite.nus.sg/SEAlinks/laos-info.html

Lonely Planet—Destination: Laos It's not the full text of a Lonely Planet guidebook to Laos, but it's a start. The site features a summary of the country's history and culture, travel tips, information about health risks (which range from cholera to dengue fever to rabies), recommendations for places to see in Laos, photos of scenes from the country, and more. ✓INTERNET→*url* http://www.lonelyplanet.com.au/dest/sea/laos.htm

soc.culture.laos (ng) You won't find many airline tickets for sale or recommendations for tours of the country, but Lao literature, language, and the survival of Lao culture are frequent topics of discussion on this newsgroup. ✓USENET→soc.culture.laos

The Internet Travel Guide—Laos Which borders are open to and from Laos? How much does it cost to eat a day? What is Laotian beer like? What are some of the health issues a traveler should be concerned about? What are the telephone numbers for foreign embassies in Laos? What should a first-time traveler read beforehand? This compact guide answers these and many other basic travel questions about Laos. ✓INTERNET...→*url* http://www.cis.ohio-state.edu/hypertext/faq/usenet/travel/laos-guide/part1/faq.html ...→*url* ftp://rtfm.mit.edu/pub/usenet/rec.travel.asia/Laos__Travel_Guide

Malaysia

List of Malaysian Restaurants When you've returned from Malaysia with a taste for Malaysian cuisine, find out where in your neighborhood it's being served with this international list of restaurants. ✓INTERNET→*url* http://walden.mo.net/~philemon/food.html

Lonely Planet—Destination: Malaysia What are the health risks for travelers? What airlines fly to Malaysia? What are the best places to see and things to do in Malaysia? ("Although pretty inaccessible, a visit to Tasik Chini in central Pahang state is well worth the effort. It's actually a series of 12 lakes surrounded by beautiful jungle territory, with great treks, and it's rumored to be the haunt of a cousin of the Loch Ness monster.") Lonely Planet maintains this site with a summary of travel information for those planning to visit Malaysia. ✓INTERNET→*url* http://www.lonelyplanet.com.au/dest/sea/malay.htm

Malaysia Homepage Just as the streets of Kuala Lumpur are clean and the waters of Penang are beautiful, this Website is a fabulous resource for the traveler to Malaysia. Click the Tourism link and head to a rich source of travel information with large directories of hotel accommodations by state, lists of places to shop and golf, an updated monthly calendar of events, maps, addresses for tourism offices, information about the country's transportation system, Web pages for Malaysia's most popular beaches, descriptions of the country's biggest tourist attractions, and much more. And Tourism is only one of several links here. Others include Government, News, and Events. ✓INTERNET→*url* http://www.jaring.my/

Malaysia Hotels A list of hotels in Malaysia with contact information. ✓INTERNET→*url* http://www.asiadir.com/Travel-leisure/Mal/Hotel.html

Malaysia OnLine Malaysia OnLine does several things at once: it serves as an index to other Internet resources about Malaysia; it features daily summaries of news from Malaysia; it carries daily reports from the Kuala Lumpur

A view of Kuala Lumpur—http://www.phlab.missouri.edu/~c579283/mly/

Stock Exchange; it provides general information about the country, such as a calendar of holidays and election results; and it offers travel-specific information in the form of an extensive directory of hotels by state. ✓ **INTERNET**→*url* http://www.mol-usa.com/

Malaysia Tourist Pages Not very glamorous, but these Web pages include a fair amount of basic tourist information for those planning trips to Malaysia. Listings for hotels and accommodations, restaurant recommendations by type of cuisine, places to shop, and even descriptions of local festivals and customs are all here. ✓ **INTERNET**→*url* http://www.iipl.com.sg/mal/text/tourist.htm

---

Penang: A Brief Introduction One of Malaysia's (and Southeast Asia's) most popular tourist destinations, the state of Penang consists of the island of Penang and a strip on the mainland known as Province Wellesley. This guide for tourists briefly describes the state and outlines the most popular tourist activities and attractions. The page links to dozens of images of Penang. ✓ **INTERNET**→*url* http://www.cs.usm.my/penang_island/tourist.html

---

The Fascinating Malaysia Promising to introduce you to Malaysia, the site features brief descriptions of Malaysian geography, history, government, and more. Its information for tourists includes dozens of photos (a fishing village in Penang, a traditional Malay house, the capital city of Kuala Lumpur, etc.), general traveling tips, a list of Malaysian overseas tourist offices, immigration information, and hotel information. ✓ **INTERNET**→*url* http://www.phlab.missouri.edu/~c579283/mly/index.html

---

Travel-Leisure on Malaysia Extensive listings for hotels and restaurants in Malaysia. ✓ **INTERNET**→*url* http://www.asiatrade.com/Travel-leisure/index.html#Mal

Taiwan

China Times Web Home Page Chinese-language Website for one of Taiwan's biggest newspapers. ✓ **INTERNET**→*url* http://www.chinatimes.com.tw/

Destination Highlights—Taipei There's more to Taiwan than importing and exporting. If you're planning a visit, check this site for descriptions of cultural events happening in Taiwan's capital that month. ✓ **AMERICA ONLINE**→*keyword* worldview→Pacific Rim→Taipei, Taiwan ✓ **INTERNET**→*url* http://nearnet.gnn.com/gnn/bus/wview/cityhigh/ch1tpe.html

---

Hotel Guide Taiwan Not only can you browse this large directory of hotels in Taiwan, but the site will also help you make reservations. Just fill out the Web form. Hotels are marked with symbols denoting whether the hotel is international class, tourist class, or budget class, and listings provide contact information and prices in NTs. Some listings even include photos. Besides hotels, the guide includes listings for restaurants, shopping centers, and transportation services (car rentals and airlines). ✓ **INTERNET**→*url* http://tradepoint.anjes.com.tw/~hotel/index.html

---

SinaNet This site runs a daily news service about events in Taiwan in both Chinese and English along with a monthly calendar of Taiwanese cultural events in both Taiwan and the U.S. ✓ **INTERNET**→*url* http://sinanet.com/bay/index.html

---

soc.culture.taiwan (ng) Should Taiwan be allowed membership to the United Nations? Does Taiwan belong to mainland China? What happened in the Taiwan Straits crisis in 1954? What are the opportunities for teaching English in Taiwan? Soc.culture.taiwan is one of the Asian newsgroup family's most contentious members. TIs (those demanding Taiwanese Independence) square off against WSRs (those Wishing to Stay a Republic), lobbing bazooka blasts across the Net with the regularity of shots fired in a free-fire zone along the Maginot Line during World War II. If you don't care about Taiwanese politics, there's discussion of Little League baseball scores and pop singers, as well as the movies of Ang Lee. The newsgroup's five-part FAQ, on the other hand, is a good resource for the traveler. It offers detailed coverage of Taiwanese culture (holidays, customs, taboos, cuisine) and tourism (where to visit, to find foreign books, to reach representatives for Taiwan in other countries, etc.). The FAQ also features general information about posting to the newsgroup, finding other sites on the Internet related to Taiwan, and making sense of political abbreviations used on the newsgroup. ✓ **USENET**→soc.culture.taiwan *FAQ:* ✓ **INTERNET** ...→*url* http://www.seas.ucla.edu/~tcyang/html/Taiwan_faq.html ... →*url* http://www.cis.ohio-state.edu/hypertext/faq/usenet-faqs/bygroup/soc/culture/taiwan/top.html

---

Taiwan Rock 'n Wall Smog. Yes. Manufacturing. Yes. Chiang Kai-Shek. Yes. But rock climbing? This site serves as a guide to rock climbing in Taiwan. Click the name of a region for descriptions of rock climbing opportunities in that region. ✓ **INTERNET**→*url* http://alpine.csie.nctu.edu.tw/rock/r1

/twnrocks.html

Taiwan Tourist Pages Listings of places to shop, eat, sightsee, and sleep when in Taiwan (or Formosa as your parents may know it). Descriptions of the country's holidays and festivals (Chiang Kai-Shek's Birthday, Sun Yat-Sen's Birthday, the Lantern Day Festival) and basic tourist information are also available. ✓ **INTERNET**→*url* http://www.iipl.com.sg/tai/text/tourist.htm

Teaching English in Taiwan If you want to spend more than a few weeks in Asia, you may have to earn some money while you're there. Teaching English is one option. This Website offers a good overview of teaching English in Taiwan with lists of schools, teaching tips, information on visas and accommodations, and more. ✓ **INTERNET**→*url* http://www.u-net.com/eflweb/taiwan0.htm

The Republic of China This is a Website for the other China. Other than the mainland, that is. It's the little island that Chiang Kai-Shek fled to when Mao came to power in 1949. And it's the little island that's been in a stand-off with its big brother to the west ever since. But back to the Website. The site offers encyclopedic coverage of the country—religions, language, currency, tipping, holidays, climate, history, telephone, and government. The traveler might appreciate the maps, embassy addresses, and the link to a Visitor's Guide to Taiwan. The Visitor's Guide features pictures and descriptions of many of Taiwan's tourist attractions, brief descriptions of Taiwan's regions, mini-guides to activities and events in Taiwan (festivals, mountain climbing, cuisine, etc.), a list of Taiwan tourist offices in Taiwan and the U.S., information about visas, and links to other tourist information about Taiwan on the Net. ✓ **INTERNET**→*url* http://peacock.tnjc.edu.tw/ROC_info.html

Travel in Taiwan This illustrated guide offers descriptions of places and events in Taiwan like Orchid Island, a small island close to the Taiwanese city of Taitung that is home to the indigenous Yamis, or the Dragon Boat Festival, a June festival held along the banks of the Hsintien River near the Chung Cheng Bridge. In addition to covering other sightseeing attractions and activities, the guide offers information on cuisine, hotels, art galleries, embassies, hospitals, banks, and airlines in Taiwan. ✓ **INTERNET**→*url* http://www.sinica.edu.tw/tit/index.html

Tibet

Free Tibet Home Page Most of the resources related to Tibet on the Internet are political, not travel-related, in nature. But despite the political agenda of this Web page, it serves as a good index for those looking to familiarize themselves with events in the isolated Buddhist nation. ✓ **INTERNET**→*url* http://www.manymedia.com/tibet/

Home Page of Tibet Sponsored by the Tibet Study Association, the site will let you take a quick, illustrated tour of Tibet, browse through a collection of pictures of the country, follow news about Tibet, and look back a few years and review the country's history. ✓ **INTERNET**→*url* http://sage.cc.purdue.edu/~wtv/tibet/

Tibetan Studies Following the Chinese occupation of Tibet, Tibetans are now a minority in their own country. But on the Web, Tibetans more than rival their Chinese neighbors for resources. This index of sites links to maps and tours of Tibet, pages dedicated to the Dalai Lama's speeches, news bulletins about Tibet affairs, information about meditation centers, reading lists, reports on Tibetan women, and much more. ✓ **INTERNET**→*url* http://coombs.anu.edu.au/WWWVL-TibetanStudies.html

Young Buddhists in Laos—http://sgwww.epfl.ch/BERGER/First/LAOS_english.html

Part 4

Australia & Oceania

Australia

While tourists are attracted by Australia's wild, wooly West, the truth about the island continent is somewhat more pedestrian. In fact, more than three-quarters of Australians live in the southeastern quadrant of the country, in the dense "Boomerang Coast" that connects Adelaide, Melbourne, Canberra, Sydney, and Brisbane. Investigate Australia's cities with **Bouldering Sites Around Sydney**, the **Melbourne Internet Restaurant Guide**, and **Brisbane—Wall to Wall Sunshine**. Learn about Aboriginal customs with **The Australian Indigenous Population**. Begin to explore the Outback with **Lonely Planet Guide to Australia** and **Wombat on the Web**. And then throw another locomotive on the barbie with **Australian Railways**.

Quintessentially Australian—http://www.wombat.com.au/wombat/

On the Net

Across the board

Australia A grab bag of information about Australia for tourists, including miscellaneous restaurant recommendations, trip reports from Internet-savvy travelers, FAQs from soc.culture.australian, and more. ✓**INTERNET**→*url* http://www.solutions.mb.ca/rec-travel/pacific/australia/

Australia and New Zealand Travel Board Lucy is going to Australia and wants to know which appliances will work in the Antipodes. Donald has an answer, and a detailed one at that: "Australian electrical supply is 220/240 V at 50 Hz. U.S. is 120 V at 60 Hz. With a step-down transformer ($50 – $150, depending on the wattage of the devices you're using), you can take most items with you. Most computer power supplies have built-in switches to adjust for voltage. Two or three dollars will buy a new power cord to match Australian outlets. The devices that won't be worth taking: televisions and VCRs—Australia uses a completely different video standard, and the frequency difference will mess with playback. Possibly CD players and tape players may work—there will probably be some sound distortion because of the frequency difference. Equipment that is normally battery-powered and used with an Australian-made A.C. adapter will work fine." (That should answer your question, Lucy.) Discuss budget airfares, popular attractions, and the finer points of travel to Australia and New Zealand on this message board. ✓**AMERICA ONLINE** →*keyword* travel forum→Travel Boards→The World Traveler→Australia & New Zealand

Australia Travel Directory Weather, visa information, and links to most of the major Australian tourist sites online, from G'Day Mate to the Lonely Planet Guide. ✓**INTERNET**→*url* http://www.anzac.com/aust/aust.htm

Australian Department of Tourism Ground zero for Australian tourism, the home page of the Commonwealth Department of Tourism includes statistics on the $11.2 billion industry, an online bookstore with downloadable pamphlets on topics ranging from ecotourism to rural tourism, and a wealth of basic information for travelers bound Down Under. ✓**INTERNET**→*url* http://tourism.gov.au/

Australian Railways Rail down under, as on any other continent, requires navigating a maze of federal, state, or local rail companies to reach your destination. The information here will help distinguish between the several public and privatized companies—when you board the tram on Collins Street in Melbourne, you won't inadvertently end up in Alice Springs. ✓**INTERNET**→*url* http://www.cs.su.oz.au/~matthew/railway/

Australian Travel and Tourism Service If you take the Indian Pacific train from Sydney at 2:20 p.m. on Monday, you can be in Perth by 7:00 a.m. on Thursday. For more information on rail travel in Aussie land and other detailed travel info, turn to this Website, where a collection of links takes you to the New Zealand home page, the Tasmanian Wildlife Service, and to virtual tours of the pubs of Melbourne and the Sydney Opera. A comprehensive source for things Down Under. ✓**INTERNET**→*url* http://www.wps.com.au/travel/travhome.htm

Australian Travel Report Plenty of Australians are touring Germany, and plenty of Germans want to go tour Australia. So in the name of international brotherhood, a student in the physics department at the University of Hamburg has created this site, which furnishes brief city guides, images, and links to Australian sites online. Before you go to Ayers Rock or Alice Springs, go to this Website, and see how one tourist fared on the great bat-shaped continent. ✓**INTERNET**→*url* burg.de/provos/australia/australia.html

Brochure Flow Home Page Greeting visitors with an authentic, hearty "G'Day," Brochure Flow bills itself as "a true Australian travel site." While it's difficult to ascertain exactly what that might mean, travelers visiting Brochure Flow will find a growing number of industry sites, including tourist agencies, resorts, airlines, cruise lines, and travel agents. Brochure Flow also includes links to other Australian travel sites on the Internet. ✓**INTERNET**→*url* http://www.broflo.com.au/

Guide to Australia Grease up those Olivia Newton-John records, pack up a bag of koala jerky, and head to the Guide to Australia, an online guidebook that dreams of being an online encyclopedia about all things Australian. With large sections on geography, politics, environment, communication, culture, and history, this is a lavish site that will keep any traveler—newcomer or veteran, casual or compulsive—up to his or her ears in things Australian. And if you want to make the acquaintance of some friendly Aussies, take a look at the Telstra White Pages, which collect residential and business listings for the entire nation. (Sadly, a residential search for "Dundee" in Queensland comes up empty—where's old Crocodile when you need him?) ✓**INTERNET**→*url* http://www.csu.edu.au/education/australia.html

Internet Directory Australia Both a business and cultural directory, Internet Directory Australia collects Websites in the land of Oz and features a special section on sports (just click on the polo ball for more information). Tourist resources include links to tour operators, transportation companies, and attractions (from the Royal Melbourne Zoological Gardens to the ironically named Sovereign Hill Gold Mining Tourist Park). ✓**INTERNET**→*url* http://www.ida.com.au/

misc.transport.rail.australia-nz (ng) Not really devoted to schedules, this newsgroup is more concerned with the culture—past, present, and future—of rail transportation in the region. But if you have a question about a late train to Canberra, ask away.

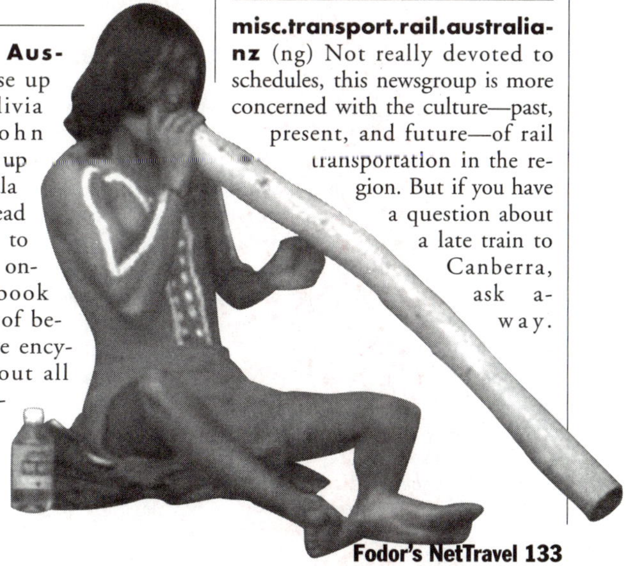

✓USENET→misc.transport.rail.australia-nz

Pacific Forum The Pacific Forum on CompuServe covers a wide variety of topics, including sports, weather, and even the Internet Down Under (which one waggish Aussie has dubbed the "Undernet"). But tourists will be most interested in the Travel Australia and Travel NZ folders, which collect budget travel tips, recommendations, and warnings from practiced Southern Hemisphere journeyers. Much of the chat is rather mundane, but every once in a while discussion erupts into something riotously aesthetic: one extended debate was over the hue of blue that fills up the New Zealand sky—is it real, or the legacy of ambitious travel photographers with polarizing filters? The libraries include a wealth of maps, images, and brief essays meant to entice you into boarding that plane bound for a Downward trip. ✓**COMPUSERVE**→*go* pacforum→Messages *and* Libraries→Travel Australia or Travel NZ

The Aussie Index What's the Aussie Index? Well, it's an index of Australian sites online. Maybe that's obvious. More specifically, the Aussie Index is a massive collection of Web pages Down Under, with sections for both commercial and non-commercial sites. The Index can be both browsed and searched; a search on "tourism" generated roughly a dozen links, including State Tourism Commissions and the National Travel Industry Awards. ✓**INTERNET**→*url* http://www.aussie.com.au/

This is Australia Sponsored by a gigantic Australian telecommunications utility, this site includes links to a variety of sites dealing with Aussie government, history, sports, education, employment, the Internet in vegemite land, and more. Travelers from abroad will be especially interested in the Tourism and Travel section, with its links to sites such as the Lonely Planet Guide, railway timetables, Qantas Airways, and virtually every large Website devoted to Australian tourism. ✓**INTERNET**→*url* http://www.telstra.com.au/meta/australia.html

Travel Downunder A general site devoted to Australian travel and tourism, with a growing list of links to other Australian travel sites, accommodations companies, weather bureaus, and tourism agencies. ✓**INTERNET**→*url* http://peg.apc.org/~gregluck/tourism/

TravelAsia Australia The two links here are both to other sites—Charles Stuart University's large Guide to Australia and the Global Network Navigator's Koblas currency converter. ✓**INTERNET**→*url* http://silkroute.com/silkroute/travel/rsrc/au.html

Womadelaide Womadelaide, the Australian alternative rock music festival, sponsors this page, which provides festival details and specifics along with basic tourist information for visitors to South Australia. ✓**INTERNET**→*url* http://www.va.com.au/womadelaide/travel_accom.html

Attractions

Australian National Botanic Gardens, Canberra The people at the Australian National Botanic Gardens want you to understand why biodiversity and conservation are essential to the survival of Australia's ecosystem, and they want you to understand with the help of the World Wide Web. Link to a description of the ANBG, explore

DETOURS

"The Aboriginal Land Rights (Northern Territory) Act was passed in 1976 by the Fraser Liberal-National Party Government. This Act resulted from the report of the Aboriginal Land Rights Commission headed by Mr. Justice Woodward, in 1974-74, and from the previous Labour Government's Aboriginal Land (Northern Territory) Bill which only failed to become law because of the double dissolution of Parliament in 1975.

"The aims of the Commission's report included:

"1. Simple justice for all people deprived of their land.

"2. The provision of a land base for an impoverished people who had no real opportunity to achieve economic equality with other Australians.

"3. The maintenance and enhancement of Aboriginal people's spiritual and cultural identity."

—from **The Australian Indigenous Population**

its governmental funding, and then link to other sites about the botanical biodiversity of Australia. And don't forget—while you're there, you can try out your new Crocodile Dundee joke, "That's not a Website—*this* is a Website." ✓**INTERNET**→*url* http://155.187.10.12/anbg.html

Australian National Parks Breathtaking photographs and friendly essays on Australia's national parks. Check out the vistas at Elebana Falls, Fraser Island National Park, and Lamington National Park. ✓**INTERNET**→*url* http://papillon.sd.monash.edu.au/~keith/national_parks/

Western Australia Maritime Museum Located in Fremantle, the Western Australia Maritime Museum comprises a number of smaller museums and institutions, including the Historic Boats Museum, the Maritime Museum, and the Departments of Maritime Archaeology, Maritime History, and Maritime Education. View a floor plan of the museum, see the current exhibit, and explore the wreck sites scattered off the coast of Perth. ✓**INTERNET**→*url* http://mm.wa.gov.au/Museum.html

Zoo Education With general information on Australian zoos and links to the major zoos of Victoria, this site allows fans of Australian wildlife to learn what national zoological gardens and sanctuaries are doing to contribute to the health and safety of the country's animals. And travelers who just want to see the animals can get addresses and phone numbers. ✓**INTERNET**→*url* http://www.vicnet.net.au/vicnet/zoo/hp1.html

Culture

Australian Television Guide If you're looking forward to an exciting trip Down Under but can't stand the thought of missing your favorite TV show, don't worry—they might be showing it in Australia, too. Check out this site, which lists the current week's programs in the country, permits both browsing and searching, and even divides shows by state. Don't expect a tremendous amount of local color, though (Kangaroo Court TV?)—much of the programming is standard American fare, with the occasional British series. And if you begin to despair for pure entertainment, just make sure you're in Queensland on Sunday at 6:30 p.m., tuning your rabbit ears to Channel 10. Because Channel 10 at 6:30 p.m. Sunday in Queensland can mean only one thing: *Baywatch*. Will Mitch and Stephanie rediscover their feelings for one another during a 24-hour Call Car shift? Be the first one in Australia to know. ✓**INTERNET**→*url* http://www.sofcom.com.au/TV/

Beat Magazine Australian rock and roll, mostly urban (Sydney and Melbourne are the two locales that merit the most coverage). Get the latest on hard rock, dance, clubs, and more. ✓**INTERNET**→*url* http://www.ozonline.com.au/beat/

DJ Neil Hume A site devoted to an Australian DJ (that's Mr. Hume) that contains some general information about Aussie nightlife. ✓**INTERNET**→*url* http://www.magna.com.au/~neilham/

Hogs Head The leading online magazine of Australian food and wine, Hogs Head includes articles on topics such as bushfoods, winemaker Marcel Guigal, and wines made from shiraz (the Australian "workhorse" vine responsible for most generic reds) and grenache (the fruity, peppery grape grown in the MacLaren Vale and the Barossa Valley). Be sure to set your Web browser window to the width of the asparagus tip, or you may miss some of the wonderful graphics at Hogs Head. ✓**INTERNET**→*url* http://www.grapevine.com.au/

Interactive Gig Listing (Australia) Where do Australian bands plug in their guitars and premiere their latest songs? At places like the Centennial Hotel in Kensington or the Guild Theatre in Melbourne. Bands post gigs

Fodor's Choice...

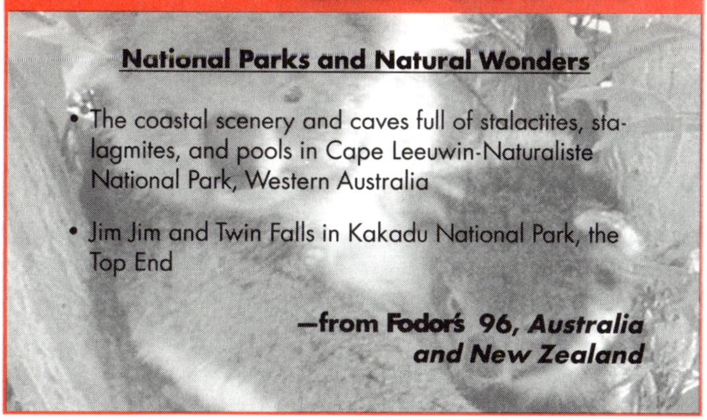

National Parks and Natural Wonders

- The coastal scenery and caves full of stalactites, stalagmites, and pools in Cape Leeuwin-Naturaliste National Park, Western Australia
- Jim Jim and Twin Falls in Kakadu National Park, the Top End

—from Fodor's 96, *Australia and New Zealand*

The picturesque city of Sydney—http://www.usyd.edu.au/su/emu/OZ/

here, so any tourists looking to be happily ensnared by Oz rock tentacles should visit this page. ✓**INTERNET**→*url* http://www.maths.monash.edu.au/~ernie/giglist/

soc.culture.australian (ng) Imagine that you've captured an Australian and you can ask him anything under the sun. "As a black American, how would I be treated in Australia as opposed to a white American?" "How do Ozzies feel about the queen?" You're probably thinking of visiting Australia, aren't you? So grill him: "Where do I stay?" "What do I see?" And, of course, "What about Oz beer?" Discussion sometimes becomes very serious—"I have another question before I actually move in late October: Is the *Star Trek* series readily available in Australia, and if so, what season are they on?" The six-part FAQ is one of the best in the Usenet world, with a full complement of essays on everything from Australian universities to native languages to quarantine policies. ✓**USENET**→soc.culture.australian *FAQ:* ✓**INTERNET**→*url* http://www.cis.ohio-state.edu/text/faq/usenet/australian-faq/top.html

Sydney Morning Herald Metro What's Metro? It's the entertainment supplement to *The Sydney Morning Herald*, with listings for music, art, movies, theater, and more, along with short features by cutting-edge Australian cultural critics. Want to explore budget restaurants in Sydney? Curious how things are going on the Sydney indie scene? Maybe you even want to learn about the ins and outs of Aussie femininity with Emma Tom's "Babewatch" column ("Exes are also dangerous. They know things about you that normal people don't. They're aware that you have pet names for your nipples.") Ah, it's nice to know that people are the same the world over. ✓**INTERNET**→*url* http://www.smh.com.au/metro

The Age *The Age* newspaper in Melbourne sponsors this site, which provides general Australian news, features, classifieds, and a special section on information technology. How will this help you if you're traveling to Australia? Not a tremendous amount, although it may be interesting to brush up on the latest developments in the ambulance union labor dispute or read a death notice of Ivan Hutchinson, Melbourne's Mr. Movies, before you board that Qantas jet. ✓**INTERNET**→*url* http://www.theage.com.au/

The Australian Indigenous Population America has Native Americans, people who existed on the land long before those of European descent arrived here, and coincidentally, the people who furnished the names for both teams in the 1995 World Series. Australia's Indians—a set of tribal groups, mostly in the northern part of the country, known as Aborigines—have an equally complex and fascinating history, and this site includes information on Aboriginal customs, history, and populations. Go on Cyberwalkabout to find out more about land rights, self-determination in Australian government, and something with the vaguely foreboding name of "cultural resilience." But be warned—knowledge is addictive, and once you start researching the Iwaidja, Waribiri, Pitjanjatara, and Wankanguru, you may never stop. ✓**INTERNET**→*url* http://www.webnet.com.au/koori/homekori.html

Guides

G'Day Mate If you're planning a trip to Australia, don't get on the plane without first visiting this site. Why? First of all, it's called G'Day Mate, and the sheer giddy joy of visiting a site with a name as silly as this one should keep you on cloud nine for the entire flight. It's better than Dramamine. But G'Day Mate is also a valuable resource for Australian travelers, with its list of festivals and events, general travel tips, and specific tourist information for each Australian state. ✓**INTERNET**→*url* http://www.ozemail.aust.com:80/~gdaymate/

Lonely Planet Guide to Australia The introduction to the Lonely Planet Guide points out that though Australia is typecast by a few icons—Ayers Rock, the Sydney Opera House—the country's richness and diversity defies easy categorization. Intended to help novices learn more about Australia, the guide includes a map of the country, basic information on history, economy, culture, holidays, and even online tips submitted by other travelers (there's free fruit and vegetables to be had for those entering the Northern Territory from Western Australia—just ask the border guards if you can have food seized for quarantine from travelers passing the other way). ✓INTERNET→*url* http://www.lonelyplanet.com/dest/aust/aus.htm

Travelling Australia Subtitled "a guide to Australian travel, holidays, tourism, and tourist operators," this site pretty much lives up to its billing, with a clickable map of the country that links to regional tourism information, and more general resources like the Guide to Australian Festivals, the Australian Shopping Directory, and even a guide to gaming and gambling in Oz (this is especially useful if you're itching to watch thousands of dollars slide through your fingertips at the Casino Canberra). ✓INTERNET→*url* http://skynet.cos.com.au:80/travel/

Wombat on the Web Travel information for Australia, particularly South Australia. Tourism resources are sparse at the moment, but they will eventually include a photo tour of the region, along with local guides for Adelaide, the Barossa Valley, Flinders Ranges, the Murraylands, and Yorke Peninsula, among other locations. ✓INTERNET→*url* http://www.wombat.com.au/wombat/

Tour operators

Australia/New Zealand Down Under Travel If you're looking for a travel agency that can help you book expeditions, walking tours, air cruises, and nature hikes, look no further. If you're looking for something slightly different, look further—this Down Under Travel is pretty much an advertisement and doesn't include any links to related travel sites online. ✓INTERNET→*url* http://Market.NET/travel/anz/

Freewheelin' Cycle Tours An advertorial site that describes three-week cycle tours all over Australia. ✓INTERNET→*url* http://www.ozemail.com.au/~traveloz/fw/fw.html

TraveLearn Australia An advertisement for TraveLearn, an educational tour company that plans trips to famous national sites such as Daintree, Ayers Rock, Hervey Bay, Cape York, and the Great Barrier Reef. ✓INTERNET→*url* http://www.ceu.uq.oz.au/travelearn/travelearn.html

Brisbane

A Day in Brisbane A diary entry from a Canadian national spending the day in Brisbane. It includes a detailed taxonomy of accents: "Every accent seems to contain its giveaway. A New Yorker says 'Caawwfee' when ordering java. The quintessential Canadian ends statements with 'eh?' The dead giveaway of an Australian is 'naaeww.' Of course, when you point this out to a local they'll deny it and in so doing prove the point: 'naaeeww I don...hmm, guess I duuheww.'" Read more of the author's observations about the city here. ✓INTERNET→*url* http://www.whistler.net/worldtour/homepage/ejournal/brisbane.htm

Brisbane City Life Consult this complete guide to Brisbane for essays on its history and climate, a listing of restaurants, and a theater, movie, concert, conference, exhibition, and festival guide. If you're looking for info on hotels and other accommodations in Brisbane, try looking under the Home Comforts section. There's even a news page to keep you abreast of the latest Brisbanian developments. ✓INTERNET→*url* http://peg.pegasus.oz.au/~maxlink/bcl/welcome.htm

Brisbane—Wall to Wall Sunshine What's the capital of the Sunshine State? No, it's not Tallahassee, not when you're talking about Queensland, Australia's Sunshine State. The magic of the Web allows you to visit Brisbane via this site, which offers essays on attractions, weather, and transportation both to Brisbane and within the city. Climb Mount Coot-tha. View the golden skyline. Marvel at the broad verandas and iron roofs of the Queenslander homes. And then think about traveling to Brisbane for real. ✓INTERNET→*url* http://www.dstc.edu.au/events/icodp95/brisbane.html

Melbourne

A Byte to Eat A Melbourne restaurant guide that lets you search by location and cuisine—more than 100 categories are identified, from Chinese-Take Out to Eclectic to Portuguese. If there's a problem with this restaurant guide, it lies in the entries themselves, which are relatively perfunctory, containing only the most basic contact data and information on liquor licensing. ✓**INTERNET**→*url* http://www.webspot.com.au/rest/

Cybernet Cafe Visit this home page for Melbourne's first cybercafé and find a brief essay on the history of the phenomenon, a collection of articles about caffeine, and a collection of links about Australia. If you're in Melbourne, drop by the Cybernet Café and check out some of the other sites listed in *NetTravel*—if it doesn't improve your Australian trip immensely, we'll buy you a baby kangaroo (yah, right, mate!). ✓**INTERNET**→*url* http://www.ozonline.com.au/netcafe/

La Trobe University Art Museum, Melbourne Online versions of the museum's current exhibitions, which showcase contemporary Australian painters and sculptors. ✓**INTERNET**→*url* http://www.latrobe.edu.au/Glenn/Museum/ArtMuseumHome.html

Melbourne Internet Restaurant Guide With more than 700 restaurants in its database, the Melbourne Internet Restaurant Guide will shock and amaze travelers who didn't even know that there were 700 restaurants in Melbourne. But if you want to find Afghani food in Fitzroy or kosher cuisine in Caulfield, just fill out the easy-to-use online form (with categories for suburb, type of cuisine, and service features), submit it, and your restaurant choices will be returned to you immediately. Descriptions include addresses, phone numbers, information on meal service, and methods of payment accepted, as well as reviews submitted by Australian diners. ✓**INTERNET**→*url* http://www.rucc.net.au/cgi-bin/melrest.cgi

Melbourne Taxi Cab Companies A list of the major Melbourne taxi companies with phone numbers. ✓**INTERNET**→*url* http://netcore.com.au/taxi.html

White Hat Tours At 1600 Pennsylvania Avenue in Washington, D.C., stands a magnificent white building, four columns out in front, a broad pediment, a fountain encircled by brilliant red flowers...oh, that's White House Tours? Hold on one moment. Okay. The person responsible for that digression has been fired. White Hat Tours is a Melbourne-based company that targets tourists, with basic information about Melbourne, walking tours of the city, and even an annotated list of 100 great things to do in Melbourne for under $10 (no, one of them is not "swallow a five-dollar bill in the middle of Fitzroy Gardens"). Want to know about restaurants, museums, festivals, historic homes, and hotels? Put on your white hat now. ✓**INTERNET**→*url* http://www.acslink.net.au/~blackbox/WhiteHat.html

Worldview—Melbourne A complete guide to Melbourne, compiled and updated by Fodor's, which has been guiding smart travelers for 60 years. Fodor's has rated hotels and restaurants, and listed tourist attractions and accommodations in dozens of other categories, including Shopping, Travel with Children, Festivals, Museums, Theater, and Dance. ✓**AMERICA ONLINE**→*keyword* world view→Pacific Rim→Melbourne, Australia

Sydney

Bouldering Sites Around Sydney Want to go rock climbing at Lindfield Rocks, Ball's Head Reserve, or Sissy Crag? Maybe you do, and maybe you don't. But you might as well be as informed as possible, and this Website, which gives directions to and descriptions of the sites, will help. ✓**INTERNET**→*url* http://www.dap.csiro.au/~cameron/climbing/syd-bouldering.html

Discover Sydney An advertorial site for a small Sydney tourism company. Visit here for descriptions and booking information for city tours, articles on cultural tourism in Australia, a list of bed-and-breakfast inns in the Sydney area, and links to other Websites. ✓**INTERNET**→*url* http://www.meetoz.com.au/g_day/

Fantasmagoric Museum An Australian cousin of Venice, California's Museum of

Jurassic Technology, the Fantasmagoric Museum collects the oddest odds and ends of art and science—alien prayer apparatuses, failed patents, and machines to help psychics straddle the line between the natural and the supernatural. Located in Sydney, the museum also has a Website, where it displays part of its collection and offers links to its parent institution, the College of Fine Arts at the University of New South Wales. ✓**INTERNET**→*url* http://hepworth.cfa.unsw.edu.au/FM/home.html

---

Living in Sydney Not really geared toward tourists—if you're living in Sydney, you wouldn't exactly be considered a tourist, would you?—this site, sponsored by Sydney University, still contains some valuable information, including a large collection of links to information about Australia. ✓**INTERNET**→*url* http://www.me.su.oz.au/sydney.html

---

Sydney Sponsored by the Faculty of Science at the University of Technology, Sydney, this page features pictures and information on the Sydney Opera House, Sydney Harbour, and other attractions in Australia's most imposing metropolis. One of the links gives Netsurfers an overview of Sydney's weather—and don't be confused by the temperatures, which are given in Celsius. ✓**INTERNET**→*url* http://www.bio.uts.edu.au/sydney/sydney.html

---

Sydney Indoor Clymbing Gym If you're in Sydney with the family and your noisy kids are driving you up the wall, relax by going up the wall again—at the Sydney Indoor Climbing Gym, which boasts more than 500 square meters of textured walls. ✓**INTERNET**→*url* http://www.dap.csiro.au/~cameron/climbing/gyms/SICG/

Sydney Party, Rave, and Club Info Find a club, take a drug, start to dance, seek a trance. It's a different kind of Down Under, and this Website will be your online guide to the rave and club scene in Australia's biggest city. Find out where the party's happening, when things are getting underway, and what you should wear (blue spiky hair is currently in mode). ✓**INTERNET**→*url* http://ion.apana.org.au/~mdagn/sydney.html

---

Sydney Weather Forecast A satellite forecast—complete with images—from the Australian Bureau of Meteorology. ✓**INTERNET**→*url* http://www.st.nepean.uws.edu.au/stuff/weather/

Worldview—Sydney This Fodor's guide is a great way to begin your exploration of Sydney. Need lists of restaurants? Want to see some theater? How about spectator sports, shopping, dance, hotels, museums, and sites geared toward children? It's all here, for browsing or for searching. ✓**AMERICA ONLINE**→*keyword* worldview→Pacific Rim→Sydney, Australia

Tasmania

Tasmania No, there's no Tasmanian devil here. But just about everything else about Tasmania is at this page, from an overview of Australia's southernmost state (and only official archipelago) to images and specific essays on Hobart, Launceton, and the Furneaux Group. There's even a .GIF of the new logo of the state (again, no devil, just a picture of the mysterious Tasmanian tiger, or thylacine, emerging from the underbrush). ✓**INTERNET**→*url* http://www.broflo.com.au/

DETOURS

"Australian Aboriginal society has the longest continuous cultural history in the world, with origins dating back to the last Ice Age. Although mystery shrouds many aspects of Australian prehistory, it seems almost certain that the first humans came here across the sea from South-East Asia. Europeans began to encroach on Australia in the 16th century: Portuguese navigators were followed by Dutch explorers and the enterprising English pirate William Dampier. Captain James Cook sailed the entire length of the eastern coast in 1770, stopping at Botany Bay on the way. After rounding Cape York, he claimed the continent for the British and named it New South Wales. In 1779, Joseph Banks (a naturalist on Cook's voyage) suggested that Britain could solve overcrowding problems in its prisons by transporting convicts to New South Wales. In 1787, the First Fleet set sail for Botany Bay."

—from **Lonely Planet Guide to Australia**

New Zealand

It's true that there are more sheep than men in New Zealand, but doesn't that make it an even more desirable vacation destination? Witness the manifold charms of this nation, favorably located in the South Pacific, at the **Gateway to New Zealand** or **Aidan's New Zealand Page**. Once you're in ol' NZ, there are many ways to explore the mountain pastures, deep lakes, and fjords—try **Mountain Biking in New Zealand**, or **New Zealand by Rail**, or take the rough road with **The Hitchhikers Guide to New Zealand**. Before you leave, don't forget to sample **New Zealand Wines Online** and get tips on sheep—er, cheap—hotels from **soc.culture.new-zealand**.

One of the North Island's many beaches— from http://www.cntraveler.com/

On the Net

Across the board

Aidan's New Zealand Page Aidan is a New Zealander, and he's started this page "so he could have somewhere to put all the shit he has collected about New Zealand, and also as a repository for any links he may come across with an N.Z. bent." At the moment, this means sites on rugby, music, cricket, and movies, all of which are enthusiasms of Aidan and many of his fellow New Zealanders. ✓**INTERNET**→*url* http://rschp2.anu.edu.au:8080/aidan/nz/nz.html

An Illustrated Tour of New Zealand/Aotearoa The virtual tour of the Land of the Long White Cloud offers literate essays and lovely visuals of Christchurch, Wellington, Auckland, and the sheep-filled countryside. ✓**INTERNET**→*url* http://www.akiko.lm.com/tour/

Gateway to New Zealand A massive site that collects information and links about New Zealand in ten categories—commerce, education, science, recreation, tourism, entertainment, news, immigration, statistics, and weather. The tourism section is especially impressive, with links to more than 20 general travel sites and a wealth of online travel agencies, publications, and hotels that specialize in travel throughout New Zealand. If you're embarking on Kiwi's Big Adventure, don't even think about missing this site. ✓**INTERNET**→*url* http://www.icair.iac.org.nz/nz/

New Zealand on the Web With a URL that gets to the point in record time (nz.com—now that's economy!), this page allows Netsurfers to take a virtual tour of New Zealand, browse the New Zealand guidebook, learn about trade and commerce, and get information on Kiwis in New Zealand and abroad. ✓**INTERNET**→*url* http://nz.com/

Culture

New Zealand—United States Dictionary New Zealanders speak English, but not exactly the same English as Americans. And some New Lelanders (that's what New Zealanders have been known to call Stanford University types, on account of the fact that the school was named for Leland Stanford) have compiled a glossary of some of the most obvious differences between English in the U.S. and N.Z. It's fairly standard British stuff—"flat" for apartment, "petrol" for gas, "bonnet" for car hood. But did you know that Kiwis have lots of other funny phrases like "ice blocks" (popsicles), "panel beaters" (auto body shops) and "Cheerios" (not the cereal, but cocktail wieners)? ✓**INTERNET**→*url* http://www-leland.stanford.edu/~jmgeorge/nzus translation.html

New Zealand Wines Online When you think of New Zealand, you probably think of sheep, or religion, or rock climbing. But not wine. Too bad, because there's a Wine Institute of New Zealand, and now the Institute has a home page with a series of informative essays on New Zealand's wines and wineries. There's even a list of United States distributors and retailers, so your knowledge won't have to be simply theoretical. Read this page, and the next time you visit New Zealand and find yourself in the midst of a romantic dinner with an attractive Kiwi, order a nice Hawkes Bay Merlot from the Heretaunga Plain. "French wines are fine," you can say, "if you like that kind of thing, but I prefer wine made in a country where the women and men have managed to strike a perfect balance between brilliance and beauty." Your date will be putty in your hands. ✓**INTERNET**→*url* http://haven.uniserve.com/~mrobins/nzwine.html

soc.culture.new-zealand (ng) Warning: Americans traveling to New Zealand should read this newsgroup to find out what they're saying about American English over there. (It's not very flattering.) Come to this newsgroup to learn which hot topics are being discussed Down Under. ✓**USENET**→soc.culture.new-zealand

Guides

Bungy Jumping in New Zealand The fact that they bungy-jump in New Zealand is heartening, because it means that the near-moronic abdication of self-preservation isn't only an American problem. This page lists destinations for bungy-jumping in New Zealand, and attempts—like every other bungy-jumping site on or off the Net—to sell the dangerous and foolhardy sport as a way of liberating the self from the strictures of an overprotective society. Life is short. Play hard. Just don't hit hard. ✓**INTERNET**→*url* http://www.clearfield.co.nz/hotpac/bungy.htm

Cybergyde to New Zealand Is New Zealand really "the way the world would have been if the human race hadn't lost the plot," as site-author David Morris suggests, or is it, rather, an oddly provincial nation of religious fanatics, as some travelers have insisted? Decide for yourself at this Cybergyde, which incorporates everything from regional essays to a gig guide for shows and concerts to special sections on skiing, diving, fishing, golf, hunting, and sailing. ✓**INTERNET**→*url* http://ihug.co.nz/kiwimall/travel/cybrgyde.html

Discover New Zealand Magazine A complete guide to New Zealand travel that moves from visa requirements through local culture to a list of activities and attractions—skiing, geyser sightings, concerts, and more. Material is updated frequently, and you can even email the editors of the Auckland-based magazine with questions. ✓**INTERNET**→*url* http://discovernz.co.nz/

Mountain Biking in New Zealand Whom can you call for advice on where to ride when you're in Wellington or Auckland? Check out the list of New Zealand Mountain Bike Association members and telephone numbers at this site. Guidebook-like descriptions of riding in Dome Valley, Rotura, and Riverhead and Whitford Forest's are also available. There's also a link to the full text of the book *Classic New Zealand Mountain Bike Rides*, which contains information on over 300 rides in New Zealand. ✓**INTERNET**→*url* http://hmu1.hmu.auckland.ac.nz:80/F212FA0D/Cmtbnz

New Zealand By Rail Timetables for trains in New Zealand, organized clearly and updated frequently. If you use this service, you'll never again feel compelled to drop to your knees in the middle of the Wellington train station and scream, "Dear God, how could I have been so stupid as to miss the Overlander again?" ✓**INTERNET**→*url* http://www.waikato.ac.nz/nz/rail/timetable.html

The Hitchhikers Guide to New Zealand An informative and irreverent guide to New Zealand written by American college students in a tone like that of some globe-trotting smarter cousins of Beavis & Butt-head. Consider this retelling of New Zealand's myth of National Origin: "Many years ago a bloke called Maui went fishing with his brothers, using his grandmother's jawbone as a fish hook (apparently his grandmother's jaw fell off through overuse, an object lesson in verbosity). He caught a big fish and hauled it to the surface. It was a big fish (man). Like, really, really big. About as big as the North Island. In fact, if the truth be told, it *was* the North Island. But that's okay, because Maui's canoe was pretty large as well, as big as The

South Island (get the picture?). Maui's brothers, seeing the size of the fish, became jealous and laid into it with their meres and axes and shit, thus conveniently teraforming it into a fairly rugged bit of heavily forested fish (or land, as geologists prefer to call it)." Filled with history, geography, and secret tips, the Hitchhikers Guide includes only one passionate exhortation—stay away from Bulls, a tiny village with a big, bad reputation. ✓**INTERNET**→*url* http://www.cs.cmu.edu:80/afs/cs.cmu.edu/Web/People/mjw/NZ/TourTravel/HitchHikersGuide.html

Travelogues

New Zealand Trip Report An extensive trip log, as well as more general observations, from an Illinoisan and world traveler who spent almost a month in New Zealand, kayaking in Milford, drinking in Westport, hearing Kiri Te Kanawa sing in Auckland, and spending Christmas in Christchurch in shorts (seasons are all topsy-turvy, remember, on account of the fact that New Zealand is all the way down there in the Southern Hemisphere). ✓**INTERNET**→*url* http://www.webfoot.com/travel/trip/trip.nz.html?Yahoo

Philip Greenspun's New Zealand Story Along with a capsule history of New Zealand, an essay on mountain biking, and images of the nation, this lengthy (and intermittently interesting) first-person travelogue frames a number of issues crucial for the New Zealand tourist, including the environment, the Internet, and racial politics. Along the way, it pauses to tackle the eternal question, "Can a German girl and a Jewish boy find happiness on the North Island?" See for yourself. ✓**INTERNET**→*url* http://webtravel.org/nz/

Bay of Plenty

Bay of Plenty A tourist site for the Bay of Plenty and Whakatane, the "sunshine capital of New Zealand." Located in the state's North Island, the region has a number of impressive attractions, including Tauranga and Mount Maunganui, Rotorua, and Opotiki. With pictures of a variety of activities—jet skiing, deep-sea fishing, and helicopter tours—this site is almost like being in the Bay. ✓**INTERNET**→*url* http://www.boprc.govt.nz/www/tourist.html

Wellington

Carter Observatory A Website dedicated to the national observatory of New Zealand, which is located in the heart of Wellington's Botanic Garden. ✓**INTERNET**→ *url* http://www.vuw.ac.nz/~bankst/carter.html

Te Papa Tongarewa Museum of New Zealand Located on Wellington's famous Buckle Street, the Museum of New Zealand houses the national painting and sculpture collection, a number of important historical artifacts—and a new museum building on the Wellington waterfront is scheduled to open to the Kiwi public in February of 1998. This Te Papa Tongarewa Website, by reproducing floor plans and excerpting from the catalogs of current exhibitions, allows prospective travelers to take a cybertour of the museum and, via links, visit other museums in New Zealand. ✓**INTERNET** →*url* http://monz.cs.auckland.ac .nz/Cmonz

Wellington City Council With a logo that looks eerily like the Parental Advisory sticker slapped on rap albums and a slogan that sounds like a beer commercial ("Absolutely Positively Wellington"), this page goes a long way toward explaining New Zealand's unself-conscious charm. Learn all about the capital of the South Pacific nation, Wellington, its government and attractions—and, if you're in the mood for an especially explosive vacation, link to the Mt. Ruapehu Eruption Pages, which come equipped with a real-time Volcano-Cam. ✓**INTERNET**→ *url* http://www.govt.nz

Fodor's Choice...

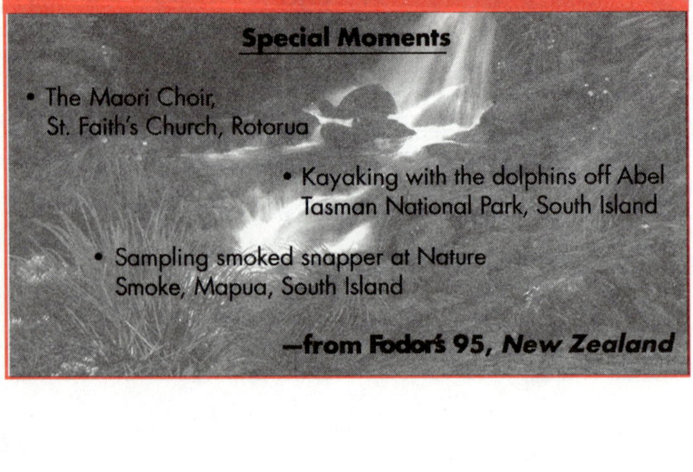

South Pacific islands

Picture yourself inside the lush, vibrant colors of a Gauguin painting...These days, you can actually get to the South Pacific—the exotic island paradises of our collective imagination—and with nary a shipwreck or mutiny. Get practical paradise planning help on CompuServe's **Pacific Chat** board or AOL's **South Pacific Board**. Don't leave without getting beneath the Disney-like stereotypes of perpetually carefree, scantily-clad natives. Search for your own Bali Hai at the **Fiji Discovey Page**, in **The Polynesian Triangle**, or on the **Tonga Page**. A virtual visit to the **Pitcairn Island Home Page** offers a history lesson on the mutiny on the *Bounty*—maybe you'll even feel a longing to overthrow the boss and hit the high seas yourself.

Neo-colonialism, holding its head high—from http://ns.gov.gu/

On the Net

Across the board

Pacific Chat When are shops open in Sydney? What are the cheapest places to visit in the South Pacific? What are the voltage differences between the United States and New Zealand? Is Bora Bora better for tourists to visit than Huahine? Get the answers to these and other questions by consulting with other world travelers in the CompuServe Travel Forum, or browse the wide selection of travelogues and amateur guides in the forum's library. ✓**COMPUSERVE**→*go* travsig→Messages *and* Libraries→Austal-NZ-S.Pacif

Pacific Island Peoples The opening screen of this page, an illustration of a scantily clad man tooting on a seashell, suggests the tone of a 1950s comic book. But a closer look at Pacific Island Peoples reveals a thoughtful, eclectic page, with a history of the 1789 mutiny on the *H.M.S. Bounty* (the inspiration for the film *Mutiny on the Bounty*) nestled along a link to the Pitcairn Island Home Page; and a wealth of Hawaiian resources counterbalancing Pacific Rim Action Alerts ("Nuclear Testing on Muraroa"). ✓**INTERNET**→*url* http://wavefront.wavefront.com/~pjlareau/pacific1.html

Pacific Islands "Things" The author of this page suggests that in the future, as information becomes less of a luxury and more of a necessity, those people living in remote corners of the world will run the risk of being left out of the loop entirely. "Nowhere, perhaps," he says, a note of earnest urgency creeping into his tone, "is this of more pressing concern than in the far-flung island states of the Pacific." With a wealth of links on nations ranging from the Solomon Islands to Tonga to New Caledonia, this massive page attempts to unite the scattered South Pacific states. Does it succeed? Was Christianity introduced to Rarotonga in 1823? ✓**INTERNET**→*url* http://www2.hawaii.edu/usr-cgi/ssis/~ogden/ogden-newpacific.html

South Pacific Board Since the days of Captain Cook, travelers have been fascinated by the constellated population of the South Pacific, the endless islands, the flawless weather, the fertile interpenetration of native languages and European tongues. On AOL's South Pacific message board, topics range from recommendations of hotels on Vanuatu to a discussion of an erotic rite performed by one vacationer and his girlfriend on Rapanui. Plenty of talk about Australia and New Zealand is also here—and don't even think about confusing Aussies and Kiwis, or you'll get the entire hemisphere's hackles raised. ✓**AMERICA ONLINE**→*keyword* travel forum→Travel Boards→World Traveler Board→South Pacific

The Polynesian Triangle Everyone knows about the Bermuda Triangle, that mysterious patch of the Atlantic Ocean that swallows planes and previously infallible seafarers. Well, the Polynesian Triangle is nothing so mysterious—it's merely a way of referring to the huge section of the Pacific that has as its three vertices Aotearoa (New Zealand), Hawaii, and Easter Island (or Rapanui). This page contains basic short, impressionistic essays on ten Polynesian locations—the Marquesas, the Society Islands, Hawaii, Baker Island, Fiji, Tonga, and more—as well as an essay on colonization strategies in the region. ✓**INTERNET**→*url* http://128.171.128.46/bishop/hawaiilo/hawup.html

Culture

Pacific (ml) For discussion of the people, culture, and news of the Pacific Islands. ✓**INTERNET** →*email* listserv@bruf pb.bitnet ✍ *Type in message body:* subscribe pacific <your full name>

Easter Island

Pictures of Easter Island One of the great enigmas of the world, Easter Island (aka Rapanui) is a Chilean dependency in the South Pacific that is most famous for its gigantic stone sculptures, or moai. See pictures of those sculptures, along with natural vistas of the island, on this page. ✓**INTERNET**→*url* http://www.tardis.ed.ac.uk/~angus/Gallery/SouthAmerica/Chile/Pascua.html

Rock Art of Easter Island A Berkeley course catalog listing for an archaeological dig on Easter Island. ✓**INTERNET**→*url* http://www.mip.berkeley.edu/urep/catalog/easter.html

Fiji

Fiji Discovery Page Fiji isn't just one place, you know—it's an archipelago of more than 300 South Pacific islands, and a complicated duplex culture, split evenly between the indigenous Melanesians and the Indians who arrived during colonial times. With links to pages about Fiji's residents, its wildlife (both airborne and aquatic), and its landscape, this page does justice to the splendor of the island. Lots of pictures here, most in brilliant color. ✓**INTERNET**→*url* http://kula.usp.ac.fj/fiji/

Fiji Page What do Germans know about Fiji? Well, they know enough to have visited it, and then to have created a home page for it. Get a map of Fiji, a brief review of the nation's history, and information about the University of the South Pacific. ✓**INTERNET**→*url* http://www.cs.tu-berlin.de/~minibbjd/fijiinde.html

Guam

Welcome to Guam The westernmost point in the United States of America, Guam is so far west it's east, more than 6,000 miles west of San Francisco and almost 4,000 miles west of Honolulu. It sits midway between Japan and Australia, in the middle of the Pacific Ocean, at the southern tip of the Mariana archipelago. With warm temperatures and two seasons—the rainy July–November fanuchanan and the dry December–June fanumangan—Guam is one of the most temperate places on the planet. Convinced yet that it's paradise? If not, visit this home page, and try to resist the onslaught of pro-Guam propaganda. Learn to speak a little Chamorro. Find out about Guam's government. And decide for yourself whether the legend of Sirena the Mermaid ("feeling unusual sensations as she swam, she soon discovered that from the waist down she had become part fish") would make good material for Disney, or at least Mrs. Paul. ✓**INTERNET**→ *url* http://ns.gov.gu/

Marshall Islands

Republic of the Marshall Islands Does the Republic of the Marshall Islands have a bit of an inferiority complex? Well, any nation with an unofficial home page that admits that "surprisingly few people outside of the Pacific know of the islands, and even fewer realize that the RMI is now independent" isn't exactly running away from the pack in the arrogance sweepstakes. But the RMI shouldn't worry. Everyone knows of the Bikini Atoll, the famous nuclear test site, even if they don't know that it's in the Marshall Islands, and anyone wanting more information will find it at this page, which has dozens of links on everything from linguistics to history to ecology to science. And don't forget to learn the catchy national anthem, which has official lyrics in both English ("I love the islands where I was born / The surroundings, the paths, and the gatherings") and Marshallese ("Il yokwe lok aelon ko ije iar lotak it / Melan ko ie, im ial ko ie, im iaeo ko ie"). ✓**INTERNET**→*url* http://www.clark.net/pub/llaack/rmi/

Micronesia

Micronesia The beautiful South Pacific paradise known as Micronesia is actually a federation of four states (Kosrae, Pohnpei, Chuuk, and Yap), and this page includes specific political information about the Federated States of Micronesia, as well as more general information about the region. Take a photo tour of Nan Madol. Download Yapese sound bites (including the lilting "Kea kireeb ea carro roeg," which means "My car is broken."). And then read the fascinating monograph entitled "Understanding Law in Micronesia—An Interpreted Approach to Transplanted Law." ✓**INTERNET**→*url* http://darkwing.uoregon.edu/~robertsr/micro.htm

Papua New Guinea

Papua New Guinea Incorporating half of New Guinea—the dinosaur-shaped island just north of Australia—Papua New Guinea also includes a string of smaller islands (Admiralty Island, New Hanover, New Ireland, New Britain, and Bougainville). This site furnishes a map, a flag, and basic information. ✓**INTERNET**→*url* http://www.tbc.gov.bc.ca/cwgames/country/Papua/papua.html

Pitcairn Island

Pitcairn Island Home Page The French Revolution wasn't the only famous uprising of 1789. The *H.M.S. Bounty*, a British ship sent to Tahiti to collect breadfruit, was shattered when a party of officers led by Master Mate Fletcher Christian overthrew the ship's captain, Lieutenant William Bligh—an event that has been immortalized on film more than a few times, with the help of actors from Marlon Brando to Mel Gibson. Six survivors of the mutiny on the *Bounty*, British crew members with Tahitian mates, fled to Pitcairn Island, a tiny South Pacific atoll, and founded a new civilization, one that survives more than two centuries later. Learn more about Pitcairn Island with this page's essays, news clippings, directory of the 50-odd permanent residents of the island, and links to related sites in the South Pacific. ✓**INTERNET**→*url* http://wavefront.wavefront.com/~pjlareau/pitc1.html

Tonga

Tonga Page Want to order some Royal Tongan coffee? How about viewing some slides of Tonga? Or maybe you'd like to download a brief biography of Taufa-ahau Tupou, the King of Tonga (hurry—he was born in 1918, and material on this page loads very slowly)? One of the only active monarchies remaining in the world, Tonga welcomes visitors, and if you're planning a trek through the South Pacific, you shouldn't miss it. Before you go, though, stop at this page, and learn all about the stick-in-the-hole game known as Heu. ✓**INTERNET**→*url* http://www.cs.tu-berlin.de/~minibbjd/tongaind.html

Vanuatu

Vanuatu: A Small Place in the South Pacific Formerly known as the New Hebrides, Vanuatu is a set of 66 Anglo-French Islands in the southwestern Pacific, roughly 1,200 miles northwest of Australia. Investigate the political history of the islands, view pictures of the nation, and learn why the author of this page considers the ni-Vans the friendliest people on earth. (Port Vila, the Vanuatuan capital, is awarded a "10 on the friendliness scale, not at all like the relatively nearby Port Moresby, Papua New Guinea, where the sane think twice about walking down the main streets in broad daylight."). ✓**INTERNET**→*url* http://www.clark.net/pub/kiaman/vanuatu.html

Western Samoa

Western Samoa Government Dubbed "the Cradle of Polynesia," Western Samoa is a set of South Pacific islands laden with palm trees and brushed by tropical winds. "Talafo lava!" That means "welcome" in Samoan, and this page welcomes all Netsurfers interested in the nation, its history, its population, and its geography. A special link on tourism lists hotels and tour operators. ✓**INTERNET**→*url* http://www.intergroup.com/interweb/samoa

The beach in Tonga—from http://www.cs.tu-berlin.de/~minibbjd/tongaind.html

Part 5

Europe

Europe

Going on the Grand Tour? It's even easier in these enlightened days of the EC and curtainless cities. But to manage all the culture—not to mention, trains, hotels, foreign menus, and funny sounding money (what is a pfennig anyway?)—you'll need some help. Start with an overview of national attractions and visa policies of the united Europe (just ignore that Bosnian thing) at the **European Community Home Page**. Once you've framed your questions, or planned an itinerary the folks at **rec.travel.europe**, eWorld's **Travel Central: Europe**, and CompuServe's **European Forum** are eager to pass on their suggestions for good pensions in Tuscany and reasonable restaurants in Provence. And avid readers can rest assured—**Bookstores of Europe** provides addresses for shops from Sweden to Spain.

Charlemagne, unifier of Europe—http://www.comptons.com/charlema.html

On the Net

Across the board

Europe Through the Back Door Rick bemoans the rising cost of Eurailpasses, while Jan wonders if the circle trip from Interlacken to Gindelwalk will be closed on account of snow in November. Brad asks anxiously if he should hug his British cousins upon first meeting them (he doesn't want to get off on the wrong foot). Anna seeks advice on finding a good salt-mine tour near Salzburg, one that's "complete with overalls and slides." All tastes, and all questions, are welcome on this board dedicated to seeing Europe. ✓**AMERICA ONLINE**→*keyword* Travel Forum→Travel Boards→World Traveler→Europe→Through the Back Door

Eurotrav (ml) The latest travel news from Europe is the focus of this mailing list. If security is beefed up at Heathrow because of a terrorist threat, if a new budget hotel has opened in Lyon, or if the requirements for acquiring a Croatian visa have changed, this mailing list will have the scoop. ✓**INTERNET**→listserv@ptearn.cc.fc.ul.pt ✍ *Type in message body:* subscribe eurotrav <your full name>

rec.travel.europe (ng) Where are the best sights in Norway? Which London restaurants serve traditional English Christmas dinners? Which hotels in Budapest are wheelchair-accessible? Are there any car-rental companies that rent to people traveling to Eastern Europe? Is Bastille Day in Paris as much an event as Mardi Gras in New Orleans? Ask your questions about travel in Europe, and you'll be answered at this newsgroup. ✓**USENET**→rec.travel.europe *FAQ:* ✓**INTERNET**→*url* ftp://rtfm.mit.edu/pub/usenet-by-hierarchy/rec/travel/

Travel Central: Europe Oh, to have such concerns as Peter, who comes to this site asking for the names of great places to eat in Tuscany next spring (Evidently there are a good number, for the question received a dozen replies). Head to any of the geographic categories on this message board to get or share advice on travel in Europe. Ask about the best pub in London (everyone knows it's the Hollywood in Chelsea), trains running from Prague to Vienna (get a couchette), how to make friends in Norway (relish smoked fish), or, if you don't have a travel question, just read and dream. ✓**EWORLD**→*go* travelers→Travelers Central→Europe

Culture

Balt-L (ml) The Baltic mailing list includes not only up-to-the-minute news postings, but also tireless dissections of moves on the international political chessboard. Conversations are often impassioned, with sentimentality colliding with calls for reform. ✓**INTERNET**→*email* listserv@ubvm.cc.buffalo.edu ✍ *Type in message body:* subscribe balt-l <your full name>

European Community Home Page The page is here, whether the Tories and the Danes like it or not. Simply click on the proper flag, and you'll be rewarded with a comprehensive list of Internet servers and a clickable map full of local information. A cultural European home page is linked to this site, where a visit to Slovenia provides ski tips, a trip to France yields a virtual tour of the Pompidou Center, and a jaunt to Germany offers a comprehensive beer guide. ✓**INTERNET**→*url* http://s700.uminho.pt/ec.ng.html

European Forum A forum with the traveler in mind. Open this site and find articles to help plan your next trip to a European country—an essay on Swiss Wine Museums, lists of vegetarian restaurants in Budapest, a story on rail travel in Ireland. Or turn to the library for tips on what to wear in Paris (for women: "To be very French, buy a lovely scarf when you arrive"), an FAQ on travel in Ireland, and much more. If you don't find the answer to your travel question in the library, the message boards are an excellent place to turn for advice. But don't be surprised if your travel query evolves into a discussion of politics and culture on both sides of the ocean: It's common for doom-mongering Europeans to worry that Americans "kill for fun, sport, and revenge." You can agree that the worst is true or instead ask, "Are Americans dysfunctional, or do they just need good haircuts?" Be prepared for threads to bounce in and out of English. ✓**COMPUSERVE**→*go* eurforum

Mideur-L (ml) A mixture of contemporary political debate, historical discussion, and ethnic bonding that will give you a taste of the region's cultural flavor. List members include scholars from around the world and middle Europeans in and outside the borders of their countries. Emotions run high during talk of current strife—Tatiana writes to a Serb about Bosnian partition, "I am pregnant as it is, so there is no need for chetniks to come here and rape me." Slovaks complain about the media's "pro-Czech" stance. Scholars step in every once in a while to moderate discussions of how hate builds over time—anti-Catholicism, anti-Semitism, and eventually anti-everything. But there is also an element of ethnic support here—a young American seeks prayers in Croatian to ease his dying grandfather's mind. ✓**INTERNET**→*email* listserv@ubvm.cc.buffalo.edu ✍ *Type in message body:* subscribe mideur-l <your full name>

soc.culture.europe (ng) Americans traveling in Europe often find themselves acting as unofficial ambassadors of their country. They are frequently called upon to explain the policies of the current administration or to defend good old American values (like the deep-rooted faith in big cars). While this newsgroup won't help Americans find a good hotel off the Asterplein in Amsterdam, it will acquaint them with current European attitudes regarding American politics and culture, and occasionally open the door for discussion of European culture itself. ✓**USENET**→soc.culture.europe

Guides

Bookstores in Various European Cities Garnered from the wisdom of bibliophiles in the rec.arts.books newsgroup, this listing will help readers get their book fix almost anywhere in Europe. Use the addresses and phone numbers at the site to buy music texts at Rae MacIntosh in Edinburgh or a popular English novel at Norli in Oslo. ✓**INTERNET**→*url* http://www.cis.ohio-state.edu/hypertext/faq/usenet/books/stores/european/faq-doc-2.html

Fodor's Choice...

Sights to Remember

France: Mont St. Michel at high tide

Greece: Sunset over the Caldera on the island of Santorini

Romania: The view from the clock tower in Sighisoara

Italy: The Grand Canal in Venice at dawn

—from Fodor's *96 Europe*

Austria

Everybody sing "Edelweiss, Edelweiss . . ." And when you're through singing the tunes of Rogers and Hammerstein, join an expedition run by **Tennengau Trekking**, listen to the lyric strains of local prodigy/bad boy Mozart, or buy some of those little candies boasting Mozart's visage that are available in Salzburg. And then choose from the ten kinds of schnitzel and 360 kinds of beer lovingly described in the **Austrian Restaurant** and **Austrian Beer Guides**. All in a trip to Austria.

The Mirabellen garden in Salzburg—from CompusServe's Graphics Corner Forum

On the Net

Across the board

Austria Trade advice about lodgings in Villach (the Park Hotel is excellent) and how to get tickets to Vienna's New Year's Eve Opera Ball (fat chance). Betsy even found out how to plan her autumn wedding in Salzburg from a Netter in the Tyrol. Come to this board to swap talk about travel and life in Austria. ✓**AMERICA ONLINE**→*keyword* travel forum→Travel Board→World Traveler board→Austria

Austria Austria is seriously wired—especially with information pertinent to visitors. Take a 20-minute virtual tour of the country, hop over to visit the polar bears in the Austrian Zoo's site, or learn about the hundreds of thirst quenchers available via the Austrian Beer Guide. ✓**INTERNET**→*url* http://ebweb.tuwien.ac.at/ortner/austria.html

General Information About Austria "Children under twelve are not allowed to sit beside the driver" in Austria—just one of the useful facts held at this site. Everything needed to have a safe and lawful trip to the land of the Von Trapps is noted: customs regulations, banking hours, ski slopes, tourist offices worldwide, the best shopping districts, and a list of phone numbers for local fire departments. ✓**INTERNET**→*url* http://www.atnet.co.at/~ed/

The Webfoot's Guide to Austria All things Austrian—Mozart, Freud, beer, and waltzing. More than a simple collection of tourist links, this site provides practical information—info on currency exchange, a dictionary, and rail and hotel guides. But the real riches are the little guides that give visitors a taste of Austria: Learn about seven different varieties of schnitzel, find out what's playing at the Opera, or discover the art galleries of Vienna. A variety of Austrian newspapers and magazines are also linked to the site. ✓**INTERNET**→*url* http:// www.webfoot.com/travel/guides/austria/austria.html

Tourism Related Information on Austria German-language tourist information illustrated with an attractive interactive map—simply *klicken Sie* on any locale for information on hotels, food, and sightseeing. ✓**INTERNET**→*url* http://www.net4you.co.at/tourism/

Virtual Tour of Austria Though this tour may take a while to complete, it takes you deep into a world of Hapsburgs and alpine slopes. A total Web tour, it links to other Austrian-related sites, featuring short illustrated essays on culture and history. Linger at the Rathouse at Night or the Spanish Riding School, or head to sites dedicated to skiing, opera, and vacation planning. ✓ **INTERNET**→*url* http://tph.tuwien.ac.at/cgi-bin/GuidedTour.pl?AustriaTour

Welcome to Austria A collection of interactive maps of Austrian provinces is the centerpiece of this site. Use the maps to access essays and pictures describing each of the provinces—from Styria to Vorarlberg. The Austrian Tourist Bureau has also prepared selected itineraries for visitors of differing temperaments—*Lifestyles of the Rich and Famous* fans might enjoy the "From Castle to Castle" tours, while those who conduct along with Zubin Mehta can follow the "Footsteps of Great Music" itinerary. And there are detours along the way—one focuses on the Viennese gentleman whose influence shadows all modern existence, Sigmund Freud. Calendars of art and music events and a list of hotels for both tourists and business travelers are here too. If you still need additional info, it's easy to email the Tourist Bureau with questions. ✓ **INTERNET**→ *url* http://austria-info.at/

ZUÖsterrich Links to Austrian news and cultural calendars in German. ✓ **INTERNET**→*url* http://bau2.uibk.ac.at/guerti/oesterreich/

Culture

Art and Music News Austria The Austrian Minister of Culture apprises visitors of not-to-be-missed festivals and exhibitions at this calendar page. Brief descriptions and contact information for events like The Cuckoo's Call (celebrating the achievements of artists persecuted under the Nazi regime), the famous Mozart festival in Salzburg, and an exhibit of German Expressionists at the Rupertinum are presented in English, German, and French. ✓ **INTERNET**→ *url* http://austria-info.at/amusa/index.html

Der Standard Keep up with the latest Austrian news with this online daily edition of the national newspaper, *Der Standard.* German speakers will find the culture, sports, and movie listings of interest. ✓ **INTERNET**→*url* http://www.derstandard.co.at/DerStandard/

soc.culture.austria (ng) A German-language newsgroup that examines issues of import to Austrians—the meaning of life, whether women are equal to men, where to get a good Sacher torte, and where local rock bands are playing. ✓ **USENET**→soc.culture.austria

Guides

Austrian Beer Guide Since there are at least 360 brands of Austrian beer, this guide will probably be appreciated. (If you're only traveling in Austria for a few days, you'll need some help pinpointing the beers you want to sample.) Contact information for all breweries is included. ✓ **INTERNET**→*url* http://www.lib.uchicago.edu/keith/austrian-beer.html

Austrian Restaurant Guide First, this guide provides a primer on Austrian cuisine—the joys of schnitzel and Viennese fried chicken (*Wiener Backhendl*). Then, the guide lists a small selection of restaurants by location—who could resist the Hänchen in Linz? A guide to Austrian wine and a link to the Austrian Beer Guide are also available. ✓ **INTERNET**→*url* http://www.lib.uchicago.edu/keith/austria/restaurants.html

Austrian Zoo If you plan on bringing *Kinder* (children) along on your tour of Austria, the zoo (Schönbrunn is the oldest zoo in the world) and aquarium described here are sure to be hits. Information, which includes admission prices, hours of operation, and special attractions, is available in both English and German. ✓ **INTERNET**→*url* http://www.luga.or.at/~hackeha/zooneu/html/zoo1.html

Salzburg

Das Monatsmagazin der Stadt Salzburg Although this monthly magazine is in German, travelers who don't speak the language can still plug keywords into the searchable calendar and get schedules of events around Salzburg. A search of Mozart brought up the address, time, and place of several concerts by local ensembles. ✓ **INTERNET**→*url* http://hirsch.cosy.sbg.ac.at/stadtleben/index.html

Salzburg There's more to Salzburg than *Sound of Music* tours according to this extensive tourism resource. An interactive map of the surrounding area gives detailed information on local recreational activities. Expect to land graylings and walleye pike in local streams, and sample spiced wine in local restaurants. ✓ **INTERNET**→*url* http://www.tcs.co.at/other.html

Tennengau Trekking This company will help you work off all the Sacher torte, Wiener schnitzel, and brew you put away in Salzburg. Get illustrated, day-by-day descriptions of its week-long alpine treks. Contact and pricing information is included. ✓ **INTERNET**→*url* http://www.tcs.co.at/guide/e_activ/trek/intro.htm

Vienna

Vienna—the cultural hotspot that gave us the waltz, psychoanalysis, and the Sacher torte—offers more than nights of high culture (and high notes) at the **Wiener Statsoper**. Enjoy Vienna's famed coffeehouses on a **Vienna City** hypertour. Discover the lively club scene or get a glimpse of the baroque majesty of the capitol of the Austro-Hungarian Empire at **ViennaSlide**, and the vibrancy of its modern art at **Museum Moderner Kunst**.

The Vienna skyline at dusk—from http://www.atnet.co.at/viennaslide/0000.htm

On the Net

Museum Moderner Kunst Among the practical information on Vienna's modern art museum is an online exhibit of some of its masterpieces—Andre Derain's *Kauernder*, Oskar Kokoschka's *Portrait of Karl Kraus*, and Magritte's *Die Stimme des Blutes.* ✓**INTERNET**→*url* http://fgidec1.tuwien.ac.at/1002situations/

Rendezvous in Vienna With a name that conjures kaffee with Ingrid Bergman and dark dealings with the Third Man, this site presents the mystique of Vienna with attractive illustrated essays on unique features of the Hapsburg capital. Visit the baroque majesty of the Ringstrasse, and be awestruck by the opulence of the Opera. Learn about famous personages, like Maria Theresa, or preview the consumer delights of Karnterstrasse. Get tips on Viennese cuisine. A list of festivals and cultural activities is provided for those who want to take the high culture road rather than explore the delights of the "Bermuda Triangle" of nightclubs. General travel information such as tourist office locations, subway and tram system plans, local banking hours, and taxi fare information rounds out the site. ✓**INTERNET**→*url* http://austria-info.at/wien/index.html

Vienna City Yet another excellent guide to the Austrian capital, with lists of sights to see and sounds to hear in an up-to-the-minute events calendar. Vienna City tells you what show's at the Österreichiches Museum, what's hot at the clubs, and what type of subway ticket is needed to reach these attractions. Youth hostels and luxury hotels are listed, with ratings and complete contact information. A pleasant addition to the site is a segment on suggested walking tours of Vienna: stroll by beautiful coffeehouses, the house where Freud lived, and many lovely gardens. The history of the Sacher torte (supposedly created on the command of Prince Metternich) is an ample dessert after this feast of information. ✓**INTERNET**→*url* http://www.atnet.co.at/Tourism/Vienna/

ViennaSlide You'll arrive in Vienna knowing the difference between Jugendstil and Art Nouveau after viewing this slide collection. The spirit of the city is expressed in annotated essays on its monuments, cafes, and culture. Special pages focus on Christmas in Vienna and shopping opportunities. ✓**INTERNET**→*url* http://www.atnet.co.at/viennaslide/0000.htm

Weiner Staatsoper An annotated version of the upcoming season's schedule for the world-famous Vienna Opera, with profiles of the principal singers, is on this Website, along with a tantalizing video of the Opera Ball. Oh, to curtsy like that. ✓**INTERNET**→*url* http://www.austria-info.at/kultur/ws-wv/

Belgium

"If it's Tuesday, it must be Belgium." In that case, better get planning, because there's a lot to do in this small country that's so rich in history. Book a hotel in Brussels through **Resotel** and then start to explore the city at **Let's Meet In Brussels. The Coast of Flanders Textural Homepage** will take you to the nightmare battlefields of World War I as well as to the home page of pleasant seaside villages. **The City of Antwerp** and the **Alternative Bruges Pages** offer the native opinion on how best to see the cities. Ensure that you don't meet your own cultural Waterloo with a visit to **Plug-In Belgium's** politeness primer.

Belgium, not unplugged—http://www.plug-in.be/plugin/

On the Net

Across the board

Belgium Forum Much of the discussion here is in French or Flemish, which proves there are real experts here to answer your travel questions. Be sure to check the English Corner topic, where you can read reviews of new plays or of museum exhibitions at the Museé d'Art Moderne. ✓**COMPUSERVE**→*go* belgium

Belgium/Luxembourg/Netherlands Johann asks the difference between two standard terms he's seen in brochures about travel in Belgium: "standard double rooms" and "fully furnished double rooms." Providing many responses, this active message board guessed it either meant that there is no reading lamp or no bath in the room. This board is an excellent place to seek travel advice from the locals and from other travelers. Desired recommendations for B&Bs comprise a large part of the traffic here, and there is no shortage of responses. Netters in Belgium are also talking about the newest cybercafés in their neighborhoods (Amsterdam's Cybercafe in Brussels gets many praises). ✓**AMERICA ONLINE**→*keyword* travel forum→travel-board→world travel board→belgium/luxembourg/netherlands

Coast of Flanders Textural Homepage Want to wander the coast of Flanders from Blakenberge to Zeebrugge? This online brochure describes the breathtaking seaside views available there and provides basic contact information for hotels along the coast. A calendar and list of local restaurants rounds out the site. ✓**INTERNET**→*url* http://www.icon.be/home_et.exe?www

Embassy of Belgium The Belgian Embassy in Washington has put together a site to help travelers prepare for a trek to the Low Countries. You can get clarification of the Belgian visa application process here and even request an application online. The site links to the home pages of Belgian cities and towns and the excellent online magazine, Plug-In Belgium. If after visiting you decide you can't leave, locate information about moving to Belgium at the site as well. ✓**INTERNET**→*url* http://www.cais.com/usa/index.html

Plug-In Belgium You'll never make a wrong turn in Brussels, thanks to this online magazine and its invaluable tips. Where else could travelers get tips on Belgian etiquette—if you're invited to a private home for dinner, arrive at least 15 minutes late. Travelers should keep change in their pockets when out on the town; it's customary to tip the doorman on the way out of a club. Beyond the Emily Post-like tips, find up-to-the-minute information on theater, music, nightclubs, and even the European Circus Festival. Take a tour of all ten provinces, or focus on select items of interest—how about the Rubens House or the Playing Card Museum? Hotels and restaurants are listed, with names, phone numbers, and brief descriptions for travel planning. Don't miss the "facts about Belgium" section—a good place to gain greater understanding of this unassuming nation. ✓**INTERNET**→*url* http://www.plug-in.be/plugin/

Culture

Belgian Rock On-Line Belgium is more than just the home of lace, chocolate, Elephant Beer, and Hercule Poirot—it's a rockin' country. Check out this site for info on upcoming gigs of local bands like Nemo and Soulwax. ✓**INTERNET**→*url* http://www.ping.be/belgian-rock/

Museé Felicien Rops Take a guided tour of the museum in Namur dedicated to the work of nineteenth-century artist Felicien Rops. Directions, admission prices, and an email link to the curator are also provided. ✓**INTERNET**→*url* http://www.ciger.be/namur/musees/rops/

Antwerp

Antwerp Zoo Head to the Antwerp Zoo for the special Mother's Day celebration—or at any other time to visit the 4,000 plus beasts that call it home. Information on parking, prices, and buggy rental is available here. ✓**INTERNET**→*url* http://www.ufsia.ac.be/antwerp/zoo.html

Digital Metropol Antwerpen This site promises to be a guide for the entire city, but the only travel-oriented info here regards the zoo. You can learn everything you need to know about that Antwerp attraction, including price info, menus for the restaurants, and even where to park your car. But for details on any other Antwerp site, you'll have to look elsewhere. ✓**INTERNET**→*url* http://www.dma.be/

The City Antwerp An introduction to the City-on-the-Scheldt, including the tale of how the city got its name. There once was a giant Druoon Antigoon who levied tolls on passing ships. If the ships refused to pay, he chopped off the crew's hands and threw (werpen) them into the sea (hand-werpen). ✓**INTERNET**→*url* http://www.ufsia.ac.be/antwerp/antwerp.html

Bruges

Alternative Bruges Page A Bruges native lists the highlights of his hometown—you must throw a coin in the Minnewater fountain with your loved one to wish for lasting happiness. Connections take you to other Bruges pages for practical information on hotels and restaurants to help you carry out the author's suggestions. ✓**INTERNET**→*url* http://www.webcom.com/~cleenwe/

Bruges Tourist Information The City Council of Bruges has made navigating the city as carefree as possible with a number of illustrated step-by-step tours. A calendar of events helps you plan evening visits to the theater or a jazz club. For more useful information, check out the shopping, public transportation, and accommodations (rated by price) recommendations. ✓**INTERNET**→*url* http://www.innet.net/brugge/toerisme/engels/hmeng.htm

Brussels

CultrAgenda Zoekmodule Search this database for listings of cultural events of all stripes in Brussels. If you don't speak Flemish, Dutch, or German, you'll have to spend some extra time figuring out the keywords you need for the search engine. ✓**INTERNET**→*url* http://www.atms.be/database/Findcultragenda. html

Hotel Métropole, Brussels Step back into time at the venerable Hotel Métropole (remember Simone Signoret walking through the lobby in *L'Etiole du Nord*?). A virtual concierge shows you to your room, which is available at a discount to Net travelers. Contact info is here for additional information. ✓**INTERNET**→*url* http://www.ib.be/metropole/

Le Meridien Bruxelles An advertisement for a new luxury hotel in Brussels; get pictures and a price list and book online. ✓**INTERNET**→*url* http://www.freesun.be/merid ien.html

Let's Meet in Brussels The Brussels Congress presents information on accommodations, transportation, dining, and sightseeing for this city that offers over 70 museums and 50 theaters. Did you know that Belgian beer comes in over 400 varieties? If you plan to sample them all during your next tour of Brussels, come to this site for help in planning your trip. ✓**INTERNET**→*url* http://www.ib.be/meet

Resotel Online hotel booking service for business and pleasure travelers to Brussels. No information on specific hotels is included—all interaction is conducted via email. ✓**INTERNET**→*url* http://www.freesun.be/resotel.html

Czech Republic

It's difficult for anyone over ten years old not to tack Slovakia onto the end of Czech.

But the Czech Republic is fast forging a unique identity that places it among the cultural capitols of Europe. (Just see what can happen when you have a playwright as President instead of an actor.) Find out what's going on in this creative stew at **Czech Happenings**—which covers everything from performance art to Parliament. **Czech Frequently Asked Questions** and **PragueTourist Information** proffer practical advice on pensions, museums, and speed limits, while **TimeOut Prague** tells you which coffee house is noted for philosophical discussion and which club specializes in industrial rock.

On the Charles Bridge—http://www.ms.mff.cuni.cz/tourist/praha/praha.en.1.shtml

On the Net

Across the board

Cesnet You don't need a passport to enter this self-proclaimed checkpoint to the Republic online. Once inside, take a virtual tour of the country with the photographs and essays housed at the Website. ✓**INTERNET**→*url* http://www.cesnet.cz/

Czech Happenings It seems as if everything happening in the Czech Republic is covered here. The national news agency provides a daily summary of the Czech press (in English), and Czech Public Radio files reports here, as does the Parliament. Cultural-events calendars give detailed synopses of what's on at the movies, in the discos, and at the theaters. (On Tuesday, Karel Capek's play, *R.U.R.*, which coined the word "robot," is being reprised in Prague.) Essays focus on famous Czechs throughout history, including the mathematician Bolzano and Czech patriot Cirmrman. You'll even find Czech recipes and the results of the Czech soccer league! Happenings is truly an all-encompassing Czech-related site. ✓**INTERNET**→*url* http://www.ios.com/~jirim/czech.html

Czech Info Center Everything is here for those on their way to the Czech Republic—current postal rates, the standings of the national soccer team, news articles from national publications, and selected pub recommendations for Prague. You can even meet the president (which you probably couldn't do anywhere else but online!). ✓**INTERNET**→*url* http://turnpike.net/metro/muselik/index.html

Information for Tourists A synopsis of Czech history, brief descriptions of sights to see, current exchange rates, and weather forecasts are available at this text overview. It also sings the praises of Czech dumplings and *silvovice*, a Moravian plum brandy that is 90 percent alcohol. ✓**INTERNET**→*url* http://www.czech.cz/tourists/tour ist.htm

Culture

About 1968 Pictures of the 1968 revolution show images of tanks, guns, soldiers, and citizens confronting the then-new reality. Many of the photographs here have been hidden for over 20 years and are receiving their first public

Prague's astronomical clock—http://www.ms.mff.cuni.cz/tourist/praha/

viewing on the Net. ✓**INTERNET**→*url* http://www.utia.cas.cz/CZrep/1968/1968r.html

soc.culture.czech-slovac (ng) This newsgroup is replete with discussions of Czech politics (most of which are about the breakup) and culture (most of which are about the perceived snobbiness of those living in Prague). Come here to acquaint yourself with the issues of import in the Czech Republic today. ✓**USENET**→soc.culture.czech-slovac

Guides

Czech Frequently Asked Questions An excellent text primer on the practicalities of Czech living and touring—the site relates that local calls cost 1.90 Kc, and 70 mph is the speed limit on four-lane highways. Annotations from recent tourists suggest prepaying car rentals in the home country but waiting to buy train tickets until near the Austrian / Czech border. Telephone numbers for everything from the American Chamber of Commerce in Prague to a nightclub in Marianske Lazne are here too. ✓**INTERNET**→*url* http://www-swiss.ai.mit.edu/czech-FAQ.html

Prague

Maps of Prague The fun-loving gang at the Division of Elementary Particle Physics has put together a collection of Prague street maps, all available as small, larger, and very large .GIFs. ✓**INTERNET**→*url* http://www-hep.fzu.cz/PragueMaps.html

Prague Grafitti Susan Farrell's photo essay on graffiti in "free" Prague, subtitled "Art Crimes." ✓**INTERNET**→*url* http://www.gatech.edu/desoto/graf/prague/Index.Prague.html

PragueTourist Information Prague has been a European capital since 870 A.D., and now it's flourishing as the post-Cold War's most luminous and energetic city. A hypertext history lesson and illustrated sightseeing tour provide background info on the entire city—from the beauty of Prazskihrad (Prague Castle) to the pathos of Zidovská ctvrt (the Jewish Ghetto). The nitty-gritty of travel is covered satisfactorily, too. Telephone numbers are included for big hotels downtown, as well as for private rooms on the outskirts of town. Local residents have kindly provided recommendations for good restaurants, all of which are noted for excellent beer. ✓**INTERNET**→*url* http://www.ms.mff.cuni.cz/tourist/praha/praha.en.1.shtml

TimeOut Prague If the press is right, everyone who is anyone in the hip world is heading to Prague—perhaps to see the Lazy Pigs at U Maleho Glena (check the nightlife events calendar here for details). Even if you never wear black or hang out in cafés for hours on end, you'll still find this online guide to Prague enlightening. *TimeOut*'s profile provides essential information for negotiating Prague—how to avoid pickpockets and where to get vegetarian food in "post-nuclear surroundings." There's even a pronunciation guide to facilitate your arrival at the pension or museum. The sightseeing highlights here point you in the right direction—see you at Wenceslas Square. ✓**INTERNET**→*url* http://www.timeout.co.uk/TO/Prague/

Fodor's Choice...

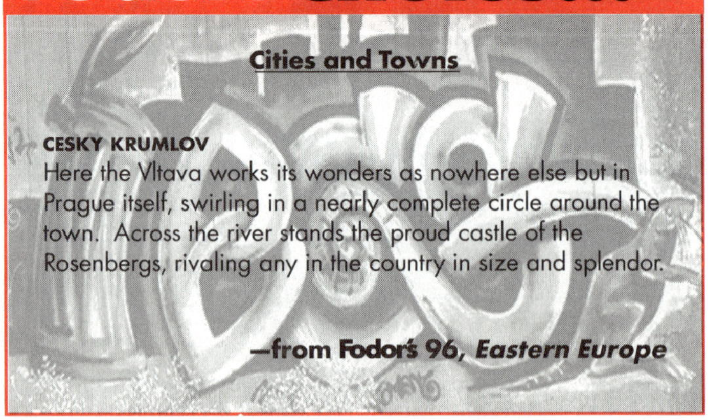

Cities and Towns

CESKY KRUMLOV
Here the Vltava works its wonders as nowhere else but in Prague itself, swirling in a nearly complete circle around the town. Across the river stands the proud castle of the Rosenbergs, rivaling any in the country in size and splendor.

—from Fodor's 96, *Eastern Europe*

Denmark

Denmark is a surprising little nation. It has a wild past—visit it at the World of the the Vikings—and apparently a wild present—there're always lots of happenings listed at **Copenhagen Party Info**. Just wait until **Copenhagen 96**, when the city is cultural capitol of Europe—festivals galore. More sedate charms are profiled in the **Museums Guide Denmark**, and **The Royal Library, Copenhagen**, where you'll discover the culture that produced *The Little Mermaid* and *The Steadfast Tin Soldier*. Take a cybertour of the historic landscape with **Denmark Info**, stopping off at the **Karen Blixen Museum** along the way to your weekend getaway at the **Falsled Kro** inn.

The ruins of Lindholm Høje, near Aalborg—http://www.iesd.auc.dk/aalborg/attr/

On the Net

Across the board

Denmark An encyclopedic text overview of Denmark that provides short essays and statistics on its population, government, and geography. Did you know that Denmark comprises a central peninsula and more than 400 islands? Check this site for interesting facts about Denmark. ✓**INTERNET**→*url* http://info.denet.dk/denmark.html

Denmark Info An excellent introduction to the country, this site offers a map with links to information on several Danish cities. Click on Ribe, for example, and learn that it is the oldest town in Denmark, dating back to at least 800 A.D., when it was an important port for the Vikings. (Today it is a more modest village with about 8,000 inhabitants.) Preview Denmark through the essays provided here. ✓**INTERNET**→*url* http://ai.eecs.umich.edu/people/skyt/DANMARK/danmark.html

Karen Blixen Museum Tour the home of the enigmatic author of *Seven Gothic Tales* and *Out of Africa*. A brief biography of the author accompanies pictures of the house, her paintings, and her beloved flowers. Museum hours, prices, and contact information are posted. ✓**INTERNET**→*url* http://www.dis.dk/dis/kultur/karenb/kbtekst.e.html

Links to Denmark Wondering what to do in Copenhagen on those nights when it gets dark in the early afternoon? You can check the Danish TV and movie listings here (in Danish) and save yourself from being bored (yes, many of the shows are in English!). Or if you prefer to be more active during your tour of the land of the Danes, come to this site and get the addresses for the Danish Royal Library and several museums and galleries all over the country. ✓**INTERNET**→*url* http:// www.infoserve.net/netquest /nordic/denmark.html

Museums Guide Denmark Click on a province for maps and descriptions of hundreds of museums—from a reconstructed seventeenth-century farm to a museum dedicated to film to the home of Hans Christian Andersen. You'll find the descriptions and admission info here translated into Danish, English, and German. ✓**INTERNET**→*url* http://www.kb.bib.dk/kultnet/museer/guideahp.htm#AMTER

World of the Vikings Good-time guys or ravaging red-haired demons? You'll have a better idea after a visit to this excellent collection of sites relating to Viking culture and Norse civilization. Get a taste for seafaring by visiting the National Museum of Denmark's home page. Or link to the Electronic Beowulf Project of the British Library to read the tale of Grendel and the monster. At other sites you can learn medieval shipbuilding and runic writing. There's even a Bryggen Runic font available for downloading, as well as the Runecaster page to tell the future. If the sea is in your blood, you might try to join the Viking Network that helps keep Vikings worldwide in touch. ✓**INTERNET**→*url* http://www.demon.co.uk/history/index.html

Hotels

Falsled Kro Use the email address here to check the availability of rooms at this inn on a Baltic island. Price and telephone information is also included. ✓**INTERNET**→*url* http://www.calvacom.fr/relais/scandinavie/falsled.html

Sonderho Kro A profile of the oldest inn on the island of Fanø. Contact the hotel, via email or phone, for further information or to book a room. ✓**INTERNET**→*url* http://www.calvacom.fr/relais/scandinavie/sonderho.html

Aalborg

Welcome to Aalborg This city by the sea has provided an extensive service for both tourists and business travelers online. Illustrated profiles of major attractions like the Tivoliland amusement park and the Viking settlement museum Lindholm Høje are linked to an area map, as are selected restaurants, hotels, and galleries. Concise traveler's tips and contact information for the tourist bureau are also included. ✓**INTERNET**→*url* http://www.iesd.auc.dk/aalborg/

Copenhagen

Copenhagen 96 Copenhagen has been designated the cultural capital of Europe for 1996, and the city is going all out to make Copenhagen a cultural showplace. Peruse the Massive Program of Events section to find activities that suit your fancy—a film festival, a Nordic Explorer exhibition, an international ballet congress, or the Rockilde rock festival. ✓**INTERNET**→*url* http://info.denet.dk/cph96/

Copenhagen Jazz House Check this site to see if jazz artists like Herbie Hancock, Betty Carter, Bill Frisell, Steve Coleman, or Joe Henderson are playing the Jazz House while you're in Copenhagen. Here you'll learn about these and other artists that have played the house as well as get a monthly schedule of performances, the cover charge for each event (how much is 50 DKK, anyway?), and directions to the Jazz House, with a map and subway instructions. ✓**INTERNET**→*url* http://www.dis.dk/dis/kultur/br-guide/jazzprae.html

Copenhagen Party Info Don't sit in your room after touring Copenhagen all day! Visit this party page and find out where the big rave, disco, and club events are happening. For each event, you'll get the address of the venue, the time things will be getting underway, and the price of admission. If you hear something you like at one of the parties, use this site's list of record stores to buy the songs that will forever remind you of your night on the town in Copenhagen. ✓**INTERNET**→*url* http://www.gbar.dtu.dk/~gc938281/Copenhagen_Party_Info.html

The Royal Library, Copenhagen You probably won't want to check out any library books on your trip to Denmark, but you might want to gather some background information on Danish culture or visit the Library's online exhibit here before you go. ✓**INTERNET**→*url* http://www.kb.bib.dk/

Creative anachronism in the Forest of Rold—http://www.iesd.auc.dk/aalborg/attr/

Finland

Finland, oh Finland, land of fish, festivals, frozen vodka, frozen toes, and fun. A trip to this northern nation offers plenty of unique travel options. **Travel in Finland** suggests a snowmobile fishing safari. **Finland Festivals** offers the calming strains of local son made good, Sibelius, and the hilarity of the **Arctic Comics Festival** ("so this reindeer walks into a bar..."). Or really get away from it all—book yourself a cottage in Lapland with **Fintrip** and watch the Northern Lights shine.

National Opera House of Finland—at http://www.hel.fi/english/

On the Net

Across the board

Helsinki for the Virtual Traveler Planning on a trip to Helinksi in the near future? Use the site's interactive map to make a virtual visit to Helsinki streets, like Marinkasemskajen, or to ride the virtual tram. After a Cyberspace jaunt around the city, travelers can look in the events guide to find out what's playing at the movies or at the Helsinki Opera. ✓**INTERNET**→*url* http://www.spellbound.com/helsinki/index.html

Travel in Finland Nearly everything at this site is related to fish, ice, or iced fish. At this collection of tourism links, travelers get information on the ice marathon (skating), a snowmobile fishing safari, and shops that sell fish smokers in downtown Helsinki. When in town, stop at the Ikaalinen Spa that's listed in the hotel guide for some herring in the hot tub. Sounds a little fishy, huh? ✓**INTERNET**→*url* http://www.travel.fi/

Culture

Aine Art Museum Take a peek at this illustrated online exhibit from a museum in Tornio that shows Finnish artwork from 1841 to the present. Its galleries boast the work of Elin Danielson-Gambogi, Esa Riippa, and Raili Tang. ✓**INTERNET**→*url* http://www.tokem.fi/av_museo/aine_egl.html

Helsinki Help yourself to Helsinki with this site's useful online guide, which tells you where to berth your yacht, rent roller skates, sweat your evening away in a sauna, or throw it away in a casino. A look at the events calendar suggests other activities: How could anyone pass up the annual Baltic Herring Market or the Finnish version of the Three Tenors, with Matti Salminen, Jaakko Ryhänen, and Johan Tilli? A set of links takes you to the home pages of the National Opera, the Finnish Film Foundation, and the State Art Museum. ✓**INTERNET**→*url* http://www.hel.fi/english/

The Finnish National Gallery Visit several galleries in one colorful online trip—the Museum of Foreign Art, the Museum of Finnish Art, and the Museum of Contemporary Arts (which, despite its name, samples works from the 13th century to the present). If you're planning to stop by any of the museums during your trip to Finland, you can find their hours and admission prices listed here. ✓**INTERNET**→*url* http://www.fng.fi/fng/html2/en/

Guides

Finland Festivals Finland is evidently a very festive place, at least according to this long annotated list of music, theater, and dance events. Highlights include the Mikkeliiv International Music Festival, the Nummirock Concert, the Savonlinna Opera Festival, chamber music at Kuhmo, jazz at Tampere, the Midnight Sun Film Festival and, of course, the Arctic Comics Festival. All venues are listed with their phone numbers and addresses. ✓**INTERNET**→*url* http://www.sjoki.uta.fi/~latvis/huvit/muut/ff_eng.html

Fintrip This all-purpose travel site lists hotels, cottages, and restaurants in Finland, with their phone numbers (in case you want to book a room at the Hotel Aurora in Helsinki). Finnish hot spots like Turku, Klaajoki, and Mikkeli, and upcoming events like the Sibelius Festival and international ski competitions are profiled here as well. ✓**INTERNET**→*url* http://www.fintrip.fi/

France

French bread, French fries and French toast—are just the tip of the huge iceberg of French culture. Get an overview at the **France Forum** on AOL or the French goverment's own **FranceScape**. The **Ministry of Culture** is exhibiting the works of the Masters, while **French Recipes** helps you recreate the works of master chefs. Charm the natives by studying **Online French Lessons**, astound them with your knowledge of **Paleolithic Cave Art**, or keep up with the Gallic social whirl at **Riveria Events**.

Mont St. Michel—downloaded from CompuServe's Graphic Corner

On the Net

Across the board

Adminet Assembled in cooperation with the French government, this full-service stop will help you plan many aspects of your trip through France. Use its collection of links to access information on government ministries, French companies, and locales from Alsace to Provence. The Entertainment section tells what's playing at the local cinema in Vichy and lists French cybercafés where travelers can go to get their Net fixes. French speakers should not miss the daily news feeds or the excellent online magazine selection here. ✓**INTERNET**→*url* http://www.ensmp.fr/~scherer/adminet/

Embassy & Consular Service in Paris A complete listing of official foreign embassies and consular services in Paris, searchable by country. ✓**INTERNET**→*url* http://www.paris.org/Addresses/Embassies/

France Forum The recent rise in terrorist activity has this message board ablaze, but most potential visitors are still lured by the siren song of French wines and cafés. Is it better to change money at home or in France? Is it true that most public toilets in France are of the "Turkish" variety? Are there tours of Monet's house at Giverny? Are formal evening clothes required in the main room of the casino at Vittel? The answers to these questions and many others are here, as are recommendations for musical theater (Moulin Rouge anyone?), barge cruises, and, of course, fine dining. ✓**AMERICA ONLINE**→*keyword* Travel Forum→World Traveler Board→France

France Forum Practice your French at this site, where most of the conversation is in the Gallic tongue. (The Tourisme category is full of French people asking advice about travel to Bali, China, and Florence.) But never fear—every English-language question or comment currently on the board received a response. Karen asks about attractions at EuroDisney—Gerrard responds that the park was renamed Disneyland Paris and that its Space Mountain ride just opened. David inquires about affordable hotels in Lyon and is treated to a long list of rooms all over town. ✓**COMPUSERVE**→*go* Frforum

FranceScape Maybe the French Government Tourist Office heard some of those rumors about their nation's hospitality, because it's created a site packed with helpful troubleshooting advice—how much to tip, where to find a good public restroom, no-smoking policies, and how to call home. There's even a special section with information for disabled travelers. A feature on cultural activities will tempt you with dreams of attending films at Cannes, hearing jazz in Montreaux, or seeing Pinnochio at the Worldwide Festival of Puppet Theaters in Charleville. For additional information, the site offers a complete list of official French tourist offices worldwide. ✓ **INTERNET**→*url* http://www.france.com/francescape/top.html

La France The big map here leads to lots of local resources. Click on any region—from Poitou-Charentes to Haute Normandie—then follow the local map and town listings and gather information on local businesses and events (a new Cajun restaurant is opening in Caen—which means it qualifies as both a local business and an event!). ✓ **INTERNET**→*url* http://www.urec.fr/France/

Les Carnet de Route de FranceWeb As its name suggests, this site is entirely in French. Francophiles will find much to please them here, with links to news services and government agencies. Links are also available for children, shoppers, travelers, and scientists—you can even link to a job bank. And the diverse cultural listings—everything from new bands to new science fiction—are not to be missed. ✓ **INTERNET**→*url* http://www.francenet.fr/franceweb/FWCarnetRoute.html

The Webfoot's Guide to France Another terrific effort on the part of the Webfoot group—this one linking cybertravelers to the French embassy, English-French dictionaries, information on exchange rates, events calendars, and the virtual Town Halls of cities from Paris to Nancy. The Paris Pages are well worth a visit, and Paris Inside Out will keep night owls happy with its What's On listings. The literati will appreciate the site's list of Parisian bookstores. And then there are the cuisine and café guides—they deserve a glance for sheer fantasy value. Hotel links, transportation maps, and a culture FAQ help Ugly Americans (or Brits or Germans) avoid annoying the natives. All that, and we haven't even mentioned the links to French literature collections, such as the Proust Page and the Siege of Paris Page. ✓ **INTERNET**→*url* http://www.webfoot.com/travel/guides/france/france.html?City

Culture

29th Montreux Jazz Festival Official Site The festival may be over, but this site goes a long way toward recreating the excitement of the event. Daily programs online feature artist profiles, complete with sound clips, of Baden-Powell, George Benson, and Sons of the Desert. From backstage come newsreels, a hall of fame, and even live feeds when the show is in progress. ✓ **INTERNET**→*url* http://www.grolier.com/festival/montreux/

Chanter-liste (ml) devoted entirely to discussion of French music, singers, and bands, including Julie Masse, Vanessa Paradis, Les Colocs, and Joe Bocan. ✓ **INTERNET**→*email* chanter-liste@wimsey.com ✍ *Email with general correspondence*

fr.rec.cuisine (ng) What other nation in the world would have a whole newsgroup devoted to food? Come here to learn about food tours of France—Jeff writes that a British agency organizes a weekend tour to Provence's famous Perigord truffle market. Get a recipe for preparing alligator meat in the French manner, or take notes on the dishes to look for on the menus of Parisian restaurants. ✓ **USENET**→fr.rec.cuisine

French Culture FAQ Gathered from the newsgroup soc.culture.french, this FAQ addresses questions on everything from good restaurants in France to citizenship requirements and tax policies. Tourists can gain useful insight from the sections on Paris and the Metro. ✓ **INTERNET**→*url* http://www.cis.ohio-state.edu/hypertext/faq/usenet/culture-french-faq/top.html

French Recipes Amaze your friends with your culinary expertise by whipping up *Le gâteau au chocolat de Xavière.* The recipe for it is here, along with connections to the French Culinary Institute in New York, sites dedicated to Alsatian and Moroccan cooking, and the archives of fr.rec.cuisine. ✓ **INTERNET**→*url* http://www.ensmp.fr/~scherer/cooking/

Le Monde Search an archive of Paris's principal daily newspaper by keyword or date. ✓ **COMPUSERVE**→*go* Le Monde

Liste de concerts de musique ancienne en France A French-language site that lists all types of musical events nationwide, from a jazz concert in Ambronay to a tribute to Gershwin in Paris. You'll only get the date, time, and location of the event, so, if you wish to attend, you'll need to do additional research for any addresses or directions you might need. ✓ **INTERNET**→*url* http://www.ircam.fr/divers/mus-anc.html

Ministry of Culture Much of the information here is in French only, which is not surprising, given the Ministry's mission to eradicate all non-French words from the nation's vocabulary. However, tourists will find plenty of useful information—Paris museum hours, directions to various monuments in Versailles, and lists of hotels and restaurants nationwide. If you speak French, you'll enjoy the many essays here on France's history and cultural offerings. ✓INTERNET→*url* http://web.culture.fr/

Online French Lessons The conversations here are very basic, but, thanks to the sound files, you won't come across as a complete fool when asking for *vin rouge* to accompany your *steak frites*. Complete sound files of simple conversations are here, as well as grammatical instruction and common French phrases—giving you something useful to do when you are just *se tournant les pouces* (twiddling your thumbs). ✓INTERNET→*url* http://teleglobe.ca/~leo/french.html

Paleolithic Cave Art Even if you can't read French, the beautiful images of paleolithic cave drawings from the Lascaux region of France are worth a cybertrip to this site. ✓INTERNET→*url* http://dufy.aquarel.fr:8001/

soc.culture.france (ng) A great place to discuss all things French—from France's nuclear policy in New Zealand to the best discos in Paris. ✓USENET→soc.culture.france

Guides

About France This French-language site is primarily commercial, boasting a "Champs Elysées Virtuels," with advertisements for fashion boutiques and gift shops. Your friends and relatives can tell you exactly what souvenirs they want with the help of this site. ✓INTERNET→*url* http://www.iway.fr/internet-way/fr/france/

Les Cybercafés in France Need to email your boss in L.A. before boarding the boat for your tour of the Seine? Even though your walking tour of Burgundy was very pleasant, do you find yourself missing the discussion of the latest *Deep Space Nine* episode on the trekkie newsgroups? Check here for the addresses, equipment types, and prices for a number of cybercafés nationwide—choose from Café Orbital, Le Web Bar, and many others to get your daily dose of Cyberspace. ✓INTERNET→*url* http://cafe.orbital.fr/cafes/

Tour de France No, this is not a bicycle race! It's a thinking person's guide to France. Pick a destination, and get an illustrated regional overview and a suggested itinerary. Practical information on trains and hotels and a suggested reading list of classic French literature accompany each entry. ✓INTERNET→*url* http://town.hall.org/travel/france/france.html

Regional info

Basque Region A lovely watercolor graces the opening page of this French-language site. Francophones will enjoy the essays on the history, culture, and traditions of the Basque region; others will be attracted by a collection of photos of resorts like Biarritz and fishing towns like St. Jean de Luz. ✓INTERNET→*url* http://wwwbay.univ-pau.fr/Basque/pbasque-page-de-garde.html

Brittany (Bretagne) Click on any Bretagne town for information on hotels, restaurants, and events. ✓INTERNET→*url* http://www.enst-bretagne.fr/Campus/bretagne/

Marseilles Hum along with the famous anthem while visiting a site that features a history and maps of the region. All information here is in French. ✓INTERNET→*url* http://www-resus.univ-mrs.fr/Fr/Marseille/index .html

Nîmes Take a look at Nimes through an historical guide that begins in Rome and ends this morning. Other links lead to guided tours of Pont du Gard and Montpellier. ✓INTERNET→*url* http://www.eerie.fr/Nimes/Nimes.html#REF_ENGLISH

Riviera Events The Riviera has long been known as the haunt of the rich and famous, and Riviera Events does much to enhance that image. Dust off your finery and head out to the Royal Regatta, the gala reopening of the Casino at Grasse, or an evening at Les Ballet Russes. Each entry lists the time and location of the event, as well as a detailed description of its offerings. ✓INTERNET→*url* http://nearnet.gnn.com/gnn/bus/wview/cityhigh/ch1nce.html

Travels in the South of France Ever since that darn book *A Year in Provence* came out, everyone's a travel writer. But this travelogue detailing the author's two weeks in the south of France does provide valuable information to help you plan your own trip—you might find it interesting to know that "Antibes is not particularly friendly to tourists because there are no no-car zones, even down near the seashore," and that a certain café in Avignon offers "a cheap prix fixee menu with chicken liver and lettuce salad, curried rabbit with noodles, and a bottle of Côtes de Rhônes." Hypertext links throughout the essay lead to price and service ratings for each hotel mentioned in the piece. ✓INTERNET→*url* http://gold.interlog.com/~lavender/france/france.htmlw

Paris

Paris—just the name is enough to send most minds wandering down romantic alleys of literature, history, and art. **The Paris Pages** will take you to the Museé d'Orsay to gaze upon Manets and to the cafés frequented by Sartre and Hemingway. Wander the same streets that Marie Antionette and Napoleon rode through in gilded carriages at the **Historical Maps of Paris** site, and ride the Art Nouveau Metro of Colette's *Claudine* by **Tracking Hector Guimard in Paris**. Zip into the 20th century with **Pariscope**'s listings of movies, theater, and music. **Restaurants & Hotels de Paris** helps you book a room on the left bank and **Jorg Zipprick's Culinary Journal** guides you to thc delights of Parisian dining. Don't worry about not speaking the language—**Paris Anglophone** provides a list of friendly ears.

The Champs-Elysées—from http://meteora.ucsd.edu/~norman/paris/

On the Net

Across the board

Paris An electronic guide to Paris with images of the city and links to information about cafes, museums, sightseeing highlights, and stores. The guide includes a Paris Glossary that describes each arrondissement, a searchable English-French dictionary of 75,000 words, and links to Paris schools. And then there are the Metro maps that will help you get anywhere you need to go within the city limits. ✓**INTERNET**→*url* http://meteora.ucsd.edu/~norman/paris/

Paris Museums, Music, Plays and Movie Halls This database is searchable by category (jazz, theater, etc.) and locale (metro stop, *arrondissement*, etc.). Knowledge (even on an elementary level) of French will help you get the most out of this exclusively French-language site. ✓**INTERNET**→*url* http://www.ircam.fr /divers/spectacles-e.html

The Paris Pages (English) The Paris Pages certainly deserve the accolades they have received—they are a complete tourist guide and the next best thing to being there. The site's interactive map links to illustrated précis on museums, monuments, and Metro stations. After viewing .GIFs of Impressionist masterpieces at the Museé de Orsay, cybervisitors can stop in at one of the popular cafés profiled—Le Deux Magots once played host to Hemingway. A culinary journal offers a gastronomic tour, and a glossary offers common French terms. The unique hypertext FAQ links visitors to hotel and hostel sites, a calendar of upcoming events, and other French Web resources. ✓**INTERNET**→*url* http://www.paris.org/

Culture

French National Center for Art and Culture Georges Pompidou Although internationally known as one of the most hideous buildings ever built, it's what's inside the Centre Pompidou that counts—and what's inside adds up to a world-famous collection of twentieth–century art. Check the Website for exhibition calendars and hours for both the museum and its film center. A French-language annotated list of links takes you to the home pages of other art museums worldwide, including The Royal Halloway Collection in London and the Tel Aviv Museum in Israel. ✓**INTERNET**→*url* http://www .cnac-gp.fr/index-e.html

Historical Maps of Paris Wandering through the twisted streets of Paris gives the impression that little has changed in the Medieval capital since the first walls went up. With the help of this collection of essays and maps, you'll find out which pre-Revolution buildings are still standing, and how Baron Hausmann shaped the city at Napoleon's request. ✓**INTERNET**→*url* gopher://gutentag.cc.columbia.edu/11 /fun/pictures/art-history

Pariscope A travel magazine in French, this site can also be enjoyed by all for its attractive presentation of the sights of Paris. Addresses and phone numbers of hotels and restaurants are also available, as are theater schedules, all linked to a map of Paris's 20 arrondissements for easy planning of nights on the town. ✓**INTERNET**→*url* http://www.pariscope.fr/

The Siege and Commune of Paris Relive the important events of 1871 through this wonderful collection of text and images. Over 1,200 photographs, 1,500 caricatures, 1,000 posters, and hundreds of books are online here. All resources are searchable by topic or by format. ✓**INTERNET**→*url* http://www.library.nwu.edu:80/spec/siege/

Guides

Bookstores in Paris An annotated list written by book lovers who indulged themselves in Paris and posted their experiences to rec.arts.books. At this section of the rec.arts .books FAQ, you'll find out what's on the shelves of FNAC (paperbacks in English), where to get cookbooks (Librairie Gourmand), and where to relax with a good novel (Tea and Tattered Pages). And, of course, there's always the jumbled joys of Shakespeare and Company of the Left Bank. ✓**INTERNET**→*url* http://www.cis.ohio-state.edu/hypertext/faq/usenet/books/stores/european/faq-doc-25.html

Nicolas Pioch's Paris Let the curator of the WebMuseum take you on an illustrated stroll around Paris. Visit the highlights of the city, and get a good historical overview (including a detailed history of the Catacombs). ✓**INTERNET**→*url* http://sunsite.unc.edu/wm/paris/

Paris Anglophone English-only tourists can breathe a bit more easily thanks to this list of English-speaking venues in the well-known capital of linguistic nationalism—Paris. It provides the addresses of businesses whose personnel speak English—from purveyors of pet food and pastries to the Paris correspondent of the British tabloid, the *Daily Mail.* Classified ads offer helpful hous-

Fodor's Choice...

Monuments

Eiffel Tower
The 10,000-ton result of a contest held to design a tower for the 1889 World Exposition, the Eiffel Tower is the most-recognized landmark in Paris.

—from Fodor's 96, *Paris*

ing connections. Every month you can enjoy a new online art exhibit and the wise words of the Anglophone opera correspondent. ✓**INTERNET**→*url* http://www.parisanglo.com/

TimeOut Paris *TimeOut* recommends the Prima Lepic in Montmarte for its value, pretty rooms, and excess of flowers, and La Bastide Odéon for an excellent Provençale dinner. This site, based on the weekly magazine of what to do and see in Paris, has done the homework for you, and its events calendar makes sure you won't miss the special character of Paris amid the crowds at the Eiffel Tower and the Louvre. ✓**INTERNET**→*url* http://www.timeout.co.uk/TO/Paris/

Hotels

Paris Hotels Four exclusive hotels—Hotel le Bristol, Hotel de Crillon, Hotel Meurice, and Hotel Ritz—post their rates, addresses, and contact information here. Put on the Ritz, and call to book the private apartment of Coco Chanel or the Windsor suite (former home of Edward and Wallis)! ✓**INTERNET**→*url* http://www.interactive.line.com/alan/lead/paris.html

Le Metro

Magic Paris Take a virtual tour of the magic of the Metro through detailed pictures of St. Michel Metro, out-of-service stations lurking empty under the busy streets, and the Louvre station, which is decorated with priceless art. ✓**INTERNET**→*url* http://www.research.digital.com/PRL/people/patat/art/paris.html

Subway Navigator This site provides maps and plots routes within the Paris Metro and RER systems—showing you where you need to make transfers, and estimating travel times—much like the electronic maps in Paris stations do. The subway navigator site (which includes cities around the world) was designed by a Frenchman. *Bien sur!* ✓**INTERNET**→*url* http://metro.jussieu.fr:10001/bin/select/english/france/paris

The Paris Metro-Tracking Hector Guimard in Paris Follow the sensuous curving Art Noveau trail of architect and decorator Hector Guimard with this lovely illustrated guide and interactive map. Start with the fluid lines adorning the entrance of Abbessess Metro station and move through Paris to the quiet grace of Hotel Particulier, 3 Jasmin Square, and other masterpieces. ✓**INTERNET**→*url* http://www.etca.fr/Users/Sylvain%20Meunier/Guimard/baladepseizeAGL/1erepage.html

Restaurants

Jorg Zipprick's Culinary Journal Jorg tells it like it is about some of the most famous restaurants in Paris—at L'Arpege he was treated to "bizarre stuff like tomatoes filled with fruits, nuts, and sugar" at an exorbitant price. Read his reviews of over 30 Paris restaurants and cafes. ✓**INTERNET**→*url* http://www.paris.org/Jorg

Paris Restaurants It is no surprise that there are numerous dining guides dedicated to the restaurants of Paris—the city is, after all, gastronomic heaven. This text file (courtesy of rec.food.restaurants) shares the experiences of an epicure who ate his way through Paris, from Jeremy's Sandwich Shop to Le Repaire de Bacchus. ✓**INTERNET**→*url* http://www.digmark.net/rec-travel/eats/ParisFrance.eats

Restaurants & Hotels de Paris Search this restaurant database by price, cuisine, location, or features (terrace, salons, music, valet parking). Then learn more about the eateries with the pictures and menus offered here. The site also provides that essential piece of info for each restaurant—what kinds of plastic they take. ✓**INTERNET**→*url* http://oda.sct.fr/

The Louvre—from http://meteora.ucsd.edu/~norman/paris/

Germany

Ever since the reunification of Germany, east and west are only words. Well, not only words—they're markers of a civilization that was torn apart and then put back together, with only the most perfunctory notice paid to the consequences. One of the most villanized nations in the history of the planet—although not without warrant—Germany is also one of the richest and proudest civilizations in Europe. Online visitors can learn about Germany's past and present at sites like the **Deutschland Online Forum** and **The Webfoot's Guide to Germany**, talk about Teutonic culture at **soc.culture.germany**, and get the latest news on Germany's pop music scenes at **VH1derland**.

On the Net

Across the board

Deutschland Online Forum Guten Tag from the gang at the Deutschland Online Forum, where people meet to discuss politics, sports, culture, and music, often in German, but sometimes in English. Check out the ongoing "I Love Deutschland" topic in the Café section, where Germans pass on their knowledge of their native land to those residing in the rest of the world. ✓**COMPUSERVE**→*go* Gerline

From http://www.bavaria.de/muenchen/english/about_munich/attractions.html

Germany William wants to know how to meet a lovely Mädchen when he takes up his post as a fitness instructor in Hanover. But most of those frequenting this board pose more conventional questions—what's a good B&B in Munich, how's the nightlife in Berlin, and how can Karen in Michigan find maternal relatives in Hamburg? ✓**AMERICA ONLINE**→*keyword* Travel Forum→Travel Boards→World Traveler Board→Germany

Germany An encyclopedic source for maps and interesting facts about Germany—did you know that 99 percent of all Germans over the age of 15 can read (although oddly, only 78 percent of all Germans over the age of 15 can read this sentence)? ✓**INTERNET**→*url* http://www.chemie.fu-berlin.de/adressen/brd.html

The Webfoot's Guide to Germany Find out which is the best beer garden in Munich, which Wagner opera is playing at Bayreuth, and where to find the Mercedes-Benz Museum. Lots of city links make planning an itinerary easy. Use the German-language dictionary, the hotel guide, and the exchange calculator to complete your plans. ✓**INTERNET**→*url* http://www.webfoot.com/travel/guides/germany/germany.html

Culture

International Short Film Festival Held in Oberhausen every April, the Festival celebrates the short-film genre with screenings, seminars, and lectures. Get info on attending the event, and read news articles about the short-film community in Germany. ✓**INTERNET**→*url* http://www.uni-duisburg.de/HRZ/IKF/home.html

Maulbronn Monastary A short virtual tour of the Cistercian monastery in Maulbronn, which was built in 1147. ✓**INTERNET**→*url* http://www.bawue.de/~wmwerner/english/maulbron.html

soc.culture.german (ng) Visit the newsgroup to discuss everything to do with Germany—from the hottest German TV shows (*Baywatch* has apparently caught on there) to the recent rise in German nationalism. The newsgroup's FAQ is an excellent resource for travelers: It lists the addresses of German embassies worldwide, explains the difference between an S-bahn and a regular Bundesbahn train (the Bundesbahn charges more for the same service), and details the many inter-city bike routes found between major cities (they are an excellent way to see the countryside). ✓**USENET**→soc.culture.german *FAQ:* ✓**INTERNET**→*url* http://grafton.darmouth.edu:8001/lrc/culture/europe/scg.faq

Suddeutsche Zeitung Search an archive of the German daily. ✓**COMPUSERVE**→*go* suddeutsche

The Week in Germany Contains news articles on cultural and political events in Germany; stories from previous weeks are archived here as well. ✓**INTERNET**→*url* http://langlab.uta.edu/langpages/GIC.html

VH-1derland The Gigs section of this site, which is brought to you by the German version of MTV, tells you where to catch your favorite acts in concert in Germany. The page posts concert dates for Die Ärtze, Simply Red, Marillion, and other international acts, up to 3 months in advance. (German ticket prices tend to be high by American standards, but the venues are smaller, and the crowds are calmer.) ✓**INTERNET**→*url* http://www.vh1.de/

Regional info

Bavaria Alpine Net Guide Come and enjoy the many attractions of Bavaria. Start with the excellent architectural tour, where a sound file plays the chimes of the bell tower in Theatinerkirche. An annotated list of museums and an opera schedule round out the culture section, each accompanied by a witty introduction by a Bavarian native. The Special Highlights section provides illustrated essays on "Mad" King Ludwig II (builder of the fairy-tale castle Neuschwanstein), Oktoberfest (including a map of all the beer tents in Munich), and rafting down the Isar (complete with prices). Additional profiles present the attractions of the Englisher Garten, beer gardens, and the Munich flea market. There are the tips on the nuances of Bavarian culture, such as how to tell the difference between Weissbeir and Dunkels and where to get the best coffee. Yankees get special attention at this site; they should be advised to bring their boots (Germans love country-western wear). And if that weren't enough, you can also get a Bavaria Net T-shirt (my parents went virtually to Bavaria, and all I got was this lousy T-shirt). ✓**INTERNET**→*url* http://www.bavaria.com/

Cologne

Zoologischer Garten Köln Leopards do not suffer in translation, neither do lemurs, and this site has full-color pictures of both. Prospective visitors to this Cologne zoo site will easily puzzle out hours and directions from the German text, and undoubtedly be very intrigued by the mention of the "Insectic Park." ✓**INTERNET**→*url* http://sunserver1.rz.uniduesseldorf.de/~nast/zoo/cologzoo/.cologzoohtml

Munich

Munich Munich is more than just the site of that yearly international beer blast called Oktoberfest (which isn't even in October, by the way). It's also the home of the double-towered Frauenkirche, of the elegant shops of Maximilianstaße, and the Englischer Garten. This Website looks at these and other highlights of the city through essays and photographs. And yes, there's also info on Oktoberfest. ✓**INTERNET**→*url* http://www.bavaria.de/Munich//

Netplace Munich Online This illustrated city portrait provides pictures of landmarks such as the Alter Peter and the Hofbrau Haus and contains a cultural calendar. Hotel and restaurant listings include prices and locations—how about a Mexikanisch dinner? ✓**INTERNET**→*url* http://www.netplace.com/netplace/munich_online.html

Screen capture from Bavaria Alpine Net Guide—from http://www.bavaria.com/

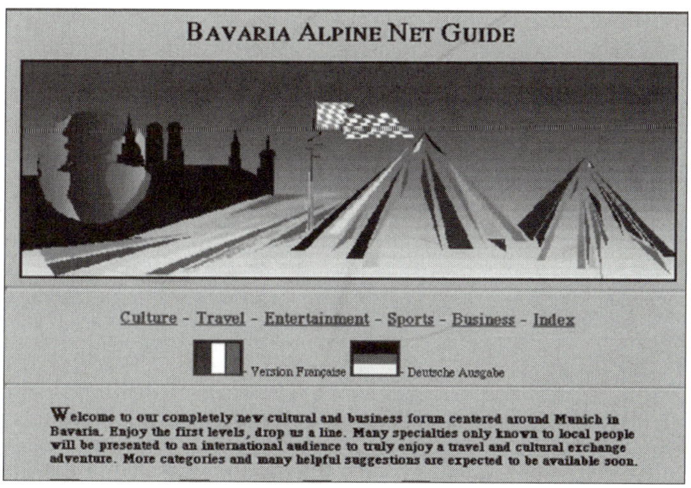

Berlin

Lincoln said that a nation divided against itself would not stand; Berlin transplanted this national aphorism to a metropolitan context and disproved it, weathering the partitioning that followed World War II and persisting, split, until 1989, when the Berlin Wall toppled and a reunified Berlin became the capital of a reunified Germany. From general sites like **Berlin** to more specific pages on everything from film (**45th International Berlin Film Festival, Kinoprogramm**) to cars (**Porsche Museum**), the Net showcases the best that Berlin has to offer.

Charlottenburg Castle—from http://www.chemie.fu-berlin.de/adressen/berlin.html

On the Net

Across the board

Berlin It takes a little traveling to get to the tourist info at this site. After reading the illustrated history of Berlin contained on the introductory page, choose the City Info topic for a citywide events calendar, city transportation maps (for the U-bahn, trains, buses, and Straßenbahn), and lists of post offices and municipal swimming pools. Other links lead to more about the "new" Berlin. ✓**INTERNET**→*url* http://www.chemie.fu-berlin.de/adressen/berlin.html

Culture

45th International Berlin Film Festival Currently, information on the 1995 Festival is found here, including profiles of films and directors like Norway's Maurius Holst and America's Robert Redford. Info on the 1996 Festival is scheduled to go up the event in February. ✓**INTERNET**→*url* http://fub46.zedat.fu-berlin.de:8080/~frs/bff-index.html

Berliner BTX-Daten Homonyms are a gift to the monolingual—they let you use this events database even though it's presented (oddly enough) in Berlin's native language. Simply plug in a date and /or a type of activity (concert, jazz, theater, etc.), and you'll soon receive a list of goings-on during your visit, plus public transportation directions to events such as the Berliner Dixieland Festival. ✓**INTERNET**→*url* http://www.is.in-berlin.de/cgi-bin/Senat-wais

Berliner Veranstaltungskalender Week-by-week listings of events across the city, including info on theater, concerts, and sporting events. The list is entirely in German. ✓**INTERNET**→*url* http://www.infopark.de/cgi-bin/veranst/in.pl

Deutsches Museum Find price information, the museum's hours, and a description of its collection at this Website for the famous museum devoted to science and technology. ✓**INTERNET**→*url* http://130.183.24.194/fdt.html

German Historical Museum, Berlin Sometimes a picture is worth 1,000 words, and if you don't speak German very well, you'll appreciate the power of the photographs at this site. Only a few of the illustrated essays, which annotate the museum's current exhibitions, are translated into English. Along with the previews of the exhibits, the Website offers museum hours and directions by subway and car. ✓**INTERNET**→*url* http://www.dhm.de/

Interactive Events Database Search this German-language Berlin events site by category—ballet, rock-and-roll clubs, etc. ✓**INTERNET**→*url* http://www.is.in-berlin.de/g-Berlin/Veranstaltungskalendar.html

Kinoprogramm Geh ins Kino with this weekly movie listing that's updated every Tuesday. You can search the database by day of show, title of film, or theater name. After you've selected a showing, the database provides directions to the theater. ✓**INTERNET**→*url* http://www.infopark.de/cgi-bin/kino/in.pl

Porsche Museum If you love fast cars, you won't make any pit stops on your way to this site, which not only profiles the history of the German car manufacturer, but also explains how to get to (and into) the museum. ✓**INTERNET**→ *url* http://192.253.114.31/Stuttgart/Porsche/Porsche_contents.html

Roman Open-Air Museum Learn about these ruins of a Roman camp that lay hidden under the dirt of Hechingen-Stein for over 1,700 years until they were discovered in 1973. Find out how to tour the site, which features a rebuilt Roman barracks. ✓**INTERNET**→*url* http://hades.tue.schwaben.de/sportrait/stein/stein_e.html

Guides

Berlin Bear Though this online magazine is in the formative stages, it already has terrific information for the Berlin-bound younger crowd. Be sure to check out their reviews of bars, cafés, and clubs before heading out for the evening—they'll tell you the best Platz for people watching and where not to go if you wish to avoid excessive numbers of teens. The restaurant guide will make you seem like a native by priming you with the name and address of the best Schnellimbiß (french fries and sausages) in town and the knowledge that Austrian cuisine is definitely not the same as German. A city guide proffers further information on everything from hotels and subways to dry cleaners and casinos. ✓**INTERNET**→*url* http://www.berlin-bear.de/

Berlin von A-Z A German-language hypertext guide to the famous sites of Berlin—Alexanderplatz, Potsdammer Platz, the Egyptisches Museum, the Reichstag. Make a list of things to see, then get subway, streetcar, and bus directions at the Website. ✓**INTERNET**→*url* http://www.informatik.hu-berlin.de/Freizeit/berlin/

Kulturbox: Tourist Highlights in Berlin and Potsdam Photos and brief annotations at this site enable prospective visitors to correctly identify landmarks such as Schloss Pfaueninsel, the TV Tower, and the modern Congress Center, called "the pregnant oyster" by the locals. ✓**INTERNET**→*url* http://www.kulturbox.de/stadt/btm/bedsehee.htm

TimeOut Berlin The people at *TimeOut* (who make it their business to know absolutely everything that's hip and happening) have turned their attention to Berlin at this site. Get with it with the help of the events calendar—how about cruising the "totalitarian" art on display at Martin-Gropius Bau, or listening to the strains of James Carter's tenor sax at The Quasimodo? Feature articles portray the life of contemporary Berlin—one focuses on Rose Zone, an "erotic contortionist" who performs for circus audiences and heads of state. And, there's the always-valuable TimeOut Guide, a must-read for all travelers, with suggestions on accommodations (from the Hotel-Pension Funk to the Hotel Inter-Continental), museums, restaurants, cafés, and clubs. If you're on your way nach Berlin, you can't ask for a better guide. After your trip, add your own recommendations to the pot by sending an online postcard to the editor. ✓**INTERNET**→*url* http://www.timeout.co.uk/TO/Berlin/

Fodor's Choice...

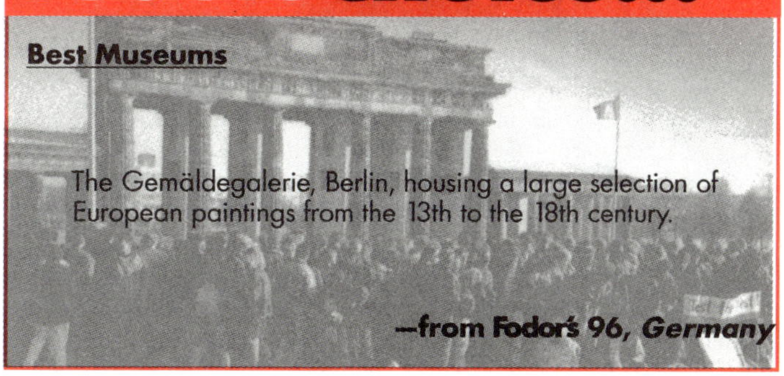

Best Museums

The Gemäldegalerie, Berlin, housing a large selection of European paintings from the 13th to the 18th century.

—from Fodor's 96, *Germany*

Greece

Without Greece, Western Civilization would be diminished to the point of invisibility, a culture with divots removed from its philosophy, literature, historiography, and medicine. Between Plato, Aristotle, and Homer, the Ancient Greeks laid the groundwork for European culture, and remnants of that glory are everywhere in the present-day nation. If travel in the Hellenic world is all Greek to you, get on the Net. Why? Well, online resources range from general discussions and guides like **Greece**, **Hellas List Home Page**, and **Greece: Travel Info** to more specific Websites like **The Island of Crete**, **The City of Thessaloniki**, and **Mount Athos.**

The Parthenon—from http://www.perseus.tufts.edu/

On the Net

Across the board

Greece Gary posts a message to this board asking for tips on where to take his new bride, Anne, for their honeymoon in Greece. Others ask for tour company recommendations or post ecstatic reviews of their trips to the jewels of the Aegean. A few helpful warnings are posted here—beware of cab drivers on the lookout for foreigners and men on the lookout for vacationing women. ✓ **AMERICA ONLINE**→*keyword* Travel Forum→Travel Boards→World Traveler Board→Greece

Greece: Travel Info Greece has 1,400 islands, and Greek mythology has nearly as many gods, goddesses and half-immortals. You'll learn about them all at this site, which provides a primer on Greek mythology, along with much-needed ferry schedules. You'll also get illustrated essays on Greek taverns and the proper tip for a taxi in Mykonos. If your thirst for knowledge about Greece is still not fulfilled, use the links to head to info on museums, a Greek-culture FAQ, Greek-language primers, and even the current Athens weather! ✓ **INTERNET**→*url* http://iris.usc.edu/home/iris/kardaras/tourist.html

Hellas List Home Page More than just a travel site with lists of hotels and restaurants, this page of links is the Web counterpart to the popular Hellas mailing list, whose logs and newsfeed are easily accessed here. Or head to soc.culture.greece for immediate discussion of important topics like "Why Greeks Hate Turks" and "Is Hellenism Racist?" Additional links allow you to make your own Greek-language calendar, contact a Greek embassy, and keep up with the Greek cartoon *Epikairo.* ✓ **INTERNET**→*url* http://velox.stanford.edu/hellas/HellasListHomePage

Culture

Architecture & Architectural Sculpture of the Mediterranean Basin An annotated catalog of more than 2,000 images of classical and Hellenistic architecture in Italy, Greece, and Turkey. ✓ **INTERNET**→*url* http://www.ncsa.uiuc.edu/SDG/Experimental/anu-arthistory/architecture.html

Hellas OnLine Greece—the home of feta cheese and Aristophanes. Learn about Greek culture while you drink in the sites at this excellent hypertext guide. Links lead to overviews of classical art and literature, a photo album of magical locales (Thessaloniki, Corfu, and Naxos), pages on sailing the Aegean and Ionian Seas, and even a homage to Greek Nobel Laureate Odysseas Elytis. ✓**INTERNET**→*url* http://www.hol.gr/greece/

Museums of Greece You'll find this a wonderful place to spend a rainy afternoon previewing the collections of major Greek museums. Take your time strolling through the online offerings of the Cartoon Museum or World War II–era photos from the Crete Historical Museum of the National Resistance. ✓**INTERNET**→*url* gopher://ithaki.servicenet.ariadne-t.gr:70/11/HELLENIC_CIVILIZATION/MUSEUMS/ART_MUSEUMS

---

soc.culture.greek (ng) Discuss and learn anything to do with Greece at this newsgroup—what wine to order with *spanikopita,* how to count to ten in Greek, which island offers the best surfing, which god turned into a bull to pick up chicks, and what *ahinos* means on a menu (sea urchin). The newsgroup's FAQ is a warehouse of useful info for travelers—you'll get restaurant, hotel, and resort recommendations, as well as a list of helpful Greek phrases, like "Miláte angliká?" which means "Do you speak English?" ✓**USENET**→soc.culture.greek *FAQ:* ✓**INTERNET**→*url* http://www.cis.ohio-state.edu/hypertext/faq/usenet/greek-faq/top.html

---

The Ancient City of Athens Maps and photographs of the remains of Greece's Golden Era. ✓**INTERNET**→*url* http://www.indiana.edu/~kglowack/Athens/Athens.html

---

Tour of Greece Improve your knowledge of Greek culture past and present at this Website. Links connect to profiles of The Greats of Antiquity—Aesop, Aeschylus, Aristophanes, Homer, etc.—and to the full text of those works that gave birth to the concept "classic." Other links lead to a history of the Olympics and to sound files of modern folk music. There's even an interactive map that serves up luscious pictures of suggested tourist venues. ✓**INTERNET**→*url* http://www.hol.gr/greece/

Guides

Sailing in the Greek Isles Sailing the deep blue Aegean from sun-drenched island to sun-drenched island...if that sounds heavenly to you, then head to this illustrated guide that tells the skipper about the winds and waves of the Aegean. Besides the purely nautical info, the site also offers indexes of estimated costs for bareboat charters. ✓**INTERNET**→*url* http://mail.eskimo.com/~dianee/greece.htm

Crete

The Island of Crete Weave your way through the ancient home of Ariadne and the Minotaur! This illustrated tourist guide to Crete describes the frescoes and mountains of this rocky island paradise. Hotel information will be available soon. ✓**INTERNET**→*url* http://www.forthnet.gr/crete/index.html

Thessaloniki

Archeological Museum of Thessaloniki An illustrated hypertext essay about Greece's second largest city, named for the sister of Alexander the Great. ✓**INTERNET**→*url* http://uranus.eng.auth.gr/museum/color/

Mount Athos Cleanse your spirit with a trip to Mount Athos (or Hagion Oros, i.e., Holy Mountain), the heart of the Christian orthodoxy. Tour the Mount with the text and photographs housed here. ✓**INTERNET**→*url* http://zeus.csd.auth.gr/athos/

The City of Thessaloniki An illustrated hypertext essay about Greece's second largest city, named for the sister of Alexander the Great. ✓**INTERNET**→*url* http://uranus.eng.auth.gr/new/eng/thessaloniki.html

Tourists crowding the Acropolis—from http://libra.caup.umich.edu/ArchiGopher/

Hungary

In Hungary, you'll need only one word: paprika. Paprika, or powdered red pepper, is everywhere—alongside the salt and pepper on restaurant tables in Esztergom, on grilled chicken in the shop windows of Budapest. Whether you're crossing the Margit Bridge from Buda or waterskiing on Lake Balaton, the tang of paprika will linger in your nostrils, on your tongue...Of course, Hungary has more to offer than a condiment. Check out **Theaters in Budapest**, the **Home Page of Nyiregyhaza**, and **Hostels in Hungary** for hints and tips on traveling in the Magyar nation.

The Parliament building in Budapest—http://www.fsz.bme.hu/hungary/

On the Net

Across the board

Hungarian Information Resources Links to all things Hungarian in Cyberspace are certain to be housed here. Travel to the Hungarian Boogie-Woogie home page for a list of clubs that feature boogie music, link to a site that offers timetables for a train trip across the country, or pick up a recipe for Hungarian cherry soup by linking to the Hungarian Cuisine page. ✓**INTERNET**→*url* http://mineral.umd.edu/hir/

Hungarian Tourist Board Don't fail to visit this site if you're planning a trip to Hungary. It holds invaluable info—the office hours and telephone numbers of train-station ticket counters nationwide, a timetable for the hydrofoil that operates between Budapest and Vienna, a map showing rest-stop locations along major Hungarian highways, plus an alphabetical list of other practical travel info that includes an events calendar, a list of cambios across the country, and a list of brochures that can be ordered from the Tourist Board for further reading offline. ✓**INTERNET**→*url* http://www.hungary.com/tourinform/

Culture

Hungarian Cuisine Explore the food of the region at this Website. Pictures and recipes for Hungarian favorites, including chitterling sausages, paprika chicken, and Budapest tenderloin steak, are available. ✓**INTERNET**→*url* http://www.fsz.bme.hu/hungary/cuisine/cuisine.htm

Hungary This illustrated essay on the joys of Hungary begins with a quote from Enrico Fermi (an Italian), whose response to the question "Do extra-terrestrial beings exist?" was "Of course, they are already here among us; they are called Hungarians." Learn more about this unique culture and its capital in the hypertext essay located here. ✓**INTERNET**→*url* http://www.fsz.bme.hu/hungary/intro.html

Hungary-L (ml) An English-language mailing list for discussion of current events and culture in Hungary. ✓**INTERNET** ...→*email* hungary@ucsbvm.bitnet ✍ *Write a request* ...→*email* listserv@ucsbvm.bitnet ✍ *Write a request*

Hotels

Hostels in Hungary An alphabetical list of youth hostels, most of which are in or around Budapest, with the phone numbers and addresses of each hostel. ✓**INTERNET**→*url* ftp://ftp.cc.umanitoba.ca/rec-travel/hostels/eu.hu.html

Budapest

Budapest The history and culture of the Hungarian capital are explored in this brief illustrated essay—learn how to make real Budapest-style goulash at home, and discover the natives' choices for the best drinks "to rinse your throat." ✓**INTERNET**→*url* http://www.fsz.bme.hu/hungary/budapest/budapest.html

Theaters in Budapest An alphabetical list of play and movie houses in the city known worldwide as the "pearl of the Danube." ✓**INTERNET**→*url* gopher://goliat.eik.bme.hu/00/hun/fali/Budapest-info/szinhaz/szinhazak.txt

Ireland

If you find yourself irresistibly drawn toward your one pair of green socks in the middle of March, you'll no doubt enjoy traveling to Ireland virtually, or otherwise. **Ireland: The Internet Collection** and **Irish and Celtic Things** are good places to start seeking little folk and tourist attractions in **CyberIreland**. Got a granny that claims to have been County Kerry gentry? Check her story through the genealogy links at the **Virtual Tourist Guide to Ireland**. Grab a pint of stout at one of the houses featured in **Chris Zimmerman's Dublin Pub Guide**, or stay at home and drink along with other online bog-men at the **Virtual Irish Pub**. The special lyricism of Ireland is held in the strains of music at **Ceolas-Celtic Music on the Internet**, and the melodious voices at **Gaelic and Gaelic Culture**.

The Dublin Castle—http://www.misty.com/ulysses/vip/tourism/dublin/dublin.htm

On the Net

Across the board

Ireland: The Internet Collection Though this collection of links has little organization, treasures are buried here if you're willing to dig. You can bone up on Irish history and culture by linking to the Irish Emigrant archives, the music archives from rec.music.celtic, the many pages dedicated to soccer scores, and even the recent Joint Peace Declaration. The Irish Law Page will help you keep out of trouble during your visit, and a trip to the Irish Genealogical Page will help you locate your ancestral home across the ocean. Gaelic speakers should jump to the library of Gaelic-L or the CURIA project to keep up on current events in Ireland. ✓**INTERNET**→*url* http://itdsrv1.ul.ie/Information/Ire land.html

Virtual Tourist Guide to Ireland Let the Web do your touring for you, by organizing the many Irish-related links in this hub. Choose a site by location, from Donegal to Dublin, or by subject—current affairs, literature, music, genealogy—and then head out into Irish Cyberspace. ✓**INTERNET**→*url* http://www.bess.tcd.ie/ireland.html

Culture

Ceolas-Celtic Music on the Internet Ceolas brags that it has the most complete collection of Celtic music information on the Net. Its many links are to online 'zines, listings of radio stations carrying *Thistle & Shamrock*, album reviews, sound clips, artist profiles, and concert listings for events worldwide. ✓**INTERNET**→*url* http://celtic.stanford.edu/ceolas.html

Gaelic and Gaelic Culture Listen to the melodious sounds of the three variants of Gaelic (Irish, Manx, and Scottish) here. Essays elaborate on the history of the Celts, and a FAQ from soc.culture.celtic answers questions about this tenacious culture. Further connections lead to the Gaelic-L library, sites dedicated to Gaelic music, online Gaelic instruction, and news sources. ✓**INTERNET**→*url* http://sunsite.unc.edu/gaelic/

Irish and Celtic Things Links to sites on Irish and Celtic things—stone circles, leprechauns, pennywhistles, and the writings of James Joyce—are offered here. Visit the Irish Soccer Homepage and get a list of matches. Or link to the Dublin Pub Guide and the Edinburgh Malt Whiskey Tour for a taste of what makes the leprechauns happy. ✓**INTERNET**→*url* http://celtic.stanford.edu/pmurphy/irish.html

---

soc.culture.celtic/soc.culture.irish (ng) Visit these newsgroups for news and discussion of Ireland and its citizens around the world—read about the Galway races, participate in The Great Debate (what's the best pub in Dublin), or get tips on where to buy a real Irish pennywhistle. ✓**USENET**→soc.culture.celtic/soc.culture.irish

---

The Irish Times Get a daily fix of things Irish with this abbreviated version of the *Irish Times*. There's the front page, of course, but the real meat lies in the home pages, football scores, and editorials—today enjoy the debate over loosening divorce laws. ✓**INTERNET**→*url* http://www.ieunet.ie/ois/irishtimes/index.shtml

---

Virtual Irish Pub It's the next best thing to being there—except, of course, virtual beer isn't nearly as delicious as the real thing. Wander into the bar, choose a table, and settle in for a chat on literature and classics, music, history, sport, and theater, or head to the live talk room for a chat. The Explore Ireland table holds a clickable map and guides to each county that contain overviews of attractions and hotel information. ✓**INTERNET**→*url* http://www.misty.com/ulysses/vip/a_vip.htm

Hotels

The Crock of Gold Tourist Information Pages A selection of pages dedicated to guesthouses, hotels, and hostels in Ireland, such as Cairbre House, built for the Duke of Devonshire in 1819, or the Rathe House Equestrian Centre. Get telephone numbers and addresses for each of the accommodations listed here. ✓**INTERNET**→*url* http://www.ripi.ie/ipi/tourism/index.html

Cork

Cork City An illustrated essay introduces prospective visitors to Cork, a city of bridges. A well-stocked visitor center provides information on transportation, exchange rates, sightseeing, selected accommodations, restaurants, and most important, pubs, which are evaluated by clientele and special attributes. Wear your Doc Martens and nose ring to the An Brog, and catch the rising stars of Irish folk music at The Lobby. ✓**INTERNET**→*url* http://symphony.ucc.ie/~niall/cork.html

Dublin

Chris Zimmerman's Dublin Pub Guide Stereotypes tell us that the Irish love their drink. (James Joyce once remarked that it was nearly impossible to walk through Dublin without passing a pub.) But who wouldn't want to spend time downing a creamy pint of Guinness in the likes of the Angler's Rest? Chris Zimmerman has assembled a collection of reviews that include price guides based on the unit of basic nutrition (pint of Guinness), as well as ratings of the musical offerings at the clubs and pubs. ✓**INTERNET**→*url* http://www.dsg.cs.tcd.ie:/dsg_people/czimmerm/pubs.html

Dublin An unannotated collection of links to Dublin resources, from the Dublin Pub Guide to Trinity University. ✓**INTERNET**→*url* http://www.bess.tcd.ie/dublin.html

---

Dublin Bedrock Theatre Company Find out what and who's playing in this group dedicated to Irish theater. ✓**INTERNET**→*url* http://www.maths.tcd.ie/~pmoloney/bedrock/

Guide to Dublin Follow in the steps of Leopold Bloom with this online map of Dublin. This site, with its comprehensive lists of hotels, businesses, and pubs, helps you decide where to stay, where to shop, and where to drink—The Brazen Head has been pulling pints for over 300 years. ✓**INTERNET**→*url* http://www.cs.tcd.ie/ud/www/dwbyrne/

Galway

The Complete Guide To Galway Galway is a university town, full of activities for all—from angling to dancing. The up-to-the-minute events calendar will keep you current on what's on at the movies and who's playing in pubs like the Pocahontas and the Furry Village. Details on yearly events such as Galway's Arts and Oyster Festivals are also included, along with guides to accommodations, eating, and shopping that offer tips on cheap places to eat and stay (check out the backpackers' guide for further information). ✓**INTERNET**→*url* http://wombatix.physics.ucg.ie/galway/index.html

Italy

The mind boggles when given the task of thinking of all the wonderful things that are Italian—calamari in red sauce, the original gladiators, family loyalty, leaning towers, long evenings drinking coffee and watching the world go by, and the Renaissance. **Windows on Italy** and **The Webfoot's Guide to Italy** help you experience these joys virtually or plan a real visit. The **Florence WWW**, **WetVenice**, and **In Sardegna Virtual** are all potent lures as well. Don't forget to dust away the ash of time at **Pompeii**, and visit **Romarch** to experience the glory that was Rome. While **Italian Nights** will show you the glory that is...Rome, Milan, and Pisa. And best of all, **Italy's Hotel Directory** can get you a room with a view.

The Coliseum in Rome—http://www.tulane.edu/lester/text/Western.Architect/Rome/

On the Net

Across the board

InItaly Online This online magazine is dedicated to "all things Italian." Choose a locale and discover a list of festivals and essays on local cuisine and culture. Or head to the message board to post questions on good honeymoon spots or car rental in Portofino. There is a resident travel agent promising bargains as well. Don't neglect the special essays on the churches of Rome. ✓ **INTERNET**→*url* http://www.lainet.com/~initaly/

The Webfoot's Guide to Italy Looking for a room with a view in Florence? Simply click on any one of six hotel directories at this site for information on accommodations nationwide. You can also find a vegetarian restaurant in Padua or get the lira exchange rate by using the links at this page. Other links to local home pages give you a feel for cities like Firenze and Trieste. And Italian speakers will enjoy the links to Italian-language newspapers and magazines. ✓ **INTERNET**→*url* http://www.webfoot.com/travel/guides/italy/italy.html

Windows On Italy This site is a large collection of bilingual links for travelers and for Italians in the homeland and on Mott Street. Many daily Italian newspapers—right, center, and left—are just a jump away, as are virtual tours of numerous cities from Milan to Naples. From here you can read essays on the wine festival in Florence and on touring the Vatican. ✓ **INTERNET**→*url* http://www.mi.cnr.it/WOI/

Culture

Il Sole 24 Hore Search an archive of the Italian daily. ✓ **COMPUSERVE**→*go* ilsole

Italia Online An Italian language site sponsored by the State University of Milan that gathers links on Italian culture, politics, and the Italian presence in Cyberspace. ✓ **INTERNET**→*url* http://www.dsi.unimi.it/Users/Students/lodi/wb-text.html

Italian Forum Come to this forum to learn up-to-the-minute travel information (if there's going to be an airline strike in Italy, the message board at this site lights up) or to peruse the traveler-friendly libraries, which are stuffed with reviews on restaurants and hotels in Italy. ✓ **COMPUSERVE**→*go* Italfo

Italian Lessons Get the most out of your trip to Italy by picking up some key phrases at this site. Each lesson consists of subject-related vocabulary instructions—learn important words to use in restaurants, train stations and at Italian customs checks. There's an interactive quiz at the end of each lesson to test your newfound knowledge. ✓**INTERNET**→*url* http://www.willamette.edu/~tjones/languages/Italian/Italian-lesson.html

Italian Nights Wonder no longer how to spend the evenings after viewing leaning towers, Coliseums, or Doge's palaces. This list of evening activities is organized by city. When in Tuscany join the crowd for music and wine at La Loggia in Pisa (address and phone number included), and when in Rome... ✓**INTERNET**→*url* http://www.cibernet.it/notti_italiane/italn.htm

Pompeii This is the closest anyone has come in the last thousand years to walking the streets of Pompeii. In this wonderful, full-color plan of the ancient city, visitors move a little figure through doorways, around corners to temples, villas, and squares—each lavishly illustrated and minutely described. You'll learn about Paganism at the altar of Diana and roofing practices through an architectural animation. It's worth several hours of exploration. ✓**INTERNET**→*url* http://jefferson.village.virginia.edu:80/pompeii/page-1.html

soc.culture.italian (ng) You'll need to know a few words in the language of love in order to enjoy the conversation at the newsgroup, which is almost exclusively in Italian (the only English-language posts are from Americans asking for help with their Italian). Perhaps more useful

Fodor's Choice...

Where Art Comes First

SISTINE CHAPEL, THE VATICAN

Under everything-old-is-new-again comes Michelangelo's awe-inspiring ceiling, freshly restored and glowing in bright colors.

—from **Fodor's 96, *Italy***

for travelers is the newsgroup's FAQ—entire sections of it are devoted to tourism, the arts, and traditional customs in Italy. ✓**USENET**→soc.culture.italian *FAQ:* ✓**INTERNET**→*url* http://www.lib.ox.ac.uk/internet/news/faq/soc.culture.italian.html

Hotels

Italy Hotel Reservation More than 2,000 hotels are listed in this database, which is searchable by price, rating, or name through a clickable map. Online booking is available. ✓**INTERNET**→*url* http://www.venere.it/home/italy.html

Italy's Hotel Directory A listing of hotels preferred by Italians themselves to permit visitors to "do as the Romans do" when they visit Bologna, Naples, Milan, and Florence, among others. Each hotel is given a star rating and telephone and fax numbers are included. ✓**INTERNET**→*url* http://www.italia.com/tradenet /HOTELS/hotel_list.html

Florence

Florence WWW Although the hotel and restaurant listing of this Website is still under construction, you will find a comprehensive listing of Florence's famous museums. There are also photo essays on the city by the Arno, a guide to Tuscany wines, and a calendar of local events (Art Garfunkel's playing in October) housed here. ✓**INTERNET**→*url* http://www.inib.it/staff/max/florence.ht

Genoa

Genoa Home Page Stroll down the streets that were home to Romeo and Juliet courtesy of this site which provides illustrated holiday suggestions as well as lists of museums, theaters, and transportation options. Stroll along the sea at Cogoleto, or join in the Mimosa Festival—the virtual tours are worth the time spent downloading the pictures. ✓INTERNET→*url* http://www.doit.it/Tourism/genova/genoa.html

Milan

La Scala Find out who's belting out arias at the world's most famous opera house with this guide to La Scala. There is a complete searchable calendar of the upcoming season and information on pricing and telephone ticket sales—a seat in the stalls for La Boheme will set you back 270,000 lire. An English-language biography of the director Riccardo Muti and plot synopsis of the house's signature opera *La Traviata* are also included. ✓INTERNET→*url* http://lascala.milano.it/

Milan The site's photo of the view from the roof of the Duomo might just sell you on a Milanese holiday. If you'd like to see the view from the Duomo yourself, check out the tourist information here for lists of four-star hotels (like Dei Cavalieri) or one-star establishments (like Casa Mia). The site also provides lists of theaters, museums, and restaurants (the price of items like *tartine*–sliced white bread is included). ✓INTERNET→*url* http://www.dsi.unimi.it/Users/Students/markus/milan/milan.html

Naples

Golfo Porte Aperte Italian-language guide to Naples including many illustrated descriptions of local attractions. Those with a modicum of initiative can puzzle out the opening times and museum content. ✓INTERNET→*url* http://www.dsnet.it/cgi-bin/cgi-gennaro/golfo.pl

History of Napoli This short text essay tells the story of the city of Parthenope from its time as a summer playground for the Roman emperors up through the present. ✓INTERNET→*url* http://sun01.iigb.na.cnr.it/napoli/neaples.html

Naples Images Enjoy a taste of Napoli with your eyes and ears through this collection of pictures and music from the southern city. ✓INTERNET→*url* http://www.na.infn.it/Images/images.html

Rome & Venice

Romarch Learn to do as the Romans did at this Website with essays on Roman life, law, and aesthetics, as well as detailed archeological reports from all corners of the formerly far-flung empire. Just choose an area like Britannia and you'll be thrown into an army encampment in the cold north near Hadrian's Wall. Or head to Gallia and explore a shipwreck off the coast of France. This is a perfect site for Roman researchers of all ages. ✓INTERNET→*url* http://www.umich.edu/~pfoss/ROMARCH.html

Spalato Exhibit Lifestyles of the rich and famous, circa 293. A virtual exhibit lets you wander the halls of this gem of late Roman architecture—through the great walls and gate, ornate entrance hall, bed chambers, and even the vaults where the Emperor Diocletian tortured his enemies. ✓INTERNET→*url* http://sunsite.unc.edu/expo/palace.exhibit/intro.html

Vatican City An amazingly rich site that opens with the full text of the latest speeches made by the city's most famous resident. The site also provides a full history of the city and .GIFs of its flag and maps of its streets. But the best part of the site is the online gallery of images from the famous museums and churches located in Vatican City—at this site you can preview over 300 images from the Sistine Chapel and close to 600 images from other selected Vatican museums. ✓INTERNET→*url* http://www.christusrex.org/www1/citta/0-Citta.html

WETVenice If you can't get to the Biennale this year, this site tells you what you're missing at the Palazzo Grassi. While you're here, take a virtual tour of eighteenth-century Venice or visit the home page of the Venice Carnival. Excellent train and hotel information is available for those traveling the old-fashioned way. ✓INTERNET→*url* http://cidoc.iuav.unive.it/wetvenice/wetvenice.html

Sardinia

In Sardegna Virtual Flip open the pages of this online magazine for illustrated essays on the island of Sardinia. Local ferry timetables and festival calendars are included. ✓INTERNET→*url* http://www.crs4.it/~cirio/ISV/

Sardinia A collection of links for prospective tourists that offers great visuals—from an annotated map to a gallery of photographs of Sardinia to a hypermedia tour of the National Archaeological Museum of Cagliari. Suggested tourist itineraries help plan days of strolling through cathedrals and eating calimari. ✓INTERNET→*url* http://www.crs4.it/~zip/sardinia/sardinia.html

The Netherlands

Holland—land of cheese and chocolate, Rembrant and red lights, windmills and the World Court. Where to begin? A journey through the canals of Amsterdam at night is a must; dinner at Excelsior's in Amsterdam, a treat (if your budget allows); an afternoon at the world-famous Rijksmuseum, a requiste (if you have any cultural pretensions at all); and a visit to a "coffehouse," a liberating experience. Bone up on sightseeing opportunities in the Netherlands with Net resources. Start with the **Netherlands Board of Tourism** and **Museums in the Netherlands.**

A windmill—from http://dru.knoware.nl/friesland/business/images.htm

On the Net

Across the board

Netherlands Board of Tourism According to this online guide, Holland has enough museums to keep a tourist busy for a decade. But not all travelers like museums. Those who prefer more outdoorsy recreation can check the helpful tips here on renting boats and bikes nationwide. Find your accommodations at this Website as well—why wait with the desperate hordes at Centraal Station's tourist window when you can reserve a room ahead of time with the help of the hotel phone numbers provided here? ✓**INTERNET**→*url* http://www.xxlink.nl/nbt /home.htm

Netherlands Forum Learn more about the Dutch in this bilingual forum. Discuss topics ranging from the Dutch language, hotel recommendations, and biking (important in Amsterdam!) to Dutch art, politics, music, and airlines. Turn to the libraries for photographs of Dutch people and places (yes, there are pictures of both little blond girls in wooden clogs and the requisite windmills). The background information about the Netherlands, provided by Dutch natives, will help your trip to the Low Country run more smoothly. ✓**COMPUSERVE**→*go* dutch→Message *and* Libraries

Netherlands Travel Board Amsterdam is probably the only city in the world with museums dedicated to Van Gogh, sex, and cigarette lighters. If you're planning a trip to this land of extreme contrasts, visit the Travel Board first for cheap airfare tips, hotel suggestions, or travelogues of other travelers' experiences. ✓**AMERICA ONLINE**→*keyword* travel forum →Travel Boards→ The World Traveler Board→Belgium/Netherlands/ Luxembourg

XS4All The Netherlands' version of Yahoo! At this collection of links, you can access local and regional news, weather, media resources, and local movie databases. Links here connect to the home pages of other XS4All subscribers and to home pages for Dutch companies, local tourist boards, community organizations, and European Community resources. There's even a link to the Dirty Dutch page, which will teach you some key Dutch phrases. ✓**INTERNET**→*url* http://www.xs4all.nl

Culture

Dick's Domain If you'd like to avoid seeing second-run American films in Amsterdam's cinemas, or you don't want to watch *Jake and the Fatman* on a Dutch TV station, here is your source for Holland's home-grown entertainment. Learn about Dutch film stars (other than Rutger Hauer and Jeroen Krabbé), tune in to *West Side Posse* on TV, and take a look at *Amsterdamned*, a gruesome murder mystery set in the official Dutch capital. ✓**INTERNET**→*url* http://www.euronet.nl/users/action/dick001.html

---

Museums in the Netherlands Rumor has it that there are two museums for each of the Netherlands' 15 million residents. Read all about museum offerings nationwide at this site, which are organized by city, province, and type. Find out also which languages are supported at each museum and which museums are handicapped-accessible. ✓**INTERNET**→*url* http://www.xxlink.nl/nbt/museums/

Neder-L (ml) Although most of the discussion on this mailing list centers around Dutch politics, travel-related topics do occasionally arise, including discussions about restaurants and museum exhibitions. ✓**INTERNET**→ *email* listserv@nic.surfnet.nl ✍ *Type in message body:* subscribe neder-l <your full name>

---

soc.culture.netherlands (ng) Discussion of issues regarding Dutch people and culture, in both the Netherlands and Belgium (the northern, Flanders region). The newsgroup's FAQ addresses tourist concerns (it gives tips on hotels and cafés), lists recipes for Dutch cuisine (including peanut sauce, a Dutch favorite of Indonesian origin), and tells you what you really need to know about driving in the Netherlands (Hint: Watch out for bikers and trams!). ✓**USENET**→soc.culture.netherlands *FAQ:* ✓**INTERNET**→*url* http://www.sci.kun.nl/scn_faq/

Alkmaar

Alkmaar Each Friday morning, the *kaasmarkt* (cheese market) is the place to see a presentation about the production of the town's most famous export—its cheese. Come to this site to pick up information about the kaasmarkt (hours of operation, directions, and cheese prices) and to read about the people who make the cheese. ✓**INTERNET**→*url* http://www.nbt.nl/holland/events/62.htm

Delft

Delft Make your way deftly around Delft with the help of this online guide to the city famous for being the source of the blue-and-white porcelain known as Delftware. A clickable map for navigating the town, photos of the city, and information from the VVV (the national tourist board) are available at this Website. ✓**INTERNET**→*url* http://muresh.et.tudelft.nl/delta/redactie/Ger-Jan/delft/delft.html

Eindhoven

Tourist Information A collection of links to the home pages of hotels, restaurants, banks, and local events around Eindhoven, including a link to the events calendar for the Van Abbemuseum. ✓**INTERNET**→*url* http://www.nbt.nl/cities/304.htmw

---

Van Abbemuseum Photography, video art, film, and paintings are the specialty of this multimedia gallery. Stills from video archives are on display in revolving shows at the site. Preview the works of many Dutch artists—Job Koelewijn, Jan Schoonhoven, and Henk Peeters, among others. ✓**INTERNET**→*url* http://dse.iaehv.nl/cultuur/musea/vanabbe/index_uk.html

Friesland

Digitale Regio Friesland This site is in a version of Dutch called Frisian as well as English. If you

Fodor's Choice...

A café—from http://muresh.et.tudelft.nl/delta/redactie/Ger-Jan/delft /delft.html

thought Dutch was rare (actually spoken by 25 million people in Holland, Belgium, Suriname, Indonesia, Aruba, and the Netherlands Antilles), Frisian is even less prevelant, spoken primarily in Friesland, a northern province, which is full of beautiful lakes and farming villages, small towns (such as provincial capital Leeuwarden), which belie the fact that the Netherlands is a densely populated country. Visit this site for more tourist information, and to see thumbnail photos of the region. ✓ **INTERNET**→*url* http://dru.knoware.nl/friesland/index.htm

Haarlem

Haarlem Not as well known as its namesake in New York City, Haarlem is an historic city less than 30 minutes from Amsterdam. Visit the Teylers Museum (online, or at Spaarne 16), the Claus Food and Fun Company, or annual events such as the Bloemencorso van de Bollenstreek (Haarlem's largest parade). Get all your information on events and accommodations here.✓ **INTERNET**→*url* http://www.xxlink.nl/cities/412.htm

Teylers Museum Info on a Dutch art and science museum located in Haarlem.✓ **INTERNET**→*url* http://www.nedpunt.nl/teylersmuseum/

The Hague

Going Out in The Hague To find out what to see and do in The Hague, turn to this page, which lists what's new in the cinemas and clubs, what touring companies are in town, and how to reach your chosen event via foot or train. ✓ **INTERNET**→*url* http://www.xs4all.nl/~ipa/

The Hague (Den Haag) Scheveningen is the location of the Kurhaus—the beach resort and casino for The Hague, which also boasts a royal palace (the other one is in Amsterdam) and events such as the North Sea Jazz Festival. Find descriptions of these attractions at the site.✓ **INTERNET**→*url* http://www.xxlink.nl/cities/den_haag

Maastricht

City of Maastricht Maastricht is a 2,000 year old city that traces its origins to Rome. Roman influence is still evident—in the architecture, the eating houses, and the people. You can take a virtual tour of the city, illustrated with colorful drawings instead of photos. ✓ **INTERNET**→*url* http://luanda.matriks.rulimburg.nl/Maastricht/index.htm

Rotterdam

Information About Rotterdam Whether you're day-tripping from Amsterdam or staying in town (lodging info is available), you'll find plenty to do. Visit the Kijk Kubis, modular cube housing turned on an angle and standing on poles, or visit the Oude Haven (Old Harbor), the only area of the city to survive the devastating bombing that occurred in 1940. Read about the city and its offerings here.✓ **INTERNET**→*url* http://www.xxlink.nl/cities/980.htm

Utrecht

ArtLab An online gallery of Dutch artists, such as Gerrit Boers, Hans Blekkink, and Brigitte Espeet. There is also a listing of local art events on the site. ✓ **INTERNET**→*url* http://dru.knoware.nl/kunst_cultuur/beeldende_kunst/artlab/nlpages/alhome .htm

Centraal Museum Utrecht Utrecht's municipal museum features paintings, sculpture, period rooms, and fashion galleries. Preview some of the art online.✓ **INTERNET**→*url* http://www.dru.nl/kunst_cultuur/centraal_museum/#gb

Filmagenda Utrecht Films and their showtimes are displayed, along with reviews (in Dutch). You're likely to find that most films are not-so-recent American movies, but, if you haven't seen *Waterworld* yet, this is your opportunity.✓ **INTERNET**→*url* http://www.nedpunt.nl/filmagenda/

Going Out in Utrecht Spend the day traveling the canals, stopping at the 13th-century wharves of the Oudegracht, and visiting the museums on the main cathedral square, then plan your evening. Although this site is available only in Dutch, the icons and the similarities between Dutch and English make it possible to decipher the information. Be adventurous and collect the addresses of restaurants, bars, and cafés all over town.✓ **INTERNET**→*url* http://www.nbt.nl/e/0/uitinutr

Amsterdam

If you're looking for the Amsterdam of tulips and Rembrandt, The Channels will take you step by step through the historic city. Get back to the future with a visit to **MySTèR 2000**, Amsterdam's own cybercafé. And check in with the present at **TimeOut Amsterdam** for welcome hints on budget dining and lodging. Amsterdam is one of the most wired cities in the world—even the Metro has an online guide.

Rembrandt's Night Watch—*from http://sunsite.unc.edu/wm/paint/auth/rembrandt/*

On the Net

Amsterdam Metro Most of your traveling in Amsterdam can be done by foot, tram, or even canal boats and watercycles. If you do take the metro (perhaps to see the Centraal Station's display of subways around the world), a map, directions, and estimated travel times are available. Or plan your trip from Schipol Airport to the city via Nederlandse Spoorwegen, the Dutch National Railway.✓ **INTERNET**→*url* http://metro.jussieu.fr:10001/bin/select/english/nederland/amsterdam

The Channels Take a tour of Amsterdam online the same way you'd do it in person: by foot, taxi, or tram (streetcar). If on foot, select an area to explore—arrows tell you the direction you are heading, photos illustrate all that you might expect to see, and annotations offer information on the area's attractions. Each of the tour's ten tram lines originates at Centraal Station—just head back there if you get lost, and start again. Or jump in a taxi, click on the street you want the driver to take you to, and you're whisked there.✓ **INTERNET**→*url* http://www.channels.nl/

Information about Amsterdam This page will help travelers find a hotel, restaurant, and suitable souvenir. Specialized links lead to sailing schools, the local gay newspaper, tips for keeping cut tulips fresh, and the Anne Frank Museum.✓ **INTERNET**→*url* http://www.xxlink.nl/cities/amsterdam

MySTèR 2000 Exploring the relationship between the mind and Cyberspace, or just checking your email while in Amsterdam? Visit this cybercafé in the heart of Amsterdam.✓ **INTERNET**→*url* http://www.euro.net/sala/myster/

TimeOut Amsterdam Essays on the latest in music, dance, theater, art, bars and clubs, film, and fashion in the capital of the Netherlands. A good source of information about local celebrities as well. Both current and past issues of the mag are available.✓ **INTERNET**→*url* http://riverland1.riv.net//yuliana/timeout/

Welcome to MoonCity Your premier guide to Amsterdam's nightlife, the city astrologically ruled by the moon. See what's happening in bars and clubs, gay or straight; on the art scene; on the rave scene; at the movies and coffee shops (yes, *those* coffee shops).✓ **INTERNET**→*url* http://www.euro.net/5thworld/mooncity/moon.html

Norway

Heinrik Ibsen and Edvard Munch's creative outpourings might make one wonder about the dark side of the land of Vikings and fish. But don't be frightened! Discover Norway's many charms with a trip to **Norwegian Travel Information Network**. Fjords, fjords, and more fjords reside at **Fjord Norway** and **Bergen—Gateway to the Fjords**, along with many other attractions like fishing streams and fish markets. But along with craggy, sublime landscapes and fish, Norway has its magical side—find it at the other-worldly flashes of the **Northern Lights Planetarium**.

On the Net

Across the board

Norwegian Travel Information Network Accommodations information here is sparse—only three hotels are listed for Kongsberg, with no addresses or telephone numbers. However, the hypertext list of tourist attractions is more complete. You'll learn that at Saggrenda you can ride a pit trail 2 1/2 kilometers into an abyss called the King's Mine. Or you can visit the city's optics museum and catch some jazz at the city's annual festival. Read information about local events like these for almost every town in Norway. And if you're tired of fish during your stay, look

The Nerøy Fjord —http://www .intercom.no/~rolfr/booking.html

in the Norwegian Dining section here for a list of alternatives—Jeppe's Pizza is open late! ✓**INTERNET**→*url* http://www.intech.no /travel/travel1.html

Tourist Information for Norway As yet, the interactive map here yields little information, but construction is underway. In the meantime, find links to the Norwegian Climbing Guide, a page about fly fishing in Norway, and the astounding Polar Regions page. Norway is certainly a hardy land. ✓**INTERNET**→*url* http://www .service.uit.no/norge/geographical .shtml

Norwegian Music Information Centre In addition to keeping the Web abreast of new Norwegian CD releases, this site provides a calendar of upcoming musical events nationwide. ✓**INTERNET**→*url* http://www.notam.uio .no/nmi/

Bergen—Gateway to the Fjords Bergen natives appear to be still smarting over the bestowing of capital status on upstart Olso, after Bergen had held the honor since the 13th century. This home page brags about Bergen's international flavor, the result of its role as a prime northern port. Walk through the city with this online tour—from the Fish Market to Bryggen (the wharf). Connections to the local tourist office will help with the practicalities of visiting Bergen. ✓**INTERNET**→*url* http://www.uib.no/guide/bergen -intro.html

Oslo Promotion When in Oslo you can visit the Ibsen Museum if you're moody, the Kon-Tiki Museum if you're adventurous, and the Munch Museum if you feel like screaming. Besides describing the museums, the site also offers advice on which restaurant serves the best herring, where to catch a performance of the Young Farmers Union dance group, and other essential experiences. ✓**INTERNET**→*url* http://www.oslonett.no/OsloPRO /index.html

Fjord Norway For those who don't know, a fjord is a long, mountainous inlet from the sea—and something Norway's creator was very good at. A consortium of hotels have put together this site, which gives seasonal room prices (you can book online) and lists local attractions (fishing and church visits among them). ✓**INTERNET**→*url* http://www.intercom.no/~rolfr /booking.html

Sørlandet, Norway Read descriptions of rafting adventures around Troll Mountain and tales of the mysteries of Mineral Park in Evje. The site's hotel list makes planning a trip to Sørlandet easy. ✓**INTERNET**→*url* http://www.oslo nett.no/home/destsor/

Northern Lights Planetarium A combination of new technology and the age-old craving for exploration has created this online tour that explores one of Norway's finest features—the Northern Lights. Get directions, show times, a QuickTime preview, and even a short lesson in physics here. ✓**INTERNET**→*url* http://www.uit.no/npt /homepage-npt.en.html

Poland

Take a virtual or real-time trip to Poland and discover that the country is really no laughing matter! Learn about Polish culture, transportation, stock options, and the Polish Pope at the **Poland Home Page**. Stop by the **Tourist Guide to Poland** to refine a travel plan to Pomerania or Silesia. **Krakow**'s home page transports you back to Poland's medieval past, while the **Centre for Contemporary Art**, in Warsaw zips you into Poland's vital present.

On the Net

Across the board

Poland Country Guide Come to this site for an online encyclopedia of all things Polish—read essays on Polish government, politics, demographics, and land use. ✓**INTERNET**→*url* http://ciesin.ci.uw.edu.pl/poland/poland-home.html

Poland Home Page Need to know when the next flight to Krakow leaves? That information is close at hand with this excellent collection of Polish-related links. A nationwide Polish railway schedule, a virtual tour of the Tatra Mountains, and the latest numbers from the Polish stock exchange are also here. There's much more of interest—daily newspapers, a cinema database, art galleries, and even a Polish TV guide. ✓**INTERNET**→*url* http://info.fuw.edu.pl/pl/PolandHome.html

From the top of the Tatras—http://www.cs.put.poznan.pl/holidays/tatry/

Culture

soc.polish.culture (ng) A bilingual newsgroup devoted to discussion of life and events in Poland. ✓**USENET**→soc.polish.culture

Tourist Guide to Poland This government-sponsored site provides a useful traveler's guide to Poland. Select a region—Pomerania, Silesia, and the Carpathian Mountains, among others—and an illustrated introduction (filled with seemingly unpronounceable words that only heighten the attraction) relates its history, geography, and culture. Travel to Wdzydze Kiszewskie to hear the strains of the native Kashubian instrument, the burczybas, at the Ethnographic Park. Special essays portray the joys of horseback riding and hunting in the famous Polish forests. Online tour suggestions guide visitors through castles, palaces, and monasteries. ✓**INTERNET**→*url* http://ciesin.ci.uw.edu.pl/poland /orbis/poland.htm

Krakow

Krakow The Kracovians responsible for this site hope that its glory shines through, although Krakow is "polluted and covered with the coating of the first capitalist years." Their illustrated offering is a good start toward dusting off the city. Get a feel for Krakow through the picture gallery and feel the magic of the city where Faustus first contacted the other world. A list of hotels in the area rounds out the site. ✓**INTERNET**→*url* http://www.cyf-kr.edu.pl/KRAKOW/index.html

Tatra Mountains

The Tatra Mountains Virtual Tourist You probably never even knew that you wanted to visit the Tatra Mountains. This virtual tour shows where this highest sector of the Carpathian Mountains resides, and it highlights a bit of its charms. An interactive map points you to mountain huts that can be reserved for cool nights. ✓**INTERNET**→*url* http://www.cs.put.poznan.pl/holidays/tatry/

Warsaw

Centre for Contemporary Art, Warsaw Modernism contrasts with the past at this multimedia site for a museum housed in a 17th century castle. Movies and images give a glimpse of the museum's permanent collection (which features many works from the Fluxus movement) and of its touring exhibitions. ✓**INTERNET**→*url* http://sunsite.icm.edu.pl /culture/csw/

Warsaw This attractive guide is a tribute to the city, lovingly illustrating the Old and New Towns, and describing its history and culture. No practical tourism information is here, only a tantalizing look at a capital long hidden from Western eyes. Links are provided to the Poland Home Page and Warsaw University. ✓**INTERNET**→*url* http://www.icm.edu.pl/warsaw/

Portugal

Europeans have long known that Portugal is a terrific (warm and inexpensive) vacation spot, and now, thanks to Cyberspace, the rest of the world is discovering Portugal, too. **Portugal's Home Page** and the **Tourist Info About Portugal** site will take you on virtual tours of the picturesque country from beaches to cathedrals—only the delicious Portuguese wine is not included. At the **Unofficial Lisbon Pages** a native offers insider's tips to enjoying the capitol, and **Portugal Online: Agenda Cultural de Lisboa** relates what's on in the city's concert halls, theaters, and clubs.

The ruins of Conimbriga—http://www.uc.pt/Conimbriga/CONIMBR.HTM

On the Net

Across the board

Portugal's Home Page The tourist information link is almost buried at the bottom of the page, but it couldn't hurt to browse through the history lessons, image collections, and even Portuguese e-zine, housed here too. The tourist information link zips visitors to the Lisbon, Braga, and Coimbra pages for local information on those locations. Visitors might also want to spend a few minutes perusing the articles on Portugal collected in the site's Electronic Newsstand. ✓**INTERNET**→*url* http://s700.uminho.pt/Portugal/portugal.html

Tourist Info About Portugal An excellent site for those considering a trip to Portugal. Find a detailed map of the country, phone numbers and addresses of Portuguese tourist offices and embassies worldwide, a list of recommended towns for tourists (which includes Caminha, Braga, and Porto), info on "natural parks" and beaches, accommodations information, and even a Portuguese-travel FAQ! ✓**INTERNET**→*url* http://shiva.di.uminho.pt/~esteves/turismo/portugal-ing.html

Culture

BurgoNews Home Page A hypertext cultural magazine composed of extracts from Portuguese media and from soc.culture.portuguese—obviously in Portuguese. ✓**INTERNET**→*url* http://leo.lnec.pt/%7Elms/BurgoNews/

Jornal de Noticias Home Page Daily edition of the Lisbon-based newspaper. If an editorial makes Portuguese-speakers boil never fear—an email connection to the staff is provided. ✓**INTERNET**→*url* http://www.jnoticias.pt/

Braga

Braga The city of Braga, in the northwest of the nation, was at various times a primary seat of government for the Romans, Suevi, Goths, Moors, and the Spanish, and it is now known as a the "Portuguese Rome." Look here for a brief overview of the city and its attractions. ✓**INTERNET**→*url* http://s700.uminho.pt/braga.html

Lisbon

Informacao sobre Lisboa Most of the info here is in Portuguese, but travelers who don't speak the language will appreciate the site for its detailed street maps. ✓**INTERNET**→*url* http://www.fc.ul.pt/lisboa.html

Portugal Online: Agenda Cultural de Lisboa A monthly calendar (in Portuguese) of happenings in Lisbon. ✓**INTERNET**→*url* http://marte.consiste.pt:80/agenda/

Unofficial Lisbon Pages From this site you'll discover important tips for your time in Portugal—some clubs that feature Fado music require a minimum consumption of four drinks! Another section of the site piques interest with its descriptions of the National Tile and Puppetry museums. Nonetheless, the real highlight of this page is the collection of images and sound clips that take you on a virtual visit of the city. There are also lists of selected restaurants and hotels to help you plan a trip to Lisbon. ✓**INTERNET**→*url* http://www.puug.pt/Lisboa/welcome.htm

Russia & the Ukraine

You've been waiting and waiting for that darned Cold War to end so that you could visit the Kremlin and Sebastopol, but now you don't know where to begin! **The Little Russia How To Page** walks you through the bureaucracy while the **Russia** hub sends you off in dozens of directions—into history and folklore at **Dazhbog's Grandchildren**, to the strains of balalaika at **Russian Music**, and the monoliths of **Moscow Architecture**. Talk some Russian at **Russian for Travelers** or talk about Russian travel at CompuServe's **Russia** forum. Find out if the Bolshoi is dancing at the **St. Petersburg Web**, or travel to the **Ukraine** site to weigh the wisdom of a post-Chernobyl vacation.

A view of Moscow at night—http://nearnet.gnn.com/gnn/wic/photo.14.html

On the Net

Across the board

A Russia Phototrack This is an absolute must-see site if you're traveling to Russia or are interested in Russian history and culture. Divided by region, the site provides extensive historical and geographical information about each area, with detailed descriptions of several cities, both major (Moscow and St. Petersburg) and minor (Tomsk and Ulan Ude). Many of the photographs of the cities are located on servers in Russia, so they may take an agonizingly long time to download. But be patient and you will be richly rewarded! ✓**INTERNET**→*url* http://nearnet.gnn.com/gnn/wic/photo.14.html

Moscow Trip "In May we went to St. Petersburg, where robbery of foreigners was practiced officially and unofficially. Last year, I remember one museum which tried charging foreigners triple admission." The author of this page tells it all in this online diary of his trip to Russia (and not just Moscow, although the title might suggest so). In addition to his helpful hints for travelers, the author provides practical info on hotels, restaurants, and attractions for people visiting the city. There's also a link here to a brief historical essay on the city. ✓**INTERNET**→*url* http://Alpha.Solutions.Net/rec travel/europe/russia/moscow.trip.efenster.html

Obtaining a Russian Visa You've booked your flight and made hotel reservations. You've even learned a word or two of Russian. So what's next? Obtaining that visa, of course, so that the Russian government won't say "nyet" to your visit. There is much useful information in this step-by-step explanation of securing a visa in Russia, including the names and addresses of Russian embassies worldwide. ✓**INTERNET**→*url* http://www.nar.com/racc/info/russian_visa.html

Russia For excellent tips from fellow travelers, visit this library, rich in the kind of insider information that will help you plan your own trip. In her article, Karen urges, "Do not leave without trying Russian ice cream. It only comes in vanilla, but oh what a vanilla. Russians eat it all year long, even when it's below freezing outside." In another article, George recommends, "Take the time, from Moscow, to book an excursion to one or more of the 'Golden Ring' towns—Sergeyev Posad (formerly Zagorsk), Vladimir, Suzdal, Rostov Veliky. Especially Suzdal, which is relatively untouched by modern times. An entire town of beautiful ancient churches." Cultivate the acquired knowledge of other travelers at this site. ✓**COMPUSERVE**→*go* Travel Forum→Libraries→Russia

Russia An excellent collection of links to help you plan your trip to Russia, including the Window to Russia page, Dazhbog's Grandchildren, Friends and Partners, and even a link to the soc.culture.soviet newsgroup. ✓**INTERNET**→*url* http://grafton.dartmouth.edu:8001/lrc/culture/europe/russia.html

Russia Culled from the rec.travel Library, the documents at this site offer an endless series of tips for the Russian traveler. Learn the finer points of spending money abroad. Get the skinny on St. Petersburg. There are also real travelogues by other brave souls who journeyed to the eastern reaches of Europe. ✓**INTERNET**→*url* http://Alpha.Solutions.Net/rec-travel/europe/russia/

Russia and the Baltics on $3 a Day Written by Rick Bakker, this document plans a budget travelogue that begins in Amsterdam (hey, wait, that's not in Russia or the Baltics!) and moves through Vilnius, Riga, Tallinn, St. Petersburg, and more, all along offering tips on saving rubles. ✓**INTERNET**→*url* http://Alpha.Solutions.Net/rec-travel/europe/russia/trip.bakker.html

Russian Resources A collection of Websites about all aspects of Russia—its universities, its government, its music, and its tourist attractions. ✓**INTERNET**→*url* http://linux1.uwc.edu/~sasha/russian.html

The Little Russia How To Page Although most of this site is devoted to links geared towards those who wish to study in Russia, some of the links are very useful for ordinary travelers as well. From this page you can jump to the Russian for Travelers Page, the Russian Consulate General in Seattle, Washington, and the State Department's travel advisory for Russia. Also at this site is a long list of shops nationwide that sell Russian books, newspapers, and videos about traveling in Russia. ✓**INTERNET**→*url* http://mars.uthscsa.edu/Russia/howto.html

Travel in Russia This Website serves as an online bulletin board where travelers can place their tips and recommendations for out-of-the-way and lesser known places to stay in Russia. For instance, one post gives the phone number and address of a private home in Moscow that will let rooms for the night. Also at the site are tips on budget tours and hints on obtaining access to the Net when in Russia. ✓**INTERNET**→*url* gopher://infomeister.osc.edu:74/00/russian/travel/travel.info

Culture

alt.current-events.russia (ng) A veritable potpourri of all things Russian, (and some not-so-Russian things) this newsgroup discusses everything from Russian techno dance parties to the O. J. verdict. Yes, they digress. In fact the digression has become the prevailing mode of conversation, with personal bickering occuring constantly. "The level of discussion has dropped very low. In fact, the name of the group no longer reflects the actual content of the postings. I suggest forming a special sub-group: alt.current-events.russia.crap." If you're looking for hotel or café recommendations, or even tips on avoiding the Russian mafia, you may want to look for a more focused source. ✓**USENET**→alt.current-events.russia

Dazhbog's Grandchildren A virtual Mecca for all things Russian! Not only does this page offer essays on Russian history, politics, and folklore, it's also packed with the full texts of Russian-language

Fodor's Choice...

newspapers and Russian literature, even Russian jokes. Much of the site is written in Russian, so, if you don't speak the language, the selection at this site will be somewhat limited. ✓**INTERNET**→*url* http://sunsite.oit.unc.edu/sergei/Grandsons.html

Friends and Partners The iron curtain is down, and communications are up! This sites opens the lines of communication between Russia and the rest of the world by promoting cultural exchange and introducing Americans and Russians to each other on the Net. People from the heart of Russia can discuss politics with people in the heart of Iowa—"They called you Reds, which is kind of funny, on account of the fact that I had a dog named Red." See what international correspondents have to say to one another about life, love, and of course, current events. ✓**INTERNET**→*url* http://solar.rtd.utk.edu/friends/home.html

Russian Daily News Extra! Extra! It's the *Russian Daily News* online. The page is short and sweet, with basic information and a link to a gopher that archives past editions. But brush up on your Russian before you check this out; all the articles are in Cyrillic. ✓**INTERNET**→*url* http://sunsite.oit.unc.edu/sergei/Daily.html

The Cathedral of the Assumption—http://nearnet.gnn.com/gnn/wic/photo.14.html

A baboshka market—http://nearnet.gnn.com/gnn/wic/photo.14.html

Russian for Travelers To get the most out of your trip to Russia, come to this site to pick up a few phrases in the native tongue. Learn how to say, "I'd like another vodka, please," and "Which way to the chess tournament?" with the help of this Web page. ✓**INTERNET**→*url* http://insti.physics.sunysb.edu/~mmartin/languages/russian/russian.html

Russian Music Ahhhhh, the universal language of music. You haven't truly experienced pop music until you've experienced it Russian-style. Discover new artists and new sounds and sing along to the Russian songs here with the help of the lyrics and sound clips. ✓**INTERNET**→*url* http://mars.uthscsa.edu/Russia/Music/

Russian Youth Hostels Seven hostels are listed here, along with their addresses, phone and fax numbers, and even email links for those hostels with Web pages. ✓**INTERNET**→*url* http://www.spb.su/ryh/ryha.html

soc.culture.soviet (ng) Igor and Mikhail, Irina and Svetlana. They all come here to talk. And talk they do—about politics, recent news events, and more, in the nation they like to call "sweet mother Russia." A trip to this newsgroup will reward you with a sample of the national culture served à la Cyberspace. ✓**USENET**→soc.culture.soviet

Window-to-Russia Did you pick up a travel brochure about Russia that contains way too many words in Russian? (Sometimes when you don't speak a language even one foreign word can be frustrating.) No problem. Check out the interactive English-Russian dictionary at this site for some help deciphering those pesky words. Other attractions here include links to virtual art exhibitions at Russian museums, business and investment information, and arts and sciences resources. ✓**INTERNET**→*url* http://www.kiae.su/www/wtr/

Tour operators

MIR Corporation You're planning that oh-so-perfect vacation. But where in the world do you go? How about Russia? MIR Corporation, a team of professional travel planners, offers several travel packages to Moscow, St. Petersburg, and the Ukraine. Read about their company and contact them with the information listed here. ✓**INTERNET**→*url* http://www.kiss.com/fr/ru_w/mir.html

---

Russia Ways Ever felt the urge to bicycle through Russia? This company will help you organize your trip. The site offers information on the company's packages—prices, itineraries, and routes, as well as contact information, are all available here. ✓**INTERNET**→*url* http://infosphere.com/clients/smallworks/russiaways/index.html

---

Russian Connections A comprehensive travel service for Russia that offers special airfares, group hotel rates, and more. As of yet, the page isn't completely built, but new links are added every week. ✓**INTERNET**→*url* http://www.magna.com.au/~hideaway/russia.html

Ekaterinburg

Ekaterinburg Whoever said there was nothing to do in the Ural Mountains? Obviously, they never stopped by Ekaterinburg. Founded in 1723 by an order of Peter the Great, the city has been through many transformations, including a name change to Sverdlovsk. In 1992, under Mikhail Gorbachev's policy of perestroika, the city's name was restored to Ekaterinburg. For a comprehensive history of the city as well as an annotated picture gallery highlighting its more popular tourist attractions, come to this Website. ✓**INTERNET**→*url* http://www.belmont.edu/BelmontHome/Homepages/Student/Sergey/Ekaterinburg.html

Moscow

Everything about Moscow Downtown Moscow never looked so good. From the Moscow subway to the Kremlin, this page illustrates some of the finer (and not so fine) points of the city through an annotated collection of pictures and maps. ✓**INTERNET**→*url* http://www.cs.toronto.edu/~mes/russia/moscow/main.html

---

Moscow Did you know that there are 160 species of birds in Moscow? Besides a list of Moscow-related trivia, this site provides names and phone numbers of hotels, restaurants, churches, and museums. ✓**INTERNET**→*url* http://www.cs.msu.su/moscow/main.html

---

Moscow With over eight million people, Moscow, the capital of Russia, count as a major international metropolis. With places to visit such as the Kremlin, Red Square, and the Hermitage, it's also increasingly a popular tourist destination. The site offers travelers some basic information about the city—with sections on Moscow's location and climate, history, museums, transportation system, restaurants, and hotels, this Web page is a must-see for those journeying to Moscow. ✓**INTERNET**→*url* http://redsun.cs.msu.su/moscow/main.html

---

Moscow Architecture Browse this library of Moscow's most famous architectural highlights—St. Daniel Monastery, the Kremlin, the Church of the Trinity, the Krutitsky Town House, and the home of V. M. Vasnetsov. The images are accompanied by brief descriptions detailing the year of the building's construction and its location. ✓**INTERNET**→*url* http://mars.uthscsa.edu/Russia/Moscow/

Moscow Kremlin On-Line Excursion Imagine you are Peter the Great or Nikita Krushchev, sauntering through the doors of the palace of power through this virtual tour. Discover the heart of

The largest cannon ever built—from http://nearnet.gnn.com/gnn/wic/photo.14.html

Moscow as you visit Red Square, the Senate Chamber, Sobornaya Ploshchad, and even the Lenin Mausoleum (it's air-conditioned!) on this illustrated tour. ✓**INTERNET**→ *url* http://www.kiae.su/www/wtr/kremlin/begin.html

Moscow Notebook On the film festival circuit, first there was Cannes, then Sundance...and now Moscow International? While not as widely known as other festivals, the Moscow International Film Festival has gained prestige since the fall of Communism. Frank Caso traveled to Moscow for last year's event, and he documents his experience at the Website: "Seeing twenty-two films in ten days is a full-time job; I managed to catch thirteen of them. I skipped the three English-language entries on purpose." Interspersed with Frank's first-hand account of the Festival, you'll find information about acquiring tickets for future festivals and recommendations of good places to stay while in attendance. ✓**INTERNET**→ *url* http://www.hear.com/rw/feature/moscow.html

Not exactly Ma Bell—http://nearnet.gnn.com/gnn/wic/photo.14.html

Moscow's Red Square—from http://nearnet.gnn.com/gnn/wic/photo.14.html

Moscow Pictures Collection Have you ever imagined strolling alongside the Moscow River with the Kremlin looming in the background? Yes? Well, then, you'll enjoy this site with its half-dozen or so photographs of the most popular tourist sites in Moscow—see impressive images of Lenin's Library, Moscow State University, and even Red Square. ✓**INTERNET**→ *url* http://www-nfcs-wane.scri.fsu.edu/~pasha/pictures.html

Moscow Railroad Trying to get from Ramenskoe to Ozyory the quickest way possible? Then consult this online subway guide for the Moscow metropolitan area to find the most direct connections. ✓**INTERNET**→ *url* http://pavel.physics.sunysb.edu/RR/Moscow-Colomna.html

Pushkin Museum of Art Preview the collection of Russia's second-best art museum at this site. See a photograph of the museum's imposing facade, and read about the treasures you'll find behind it—*The Satyre and the Peasant* by Jacob Jordans, *Breakfast Piece*, by Peter Claesz, and *Betrothal of the Doge and Sea* by Canaletto, are all online here. ✓**INTERNET**→ *url* http://www.rosprint.ru/art/museum/pushkin/

St. Petersburg

St. Petersburg Web St. Petersburg sounds so much friendlier that Leningrad, right? The Russian Internet provider, Relcom, has created a virtual city café here—complete with copies of the English-language paper, a hip Russian magazine entitled *Beat?*, and a weekly culture, restaurant, and bar guide that can't be beat. Russians living aboard will appreciate the taste of home provided by the cartoons of Victor Borgorad and short stories about life in the city of the tsars. ✓**INTERNET**→ *url* http://www.spb.su/

The Ukraine

Ukraine Since its independence in December 1991, the Ukraine has continued to flourish as one of the more popular states of the former Soviet Republic. Nestled between Russia and the eastern European countries, the Ukraine is the second largest state in Europe (and the leading one in radioactivity, given that it's the home of the infamous Chernobyl nuclear power plant). This page is packed with historical facts, vital statistics, and links to other Ukraine and Ukraine-related pages. ✓**INTERNET**→ *url* http://www.physics.mcgill.ca/WWW/oleh/ukr-info.html

Spain

Don Quixote was from Spain, as was Picasso, and Hernan Cortés, and millions of other explorers, whether fictional, artistic, or imperialistic. From the dense metropolitan splendor of Madrid to the beauty of Barcelona, from the Malaga to Gibraltar, Spain has pieces of dozens of cultures lodged within its brilliant mosaic—there are Moors and Catholics, Basques and Catalunians. Discover Spain at **Discover Spain**; say yes to further exploration at **Si Spain**; and then explore history, cuisine, and culture at sites ranging from **Basque Country** to **The Spanish Wine Page** to **Bilbao, An Open City**.

On the Net

Across the board

Discover Spain Sponsored by the Tourist Office of Spain, the site features an incredible amount of information for travelers, including detailed profiles of Spanish towns—from the metropolis of Barcelona to the seaside town of Costa Del Sol. Transportation and hotel info is available, as are explanations of social customs and a wealth of images of Spain. Check out the essay on social customs, which explains siesta hours, or pick up some recipes for gazpacho and paella. ✓**INTERNET**→*url* http://www.ozemail.com.au/~spain/

The Running of the Bulls—http://yago.eunet.es/InterStand/cyberagentes/cyber_14/

Si Spain The Spanish Embassy in Canada reminds all tourists that dinner is not served until 8:30p.m. in Spain, but there is much to do to occupy the early evening—like a stroll in the nearest palacio. In addition to the expected information on accommodations, tourist attractions, and visa requirements, you can find in-depth looks into Spanish culture at this site; read about the changing role of women, Spain's Moorish past, or about Spain's national sport, bullfighting. ✓**INTERNET**→*url* http:// www.civeng.carleton.ca /Si Spain

The Webfoot's Guide to Spain Quick, what numbers do you dial to phone Maria in Madrid? This huge resource has the answer to that and many other questions about Spain. Links lead to exchange-rate pages, the Spanish Embassy, the home page of the city Bilbao, a map of the Barcelona subway, and even introductory Spanish lessons. ✓**INTERNET**→*url* http://www.web foot.com/travel /guides/spain/spain.html?City

TimeOut Madrid *TimeOut Madrid* can tell where the best tapas bars are, or it can bring you face to face with Velasquez at the Prado through its excellent city guide and calendar. The unexpected is plentiful here—whether it be a celebration of Basque fashion designer Balenciaga, a look at the thriving culture of machismo, or a tour of the bull rings of Spain. The only thing this site doesn't do is teach you how to flamenco! ✓INTERNET→*url* http://www.timeout.co.uk/TO/Madrid/

Culture

Basque Country Did you know that the Basque language is totally unrelated to any other European tongue? Find out more about this non-Indo-European language and the culture that surrounds it. A lyrical essay by writer Manuel Leguineche opens this exploration of Basque towns, people, and culture. Read on to discover unique facets of Basque life—during the celebration of Easter, effigies of Judas are burned, after which people sit down to a delicious meal of angulas (baby eels in garlic and squids in black ink). You'll have to plan your journey into the Basque world by yourself—no travel connections are provided. ✓INTERNET→*url* http://www.we.lc.ehu.es/Basqu eCountry/PaisVasco.html

Espana-L (ml) English-language discussion of Spain and its people. ✓INTERNET→*email* espana-l@uacsc2.albany.edu ✍ *Type in message body:* subscribe Espana-L <your full name>

soc.culture.spain (ng) Just exactly what are tapas anyway? Post a query at this newsgroup and find out. Pose any of your Spanish-culture questions here, and expect answers in Spanish and English. ✓USENET→soc.culture.spain

Cities & regions

The Spanish Wine Page This handy guide ranks Spanish wines by region and year. The names and phone numbers of wineries are included for those who want to indulge in some serious tasting. ✓INTERNET→*url* http://www.eunet.es/InterStand/vino/es_vino.html

Barcelona See pictures of places to visit in Barcelona (Sagrada Familia, Barri Gotic, and the Placa del Rei among others), take a virtual tour of the Barcleona Pavilion (designed by Mies van der Rohe), and link to the Barcelona City Hall. ✓INTERNET→*url* http://www.ac.upc.es/Barcelona.html

Barcelona City Hall A wealth of illustrations introduces cybertravelers to its charms, while the accompanying text offers an historical perspective of the sites and gives practical hints for planning a visit to them. So sit back and take a virtual tour that spans the last two millenia. ✓INTERNET→*url* http://www.bcn.es/

Barcelona Info Divided into easy-to-find sections such as Annual Events & Festivals, Shopping, Restaurants, and Museums, this site offers comprehensive lists and reviews of fun things to do and enjoy around the city of Barcelona. ✓INTERNET→*url* http://www.gol.com/spain/barcelon.htm

Visita a Galicia You might not be able to read about the many attractions, restaurants, and the history of this area since all the information at the site is in Spanish. But you can find a little piece of Galicia in the sound files. ✓INTERNET→ *url* http://sol.des.fi.udc.es/cgi-bin /limita/

Gijón Gijón is the capital of the Costa Verde, perched atop Santa Catalina Promontory. Check this site for suggested tours of the city, from the Bagpipe Museum to La Semana Negra, a Whodunit Week dedicated to crime fiction. Gijón appears to be a haven for the unusual—though you'll have to contact a travel agent for specifics. ✓INTERNET→*url* http://www1.uniov.es/asturias/gijon_i.html

Pamplona's Running of the Bulls Online Experience the ultimate in machismo from a safe distance. After reading a eulogy to Mathew Tassio (the last man to die running), listen to the San Fermines' song to get your blood stirring, and then plunge into the swirling mass of men by clicking on the MPEG video file. Hey Toro—what're you lookin' at? ✓INTERNET→*url* http://yago.eunet.es/InterStand/cyberagentes/cyber_14/s_fermin.htm

Fodor's Choice...

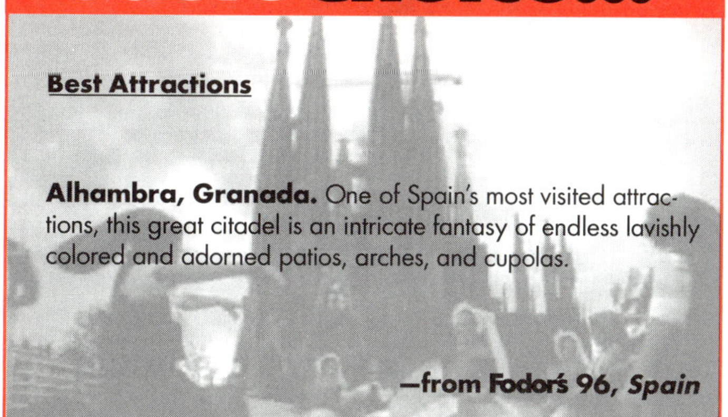

Best Attractions

Alhambra, Granada. One of Spain's most visited attractions, this great citadel is an intricate fantasy of endless lavishly colored and adorned patios, arches, and cupolas.

—from Fodor's 96, *Spain*

Sweden

Does the idea of herring—creamed, smoked, or pickled—make you go weak in the knees? Are the names Norrköping and Valdermarsvik music to your ears? Want to spend you vacation running with the reindeer? If so, Sweden is the place for you. However, **Virtual Sweden** and **The Swedish Smørgasbord** show that it's also a great place for people seeking stunning scenery, clean cities, cultural festivals, and, incidentally, blondes. Visit the capitol at **Stockholm: Beauty by the Water** and enjoy its cosmopolitan wares at the **Royal Swedish Opera House** and its avant guarde scene at **ArtBin** and **Kultur. Welcome to Stockholm** greets aspiring tourists with long lists of lodging and dining options. Or head for the bucolic joys of **Kinda** and **Uppsala**.

Stockholm's Drottningholm Castle—http://www.westnet.se/sweden/provincial/

On the Net

Across the board

The Swedish Page Sweden has an astounding number of Net sites, organized for easy use in this large collection of links. Choose from information about upcoming events, connect to the home page of the national library, see who's singing at the Opera House, or check the price of sardine stocks on the Stockholm Exchange. Those who read Swedish will enjoy links to the press and even a collection of computer magazines. Tourists should head for Virtual Sweden, where it seems as if every town in the country has a page online and in English, each singing the local praises. A link even takes you to the Nobel Academy—study hard and pick up some pointers on winning. ✓**INTERNET**→*url* http://www.algonet.se/~nikos/swedish.html

The Swedish Smørgasbord A friendly virtual moose welcomes visitors to this "smørgasbord," which is full of tantalizing Swedish links rather than creamed herring. Head to the tourism section of the site for profiles of Swedish provinces and cities. You'll also find essays on Swedish culture, religion, and the "national character" ("Swedes consider the concept of social class outdated ... Another characteristic of the Swedish mentality is the urge to agree on things.") After you've read about what makes Swedes tick, turn your attention to descriptions of Swedish music, food, film, literature, and museums, and learn about tiled stoves and the Nobel Prize. Practical tourist information is also presented at the site, including embassy addresses, lodging suggestions, driving instructions, and tips for disabled visitors. There's even a tip on drinking Swedish water—the water there is so pure, you are invited to drink from lakes and streams! ✓**INTERNET**→*url* http://www.westnet.se/

Virtual Sweden The number of local Swedish tourist pages listed here is nothing short of phenomenal—there are over 180. Stockholm alone has 30. Organized by province, most pages are presented in both Swedish and English. Resources vary, but, at the minimum, visitors will receive an illustrated overview of each town, often accompanied by information on accommodations, dining, and other tourist endeavors. So it's off to Motala or Norrköping or Vadstena or Valdermarsvik or Ydre... ✓INTERNET→*url* http://www.algonet.se/~nikos/wwwreg/sverunt.html

Culture

Kultur A Swedish-language directory of the arts. Nine sites alone are dedicated to performance art, and eleven to something called *Föreningar och sällskap*. A link leads to *Den digitala salongen*, where Swedes meet to discuss the arts in a virtual salon. ✓INTERNET→*url* http://www.sunet.se/sweden/art-sv.html

The Art Bin Homepage Come face to face with the avant-garde of the far North in this online arts magazine, which features articles on new gallery shows, performance art, and even Net culture. View pieces of classic and modern art at the online gallery. ✓INTERNET→*url* http://home.netscape.com/home/internet-direc

Kinda

Kinda Kinda is a pleasant district in the southern part of Östergötland. This home page tells the region's story from the Stone Age to the Net Age and offers sightseeing and lodging suggestions. A special section describes Kinda's opportunities for adventure tourism—learn rock climbing at a local climbing school; investigate the Trollegater (the Trolls' Cave) if you dare; or hike through Helvetets Portar (Hell's Portals) along the path of King Karl XI. The Kinda Tourist Office can help book all three tours. ✓INTERNET→*url* http://www.lio.se/(en)/kinda/

Stockholm

Museums in Stockholm A hypertext map makes planning cultural excursions in Stockholm easy. Head from the Royal Palace to Hallwyll Museum to the Music Museum. Some museums offer full-page descriptions of their collections. ✓INTERNET→*url* http://www.sunet.se/stockholm/museums/museums.html

Canoeing the Kinda Canal—http://www.lio.se/(en)/kinda/turism.html

Royal Swedish Opera House Find out what the Royal Swedish Ballet has in its repertoire for the current season with this complete schedule. Also online is a brief history of the company that nurtured talents like Marie Taglioni, and a photographic tour of the House (where King Gustav III was assassinated in 1792). Ticket information, a seating chart, and even a virtual gift shop are here as well. ✓INTERNET→*url* http://soho.ios.com/~gberkson/operan/

Stockholm '98 Plan well ahead—choose to visit Stockholm in 1998 when it will serve its term as Europe's cultural capital. Previews of the many events and exhibits are presented here. ✓INTERNET→*url* http://www.sunet.se/stockholm/kultur98/home.html

Stockholm: Beauty by the Water Discover the attractions of Stockholm at this full-service home page. There are boats to sail, museums to visit, gardens to meditate in, and fish to eat at fancy and home-style restaurants. Find out details from this well organized home page, which provides basic info for planning a trip to Stockholm, as well as a list of Swedish tourism offices worldwide. (Don't miss the Wine and Liquor Museum—bottoms up!) ✓INTERNET→*url* http://www.westnet.se/sweden/provincial/stockholm/

Welcome to Stockholm Take a virtual tour of the archipelago, wander through the city's art galleries, or visit the famous Stockholm steamships. The comprehensive hotel and dining guide will help you plan your vacation. ✓INTERNET→*url* http://www.city.net/countries/sweden/stockholm/

Uppsala

Uppsala An irreverent essay introduces this Swedish city to Web travelers ("Academic studies have been practiced here since Christopher Columbus was nothing but a little brat running around in shorts [1477]"). Read about some of Uppsala's attractions (grave mounds will pique the interest of the morbid). The responsibility for planning a trip to Uppsala rests on the viewer, however; no practical tourist information is included. ✓INTERNET→*url* http://www.csd.uu.se/uppsala-student/upsalaguide/guide.html

Switzerland

Wonder what Heidi and Peter are up to these days? It's entirely possible that they're spending the midnight hour at one of the nightclubs listed at the **Rave in Switzerland** site. If raving isn't you thing, never fear, the Switzerland you read about in story books is still around too (they can't really move the Alps you know). Head to **SwissInfo** or the **Berne** page for spectacular views of the mountains and to **Ticino: The Italian Switzerland** for picturesque little farms along deep blue lakes. Switzerland, in addition to being beautiful, is expensive, and **Hotel+ (The Swiss Hotel Index)** can help locate the right hotel for any budget.

Geneva's Promenade des Bastions—http://is.eunet.ch/GenevaGuide/tourfil/visit0.html

On the Net

Across the board

Information About Switzerland If you're writing a social studies report about Switzerland, this site has everything you'll need—maps, population figures, form of government, and principal cities. Its primarily text-based information is much less useful for prospective tourists, although you will be able to impress patrons in any bar in Zurich by naming the nation's primary industries. ✓**INTERNET**→*url* http://www.ethz.ch/swiss/Switzerland_Info.html

SwissInfo An encyclopedic essay about the history of Switzerland opens this page. Learn about the Swiss principle of neutrality, but not where to stay for the night. Links lead to lists of upcoming concerts and art exhibitions in Zurich; however, tourist information ends there. ✓**INTERNET**→*url* http://www.swissinfo.ch/swissinfo/general.html

Cinet Switzerland A weekly listing of movie releases, reviews, box office charts, pictures, and theater listings for movie houses in the German-speaking section of Switzerland. ✓**INTERNET**→*url* http://kino.ch/

Museums and Exhibitions This searchable database, the effort of the Swiss Academy for Humanities and Social Sciences, presents information on the collections of every museum in the nation. Visit the William Tell Museum in Berglan (apples and arrows available in the gift shop). Or the home of Heidi's creator, Johanna-Spyri, in Hirzel (goats no extra charge). Near Reichenbach Falls, where the super sleuth met his death (supposedly), find the Sherlock Holmes Museum. And, of course, there's the Museo del Cioccolato in Caslano, dedicated to the food of the gods, chocolate. ✓**INTERNET**→*url* http://www.dsk.ch/guide/guide.htm

Rave in Switzerland Pick up tips on partying in the Schweiz at this Website, which is full of the information needed to get you there—descriptions of the main scenes, a comprehensive list of events (along with .GIFs of flyers), a directory of nightclubs (including discos and after-hours clubs), and even files on special events in other countries like Italy and Germany (which might come in handy if you're continuing your tour of Europe through those countries). ✓**INTERNET**→*url* http://hector.unil.ch/~94411071/rave.htm

Hotel + (The Swiss Hotel In-

dex) Bare-bones information on hotels throughout the country, with addresses and telephone and fax numbers. ✓**INTERNET**→*url* http://is.eunet.ch/Swisscom/hotcom.html

---

Basel The Basel home page reflects the special nature of the mountain republic—it is very, very organized. Information on hotels and restaurants is presented clearly and rigidly in tabular form. Further terse entries cover entertainment opportunities, cultural listings, local businesses, and even the Basel flora and fauna. ✓**INTERNET**→*url* http://www.urz.unibas.ch/basel/basel.htm

---

Berne The name of the city is derived from the German word for bear—that's why you'll see likenesses of the furry creatures all over the city (there's even a bear on Berne's coat of arms). The Website takes you on a virtual airplane ride over the city, where you see spectacular bird's-eye views of the ancient city walls. After your flight, travel up the Swiss Alps through a video clip taken from a cable car going up from Mürren to the Schilthorn. Enjoy sound clips of local musicians playing folk tunes, city maps, and short descriptions of some of the city's finer features, which include the famous Clock Tower and more than 100 fountains. And, of course, there are lots of pictures of bears here, too. ✓**INTERNET**→*url* http://www.vptt.ch/bern-page.html

---

Geneva Welcome to a page dedicated to the birthplace of the World Wide Web. Befitting the city's status, this guide is appropriately electronically impressive, loaded with a virtual art gallery, a guided tour of Geneva, and even an online hotel reservations service. Guides to bars and discos and a cultural calendar are in the works. ✓**INTERNET**→*url* http://www.eunet.ch/GenevaGuide/

International Automobile Museum If you'd rather be looking at Porsches instead of Picassos, this is the museum for you. Get admission hours and prices here, and preview the museum's collection of Auburns, Bugattis, Cadillacs, and Ferraris. ✓**INTERNET**→*url* http://www.fastnet.ch//LSNE/ARTCUL/MUSEE/musauto.html

---

Cinema Listing An alphabetical list of movie theaters in the Lausanne area. Get current show schedules, addresses, and telephone numbers for each of the more than 30 houses listed here. ✓**INTERNET**→*url* http://litwww.epfl.ch/~vandel/cinema.html

---

Ticino: The Italian Switzerland Climb aboard the William Tell Express in Lucerne and head for the bucolic pleasures of Lugano and Ticino. After perusing the illustrated essays on the lakes, picturesque towns, and alpine pastures, you'll be ready to seek accommodations using the list included here. Choose from a four-star hotel, or go the more romantic route and rent a *rustico*, a 200-year-old-plus stone farmhouse along a mountain path. Addresses of tourism offices and travel providers are included. ✓**INTERNET**→*url* http://www.tourism-ticino.ch/

Concerts in Zurich Discover what's going on in film, theater, dance, art, and music throughout the Swiss nation. It's not all chamber music in fastidious concert halls—the Greasy Miss Show is slated for next Monday. ✓**INTERNET**→*url* http://ezinfo.ethz.ch/eth/chconc/concerts.html

---

Zurich A brief essay on Switzerland's largest city. Impress the city's 400,000 natives with your detailed knowledge of their hometown—it's serviced by more than 150 airlines, and it's the economic heart of Switzerland, with over 350 banks and the Zurich Stock Exchange. For more information about visiting Zurich, call the local tourist office, whose number is listed here. ✓**INTERNET**→*url* http://josef.ifi.unizh.ch/groups/dbtg/vldb95/zh.html

---

Zurich Guide Also known as Europe's "Little Big City," Zurich has much to offer to travelers, and this site details some of those offerings. Learn about the area's climate (temperatures are given in both Celsius and Fahrenheit); Zurich is famous for its mild summers. A whole section of the site is devoted to public transportation in the city, complete with hours of operation and estimated prices for some trips around the city by streetcar and bus. Also get a list of places to go in Zurich—each attraction, from the Schauspielhaus to the Clock Tower, is profiled with a short essay and a photograph. ✓**INTERNET**→*url* http://www.eunet.ch/swissinfo/local/zh/zh.html

---

La Place du Bourg-de-Four in Geneva —http://is.eunet.ch/GenevaGuide/

Turkey

Discover the true meaning of Turkish Delight through a visit to the millennial empire itself. A hypertour of 10,000 years of Turkish history sets the stage at **EBB: Hotel, Travel and Translation Services in Turkey.** Curiosity piqued? **All About Turkey** and the **Turkey Home Page** offer lots of nuggets on Turkish culture, travel, food, and even humor. Wander into the coffee houses at **Istanbul,** or head to **TimeOut Istanbul** for up to the minute events listings. Then head to **soc.culture.turkish** to discuss that cup of Turkish coffee.

Bergama, Izmir—from http://www.ege.edu.tr/Turkiye/InPictures.html

On the Net

Across the board

All About Turkey This collection of links connects to almost everything about Turkey on the Web. From here those with an Indiana Jones complex can visit several archeological sites. For a feeling for the Turkish sense of humor, head to the Turkish Comics Collection and the Turkish Humor Page. The strains of Turkish music are available from sound files on several pages, as are poems, a treatise on Karagoz (Turkish Shadow Theater), and film reviews. And then there's the real Turkish delight—no fewer than three pages dedicated to Turkish cuisine. Turkish government, religion, and news sites are also just a jump away. ✓**INTERNET**→*url* http://www.ege.edu.tr/Turkiye/

Turkey Home Page A complete travel guide to Turkey, this site offers tips on where to stay, what to pack, and how much a phone call costs. It also features links to illustrated tours that allow you to experience Ankara, Istanbul, and the Inlara Valley in virtual splendor. Additional links highlight Turkish history, theater, cinema, and yachting. ✓**INTERNET**→*url* http://www.metu.edu.tr/~melih/turkeyhome.html

EBB: Hotel, Travel and Translation Services in Turkey The title of this site is somewhat misleading—as yet there is only one hotel listed. But that doesn't mean that the site isn't worth a visit! Here Turkey meets *Star Trek* in a "warp speed" interactive tour of 10,000 years of Turkish history. Other sections of the site display the treasures of Anatolan culture, photos of the country's landscapes, and glimpses of the wide scope of Turkish culture (music, cinema, poetry). If you don't need to spend the night, don't miss this site. ✓**INTERNET**→*url* http://www.xmission.com/~gastown/ebb/index.html

soc.culture.turkish (ng) Topics at this newsgroup run the gambit—from discussions of current politics to tips on good Turkish pop music sites on the Net. For travelers, the newsgroup's FAQ is invaluable—learn where to get cheap tickets to Istanbul and where to stay once you get there. ✓**USENET**→soc.culture.turkish *FAQ:* ✓**INTERNET**→*url* http://www.eecs.nwu.edu/~yusuf/FAQ/s.c.t-FAQ

Istanbul

Istanbul An illustrated overview of the only city in the world built on two continents. You'll learn about the Bosphorus, the Golden Horn, and the Hagia Sophia. Smaller features provide suggestions for sightseeing, outdoor activities, and shopping. See you on Sogukcesme Street. ✓**INTERNET**→*url* http://www.metu.edu.tr/~melih/turkey/marmara/istanbul/istanbul.html

Time Out Istanbul Choose a starting point for a hypertext tour of Istanbul—Sultan Ahmet Square, Tokapi Palace—and you're off on a 48 stop tour of the city. Choose departure and destination points and experience a leisurely stroll through an ancient, exotic world. Well worth a visit. ✓**INTERNET**→*url* http://www.duke.edu/~emin/ISTANBUL/

The United Kingdom

Pints of beer, pots of tea, Wellingtons, Paddingtons, bad teeth, and quirky humor.

Those darn Brits are busy creating an empire again, this time in Cyberspace. One-stop accommodation and itinerary planning to the sceptered isle is available on CompuServe's **Travel Britain Online.** But then you'd miss the joys of virtual visits to **Brighton**, **Cambridge**, and **Liverpool**. Those who seek the Britain of Chaucer would do well to head to the virtual **Canterbury**; those who seek the Britain of Johnny Rotten should try the **Knowhere Alternative Guide to the U.K.** Take **A Tour of Wales** and encounter memories of Merlin and Dylan Thomas. And now that peace has broken out, the information at the **Northern Ireland Information Centre** is alluring. Of course, if it's Di you want to dish, speak your piece at the **UK Forum** on CompuServe.

A bird's-eye view of Canterbury—http://www.cs.ucl.ac.uk/misc/uk/canterbury.html

On the Net

Across the board

Hotels and Resorts in the United Kingdom Search the listings by region for information on a wide range of accommodations—from Country Houses in Buckinghamshire to a B&B on the outskirts of Edinburgh. Links to hotels with Web pages are provided. ✓**INTERNET**→*url* http://www.webscope.com/travel/uk.html

Knowhere Alternative Guide to the U.K.: No Kilts, No Leeks and Not a Thatched Cottage in Sight Gen X'ers, skateboarders, and junk-food eaters—here's a guide for you! Find out where the boarders meet, where the best munchies can be found, and which bands are hot in towns from Inverness to Bristol. ✓**INTERNET**→*url* http://www.state51.co.uk/state51/knowhere/

PA News Come here for British news hot off the wire. ✓**COMPUSERVE**→*go* pa

Travel Britain Online Thanks to the British Tourist Authority, which sponsors this up-to-the-minute online guide to "events, anniversaries, customs, carnivals and fairs, dance and drama performances, exhibitions, music, and sport." Each listing includes admission prices, and the U.K. What's On Guide even lists the movies playing in London cinemas. ✓**COMPUSERVE**→*go* tbonline

Travel in the U.K. The author of this page has assembled an impressive collection of tourism links about the U.K. Begin with his virtual pub guide—The Shoulder of Mutton in Buckinghamshire sounds intriguing. A number of links provide information on places to stay—from the Savoy to a B&B on the Isle of Bute. A trip to the London Mall site tells you what's hot in the clubs and in the West End theaters. ✓**INTERNET**→*url* http://www.neosoft.com/~dlgates/uk/uktrav.html

U.K. Accommodation & Travel Services This service contains a number of useful features for those touring the United Kingdom. The Automobile Club's rat-

A view of Cambridge—http://www.cs.ucl.ac.uk/misc/uk/cambridge.html

ings of restaurants may help you avoid the notorious plague of the English (bad food). In fact, each restaurant entry is extremely detailed, down to price range, seating capacity, the best entrees, and even the best sauces. The site also rates British hotels and inns, golf courses, and outings. And soon to come: AA Roadwatch, an up-to-the-minute advisory service for all British roadways. ✓**COMPUSERVE**→*go* ukaccomm

U.K. and Ireland Guide Yet another excellent collection of resources on the U.K., this time presented in an interactive map. Click on Glasgow, and an introduction to the country from the University of Glasgow's gopher pops up. Choose the coast of Cornwall, and get a tour of King Arthur's Britain. You get the idea. ✓**INTERNET**→*url* http://www.cs.ucl.ac.uk/misc/uk/intro.html

UK Forum Americans reading the Politics section here might think they stepped into a parallel universe, where the Clinton health plan has passed and is running as smoothly as the post office; where Social Security is for some reason called national insurance; and where elected officials actually participate in political discussions on the Internet. Don't worry: It's not the future; it's just Britain. In Rover's Return Pub, Brits pretend to be drunk and fondle each other boozily. Recently, forum members met offline in Manchester, London, and Los Angeles. Tourists share tips on places to visit, such as the Dylan Thomas house in Wales and the hedge mazes at Hever Castle, or arrange to rent a converted barn in Cornwall. Oddly, John Cleese's name pops up in nearly every thread. ✓**COMPUSERVE**→*go* ukforum

England

Brighton A virtual tour of Brighton and neighboring Hove, a conurbation nicknamed London-by-the-sea. The ornate Royal Pavilion is here of course, as well as photos of the Palace Pier, the Lanes (shopping district with passageways only three feet wide!), Queen's Park and views of the historic Regent architecture. Tourist information is provided on local hotels, pubs and restaurants, and activities throughout East Sussex. ✓**INTERNET**→*url* http://www.pads.co.uk/vbrighton/

Cambridge The beautiful medieval seat of learning on the banks of the river Cam is actually very well wired. Turn here for historical overviews of the city, illustrated walks through its streets, and information on book shops, bike hire, theaters, and B&Bs in town. Further links lead to the online events calendar, What's On? in Cambridge, and not unexpectedly for a college town, to a detailed pub guide. ✓**INTERNET**→*url* http://www.cs.ucl.ac.uk/misc/uk/cambridge.html

Canterbury Modern-day pilgrims should start their trek at this site, with its links to an interactive map, the University of Canterbury home page, and to a very amusing tourist guide that begins, "Canterbury is a Mecca for tourists. Early tourists included Caesar J. and Claudius I. They came, saw, and conquered. When they discovered all the deck chairs were taken, they disappeared back to Rome to change out of their swimming

Fodor's Choice...

Stately Homes

Blenheim Palace, Thames Valley

Britain's largest stately home and the birthplace of Winston Churchill, this early 18th-century Italianate mansion in Woodstock stands majestically in 2,000 acres of parkland and exquisite gardens landscaped by Capability Brown.

—Fodor's 96, *Great Britain*

things." After chuckling over the history lesson, be sure to take the guide's illustrated tour, which actually walks visitors through Canterbury from gate to gate. ✓**INTERNET**→*url* http://www.cs.ucl.ac.uk/misc/uk/canterbury.html

Gidleigh Park Promotional page for a "luxury" hotel in Dartmoor National Park run by Americans! (Dartmoor is not just a place where they send criminal lunatics!) ✓**INTERNET**→*url* http://www.calvacom.fr/relais/uk/gidleigh.htm

Hadrian's Wall Hadrian enslaved Celts just to build it; at least you could go and look at it! Find here an informative guide to one of the most important archeological sites in the U.K., as well as suggestions for other things to do in the neighborhood, and info on how to get to and where to stay around the old pile of rocks. Just catch the Haltwhistle bus from Hexam. ✓**INTERNET**→*url* www.demon.co.uk/tynedale/

Jersey Zoo When was the last time you saw a reticulated poison arrow frog? Well, there are now eight in residence at this zoo. Find out all about the zoo's growing collection, which includes partula snails, a Livingstone's fruit bat, and pink pigeons. Admissions info is provided as well. ✓**INTERNET**→*url* http://www.cc.columbia.edu:80/cu/cerc/WildOnes/zooNews.html

Liverpool Everyone in the world knows this town's chief cultural export—the Beatles! The town that spawned the Fab Four also sponsors this Website, which provides a virtual tour of the city. You'll stroll past churches, shops, and monuments—the only place it doesn't take you is down to the docks for a drink—but you can probably manage that on your own with the maps and lists of cafés provided here. ✓**INTERNET**→*url* http://www.csc.liv.ac.uk/users/webtour/city/tour.html

The Liverpool skyline at night—http://www.csc.liv.ac.uk/users/webtour/city/tour.html

Oxford Don your gown (an Oxford pun!) and head for what is probably the most famous university town in the Western world. This full-service guide will help you find a hotel room, bookshop, and even your friend James at Christ Church. (It can't, however, tell you how to pronounce Balliol.) ✓**INTERNET**→*url* http://www.comlab.ox.ac.uk/archive/ox.html

South East England Tourist Board Internet Covering East Sussex, Kent, Surrey, and West Sussex, this site offers an interactive accommodations map and a central booking agency. Look here for addresses of local tourist boards (very useful in booking B&Bs). ✓**INTERNET**→*url* http://www.se-eng-tourist-board.org.uk/seetb/

South West of England Wander along the cliffs of Lyme Regis with this site covering Avon, Cornwall, Devon, the Isles of Scilly, Somerset, and Wiltshire. An illustrated guide to attractions like Stonehenge, Glastonbury, and Tintagel is bound to intrigue you. A Trencherman's guide lists 35 restaurants in the area, and a section on local accommodations helps you locate a hotel for your stay. ✓**INTERNET**→*url* http://www.dcs.ex.ac.uk/wcol.html

Virtual Blackpool Smell the cotton candy and the brine of the sea—that's right, you're at Virtual Blackpool. Visit the Tower, the Golden Mile, the Pleasure Beach, and the Sandcastle through the pictures and text at this site. If you're longing for fun and sun, try the links here to vacation-planning resources. ✓**INTERNET**→*url* http://www.digitalresorts.co.uk/uk/blackpool/

York Visitors to York can actually visit a real-life shambles—a medieval butchery that gave the language a favored descriptive word. According to this small text guide, they can also eat Chinese at Kings Castle in Swinegate, watch a soccer match, and take a Ghost Walk after dark (prices and contract information for a variety of tours is included). ✓**INTERNET**→*url* http://www.york.ac.uk/york

Northern Ireland

Armagh: City of Saints and Scholars A regional map gives potential visitors the coordinates of historical sites, equestrian centers, and excellent fishing spots in the vicinity of Armagh. ✓**INTERNET**→*url* http://home.netscape.com/home/internet-se

Northern Ireland Information Centre Tourism is booming in Northern Ireland, so travelers will appreciate this guide that presents colorful tours of the Mourne Mountains, Armagh, Derry, and Belfast. Learn more about Irish history and culture through links to the Celtic Music archive, the Gaelic Games home page, and the North of Ireland Family History Society. ✓INTERNET→*url* http://www.gpl.net/niic/

Northern Ireland Travel Guide A series of interwoven pages takes cybertourists on a visual tour of the charms of Northern Ireland. Although there is no information on lodging or dining, you might want to check the list of pubs that feature traditional music in Belfast and the info on touring the homes of the leprechauns in the Glens of Antrim. ✓INTERNET→*url* http://www.interknowledge.com/northern-ireland/index.html

Wales

A Tour of Wales Although it takes a long time to get through this online tour of Welsh history, it pays off. You'll see pictures of some of the country's most important historical sites (Pentre Ifan Cromlech, Aberystwyth Castle, and Cwmystwth Mines are among them) and read essays on their importance. Names of the sites are listed in English and Welsh—click on the sound clip to hear the names spoken in Welsh. ✓INTERNET→*url* http://www.ihi.aber.ac.uk/Wales/wales.html

A Welsh Course Only a few hundred thousand people in the world speak Welsh as their first language. You can speak at least a few words of Welsh with the help of this site. This online course doesn't assume any former knowledge of the language, so you'll start with very simple words and phrases to use during your travels—like "please," "Thank you," and "How much does it cost?" In addition to the language lesson, this site also offers an interesting FAQ that addresses one very important question—"Is Welsh a dying language?" This Website assures that the language will be alive a while longer. ✓INTERNET→*url* http://www.cs.brown.edu:80/fun/welsh/

Great Little Trains of Wales A site that offers train schedules for the major lines in Wales—including the Talyllyn Railway, the Llanberis Lake Railway, and the Welshpool Railway—as well as a brief illustrated history of each of the lines and photographs of some train stations along their routes. ✓INTERNET→*url* http://www1.roke.co.uk/WHR/whr64/gltw.html

soc.culture.welsh (ng) Not only can you post in English here without fear of flames, but Cornish and Breton are equally welcome. A heated discussion is underway on the derivation of the derogatory term "welsher." But there's plenty of talk about the fate of the National Football team and the underappreciated appeal of Cardiff, too. ✓USENET→soc.culture.welsh

The Cymdeithas Madgo Home Page This is the home page of a society dedicated to the preservation of the Welsh language. Stop here for insight into Welsh culture, and for the society's eight-day course, which will have you talking like a native in a very short time. Links to other Welsh-related resources are also online here. ✓INTERNET→*url* http://tpowel.comdis.lsumc.edu/cymraeg/madog.htm

Welsh WWW Home Page There might be more virtual Welsh citizens than actual Welsh in Cardiff—the sheer number of links at this very large site points that way. Try Curiad for updates on the Welsh music scene, or jump to *DELTA*, a magazine that details the latest achievements in the Welsh science world. You could also head to soc.culture.welsh for discussion of all things Welsh—from coal to Celts—or pay a visit to the Virtual Welsh Community Book, which keeps track of the Welsh presence on the Web—add your own name if St. David is your patron. ✓INTERNET→*url* http://alife1.cs.man.ac.uk:80/welsh/

Wales's Pentre Ifan Cromlech—http://www.ihi.aber.ac.uk/Wales/wales.html

London

They're changing guards at Buckingham Palace...but what time? A quick trip to TimeOut London will tell you precisely the minute that the horseguards leave St. James. You might also try to get a glimpse of Her Majesty during a visit to **The Queen's Gallery** and **Windsor Castle**. You are certain to see her, and Charles and Di and Jack the Ripper, at **Madame Tussaud's**. But there's more to see in London than waxworks, royal or not. There are the plays listed in the **London Theatre Guide**, the dancing delights of the **London Club Guide**, and of course, the manifold pleasures of **London Pubs**. So book yourself a B&B (in a country where the number of slices of toast per guest is mandated by law) with the **Hotel Guide**, and the gang will save you a stool down at The Rose and Crown.

Now THIS is London!—http://www.cs.ucl.ac.uk/misc/uk/london/

On the Net

Culture

British Library Wander into the seat of knowledge of the British Empire. You can't take out the books, but with the help of the online catalog, you can at least see if Danielle Steele is on the shelf. Current library exhibitions are profiled, which makes this site well worth a visit. ✓**INTERNET**→*url* http://portico.bl.uk/

London Theatre Guide Reviews of shows currently doing their runs of theaters in London. Each show is reviewed in full with cast lists and clippings from the local press. After selecting a show, find information about its venue here. ✓**INTERNET**→*url* http://www.demon.co.uk/dalglish/theatre/

London Transport Museum This home page promises that you'll "See shiny buses and trams, hear the hiss and thump of points changing and experience the smell of hot oil, steam and stables!" If you haven't had enough of the Tube after a ride from Liverpool Street to Sloane Square, this is the museum for you. ✓**INTERNET**→*url* http://www.cs.city.ac.uk/london/entertainment/museums/lt/lt.html

Madame Tussaud's When she was just a little girl in Strasbourg, France, Madame Tussaud knew that the world needed a chamber of horrors (as a child she made wax molds of post-guillotined heads). Now her vision has evolved into one of the most famous horror museums in the world. Read about the museum's history and recent technological advances at the museum that make the exhibits even more convincing. The museum's hours and admission prices are included in case this virtual tour intrigues you. ✓INTERNET→*url* http://www.illumin.co.uk/illumin/interac/tuss.html

Museums in London A comprehensive list, with links to the actual tombs of erudition where possible. The martial in nature should not miss the Imperial War Museum, while others must patiently wait until the Victoria and Albert (V&A)'s domestic treasures are available on the Net. Hours, prices, and addresses are included for all the museums listed here. ✓INTERNET→*url* http://www.cs.ucl.ac.uk/misc/uk/london/museums.html

Royal Botanic Gardens If you're planning to visit London in November, remember to check in here to see why you should have traveled in June. In addition to the glorious .GIFs of the gardens, find information on the research and educational programs taking place at the gardens. ✓INTERNET→*url* http://www.rbgkew.org.uk/

The Queen's Gallery, Buckingham Palace The collection of the Queen's Gallery was created by Anthony Blunt, the Queen's official curator and the infamous fourth man in the Burgess / McClean / Philby spy ring! So visit this site for a look at the kind of paintings royals and traitors prefer. Details of current exhibits are presented here. ✓INTERNET→*url* http://www.u-net.com/hotelnet/palace/gallery.htm

Windsor Castle Visit the Royal residence virtually—the state apartments, the Queen's presence chamber, St. George's Chapel, and Queen Mary's doll house. Opening hours and a map are included to ensure that you don't surprise the royals in their jammies. ✓INTERNET→*url* http://www.u-net.com/hotelnet/windsor/home.htm

The Tower Bridge at night—from http://www.cs.ucl.ac.uk/misc/uk/london/

Guides

London Club Guide Do you wear Doc Martens at the Colherne in Earls Court or a twin set and pearls? This guide will help you avoid embarrassing social faux pas while touring the big city. Each club listing details the spot's hours, music style, cover charge, and clientele. ✓INTERNET→*url* http://www.londonmall.co.uk/londonclubguide/

London Pubs According to this guide Ye Olde Surgeon in Bloomsbury serves an excellent pint of bitter. However, if you're looking for a pub lunch, The Rose in the Fulham Road is a better bet. Choose by location or by name (The Frog and Nightgown sounds appealing). Or dispense with the guide altogether and do a crawl from block to block! ✓INTERNET→*url* http://www.cs.ucl.ac.uk/misc/uk /london/pubs/index.html

TimeOut London The events calendar here provides in-depth listings of events designed to appeal to every interest group from children to technopunks to gays and lesbians to football fans. A Student Guide caters to the terminally poor and earnest crowd. Also find accommodation, dining, and sightseeing suggestions and London travel tips. The current Best Of Guide tells you where to get the best Tex-Mex in Kensington and the best pint of Bass. ✓INTERNET→*url* http://www.timeout.co.uk/TO/WorldMap.html

Hotels

Hotel Guide Get a short description of the services, price structure, and location of over 75 hotels in the metropolitan area. Phone numbers are provided if you wish to make a reservation. ✓INTERNET→*url* http://www.u-net.com /hotelnet/london.htm

The Vicarage Hotel Promotional site for a B&B in the West End. ✓INTERNET→*url* http://wworks.com/~deadlock/

Scotland

"Och Aye, I'll have another wee dram of that whiskey lassie!" That's what you'll be saying after you've traveled to Scotland Information and have wandered the Malt Whiskey Trail. Of course, there's more to Scotland than malt whiskey, men in skirts throwing large logs for fun, and stuffed sheep stomach for breakfast. There's golf—at **Letham Grange Hotel and Golf Courses.** There's the avant-garde cosmos of the Fringe Festival, detailed at **Edinburgh—The Capital of Scotland.** There're the Highlands, the Islands, and the Great Glen, and **Scotland Travel and Accommodation** can help you find a B&B in any of them. Chat up some Scots virtually about their favorite plaids on **soc.culture.scottish** or meet the country's own cyberpopulace in person at **Web 13—The Internet Cafe.** Of course, that still leaves Scotland's most famous resident out of your travel plans (no it's not Sean Connery), so spend a little time visiting **Nessie on the Net.**

The Eilean Donan, near Kyle of Lochalsh—http://www.cs.ucl.ac.uk/misc/uk/scotland.html

On the Net

Across the board

Scotland Should anyone really go to Fife in February? Greg asks where in the cold, cold north should he and his wife spend Valentine's Day (perhaps the romantic banks of the Clyde?). Among the predictable queries for B&Bs and world class golf courses are those seeking advice on a traditional Highland wedding (both bride and groom in skirts). Ask anything, the Scots can take it. ✓**AMERICA ONLINE**→*keyword* travel forum→message boards→world traveler→Scotland

Scotland Home Page Scotland's Web sites all seem to sport .GIFs of cows. In addition to cow snapshots, this hypertext overview walks visitors over the hills and dales while feeding them with useful tidbits of information—Scotland includes 787 islands; the drink Rob Roy was named after an actual person, etc. Lurking at the end of the introduction is an excellent collection of links to pages dedicated to examining Scottish cuisine and to explaining the national need to wear plaid. ✓**INTERNET**→*url* http://www.geo.ed.ac.uk/home/scotland/scotland.html

Scotland Information Ah, finally a site after a Celt's own heart—this collection of links heads straight to the pub with a link to the Malt Whiskey Tour, which rates distilleries, details their histories, shows their locations on interactive maps, and even lets you order their wares online! But there's more to culture than a good drink, so visit the other links held here that take you to the world of Robbie Burns, explain the Clans, and even strive to make haggis appealing. ✓**INTERNET**→*url* http://www.cs.ucl.ac.uk/misc/uk/scotland.html

Scottish Tourist Board The "official" tourism hub for Scotland offers info on bargain travel packages, tips for skiing in Scotland, and feature articles on subjects like the "Kilt Movies" that have been making skirt-wearing guys into international sex symbols.✓ **INTERNET**→*url* http://www.scotourist.org.uk/stb/

Tweednet Warning: this is a tartan-free zone! There are thousands of sites linked to Tweednet, including organizations dedicated to restocking the salmon in the Tweed, a guide to national poet Robbie Burns, and a business directory. Further links take visitors rock climbing and stargazing at the Royal Observatory. Head to The Internet Cafe for updates on the Edinburgh Fringe Festival. ✓ **INTERNET**→*url* http://www.scotborders.co.uk/

Culture

Nessie on the Net You might want to head straight to the gallery of sheep photos, but then you'd miss the pictures of the big highland bulls. Whiskey, salmon, tossing really big sticks, and smoking are the other hallmarks of the highlands explored here, except, of course, Nessie. No, there isn't any definitive proof here, for that you must visit her home (directions included).✓ **INTERNET**→*url* http://www.scotnet.co.uk/highland/

soc.culture.scottish (ng) Ever wonder what makes a Scotsman a Scotsman? Is it the skirt wearing, the love of golf, or the curling? There may never be a definite answer to this question, but one thing's certain—the Scotsman wonders the same about his American counterpart—is it the jeans wearing, the love of baseball, or the watching of *Happy Days*? Post to this newsgroup to discuss Scotland with the natives.✓ **USENET**→ soc.culture.scottish

Guides

Scotland Online This guide tells you everything you need to know about visiting Scotland, from hotel listings to restaurants, to suggested sightseeing stops. After your trip, visit the Reader's section of the page to share your experiences with other Netters.✓ **INTERNET**→*url* http://www.ibmpcug.co.uk/~ecs/

Scotland Travel and Accommodation The ferry from the Isle of Bute to Rothesay takes 30 minutes and it runs every 45 minutes. This site tells not only how to get to the ends of the Scottish earth, but where to stay once you arrive. With its listings of hotels, restaurants, and pubs, it's a comprehensive travel site. (Try the Fernie Castle Hotel in Cupar, or the much less expensive Royal Hotel in Dysart when heading toward Fife.) Email connections to all lodgings are provided.✓ **INTERNET**→*url* http://www.ftech.net/~milford/scotland/scotland.html

Virtual Inn Check in here before you check in at the Tartan Arms in Glasgow. This huge list of hotels, pubs, and restaurants (over 7,000 in all) will help ensure that you only wake up to a breakfast of haggis if you really want it.✓ **INTERNET**→*url* http://www.virtual-inn.co.uk/

Hotels

Letham Grange Hotel and Golf Courses Golf fanatics have a deep longing to hit little white balls on the green turf in the home of the game. This hotel is longing to make those dreams come true. Find out about its accouterments and rates here.✓ **INTERNET**→*url* http://www.webcom.com/~tli/uk-golf/letham.html

Edinburgh

Edinburgh—The Capital of Scotland From Arthur's Tor to Princes Street, the gray stone city is here, in an online version of the "official" city guide. Annotated photo essays describe local attractions—don't miss the bloodstain on the floor of Holyrood where Rizzo was stabbed 57 times in front of Mary, Queen of Scots. An interactive map helps walkers plan their tour of the sites on foot (24 hour toilets are marked on the map). Link to the Edinburgh Tourist Board for information on restaurants, hotels, local attractions, and events.✓ **INTERNET**→*url* http://www.efr.hw.ac.uk/EDC/Edinburgh.html

Web 13—The Internet Cafe Web 13 is Edinburgh's "official" Website, and it lists info on upcoming local events, be it the Edinburgh Fringe Festival or the Highland Traditional Music gathering. This all-purpose tourism site offers the details on galleries, accommodations, and bus tours of Edinburgh. What's on in the theater, cinema, and clubs is logged in at the site's Entertainment section. ✓ **INTERNET**→*url* http://www.presence.co.uk/index.html

Glasgow

The Unauthorized Glasgow 1999 Homepage Voted Great Britain's City of Art and Architecture for 1999, Glasgow shows off its architectural savvy at this site. Preview controversial building proposals, visit online galleries, or enter the fray yourself via the Glasgow School of the Arts' design competitions.✓ **INTERNET**→*url* http://www.colloquium.co.uk/www/eponym/glasgow_1999/intro.html

Across Europe

All too often, the modern-day European tour is like a recap of the day's NBA action—all highlights. But there are more than two dozen nations in Europe, and most of them have their own secret treasures for ambitious travelers. Delve into the lesser-known corners of Europe with the **Albania World Wide Web Home Page, Iceland Info**, the **Luxembourg National Museum of History and Art**, and more.

Take a stroll through Iceland—from http://www.infinet.com/~leep/images/

On the Net

Albania

Albania World Wide Web Home Page Chock-full of information about the land of the double-headed eagle—from a sound file of the national anthem to the 1992 election results. A virtual tour stops at the major cities of the formerly curtained country—Tirana, Shkdora, Gjirokastër, and the ruins of the 4th-century-B.C. fortified city of Butrinti. Other features of the site profile the Albanian people and culture—including famous Albanians like King Farouk of Egypt and Mother Theresa.✓ **INTERNET**→*url* http://www.ios.com/~ulpiana/Albanian/index.html

Andorra

About Andorra For a country of only 468 square kilometers, Andorra has a lot to offer tourists. This site informs the curious about history and culture, art, gastronomy, handicrafts, exhibits, festivals, snow, fauna and flora, sports, fairs, and conventions in Andorra. After a stop here, one knows that the country was founded by Charlemagne, is famous for its pork products, has 30,000 hotel rooms, has ski slopes open six months a year—and that's without even mentioning the wild boars!✓ **INTERNET**→*url* http://www.xmission.com/~dderhak/andorra.htm

Introduction to Catalan Catalan is the national language of Andorra, a large part of Spain, and a region of France. Get a brief text overview of Catalan language and culture here.✓ **INTERNET**→*url* http://www.willamette.edu/~tjones/languages/Catalan/webcat1.html

Josh's Andorra Page Head to this hypertext overview for insight into modern Andorran politics, economics, and culture. Josh also provides links to other Andorran sites.✓ **INTERNET**→*url* http://cristal.icp.grenet.fr:8080/~jordi/Andorra_Eng.html

Skiing in Andorra Get the scoop on the joys of skiing in Andorra—including trail-difficulty assessments and maps and guides to the lodges with the cheapest beer.✓ **INTERNET**→*url* http://rmd-www.mr.ic.ac.uk/snow/reports/andorra.html

Armenia

Armenian Home Page Find links to Armenian newspapers, a number of mailing lists, several newsgroups, and an IRC channel for discussion of all things Armenian. For tourists and the curious, links to visa requirements, travel information, maps, and suggested tours are here to provide practical assistance. There's even a link to a large collection of Armenian jokes—tell the one about the Armenian, the Georgian, and the Russian at a bar in Yerevan and make some new pals. ✓**INTERNET**→*url* http://wotan.wiwi.hu-berlin.de/~houssik/armenia.html

---

Window to Armenia The history of Armenia is long—the lesson here begins a millennium before the birth of Christ. The country's culture is rich and tenacious, surviving years of oppression; learn about it here through online galleries displaying visual and performing arts. Virtual tours take Net travelers down Mashdots Avenue in Yerevan, to the site of the Battle of Ssardarabat, the heights of Echmiadzin, and the resort of Dilijan. All combined, the resources succeed in making Armenia an intriguing travel destination. ✓**INTERNET**→*url* http://www.darmstadt.gmd.de/~baloian/armenia.html

Belarus

Virtual Guide to Belarus Dimitry Zelenko has assembled a collection of links to info on his home country, including connections to an illustrated multi-century national chronology, cultural overviews highlighted by sound files of folk songs, and galleries of national costumes and textile patterns. For tourists he has tendered a list of "possible attractions," full of city guides for Minsk, Harodnia, and other Belarusian towns, and an Advice for Tourists section with gems like "Beware of the guys in sports suits and with short haircuts. These are potential hunters for simple-minded foreigners." Also online here is a poignant apologia of "the balloon incident." The author's plea that it be the last incident in the Cold War even received a forgiving and empathetic response from one of the dead pilot's brothers. ✓**INTERNET**→*url* http://faraday.clas.virginia.edu/~ana4a/Belarus.html

Bulgaria

All About Bulgaria Bulgaria. Perhaps it's not the first destination to come to the mind of travelers, but a trip to this site is certain to make even the most weary jet-setter stand up and take notice. The immense hypertext FAQ here displays the richness of Bulgarian culture—choose from history lessons, online newspapers, recipes for Bulgarian-style baklava, essays on Bulgarian music and dance, Cyrillic fonts for reading Bulgarian text, and a Bulgarian soccer-club schedule. But that's not all—travelers also get phone numbers for hotels, hospitals, and nightclubs nationwide. Even popular proverbs are included—"All diseases are caused by not drinking regularly." ✓**INTERNET**→*url* http://www.cs.columbia.edu/~radev/bulginfo.html

---

Information about Bulgaria Start with a picture essay on the Bulgarian royal family and His Royal Majesty King Boris III. After paying homage to the royals, continue with an article on Bulgarian dances, pictures of current bank notes, and links to Bulgarian FAQs and newsgroups. Anyone looking for a summer home would do well to check the privatization information provided at this site by the government. ✓**INTERNET**→*url* http://pisa.rockefeller.edu:8080/Bulgaria/

Croatia

Croatia Understandably, the Croatian tourist industry has been suffering of late, but this site is certainly a good substitute for being there. A clickable map takes travelers to a number of Croatian cities—Zagreb, Split, and Dubrovnik, among others. Photos and sound files bring the page alive, and articles on culture and politics give foreigners a grounding in the nation's long history. Text of news stories from Croatian radio and photographs of the war zones keep Web travelers on top of the political situation. Those who wish to explore Croatia for real will find a Croatian phrase guide, a weather guide, and practical information on customs and money. ✓**INTERNET**→*url* http://tjev.tel.etf.hr/hrvats ka/HR.html

Fodor's Choice...

Romania's Mogosoaia Palace—http://www.cs.jhu.edu/grad/mihai/bucharest/

Cyprus

Cyprus This island state has an impressive cyberpresence. Each town is lovingly profiled with an illustrated guide to its history, culture, and accommodations, as well as feature articles on subjects like "The Antiquities of Turkish Nicosia." Links lead to guides for Cypriot dance and poetry and an online Cypriot arts museum. Under the deceptive heading "Other" lurk treasures like an illustrated essay on the wild donkeys of the Karpaz Peninsula and *National Geographic* photos of Cyprus from a 1928 issue. ✓**INTERNET**→*url* http://force.stwing.upenn.edu:8001/~durduran/cyprus.html

North Cyprus Home Page A site dedicated to Turkish North Cyprus covering all aspects of the society, with essays on everything from history (with a decidedly Turkish slant) to local traditions and cuisine. Text documents answer basic tourism questions (they drive on the left) and list tour operators who specialize in travel to North Cyprus. The portraits of attractions like Othello's Tower or the 700-year-old fig tree at the Lala Mustafa Pasha Mosque are enticing. ✓**INTERNET**→*url* http://www.brad.ac.uk/~yysentur/.ncyprus/doc2.html.

Republic of Cyprus (Pitas) Welcome to the Republic of Cyprus home page, the other side of the story, which comments that Nicosia and Limassol "have been under Turkish occupation since 1974 and are inaccessible to visitors." Like the North Cyprus home page, a very politicized historical essay is a prominent feature. Tourist information is scant at present, but the town profiles are useful. ✓**INTERNET**→*url* http://www.ucy.ac.cy/cyprus/cyprus.html

Estonia

About Estonia The strains of the Estonian national anthem welcome browsers to this all-purpose site. Links here lead to Estonian news services, an English-Estonian dictionary, and a guide to doing business in the newly capitalist republic, among other sites. ✓**INTERNET**→*url* http://www.eenet.ee/english/intro.html

Estonia Country Guide An online textbook begins Estonian history in the eighth millennium B.C. Other hypertext articles discuss the Estonian people, nature (kukersite is an important mineral resource), and culture (upcoming St. John's Day celebrations and the Vijandi Early Music Festival are profiled). Links to news sources about Estonia and other Baltic states are also available. ✓**INTERNET**→*url* http://www.nlib.ee/ESTCG/

Institute for Baltic Studies A participant in the Globewide Network Academy, this site offers a broad introduction to Estonian politics and culture through sources like the epic poem *The Kalevipoeg*, a monograph on Estonian theater, and the manifesto of the guerrilla independence movement. ✓**INTERNET**→*url* http://www.ibs.ee/

The Baltics Online Daily news from the Baltic republics. ✓**INTERNET**→*url* http://www.viabalt.ee/

Iceland

A Guide to Iceland Updated every Monday, this guide brings the latest on "Iceland and its people" through articles on history, government, and economy. A fascinating FAQ proffers informative tidbits—for 20 years there was no TV on Thursday in Iceland; more than 70 percent of newborns are illegitimate, and the sale of M&Ms is illegal in Iceland. For practical info on travel in the country, turn to the site's list of tourist attractions, local events, accommodations, and up-to-the-minute weather. A phrase book reads like a guide to picking up chicks, instructing not only how to ask for the restroom, but also spelling out, "You are an angel fallen to earth" and "I have never seen a woman more lovely" in the native tongue. ✓**INTERNET**→*url* http://www.primenet.com/~peetah/iceland/Islandia.html

Iceland How can you help but love a country that boasts Santa Claus as a tourist attraction? The Website's photographs of the island nation are breathtaking, and the information on hotels, golfing, fisheries, and museums is useful for all tourists. You can even sign up for a barhopping tour of Reykjavik! The section on Hafnarfjodur, "the home of Vikings, elves, and hidden people," is highly recommended. ✓**INTERNET**→*url* http://rvik.ismennt.is/~thorthor/iceland.html

Iceland Info Click on a map of Iceland, and take a short photographic tour of this small nation. ✓**INTERNET**→*url* http://www.rfisk.is/english/iceland/rest_of_iceland.html

Lose some money at Monaco's Monte Carlo casino—http://www.monaco.mc/monaco/

Latvia

Latvia Facts and News For those who still need help untangling the remains of the USSR, this site offers general information about the nascent republic and links to Latvian news agencies. ✓**INTERNET**→*url* http://www.vernet.lv/latvia/

Travel in Latvia (Latvian Tourist Board) The tourist board has an impressive presence here. Prospective travelers will get help obtaining a visa and finding a good restaurant (how about Mazabele in Skrunda) and a dry cleaner to get the spot of Black Balsam (a Latvian alcohol whose secret recipe includes oak bark and orange peels) out of their ties. Consult hotel listings for all large towns and a calendar of upcoming events. For those interested in the great outdoors, this site provides contact information for adventure-tour providers as well. ✓**INTERNET**→*url* http://www.vernet.lv/latvia/travel/

Go to Iceland, climb a glacier—http://rvik.ismennt.is/~thorthor/myndir/

Welcome to Latvia Introducing the ancient cultural community of Latvia is a brief hypertext essay—complete with pictures of Riga and sound files, font files, and tutorials in the Latvian tongue. Further pointers lead to sites dedicated to other Baltic nations and facts about the country. ✓**INTERNET**→*url* http://www.latnet.lv/

Lithuania

Welcome to Lithuania A page dedicated to the people, culture, language, and politics of Lithuania. ✓**INTERNET**→*url* http://neris.mii.lt/

Luxembourg

Luxembourg Discover this small nation with a pleasant overview of the land under the rule of Grand Duke Jean. Special pages are dedicated to attractions like Luxembourg City, Vianden, "Luxembourg's Switzerland," and the valley of the Black Ernz. ✓**INTERNET**→*url* http://rzstud1.rz.uni-karlsruhe.de/~ujiw/lx.html

Luxembourg National Museum of History and Art Visiting Le Musée National d'Histoire et d'Art will expand your knowledge of the tiny Grand Duchy, a nation roughly the size of Jacksonville, Florida. The site's elegant entry hall leads to exhibits on the art and lifestyles of Luxembourgers. Special exhibitions include the collection of the Prince of Liechtenstein. (Liechtenstein is a European nation even tinier than Luxembourg.) Links connect to several other online museums worldwide. Some information at this site is only in French. ✓**INTERNET**→*url* http://www.men.lu/~fumanti/LuxMusee.html

Monaco

Monaco The Net has one definitive site about Monaco, and this is it. You'll find everything you need to know about this tiny nation famous for its income tax (or lack of it), its casino, and its royalty. A brief intro lists What's Cool in Monaco—arriving by helicopter from Nice Airport and spotting Princess Caroline are on top of the list. Then a FAQ provides interesting tidbits about the mountainous country—at points, Monaco is only 350 meters wide. But the real meat of the page comes with an events calendar (with dates and details on the Grand Prix, the Red Cross Gala, and other notable happenings), a history of the country, lists of hotels (from six-star hotels to those with only four), and a description of Prince Rainier III's collection of antique automobiles. Read the section called Monegasque Traditions before honeymooning in Monaco—they practice *ciaraviy*, which entails an all-night-long serenade under the windows of newlyweds. (Wonder if Grace Kelly and Rainier received that treatment?) ✓**INTERNET**→*url* http://www.monaco.mc/

The Monaco Grand Prix Relive past racing seasons here through photos from the pit and the winner's circle. Real racing aficionados will enjoy the profiles of men and machines that win and the article on the new Formula1 rules. Info on next year's schedule and ticket purchase is also provided. ✓**INTERNET**→*url* http://www.monaco.mc/monaco/gprix/index.html

The former crash pad of Dracula—http://www.embassy.org/romania/travel/

Armenia's Goshovank Monastery—http://www.darmstadt.gmd.de/~baloian/

Macedonia

Republic of Macedonia Information An all-encompassing page that takes you on virtual tours of major cities like Skopje, Ohrid, and Prilep; acquaints you with the national flag, anthem, and constitution; and even offers an interview with Milcho Manchevski, director of *Before the Rain*. ✓**INTERNET**→*url* http://asudesign.eas.asu.edu/places/Macedonia/republic/

Virtual Macedonia More than just a great collection of photographs of the Macedonian countryside, this site offers a real slice of Macedonia culture—pick up some Macedonian Lenten recipes, read a short history of the nation, and even read stories on current events in the Republic. ✓**INTERNET**→*url* http://www.rit.edu/~bvs4997/Macedonia/

Romania

Bucharest This site relies on the *Encyclopedia Britannica* for historical background, but it's put together its own virtual tour to lure visitors with a glimpse of the Cotroceni Palace and Herastrau Park. Also here are lists of restaurants, hotels, clubs, and museums to serve all tourist needs. Links to airlines that fly to Bucharest make planning travel to the capital easy. ✓**INTERNET**→*url* http://www.humnet.ucla.edu/hcf/staff/andrei/bucuresti.html

Embassy of Romania The embassy's pages proudly point out the highlights of the nation—Romania's Riviera, Bucharest, wildlife on the Danube, Roman spas, and the gothic charms of Transylvania—in an informative graphic essay. Basic tourism info is provided, although one wonders about the national passion for "battered brains" in Dracula's homeland. The embassy also publishes an online English-language newsletter called *Romania Today*. ✓**INTERNET**→*url* http://www.embassy.org/romania/

Romanian for Travellers Use the sound files to ensure that you are polite when traveling in Romania. "One ticket please" is *Un bilet pentru..., va rog in Timisoara.* ✓**INTERNET**→*url* http://insti.physics.sunysb.edu/~mmartin/languages/romanian/romanian.html

Romanian Tourist Information Romanians are very practical people according to this site, which will point you to tourist agencies and embassies aching to help you plan a trip there. The attractions of this country have their own flavor—how about a weekend at a Black Sea resort or a week following in Dracula's footsteps (via coach tour, of course). Staying in a four-star hotel in Bucharest will only set you back $80—let's pack! ✓**INTERNET**→*url* http://www.qqq.com/romania/

Slovakia

Interactive Slovakia Slovakia certainly wins the prize as the most wired of the former Eastern Bloc countries, by virtue of its virtual tours of almost every nook and cranny of the country. See the ominous gothic castle looming over Bratislava and the town walls of Kezmarok in the High Tatras. You can even rent a cottage in the Kremnicke Vichy online! Nonetheless, it hasn't (yet) been shown that taking a virtual spa treatment will help with lower back pain. ✓**INTERNET**→*url* http://www.savba.sk/logos/interactive/list.html

Slovakia Online Enter Slovakia via this virtual gateway that leads to info on Slovakian music, art exhibits, and even theater programs. After taking a quick read through *The Bratislava Medical Journal*, relax and tune your short-wave radio into Radio Ragtime Bratislava (its frequency is listed here, too). ✓**INTERNET**→*url* http://savba.savba.sk/logos/list-e.html

Slovenia

Slovenia Guide Not to be confused with Slovakia, Slovenia used to be part of Yugoslavia, but in 1990, "the year of the horse in the Chinese horoscope, which brings great changes," it became independent. This hypertext essay lovingly describes its verdant landscape and deep, cool caves. Also find here a wealth of specific travel information and cultural delights such as recipes for Slovenia's wild mushrooms or a peek at the spas dotting the landscape (how about a slimming course at Dolenjske Toplice?). ✓**INTERNET**→*url* http://www.ijs.si/slo.html

DETOURS

"Yup, there are caves in Luxembourg. They are called the Casemates. Don't ask me what that means. They have been hewn out of the rock face and could shelter an army as well as a bunch of cannons. I think they helped the Luxembourgeois defend the city a number of times. You can also take an elevator to the Grund (ground) where the rest of the 'old city' is/was (we didn't go there because of time constraints). BTW they are right 'in town' so they are easy to find and get to (if I remember correctly they are fairly close to a parking garage!). Luxembourg is a delightful city, very fairy-tale like and lots of nice places to wander through -- for about a day. It is also the only country that actively commemorates (in my opinion) America's contribution to the liberation of Europe (by the Allied forces). I think the Battle of the Bulge was fought on Luxembourg soil, and you see tanks and other statues and reminders of the war in many small towns."

—from **Luxembourg**

Part 6

Latin America & The Caribbean

Mexico

Discover the beaches of Cancun, the ruins of the Yucatan, or the vibrant streets of Mexico City. Find out what others have enjoyed by tuning into CompuServe's **Mexico Forum** or AOL's **Mexico** bulletin board. Worried about the water? One look at the **Cancun Online** proves that the blue-green waters of Mexico are in good shape. A trip to the **Indigenous Peoples of Mexico** site reveals that Mayan culture is still alive and well. The **soc.culture.mexican FAQ** answers troubling questions about the origin of burritos and the real meaning of the word gringo. Get a taste of the culinary treats of Mexico at **Mexican Cuisine**, and dance off the calories to the sound files of the Mexican national music—**Mariachi**.

The ruins of Chichén Itzá—http://www.wotw.com/wow/mexico/cancun/chichen.html

On the Net

Across the board

Mexico There's something to please all sorts in Mexico, as the variety of postings to this board ably demonstrates. Edie wants to know about a sun-and-shopping trip to Puerto Vallarta, while Brian wants to study Spanish in Cuernavaca and seeks cheap rent. The traffic is heavy here, so you'll get answers in no time flat, whether you're asking about the condition of Cozumel's reefs (they're underwater) or bargain airfares to Cancun (they're not). ✓**AMERICA ONLINE**→*keyword* TravelForum→message boards→world traveler→Mexico

Mexico Forum The huge tourism section here is packed full of recommendations for Cancun resorts, condo rental offers, and discussions of Mayan ruins. And because of the number and demographic diversity of the contributors, someone is bound to know the current price of Pemex gas or the location of the annual Cervantes festival (Spain, perhaps?). The libraries provide a wealth of files on Mexico, including accommodations guides, maps, and the occasional first-person travelogue. ✓**COMPUSERVE**→*go* mexico

Mexico-L (ml) Mexico is one of the most popular destinations for U.S. tourists, and this mailing list discusses the highlights of the nation, from Mexico City to Mayan ruins. ✓**INTERNET**→*email* listserv@tecmtyvm.mty.itesm.mx ✍ *Type in message body:* subscribe mexico <your full name>

Mexico-Related Links Hop off this collection of links to discover the current peso exchange rate (it can only get better) or to read a FAQ from soc.culture.mexican. If you can handle large .GIF files, there are scans of several daily newspapers' front pages. And then there are the political commentaries, the Ballet Folklorico, and the Indigenous Peoples network. Travelers aiming for Mexico can learn basic Spanish, find out where to get a visa, or prepare for their trip with historical essays. Get busy. ✓**INTERNET**→*url* http://www.eden.com/~tomzap/links.html

rec.travel Library Mexico A small selection from the popular rec.travel newsgroup. Find out if Bruce enjoyed his motorcycle trip or what Jim found in Mazatlan (not himself, and not true love, but plenty of other things to hold his interest). The soc.culture.mexican FAQ is also housed here. ✓INTERNET→*url* http://www.digimark.net/rec-travel/north_america/mexico/index.html

soc.culture.mexican FAQs After listening to greetings in Spanish, Mayan, Nahuatl, and Zapoteco, visitors to the soc.culture.mexican FAQs can browse the 50 short documents that profess to answer the basic questions about Mexico and Mexicans. The FAQs cover a surprisingly broad range—not only will you learn how to interpret Mayan calendars and the origin of the term "gringo," but you'll get information on the Indian population, the Mexican Internet, and whether or not burritos are authentically Mexican. Unfortunately, all answers are not in English, so you may be left puzzling over ominous phrases like "el gigante imperialista McDonald's." ✓INTERNET→*url* http://www.public.iastate.edu/~rjsalvad/scmfaq/faq index.html

TravNet! Mexico Maps, cultural overviews, and visa information, as well as a telnet connection to the travel agency sponsor.✓INTERNET→*url* http://www.sky.net/~eric/t/tnmex.htm

Web Turistico de Mexico Get hotel and dining information for all of Mexico's provinces, along with short essays on historical attractions. And though descriptions are in Spanish, the star-ratings system, addresses, and phone numbers need no translation—so jump right over, ahora. ✓INTERNET→*url* http://ss20.mty.itesm.mx/turweb/

Windows on Mexico The perfect starting place for Mexican tour planning. The illustrations themselves are a tantalizing lure, but it's the services offered by Windows on Mexico that elevate this site over the competition. Choose a travel theme—beaches, spas, archeology, ecotourism, and so on—and you'll get a comprehensive portrait of Mexico through the lens of that theme, as well as a large list of tour operators and resorts. After you've chosen your resort, the events calendar tells you how to spend all that extra time available after snorkeling, sunning, and exploring. And the page comes complete with a link to the Mexican Tourist Bureau and other Mexico sites online. ✓INTERNET→*url* http://www.wotw.com/wow/mexico/mexico.html

Worldview—Mexico While some of the destinations represented here aren't Mexican—Rio de Janiero, San Jose, Buenos Aires—more than a dozen are, from Acapulco to Cancun to Cozumel to Guadalajara to Mexico City. Each Worldview folder contains information on festivals, hotels, museums, restaurants, and shopping, as well as special features on selected attractions (Oaxaca's Planetarium Nundehui, Puerto Vallarte's Museo del Cuale). ✓AMERICA ONLINE→*keyword* worldview→Latin America

Culture

Cinco de Mayo Want to know why the fifth of May is so darn fun in Vera Cruz? Look here for a brief history of Mexico's national holiday, and then hum the Liz Phair song to yourself as you browse. ✓INTERNET→*url* http://latino.sscnet.ucla.edu/demo/cinco.html

Indigenous Peoples of Mexico The quotation that opens this page clearly expresses its political perspective: "Every mestizo is one less Indian—or one more Indian waiting to re-emerge." And it is here you will find the long-suppressed voice of the indigenous. Resources include a native-languages database, excellent illustrated ethnographic profiles from NativeNet, and an archive of poetry, songs, and legends. Divided both by ethnic groups and by region, the site is relatively comprehensive, and the Chiapas menu holds a number of sources on the current peasant uprising. ✓INTERNET→*url* http://kuhttp.cc.ukans.edu:80/~marc/geography/latinam

Fodor's Choice...

Worth Seeing

Mexico City. The Zócalo—officially called the Plaza de la Consitución—is the largest plaza in the Western Hemisphere. The word "zócalo" actually means "pedestal." In the 19th century there were plans to build a monument to Mexican Independence in Mexico City's main Plaza. For whatever reason, the monument was never built, and all that remains of those designs is the name for the base of the monument—the pedestal—that never came into being. The misnomer stuck and is now the term applied to the main plazas of most Mexican cities.

—from Fodor's *Mexico on the Loose 1995*

Enjoy unbridled hedonism in Cancun—http://www.wotw.com/wow/mexico/cancun/

/mexico/mex_main.html

Mariachi A Spanish explanation of the appeal of the "national" music of Mexico. ✓**INTERNET**→*url* http://mexico.udg.mx/Udg/Extuniv/mariachi.html

Maya Adventure Pack your explorer's kit and head for the Mayan ruins of the Yucatan. Choose a magically named site from the map—Chichen Itza, Tikal—and explore the arts, architecture, culture, and religion of this age-old culture. A tour takes the intrepid traveler through eight sites, each with a different focus, such as the textile-arts industry or altars of sacrifice. ✓**INTERNET**→*url* http://ties.k12.mn.us/~smm/

Mexican Cuisine Step into the cocina (kitchen), and you'll be greeted by loads of recipes and an explanation of proper cooking techniques, as well as descriptions of 10 types of chiles. Pre-Columbian delights include Maguey's worms and escamoles (ant eggs). ✓**INTERNET**→*url* http://csgwww.uwaterloo.ca/users/dmg/mexico/cocina/cocina.html

soc.culture.mexican (ng) Discussion here is in both English and Spanish and is often focused on politics, the troubled economy, and the Chiapas rebellion. But avid travelers do use the group to ask for recommendations on good hotels and the "best" ruins to visit. ✓**USENET**→soc.culture.mexican

The World of Mayan Culture Many think that Mayan culture is limited to the crumbling monoliths of the Yucatan and Tikal. This excellent site disproves this preconception with great tours of the Mayan world, both ancient and modern. Learn about recent archeological discoveries or Maya cuisine. Read tourism suggestions. And then jot down the contact numbers for travel planning, tours, and accommodations. ✓**INTERNET**→*url* http://www.yucatan.com.mx/mayas/mapaengl.htm

Regional info

Bel-Air Resorts Mexico Promotional site for resorts in Costa Careyes, Puerto Vallarta, and Tamarindo. ✓**INTERNET**→*url* http://www.wotw.com/wow/situr/bel-main.hml

Cancun and Mayan Coast The focus here is on hedonism, all made possible by the marriage of the Caribbean sun and sea and a highly developed tourist infrastructure. Wander through resorts like Hotel Costa del Mar and Posada Captain Lafitte; accommodations profiles are organized by locale, and contact information is included. ✓**INTERNET**→*url* http://www.pic.net/uniloc/mexico/

Cancun Online Head to American teens' favorite south-of-the-border hotspot. It's all here, from lists of hotels and restaurants to entertainment calendars to train schedules. In case you thought Cancun was all about sex, drugs, and suntans, think again—you can gamble, visit rustic villages, or ponder nearby Mayan ruins. Added plus: travel can be booked online! ✓**INTERNET**→*url* http://www.cancun.com/color.html

Chihuahua Discover the province whose name now conjures up images of lap dogs. Read about Chihuahua's interesting attractions; unfortunately there's no hotel or restaurant info here. ✓**INTERNET**→*url* http://cs.utep.edu/chihuahua/main.html

Pacific Coast of Oaxaca, Mexico Oaxaca's average fall water temperature is 98 degrees. But its attractions aren't limited to body-hot water—there's the majestic Palacio del Gobierno and the beautiful Teatro Mecedonio de Alcala. And this Website isn't limited to Edenic rhapsodizing. Get articles from popular magazines, check hotel prices and tour operators, and learn which cash machines give the best exchange rates. There's even an archive of travelogues posted at the site, so you can learn from those who went before you. ✓**INTERNET**→*url* http://www.eden.com/~tomzap/index.html

Latin America

Salsa—it's both a dance and a spicy condiment, and both hint at the special lively bite of their Latin American home. Get a taste of culture south of the border at **Things Latino—CyberRaza from EgoWeb** or **Latino-Link.** Plan your own journey of discovery with advice from **rec.travel.latin-america** or CompuServe's **Mexico / Central America** board. **AmeriSpan Unlimited** will teach you how to converse though its immersion (in culture, not water) programs. Use your newfound language skills talking with actual Latin Americans on **soc.culture.latin-america** or reading the daily papers like *El Norte* and *Dairio de Hoy* at **News and Electronic Forums** while drinking a cup of Colombian coffee. And yes, put on your red dress and head to **Salsa Basic** to ensure you're a hit on the dance floors of Mexico City.

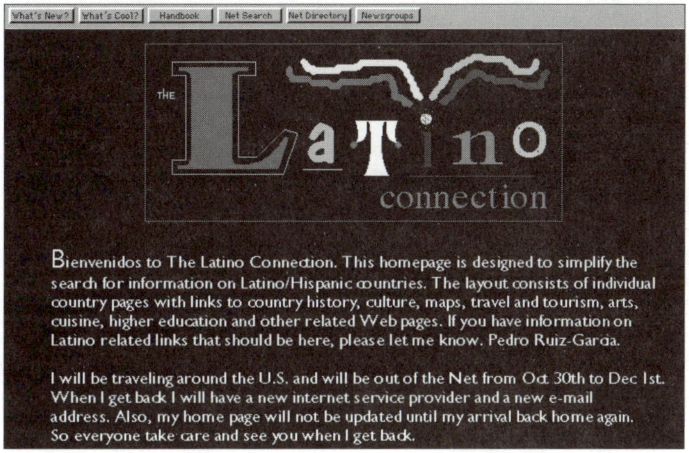

Welcome to the Latino Connection—http://www.webspace.com/~pedro/index.html

On the Net

Across the board

Latin America Worldview Comprehensive guides for a variety of Latin American cities, from Cancun, Mexico to Santiago, Chile. ✓**AMERICA ONLINE**→*keyword* worldview→Latin America

Latin American Information Network This index is an excellent starting point for Latin American exploration. Sites are organized by country or by topic—music, anthropology, news, etc. Travelers will feast on the links to the big sites, like rec.travel archives or the Virtual Tourist, and be charmed by the little sites that didn't slip through the cracks, like the Tango Server and the Chilean Sky Guide—they'll help you dance under the Southern stars with ease. ✓**INTERNET**→*url* http://lanic.utexas.edu/

LatinoLink Open the pages of this weekly e-zine to find timely hypertext news articles and political commentary in English and Spanish. But all is not politics here—links connect to lifestyle, travel, and entertainment pages that provide excellent diversions, with stories about the struggle over Eva Perón's remains, the Tejano music boom, and the documentary *Carmen Miranda: Bananas Is My Business.* ✓**INTERNET**→*url* http://www.latinolink.com/

LatinoWeb Some of the diverse links here take cultural explorers to the Andean Music page or the Ballet Folklorico. No fewer than six sites hold recipes for chimichangas and psole—but if you decide that money's more important than food, the *Wall Street Journal* and *Las Journada* are just a jump away. ✓**INTERNET**→*url* http://www.catalog.com/favision/latnoweb.htm

Mexico/Central America Mary sings the praises of Guatemala, as do 14 others. Helene wants a romantic hideaway in Mexico, and Carlos points her to a hotel in Ixtapa. Participation is broad; one person quotes Simone De Beauvoir in an ongoing debate on money smuggling. Others enjoy comparing the benefits of resorts, or wondering aloud if Costa Rica is really appropriate for a couple toting an infant. ✓**COMPUSERVE** *go*→travsig→Message Boards→Mexico/Central America

rec.travel.latin-america (ng) Barbara is desperately seeking a reasonable hotel in Cabo San Lucas. Jed wants to know about rafting opportunities in southern Mexico. Marc is eager to hear from anyone who's traveled to Guyana. And Bill is looking for the best restaurants in Zihuatanejo. What do they have in common? They all turned to rec.travel.latin-america for answers, and they got them. ✓**USENET**→rec.travel.latin-america

The Latino Connection Start exploring Latin Cyberspace here, with loads of links sorted by country. At the minimum you'll find basic political information, maps, and online guidebooks about the nation of choice. But there's always more—travelogues, cookbooks, newspapers, music sites, mailing lists, and millions of pictures. ✓**INTERNET**→*url* http://www.webspace.com/~pedro/index.html

Things Latino—CyberRaza from EgoWeb Felipe, the creator of this vast collection of Latino links, has assembled a "discovery point" for cyberexplorers. Country-specific links transport visitors and expatriates to virtual Guatemala, Peru, and other nations. And then there are the online meeting places—the Latino Connection, El Mundo Latino, and Hispanic.Com offer Spanish-language discussions. Political links, history links, and music and art links round out the resources here. End the day with a samba at Alberto's Nightclub. ✓**INTERNET**→*url* http://edb518ea.edb.utexas.edu/html/latinos.html

Culture

Hispanic/Latino History What were the flour wars? Find out about the "near apocalyptic" pre-Columbian feud in the Aztec Empire from a hypertext essay. The long, variegated history of Spain in the New World is attractively presented in the Library of Congress exhibit, "1492: An Ongoing Voyage." Other links lead to mission churches in California, the Alamo, and a Mayan museum. ✓**INTERNET**→*url* http://latino.sscnet.ucla.edu/research/history.html

News and Electronic Forums Prospective visitors will do well to check out this news center. Daily issues of many foreign papers can be reached from here—Colombia's *Diario Estrategia*, Ecuador's *Diario de Hoy*, and Mexico's *El Norte*, among others. General news links proffer the world view of El Comercio Asturias in Spain, CNN, and Freedom Forum. And after you read the news, debate its importance by linking to the newsgroups dedicated to each country. ✓**INTERNET**→*url* http://lanic.utexas.edu:80/la/region/news/

Salsa Basic Want to impress the locals with your grace and rhythm? Now you can learn to salsa with this online dance lesson, which comes complete with sound, text instructions, and your choice of male or female instructor. And when you're done with salsa, link to the Virtual Ballroom to learn the mambo. ✓**INTERNET**→*url* http://www.cts.com/~danclink/salsabas.html

soc.culture.latin-america (ng) This grab bag of English and Spanish postings is just as likely to offer a review of a new Brazilian Web page or a Spanish Art Exhibit in New York as to discuss poverty, Mayan astronomy, or land development in Brazil. Tourist questions are welcome; if your tone achieves the right mix of curiosity and seduction, you might even end up with a travel partner. ✓**USENET**→soc.culture.latin-america

Ecotravel

El Planeta Platica This newsletter focuses on ecotravel in Spanish-speaking countries—in other words, ways that travelers can use their time and money to save the planet. With a plethora of links—not only to articles on the environmental effects of oil and coffee, an ecotravel contact list, and book reviews, but also to destination reviews for the Mexican interior, Central America, and South America—this is the foremost site online for environmentally minded travelers. If you think "sustainable development" refers to a Fotomat, don't come here. Otherwise, do. ✓**INTERNET**→*url* http://www.versa.com/mader/ecotravel/ecotravel.html

Services

AmeriSpan Unlimited AmeriSpan sponsors immersion Spanish-language programs in 12 locations. The linguistically ambitious can get prices and course descriptions here, but all travelers will enjoy the travel tips, country guides, and links to sites from Costa Rica to Chile. ✓**INTERNET**→*url* http://www.amerispan.com/

Latin American Travel Consultants (LATC) LATC helps people plan travel to Latin America with guidebooks, guide services, and local offices in most countries. Get more information by reading this online brochure. ✓**INTERNET**→*url* http://www.amerispan.com/latc/

Central America

These days, visitors other than Contras are heading for Central America in droves. The Green Arrow Guide to Central America points tourists in the direction of ecotours, the Honduran rainforest, and the volcanoes of El Salvador, while AOL's **Central America Board** provides experienced advice on dealing with the slight insect problem and offers tips on good hotels. Divers desiring an up-close-and-personal adventure with our underwater friends should check out the **Belize Online Tourist Guide, Scuba Diving in Panama,** and **Bay Island Tours.** You are sure to get away from it all at **The Inn of the Last Resort,** but remember, you can always check your email at **Rock Olas,** in San Jose, Costa Rica.

A beach-front shack in Belize—from http://www.belize.com/caulkph2.html

On the Net

Across the board

Central America Steve and two Swiss friends are planning an eight-month bicycling tour of Central America. Are there any places they should skip entirely? One experienced traveler warns of political turmoil in El Salvador, but most of the posters are more worried about the insect population than the human one (use industrial strength DEET or Avon's Skin So Soft!). People here ask, and offer, advice on scuba diving, sightseeing, parking a "luxury RV," and just plain relaxing in the warm Central American sun. ✓**AMERICA ONLINE**→*keyword* travel forum→Message Boards→World Traveler→Central America

Guides

Green Arrow Guide to Central America Green Arrow has found its niche—providing tourist guides for newly desirable destinations in Central America. Use the country guides for Costa Rica, Panama, Guatemala, Honduras, Belize, Nicaragua, and El Salvador, or browse by category (ecotourism, adventure sports, honeymoon destinations, Mayan world, or sport fishing). Yuppies might enjoy the Tawahka Anthropological Reserve, where entire days are spent building balsa rafts (just like the natives). And surfers looking to conquer new territory will be thrilled to learn that El Salvador has waves to spare. ✓**INTERNET**→*url* http://www.greenarrow.com/welcome.htm

Belize

Belize Yet another visitor is wondering what to do on a honeymoon in Belize (you need instructions?) other than visit the ruins at Tikal and the baboon sanctuary, and go snorkeling and horseback riding. He's told to plan for a riverboat ride and a drive down the Hummingbird Highway. Turn here for expert advice on everything from exploring the Mayan past to viewing the underwater present (and even renting cars). ✓**AMERICA ONLINE**→*keyword* travel forum→Message Boards→World Traveler→Belize

Belize Online Tourist Guide Endorsed by the Belize Tourism Industry Association and the Belize Tourist Board, this site has a range of info for the traveler: maps, photos, event calendars, regional profiles, etc. In a hypertext essay on the Ambergris Caye, for instance, visitors can view a large moray eel, and then if they still want to go diving, they can check out the transportation and hotel information. ✓INTERNET→*url* http://www.belize.com/

Green Arrow Guide to Belize Belize, this guide warns, is not a shopping place—except for bugs, who shop for blood so ferociously your repellent may not be enough to keep them at proboscis's length. But Belize is the home of the Community Baboon Sanctuary, actually populated by black howler monkeys. And it's the former home of huge Mayan cities like Xunantunich. Learn more about Belize's attractions, but little about its accommodations here. ✓INTERNET→*url* http://www.greenarrow.com/belize/belize.htm

Costa Rica

Costa Rica A family of 19 is seeking accommodations for Christmas week and gets numerous suggestions from board members. All types are served by this board—James is seeking a luxury resort for a winter getaway, while Karen wonders how prices for Costa Rican rafting expeditions compare with those in Mexico and Guatemala. ✓AMERICA ONLINE→*keyword* travel forum→Message Boards→Travel Boards→World Traveler→Costa Rica

---

Costa Rica Expeditions A promotional site describing the variety of expeditions available—from a visit to the Monteverde Cloud Forest and Butterfly Garden to a rain forest workshop (a nine-day educational program for the environmentally earnest). Booking information is included. ✓INTERNET→*url* http://www.cool.co.cr/crexped.html

Costa Rica General Info and Travel Half informational site and half promotional brochure for the Changes in L'Attitudes travel agency, this page includes great illustrations (including maps) and interesting information. After boning up on Costa Rican history (Costa Ricans take pride in their European heritage) and geography (Costa Rica is divided into seven provinces or states), take a look at the suggested itineraries. For further information, contact the sponsor via email. ✓INTERNET→*url* http://www.costa-rica.com/Costa/

Costa Rica Handbook This 100-page excerpt from a Moon Travel guide offers a tantalizing view of the nature and culture of Costa Rica. The author waxes eloquent on the beauty of jungle insects, including those too small to see (like the hummingbird flower mite, which is less than one-hundredth the size of the period that follows this rather unwieldy sentence). Unfortunately, the practical tourist information—hotels, restaurants, tour operators, and Spanish-phrase books—can only be found in the actual handbook, which can be ordered online. ✓INTERNET→*url* http://webtravel.org/cr/moon/cr-handbook.html

---

Costa Rica Tourism by Inter@America Information here is easily manageable, providing a nicely illustrated country overview and then the real meat of travel—a FAQ, suggested attractions, and a hotel database. Search for lodging by price or locale—some established hotels even have their own home pages. How about a night or two at the Corcovado Lodge Tent Camp? ✓INTERNET→*url* http://www.cool.co.cr/cgi–bin/turismo

---

Costa Rica TravelWEB The emphasis at this site is less on cyberwandering than nailing down the details of a trip to Costa Rica. To that end, TravelWEB is inaugurating an interactive travel agency to answer questions and book travel arrangements online. Featured destinations are explored in illustrated articles, complete with recommended hotels and tour operators—in Manual Antonio National Park, visitors can stay at the Tulemar Bungalows before taking a mangrove trip with Iguana Tours. The level of detail makes this a useful site for starting your

Fodor's Choice...

Tikal, Guatemala

A visit to the country's most famous ruin will leave you in no doubt as to the extraordinary accomplishments of the Maya; this vast array of awe-inspiring temples and intricate acropolises was once a teeming metropolis with a population of nearly 200,000.

—From Fodor's 96, *Costa Rica, Belize, Guatemala*

The Costa Rican jungle—http://webtravel.org/cr/tortuguero.html

travel planning. ✓**INTERNET**→*url* http://magi.com/crica/

Dairo La Nacion Online version of the daily from San Jose, Costa Rica, in Spanish. ✓**INTERNET**→*url* http://www.nacion.co.cr

Green Arrow Guide to Costa Rica *Hola Costa Rica*, an attractive Internet magazine, has profiled the nation's rain forest and beaches. After exploring the charms of national parks and ancient civilizations, you might want to read about a romantic getaway at Finca Rosa Blanca, known for its "spectacular bathroom...complete with a mini-waterfall." Best news: you can book it online. ✓**INTERNET**→*url* http://www.greenarrow.com/costa/cr.htm

Philip Greenspun's Web Travel Review on Costa Rica Here Philip Greenspun, the renowned online travel writer, takes people on a virtual tour of Costa Rican highlights—the sloths and iguanas of Tortuguero, the spectacular Monteverde Cloud Forest, and Arenal Volcano, one of the world's most active volcanoes. Greenspun also provides tips for those who are inspired to "really" go—those travelers willing to go all-out spending money, booking hotels, and arranging for spectacular photography. And he even includes a list of "next time" attractions, since the country is worth more than one visit. ✓**INTERNET**→*url* http://webtravel.org/cr/

Rock-Ola's Travel can be broadening, but it can also show just exactly how small the world has become. This San Jose bar specializes in oldies, rock 'n' roll memorabilia, and vinyl. Bury yourself in the past, or embrace the present—Rock-Ola's is also a cybercafé. ✓**INTERNET**→*url* http://www.cool.co.cr/usr/rockolas/index.htm

Tico Times Online Read excerpts of the English-language weekly before boarding at JFK. ✓**INTERNET**→*url* http://magi.com/crica/ttimes.html

Welcome to Costa Rica According to the site's FAQ, the best time to visit Costa Rica is from December through April (unless, of course, you are coming for the Atlantic Green Sea turtle nesting that takes place from June through September). The FAQ also offers information on road conditions and nightlife, and a hotel database makes finding accommodations easy. ✓**INTERNET**→*url* http://merica.cool.co.cr/cgi-bin/turismo/

El Salvador

Green Arrow Guide to El Salvador Green Arrow assures that the active volcanoes haven't blown since 1957; however, they can't say the same for the civil war. Hotel reviews and pictures of surfing along the coastline and relaxing at the resorts at Lago del Coatepe don't allay misgivings. Especially since the item preceding "souvenirs" in the travel checklist is "war." ✓**INTERNET**→*url* http://www.greenarrow.com/salvador/salvador.htm

Travel Information El Salvador Ah, the ironies of the global marketplace—"El Salvador has a developing economy. Its tourism facilities are not fully developed. Credit cards are widely accepted." This information package is not designed to reassure those to whom El Salvador means murdered priests and military juntas. It reminds potential travelers that

The Mayan temple at Uaxaltun—http://udgftp.cencar.udg.mx/ingles/Precolombina/

crime is prevalent and that U.S. citizens are often the preferred victims of street thugs. If you still want to go, be sure to contact the authorities listed here before you leave. ✓INTERNET→*url* http://www.ct.com/travel/usstate/ta59.html

Guatemala

Green Arrow Guide to Guatemala Green Arrow's guide recommends bringing rubber boots—they are a scarce commodity in Guatemala City. Along with providing such useful travel tips, this guide divides the country into five distinct vacation areas and experiences. Enjoy the juxtaposition of old and new in the capital; encounter living Mayan culture in the highlands; go back in time at the Mayan ruins of Tikal; relax on unspoiled, rugged beaches on the coast; or explore the isolated rain forest in Alta. As yet the practical information is limited to addresses of three tour companies and two resorts—but that's never stopped a real traveler before. ✓INTERNET→*url* http://www.greenarrow.com/guatemal/guatemal.htm

Guatemala This is a truly lovely site, almost as good as a documentary—with sections on culture, history (Mayan to modern), and ecology, all accentuated with glorious photographs of Tikal and Chichicastenago. The travel information is in its formative stage—connecting airlines and car rental information is online, while accommodations are yet to be added. ✓INTERNET→*url* http://www.neptune.com/guatemala/guatemala.html

Guatemala Just how good is the Green Tortoise bus tour of this Central American nation? You'll get the answer here. Safety questions are often posted to this board, so it's a good idea to check in here and with the consulate before you head out. But there are also Guatemalan natives in residence on this board who let prospective travelers in on the real secret gems of their native land. See you at the Villa Maya near Tikal. ✓AMERICA ONLINE→ *keyword* travel forum→Message Boards→Travel Boards→World Traveler→Guatemala

Guatemala WWW Home Page The gorgeous photos here make this site a virtual *National Geographic*. Learn about Guatemala's history with essays on ancient, colonial, and modern times. After you've visited the Mayan ruins, take a look at the flora and fauna. ✓INTERNET→*url* http://www.ualr.edu/~degonzalez/Guatemala.html

Honduras

A Walkabout in the Rio Platano Biosphere, La Mosquitia Come face to face with the Biosphere in this ecotourist travelogue. This reserve is in grave danger of being commercially developed, and this description functions as a battle cry for its preservation—it even provides the Honduran president's fax number so you can complain to the highest authority! ✓INTERNET→*url* http://www.cam.org/~derekp/index.html

Green Arrow Guide to Honduras Visit the Mayan ruin at Copan, recently declared a World Heritage Site, or relax in the thermal springs at Auga Calinete. After a day of river rafting, head to Alejandros, the capital's sole disco, and dance the night away. In addition to making these excellent vacation suggestions, this guide profiles the Bay Islands, former home to pirates. ✓INTERNET→*url* http://www.greenarrow.com/honduras/honduras.htm

Honduran Notebook Get the inside scoop on the youth travel scene through this rather self-satisfied journal. You will get tips of some value—Honduras is one of the cheapest places in the world to get a scuba certification, and always order the red snapper. (Unless, of course, you're consuming pizza at the Mermaid Inn.) ✓INTERNET→*url* http://oeonline.com/~sgoodf/honduras/hondu1.html

A Honduran beach—from http://www3.islands.com/coral/resorts/innlast.html

Tourists lunching in the rainforest—from http://webtravel.org/cr/tortuguero.html

Honduras Pictures, literature, music, and even a link to the school of agriculture in Zamorano make this one of the best sites for those wishing to acquaint themselves with the Central American nation of Honduras. Tourists will appreciate the list of Honduran organizations in the U.S. and the handful of travelogues presenting real-life Honduran adventures in the waters and jungles of the Mosquito Coast. ✓**INTERNET**→*url* http://www.gl.umbc.edu/~apined1/English/EngIndx.html

Honduras Travel Tips Learn about currency, visas, camping, adventures, and live-aboard boats in Honduras. Interesting digressions from the norm include the address of Honduras's only nudie bar and the sad knowledge that blackjack is not an option at the many casinos constellating the countryside. ✓**INTERNET**→*url* http://www.amerispan.com/ameri.v0/ht_4_95.html

The Inn of Last Resort No, this isn't either the couch in your parents' den or Club Med Sarajevo; it's a luxurious beachfront spa in Roatan, Bay Islands, Honduras. Get an online brochure and contact info here. ✓**INTERNET**→*url* http://www3.islands.com/coral/resorts/innlast.html

Nicaragua

Careli Tours: The Tour Operator of Nicaragua Description of a variety of tours—rain forests or beaches—offered by this Managua-based agency. ✓**INTERNET**→*url* http://www.greenarrow.com/nicaragu/adcareli.htm

Green Arrow Guide to Nicaragua Green Arrow assures prospective visitors that the only loud noises they'll hear are those from thousands of squawking parrots disturbed by church bells. After all, the army has shrunk from 100,000 to just...10,000! Feature articles here attempt to eradicate all mental pictures of Sandinistas, Contras, and the late unpleasantness with visions of sport fishing on Lake Nicaragua and bargain hunting in the markets of Managua (disarmed grenade, anyone?). Contact information for several hotels and tour operators is listed. Try Charly's Ye Ye restaurant for a good rum drink. ✓**INTERNET**→*url* http://www.greenarrow.com/nicaragu/nicaragu.htm

Lonely Planet: Destination Nicaragua Lonely Planet takes a political stance here—disapproving of U.S. interference in a popular revolution. A tourist guide can hardly ignore a war that has "obliterated" much of the cultural heritage of the nation. Yet, there are still off-the-beaten-track suggestions that sound intriguing, like exploring some of the 365 islands offshore from Granada or hiking among the volcanoes of the Volcan Masaya. ✓**INTERNET**→*url* http://www.lonelyplanet.com/dest/cam/nic.htm

Nicaraguan Refried Beans Cyndi learned this recipe while living in Nicaragua, so it's bound to be authentic. Lime and lard make these beans stand out from the crowd. ✓**INTERNET**→*url* http://www.honors.indiana.edu/~veggie/recipes.cgi/Beans/beans9

Panama

Focus on Panama Will Americans be wary of traveling to a former war zone and protectorate of a drug-smuggling strongman? The creators of this page hope not, and that's why they've designed this colorful national advertisement, complete with a less-than-impressive introduction ("Contrary to what you may think, Panama is one of the top three Latin American countries in standard of living, life expectancy, and quality of life."). Dozens of photos of the canal, beaches, and local handicrafts are embedded in a hypertour. Short essays furnish a few actual names of restaurants and clubs (Thursday is Ladies' Night at Bacchus disco). Beach resorts get more detailed descriptions. ✓**INTERNET**→*url* http://www.iaehv.nl/users/grimaldo/panama.html

Green Arrow Guide to Panama No Noriega in fatigues here. A photo of a tanned beauty in a bikini graces the Top Tourist Attractions section, which praises the islands off the Caribbean coast. Attempting to appeal to the save-the-planet set, another feature describes Panama City as "the rain forest capital;" yet another lists tour operators and hotels. All in all, this is a solid (and improving) page devoted to Panamanian tourism. (New Yorkers who visit the site should laugh cynically at the mention of the *agouti*, a large jungle rodent, and say to the New Yorker nearest them, "Sounds to me like a subway rat with a pedigree.") ✓**INTERNET**→*url* http://www.greenarrow.com/panama/panama.htm

Panama Home Page (Panama-L) It's okay to drink the water in Panama, and wearing miniskirts is fine, too. This site is packed with such useful information, as well as interesting side trips of sound clips and photo galleries. But entering the nation in a car means mandatory fumigation, and you'll also have to prove that you don't plan to make a mint selling the car and flying home. If you have any other questions, this full-service site will help point you toward the Panamanian official nearest your home. Turn to the culture page to preview food and folklore—have a glass of Seco and join the dance. ✓**INTERNET**→*url* http://holly.colostate.edu/~panama/panama.ht

Panama Info Take the time to look at the image archive here. The vivid colors of the Gaucamaya parrot ($3,000 in a U.S. pet shop) are a potent lure to the wild rain forests where they fly free. The other resources and links here, including the CIA World Fact Book and a news archive, provide a useful overview. ✓**INTERNET**→*url* http://www.iaehv.nl/users/grimaldo /panama2.html

Panama Page Come to this hub for all manner of links Panamanian. An image archive presents Panamanian beauties, while an informative article explores the twists and turns of U.S./Panama relations. Current weather in Panama City is just a click away, as are several daily newspapers. Travelers will undoubtedly wander further afield after linking to the Latin American Network of the Rec. Travel Library. ✓**INTERNET**→*url* http://leviathan.tamu.edu/panama/panama.html

Panama: Places, Festivals, and Museums Just click on a map, and find out what's happening in Panama. A hypertrip to Chiriqui brings links to a scuba site, museums, and local newspapers. The festival list is intriguing—in Colon they celebrate the Cristo Negro (Black Christ) in October, while Las Tablas's Carnival is said to be the best in the nation. ✓**INTERNET**→*url* http://gringo.ent.ohiou.edu/~medina/panama.html

Scuba Diving in Panama This text essay rhapsodizes about the underwater sights of Panama and offers sightseeing hints for "land lovers." Highlights include the original Chiquita banana farm and a chocolate plantation near Boca del Drage ✓**INTERNET**→*url* http://gringo.ent.ohiou.edu/~medina/scuba.html

Some WWW Locations with Information about Panama Brief descriptions here will help you navigate through Panamanian cyberspace. Link to Felipe Tribaldo's page for .GIFs of flora, or turn to Enrique Medina's Panama page for folklore and museums. Azael Barrera's page is listed as a must-see, while the University of Panama's gopher is a good starting place for either a term paper or travel planning. ✓**INTERNET**→*url* http://www.iaehv.nl/users/grimaldo/guest.html#panama

An idyllic Costa Rican glade—from http://www.cntraveler.com/

South America

South America—land of ghostly Incan cities, unexplored Amazon jungles, snow-covered peaks, and modern cities. You might need some assistance navigating the continent. For personal advice turn to CompuServe's **South America** board or the true-to-life experiences of travelogues like **Journey to Where the Land Ends**. Visit the wonders of the Andes with the cybertrips available at **Bolivia's Experimental Home Page**, or jump to the **Chilean Ski Guide** while sipping **Coffees of Columbia.** Wander into the steamy jungle at **Ecuadorian Amazon** or delve into the secrets of Machu Picchu at **Red Cientifica Peruana**. Save the planet and have an adventure with the help of **South American Explorers Club** and **Hike the Andes**. Or just contemplate the sensuality of Brazil at the **Tango Server.**

Angel Falls, the highest in the world—http://www.relevantum.fi/demot/putous.html

On the Net

Across the board

Hotels of South America Contact information for selected hotels in South America. One caveat: don't look for much local character, since many of the properties listed belong to international chains. ✓**INTERNET**→*url* http://www.digimark.net/dundas/hotels/samerica/

South America Randy wants to know where to play some polo in Argentina, and Sharon is seeking a $50 per night room in Santiago. They both asked for, and got, answers from this busy message board, which covers the whole range of South America, from the heights of Cuzco to the Amazon basin. ✓**AMERICA ONLINE**→*keyword* travel forum→Message Boards→World Traveler→South America

South America Jane wonders if she should bring her wet suit for snorkeling in the Galapagos. Steve answers emphatically: "Yes, Jane, yes!" Chris posts a query about the stability of Peruvian currency, while Liza seeks a room with a view of Igautu Falls. The topics may sound exotic here—Chilean fjords, Amazon canoe trips—but feel free to post any comment or question. ✓**COMPUSERVE**→*go* travsig→Message Boards→South America

South American Explorers Club Dedicated to aiding climbers and other adventure travelers in Ecuador and Peru, the South American Explorers Club has posted membership info, contact information, and destination guides online. ✓**INTERNET**→*url* http://www.digimark.net/rec-travel/south_america /s_am_explorers_club

Argentina

Argentina A Spanish-language list of WWW sites dedicated to Argentina. Links lead to sites on politics, history, music, tourism, and tango, and the site is well worth a visit even by non–Spanish speakers. You may very well end up on the summit of Aconcagua or dancing in Buenos Aires. ✓**INTERNET**→*url* http://arcadia.informatik.uni-muenchen.de/rec/argentina/

Buenos Aires From the Plaza de Mayor to the Calle Lavalle, from the Cementerio Recoleta to the Avenida Nueve de Julio, Buenos Aires sparkles like a gem in the somewhat tarnished setting of Argentina. One of the largest cities in South America, it's also one of the most satisfying for American travelers—especially travelers who have access to Fodor's Worldview. And if you save up your pennies, you can eat at Yuki, El Repecho de San Telmo, and Tomo I, and then retire to your room at the Claridge, Panamericano, or the Libertador Kempinski. ✓**AMERICA ONLINE**→*keyword* worldview→Latin America→Buenos Aires

Buenos Aires Graphics of an accordion and of a tangoing couple welcome visitors to the Buenos Aires page. Material is organized into historical, geographical, cultural, sporting, and gastronomic references, and each neighborhood is described in lavish detail, right down to the addresses and phone numbers for hotels. ✓**INTERNET**→*url* http://www.secyt.gov.ar/bue/buei.html

Los Notros, Argentina A promotional site for a luxury hotel on the banks of the Perito Moreno Glacier, in the heart of a national park. Find out how to book at this site. ✓**INTERNET**→*url* http://www.opendoor.com/patagonia/ntros.html

soc.culture.argentina (ng) Argentinean politics, soccer, and rock 'n' roll, as well as the occasional question from a gringo traveler who has spent time in Argentina's cities and wilds. ✓**USENET**→soc.culture.argentina

Tango Server Feel the heat of Buenos Aires and go with it. All one needs to learn the dance is here: history, lyrics, music, theory, and instructional movies. You need only supply the rose, the teeth, and the Addams Family videotapes. Cara mia! ✓**INTERNET**→*url* http://litsun.epfl.ch/tango/index.html

Tapa de la Guia del Mercosur A Spanish-language site that covers Argentina province by province. ✓**INTERNET**→*url* http://www.megasur.com/arg/index.htm

The Lonely Planet: Destination Argentina Argentina is presented in all its glory here—with tangos, gauchos, Magellanic penguins, and soccer fans. Check out the slide show, and bone up on the history of Evita's homeland. Although this online version of the guide won't tell you where to stay, it does provide helpful hints about Argentina (on menus, meat invariably means beef). ✓**INTERNET**→*url* http://www.lonelyplanet.com/dest/sam/argie.htm

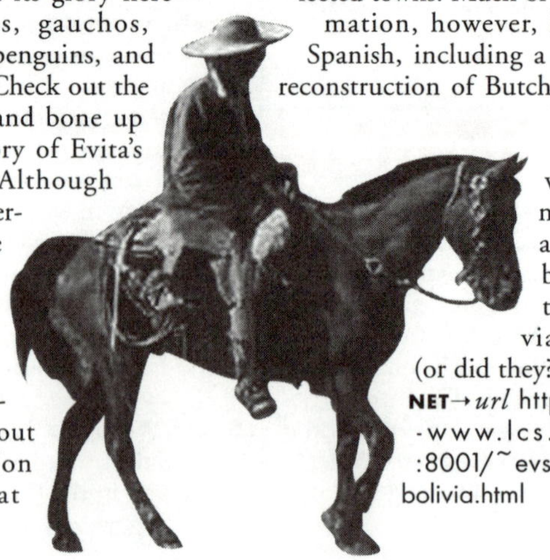

TravNet: Argentina TravNet sites are still under development, but they promise everything from hotel links to custom-made cybertours of attractions. Now you can be assured of good general information, courtesy of the State Department; travel tips; and a link to the chat of soc.culture.argentina. ✓**INTERNET**→*url* http://www.sky.net/~eric/t/souarg.html

Bolivia

Bolivia Travel Trip This travelogue dates from the summer of 1993, but some of the information is timeless. The author advises women that the high altitude will "play merry hell" with them. And, certainly, the tips on the proper way to chew coca (30 leaves with a little bit of ash) are just as relevant as ever. ✓**INTERNET**→*url* http://www.digimark.net/rec-travel/south_america/bolivia/trip.tinsley

Bolivia's Experimental Home Page This richly illustrated site takes cybervisitors on a tour of Bolivia, even providing a few suggestions for hotels in each of nine selected towns. Much of the information, however, is still in Spanish, including a historical reconstruction of Butch Cassidy's final years, which culminated in a bloody battle with the Bolivian army (or did they?). ✓**INTERNET**→*url* http://larch-www.lcs.mit.edu:8001/~evs/bolivia/bolivia.html

Bolivia's World Wide Web Site Although the tourism information here is limited to brief essays on culture and history, there is much to learn. The hypertext leads potential visitors on a virtual tour from the world's highest freshwater body, Lake Titicaca, to the depths of the Potosi silver mines. Daily news in Spanish, and even investment opportunities, are presented here too. ✓**INTERNET**→*url* http://jaguar.pg.cc.md.us/bolivia.html

---

Gateway of the Sun A small selection of the variety of Bolivia, from the colonial legacy of San Felipe Neri to the natural majesty of the jungle leopard. ✓**INTERNET**→*url* http://falcon.cc.ukans.edu/~bolivia/

Lonely Planet: Destination Bolivia Another good excerpt from the guide series, leaving out, of course, the much-needed accommodation information. What is here is an excellent overview of Bolivian culture, suggestions for outdoor expeditions, and a meditation on the sounds of the jungle, from crunching leaves to chirping insects. ✓**INTERNET**→*url* http://www.lonelyplanet.com/dest/sam/bolivia.htminfo,slides and map

---

soc.culture.bolivia (ng) "What has Andean peaks and starred in *Grease*?" "Bolivia Newton-John." This joke isn't here, but plenty of other discussions about Bolivia are, on topics ranging from violence in the Amazon basin to modern literature. ✓**USENET**→soc.culture.bolivia

---

The Bolivian Music Page Those blessed with a sound card will enjoy the drums and flutes of a Morenada clip that accompanies the pictures and text describing Andean traditional music. The Andean Folkloric Journal also calls this page home, and traditional bands are welcomed to register online—so check here for places to enjoy the haunting music far away from the high hills. ✓**INTERNET**→*url* http://www.ping.be/belgian-rock/

Brazil

Art Gallery This excellent online exhibit drops you into the rain forest, where you can cavort among the native tribes, colorful birds, and deep, deep green. ✓**INTERNET**→*url* http://www.deltanet.com/brazil/ag/ag.htm

---

Bahia Info This site is dedicated to Lemanja, the goddess of the sea who rules over the glorious stretches of sand at Bahia. The unique Afro-Portuguese sensibility of Bahia informs this Website, which not only recommends beaches and restaurants, but also offers a direct email connection to Dona Vani, a registered tour guide waiting to show you this coastal paradise. ✓**INTERNET**→*url* http://sensemedia.net/sprawl/21672

Bem Vindo & Welcome to Brazil A jaunt to Rio from this Website includes a sound file of "The Girl from Ipanema" (just to get you in that Carnaval mood), a virtual tour of a street market, and info on the four local football (that's soccer) teams. Other virtual tours take you to the ancient city of São Paulo or into the Amazon jungle. Each illustrated hypertext essay includes practical tourism information and a special guide for business visitors. ✓**INTERNET**→*url* http://darkwing.uoregon.edu/~sergiok/brasil.html

---

Brazil Flying down to Rio? If so, pick up some travel tips at this active board first. Melanie inquires about wheelchair access to Iguacu Falls, while Tom worries about the ticket he just purchased from a ticket consolidator. And the board is just full of useful items like the dates for Carnaval and the name of a good, reasonable hotel in São Paulo. ✓**AMERICA ONLINE**→*keyword* Travel Forum→Message Boards→World Traveler→Brazil

---

Brazil Embratur Brazilian Tourist Web You might win a free trip after taking this site's tourist poll. But even if you don't

---

Fodor's Choice...

Special Attractions

Argentina
Attending the Sunday flea market in the San Telmo district in Buenos Aires.

Colombia
Watching the cutting and polishing of rough emeralds at Sterling Joyeros in Bogotá.

Chile
White water rafting in the rivers around Pucon.

—from Fodor's *South America*

---

get to fly down to Rio, this page will make you feel as if you've been to Brazil, with excellent presentations on each state and city, accommodations guides, and even a calendar of upcoming events. See you at the Antontawa Rodeo. ✓INTERNET→*url* http://www.embratur.gov.br/sBook/Poll/Lottery

Brazil in Brief Come here for capsule articles on geography, government, and culture. Worth special mention are the illustrated essays on the Amazon—did you know that much of the basin has never, ever been explored? ✓INTERNET→*url* http://www.demon.co.uk/Itamaraty/bb.html

Carnaval in Brazil Catch the party spirit from this collection of pictures. Doesn't the goddess Jaci remind you of someone? ✓INTERNET→*url* http://darkwing.uoregon.edu/~sergiok/brasil/carnaval.html#start

Hostels in Brazil A long list with addresses, phone and fax numbers, and international hostel affiliations. ✓INTERNET→*url* http://www.solutions.net/rec-travel/hostels/sa.br.html

Museums—USP A Portuguese-language list of Brazilian museums. ✓INTERNET→*url* http://www.usp.br/cultura/museus/museus.html

Rio de Janeiro Let's go to Rio... walk though the city's many neighborhoods or look into the local picks of hotels, restaurants, and shops. Contact info for several travel agencies specializing in Rio is provided. ✓INTERNET→*url* http://www.deltanet.com/brazil/rio/rio.htm

soc.culture.brazil (ng) A mixture of Portuguese and English chat is here, ranging from complaints about portrayals of Brazil in mass media to requests for English translations for common fish names. And political debate is, of course, ever present. ✓USENET→soc.culture.brazil

Indigenous Brazilians—from http://www.deltanet.com/brazil/ag/ag.htm

Taste of Brazil Learn how to make the delicacies of Brazil. Start with *sopa de milho* (corn soup), and move on from there, rubbing your stomach at intervals to remind yourself how lucky you are. ✓INTERNET→*url* http://pasture.ecn.purdue.edu/~agenhtml/agenmc/brazil/recipes.html

The Brasil Page This highly rated page shows that the Brazilian spirit is international. Not only can one keep up with the soccer scores, look at the offerings of Brazil's many museums, find an investment opportunity in Rio, or check up on the former leader's trial, but you can also link to the Samba in Sweden site or sign up for lessons at Edinburgh's dance school. ✓INTERNET→*url* http://charlotte.acns.nwu.edu/rio/brasil.html

The Brazilian Society Web Page From the faraway shores of Wales comes an excellent resource on Brazil. Travelers can skip the list of upcoming activities of the Cardiff Brazil Society and head right for the country profiles and travel and tourism information. Find out what's happening in the clubs and galleries of São Paulo and Rio, and where to find a hostel countrywide. ✓INTERNET→*url* http://www.cf.ac.uk/uwcc/suon/brazil/braz-soc.html

Chile

Anden Chile This Spanish language site offers connections to Chilean newsgroups, mailing lists, and home pages. Several collections of poems by Pablo Neruda highlight the literature offerings. ✓INTERNET→*url* http://www.eden.com/~carlos/anden.html

Chile Page Some of the large holdings here are in Spanish, but that shouldn't deter prospective tourists from stopping in. You can read Darwin's original travelogue of the Galapagos, *The Voyage of the Beagle* (in English). Links connect to home pages of Chilean rock groups, a Chilean observatory, and an article on how to work or study in Chile. There's even a Turismo section, which points visitors toward the Lonely Planet guide, Chile's beaches and rivers, the Atacama Desert, the ski slopes, and the ever-mysterious Easter Island—which is in the South Pacific but belongs to Chile, and that's not even the reason it's mysterious. ✓**INTERNET**→*url* http://sunsite.dcc.uchile.cl/~mvasquez/chile/

Chile-L Homepage Home for the Spanish discussion of Chilean politics and culture. Subscription instructions for the CHILE-L mailing list are here, as is a link to soc.culture.chile newsgroup for cybertalk on current events. Additional links lead to such diverse resources as the Chilean Ski Guide and a cookbook packed with traditional recipes. ✓**INTERNET**→*url* http://sunsite.dcc.uchile.cl/soc.culture.chile/

Chilean Rivers Part political pamphlet, part adventure-travel guide, this site not only describes the joys of rafting on the Rio Bio and the Futaleufu, but tries to enlist aid in preserving them from development. The online guide by Lars Holbek describes navigating the rivers, as well as sleeping, eating, and driving in Chile. Maps are included. ✓**INTERNET**→*url* http://www.rahul.net:80/fallside/awa/river_project/Chile/

Chilean Ski Guide Watch out for that mogul, and keep your knees tucked when you schuss. This very detailed guide, which profiles many resorts and runs and keeps snow worshipers up-to-date on slope conditions, also offers basic suggestions for trouble-free travel in Chile. ✓**INTERNET**→*url* http://clubmidd.middlebury.edu/Courses/internet/students/passikof/final.html

Destination Chile & Easter Island "Like a phoenix rising from the flames of political turmoil, Chile is once again a popular destination." Thus begins the Lonely Planet guide, with prose as portentous and purple as the rhetoric of the Allendes during the wane of their dictatorship. But like a phoenix, Chile rises above this bad writing and acquits itself on the strength of its magnificence. The slide show of Chile's natural attractions is nothing short of spectacular, and the profile of Easter Island, the world's most remote inhabited spot, makes the minimum 1,900-mile trip seem worthwhile. Turn to a tourist agent for practical details, or shell out for the hard copy of the Lonely Planet guide. ✓**INTERNET**→*url* http://www.lonelyplanet.com.au/dest/sam/chile.htm

---

Journey to Where the Land Ends An illustrated travelogue by Adrienne Shaine Clermont about her expedition to Chile to study the Chinchorro mummies. All is not anthropology here—Adrienne takes us along with her from airport security to Easter Island, tossing in interesting facts and fables and even excerpts of history books as she sees fit. (Did you know that eighteenth-century Dutch explorers say that the famous stone heads once wore jaunty tall red hats?) ✓**INTERNET**→*url* http://teddy.law.cornell.edu:8080/chile/chile.htm

---

Santiago A hypertext essay describing the beauties of a capital that boasts both ski slopes and beaches nearby. Take a hypertour of the city center, and learn about Santiago's history. Special sections discuss cultural, eating, shopping, and outdoor opportunities (although lists of restaurants and hotels are scanty). ✓**INTERNET**→*url* http://sunsite.dcc.uchile.cl/chile/turismo/santiago.html

---

soc.culture.chile (ng) Spanish-language discussion of politics and culture. ✓**USENET**→soc.culture.chile

---

The Corner of the Chilean Country Music An expatriate Chilean languishing in Sydney, Australia, has collected here lyrics of traditional songs, cuecas, tonadas, etc., to help others retain contact with home. Sing along with "El Ay Ay Ay." ✓**INTERNET**→*url* http://www.zip.com.au/~mgiuras/english_version .html

Colombia

Basic Colombia Start exploring Colombia through this small collection of links. Online here is basic national data, including a provocative essay entitled "A Daring Synthesis of Character." Further links lead to tourism info in Spanish, Colombian news sources, other Colombia home pages and, of course, a site giving homage to the champion Colombian soccer team. ✓**INTERNET**→*url* http://www.univalle.edu.co/~servinfo/colombia.sp.html

---

Coffees of Colombia Find out here if Juan Valdez really does personally harvest every bean that comes out of Colombia. (Although Colombia is second to Brazil in coffee production, "Colombia is known to produce a much finer coffee than Brazil.") Caffeine junkies will go weak in the knees with the pictures and elegant descriptions of Colombian coffee varieties and will want to follow the links to other Web coffee stops. ✓**INTERNET**→*url* http://www.primenet.com/bid/coffeeworld/colombia.html

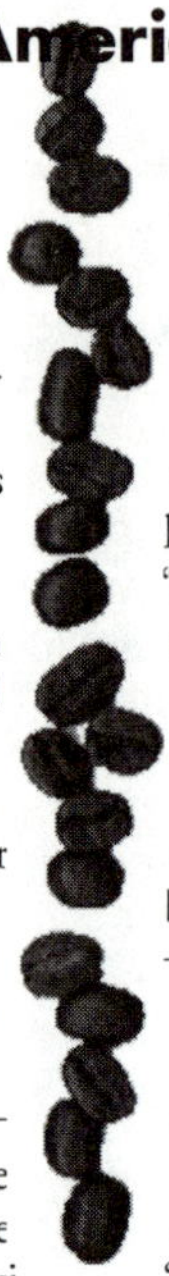

Colombia Learn all about the land of cartels and coffee here Explore history, literature, environment, music, sports, and government. Though there is little of value to real—rather than virtual—tourists, the site does offer an online phone book, which provides connections to many other information sources in Colombia. ✓**INTERNET**→*url* http://www.sangamon.edu/colombia

Colombia Turismo A Spanish-language site that holds nationwide information and caters to the adventure tourism crowd. Contact numbers for in-country tour agencies are included. ✓**INTERNET**→*url* http://www.uniandes.edu.co/Colombia/Turismo/turismo.html

Republic of Colombia A very basic site providing an encyclopedic profile, accompanied by a list of consular offices worldwide. ✓**INTERNET**→*url* http://www.colostate.edu/Orgs/LASO/Colombia/colombia.html

Ecuador

Ecuador Want to know what the snow conditions will be for an assault on Chimborazo in November? You'll be sure to get some advice, as do those who post queries about renting cars in Quito, and the pros and cons of taking an infant to the Galapagos. A post is even here about the availability of "feminine hygiene products" in the capital (an Ecuador-bound woman has promised to investigate). ✓**AMERICA ONLINE**→*keyword* Travel Forum→Message Boards→World traveler→Ecuador

Ecuador The gems here are the travelogues of modern-day explorers. These illustrated accounts reek of new kinds of adventure—exemplified in "World Peace Through Frisbee" and "Ecuador: Jungle, Andes, and Galapagos with a Toddler." Links lead to other Ecuador resources and organizations that sponsor learning programs and group tours. ✓**INTERNET**→*url* http://homepage.seas.upenn.edu/~leer/ecuador/

Ecuadorian Amazon Most of the documents housed here discuss the impending development of Ecuador's Amazon basin. Ecotourists may well find hot spots to protect, or at the very least visit before the oil rigs sludge in. ✓**INTERNET**→*url* http://ukanaix.cc.ukans.edu/~marc/geography/latinam/ecuador/amazon/ecuador.html

French Guiana

Lonely Planet: Destination French Guiana Like their books, Lonely Planet's online guides offer hard facts, down-to-earth tips, and unbiased tourism information for independent travelers, in this case about travel in French Guiana. ✓**INTERNET**→*url* http://www.lonely

DETOURS

On Iguazú Falls:

"Situated in the Parque Nacional Iguazú near Puerto Iguazú, these spectacular falls lie just east of the confluence of the Iguazú and Paraná rivers. At least 5,000 cubic meters of water per second plunge the 70 meters into the abyss below.

"If the Iguazú Falls look familiar, it's because they were the 'supporting actors' in the film *The Mission*—they were the backdrop for many of the movie's scenes. Appropriately, the area has historic ruins of Jesuit missions which also draw many visitors. San Ignacio Miní, built in a style of architecture known as 'Guaraní baroque', is especially popular.

"Above the falls, the waters are suitable for canoeing, kayaking and other water sports. The surrounding park is home to 55,000 hectares of pristine subtropical rainforest, with abundant wildlife and plant species."

—from **Lonely Planet: Destination Argentina**

Her name is Rio, and she dances…—http://www.deltanet.com/brazil/rio/rio.htm

planet.com.au/dest/sam/fgu.htm

Paraguay

The Absolutely Unofficial Home Page of Paraguay You will find little of practical tourist value at this site dedicated to the landlocked Latin American gem, but it does provide a nicely illustrated overview of history and culture, and the latest news and football scores. ✓**INTERNET**→*url* http://mail.eskimo.com/~krautm/index.html

Peru

Hike the Andes People who've actually been to Machu Picchu tell you how to do it. Find here suggested routes, maps of peaks to be conquered, high hotels catering to hikers, and, most important, in-country contacts expert in facilitating treks. ✓**INTERNET**→*url* http://www.wp.com/andes/

Observación de la Naturaleza—Ecoturismo This Spanish-language site promotes ecotourism in Peru. See the Empire of the Incas and the many national parks while supporting environmental protection. ✓**INTERNET**→*url* http://www.rcp.net.pe/peru/ecoturismo.html

Peru Mark is just back from an Amazon River cruise and is very eager to share his experience. An aspiring ecotourist seeks a nature-sensitive tour operator. And many want to know what in the world the weather will be like at Macchu Picchu in December. If following the Inca trail sounds like a dream come true, as it did to two college friends who posted recently, begin planning with the help of amateur experts here. ✓**AMERICA ONLINE**→*keyword* Travel Forum→Message Boards→World Traveler→Peru

Red Cientifica Peruana Like Pizarro, you'll have to be an intrepid explorer to conquer this massive collection of Peruvian links. However, as this is the only really comprehensive Peruvian site, a visit is almost a must. The index is searchable, but you might want just to wander through the About Peru section with its interactive map, lovely picture gallery, and selection of haunting flute music. For Spanish speakers the travel information contained within the map is excellent. ✓**INTERNET**→*url* http://www.rcp.net.pe/index-ing.html

Suriname

SML-Suriname Mailing List (ml) Mailing list and newsletter for discussion of Surinamese issues. ✓**INTERNET** …→*email* suriname-request @cp.tn.tudelft.nl ✍ *Type in subject line:* subscribe …→ suriname-n-request@cp.tn .tudelft.nl ✍ *Type in subject line:* subscribe *Info:* ✓**INTERNET**→*url* http://www.cp.tn.tudelft.nl/L.C.Breebaart/sml.html

Suriname Suriname was once part of the Netherlands, known as Dutch Guiana. These pages contain tourist resources, as well as information on the people; the capital, Paramaribo; a tour of the Amazon interior and rain forests; and links to tourist guide (such as the Lonely Planet) pages for Suriname. Information here is in Dutch and English. ✓**INTERNET**→*url* http://www.xs4all.nl/~ldirksz/index.html

Uruguay

Uruguay Maintained by a college student in Uruguay, this site includes information on Uruguay's history, geography, climatology, economy, and population. ✓**INTERNET**→*url* http://bilbo.edu.uy/uruguay.html

Uruguay's Hostels A list of hostels, along with addresses, phone numbers, and affiliation codes (if any). ✓INTERNET→*url* http://www.hostels.com/hostels/sa.ur.html

Welcome to Uruguay You haven't really arrived in Uruguay; it's only the Uruguay home pages, a collection of articles and links about the nation. Learn how many people are in Uruguay (just over three million permanent residents), what percentage of the nation's export revenue is earned from beef (31 percent), and why international travelers flock to the Rio de la Plata. You can also link to other Uruguay sites online. ✓INTERNET→*url* http://www.funcity.com/uruguay

Venezuela

Embassy of Venezuela Once you get past the polite political introduction, you'll find much of interest here. Check out the online publications such as Venezuela Revisited and El Dorado, which provide a native's perspective on contemporary Venezuela. Political, economic, and cultural affairs sections are updated frequently. Contact information for Venezuelan embassies worldwide is here too. ✓INTERNET→*url* http://venezuela.mit.edu/embassy/

GORP Venezuela Resource Listings Connect to the Venezuelan great outdoors courtesy of GORP's collection of links, including several to area tour specialists. After exploring the Venezuelan parks and rivers in Cyberspace, head to the Adventure Travel Bookstore to purchase maps and guidebooks online. ✓INTERNET→*url* http://www.gorp.com/gorp/location/latamer/venezuel.htm

La Pagina de Venezuela This site has a lot to offer tourists—basic info from the CIA, links to universities and other Venezuelan pages, and a nice collection of images and maps. Few frills, but good solid information. ✓INTERNET→*url* http://www.cheme.cornell.edu/~abelloso/Venezuela.html

soc.culture.venezuela (ng) Almost invariably in Spanish, the chat here frets over Amazon-basin violence, provides a venue for political grandstanding, and is quick to point out developments in Cyberspace of interest to virtual Venezuelans. ✓USENET→soc.culture.venezuela

The lost city of Machu Picchu—from http://www.aboveall.com/

Torcaza Trails Environmentally and politically correct tours of the Sierra Nevada National Park in the Venezuelan Andes. (They promise that their treks have "minimum impact on both the environment and the traditions of the local people.") Get contact info and descriptions of their adventures (fishing for and frying piranhas for lunch is the highlight of day three). ✓INTERNET→*url* http://venezuela.mit.edu/tourism/torcaza/torcaza1.html

Venezuela How could one not respond to a query titled "Help With Angel Falls!!!" Although Lisa is working in Venezuela, she couldn't get information about Angel Falls locally, so she turned to the Net for help. Other Netsurfers were happy to reply, whether making recommendations (the resort at Margarita Island comes up quite often) or asking questions ("Are the prices as low as people say?" asks Ron). Turn here for further info on bargains way below the equator. ✓AMERICA ONLINE→*keyword* Travel Forum→Message Boards→World Traveler→Venezuela

Venezuela is Beautiful Loaded with pictures, this 60-page brochure explores the coral beaches, rain forests, and mountain peaks of Venezuela. The guide is organized by locale and, though it doesn't contain specific travel info, it is well worthwhile for travel inspiration. Be patient as the pictures load; you won't be disappointed. Transportation tips help you explore non-virtually. ✓INTERNET→*url* http://venezuela.mit.edu/tourism/brochure/

The Caribbean

Sun, surf, rum drinks, and steel drums—the Caribbean really does have everything. But how to choose between the hundreds, nay thousands, of islands and atolls lying in wait for tourists in the warm, blue-green waters? Start the narrowing process with the **Caribbean Guide** or **CaribWeb's** massive offerings. Refer to the island profiles at **CaribWeb**. Or just ask whether the Bahamas or Barbados has better beaches on AOL's **Caribbean Traveler's Board**. Those with a proven propensity for wearing plaid shorts and white loafers should head directly to **The Bermuda Golf Home Page**, while those with Robinson Crusoe fantasies should check out Bequia Island, St. Vincent, and the Grenadines. Confused? Relax and everything will be Irie.

A beach on Barbados—from http://www.cntraveler.com/

On the Net

Across the board

Caribbean Board Want to know why Negril's beach is called the "Seven-Mile Beach" when it's only five miles long? Heading to the Dorado casino in Puerto Rico and need to know if a jacket is required in the main playing rooms? Looking for pictures of scantily-clad couples strolling on beaches, information on the parliamentary system in Bermuda, or a travelogue of a one-day trip to Saba? Come to the message board and libraries here to exchange all manner of information related to travel in the Caribbean. ✓**COMPUSERVE**→*go* travsig→Messages *and* Libraries→Caribbean

Caribbean Guide Written by nationally-syndicated travel columnists Shirley Slater and Harry Barsh, the Guide is an excellent resource for discovering the 37 islands of Caribbean. Use the cross-linked sections of the Guide to find the restaurant, hotel, shopping, and attraction information you want for any of the islands. To locate info on an island by region, select the Island Maps section, then choose an island by name from the regional map. If you're searching for an island by type of attraction, then choose the Island Features topic, which allows you to browse lists of islands offering attractions like out-of-the-ordinary diving opportunities or outstanding wedding and honeymoon resources. If you already know which island you'd like to visit, hit the Index of Islands and go directly to current tourism info for your desired destination. Selecting Aruba, for instance, yielded brief essays on what to do on the island (try dune-sliding at Boca Prins), a list of high-end and moderately priced hotels, and a list of recommended restaurants (Mi Cushina lets you sample funchi, which is Aruban cornmeal mush). Information on Cuba and Haiti is currently not included in the Guide, but this is an excellent place to begin researching a vacation to any of the other Caribbean islands. ✓**PRODIGY**→*jump* travel→caribbean guide

Caribbean Internet References For geographic, historical, and economic profiles of the Caribbean Islands, turn to this Website. You'll also get info on tourism and sailing in the area as well as links to pages about specific islands like St. Lucia, Barbados, and Grenada. ✓**INTERNET**→*url* http://www.freenet.hamilton.on.ca/~aa462/carib.html

CaribWeb Billing itself as "The source for Caribbean travelers and explorers," this Website is indeed a comprehensive source of info about the area. Visit this site for trip reports that detail accommodations, restaurants, beaches, and other attractions for islands from Bermuda to St. Bart. Use the CaribSearch database to find hotel and restaurant listings for specific islands, or scan CaribMoon for tips on planning a Caribbean honeymoon or wedding. You can also discuss travel in the Caribbean on a bulletin board where Caribaphiles exchange travel tips on good hotels and restaurants. ✓**INTERNET**→*url* http://www.caribweb.com/caribweb/

CPSCaribNet Your gateway to exploring the Caribbean. This mammoth site offers information about various Caribbean islands—each island is profiled with a map and essays on its geography, history, government, economy, and transportation systems. After choosing an island for your next vacation destination, check this site for the names and phone numbers of companies that specialize in Caribbean golfing, honeymoon, scuba, and yachting tours. ✓**INTERNET**→*url* http://www.cpscaribnet.com/

Destinations in the Caribbean Brief text descriptions of various island destinations. Browsing the Aruba topic here leads to information (including local telephone numbers for additional info) on tours of Fort Zoutman, the Aruba International Dance Festival, and the Bon Bini Festival (which celebrates Aruban folklore). ✓**INTERNET**→http://gnn.digital.com/gnn/bus/wview/cityhigh/carib.html

InterKnowledge Travel Network For each island InterKnowledge Travel Network has assembled detailed information about general culture, points of interest, activities, travel tips, transportation, accommodations, restaurants, and nightlife. Clicking on Curacao yields information on the International Blue Marlin Tournament held yearly in March, pictures of a turn-of-the-century plantation, a list of travel agents offering special packages to Curacao, and travel tips (most hotels in Curacao routinely add between 10 and 12 percent service surcharge to your bill, so there's no need to tip the maid.) ✓**INTERNET**→*url* http://www.interknowledge.com/

MIT Caribbean Home Page This site is an immense collection of links to various Caribbean-related resources. Stop at De Shop Corner to get in touch with other Islanders. From there it's just a jump to Caribbean-related newsgroups. Turn the corner to a list of home pages maintained by West Indians. The Caribbean Contact Point lets Caribs and others with an interest in the Caribbean add their names and personal and professional information to a searchable database. As MIT's party line goes "the members of the MIT Caribbean community actively maintain this collection of links so you can expose yourself to the exotic culture, pulsating rhythms, mouth-watering delights, nostalgic vistas and cosmopolitan people of the Caribbean region." Enjoy the view from their window. ✓**INTERNET**→*url* http://caribbean-www.lcs.mit.edu/caribbean-www/

rec.travel Library—Caribbean Open this site for an alphabetical list of files on major Caribbean islands like Aruba, the Bahamas, St. Bart, and Trinidad. You'll be teased with sections called Travel Tips, Special Events and Festivals, and Travelogues that unfortunately don't contain any information. All you'll find in each island's file are links to other Caribbean sites, like those at GNN and InterTravel. ✓**INTERNET**→*url* http://www.solutions.mb.ca/rec-travel/caribbean/

The Caribbean Traveler Board Netters share their island experiences on the board, which is neatly organized into topics like Hotels, Bad Places to Stay, Best Island Restaurants, and Sailing Tips. There are also permanent discussions devoted to specific islands—like the Tobago topic, where Lorraine can ask what to do when she's there and someone else can recommend tasting shrimp creole on the island (Gemma's is not to be missed). Whether seeking knowledge, or passing on your wisdom to others, the board offers invaluable first hand information on the Caribbean. ✓**AMERICA ONLINE**→ *keyword* travel forum→Travel Boards→The Caribbean Traveler Board

The Civilized Traveler A general Caribbean travel site containing numerous links, including links to discount brokers for travel and hotel reservations. This is a really good source of information on St. Bart and the French West Indies. ✓**INTERNET**→*url* http://www.crl.com/~philip/trinfo3.html

Culture

Afro-Caribbean Music Available in English and French, the Afro-Caribbean Music Guide provides exhaustive listings of Caribbean-music resources indexed by country, style, artist, and recording label. The Website also offers a bibliography for further reading and links to other Caribbean-music sites, like the Cuban Music Page. ✓**INTERNET**→*url* http://www.ina.fr/Music/index.en.html

Caribbean Art Gallery The work of such Caribbean artists of note as José Morales, Guillo Pérez, and Diógenes Ballester are exhibited in the gallery. Spanish-language interviews with the artists offer glimpses into the creative process. ✓**INTERNET**→*url* http://www.nando.net/prof/caribe/Caribbean_Art_Center.html

Caribbean Corner A page by a Trinidadian with information on several of the islands, including links to island-specific news and to music and video clips. ✓**INTERNET**→*url* http://www.catalog.com/caribco/

Caribbean Religions Focusing on voodoo and santeria, this site shows pictures of altars to voodoo deities and provides a dictionary of voodoo and santeria terms and gods. Both religions are highlighted in an essay about the magical frenzy of Carnival on the Islands. ✓**INTERNET**→*url* http://www.nando.net/prof/caribe/caribe.com.html

clari.world.americas.caribbean (ng) This is a low-traffic, unmoderated list and the home of heavy political discussions between disgruntled grad students and political extremists. Look through it to remember what it is you're going on vacation to forget. ✓**USENET**→clari.world.americas.caribbean

Hibiscus Records For island music lovers. *En Francais seulement. "Les Hits les plus chaude de la Caraïbe."* A catalog of the hottest hits of the Caribbean music scene, both audio and video. Audio files are available for such stars as Kwak, Eugène Mona, and Palaviré. ✓**INTERNET**→*url* http://www.ina.fr/Music/Labels/Hibiscus/

soc.culture.caribbean (ng) Mary reminds everyone that the Boston Carnival is on August 19 this year. Dan posts addresses for two more sites for watching the Chance's Peak volcano in Montserrat. The debate rages in Spanish over Cuba, and Foster seeks other Vincies (those from St. Vincent) for a discussion of the homeland. Lots of islands, lots of people, and a wide range of topics are discussed here. ✓**USENET**→soc.culture.caribbean

Hotel & resort guides

Caribbean Home Page A fairly complete online guide for resorts and hotels in the Caribbean. Whether you are an individual interested in finding an island hideaway, or a travel agent interested in visitor recommendations, you will find this guide a valuable source of information. Search the database by island name or topic for price info and service descriptions for over 220 Caribbean resorts and hotels. ✓**INTERNET**→*url* http://www.christwh.com/islands/index.html

Caribbean Information Office This site is an index of hotels and their phone numbers listed by island. ✓**INTERNET**→*url* http://www.caribbeans.com/

Chillin' on Tobago—from http://www.cntraveler.com/

Tour agents

Advance-Damron Vacations This company features Caribbean vacation packages that cater to gay men. Email or phone the company for additional info on its packages. ✓**INTERNET**→*url* http://www.advance-damron.com

Beau Travel A folksy site from a travel agency specializing in trips to the Caribbean and (incongruously) New Hampshire. Find information about Jamaica and Barbados, including spotlights on local food, arts, sports, shopping, and a description of the main resort areas. Of course there's also an ad for the company's many tours leaving from New York or Boston. ✓**INTERNET**→*url* http://www.mv.com/biz/beautravel/

Caribbean Specials Descriptions of tours to the Islands. ✓**INTERNET**→*url* http://www.hardiman.com/malls/rmcm/travel/carribean/special/

Island Hideaways An advertisement for a company that specializes in Caribbean vacations and travel packages. Get information

Fodor's Choice...

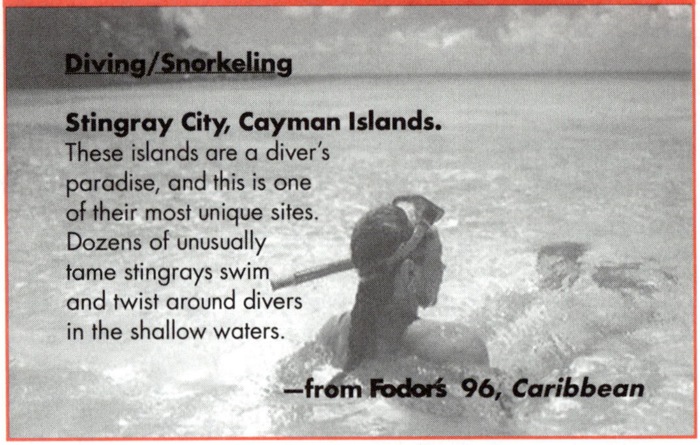

Diving/Snorkeling

Stingray City, Cayman Islands. These islands are a diver's paradise, and this is one of their most unique sites. Dozens of unusually tame stingrays swim and twist around divers in the shallow waters.

—from Fodor's 96, *Caribbean*

on their villa rentals and resort accommodations. ✓**INTERNET**→*url* http://www.islandhideaways.com/

Anguilla

Anguilla Home Page When traveling in Anguilla, don't get too close to manchineel tress (the ones with the green apples)—their sap can burn and irritate the skin. The official home page for Anguilla, a small British dependency located at the northern end of the Leeward Islands, is chock full of practical tips for visitors. (Bring proof of prescriptions for any medicine you pack; Anguilla is aggressive about keeping drugs off the island.) The site also offers information on local lingo, public holidays, and taxi rates, as well as information about local history, tourist attractions, and resources. The site links to hotel and restaurant listings at other Caribbean sites. ✓**INTERNET**→*url* http://galaxy.cau.edu/Anguilla/anguilla.html

Anguilla Home Page Read about Anguilla's zero-tax jurisdiction and the resulting tax-haven industry there. Or for lighter fare, look at the gallery of photographs featuring the colorful stamps of Anguilla. ✓**INTERNET**→*url* http://www.offshore.com.ai/anguilla/

Antigua & Barbuda

Antigua & Barbuda Today This list of resources on the two islands covers all kinds of necessities, including the names and addresses of restaurants, hotels, grocery stores, liquor stores, hair salons, car and bike rental agencies and banks. Also get an overview of the history (Christopher Columbus discovered Antigua in 1493) and geography (the islands boast 365 beaches between them) of the region. ✓**INTERNET**→*url* http://www.interlog.com/~observer/antigua/hcontents.html

Antigua Facts Useful, if terse, information about the geography and history of the largest of the Leeward Islands. Don't leave this site without strolling through the dazzling picture gallery. ✓**INTERNET**→*url* http://acorn.educ.nottingham.ac.uk//SchEd/pages/elizat/

Barbuda Pigeon Cliff. Codrington Shoal. Cocoa Beach. These are all names of some of the many geographic highlights of this island which lies 30 miles north of Anguilla. Pick up a very detailed map of and read a short essay about this island almost entirely surrounded by coral reef. ✓**INTERNET**→*url* http://www.candw.ag/barbisl.html

Aruba

Aruba On-Line A semi-official guide to Aruba (it's partly sponsored by the Aruba Tourism Authority), this Website provides a comprehensive guide to travel and attractions in Aruba, complete with phone numbers for everything from dive shops to deluxe resorts. The page claims to list all information on all known resorts on the island. It also offers links to local car rental companies. ✓**INTERNET**→*url* http://www.shore.net/olm/aruba

Aruba—One Happy Island Mike Saperstein is a self-proclaimed expert on touring Aruba, and he gladly lists his reviews of his favorite hotels, casinos, restaurants, shopping stops, tours, and more. If you choose to follow Mike's tips on your next trip to Aruba, you'll need to ask the concierge for directions to his recommended spots—no addresses or telephone numbers are listed here. ✓**INTERNET**→*url* http://www.solutions.mb.ca/rec-travel/caribbean/aruba/mike-saperstein.html

Windsurf Village Aruba A promotional page for this company that offers accommodations in Aruba that cater to windsurfers. Average year-round wind speeds that clock in at 20 knots, and increase to 25 to 35 knots during spring and summer, perpetuate Aruba's status as one of the windiest spots in the world. ✓INTERNET→*url* http://www.sccsi.com/Club_Mistral/aruba.html

The Bahamas

Bahamas Condo & Villa Vacations Tired of lodging with the hoi polli? You can rent a private condo, villa, or penthouse when vacationing in the Bahamas. This company will show you how. ✓INTERNET→*url* http://www.com/softek/bvilla.html

Bahamas On-line "The Bahamas' First WWW Server" is a feel good site that promotes the local culture of the Bahamas with information on Nassau, Paradise Island, Cable Beach, Goombay punch (a rum-laden beverage), and "the friendliest people you'll ever meet." A wide range of topics, including Bahamian history, accommodations, restaurants and bars, banking, duty free, fishing info, and museum tours is covered. ✓INTERNET→*url* http://TheBahamas.com/

Lucayan Beach Resort & Casino Information about Grand Bahamas only beach front resort and casino. ✓INTERNET→*url* http://www.iisys.com/www/itg/bahamas/hotels/lucaya/lucaya.htm

A scene from Anguilla—from http://www.cntraveler.com/

Luxury Dive Yacht Ever fantasize about acting like Donald Trump for a day? If you have, why not rent your own ostentatious mode of transportation and fulfill a dream. You can rent this 125 ft. Ballymena Luxury Dive Yacht and tour the Bahamas. Contact the owner through the telephone number listed at the Web page. ✓INTERNET→*url* http://www.aksi.net/rnr /ballymena.html

The Bahamas Did you know that the Bahamas are comprised of over 700 distinct islands? Or that the Flamingo is its national bird? That the Bahamian national holiday is celebrated on July 10th? Come to this site for background info on the exotic islands—get a history, lots of trivia, and some pictures. ✓INTERNET→*url* http://w3.gti.net:80/bahamas/

Water Sports Information This is an informal guide to companies involved in watersports on the island. Learn about the services, office hours, and price ranges of companies in the scuba, diving, snorkeling, fishing, and parasailing industries. ✓INTERNET→*url* http://www.magicnet.net/cge/uts/1702/scubinfo.html

Barbados

Barbados Barbados—or B'dos, as the locals say—is well represented at this site. You'll find listings for events, logistical information, a map, and pictures as well as tips on understanding the local lingo. Follow the link to the Barbados Selection Page for various other information sources of interest to travelers. ✓INTERNET→*url* http://mrlxp2.mrl.uiuc.edu/~stuart/barbados/index.html

Barbados This is a charming site, although it's still in development. There are links to hotels (only two listed as yet), restaurant home pages, sports facilities, and nightlife opportunities. The descriptions are enthusiastic but not overblown, and you also get practical price information for most of the services. ✓INTERNET→*url* http://www.caribsurf.com/barbados/bar_home.html

Barbados Home Page This online guide provides info on Barbadian beaches (the biggest waves are at Bathsheba Beach), golf courses (there are hundreds of them), pirate ship cruises (bring your own bottle of rum), and local church schedules (for after the pirate ship cruise). The essays here are a pleasure to read and can be enjoyed even if you're only armchair traveling to Barbados. ✓INTERNET→*url* http://www.fleethouse.com/barbados/barb-hom.htm

Barbados Hotel & Tourism Association This is an excellent site to begin your research of Barbados hotels. For each of the over 40 hotels listed here, you'll learn how far it is from the airport, how many pools, rooms, and restuarants it has, and whether it offers services for business meetings. You'll need to fill out and submit the online form for rates information (it changes with the seasons, of course). ✓INTERNET→*url* http://www.bajan.com/barbados/

Visit the Islands of Sun & Fun Travel information about the island of Barbados. Read short descriptions of local sites like the St. Nicholas Abbey, which was built in 1650, and the Farley Hill National Park, which offers a view of the entire Scotland District from 900 feet above sea level. The site also offers the names and phone numbers of a handful of selected hotels. ✓**INTERNET**→*url* http://www.ndl.net/~carib/

Bequia Island

Bequia Island, St. Vincent and the Grenadines Written in FAQ style, this site answers questions like "Why Bequia Island?" (Possibly for the "tropical blue waters.") "What's there to do there?" (Eat lobster pizza, for one.) "Are there guest houses there?" (Yes, and the site lists the names, addresses, and phone numbers for 15 of them.) Read about the island's famous white coral sand and black sand volcanic beaches and get practical information about flight schedules, hotels, and restaurants here. ✓**INTERNET**→*url* http://www.freenet.hamilton.on.ca/~aa462/bequia.html

Bermuda

Bermuda Diving Your one stop WWW page for all the information you need about recreational scuba diving in Bermuda! Get a list of dive shops (with telephone numbers, addresses, and service descriptions), info on a number of diving sites, and even a short essay on the Bermuda Aquarium. ✓**INTERNET**→*url* http://turnpike.net/emporium/D/diving/

Bermuda Triangle A funky page investigating the mystery of the infamous triangle where everything to single engine fighters to Elvis have either been lost or seen. Give yourself goosebumps by reading the myth of Flight 19 when six planes and 27 men disappeared into the magical waters of the Triangle. ✓**INTERNET**→*url* http://tigger.cc.uic.edu/~toby-g/tri.html

Bermuda-L (ml) A mailing list devoted to any subject that relates to life in Bermuda—including discussions of its society, culture, politics, history, people, and economy. ✓**INTERNET**→*email* request@bercol.bm ✍ *Type in message body:* subscribe bermuda-l

Bio Station Weather Your one-stop shopping source for detailed Bermuda weather info. ✓**INTERNET**→*url* http://www.bbsr.edu/weather.html

Forbes' Bermuda Online An excellent library of facts about the island, Bermuda Online is a virtual Bermuda FAQ, with business-oriented information regarding tourism, telecommunications, and meeting places. ✓**INTERNET**→*url* http://www.microstate.com/pub/micros/forbes/

Information About Bermuda Provided by Bermuda College, this page contains a wealth of resources, including visual images of Bermuda as well as general info about the history of the island. The site goes on to list a variety of statistics about the island, like the number of fires on Bermuda attributed to "malicious" intentions over the past three years. ✓**INTERNET**→*url* http://www.bercol.bm/Bermuda/Bermuda.HTML

The Bermuda Connection A large collection of links to the home pages of Bermudians on the Web, Bermuda Online, the Bermuda-L Home Page, The Bermuda Golf Page, and many, many more sites. ✓**INTERNET** →*url* http://coos.dartmouth.edu/~aer/

The Bermuda Golf Home Page Bermuda: the word conjures up many images of beaches, friendly people, and quaint houses, but one thing stands above all else (apparently)—Bermuda golf. Bermuda's 8 full courses give it the most golf courses per square mile of any country on earth, and they are all covered in exhaustive detail here. The greens and fairways are, naturally, covered with Bermuda grass, but at certain times of the year, the greens are overseeded with either rye or a mix of rye and other grasses. Bring your 1 iron! ✓**INTERNET**→*url* http://coos.dartmouth.edu/~aer/GOLF/

Bonaire

Official Guide to Bonaire (Netherlands Antilles) A hypertext guide to Bonaire that describes the past and present of this small island off the coast of Venezuela. Contact numbers for restaurants and hotels are online. ✓**INTERNET**→*url* http://www.interknowledge.com/bonaire/index.html

Welcome to Bonaire The maps at this Website show the location of Bonaire in the Caribbean and highlight the attractions on the island itself (like Washington Slagbaai National Park). Helpful subject files offer info on diving, cycling, accommodations, restaurants, and local events. You can also explore the history, culture, and language of the island. (In Papiamentu, "thank you" is said "*Danki.*" *Ayo*!) ✓**INTERNET**→*url* http://www.interknowledge.com/bonaire/index.html

British Virgin Islands

Bareboat or Crewed Charters Get rates, photos, and descriptions of charter tours serviced by this company. Sailing lessons are also available through Bareboat or Crewed Charters. Contact them with the information listed here. ✓**INTERNET**→*url* http://edu mall.com/users/sailing/wildcat.htm

Catamaran Notes: Ginny's Sailing Guide to the British Virgin Islands Ginny just loves to sail in the British Virgin Islands, and she encourages you to do the same with her page full of hints for anchorages, restaurant recommendations, snorkeling tips, and more. ✓**INTERNET**→*url* http://edumall.com/users/sailing/bvi notes.htm

Official Online Tourist Guide to the British Virgin Islands This site invites you to discover nature's little secrets on the British Virgin Islands. For descriptions of local hotels and restaurants, check into this page. ✓**INTERNET**→*url* http://www.cm.cf.ac.uk/User/P.S. Braendgaard/bvi/home.html

The Webfoot's Guide to British Virgin Islands A comprehensive collection of links that will take you to an events calendar and general tips for travelers. ✓**INTERNET**→*url* http://www.webfoot .com/travel/guides/bvi/bvi.html

Cayman Islands

Cayman WebGuide The online source for information about the Caymans. The site details information on travel, business opportunities, real estate, diving and watersports, accommodations, restaurants, car rental, and nightclubbing in the Caymans. Some of the hotels listed at the site offer links to virtual tours of their grounds. ✓**INTERNET**→*url* http://www.wweb .com/cayman/

Enterprise Bed and Breakfast Proof that the *Star Trek* cult is deeply rooted, the Enterprise Bed and Breakfast in Grand Cayman offers affordable, world-class diving and snorkeling, as well as rooms decorated completely in *Star Trek* motifs. The B&B is located six minutes from the heart of Georgetown, seven minutes from Seven Mile Beach, and light years from hotel-chain prices. Beam me up, Scotty. ✓**INTERNET**→*url* http://www.earthlink.net /~enterprise/

Cuba

Cuba-L (ml) For discussion of current Cuban culture, politics, and general news. ✓**INTERNET**→*email* listserv@unmvma.unm.edu ✍ *Type in message body:* subscribe cuba-l <your full name>

Cuban Internet Resources The creator of this page seems to have linked to every Internet site that mentions Cuba, so the pickings are eclectic, from a .GIF of the sheet music for Irving Berlin's "I'll See You in Cuba" to a section of the World Sex Guide. There are also some travel-related links—if you take time to sift through the offerings, you'll find links to Scuba Cuba, Discover Cuba, and the Caribbean Religions home page. ✓**INTERNET**→*url* http://ix.urz.uni -heidel berg.de/~pklee/Cuba/

Discover Cuba A short list of facts about Cuba constitutes this Web page. Did you know that Cuba has over 280 natural beaches, and that it's the largest of the Caribbean Islands? Come here to bone up on your knowledge of the island nation. ✓**INTERNET**→*url* http://www.its.net/its/alljamaica /cuba.htm

soc.culture.cuba (ng) Discuss Cuban culture, society, and politics at the home of bilingual anti-Castro rant. There isn't much

DETOURS

"Bob and I walked past four beautiful-houses down the beach and boarded Fergie's water taxi that took us out to a sand bar in the middle of the reef-protected sound. As soon as we dropped anchor, at least 20 Southern Sting-rays thronged the boat.Needless to say, we were in the water quickly to get an up-close-and-personal look at our new friends.

"Fergie...got into the one-meter deep water and picked up a ray four feet across in his arms to show us the mouth, which was about six inches back from the snout on the underside of the ray. 'Just keep a piece of squid in your fist and they'll come to you,' Fergie instructed, 'When you want to give up the squid, just open your fist and she'll suck up the food. They've got no teeth, but they generate more suction than a Hoover.' After I got a good look at her, I opened my hand, and within seconds the ray had captured the morsel and was gone."

—from **rec.travel Library—Caribbean**

practical travel info here, but the newsgroup might prepare you for some conversation topics that could come up while you're visiting the island. ✓**USENET**→soc.culture.cuba

The Cuban Music Page Cuba has been listening to the music of the rest of the world. What has evolved is a rich mixture of rock, tropical, Caribbean, and easy-listening love songs. The mix of styles is broadcast all day, every day, to the people of Cuba and those lucky enough to be passing time in the Keys. This site gives Web explorers a chance to hear some of this wonderful music by downloading MIDI files. ✓**INTERNET**→*url* http://itre.uncecs.edu/music/cuban-music.html

Curaçao

Curaçao Homepage If windsurfing in virgin waters sounds good to you, then Curaçao might be a Caribbean Island you'd like to visit. Curaçao also has some adventures to offer landlubbers, like the Christoffel National Park where wild donkeys and deer mingle freely with iguanas. You can read about the various attractions of thc island and get a list of Curaçan tourism offices in the United States. ✓**INTERNET**→*url* http://huizen.dds.nl/~curacao/

Dominican Republic

Dominican Republic (AAArt) Currently this site features contact information for two resorts in the Republic, but it promises more cultural and commercial information soon. ✓**INTERNET**→*url* http://www.AAArt.com/domrep/

Republica Dominicana The government tourism department sponsors this site and provides info on travel in the Dominican Republic, with detailed information on everything from reserving hotel rooms and renting private villas, to tips on navigating crowded Dominican streets. There's also a clickable map of the Dominican Republic and a virtual tour of the island's world renowned Amber Museum. ✓**INTERNET**→*url* http://www.qqq.com/dominican/index.html

A Bermuda cove—from http://www.cntraveler.com/

soc.culture.dominican-rep. (ng) You'll need to *habla* a little *Español* to get much out of this newsgroup which discusses current events and culture in the Dominican Republic. ✓**USENET**→soc.culture.dominican-rep.

The Dominican Republic North Coast Home Page This is the territory that caused Columbus to exclaim "Hispaniola! The most beautiful island I have ever seen!" This promotional page features a full-color map showing the locations of the companies advertising on the site, which include the Sea Horse Ranch, Casa Don Fello Villas, Trade Winds Resort, and Melissa Tours. ✓**INTERNET**→*url* http: //156.34.233.33/index.htm

French West Indies

French West Indies Caution: The beaches of the French West Indies (namely those of St. Bart, Martinique, and Guadeloupe) are all optional-topless beaches! If that doesn't frighten you off the idea of visiting, check this site to read about the "world-class" dining opportunities of St. Bart, including the house-specialties of selected restaurants and their infamous price lists ("Eating out in St. Bart is an adventure in paying"). This type of detailed info makes the page worth a visit. ✓**INTERNET**→*url* http://www.crl.com/~philip/fwi.html

Grenada

Grenada Kevin's parents grew up in Grenada, and he assembled this site to learn more about their heritage. He has assembled many beautiful photographs of the island along with reviews of local events, like the Grenada Carnival. Kevin also prints digests of local news stories at his site. ✓**INTERNET**→*url* http://watt.seas.virginia.edu/~krf2w/grenada.html

Haiti

Haiti or Quisqueya or Bohio Stroll through virtual galleries of contemporary Haitian art by Saint Suran, or read about the making of Barbancourt, Haiti's most famous rum. If you're wondering what compas and voodoo rock

A Jamaican cove—from http://www .cntraveler.com/

sound like, download the soundfiles of noted artists here. Besides offering its own resources on Haitian culture, this page also links to The Voodoo Server and to the newsgroup soc.culture.haiti. All of the info here is tendered in English, French, and Kreyol. ✓**INTERNET**→*url* http://www.primenet .com/~rafreid/

soc.culture.haiti (ng) French-language discussion of issues relating to Haiti. ✓**USENET**→soc.culture .haiti

Jamaica

Jamaica Jamaica's secondary industries are sugar, citrus fruits, bananas, spices, and its world-famous Blue Mountain coffee. If you're planning to participate in its primary industry, tourism, check into this site which has a historical essay on the island, some tips on things to know before you head there (it rains the most in October), and descriptions of major cities like Mobay. ✓**INTERNET**→*url* http://www.webcom.com /~travel/jam1.html

Jamaica Tourist Board Changes in L'Attitude and the Jamaican Tourist Board sponsor this site with its well-designed pages and enticing photos. It covers the major resorts, sports, and honeymoon spots in incredible detail, down to how much to tip your manicurist at the Grand Lido Resort. The General Information at the Website page gives helpful information on local driving, gambling, electrical systems, and more. But there is unfortunately no info here on the island's native population or their culture. ✓**INTERNET**→*url* http://www.jamaicatours.com /Jamaica/

Jamaica's South Side An illustrated essay about Jamaica's picturesque South Side, done in *National Geographic* style. Don't leave the site without seeing the photo of the mullet fishermen stringing their nets across Alligator Pond River. ✓**INTERNET**→*url* http://www .rsmas.miami.edu/sea-frontiers /spring-95/ja maica.html

Netherlands Antilles

antilnet.com Welcome (or *bon bini* as the locals say) to the home page of the Dutch Caribbean, which holds information about the Netherlands Antilles in general, with links to more specific information about Aruba, Curacao, Bonaire, St. Maarten, Saba, and St. Eustatius (also known as Statia). The site's general information about the Netherland Antilles includes history, economic trends, climate, geography, and more. Links to pages for each island provide pictures, tourist information, investment guides, and other resources. ✓**INTERNET**→*url* http:// www.antilnet.com/

Puerto Rico

Puerto Rico This Caribbean Island is roughly the size of Connecticut, and they use American greenbacks there just like in Connecticut. But that's where this island's resemblance to the Nutmeg State stops. Puerto Rico's average annual temperature is 78 degrees, and it's known to be the birthplace of the Pina Colada. Read more about the island and its culture at the Website. ✓**INTERNET**→*url* http://hpprdk01.prd.hp.com/

Puerto Rico Outdoor Resources There's more to do in Puerto Rico than sit on the beach and drink Pina Coladas! Read about the wildlife of the Caribbean National Forest located in the rugged Sierra de Luquillo, 40 km southeast of San Juan. ✓**INTERNET**→*url* http://www.gorp .com/gorp/location/pr/pr.htm

soc.culture.puerto-rico (ng) Spanish-language discussion of life and events in Puerto Rico. ✓**USENET**→soc.culture.puerto-rico

Saba

Saba The island of Saba—which is actually an inactive volcano—has the shortest commercial runway in the world. But volcano or not, Saba is a lot of fun. Hitchhike with friendly Sabans along The Road to The Bottom for local shopping and nightlife or enjoy the great diving opportunities. If you plan on staying the night, check this Website for hotel listings. Yes, there's more than one. ✓**INTERNET**→*url* http://www.digi mark.net/dundas/sabadeep/

St. Kitts

Welcome to St. Kitts & Nevis If you want to shipwreck yourself on the beaches, head to the accommodations page of this illustrated hypertext introduction to "The Secret of the Caribbean" for room rates in hotels all over the island. The over 400 sunken ships off the coast of St. Kitts and Nevis make it one of the world's premier diving sites. ✓**INTERNET**→*url* http://www.interknowledge.com/stkitts-nevis/index.html

St. Lucia

Saint Lucia Vacation Rental "Saint Lucia, West Indies, location: three bedrooms, two baths, kitchen, dining room, living room, porch with view, three-minute walk to beach, five-minute walk to tennis courts, nine-hole golf course, horseback riding. Maid included in rental price." This is just one sample of the rentals available through this service. Read about their properties and contact them with the info listed at the Web page. ✓**INTERNET**→*url* http://branch.com:1080/lucia/lucia.html

St. Maarten

Welcome to St. Maarten (Netherland Antilles) View the info at this page by clicking on the highlighted topics—city sights, beaches, hotels, shopping, restaurants, sights. The text descriptions are augmented by lush photography that is meant to show "the beauty of this island to anyone considering a visit or as an alternate vacation spot to other tropical islands." ✓**INTERNET**→*url* http://199.170.0.111/

St. Vincent

St. Vincent & the Grenadines These islands are often mentioned as the best place in the world to sail—nice breezes, moderate temperatures, beautiful islands. This page with a nice map and a photo of a harbor in Bequia. The descriptions of the islands are complete with listings of lodgings, restaurants, and local attractions. ✓**INTERNET**→*url* http://www.ualberta.ca/~amitchel/stvg.html

Islanders Provides information about music, art, events, and the people from Trinidad and Tobago. ✓**INTERNET**→*url* http://webcom.net/~island/

Trinidad and Tobago The site makes planning a vacation on either Trinidad or Tobago much easier by providing recommendations for good (and often inexpensive) hotels and restaurants as well as linking to several Websites with info on the islands. ✓**INTERNET**→*url* http://www.ugcs.caltech.edu/~benedett/trinidad/trinidad.html

Turks & Caicos

Eagles Rest Villas T&C A villa rental company with rates and contact numbers at its site. ✓**INTERNET**→*url* http://www.fortmyers.com/caicos.htm

U.S. Virgin Islands

America's Caribbean Paradise, U.S. Virgin Islands An excellent list of each island with hotel, cottage, and guest house price info. You'll also be treated to gorgeous pictures of beaches and people. ✓**INTERNET**→*url* http://www.usvi.net/

Caribbean Villas and Resorts Contact info for this company that rents villas and cottages on the U.S. Virgin Islands. ✓**INTERNET**→*url* http://east_coast_ani.cybernetics.net/vi/VIRGIN.htm

Historic Puerto Rico—from http://www.cntraveler.com/

Part 7

North America

The United States

It's a big country—somebody's got to visit it. Don't sit around pining after the culture of Paris when San Francisco's just a few states away. There's no need to head for the Seychelles when the Florida Keys don't even require a visa. **Destination Guide U.S.A.** on AOL will overwhelm potential tourists with the number of things to do and see in the most unexpected of places—North Dakota, West Virginia, and even New York City. At the **U.S. Travel Board** forum, thousands of happy U.S. travelers proffer advice on the best B&Bs on Cape Cod, and the best salmon fishing near Seattle. If you know you're heading to Milwaukee for Christmas, why not check in with **Tourist Offices of the United States** for info on attractions along the way? The travelogue **U.S.A. from Coast to Coast** will remind you that this land is indeed your land, so go out and conquer it, Holiday Inns, diners, and all.

Mt. Rushmore—from http://anansi.panix.com:80/~wizjd/cgi-bin/getphoto.cgi/

On the Net

Across the board

Destination Guide U.S.A The United States is in many ways a collection of nations with distinct cultures, traditions, laws, and topography. It's hard to believe that the lush forests of the Hawaiian Islands are part of the same country as the plains of Wyoming; Nebraska and Wisconsin are both Midwestern states, yet the former is very conservative, and Wisconsin has a Socialist governor. Even within states there are extremes, as any rural farmer near the Thousand Islands will tell you when he relates the story of his first trip to New York City. Start to make sense of this diverse and complex country with the help of this Website, which profiles each state with geostats, demographics, and economic statistics. For those planning to tour America, there are listings of events for each state and descriptions of attractions that cover everything from museums in urban areas to wine festivals out in the country. Dos and don'ts are listed for each state—most describe places or activities that are musts to enhance your visit; others are cultural or practical warnings: don't underestimate driving times in western states—they are quite vast; do try chocolate-covered huckleberries, a Montana delicacy; don't judge New Jersey by the Turnpike. Do stop by this site if you're planning a trip in or across America. ✓**AMERICA ONLINE**→*keyword* Traveler's Corner→U.S. Profiles ✓**EWORLD**→*go* traveler→destination guide→U.S./Canada Profiles

Tourist Offices for the United States Contact information is provided for each state's tourism office, which supplies free maps, tour guides, lists of restaurants and hotels, and event calendars to visitors. ✓**AMERICA ONLINE**→*keyword* travel forum→Tourist Offices for the

United States

U.S. Travel Board More than 23,000 postings on the United States are to be found here; chances are that your destination will be included. All 50 states appear, as well as the national parks and Disney World (a world unto itself). Maine, Tennessee, and Virginia seem to elicit the greatest number of postings, Oklahoma and Delaware the least. A poster in the Minnesota forum named GiveMeJava laments that ethnic restaurants in the Twin Cities aren't authentic. ("The Mexican food tastes like frozen dinners.") Plenty responded with their recommendations for other eateries. Use this board to post your questions about travel in the U.S. or to share your expertise with other travelers. ✓**AMERICA ONLINE**→*keyword* travel forum→The Travel Board→U.S.→Traveler Board

Culture

soc.culture.usa (ng) Where to begin? A country as diverse as the United States will undoubtedly have a newsgroup that's all over the place. Everything American, past and present, makes a showing here. The Million Man March in Washington D.C. is a hot topic, with much focus on Louis Farrakhan (whether or not he is conservative, and if he should be feared). The Persian Gulf War is still being discussed—mostly from the point of view of Iraqi expatriats. Since the U.S. is a "melting pot," much discussion is about other nations: Is Greece truly a democratic country? Is Haiti becoming a new type of dictatorship? Jump into the thick of things in this wide-open newsgroup; as our television talk shows illustrate, no topic is too trivial, outrageous, or outdated to be discussed. ✓**USENET**→soc.culture.usa

Services

Ticket Trader Find out prices and ticket availability of concerts, sports events, and theatrical performances around the country. Listings are by event or artist, and seating charts for the venue are included. Contact information for registered ticket brokers (some online) is provided. ✓**INTERNET** ...→*email* marty@tickettrader.com ✍ *Write a request* ...→*url* http://www.tickettrader.com/

United States Chamber of Commerce You can obtain the latest on travel news, information, resources, and events from this federation of businesses, chambers of commerce (at the local and state levels), and American chambers overseas. ✓**INTERNET**→*url* http://www.uschamber.org/chamber/

Travelogues

Three Dudes Tour the USA Andy, Jeff, and Pete, three University of Illinois dudes, set out to explore America from the Midwest to the Southwest in an old Olds, with not too much cash and even fewer rules (no chain restaurants, no TV). They lived to tell the tale, and they do so at this page. Along the way they provide you with lots of photos; odd details of the hotels they encounter, places that suck (Oklahoma), and rules they break (a Denny's breakfast in Tennessee); as well as personal status reports on their sunburns, cleanshavedness, and car counts on the open road. Join them as they relive their journey, and plan the next one. ✓**INTERNET**→*url* http://www.students.uiuc.edu/~pzurich/intro.html

Drive through a tree—http://www.cmp.ucr.edu/exhibitions/netex_history_intro.html

To the Grand Canyon Three guys (Don't women other than Thelma and Louise take road trips?) chronicle their journey from Toronto to the Grand Canyon. A frightening photo shows them all asleep in the car at once! Read this travelogue of their sometimes scary trip across 13 of America's great states. ✓**INTERNET**→*url* http://www.inforamp.net/~kfair/gcanyon.htm

U.S.A. From Coast to Coast Three men from Denmark descend upon the U.S. and cross the country. They travel mostly along U.S. Route 80, making detours through the Rockies, to the Grand Canyon, and up to San Francisco before ending their trek in Los Angeles. For each of the eight regions they visit, they tell which hotels they stayed in (Vanderbilt YMCA in New York, for example), as well as what tourist attractions they visited, the best places to dance, and their secret discoveries of the best food and sinful desserts (that's what they said). It may take time to browse through their pages (the site is in Denmark), but it's well worth the wait and will entice you to head for the nearest gas station with your suitcases packed. ✓**INTERNET**→*url* http://www.diku.dk/students/peer/

U.S. Guide

ALABAMA

The Birmingham Web: The Matrix Everything in Birmingham seems to be wired—from the art museum to the Baptist churches, the zoo to the sheriff's department—they all have links to this page. This very organized site guides visitors to current events in town, the local media, and to tourist attractions, such as the Jazz Hall of Fame, the Civil Rights Institute, and Helen Keller's home. ✓**INTERNET**→*url* http://www.the-matrix.com/

The Birmingham Zoo Visit the zoo online with this annotated collection of pictures featuring elephants, polar bears, lions, and, of course, alligators. If you prefer to visit in person, the site also details the zoo's schedule and location and its educational programs. ✓**INTERNET**→*url* http://www.bhm.tis.net/zoo/

Welcome to Huntsville NASA's first rockets were produced here, which explains why Huntsville is often called Rocket City. Learn about the city's aerospace heritage at the site, where you can also plan your flight to Huntsville (not in a rocket), scan a list of local hotels, and read about attractions like the NASA Space Flight Center and a Huntsville hardware store that's been in business since 1897. ✓**INTERNET**→*url* http://iquest.com/~cvb/

Montgomery Magazine HyperCalendar If you'd like to know what's going on in the capital city—sports events, bookstore readings, and the local weather—find out here at this monthly calendar of events. ✓**INTERNET**→*url* http://www.wsnet.com/~jtu3/index.html

ALASKA

Alaska Internet Travel Guide A comprehensive travel guide to the state—in addition to the basic hotel, restaurant, and popular tourist attraction listings, get beautiful photos, a primer on Alaskan lingo (a cheechako is a newcomer to Alaska; sourdough is an old Alaskan), hunting and sports links, and tips on staying in an igloo (they really do exist). Links lead to local travel agents and tour companies, as well as to Alaska-related Websites. ✓**INTERNET**→*url* http://www.Alaska-Online.com/travel/alaska.htm

---

Alaska Marine Highway System Because the Alaska Railway and road systems are snowed under at times, the most reliable means of transporting people, mail, and cargo remains the Marine Highway System. Its ships resemble small luxury liners, but they are actually ice-breaking ships that link the cities and towns of Alaska—from Juneau, the small southern capital, to remote Nome, which is closer to Russia than to Anchorage. Vessel information, photos, maps, and schedules are included. ✓**INTERNET**→*url* http://www.dot.state.ak.us/external/amhs/home.html

---

Alaska Railroad Watch whales spout and glaciers roll by! The railroad serves travelers with tour and ferry packages; some tours are on special sightseeing trains. Stop at this online station for fares and schedules. ✓**INTERNET**→*url* http://alaskan.com/akrail.html

---

alt.culture.alaska (ng) For discussion of life in Alaska. Come here to learn about out-of-the-way places in this remote state—like Anaktuvuk, where a small museum is hidden deep within the local forest. The newsgroup's FAQ lists the phone numbers and addresses of local businesses (including ho-

Fodor's Choice...

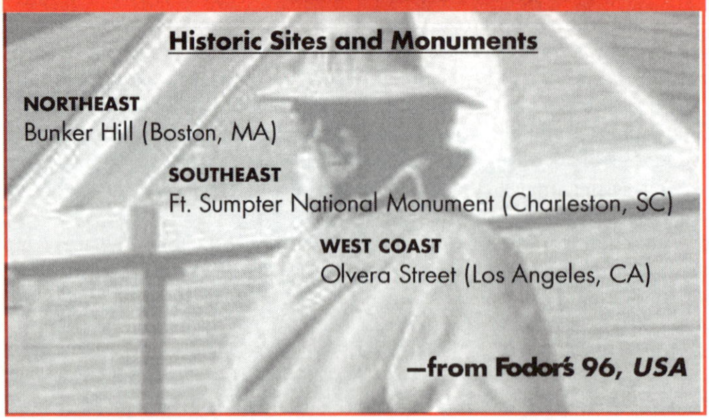

Historic Sites and Monuments

NORTHEAST
Bunker Hill (Boston, MA)

SOUTHEAST
Ft. Sumpter National Monument (Charleston, SC)

WEST COAST
Olvera Street (Los Angeles, CA)

—from Fodor's 96, *USA*

tels, restaurants, and government offices) and tells tales about real northern exposure. ✓USENET→alt.culture.alaska *FAQ:* ✓INTERNET→*url* http://camelot.acf-lab.alaska.edu/~fsdpr/akfaq/index.html

Grandview Lodge—Mt. McKinley The highest peak in North America at over 20,000 feet, Mount McKinley is visited by thousands who trek to Denali Park each summer. This online brochure features lovely scenic views of the big mountain, along with tour prices, historical information, and events listings. Contact the Mount McKinley rangers from here for reservations or additional information. ✓INTERNET→*url* http://www.alaska.net/~grandv/

Anchorage CityLink Anchorage's many attractions are highlighted at this Website—like Earthquake Park, which is devoted entirely to a quake in 1964 (at 9.2 on the Richter scale, it was North America's most powerful to date). Great tips on local artisans, eateries, and hotels as well. ✓INTERNET→*url* http://www.neosoft.com/citylink/anchor/

ARIZONA

Arizona Destinations Web Pick a city on the map here, and then click for listings of all that you'll want to see and do in that location. If you pick Lake Havasu City, you'll be rewarded with a description of the London Bridge tours offered there. Or if you're a virtual traveler looking for a taste of the region, you can shop for Southwestern-style rugs or clothing in the Southwestern Mall here. ✓INTERNET→*url* http://www.amdest.com/

Grand Canyon National Park Current weather reports, trail descriptions, safety alerts, maps, and listings of special events in the Canyon. Also find geological info on the formation of the Canyon, a FAQ, and tips on additional reference materials. Happy trails! ✓INTERNET→*url* http://www.kbt.com/gc/gc_home.html

The Grand Canyon—from http://www.panix.com/~wizjd/photo/

Grand Canyon Tour This site offers a whole lot of info on Arizona's great big canyon. Veteran hikers share their tips on supplies to bring, books to read for info, and trails—scenic, safe, and daring routes—it's your choice. Their list of Canyon common occurrences (finding a scorpion under your sleeping bag, pumping water, watching the cactus bloom) makes this online tour as virtual as possible. ✓INTERNET→*url* http://metro.turnpike.net/H/hud/CANYON.HTM

The ArizonaWeb Enter the great state of Arizona at this Website. Cross the state line with this collection of links to pages on dozens of tourist destinations, as well as on businesses, government offices, and local radio and TV stations in Arizona. ✓INTERNET→*url* http://arizonaweb.org/enter.html

Flagstaff Infoguide A site replete with descriptions of Flagstaff city attractions—including the Lowell Observatory, North Arizona University, and historic downtown—plus links to info on the Grand Canyon, Native American communities, and the nearby Kaibab and Coconino National Forests. As if that weren't enough, there's also a calendar that lists local symphony performances and rodeos. ✓INTERNET→*url* http://www.primenet.com/~iink/flag/mm.html

Heard Museum Phoenix's contemporary and historical Native American and Southwestern art museum is available to you online. Preview their collection of Native American artifacts, which includes beautiful woven baskets and buffalo capes worn during ritual dances. ✓INTERNET→*url* http://hanksville.phast.umass.edu/defs/independent/Heard/Heard.html

Phoenix at your Fingertips Everything you ever wanted to know about Phoenix—from Super Bowl XXX information to the requisite art, culture, hotel, and restaurant listings. So much about Phoenix is here that travelers can skip over the info on when to put their trash out and head straight for the description of the Museo Chicano. ✓INTERNET→*url* http://www.ci.phoenix.az.us/

Scenic Tucson When you visit this site, forget that Tucson is a sprawling city in a growing state. Instead, immerse yourself in pictures of the desert's flora and fauna, retreat to a reservation through essays on Native American culture, virtually scale a mountain, or watch the sun come up over the Catalina foothills. If the site convinces you to pack up and head for those Catalina hills, you'll have to research hotel and restaurant info elsewhere. ✓INTERNET→*url* http://www.brainlink.com/~tucson/scenic/index.html

ARKANSAS

Arkansas Rivers Whitewater is not just the name of a troublesome financial deal; it's also one of Arkansas's most beautiful natural resources. Dive in to this page just brimming with Arkansas river statistics, which are accompanied by detailed descriptions and action-packed photos of each waterway. ✓INTERNET→*url* http://www.rahul.net/fallside/awa/river_project/Arkansas/

Little Rock If you're in the state capital, the former (and possibly future) home of the current U.S. president, there are plenty of distractions to keep you occupied, including a tour of the Villa Marre, whose facade was featured in the TV series *Designing Women.* Click on the appropriate buttons for dining and lodging options in addition to tourist site information. ✓INTERNET→*url* http://www.neosoft.com/citylink/lit-rock/

Welcome to Mountain Home, Arkansas You can't help but be drawn to a place called Mountain Home—just hearing the name inspires warm feelings. Where to stay, what to do, when to take Ozark Mountain tours, and how to make Mountain Home your mountain home away from home can all be learned at this site. ✓INTERNET→*url* http://www.crl.com/~ozark/mtnhome/index.html

CALIFORNIA

For Los Angeles sites, see page 247.

California Forum Afraid you won't be able to communicate with the natives? Talk to some first with a visit to this active forum, where Californians and visitors exchange info on romantic getaways, local bands, and good restaurants in towns from Eureka to San Diego. ✓COMPUSERVE→*go* california

The California Page Search the database at this page for city-specific info on local California businesses and attractions. Or download any one of the numerous city and regional maps here. ✓INTERNET→*url* http://www-ca.llnl.gov/california/servers.html

Virtual Tourist California Famous for its cloverleafs and highways, this state has jumped on the information highway in a big way. Search hundreds of links here for specific locales and services, or browse through pictures, virtual tours, and calendars of events. If you can't afford the price of a plane ticket, consider a virtual drive up the 49-mile scenic stretch of the lovely California coast—you'll see Alcatraz, Disneyland, the San Diego Zoo, and Death Valley, which all have home pages just a jump away from this site. ✓INTERNET→*url* http://www.research.digital.com/SRC/virtual-tourist/California.html

DETOURS

"The first time I saw it happen nothing registered on my conscious mind, because it all seemed so natural—as the car in front turned down the off-ramp of the San Diego freeway, the girl beside the driver pulled down the sunvisor and used the mirror on the back of it to tidy her hair. Only when I had seen a couple more incidents of the kind did i catch their import: that coming off the freeway is coming in from outdoors. A domestic or sociable journey in Los Angeles does not end so much at the door of one's destination as at the off-ramp of the freeway, the mile or two of ground-level streets counts as no more than the front drive of the house.

"In part, this is a comment on the sheer vastness of the movement pattern of Los Angeles, but more than that it is an acknowledgement that the freeway system in its totality is now a single comprehensible place, a coherent state of mind, a complete way of life"

—from **Virtual Tourist California**

(cont'd pg. 250) →

Los Angeles

Even if you're not ready for your close-up, Los Angeles can be a fun place to visit. Sure, you might want to visit a tanning salon first and practice "lunching" or "dialoguing" and dust off your inner child. But once ready, **@LA** and **Los Angeles Superstation** will help you slide right in to the local scene. Get around (from Century City to Santa Monica) thanks to **Los Angeles Subways**, or more realistically, with the help of the Los Angeles **Real-Time Traffic Report**. As for attractions, there's the **Los Angeles Zoo** (home to baboons and failed sitcom actors), or **The George C. Page Museum of La Brea Discoveries** (i.e., tar pits—the perfect place to dispose of the kids for the afternoon). Visit Nixon's haunting grounds at **San Clemente** or Walt and Mickey's at **Disneyland Park**. If that's not enough fun, the **LA Weekly Essential Guide to LA at Night** tells you where all the young starlets will be hanging out for the evening. Have a blast!

Mann's Chinese Theater—http://www.geopages.com/cgi-bin/main/Hollywood/gallery.html

On the Net

Across the board

Fodor's Destination Highlights—Los Angeles Weekly events listings for the city are here, along with dining and lodging options, searchable by price. ✓**E-WORLD**→*go* fodors→Destination→Highlights→Usa→Los Angeles

Fodor's Worldview—Los Angeles Whether you're a business traveler, or in town to take a sightseeing tour, you'll find things of interest here. Hotels and motels are recommended, and choice dining spots, stores, museums, nightlife spots, and recreation are described for visitors. Practical information about city transportation, currency exchange locations, emergency services, and important phone numbers is included. ✓**AMERICA ONLINE**→*keyword* worldview→Usa→Los Angeles

@LA A hubsite for all types of community and visitor resources in the Greater Los Angeles area (and it's a big area—larger than the state of Rhode Island). The site is truly massive; hundreds of links take you to a wide variety of sites, including the Natural History Museum of Los Angeles County, Santa Monica Coffee Houses, and the L.A. County Court House. ✓**INTERNET**→*url* http://emporium.turnpike.net/A/atLA/index.htm

Los Angeles Superstation The cool site to all that's going on in L.A. See what the city looks like with the photo page, get the lowdown on the earthquake situation, and meet Angelenos through their home pages. All sorts of visitor information is available for tourists, and you even get to meet Fantasia Darling! Never heard of him? Now's your chance. ✓**INTERNET**→*url* http://www.fountainhead.com/super.html

Culture

Los Angeles County Museum of Art This site is filled with artistic masterpieces from L.A.'s premier art museum, including selections from the Eastern Art, Decorative Art, Costumes, and Textiles Galleries. The museum's aggressive exhibition schedule has been scaled back recently due to funding cuts, but the LACMA still offers a wide variety of shows as diverse as a collection of ancient Chinese ritual robes and a retrospective of Roy Lichtenstein's work. Visit the Website for a current schedule of events and general museum info. ✓**INTERNET**→*url* http://www.lacma.org/

Los Angeles Murals Homepage SPARC (The Social and Public Art Resource Center) will take you on a tour of the spectacular murals of Los Angeles. View with wonder the art that started as political protest and ended up bringing beauty to the community. ✓**INTERNET**→*url* http://latino.sscnet.ucla.edu/murals/index1.html

---

Los Angeles: Revisiting the Four Ecologies L.A.'s architecture reflects social and environmental issues more clearly than most cityscapes. At this site explore surfurbia (the coastal suburbs), downtown and midtown L.A., the foothills surrounding the city, and autopia (the infamous L.A. freeway system). This site is not a virtual tour of Los Angeles; it examines specific design issues and their relationship to aspects of the city. ✓**INTERNET**→*url* http://www.cf.ac.uk/uwcc/archi/jonesmd/la

---

Los Angeles Zoo The gallery of images here showcases the Zoo's animal attraction. Some of the photos are huge (312K), but so are the animals—for example, the Zoo's prized hippo, Bertha, is not to be played with. If you'd like to visit the Zoo in person, it's in Griffith Park; all directions, hours, event information, and FAQs you'll need to plan you visit can be found here. ✓**INTERNET**→*url* http://www.ci.la.ca.us/dept/ZOO/

Route 66 Los Angeles Webstation Your complete movie guide for L.A. Find out what's in the cinema as well as on TV and newly released on video. ✓**INTERNET**→*url* http://www.losangeles.com/

The George C. Page Museum of La Brea Discoveries (La Brea Tar Pits) If you saw the L.A. cult film *Miracle Mile*, you know that the La Brea Tar Pit is an important locale. Read all about the location's fossils, its permanent collection, and how you can visit it. Unfortunately, there are no images to view here; you'll have to contain your excitement until you arrive. Advice: Don't rent *Jurassic Park* before your visit. ✓**INTERNET**→*url* http://cwis.usc.edu/lacmnh/page/

The LA Weekly Essential Guide to LA at Night You've got one night in L.A.—where do you go? If you're dancing, where else but Saturday Night Fever? Unless you're a lesbian; then the Palms might be more fun. The Dance listings here won't tell you when the Joffrey is in town, instead it points to places shakin' when the earth's not quakin'. Music, eats, bars, games, piercing and tattoo shops (go to Cliff Cadaver), and comedy clubs are listed here. The site lets you link to the New York version of the Guide, so you can see which scene is hotter on any particular night. ✓**INTERNET**→*url* http://mosaic.echonyc.com/~voice/latit.htm

Restaurants & cafés

Chris Richter's Los Angeles Restaurant Reviews A personal collection of L.A. restaurant reviews, organized by how often Chris Richter eats there. ✓**INTERNET**→*url* http://www.earthlink.net/~crichter/goodeats.htm

---

The World Café You've just spent the last week navigating old Route 66 and you're finally in San-

Fodor's Choice...

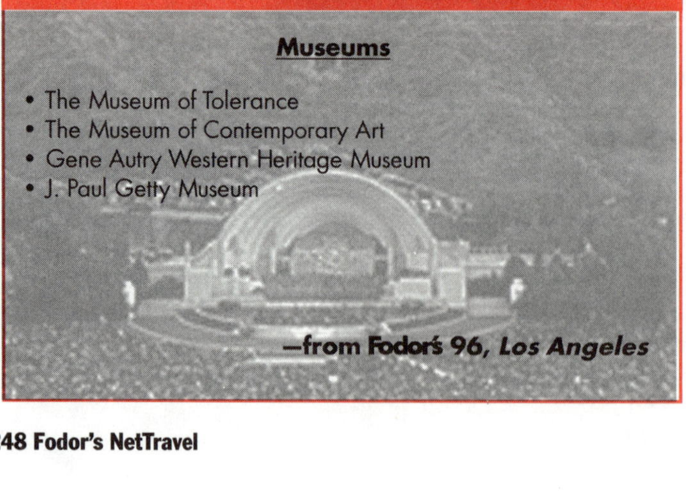

Museums

- The Museum of Tolerance
- The Museum of Contemporary Art
- Gene Autry Western Heritage Museum
- J. Paul Getty Museum

—from Fodor's 96, *Los Angeles*

ta Monica! You can probably use some coffee. Check in to this cybercafé for a drink, and to see what new book has just been added to the Net Books Website. ✓ **INTERNET**→*email* teck@extremes.net ✍ *Email with general correspondence*

Transportation

Los Angeles Real-Time Traffic Report Why get stuck on one of those frantic freeways? Check the up-to-the-minute traffic reports here to see if you should take the subway instead. If you're driving from L.A. to another city, say, San Diego or Milwaukee, you can check their traffic here also. ✓ **INTERNET**→*url* http://www.scubed.com/

Los Angeles Subways What do you get when you cross the London bus system with New York's subway? The double decked trains of the Los Angeles Metrolink. Yes, L.A. has a subway now (you pay fares on the honor system!), and it even takes you to the airport (the Green Line). This page tells you everything you need to know to use it. ✓ **INTERNET**→*url* http://ucs.usc.edu/~ertrinid/larail.html

Catalina

Catalina Island Guide The contestants on TV's *Love Connection* always seem to come here for their dates. What's the attraction? Twenty-two miles out in the Pacific is the perfect outdoor lover's paradise. Included here are resources to aid people who are here for a day trip, renting for the summer, or getting married. At the Website access a huge island map (143K) with a guide to the Island's main town, Avalon, excerpts from local newspapers, and numerous lodging, dining, and sports equipment rental listings. A visit to Catalina Island might prove to be the ideal way to get away from it all while still staying within Los Angeles County. ✓ **INTERNET**→*url* http://www.deltanet.com/guide/

Orange County

About Anaheim, Orange County, And The Los Angeles Area Orange County houses Disneyland, and surprisingly, much more. Visit the rest of Anaheim, bike around Orange County, and see this entire area virtually if you desire. If you absolutely can't stay away from amusement parks, visit VirtualWorld in Costa Mesa or Yesterland—an online amusement park composed of discontinued Disneyland attractions. ✓ **INTERNET**→*url* http://sundry.hsc.usc.edu/lacon3-info/www/Anaheim/anaheim.html

Disneyland Park If you can't travel to Neuschwanstein in the Alps, how about Cinderella's castle and Space Mountain? Everything Disney is located here—maps of the park, descriptions of the attractions and rides, and an entertainment schedule (Fantasy in the Sky with Tinkerbell) are all here online. ✓ **INTERNET**→*url* http://www.best.com/~dijon/disney/parks/disneyland/

Orange County Restaurant Review A wide variety of reviews are here—from praise the of the Scottish Bridie at the Olde Ship to a luke-warm reception of the take-out Turkish pita sandwiches from Ferdussi. Some of the reviews are linked to restaurant home pages (in case you like what you read about them), and the reviews come complete with price guides. ✓ **INTERNET**→*url* http://www.gordian.com/users/daniel/restaurant/reviews.html

San Clemente: Spanish Village by the Sea Break away from the big cities for a visit to this Orange County seaside resort. You won't have trouble finding food—the restaurants outnumber the residents. For dates of local events and a list of the best places to surf, drop in for a visit. ✓ **INTERNET**→*url* http://www.mind.net/bba/SC/index.html

Venice Beach

Venice Beach Flex your muscles on the beach here with the other surfers, skaters, jugglers, and freaks who comprise the daily scene here at the pier. Find out all that's happening in Venice—and by the way, where the heck is it, anyway? There are pointers to other tourist destinations in the area, including Sin City itself: Los Angeles. ✓ **INTERNET**→*url* http://www.mediaonline.com/bizads/venicebeach.html

The famous Hollywood sign—http://www.geopages.com/cgi-bin/main/Hollywood/gallery.html

California Beach Apartments A promotional page featuring photos of fully furnished beach-front apartments for rent through this company. ✓**INTERNET**…→*email* BeachApts@aol.com ✍ *Write a request* …→*url* http://www.best.com/~travel/ca-beach.html

---

Inn Access Looking for that perfect California inn? Will it be the beach or the desert? Find them here at the CABBI (California Association of Bed & Breakfast Inns) site. Click on the map or letter of the city; download the online brochures to help with your selection. ✓**INTERNET**→*url* http://www.mcn.org/B&B/B&B.html

---

City of Berkeley Home Page Tourists can use this collection of links to access listings for any number of events, museums, and theaters that flourish in this famous college town. There's even a link to UC at Berkeley here to aid those traveling to the city on academic matters. ✓**INTERNET**→*url* http://www.ci.berkeley.ca.us/

Restaurants in the Berkeley Area A list of restaurants in Berkeley from Crepes-A-Go-Go to New Dehli Junction, organized by location or alphabetically, with short reviews, addresses, and phone numbers. ✓**INTERNET**→*url* http://sseos.lbl.gov/Restaurants/Restaurants.html

---

Napa Valley Virtual Visit Napa Valley is synonymous with wine country, so you won't be surprised that the beverage is the focus of this Website. The QuickTime videos and sound clips that pepper these virtual vineyard tours will make you wish you were in the Valley sipping wine samples. If you can't drop everything and make your way to Napa, you'll be happy to know that the site also lets you order wines online. ✓**INTERNET**→*url* http://www.freerun.com/

Welcome to Monterey Peninsula If you'd rather be hot-air ballooning, strolling through quaint villages, or mountain biking than battling traffic in L.A., then a trip to the Monterey Peninsula may be in order. Located between Los Angeles and San Francisco, the Peninsula offers another view of California. Come to this site to tour the area through photographs and essays. If you wish, you can also reserve a hotel online and read local restaurant menus. ✓**INTERNET**→*url* http://www.monterey.com/california/

Death Valley, California—from http://anansi.panix.com:80/~wizjd/cgi-bin/getphoto.cgi/

Artdirect's San Diego Homepage San Diego's museums can be enjoyed even by those who aren't in Balboa Park. See online versions of several collections—if you're interested in Rubens, El Greco, or Juan Sanchez, don't miss the online version of the San Diego Museum of Art. A visit to this page will also reward you with half-price tickets for performances at the Old Globe Theatre, performance schedules for the California Ballet company, and lists of festivals that make the streets of San Diego come alive. ✓**INTERNET**→*url* http://www.artdirect.com/california/san.diego/homepage

---

City of San Diego The San Diego Website is among the more organized you'll find—clicking on one of 30 buttons will direct you to info on specific features of the city, including the famous zoo (the city's pride and joy), restaurants, hotels, and transportation (ride the red trolleys to Tijuana!). ✓**INTERNET**→*url* http://www.nosc.mil/planet_earth/sandiego.html

---

Westgate Hotel Make reservations online for this classic hotel in downtown San Diego. ✓**INTERNET**→*url* http://www.sddt.com/~westgate/

Bay Area Restaurant Guide Some of the best restaurants in San Francisco, East Bay, and Marin County have links to this page. Others are listed only in the site's database. Search for a particular restaurant by cuisine or location, or scan the entire list and fantasize about fresh seafood and

Napa Valley wines. After selecting a restaurant, read the reviews here to be certain you've made the right decision. ✓**INTERNET**→*url* http://www.w3.com/bayfood/

Q San Francisco: Gay Guide These pages list hundreds of lesbian and gay resources in the Bay Area, and the site's by no means a complete list! Gay-friendly lodgings, bars and clubs, restaurants, museums, walking tours, churches, health clubs, theaters, and even gay and lesbian events are listed here. ✓**INTERNET**→*url* http://www.qsanfrancisco.com/qsf/guide/contents.html

San Fran Subway Navigator Let's get this straight—there's BART, which runs underground, but it's not the subway, which is MUNI, but MUNI surfaces and becomes a trolley, but it's not the same as the cable cars, and what the heck is a trolleybus? Make sense of San Francisco's multifaceted public transportation systems with the help of this site. ✓**INTERNET**→*url* http://metro.jussieu.fr:10001/bin/select/english/usa/san-francisco

San Francisco Artdirect A complete guide to the arts in San Francisco. Exhibitions, musical performances, architecture of note, and local universities are among the listings. You can also visit the Art Explosion Gallery online, as well as the San Francisco Museum of Modern Art and the Ansel Adams Center of Photography. ✓**INTERNET**→*url* http://www.artdirect.com/california/san.francisco/homepage

San Francisco Examiner and San Francisco Chronicle See what's going on in the Golden Gate city tonight by reading the full text of the papers at this site. ✓**INTERNET**→*url* http://www.sfgate.com/

San Francisco Hotel Reservations Search hotels by location, price, type (luxury, high-rise, small inn), and then check availability. Book your reservations online. Descriptions are provided to ensure that you aren't housing your CEO in a motel in Haight-Ashbury. ✓**INTERNET**→*url* http://www.hotelres.com/

San Francisco Museum of Modern Art The new museum building, designed by Hellmuth, Obata, and Kassabaum, is as much a work of modern art as the collections within. Tour the museum's permanent collection and special exhibitions (one show recently featured Willem De Kooning's late paintings), shop in the museum store, and browse information about educational programs. ✓**INTERNET**→*url* http://www.sfmoma.sf.ca.us:1995:/galleries/galleries.html

San Jose Living Online Guide Do you know the way to San Jose? Well, finding directions might be easier than you think—just get online and visit this site. Once in virtual San Jose, visit the galleries of de Saisset Museum at Santa Clara University, tour the local wineries, see the Giants play, or read the full text of the Mercury News. A section of the site offers excerpts from *Out NOW!* (gay weekly) that tell what's hot and what's on in the San Jose gay community. ✓**INTERNET**→*url* http://www.acoates.com/sjliving

Santa Cruz Page What else is in Santa Cruz besides that quirky university? See for yourself—plenty of photos of the city are at this site, along with a description of the Marshmallow Peanut Circus, a list of local bookstores, and a link to the local Pizza Hut. (Yes, you can order a slice online!) ✓**INTERNET**→*url* http://www.human.com/scruz.html

Santa Cruz Surfer's Corner Surf's Up! Or is it? Check local conditions daily, and best of all, visit the online surfer's museum, which features pics of vintage surfboards and profiles of local surfing legends. Did you know that surfing was introduced to Santa Cruz by David Kawananakoa, nephew of Queen Liliuokalani of Hawaii? ✓**INTERNET**→*url* http://www.cruzio.com/~sconline/surfpg.html

COLORADO

Colorado Resort Net Organized by city, Resort Net provides great ski-condition info during the season and a comprehensive guide to Colorado hotels, but it comes up short when the subject is restaurants—there were no food listings when we checked. To make up for it, Resort Net features a nifty electronic form that lets you enter keywords describing your perfect vacation. Send in the form, and Resort Net matches your requirements with resorts that fit your needs—and then sends you back contact info. ✓**INTERNET**→*url* http://www.toski.com/CRNMAIN.HTM

Colorado Virtual Tourist Links here lead to home pages that address every facet of Colorado life—sports, government, parks, lodging, airports, food, schools and libraries, cultural attractions, clubs, and businesses. The collection is organized by city. ✓**INTERNET**→*url* http://www.capcon.com/virtualtourist/

Colorado Web Come to this collection of links and visit the Ghost Town Wild West Museum and the Garden of the Gods, join the Colorado Rocket Society, consult the Intellicast Ski Report, root for the Denver Grizzlies, explore Montezuma County, and find the best B&B that Boulder has to offer. A great place to start your Colorado vacation. ✓ **INTERNET**→*url* http://www.rmii.com/colorado/info.html

Colorado's Best Bed and Breakfasts, Inns, and Small Hotels Pick a charming B&B from this guide that gives detailed descriptions of the history and "atmosphere" of the lodging and surrounding area, as well as contact information for each B&B. ✓ **INTERNET**→*url* http://www.virtualcities.com/~virtual/ons/co/r/co35r01.htm

The Source for Rocky Mountain Restaurants More than 15,000 restaurants located throughout Colorado are listed by city, cuisine, price, and name. The site's definitely the best Colorado dining index on the Net, answering all your questions except whether to eat Chinese or Italian. ✓ **INTERNET**→*url* http://www.mtt.com/theSource/rockyMountain/

Colorado Springs A site featuring facts and figures about Colorado and Colorado Springs, a small reference page detailing handicap facilities around the state, and a What's New section that gives you the latest on what's happening in the area. ✓ **INTERNET**→*url* http://www.usa.net/cscvb/default.html#6385

Denver CityLink Although information here is limited to the essentials (phone numbers and addresses), it's still a fine place to get an overview of Denver's attractions—from Michael Garman's Magic Town to Buffalo Bill's Memorial Museum and Grave. There's also info on places to stay, including listings for large hotels (Embassy Suites Hotel) and smaller hotels (the Cherry Creek Inn). ✓ **INTERNET**→*url* http://www.neosoft.com/citylink/denver/

CONNECTICUT

Connecticut Restaurants More than 230 restaurants are listed in the guide for western and southern Connecticut (the wealthy suburbs closest to New York City). They can be cross referenced by location, price, or cuisine. Reviews of each establishment will help you make a selection. ✓ **COMPUSERVE**→*go* zagats→Access Restaurant Listing→Connecticut

Liquid Arts: Connecticut Restaurant Guide Details on restaurants throughout the entire state are easily accessed at this listing that is organized by type of cuisine and restaurant location. ✓ **INTERNET**→*url* http://liquid.neca.com/liquid/food.html

The Connecticut Homepage Each week this site highlights specific regions, towns, and attractions with virtual tours. A recent week featured the town of Wilton, the Housatonic Valley (where Danbury is located), and the Mark Twain House. Connecticut's parks and forests are also featured, with listings of campgrounds along the Connecticut River Valley. The site even lists historic places to visit and a calendar of events for the state. Plenty of maps help you find your way; if you're hopelessly lost, however, browse the real estate listings and make this your home. ✓ **INTERNET**→*url* http://www.connecticut.com/

The Connecticut Tourism Guide Although the state is small enough to drive through in an afternoon, it comprises many distinct regions: the coast, the Connecticut River Valley, the Gateway to New England (the cities and suburbs adjacent to New York), and the rural region in the northeast. Click on the map at this site to visit each region. You can then glimpse photos of fall foliage, covered bridges, Mystic seaport, Yale University, and other Connecticut attractions. Listings of B&Bs, restaurants, parks, and cultural events are accessible with just a click. ✓ **INTERNET**→*url* http://ctguide.atlantic.com/vacguide/

Welcome to Hartford, Con-

Rocky Mountain high—from http://anansi.panix.com:80/~wizjd/photo/

The Capitol Dome at night—http://www.cs.virginia.edu/~rdc8a/photos/washington.html

necticut This growing Website will dispel rumors that Hartford is just a boring capital with lots of insurance companies. The performing arts do flourish here, and the numerous college campuses ensure a nightlife scene. Check out this page for more details. ✓ **INTERNET**→*url* http://www.hartford.edu/city/hartford.html

Yale University Art Gallery Let your mouse be your guide to the impressive collections of the university's museum, which is online here. See exhibits of pre-Columbian sculpture and galleries of African, American, Asian, early modern, and contemporary art, including works of artists such as Piet Mondrian, Pablo Picasso, and Vincent van Gogh. ✓ **INTERNET**→*url* http://www.cis.yale.edu/yups/yuag/

DELAWARE

Big Shout Magazine To find out what's on in the Delaware Valley region, pick up this weekly online magazine. Current and back issues are available, and each has a different theme (Delaware restaurants, beaches, and pubs). ✓ **INTERNET**→*url* http://www.magpage.com/bigshout/

Delaware Tourism A page devoted to the merits of this tiny state often overlooked by tourists. Read about scenic towns like New Castle, where most homes resemble period museums; the excellent collection of the Delaware Art Museum in Wilmington; Nemour Mansion and Gardens; and the beautiful seashore at Rehoboth. Access information also on Delaware's state parks, performing arts, and other pertinent visitors' resources. ✓ **INTERNET**→*url* http://167.21.1.11/tourism/intro.htm

DISTRICT OF COLUMBIA

Cheap and Safe D.C. Tips on free or almost-free attractions in the Capital City: the Smithsonian (free!), the White House (free!), the National Zoo (no, not Congress), and the Old Town Alexandria walking tour (also free) ✓ **INTERNET**→*url* http://www.cais.com/npacheco/dc/dcfree.html

Subway Navigator Washington, D.C. If you're planning a night on the town in Washington, and you're using the subway to get around, you should definitely consult this guide before starting your evening. The Metro closes at midnight, so there's no time for botched connections! ✓ **INTERNET**→*url* http://metro.jussieu.fr:10001/bin/select/english/usa/washington

The District Area Dining Directory This dining directory is the closest thing to a slot machine you'll find in D.C. There are three scroll bars: first, select cuisine (for instance, Irish), then the type of dining you prefer (coffeehouses), then the desired area of the city (Dupont Circle). Then click Find and voila! Well, nothing fits these particular criteria, but when you do luck out, you get a description of the restaurant, its address and phone number, and a list of credit cards accepted. ✓ **INTERNET**→*url* http://dc.myhouse.com/

The White House Our President's home, also a favorite attraction of Americans with guns, is online with a recorded greeting from the President, a tour of the grounds, a history of the building, and info on visiting America's casa blanca. ✓ **INTERNET**→*url* http://www.whitehouse.gov/

Traveler's Edge—Washington D.C. The Traveler's Edge simplifies the city for you, telling you how to get in touch with Old Town Trolley Tours, where the funniest comedians perform, what government attractions (such as the White House, the Capitol, the Library of Congress) are open to the public, and how to get to them. ✓ **EWORLD**→*go* travelers→city files→u.s. cities→washington d.c.

Washington D.C. Visitors' Guide Visiting our nation's capitol? Come to this site and find Metro maps to get you into the city, hotel listings to help you find a place to stay, and phone numbers of car rental agencies to help you tour the city. The site's map shows you how to get from the Capitol to the Smithsonian. Still not satisfied? Then go to the Mall section, which lists all the shops in Union Station. That's it—you're on your own from here. ✓**INTERNET**→*url* http://www.proxima.com/dc/tourist/

FLORIDA

For more Disney sites, see page 308.

Destination Florida Thanks to its theme parks, sun, sea, and space center, Florida has always been a hotspot for visitors from all over the world. Now, you can search a large database of travel accommodations for the Sunshine State and purchase tickets to hundreds of cultural and sporting events through an online link to Ticketmaster. ✓**COMPUSERVE**→*go* florida

Florida Destination Guide The entire Sunshine State is covered here—what to do for fun (hint: Disney is in Florida), geostats (did you know that the nation's oldest city is St. Augustine?), and dos and don'ts (don't look for a police station in the small Panhandle town of Carrabelle—it's a phone booth; don't expect to see flamingos roaming freely in Florida—they're not native to the state). ✓**EWORLD**→*go* travelers→Destination Guide→U.S./Canada Profiles→States A-F→Florida

Florida Forum By far the most frequented topic on this message board is Disneymania. Check here for tips on the best time to head for the Magic Kingdom or to compare the relative merits of touring MGM and Universal. Those "other" parts of Florida are covered as well, and the locals are willing to help visitors find the perfect condo rental or scuba instructor. ✓**COMPUSERVE**→*go* Florida sig

The "Mural" building in Miami—http://www.period.com/travel/usa/usa02.htm

Florida Infoguide Boasting more than 15,000 restaurant and 2,600 hotel listings, this searchable database puts you in touch with the resources you need to enjoy Florida. ✓**INTERNET**→*url* http://infoguide.com/

Boca Raton Stimulate your senses with this virtual tour of Boca Raton on the Web—listen to music from the Harid Conservatory, stroll around the city admiring the famous Art Deco architecture, and read a brief history of this enchanting locale. For real-life visitors, the site offers listings of what to do and where to stay when you're done doing it. ✓**INTERNET**→*url* http://bocaraton.com/

Daytona Beach, Florida Daytona Beach is the new vacation spot for college students now that Fort Lauderdale has pulled in the welcome mat. You'll find here a tame tourist site listing places to eat, sleep, and be merry. Don't miss the Daytona Speedway, Sugar Mill Gardens, or the newest attraction, Angell & Phelps Chocolate Factory. Details on reaching these and more sightseeing highlights may be found here. ✓**INTERNET**→*url* http://www.charm.net/~ibc/daytona/

Discover Key West The southernmost point in the U.S. and the end of Route 1, Key West actually seceded from the U.S. in 1982. Come to this site to learn why and to access info on the sizable Key West gay community, local events, hotels and B&Bs, and restaurants (including where to get the best conch in the self-titled Conch Republic). ✓**INTERNET**→*url* http://discover.key-west.fl.us/

Florida Keys On-Line Guide A general guide to the 110-mile-long string of Keys. Did you know that there's an underwater hotel in the Keys? It's called Jule's Undersea Lodge. Or you can stay on land if you prefer; arrange it with the substantial hotel listings provided here. Links connect to art galleries, local news, and sporting resources for boaters and divers. ✓**INTERNET**→*url* http://Florida-Keys.FL.US/

Sanibel—Captiva Island Discover the charm of these uncrowded little islands. Known for good beachcombing for seashells (especially after a storm), Sanibel also has charming shops and galleries on Periwinkle Way. Hotel and restaurant listings are here for you—also find links to resources on boating or fishing in the Gulf. ✓**INTERNET**→*url* http://www.coconet.com/sanibel-captiva/info.html

Greater Miami Convention and Visitors Bureau Introduce yourself to Miami's neighborhoods: Little Havana, Overtown, Coconut Grove, and South Beach. With detailed descriptions of the city's arts, festivals, and nightlife, as well as maps, shopping guides, and lodging and dining suggestions, this is the most comprehensive source on Miami on the Net. ✓**INTERNET**→*url* http://www.neptune.com/bureau/bureau.html

Virtually South Beach If a New Yorker tells you they're flying to Warsaw, they're probably referring to one of Miami Beach's hottest clubs instead of Poland's capital. Your mouse is your guide to accessing info online on the hotels, restaurants, and fabulous beaches of South Florida. ✓**INTERNET**→*url* http://sobe.com/

Orlando Orlando is online at this page. Head to info on Church Street Station, an old railroad terminal that's now an entertainment complex with live-music clubs, restaurants, bars, and great mall-type shopping. Perhaps you'll take a trip to Parliament House. Or visit SeaWorld to pet the dolphins and get your feet wet. Are there links to any other famous Orlando attractions here? Of course—you can jump from here to the Disney World page as well. ✓**INTERNET**→*url* http://intpro.com:80/orlando/

Walt Disney World Resorts and Theme Parks Reservations and ticket info for hotels and restaurants in the Magic Kingdom, Epcot Center, and Disney-MGM Studios is at the site. ✓**INTERNET**→*url* http://www.travelweb.com/thisco/wdw/wdwhome/wdw.html

Tampa There's more to Tampa beyond the fantastic airport. In Ybor City, visit the restored Cuban cigar factory at Ybor Square, dance the night away at Tracks, or take the tram to Harbour Island for shopping in a brand–new community. Perhaps you'll visit the Dali Museum in nearby St. Petersburg, or take the trolley over to The Pier, a five-story entertainment complex. Busch Gardens, the Florida Aquarium, and the Tampa Museum of Art are all within a short drive. It's an even faster trip to them all at this Website. ✓**INTERNET**→*url* http://www.neosoft.com/citylink/tampa/

GEORGIA

For Atlanta sites, see page 256.

Georgia Bed and Breakfast Database Listings of small inns and B&Bs throughout the state may be accessed here; this site may be essential if you're attending the upcoming Olympics, as most accommodations in Atlanta have been reserved for Olympic personnel and athletes. ✓**COMPUSERVE**→*go* inns→Databases→location→city and state→GA

GO-Georgia Online Network Of course, you can't read anything about Georgia these days that doesn't mention Atlanta and the Olympics. This page is no exception—there are links here to the Atlanta Olympics FAQ and the Welcome Atlanta page. But you'll also get a tour of the rest of Georgia, with virtual visits to Murray County, the Sea Isles, national parks and forests, Zoo Atlanta, and Stone Mountain. Come to this site for a taste of the Peach State. ✓**INTERNET**→*url* http://www.State.Ga.US/

Athens Known as the home of R.E.M. and the B-52's, Athens is booming with hip culture. But there's more to Athens than rock and roll, and a visit to this site will prove it. Link to the home page of the University of Georgia and to essays and photographs of Athens' famous Federal, Greek Revival, and Victorian-style houses. And, of course, there are links to the home pages of those famous Athens' bands as well. ✓**INTERNET**→*url* http://www.grady.uga.edu/Athenstown/Classic.html

Golden Isles at a Glance A page dedicated to Georgia's coastal islands. Read about places to visit (Fort Frederica, Jekyll Island Historic District, the Mary Miller Doll Museum) and things to do (the Brunswick Civic Orchestra is in its 13th season). If you're into the outdoors, the site offers guides to local fishing holes and to runners' trails. ✓**INTERNET**→*url* http://www.webrunner.com/webrun/lcmn/lcmn.html

Cruising the Delaware Memorial Bridge—http://cnj.digex.net/~jimh/photo/

(cont'd pg. 258) →

Atlanta

Watch out! Atlanta is burning again. But this time it's burning with excitement. The Peach Tree State's first city is gearing up for a influx of glorious (albeit sweaty) specimens of human development for the 1996 summer Olympics. AOL's **1996 Olympics** site gets into the spirit months ahead of time. There you can speculate on the discus champs—will it be the Romanian women or some tough little blonde from Iceland? The **Atlanta Olympics FAQ** will answer the more practical questions—like is there any possibility for getting a gymnastics ticket? (No.) But if the grunts and groans of competitive sports aren't your cup of tea, try the cultural joys of the **High Museum of Art** or choose an eatery from the **Atlanta Restaurant Guide** and do your own carbo packing. A stop at **Welcome to Atlanta** ensures that you'll get a hotel room and street map, no matter what draws you to Scarlett's home town.

The Atlanta skyline at night—http://zaphod.cc.ttu.ee/vrainn/Atlanta/ahome.html

On the Net

Across the board

Atlanta Convention & Visitor's Bureau If you're planning your own personal march through Atlanta, stop by this Website first for a calendar of events, a city history (no, *Gone with the Wind* was not completely fictional), cultural information, a list of convention facilities and services information for business travelers, as well as recommendations on lodgings, dining, and clubs. ✓ **INTERNET**→*url* http://www.com/acvb/

Traveler's Edge—Atlanta Basic travel suggestions for the city, including business listings, city attractions, a nightlife guide, and history. No specific Olympic information here yet. ✓ **EWORLD**→*go* travelers→U.S. cities→Atlanta

Welcome to Atlanta So what's new in Atlanta? Well, only that the world is visiting for the Olympics in 1996. That's the big event which dominates the city as well as this site. There are FAQs on Olympic events, ticket purchasing, the new Olympic stadium and other sports venues as well as more general tourist info like lodging information (in and around the city, and in neighboring states!), and transportation and safety suggestions. The page also takes you on a photographic driving tour to visit Underground Atlanta (a vintage old network of underground brick streets, ornamental facades, and tunnels now housing shopping and entertainment), the High Museum, and the Coca-Cola headquarters. Get to know the city and its highlights here. ✓ **INTERNET**→*url* http://www.ajc.com/atl/welcome.htm

Guides

Atlanta Restaurant Guide You'll probably work up quite an appetite with your search for a hotel room in Atlanta, especially during the Olympics. Luckily this restaurant database will take the work out of finding a good place to eat. Just choose the type of cuisine and general location you're looking for, and the database provides a list of establishments that suit your criteria. ✓ **INTERNET**→*url* http://www.w3.com/atlanta/

Subway Navigator While this site won't tell you about the public library branches in the stations, you will get a map of the MARTA rapid rail system, illustrating the trip from the airport and suburbs to downtown. The Welcome to Atlanta site provides detailed subway directions to Olympic venues. ✓ **INTERNET**→*url* http://metro.jussieu.fr:10001/bin/select/english/usa/atlanta

Museums

High Museum of Art Nestled on one of Atlanta's 23 Peachtree Streets is the High Museum, famous for its diverse collection of traditional and contemporary European and American art. The home page teases you with an image of the museum's acclaimed facade; unfortunately, the graceful interior is currently not displayed. The online galleries sample the permanent collection—from the work of the Italian Renaissance masters (Bellini's *Madonna and Child*) to modern artists (a Warhol silkscreen of Marylin Monroe). Pieces from the furniture galleries are also represented. Special exhibitions have featured Jacob Lawrence's *Migration Series* and "The Treasures of Venice." ✓ **INTERNET**→*url* http://isotropic.com/highmuse/highhome.html

Michael C. Carlos Museum, Atlanta, Georgia You can take a self-guided tour through Emory University's museum on campus. If you'd rather avoid students and tourists, do it from your computer. Mostly ancient civilizations are represented; a recent exhibition here was "Reflections of Women in the New Kingdom—Ancient Egyptian Art from the British Museum." Michael Graves designed the museum, making it a work of art itself and well worth a visit. Learn the museum's hours and admissions prices at the Website. ✓ **INTERNET**→*url* http://www.cc.emory.edu/CARLOS/carlos.html

The Olympics

1996 Olympics Gear up for the Olympics at AOL's fantastic site. Log on and get worldwide news about nations preparing for the games, find out where the Olympic torch is today, or get ahead of yourself and see who's bidding for the 2004 games. Updates on Atlanta's ongoing preparation are here as well as an Olympic trivia quiz. Many images are here also, including several from the 1995 Olympic Festival. And if you won't be able to attend the Atlanta games, the site's Olympic Shop section allows you to purchase "official" Olympic sportswear (which might lessen the blow of not actually being there). ✓ **AMERICA ONLINE**→*keyword* Olympics

Atlanta Olympics FAQ A great place to help you get through the Games smoothly, the site offers a schedule of events for each Olympic sport, information on working for the Games (which you may need to do in order to see the events if you've waited too long to arrange tickets), tips and contact numbers for renting your home, a guide to getting there and around the city, and hints on scrounging for tickets and accommodations (good luck!). Links to other Olympic Websites as well as to local newspapers are also located here. ✓ **INTERNET**→*url* http://WWW.CIS.Ohio-State.Edu/hypertext/faq/usenet/1996-olympics-faq/faq.html

DETOURS

"So, it feels as if the public is being squeezed out of the Olympics? Well, consider how much room must be made for the ever-growing Olympic family before the average spectator gets a crack at tickets, rooms and parking spaces.

During the Games, an army of more than 160,000 will be filling the hotels. They've purchased more than a third of the tickets and reserved more than half the city's hotel rooms.

The tightest squeeze is on accommodations. On top of 30,000 hotel rooms for the family, Atlanta Olympic organizers have leased more than 10,000 beds in a dozen college dormitories and come up with another 1,370 beds in such unlikely locations as the Atlanta Union Mission. And the Olympic Village at Georgia Tech will house 15,000 athletes and officials. Another 2,000 officials will be put up elsewhere."

—from **Welcome to Atlanta**

Savannah Online Planned on a grid system, Savannah's historic district is punctuated by dozens of elegant squares. Unfortunately, few of the colonial-era homes, forts, and museums can be previewed here; you'll have to visit in person. To help you explore Savannah, the site provides info on lodging, dining, entertainment, recreation, and shopping. ✓ **INTERNET**→*url* http://www.catalog.com/cgibin/var/savannah/welcome.htm

HAWAII

alt.culture.hawaii Web Page This home page offers much more concrete information on Hawaii than its namesake newsgroup. Don't miss the recipes for kine (for a taste of the islands when stuck in Cleveland) or the subscription information for the newsletter Hawaii, which offers daily updates on the weather, politics, and events on the islands. ✓ **INTERNET**→*url* http://hookomo.aloha.net/~prophet/ach.html

Hawaii This Prodigy guide introduces you to each of the eight islands that form the state, provides maps of the tourist attractions, lists the best beaches in each location (Kailua Beach on Oahu and Kalikiwai Beach on Kauai are noted), and links to the Compton's Online Encyclopedia's Hawaii listings. ✓ **PRODIGY**→*jump* travel→regional guides→hawaii

Hawaii Forum If you would like advice on where to stay, on restaurants where German is spoken, or on unusual places to visit, go to the Hawaii Forum, a comprehensive source for info on Hawaii. See photos of the glorious Hawaii landscape, or post questions and comments and have them answered by fellow travelers and native Hawaiians. ✓ **COMPUSERVE**→*go* hawaii→Messages *and* Libraries

Tunnels Beach in Hawaii—from http://www.safariair.com/

Hawaii Home Page While primarily serving residents with links to community resources and government pages, this site also connects to advertisements for various beach resorts, home pages for individual islands, tourist info pages in Japanese and German, and a virtual tour of Hawaii. ✓ **INTERNET**→*url* http://www.hawaii.net/

Kailua and Lanikai Beach Vacation Rentals A promotional page for this company with properties for rent. ✓ **INTERNET**→*url* http://opendoor.com/rentals/AllHI.html

Outrigger Hotels Come here for reservations information for this hotel chain in Hawaii. ✓ **INTERNET**→*url* http://www.outrigger.com/infoweb/

Planet Hawaii Preview the attractions of the islands by watching the volcanoes bubble at Hawaiian Volcanoes National Park. Or learn to speak pidgin English so you can fit in at the luau. Each month the site places a camera at a different location in Hawaii and lets Netters watch the action as it happens. ✓ **COMPUSERVE**→*go* Hawaii→Messages *and* Libraries ✓ **INTERNET**→*url* http://www.outrigger.com/index.html

Polynesian Cultural Center Sound files of Polynesian salutations (from Maori to Tahitian) welcome you to the site ("Aloha!"). Founded by Mormons, the Cultural Center serves as an archive of information on Polynesian societies. Lavishly illustrated profiles of each island and its people will help you decide which areas to visit on your vacation. ✓ **INTERNET**→*url* http://center.byuh.edu/

Three Shields Hawaii Prepare Hawaiian dishes such as manapua, char siu bao, or spam musubi with the help of the recipes at this page. Or if you're not feeling that ambitious, but you'd still like to sample the flavor of the islands, check out the site's guide to Hawaiian restaurants in the continental U.S. Or if nothing less than eating Hawaiian food in Hawaii will do, use the airline listings for trans-Pacific, as well as interisland, flights; the nightlife recommendations; and the hotel and shopping resources at the page to plan your trip. ✓**INTERNET**→*url* http://www.aloha.com/~curran/

Traveler's Corner Hawaii Find a list of activities for tourists on various islands, as well as historical information, statistics on the islands, and a list of dos and don'ts. (Do purchase a lei upon arrival to start your trip off right, but don't say "back in the States" when referring to the U.S. mainland—Hawaii is a state also.) ✓**AMERICA ONLINE**→*keyword* traveler's corner→us profiles→g-k→hawaii

Virtually Hawaii: Virtual Field Trips Are you sitting in your apartment in Ottawa dreaming of tropical weather in Maui? Use the Net to realize your dream! Tour a volcano on the Big Island, a beach on Maui, the streets of Waikiki, or the forests of Molokai, among other stunning places. Feeling warmer now, eh? ✓**INTERNET**→*url* http://satftp.soest.hawaii.edu/space/hawaii/virtual.field.trips.html

Your Hawaiian Name Enter your name into this database and learn the native Hawaiian version of your tag. The name John came back as the slightly more exotic Keoni! ✓**INTERNET**→*url* http://hisurf.aloha.com/Find.html

Kauai Vacation Planner Home Page A lesser known but no less beautiful island in the chain, Kauai features the lovely beaches, fascinating wildlife, and unique history that make Hawaii a special state. Take an island tour, and visit hotels and restaurants; then don a virtual bikini, and click on activities to enjoy on Kauai—surfing is on the top of the list. ✓**INTERNET**→*url* http://hoohana.aloha.net/~hspub/kvp/

Maui On-Line Home Page Click on the hula skirt icon for a list of entertainment options on Maui, Hawaii's second-most-popular destination (Honolulu is the most popular). Look at classified ads here for vacation rentals or employment, see what you're missing on the Maui videotapes (they include Seascapes and Sunsets, The Humpback, and Secrets of the Hidden Valley Isle), and read about local lodging, dining, and shopping. ✓**INTERNET**→*url* http://maui.net/~mol/molhome.html

IDAHO

Idaho Microbreweries Hypertext information on beer-brewing tours. No large label names, like Budweiser or Miller, are on the list—instead you'll see local beverages such as T.W. Fisher's Cream Ale and Sun Valley Blonde in the making. ✓**INTERNET**→*url* http://www.csn.net/~scotto/id.html

The Unofficial Idaho The unofficial page does have the official information: learn that Idaho is the Gem State, Boise is the capital, the state bird is... well, you get the idea. And the page has the lowdown on state parks and natural resources, Idaho's other (than Boise) cities, local media, weather, and other resources. ✓**INTERNET**→*url* http://www.cs.uidaho.edu/~beers/Idaho/

Yellowstone National Park The world's first national park is partially situated within Idaho. You can see the park's beauty in breathtaking .GIFs of Norris Basin, Yellowstone Falls, the Mammoth Hot Springs, Old Faithful, and other feats of nature. This virtual tour is surpassed only by an actual visit. ✓**INTERNET**→*url* http://www.forestry.umt.edu/yellowstone/

Cybertaxi Home Page In addition to advertising Don Nineteen's taxi service in Boise, the page offers a cybertaxi ride through the city, with pictures of its streets, shops, and government buildings. Links connect to other Idaho Websites, including the Official Idaho Page. ✓**INTERNET**→*url* http://www.cyberhighway.net/~taxi/

ILLINOIS

For Chicago sites, see page 260.

Champaign-Urbana Conven-

Fodor's Choice...

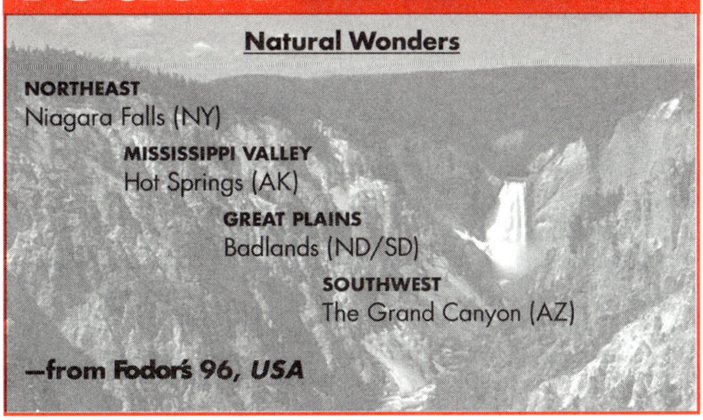

(cont'd pg. 263) →

Chicago

Many people in Chicago believe six impossible things before breakfast every morning.

Two of which are that the Cubs will win the World Series and that politicians never lie. You'll have to visit the Windy City to learn what the other four are, and a visit to **This is Chicago!** and eWorld's **Traveler's Edge—Chicago** will help you plan your trip. Before you go, discover the rhythms of Chicago at **Chicago Soundweb,** and get some Polish potato pancakes to go along with the brew at the **Chicago Ethnic Dining Guide**.

Downtown Chicago—downloaded from CompuServe's Archives Forum

On the Net

Across the board

alt.sports.baseball.chicago-cubs/alt.sports.basketball.nba.chicago-bulls/alt.sports.football.pro.chicago-bears (ng) The best way to befriend a Chicagoan is to be able to talk sports. Check the postings here so you'll know what you're talking about; but for heaven's sake don't root for the White Sox while in Comiskey Park! ✓ **USENET**...→alt.sports.baseball.chicago-cubs...→alt.sports.basketball.nba.chicago-bulls...→alt.sports.football.pro.chicago-bears

Chicago! At this Website Chicago is referred to not as the Windy City, but as the City of the Big Shoulders. The city needs to have big shoulders to support the amount of info listed at this page. You'll find a large JPEG (295K) of the city skyline, a listing of numerous bars and clubs on Rush Street, info about the local gay / lesbian scene, a schedule for the local comedy scene, and links to schedules for the Cubs, White Sox, Bears, and Bulls. If those resources don't tell you what you need to know, check the links to other collections of Chicago links. ✓ **INTERNET**→*url* http://www.tezcat.com/web/chicago.html

Chicago City Guide Prodigy members select the best and worst of Chicago here; see how their findings compare to your own experiences. ✓ **PRODIGY**→*jump* travel→City Guides→Chicago

Fodor's Worldview—Chicago Fodor's guides you around the Second City. Take a look at sightseeing suggestions (you've got to tour the city in one of the red double-decker tour buses), tips on where you might stay to be close to the great array of restaurants, and recommendations on what to see in Grant Park's museums, theaters, and aquariums. ✓ **AMERICA ONLINE**→*keyword* worldview→USA→Chicago

This is Chicago! If you want to attend a performance at the Goodman Theatre in Grant Park or visit The Art Institute of Chicago, and you're curious how close they are to your Michigan Avenue hotel, this is your source. All the Windy City's sights, such as the Sears Tower, Shedd Aquarium, Lincoln Park, and the Historical Society—plus restaurants, nightclubs, and services for foreign tourists—are listed here, some with direct links. ✓ **INTERNET**→*url* http://www.ncsa.uiuc.edu/SDG/IT94/Venue.html

Traveler's Edge—Chicago A quick-reference guide to the Windy City, especially useful for business travelers—find out where to rent a laptop, cellular phone, or conference room. The site also describes the city's attractions in a nutshell, and includes an essay on Chicago's wealth of outdoor sculpture by renowned artists (the works of Picasso, Henry Moore, and Botero can be found throughout the city). The sightseeing pages briefly list other city highlights to help you plan your day's tour. ✓ **EWORLD**→*go* travelers→City Files→U.S. Cities→Chicago

Nightlife

Chicago Jazz The hippest places to hear jazz and the blues in Chicago are listed here. You might like Dick's Last Resort, which features top-name acts but doesn't charge a cover. Or maybe the blues / rock-and-roll crossover artists at the Bulls Club uptown are more your style. Read the reviews at this page and decide for yourself, then use the addresses and phone numbers listed here to get to the club of your choice. ✓ **INTERNET**→*url* http://www.tez cat.com/~jmiles/

Chicago Soundweb Your quick-reference guide to the hottest dance clubs around the city. Includes contact information to find out about live acts and special performances. ✓ **INTERNET**→*url* http://www.soundweb.com/Dirs/dance.html

Oak Park

The Oak Park Tourist Just to the west of Chicago, Oak Park is a community noted for its diverse population, beautiful homes, and lovely lawns. It also has one of the largest concentrations of Frank Lloyd Wright architecture in the nation. You can tour the area from the Oak Park Visitor's Center (contact information is here) or online. You can also take a virtual tour of Wright's Prairie-style homes online, or a rollerblader tour offline. Get there via the CTA Blue Line or on the Net. ✓ **INTERNET**→*url* http://www.math.uic.edu/oakpark/

Restaurants & cafés

Chicago Ethnic Dining Guide A phone number and address for Chicago restaurants serving every imaginable kind of cuisine (from Afghan to Vietnamese), including a vegetarian restaurant for stranded travelers at O'Hare Airport. ✓ **INTERNET**→*url* gopher://gopher.uchicago.edu/00/chi/food-ch

The Sears Tower—downloaded from CompuServe's QPics Forum

Urbus Orbis Chicago-area residents can now surf the Internet, participate in online chat discussion groups, play games, and get some work done, all with computers hooked up at the Urbus Orbis, located in the heart of Chicago's Near North area. In addition to getting online, patrons can enjoy light meals or entrees, as well as musical and theatrical performances. ✓ **INTERNET**→*url* urborb@well.com ✍ *Email with general correspondence*

Transportation

Chicago Rapid Transit In Chicago, you can take the subway to and from both airports, hop aboard the Evanston Express to tour the northeastern suburb that houses Northwestern University, and travel around the Loop that gives the downtown area its name, or hop on and off at three stops within one long station. ✓ **INTERNET**→*url* http://metro.jussieu.fr:10001/bin/statmap/english/usa/chicago

Fodor's Choice...

Special Moments

- Feeding time at the coral reef of the John G. Shedd Aquarium
- The skylit sculpture court at The Art Institute of Chicago
- The winter orchid show at the Chicago Botanic Garden

—from Fodor's 95, *Chicago*

tion & Visitors Bureau This page has great tourist info concerning hotels and restaurants in the area, complete with addresses, phone numbers, and the types of credit cards accepted at each place. Also, something for those individuals seeking a little respite from traveling—a full list of local churches and temples, with service and prayer times noted. ✓**INTERNET**→*url* http://www.prairienet.org/community/convention/home.html

Krannert Art Museum, U of I, Urbana-Champaign An online sampling of the museum's holdings, including the works of Gabrielle Münter, Yves Tanguy, and Camille Pissarro. ✓**INTERNET**→*url* http://www.art.uiuc.edu/kam/Misc/kam.toc.html

Southern Illinois Tourism Council This major directory of visitor information is a buffet of links to other sites that highlight attractions, history, parks, weather, and accommodations in the region. Free maps and guides to adventures in southern Illinois are available from this page. ✓**INTERNET**→*url* http://www.intrnet.net/~sitc/index.html

State of Illinois A large collection of links to sites about the state that gave America the hog-butchering capital of the world, Abraham Lincoln, and the Art Institute of Chicago. Organized alphabetically by site name, the links access a number of pages directly related to tourism (the home pages of The Field Museum and Tourism Chicago) and pages not so directly tourism related (the Teachers' Retirement System page and the Bureau of Warehouses). ✓**INTERNET**→*url* http://www.state.il.us/

Western Illinois Browse this guide to resources for 13 counties in the western part of the state. The site lists hotels and restaurants (with their phone numbers) from Adams to Warren County, as well as local attractions (you can tour Wyatt Earp's birthplace in Warren County) and specialty stores (antiquing seems to be popular in western Illinois). ✓**INTERNET**→*url* http://www.outfitters.com/illinois/

INDIANA

Indiana Register A compact fact sheet focused on Indianapolis. Learn some fast facts about the city (it's the 12th-largest city in the U.S.); get phone numbers and addresses for restaurants, hotels, and cab services; and scan a list of available activities (shopping and attending sports events seem to be very popular). Everything you'll need to know while attending the Indy 500 is here. ✓**INTERNET**→*url* http://www.inetdirect.net/indianapolis-register/about-indy.html

Indianapolis Museum of Art Click past the famous Love sculpture by Robert Indiana that opens this site, and preview images of the museum's special exhibitions. Works in the permanent collection are also online here, including El Greco's St. Matthew. The museum's hours and admission prices are listed at the Website. ✓**INTERNET**→*url* http://otisnet.com/IMA/ima.htm

Indianapolis Symphony Orchestra Get a monthly calendar for this orchestra that performs in the heart of downtown Indy, right off Monument Circle. ✓**INTERNET**→*url* http://www.in.net/iso/

IOWA

Iowa Virtual Tourist Oddly, Hollywood has been a catalyst for the Iowa tourist industry over the past ten years. Not that the state

DETOURS

"The Kingdom of Calhoun (or Calhoun County, Illinois, USA) is a long peninsula between the Mississippi & Illinois Rivers. Much of the Kingdom of Calhoun is virtually an island between two great rivers. The northern border to the "mainland" is less than 17 miles wide. The only other connections are the lone bridge from Hardin to East Hardin, Illinois, and three ferry routes.

"Calhoun County was named after a great American spokesman. John Caldwell Calhoun [1782-1850] was a lawyer and statesman. He served as a US Representative and a US Senator from South Carolina,and Vice-President of the United States[1825-1832] under US Presidents John Quincy Adams and Andrew Jackson. Calhoun is recognized as the "Father of Nullification" [States Rights], a political idea that any state could nullify any federal law that the state felt was unconstitutional."

—from **Western Illinois**

didn't have lots to offer before—beautiful farmland and nice folks, but due to the recent movies that have capitalized on the image of the hometown, Iowa has become a not-too-uncommon vacation locale. (If Hollywood makes a movie, they will come.) ✓**INTERNET**→*url* http://www.netins.net/ivt/

Cedar Rapids, Iowa Not just another sleepy little town, Cedar Rapids is a major center for commerce and cultural life in Iowa. This Web page displays a number of links to businesses and attractions around Cedar Rapids. For example, you can connect to the Cedar Rapids Symphony's home page to download sound clips of the *Flight of the Bumblebee* or browse the art work at Gallery Lainzberg, one of the local galleries. For community information this site is like a town meeting. ✓**INTERNET**→*url* http://www.biz.uiowa.edu/iapages/cedarrap

Des Moines Net This is the Internet representative for the capital city. The page supplies useful information concerning logistics and the usual tourist resources like hotels and dining directories, along with coverage of Des Moines' biggest claim to fame. First there was a bridge, then a book, then a movie—now there's an ice cream flavor named after Francesca and her lament. When visiting Des Moines, don't miss what all the crying was about and see Robert James Waller's inspirations in real life. ✓**INTERNET**→*url* http://www.dsmnet.com/

KANSAS

Kansas Sights A page dedicated to ridding travelers of the idea that Kansas is just a state to drive through on the way to Colorado or Missouri. According to this site, there's plenty to do and see in Dorothy and Toto's home state—a visit to the Robinson Observatory for some stargazing in very clear skies, or an afternoon of bird watching at the Prairie Falcon Range might just suit your fancy. Besides listing Kansas attractions, the Website also introduces you to some of the natives, including representatives of the Kaw Nation and good 'ol Bob Dole. ✓**INTERNET**→*url* http://falcon.cc.ukans.edu/~nsween/europa.html

Dodge City Throw on your hip belt and kick the dust off your boots before you go to Dodge City, because its citizens take the Wild West very seriously. If Doc Holliday and Wyatt Earp were your heroes as a kid, in Dodge City you can see their likenesses in wax, and then buy every souvenir with a renegade motif for the loved ones back home. Get information on the attractions of the city at this site, where there's even a Gun Toters Anonymous Hotline number listed for those with itchy trigger fingers. ✓**INTERNET**→*url* http://www.neosoft.com/citylink/dodge/

A Kansas prairie scene—http://euphony.com/euphony/articles/35/Interior/Interior-RG.html

Calendar of Kansas City Area Music A guide to rock-and-roll bands playing in Kansas City. The site's author must be a fan of grungy music; the site tends to favor bands like Elastica, Green Day, and Urge Overkill. ✓**INTERNET**→*url* http://www.sky.net/~eml/kcmusic.html

Kansas City "I'm going to Kansas City. Kansas City, here I come...They've got some pretty little women there, and I'm gonna get me one." Kansas City has more to offer than its female population, such as a variety of restaurants and art boutiques. Investigate this Website for more select tourist info. ✓**INTERNET**→*url* http://www.sky.net/~mgh/

Kansas City MenuNet Addresses and telephone numbers of every restaurant in town. Unfortunately, there are no reviews, and the restaurants are listed alphabetically—making it difficult to locate restaurants in a particular part of town. ✓**INTERNET**→*url* http://www.fileshop.com/personal/jmcclure/menunet/menunet.html

Topeka Zoo The natives are restless in Topeka, and nobody seems to mind. Really, the monkeys have their own keys to the park, golden eagles flourish in captivity, and the gorillas are so close even Diane Fossy would be jealous. Find out the other reasons why the Topeka Zoo calls itself "the world's most famous" at this home page. ✓ **INTERNET**→*url* http://lawlib.wuacc.edu/topeka/zoo/zoo.html

KENTUCKY

Kentucky Atlas & Gazetteer Maps of the Commonwealth, its cities, and the topography are complemented by historical data and interesting statistics (Did you know that all of Kentucky was once a single county of Virginia?). Also find here scenic images and an audio clip (219K) of the state song, "My Old Kentucky Home, Good-Night!" ✓ **INTERNET**→*url* http://www.uky.edu/KentuckyAtlas/kentucky.html

Kentucky Resource Listings Native Americans lived here, Daniel Boone explored here, and now you can also commune with nature in the state parks and national forests of Kentucky. With several mountain ranges and dozens of rivers, the state offers a variety of choices to the outdoor enthusiast. Directions, facility descriptions, and a link to the Adventure Traveler's Bookstore will assist with planning your visit. ✓ **INTERNET**→*url* http://www.gorp.com/gorp/location/ky/ky.htm#attraction

Lexington There is plenty to do in Louisville's cross-state rival; hypertext listings of things to see and do, hotel and restaurant recommendations, and other Kentucky links can be found here. ✓ **INTERNET**→*url* http://www.neosoft.com/citylink/lexing/

Louisville Visitor Center Your source for comprehensive listings of places to stay and things to do in Louisville (pronounced loo-uh-vul in Suthun'). Click on the city skyline image for listings of the best restaurants by cuisine; visit the J.B. Speed Museum for the fine collection of Dutch and American art; and, if the Kentucky Derby is over, see the city via a romantic horse-tram tour. Mostly hypertext listings, but very thorough. ✓ **INTERNET**→*url* http://www.iglou.com/lou/lou_main.html

Louisville Zoological Gardens "Unofficial" HomePage No photos of the animals are here, but you are told their names and ages (Neal the warthog sounds interesting). The zoo's schedule and educational programs are provided at the page. ✓ **INTERNET**→*url* http://www.iglou.com/members/falco.html

The Kentucky Derby Drawing thousands to Churchill Downs in Louisville every May, this two-minute event generates much excitement, pride, and income for Kentucky. It has been going strong for 120 years—not even world wars managed to interrupt the tradition. You can place a bet on your favorite horse at the Website, but if you want to see it run in person, stop here for information about acquiring tickets to next year's race. ✓ **INTERNET**→*url* http://www.inslab.uky.edu/~stevem/horses/KyDerbyInfo/kyderby.html

LOUISIANA

For New Orleans sites, see page 266.

Louisiana Home Page Lost for hours at least, or even days—that's what you'll be after entering this Louisiana net megalopolis. Interesting links galore are here, and the collection is updated frequently, so don't forget to check in at What's New. Follow your heart's desire to the Cajun Cooking pages, a B&B list, and sites dedicated to sport fishing in the Gulf or jazz on Bourbon Street. ✓ **INTERNET**→*url* http://www.accesscom.net/la/la1.htm

Re-enacting the Civil War in Kentucky—http://www.state.ky.us/tour/bluegrass.htm

Louisiana Office of Tourism Welcome to the home of kudzu, gators, red beans and rice, and rum drinks. A load of tourist info is online here, broken down by locale and activity. Tour the plantations along the River Road, land a big fish, or kick back in Cajun country. After perusing the illustrated introduction to each area, check out the dining, lodging, and activity information for nearly every town in the state. But that's not all—there are links to a good history of Louisiana, the state B&B association, and many other travel resources. ✓ **INTERNET**→*url* http://www.state.la.us/crt/tourism.htm

Louisiana Profile The best feature of this site is a list of Louisiana dos and don'ts—maintain composure when confronted by the strip clubs along Bourbon Street, and definitely visit the Creole Nature Trail. The list of attractions is comprehensive, pointing out the charms of plantation tours and cities like New Iberia, home to the Jungle Gardens and McIlhenny tabasco sauce. You'll have to look elsewhere for lodging and restaurant info, however. ✓E-WORLD→*go* Travelers→Destinations→U.S. profiles

---

Louisiana State Parks This site will help those interested in doing something other than consuming jambalaya or drinking Hurricanes while in Louisiana. Each park profile tells of the glories of nature to be found there, as well as where to pitch your tent. ✓INTERNET→*url* http://www.state.la.us/crt/spintro.htm

---

The Cajun and Creole Pages Cajun and Creole are much more than types of cuisine. Learn exactly what they are from actual members of each culture. ("Cajun" most often refers to someone of French descent, while "Creole" is associated with the mixture of races and cultures around the Delta.) Read more about Cajun and Creole history, culture, and music, and even connect with other cyberCreoles and cyberCajuns. ✓INTERNET→*url* http://http.tamu.edu:8000/~skb8721/

The Greater Baton Rouge Home Page "Welcome to the capital of Louisiana!" proclaims this page, reminding everyone that New Orleans isn't the only game in the state. Learn more about Baton Rouge with the site's history lesson, and lodging and dining suggestions. ✓INTERNET→*url* http://www.tyrell.net/~aevinc/aev2gbr.html

---

The New Orleans and Cajun Country Newsletter Every month or so the tireless editors of this newsletter gather information on the wide variety of things happening in Louisiana. There's the annual Swamp Festival, the St. Martinville Pepper Festival, and the 50th Annual Yambille (all things sweet potato). Get complete details on these events, and read columns on local humor, culinary attractions, and Louisiana folklore. ✓INTERNET→*url* http://www.noconnect.com/forms/cajunews.htm

MAINE

Maine Brew Page What a great idea! A Ski & Brew Festival! Why haven't more people thought of getting folks tipsy and sending them careening down a mountain at 75 mph? Really, read about the Ski & Brew Festival and Maine's home-grown suds at this site. Anyone for a Thunder Hole Ale? ✓INTERNET→*url* http://w3.maine.com:80/brew/

Maine Profile There's good advice here to help you find activities off the beaten track—such as taking the 1914 steamer Kate for a ride on Moosehead Lake. Tips for tenderfeet are also included—"Don't honk or otherwise annoy a moose." Words to live by. ✓EWORLD→*go* travelers→destinations→ U.S. profiles→Maine

---

Maine: Region by Region Visit Maine region by region here—it's not just lobsters, moose, and trailer parks, you know. Use the page's accommodation and attraction information to arrange a trip—knowing that you've got a bungalow reserved at Gray Ghost Camp will be a comfort after a long day of hiking or canoeing. Several tour services have promotional pages here, too. ✓INTERNET→*url* http://www.maineguide.com/region/region.html

---

Maine Sportsmen's Guide Besides a nice picture of a big, hunter-enticing moose, the Web page offers details on various hunting seasons and on how to get a fishing license from out of state. For the less bloodthirsty, there is information on camping, hiking, and canoeing, including contact information for several guide services and sporting-goods outlets. ✓INTERNET→*url* http://www.maine

The New England countryside—from http://www.cit.state.vt.us/vtlife/fall95/dedcrek.htm

(cont'd pg. 269) →

New Orleans

Hey, where y'at? If you're really lucky, the answer will be in New Orleans—the promised land for those who love food, music, history, and a really, really good time. **New Orleans Information**, the **Big Easy**, and **Virtually New Orleans** are all terrific places to start exploring. **The French Quarter** takes you down the raucous blocks of Bourbon Street and into the quiet courtyards once frequented by Creole aristocracy. Don your rhinestone bikini and head for **Mardi Gras CityLink** for the complete schedule for this year's upcoming bash (hangover cures not included). Or head downtown to Tipitina's and the **New Orleans & Louisiana Music Pages** for music to sear your soul. Picking a goal to aspire to is to be admired. How about **Eating Your Way Around New Orleans**?

Mardi Gras—downloaded from CompuServe's Travel Forum

On the Net

Across the board

Big Easy Another excellent source of New Orleans info—tourists should turn here for B&B suggestions, restaurant reviews, and an admirably complete schedule of local events encompassing everything from a 19th-century cooking demonstrations at the historic Hermann-Grima house to a golf expo to a Diana Ross gig. ✓**INTERNET**→*url* http://www.big-easy.com/

New Orleans Connection Of greatest interest to travelers here is the Tour section that outlines bus excursions, plantation romps, and swamp tours. Just push the help button to make reservations for any of the tours. A few hotels also use this site for online booking. Local information includes a dictionary of New Orleans lingo and the winning lottery number. What would any trip, virtual or otherwise be without souvenirs? You can get a taste of the Big Easy by ordering Zapp's potato chips, hurricane glasses from Pat O'Brien's Bar, or chicory coffee from Cafe Du Monde online. ✓**INTERNET**→*url* http://www.noconnect.com/

New Orleans Information Look here for online booking and deals with many of the larger hotels. The site's guide profiles attractions as diverse as riverboat gambling and the Urseline Convent Museum. You can also get information on the New Orleans Jazz Festival where Ray Charles and Snooks Eaglin grace the stage. Check for each year's schedule and booking info here. There's a food primer that defines andouille and beignet, but you really have to experience them to understand their true meaning. Filling out an email request form returns more information. ✓**INTERNET**→*url* http://www.neworleans.com/

Virtually New Orleans Get the up-to-the-minute low down on New Orleans here—online hurricane updates, weekly photo features, and news. Travelers will especially appreciate the transit information, which provides maps of streetcar and bus lines as well as bike and car rental info. In addition to guides to the primary motivations of New Orleans tourism—eating, sightseeing, and music—Virtually New Orleans has good suggestions for the fourth joy of the Big Easy—shopping. ✓**INTERNET**→*url* http://yatcom.com/neworl/vno.html

Attractions

New Orleans Cemetery Images In the Delta, coffins buried underground have an unpleasant tendency to rise back up and float round town. Take a tour of the famous gothic above-ground tombs of New Orleans Cemetery. ✓**INTERNET**→*url* http://www.webcorp.com/images/nocemtnt.htm

Culture

House of Blues Join Jake and Elwood for a few beers and a mind-bending version of "Soul Man" at this new venue. Club listings and directions are provided. ✓**INTERNET**→*url* http://www.underground.net/HOB/

New Orleans & Louisiana Music Pages They're all here—from Johhny Adams to Buckwheat Zydeco and all the Marsalises and Nevilles in between. The Website offers biographies of the local talent and links to pages dedicated to the many genres that can call New Orleans home. Each artist profile contains reviews, photos, a discography of and often a sound clip or two from current releases of "New Orleans" artists. Be sure to stop in at this site before you hit Bourbon Street so you'll know which new talent or old pro to catch. ✓**INTERNET**→*url* http://www.geopages.com/SunsetStrip/1202/nomusic.htm

French Quarter

The French Quarter The French Quarter welcomes visitors with the sounds of a block-long walk in Jackson Square—a horse-drawn buggy, jazz, and street dancers. Once you're properly in the mood, head to the meat of this travel planning site—suggestions on everything from how to choose a French Quarter hotel to where to hear the best jazz and eat the most crawfish. Special sections detail free activities throughout the city and address resources provided in New Orleans for the disabled. An events calendar notes the "scheduled" events (as opposed to the

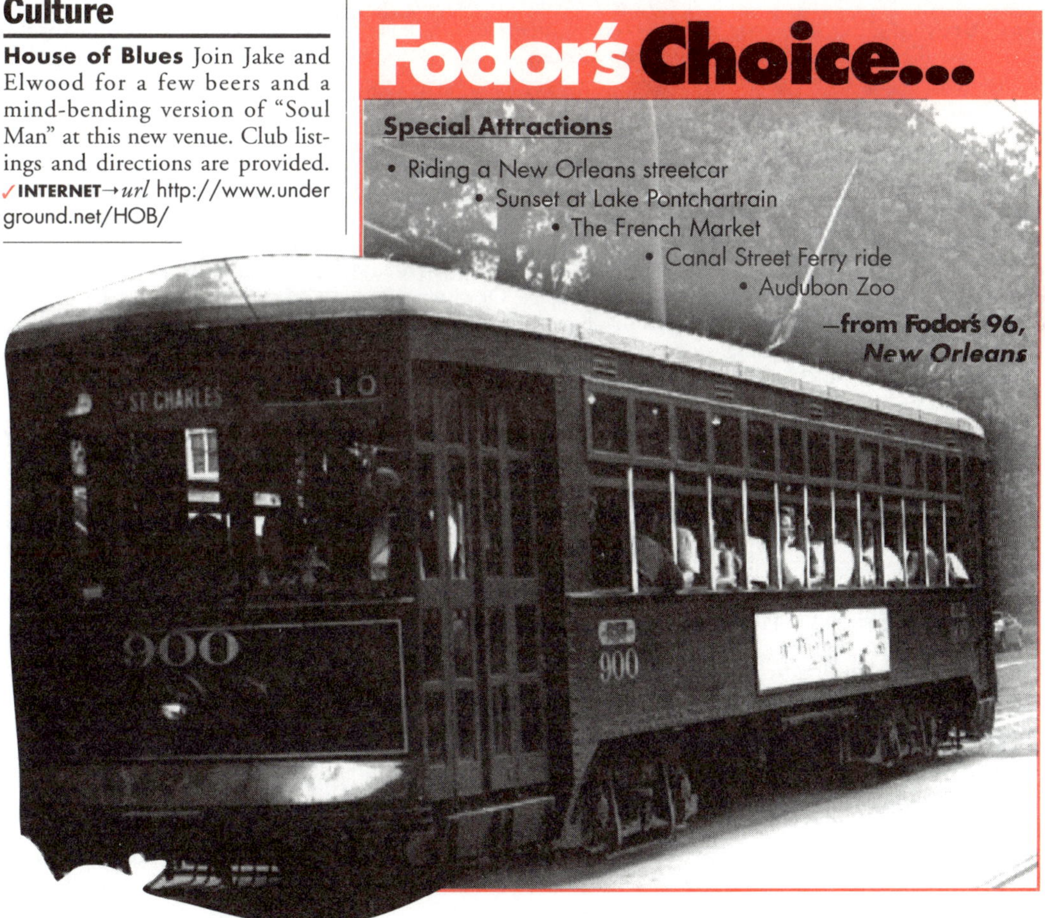

spontaneous happenings common there), and every museum from the Voodoo to the Confederate is profiled. Then take that walk through the Vieux Carré courtesy of a illustrated hypertour. Wander through this famous neighborhood—hear the strains of jazz along Bourbon Street, smell the beignets and chicory at Cafe Du Monde, open the door into the gentile past at Hove Parfumier on Royal. If you've just returned from New Orleans, you can even add your memories to the collection here. ✓**INTERNET**→*url* http://www.frenchquarter.com/

Mardi Gras

Mardi Gras CityLink Don your finest, loose that gloom and head for the 140th Mardi Gras celebration. This "official" site offers schedules of the "twelve days of merriment and madness" as well as much needed assistance (in the form of an 800 number and all online booking link) in getting a room during the festivities. Sound files offer up a bit of the spirit of Mardi Gras, and a dictionary puts you in the know about bouef gras. Have your own Mardi Gras at home, or just get your souvenirs in advance—this site also sells everything from King Cake and t-shirts to candy doubloons and beads—a virtual Bourbon Street. ✓**INTERNET**→*url* http://www.neosoft.com/citylink/mardigr/default.html

The Carnival FAQ You'll appreciate the Website for its handy list of dos and don'ts. Do "feel free to imbibe and enjoy your favorite beverages of all kinds." Don't "carry more than $20.00 at a time—pickpocketing is a major industry during Mardi Gras." After reading the site's good advice, stop by and check out the Mardi Gras calendar, history, and travel planner. ✓**INTERNET**→*url* http://www.webcom.com/~gumbo/carnival-faq.html

Restaurants

Eating Your Way Around New Orleans This text file, written by a dedicated gourmand for rec.travel, contains the astonishing information that fully one-half of all the restaurants listed in the WPA (Works Progress Administration) Guide to New Orleans written in 1938 are still around. Good food never gets old. So get the skinny on the best pecan pie, bread pudding, and crawfish etouffé here. ✓**INTERNET**→*url* http://www.digimark.net:80/rec-travel/north_america/usa/louisiana/new_orleans

Mike Perry's New Orleans Area Restaurants Mike breaks down eating into categories. For those misguided souls who want a burger or, heaven forbid, health food, in the gastronomic paradise of New Orleans, he's provided some suggestions. Or choose by location—spending the evening out in Metaire?—he's got a restaurant for you. Each entry describes the menu, service, and even dress requirements. Phone numbers and hours make reserving a quiet table for two a breeze. ✓**INTERNET**→*url* http://www.wisdom.com/la/rg/rmenu.htm

New Orleans Restaurants This text guide from rec.travel.north-america details the opinions of a frequent New Orleans visitor. Places outside the Quarter (that means cheaper) are well represented. Try Visko's for great crawfish. ✓**INTERNET**→*url* http://www.digimark.net:80/rec-travel/north_america/usa/louisiana/new_orleans.eats

DETOURS

A New Orleans Dictionary:

"DAWLIN' - A universal form of address. Women use it universally to both sexes, men use it toward women.

DEM, DESE, DOSE - Them, These, those.

DIS - This.

DRESSED - When ordering a po-boy, "dressed" indicates lettuce, tomatoes, pickles and MYNEZ, on it. (See NUTTINONIT)

EARL -
1. A vegetable product used for cooking, sautéing, making roux, etc.

2. A petroleum product used to lubricate the engine of your car.

3. Your Uncle Earl. (Most New Orleanians have an Uncle Earl; I do.)

ELLESHYEW - Louisiana State University, Baton Rouge. Occasionally preceded by the term, "Go ta hell ..."

ERSTERS - Oysters."

—from **The Gumbo Pages**

A Nantucket lighthouse—http://www .mcs.net/~jjudy/pictures.html

guide.com/sportsmen/sprtguid.html

Maine Tourism Web Definitely a good place to be planning a trip Down East, this site provides links to a wide variety of pages in Maine—from online purveyors of Christmas wreaths to tour operators that specialize in moose safaris. Unfortunately, much of the information lacks detail—but the numbers and addresses of virtually every Chamber of Commerce in the state are listed here, along with several travel agents. Or head to the online chat room and say Aayuh. (There's a freewheeling exchange on B&Bs, mountain biking, and L.L. Bean going on at all times.) ✓**INTERNET**→*url* http://www .state.me.us/decd/tour/

The Collier House Promotional site for a nineteenth-century summer "cottage" turned B&B. ✓**INTERNET**→*url* http://www.acadia .net/w95024/

TravelMaine This Website's essays explain how to book a room in Bar Harbor in August, where to get the best lobster roll in Damariscotta, and where to spot a bear in Aroostook County. ✓**INTERNET**→*url* http://www.source maine.com/TravelMaine/

Bar Harbor Navigate the crowded waters of Maine's top tourist town with the help of this little guide. A hypertext document lists several hotels and restaurants and briefly profiles Acadia National Park. ✓**INTERNET**→*url* http://bar harbor.com/

L.L. Bean L.L. Bean used to be a tiny sporting-goods store in the tiny town of Freeport. Now it's one of Maine's premier tourist attractions, a megalith presiding over an outlet-shopping mecca. Find out about the store and its wares here. You can even order online so you look like a Mainer before you cross the New Hampshire border! Spend some extra time exploring this site's excellent outdoor resources, which cover every park, state and national, in the country. ✓**INTERNET**→*url* http://www.llbean .com/

The Inn at Goose Rocks, Kennebunkport An advertisement for a hotel to stay in after spending an afternoon trying to spot George Bush. Find out more at this promotional page. ✓**INTERNET**→*url* http://www.cybertours .com/innatgrb/home.html

Greater Portland Area Resource Guide This little guide tells out-of-towners how to reach and enjoy this city that retains enough Maineisms to be charming, without forcing culture shock. As yet, the pickings here are slim but give them a chance to grow on you. ✓**INTERNET**→*url* http://www .maineguide.com/portland/port land.html

MARYLAND

Great Oak Manor Bed & Breakfast A promotional page for the B&B that lets you meet the Cantors, your hosts, visit some of the rooms, and find out about recreational facilities and attractions in the vicinity. ✓**INTERNET**→*url* http://www.covesoft.com /great_oak/

MARC Train Service Travel between the suburban areas around Baltimore, the Baltimore-Washington Airport, and Washington, D.C., on this efficient rail line. Schedules and maps are available here. ✓**INTERNET**→*url* http://www .libertynet.org/~dvarp/MARC/

Historic Annapolis Information on and illustrations of historic homes grace these pages, and descriptions of numerous hotels and B&Bs and fine restaurants are also available for those planning a visit. ✓**INTERNET**→*url* http://www.umcp .umd.edu/CampusMaps/Annapolis /Welcome.html

Virtual Annapolis Start at the City Dock downtown, click anywhere on the map, and take a virtual tour of this colonial capital. Visit the Naval Academy, St. John's College across the street (founded in 1696, it's the third-oldest college in the country, after Harvard, and William and Mary), the town green, and fine restaurants and antique shops. Some of the images are quite large; patience will be necessary. ✓**INTERNET**→*url* http://www.infi.net/capital/tour /index.html

Baltimore With Johns Hopkins University, a variety of museums, the bustling nightlife of the Inner Harbor, the grand, new Orioles stadium at Camden Yards, and a thriving local music scene, Baltimore now actually draws people from nearby Washington, D.C. At the Website, access listings of ho-

The Boston skyline at dusk—from http://msia02.msi.se/~apollo/apollo/Boston/

tels, where you receive detailed descriptions of the accommodations and facilities and can make your reservations online for individuals or groups. ✓**INTERNET**→*url* http://www.baltimore.com/

The Baltimore Beer Guide A college town by definition has dozens of bars, but Baltimore may rival Milwaukee as the beer capital of the U.S. Maps, photos, and reviews of beers and ales made right in Baltimore are available at the site. (The photos are especially helpful; they'll remind you of where you've been after the brewery tour samples have taken their toll.) ✓**INTERNET**→*url* http://www.charm.net/~stevens/BBG.html

MASSACHUSETTS

Massachusetts Diner Directory If you're a college student in Worcester (or even a tourist!), cheap eats might be important. This growing, statewide diner guide has mostly Worcester (pronounced "woo-ster") listings, but you'll find listings for Northampton, Westfield, Boston, and other cities as well. These are traditional diners, art deco, trailers with long-counters; choose a favorite from the images here. ✓**INTERNET**→*url* http://www.neb.com/noren/diner/MA_diner_dir.html

The Big Mamie Home Page "Big Mamie" is the Battleship Massachusetts, and a photograph of her at dock opens up this collection of links to maritime-theme tourist attractions. Link from here to schedules and admission prices for tours of the Marine Museum, home of the world's largest Titanic exhibit; the replica of the H.M.S. Bounty; and, of course, the Massachusetts. Also find links to the Old Colony Railroad Museum and to the Heritage State Park page. ✓**INTERNET**→*url* http://www.pictac.com/~jack/MAMIE/

Boston City Guide Grab a Fodor's guide here, and click your way to a Boston hotel that fits your budget; find details on getting there and getting around; and peruse a comprehensive listing of restaurants, festivals, attractions, and night spots to visit. For a small price, you can order travel updates for the specific time you'll be in Beantown (but don't let a resident hear you call it that). ✓**AMERICA ONLINE**→*keyword* world view→usa→boston

Boston Online A comprehensive Website guiding you to most of the resources a visitor or resident will likely need. If you want to locate a place to stay, find out what to do for fun, get maps, learn about gay/lesbian clubs and organizations, or visit the Boston Museum of Fine Arts, you can find guides for all of those things and more at this page. ✓**INTERNET**→*url* http://ftp.std.com/NE/boston.html

Museum of Science, Boston Located on the Charles River Dam between Boston and Cambridge, this museum can be toured in three ways online: a clickable map; a guided tour that lets you control the pace (stopping where you need to); or, if you're using Netscape, an automated tour that takes just under ten minutes. See elements of the permanent collection and also of visiting exhibits, such as "Square Wheels: Driving Science Home, and Hunters of the Sky." ✓**INTERNET**→*url* http://www.mos.org/

New England Aquarium The aquarium's hours, location, and admission prices can be found here, but not a single fish is pictured. You'll just have to visit in person to see our finned friends, but the Whale Watch and Science at Sea schedules will ensure that you don't miss a minute of the action. ✓**INTERNET**→*url* http://ftp.std.com/homepages/std/otherent.html#aqua

Subway Navigator-Boston Boston's subway system is the oldest in the United States, built in 1897. Use this site to find your way around town from the first station, Park Street. ✓INTERNET→*url* http://metro.jussieu.fr:10001/bin/select/english/usa/boston

Virtual Freedom Trail Discover America's early history on the Freedom Trail. Some of the sites along the trail are illustrated here, including the State House, the Old North Church, and Paul Revere's House. The site's map will help you avoid getting lost (the red lines on the sidewalks are another safegaurd against losing your way). Links connect to the Black Heritage Trail in Boston and to the Museum of African-American History. ✓INTERNET→*url* http://ftp.std.com/homepages/std/free dom.trail.html

City of Cambridge Situated across the Charles River from Boston, and home to Harvard and MIT, Cambridge is quite a city in its own right. If you're planning on exploring Cambridge, you may want to visit this site for museum listings (both on and off the college campuses), a history lesson on the city, and an events calendar for the goings-on around Harvard Square. Excellent city maps detail the locations of hotels, colleges, mass transit stops, and other points of interest. ✓INTERNET→*url* http://www.ci.cambridge.ma.us/

Bed & Breakfast Cape Cod A reservation service aiding travelers desiring to B&B on the Cape. ✓INTERNET→*url* http://www.shore.net/olm/bnbcc.html

Cape Cod Travel and Tourism If you want a head start planning your vacation on the Cape, check this site for hotel listings, travel guides, local town info (should you poop out prior to Provincetown), and tips on the best places for lobster dinners. Maps and photographs are here for reference. ✓INTERNET→*url* http://www.dmc.oa.net:8001/

Martha's Vineyard Home Page Sail over to Martha's Vineyard any time of the year (easy to do online) to appreciate the beautiful beaches, quaint towns, and charming B&Bs of the area. Find out what it looks like, how to plan a vacation on the island, and how to get there. ✓INTERNET→*url* http://challenge.tiac.net/users/prowten/index.html

Nantucket This site's photographs of and historical information about Nantucket may make you want to visit, so you'll be happy to find a listing of private homes that can be rented directly from the owners. Also here is a directory of inns, and lists of literature (travel-related and of general interest) about Nantucket—but don't expect any limericks. ✓INTERNET→*url* http://oneweb.com/infoctrs/NIIC.html

Destination Plymouth Visit this site in late November for a lesson on the first Thanksgiving. Or plan a trip to the town with the site's vacation planner, which offers info on local hotels and museums, and maps showing how to get to Plymouth Rock. ✓INTERNET→*url* http://media3.com/plymouth/

Welcome to Salem, Massachusetts Salem hasn't had a moment's peace since the infamous witch trial in 1692. When you visit, in person or online, you won't be surprised to see witch icons everywhere—on street signs, schoolhouses, even menus. Check out the Haunted Happenings section; you'll visit the Witch Museum, the Witch's Dungeon Museum, and other witchy sites. If

DETOURS

"Thanksgiving and the Pilgrims seem to go together, just like Christmas and Santa Claus—but the truth is, the Pilgrims never held an autumnal Thanksgiving feast. Before you cancel the turkey, take a look at the origin of that particular myth. In some ways, the truth is even more intriguing.

"The Pilgrims did have a feast in 1621, after their first harvest, and it is this feast which people often refer to as "The First Thanksgiving". This feast was never repeated, though, so it can't be called the beginning of a tradition, nor was it termed by the colonists or "Pilgrims" a Thanksgiving Feast. In fact, to these devoutly religious people, a day of thanksgiving was a day of prayer and fasting, and would have been held any time that they felt an extra day of thanks was called for...it's possible, even probable that turkey found its way to the table."

—from **Destination Plymouth**

witches aren't your cup of tea, hop off your broomstick and visit the Peabody Essex Museum to preview its fine art collection. You can pick up dining, lodging, and entertainment listings for Salem. ✓INTERNET→*url* http://www.star.net/salem/

Berkshire County Thinking about a visit to the Berkshires in Western Massachusetts conjures up images of summer stock theater groups, Tanglewood (the summer home of the Boston Symphony), cross-country skiing, and quaint inns near the forest. Tourist and event information may be found here for year-round happenings. ✓INTERNET→*url* http://www.ultranet.com/~isite/berkshire.html

MICHIGAN

Keewenaw Traveler The Keewenaw Peninsula has historic towns and National Parks for sightseeing. Visit Isle Royale for a glimpse of Michigan's only wilderness park—and be sure to read the advice about the moose and black bear. Read here about finding agates on nearby beaches, and about historic buildings, such as the Douglass House (once an elegant hotel) in downtown Houghton, and several old lighthouses. Photos illustrate a nostalgic beauty. Complete tourist information is here, should you wish to visit in person. ✓INTERNET→*url* http://www.portup.com./traveler/home.html

mi.misc (ng) Under discussion here are local events, such as the Ann Arbor Film Co-op schedule, neighborhoods, the Michigan Lotto, and current events in the state, for example, the Michigan Telecommunications Act. Most postings in this newsgroup are under the thread called For Men Only!, which focuses on the (heterosexual) pickup scene—the best pickup lines, how women harass men in bars, and 900 telephone lines. That's Michigan! ✓USENET→mi.misc

A Cape Cod harbor—from http://www.capecod.net/web_pages/photopage3.html

Michigan: Great Lakes State Visit towns all around the state with the collection of city home pages located at this Website. A trip to the Holland page rewards you with a lesson on that city's Dutch heritage, its Calvinist traditions, and its tulip festival, which is the largest celebration of the flower held outside the Netherlands. Or visit Mackinack (pronounced mak-i-naw) Island in the upper peninsula, a great resort town. Bloomfield Hills is not just the home of Aretha Franklin; it's also the location of Cranbrook Academy, an art/architecture school designed by Eero Saarinen, featuring sculpture by Charles Eames. There's Saugatuck, a popular gay resort in the north; Ann Arbor; Detroit... Plan your Michigan vacation here. ✓INTERNET→*url* http://kalamazoo.inetmi.com/mihmpg.htm

Northern Michigan Connection Think golf (Traverse City), think art (Interlochen Arts Festival), or think skiing (Cadillac and Crystal Mountain). Here you can see photographs and read descriptions of these and other attractions in the area. ✓INTERNET→*url* http://www.iquest.com/michweb/

Living In Ann Arbor Ann Arbor is one of the great progressive college towns (it's home to the University of Michigan); people often decide to stay on in Ann Arbor after graduation. The university ensures that there are plenty of activities, as well as art, culture, and many visiting performers drawn in by the sophisticated audience. Find out all there is to see and do, where to bunk down, and what's happening at U.M. here; this page is for students, townies, and tourists alike. ✓INTERNET→*url* http://www.gisd.com/SGIpublications.html

Virtual Ann Arbor The JPEGs here allow you to tour the city and the University of Michigan campus, visit restaurants and bookshops, and meet students and residents. ✓INTERNET→*url* http://www.sils.umich.edu/AnnArbor/

Detroit City Link Discover Detroit City with the help of this guide featuring events listings, descriptions of local attractions (lots of them free), and hotel suggestions. ✓**INTERNET**→*url* http://www.neosoft.com/citylink/detroit/

Detroit Institute of Arts There's more to the Motor City than cars and Motown, as the DIA artfully demonstrates here. Almost every period of Western art is represented at this small but growing site. Click on any of the images to reveal the artist, period, and medium of any painting in the exhibit. Information on museum-sponsored events is also available. ✓**INTERNET**→*url* http://205.199.95.66/~dia/home.html

---

Detroit Restaurant Recommendations The best of Detroit dining, from people in the know. Send in your recommendations, or find a place here to satisfy your cravings. ✓**INTERNET**→*url* http://www.digimark.net:80/rec-travel/north_america/usa/michigan/detroit.eats

---

Detroit Zoo Actually in suburban Royal Oak, the Detroit Zoo is featured at this site, with hypertext information about the animals, hours of operation, and the Zoo's educational programs. ✓**INTERNET**→*url* http://www.ring.com/zoo/overview.htm

---

Travelers Edge–Detroit A popular T-shirt boasts, "I'm so bad, I vacation in Detroit." Detroit has certainly seen better days, but a visit there is not necessarily a joke. With a lively theater district (on Woodward Avenue, anchored by the Fox), great ethnic restaurants, Motown, the Renaissance Center, Greenfield Village, the Henry Ford Museum, and Detroit's status as international gateway for Northwest Airlines, the Motor City is starting to get the boost it needs. Find here listings of sightseeing attractions in and around the city—the People Mover monorail is a great way to see downtown. ✓**EWORLD**→*go* travelers→city files→Detroit

MINNESOTA

Bend of the River Bend of the River is a collection of links to resources for South Central Minnesota. Connect with an events calendar, Minnesota Public Radio, and the Southern MN Online Art Gallery, for starters, and, if you really want to do your homework on Minneapolis, check out the extensive directories of universities, school boards, and libraries in the area. ✓**INTERNET**→*url* http://www.mankato.mn.us/

Fun Things to Do In Minnesota What could be more fun than the Mall of America? Imagine an indoor, climate-controlled warehouse of fun and capitalism. After racing down the log-flume, you can pick up one of the new tunics from The Limited, see the daily fireworks display, and meet your friends at Fat Tuesday's for Parrot Punch. Besides all this fun and profit, the page highlights other Minnesotan attractions, like the Science Museum, the Como Conservatory, and the Children's Museum. ✓**INTERNET**→*url* http://www.primenet.com/~kennyb/mn-fun.htm

---

Minnesota Star Tribune So what do you care about the news in Minnesota? Don't scoff too soon—this Website for the *Tribune* online provides links to tourism pages like the Greater Minneapolis Convention and Visitors Association and the Minneapolis / St. Paul Map & Travel Center. ✓**INTERNET**→*url* http://www.startribune.com/

Minneapolis Home Page The Twin Cities are online at this page, which is full of helpful tourist listings. There's info on the big three—shopping, lodging, and dining—as well as a personal welcome from Sharon Sayles Belton, the current mayor. Mayor Belton even suggests some exciting things to do during your stay in Minneapolis, such as taking a walk through the city's sculpture garden, renting a canoe on Lake Cal-

---

Fodor's Choice...

Viewpoints

NORTHEAST
World Trade Center Tower (New York)

MIDWEST
Chicago from a boat on the river (IL)

SOUTHWEST
Dead Horse Point (Moab, UT)

PACIFIC
Calving tidewater glaciers from the deck of a cruise ship (AK)

—from Fodor's 96, *USA*

houn, or attending a play in one of the city's acclaimed theaters. (Prince fans may be disappointed to learn that the artist hasn't opened his home to the public yet.) An events calendar rounds out this extensive site. ✓INTERNET→*url* http://www.designstein.com/gmcva/

Minneapolis Institute of the Arts The museum, housing more than 85,000 objects spanning 4,000 years of world history, spotlights some of its more famous pieces at this Website. View pieces by Georges Braque, Walker Evans, and Wassily Kandinsky. ✓INTERNET→*url* http://www.mtn.org/MIA/

Minneapolis Restaurant Recommendations What's the best Ethiopian restaurant near the university? And where's the best cup of espresso in town, for a follow-up to that Ethiopian food? The answers to these questions and many others can be sought and found here. ✓INTERNET→*url* http://www.digimark.net:80/rec-travel/north_america/usa/minnesota/Eats

City of St. Paul This is a great Website for visitors to St. Paul—it is chock-full of information on breweries, accommodations, and restaurants. When looking for fun stuff to do in St. Paul, the name "Ordway" seems to come up often. Support St. Paul's cultural legacy by checking out the Ordway Music Theatre, which features big shows like Damn Yankees! and Showboat, or the Ordway Japanese Garden. ✓INTERNET→*url* http://www.stpaul.gov/

MISSISSIPPI

Mississippi Gulf Coast Over 80 links to listings and home pages for the best the Gulf Coast has to offer—lodging, food, shopping, casinos, recreation, and more. Park your RV at the Mazalela Travel Park, then take the kids to Slippery Sam's water park; or take the Happy Hooker out to snag some swordfish, then head over to the Copa for a game of blackjack. Take your winnings and treat your significant other to a dinner at Germaines Restaurant, and end the day by kicking back for some blues at the Bait House. ✓INTERNET→*url* http://www.gulfcoast.com/

The Center for the Study of Southern Culture What is Southern culture? Well, according to the Center, it's everything from The Last Picture Show to yard art, from a lecture on Brazil and the Confederate Community to the 1995 International Conference on Elvis Presley. This site offers links to lecture and festival schedules, periodical and newsletter archives, and order forms for books and videos produced by the Center. ✓INTERNET→*url* http://imp.cssc.olemiss.edu/

Biloxi You'll never get the blues in Biloxi, there's so much to do—Magic Golf! Mad Potters! Wet Willies! The world's largest rocking chair! This page offers links to basic info on lodgings, food, and thrill-a-minute activities. ✓INTERNET→*url* http://www.neosoft.com/citylink/biloxi/default.html

Jackson Zoological Park Have you ever seen a loxodonta africana? How about a pan troglodyte or an acinonyx jumbatus? Actually, you probably have, because those are just the zoological terms for elephant, chimpanzee, and cheetah, respectively. They may be zoo staples, but they are also endangered species, and you can find them, along with hundreds of other animals, at the Jackson Zoological Park. This site is home to about two dozen animal images, along with general info on the zoo's location and hours. ✓INTERNET→*url* http://www.mindspring.com/~zoonet/jackson/

Biedenharn Candy Company and Museum of Coca-Cola Memorabilia In 1894, the first bottle of Coca-Cola went down the assembly line in Vicksburg, Mississippi. See where it all began at this site, which gives images and abstracts of the major exhibits, and general museum information. You know cocaine was an actual ingredient in the syrup back then. And Coke grew to become the most popular soft drink in the world. Go figure. ✓INTERNET→*url* http://www.kcom.com/travel/company/0060/main.htm

Vicksburg This page provides links to text, images, and a handful of home pages showcasing lodging, dining, recreation, and cultural attractions for the city known as "the small town with the big city attitude." The page succeeds at portraying Vicksburg as both charming and cosmopolitan. Its Southern grandeur is very accessible—the section on historical homes looks suspiciously similar to the B&B section. ✓INTERNET→*url* http://www.southernnet.com/vicksburg/cvb/index.htm

MISSOURI

Destination Guide—Missouri Statewide information is provided here, a great deal of which is about major cities: St. Louis, Kansas City, and Branson. The dos and don'ts entries make note of Missouri's many caves, such as Crystal Cave in Springfield and Boone Cave in Rocheport; part of the Ozark mountain range is also located in the state, providing great outdoor opportunities. ✓AMERICA

ONLINE→*keyword* Traveler's Corner→U.S.Profiles→States L-Q→Missouri ✓**EWORLD**→*go* Travelers→U.S./Canada Profiles→States L-Q→Missouri

Lake of the Ozarks The location isn't as bucolic as its name suggests—this tourist area features a strip with arcades of novelty stores, shops, bars, and restaurants. There is also a lake there, by the way; Purists can rent a boat for the day. If you prefer getting water in a different setting, the Wet N' Wild amusement park is nearby. This Website details all there is to do in the area and provides contact information. Curiously, there doesn't seem to be any lodging information; however, the local tourist board number is included for recommendations. ✓**INTERNET**→*url* http://www.odd.net:80/cgi-win/loto.exe

State of Missouri Home Page Link from here to city home pages and to descriptions of recreational, educational, and cultural offerings throughout Missouri. The site also provides a detailed state map. ✓**INTERNET**→*url* http://www.ecodev.state.mo.us/

The St. Louis Homepage Grab your camera and head for St. Louis! The first thing you'll do is ride the little pods to the top of the Gateway Arch—600 feet over the Mighty Mississippi! When you're back down on earth, you'll discover the long list of other tourist attractions available for you here. Visit Forest Park, where the St. Louis Science Center, Art Museum, and Zoo are located; you might also enjoy St. Louis's Missouri Botanical Gardens, riverboat casinos, wineries, the nightlife at Laclede's Landing or in the Central West End, and the Fox Theater. See the Cardinals play at Busch Stadium, in the middle of downtown. Be sure to visit the exhibits at the Museum of Westward Expansion. If you've brought the tykes with you, check the section here about activities that might appeal to them, such as the Forest Maze and the Video Game Museum. You can explore most of these attractions online. Getting from the airport to and around St. Louis is easy because of the new Metrolink trams, which you can read about in the Website's extensive section on transportation. ✓**INTERNET**→*url* http://www.st-louis.mo.us/

A misty Midwestern morn—from http://sapphire.surgery.wisc.edu/barns.html

Hannibal, Missouri Nicknamed "America's Hometown" (wait—isn't that Cleveland's slogan, too?), and the boyhood home of Mark Twain, Hannibal makes a great excursion from St. Louis, only two hours south of the metropolis. Information is provided about Tom Sawyer Festival Days, historic downtown tours, and visits by queens: not Queen Elizabeth II of England or Queen Beatrix of Holland, but the Delta Queen steamboat cruisers that ply the Mississippi. ✓**INTERNET**→*url* http://www.webcom.com/~twainweb/

Kansas City BBQ Connection For the best in French cuisine, fly to Paris. For the ultimate in barbecue, Kansas City is the destination you want. Restaurant reviews, information about barbecue products, and the story of KC's barbecue heritage can be accessed here. ✓**INTERNET**→*url* http://www.rbjb.com/rbjb/bbq.htm

Kansas City Visitor's Bureau No fair! This site describes all there is to do in Kansas City and how beautiful the city is, but cruelly provides no images. You'll have to imagine the 200+ fountains (more than in any city except Rome); the wide, green boulevards (more than in Paris); the revitalized art deco downtown, with the Garment District; and the splendid museums. Visit the "Brooklyn Bridge" at the Bartle Convention Center, or take in a show at one of the more than 100 theaters in the city—in a theater district known as Avenue of the Arts. Country Club Plaza, the nation's oldest shopping center, provides plenty of shopping opportunities, there is a big jazz scene that rivals New Orleans's, and the city is known for its barbecue cuisine. Besides the lengthy descriptions of the town, you'll find schedules of many annual festivals, and information on the grand, new Kemper Museum of Contemporary Art & Design. As the song says, "Everything's up-to-date in Kansas City." ✓**INTERNET**→*url* http://www.sky.net/~kcom/cv/cvhome.html

MONTANA

Maps of Montana Montana is one of the largest states in the nation. If you decide to tour it by car, a good map is essential. View several types of map, including county, city, railroad, highway, Indian reservation, forest, and National Park maps. ✓**INTERNET**→*url* http://nris.msl.mt.gov/gis/mtmaps.html

---

Missoulian Online Missoula, the progressive city where the University of Montana is located, is also home to the state's principal newspaper, *The Missoulian*. The full text of the paper is here, with listings of local events, a movie guide, photos of the town, and even a local weather report. ✓**INTERNET**→*url* http://www.missoulian.com/

Treasure State Outfittin' Contact information and package descriptions for this company, which offers to guide you to the fishin' and huntin' in Montana. ✓**INTERNET** ...→*email* montana@libby.org ✍ *Email with general correspondence* ...→*url* http://www.libby.org/TSO/montana.html

NEBRASKA

Nebraska Game and Parks Commission Johnny Carson's from Nebraska, although he doesn't count as Nebraska wildlife, or at least not in the same way as the sandhills goose or the bull moose. Goose, meet moose. Moose, meet goose. Ed, stop laughing. If you're interested in nocturnal quadrupeds rather than late-night network bipeds, come to this page, which contains a network of links that will give travelers keys to unlock the great Nebraskan outdoors. With resources on fishing, boating, hunting, and camping, this is a comprehensive page, and one that even allows for Netsurfers to post compliments and criticisms. ✓**INTERNET**→*url* http://ngp.ngpc.state.ne.us/

Nebraska Travel & Tourism Governor Ben Nelson welcomes you to this site, saying, "You're all invited to Nebraska, a state that's been called a 77,000-square-mile museum without walls." Ben goes on to counter Willa Cather's description of the state as "land as bare as a piece of sheet iron" by celebrating the buttes, canyons, rolling hills, fertile crop lands, and endless ranchlands. Ben's message ends, but the Website goes on, offering guides to motels, hotels, ranches, B&Bs, mountains, and more. There's an archive of Nebraska-related information that includes a wealth of detail on state symbols, history, government, economy, education, and climate. This is a proud state with a great heritage, breathtaking beauty, and the world's largest railroad classification complex. ✓**INTERNET**→*url* http://www.ded.state.ne.us/tourism.html

---

Nebraska WWW Resources A large list of Nebraska Websites, including many that won't appeal to travelers (higher education, telephone utilities) and a few that will (sites dedicated to specific towns and cities, from Beatrice to David City to Papillion to Omaha to Lincoln). ✓**INTERNET**→*url* http://www.ded.state.ne.us/neweb/neweb.html

---

Cook, Nebraska—The Best Small Town in America Although there are only 333 people in Cook, Nebraska, they're all incredibly friendly—except for one guy, and he never comes out of his house anyway, preferring instead to sit inside and whittle tiny figures of Isadora Duncan out of soap. If you visit the Best Small Town in America online, you may be enticed into visiting it off-line, especially during July's Windmill City Days, which celebrate the giant, four-armed devices that once pumped water from artesian wells beneath the town. ✓**INTERNET**→*url* http://www.infoanalytic.com/cook/index.html

---

Lincoln Online Billed as "your hyperlink to Nebraska's Capital City," this page includes information on government, education, arts and entertainment, food and lodging, news, weather, shopping, and tourism, and even links to a city map, so you won't get your South Street crossed with your Vine Street (they're parallel). ✓**INTERNET**→*url* http://www.inetnebr.com/

The Omaha Page Remember when Mutual of Omaha used to sponsor "Wild Kingdom", and Marlon Perkins talked about actuarial tables to lions, who usually responded by biting off his hand at the wrist? (Oddly, each week the hand had regenerated.) Well, Omaha is more than just a punchline in an insurance joke—it's also one of the largest cities in Nebraska. Get information on local arts and entertainment, recreation and parks, and attractions, including Fontenelle Forest, the Ak-Sar-Ben

A view of Montana's Glacier National Park—http://www.ganson.com/jganson/glacier.html

Aquarium, the Black Americana Historical Museum & Rainbow Gallery, Boys' Town, and the Gerald Ford Birthplace Museum. ✓**INTERNET**→*url* http://www.novia.net/~cmeyers/omaha.html

Papillion Papillion means "butterfly" in French, more or less, but in Nebraska Pappilion means the Crossroads of Sarpy County, the fastest-growing city in Nebraska. And on the Web, Papillion means an essay and a link to the city's own telnet connection, which includes information on events and accommodations. ✓**INTERNET**…→*url* http://www.papillion.ne.us/ …→*url* telnet://bbs.papillion.ne.us/

NEVADA

Nevada State Fair Held at the Livestock Convention in Reno, the state fair is fun for fans of bovine creatures and cotton candy, but probably few others. However, to be fair, the Nevada State Fair boasts an unusual event that appeals to the multitudes—the annual Spam Cook-Off. From this Website, collect Spam cooking, eating, and wearing suggestions (yes, if it's good enough for your belly, it's good enough for your back). Sign up now online to see Spam cubed, sautéed, and bronzed at the Nevada State Fair. ✓**INTERNET**→*url* http://www.aztech-cs.com/nsf/y-home.html

Nevada Travel Parks Association Tired of hemorrhaging money while playing the one-armed bandit? Blasé about naked women? Disgusted by Tom Jones? Try exploring some of Nevada's other resources—like Death Valley, the Lehman Caves, and Hoover Dam. Access a directory of campgrounds here, which you are organized by special interest, like laundry, pet acceptance, and handicap accessibility. ✓**INTERNET**→*url* http://www.campgrounds.com/ctpa/

Prostitution in Nevada Read tips from a former prostitute, download legal statutes, and find a straightforward tour of truck stops, rest stops, and hotels catering to the oldest profession. For example, when in Welles, remember "Donna's and the Hacienda, across the railway tracks on 10th street on the north side of town, right beside each other. They're somewhat upscale compared to the houses in Elko and Winnemuca, but since Wells is pretty much a truck stop, what you tend to get there is your standard truck-stop-brothel-working-girl." ✓**INTERNET**→*url* http://www.paranoia.com/faq/prostitution/Nevada.html

Carson City, Nevada The capital city averages 266 days of sunshine a year and is owned by former talk-show host Johnny Carson. This Website showcases various facts about Carson City and includes a look at frontiersman Kit Carson. ✓**INTERNET**→*url* http://www.sierra.net/NV4Sale/carson.html

Las Vegas Leisure and Travel Guide Another major collection of links to hotels and casinos in Las Vegas, all of which promise to provide you with the most stupendous vacation of your life. However, if high-rolling isn't your only objective, this Website offers information on boat tours of the Colorado River and day trips to Laughlin and Stateline. Billions of telephone numbers to sightseeing companies are here, too. ✓**INTERNET**→*url* http://www.pcap.com/

Las Vegas-Reno-Lake Tahoe-Laughlin Room Reservations Bureau This site displays one very important number that lets you make reservations at all the palaces of pleasure and pain in Nevada. The MGM Grand, Bally's, Stardust, Ceasar's, and the Sahara, just to name a familiar few, accept reservations from this room-and-travel coordinator. ✓**INTERNET**→*url* http://www.lv.com/Paradice/index.html

Vegas.com Is that IRS return check burning a hole in your pocket? Does lap dancing suddenly seem like viable entertainment? The only way to get a handle on your hedonism may be to go out to Las Vegas and try your luck. For the most comprehensive information on visiting Vegas, don't miss this Web page, offering links to everything from pet hospitals (for puppy emergencies) to all-night jacuzzi chapels. Vegas.com is a major collection of links to glitzy hotels, casinos, and clubs, allowing you to make reservations online before you touch down in the desert oasis. ✓**INTERNET**→*url* http://www.vegas.com

NEW HAMPSHIRE

New Hampshire's Lodging Resources Links to contact information for B&Bs, hotels, and camping grounds in the Monadnock, Lakes, White Mountain, and Seacoast regions. ✓**INTERNET**→*url* http://vintagedb.com/guides/lodging.htm

---

NH Restaurant Menu Index A Van Gogh landscape welcomes you to this little Website, which gives city-by-city listings for hundreds of New Hampshire's restaurants. So far, the site offers only contact information and addresses, but it promises online menus soon. ✓**INTERNET**→*url* http://www.ultranet.com/~iw/rest/rest.htm

---

Seacoast Online Browser A collection of links to a history of the coast and to basic information about dining, entertainment, lodging, and shopping at the shore. You'll also find sun-drenched images of and details about the many beaches and parks in the region. ✓**INTERNET**→*url* http://www.sob.com/

The Story of Lucknow Use the tour schedules at the Website to visit this grand New Hampshire estate, which sits atop Ossipee Mountain, surrounded by 4,000 acres of forest land. ✓**INTERNET**→*url* http://www.kaiwan.com/~lucknow/lucknow2.html

---

The Unofficial New Hampshire Home Page "Tax free shopping" flashes on every page of this travel guide, but there is more to New Hampshire than good bargains. Go antique-hunting or cross-country skiing in Monadnock, do some hiking in the White Mountain region, take in some theater, visit the historic sites in the Dartmouth-Lake Sunapee area, spend the day on the links in Merrimack Valley, or go whale-watching in the Seacoast region. This site links to basic regional info on attractions, sights, and accommodations all over the state. ✓**INTERNET**→*url* http://VintageDB.com/guides/

What, Where, When New Hampshire The Granite State entreats you to visit at this page. Available in both German and English, this site will show you the best of New Hampshire, with links to home pages and texts on local attractions and services. Most of the collections deal with the multitude of natural resources and activities, from horseback riding to mountain climbing, but events calendars, lodging reviews, and virtual tours of historic districts and covered bridges are also available. ✓**INTERNET**→*url* http://newww.com/

NEW JERSEY

100% Smokefree Dining in New Jersey A dining guide with a twist—no smoking is allowed in any of the restaurants on this list. Sponsored by New Jersey GASP (Group Against Smoking Pollution), the guide provides listings by city and county of hundreds of restaurants (and names of fast-food chains) where you can avoid cigarette smoke while dining. ✓**INTERNET**→*url* http://www.ezweb.com/gasp/

A New Jersey chapel—http://cnj.digex.net/~jimh/photo/

New Jersey Transit Getting around the Garden State without a car is easy if you've got the right information. Schedules and maps for commuter trains, subways, PATH trains, airport buses, ferries, and trolleys throughout New Jersey are featured, as are directions to neighboring New York City and Philadelphia. ✓**INTERNET**→*url* http://www.eclipse.net/~scheurle/njt/

World of Interest—of New Jersey Interest Access lottery results, local church schedules, and weather reports at this site. You can even visit the NJ Devils, Nets, and other sports teams (maybe the Yankees, by next year) with the links provided here. At Atlantic City's section of the site, play the slots or blackjack online, or get hotel and casino addresses to gamble in the flesh. You can even meet this year's Miss America contestants and read up on past winners and Pageant history. ✓INTERNET→*url* http://woi.com/woi/indexnj.html

New Jersey State Aquarium A gopher menu for information on admission and events at the magnificent aquarium. ✓INTERNET→*url* gopher://crab.rutgers.edu:70/11/camden/Camden_Community_Events_and_Information/New_Jersey_State_Aquarium

Cape May County, NJ New Jersey has its own cape, with wide sandy beaches, hundreds of Victorian inns, quaint towns, and working farms. From here you can visit Cold Spring Village, a living museum dedicated to life in New Jersey before 1900; Wildwood, known for its amusement piers; and Cape May itself, where gingerbread Victorian homes, gas street lamps, and colorful stained glass abound. The city, a National Historic Landmark, hosts an annual Tulip Festival, Victorian Week, and Christmas in Cape May—all attended by thousands each year. If you're still not sold, the images here should inspire you to pack. ✓INTERNET→*url* http://www.beachcomber.com/Capemay/tourism.html

HobokenX A hypertext guide to the dozens of bars, restaurants and clubs in this Mile Square City on the Hudson. See independent films at Projected Images, or hear new and popular bands at Maxwell's. The works of local artists are featured online; you'll also find listings of resident theater companies. ✓INTERNET→*url* http://www.stevens-tech.edu/hobokenx/

Liberty Science Center—Jersey City Downtown Jersey City's sparkling new Science Center is now online! Featuring the self-proclaimed "yuckiest site on the Internet," the current exhibit is Cockroach World! Yuck! It's not a New York City apartment, but an exhibit on the Environment floor. The center also features the world's second largest Omnimax Theater, an 3-D theater, a cafe with panoramic views of nearby Statue of Liberty and Ellis Island and New York. ✓INTERNET→*url* http://www.lsc.org

Montclair Home Page Montclair is a beautiful township in suburban northern New Jersey, with a diverse population and a beautiful Tudor-style downtown district. Several films have been made in or about the town, which has earned the nickname, "Hollywood of the East." At the Website find links to the Montclair Art Museum online and Montclair State University. Also enjoy an events calendar, which highlights musical performances, and read about famous Montclair citizens, recreation opportunities, local B&Bs, and shopping. ✓INTERNET→*url* http://www.interactive.net/~upper/

Ocean City Listings of things to see and do in Ocean City, whether it's visiting the local museum, historical lighthouses, or the huge, newly restored beach and boardwalk with amusement pier. It's a popular summer resort, and the many Victorian B&Bs and hotels fill up quickly. ✓INTERNET→*url* http://www.Neosoft.com:80/cityink/oceancty/default.html

Princeton Online A community-based online service, which has links to its famous university, an events calendar (featuring the McCarter Theater's new season), historical information about locals such as Thomas Edison and Albert Einstein, listings of wineries in the area, and other Mercer and Middlesex County resources. ✓INTERNET→*url* http://www.princetonol.com/

Trenton The state capital historically has not been a tourist destination as much as the butt of jokes. Now, with its own airline (Eastwind), the State Museum and Planetarium, newly popular Trenton State College, and dozens of hip shops and antique galleries,

The Alpine boat basin in New Jersey—from http://cnj.digex.net/~jimh/photo/

the city is becoming increasingly appealing. Restaurants, cultural events, and area attractions, along with airline and train schedules, are found here. ✓**INTERNET**→*url* http://www.prodworks.com/trenton/

NEW MEXICO

Bienvenidos a Nuevo Mexico A terrific feature of this site is the mileage calculator that lets you compute your distance from wherever you are to the Land of Enchantment You can also learn about local culture, history, cuisine, and style here. (No, the dreaded Santa Fe style isn't "real" —real Santa Feans are nauseated by pastels.) Special sections are geared toward the needs of international, senior, family, and disabled travelers, to make sure everyone has the optimum good time. ✓**INTERNET**→*url* http://www.nets.com/newmextourism/

Images of New Mexico Phillip Greenspun's photo essay on the dwellings of New Mexico. Enjoy the glorious pictures of adobe homes, Carlsbad Caverns, and wide open spaces. ✓**INTERNET**→*url* http://www-swiss.ai.mit.edu/philg/new-mexico/album.html

---

New Mexico Head to the New Mexico home page for the big enchilada of tourism information. Learn where to stay, what to do, and most important, where to eat in the Land of Enchantment (there are also recipes!). Take a walk through Georgia O'Keeffe's red rock country, or view ancient Anasazi petroglyphs: the virtual trips alone are worth a visit to this site. ✓**INTERNET**→*url* http://www.viva.com/nm/nmhome.html

---

New Mexico Information This site provides exactly what it promises—information about New Mexico. Link from here to the University of New Mexico, the state government, and home pages for towns from Las Crucas to Pojaque. Pick and choose among sites dedicated to everything from the social whirl of Las Vegas (that's Las Vegas, New Mexico) to the New Mexico Museum of Natural History—they're all here. ✓**INTERNET**→*url* http://128.165.127.126/NewMexico.html

---

New Mexico Profile New Mexico offers more than cactus and cowboy boots. Find out about the state's big attractions—Carlsbad Caverns and Santa Fe—as well as the lesser-known treasures of Grand Quivera and the mountain road through Truchas. ✓**EWORLD**→*go* travelers→U.S.profiles→New Mexico

---

White Sands National Monument Nothing is quite as surprising as coming upon a field of white in the hot, dry desert. No, it's not a hallucination induced by too much heat or too much tequila—it's the crushed gypsum dunes of White Sands. The Website offers details about this National Monument and an email address to contact the rangers for additional info. ✓**INTERNET**→*url* http://speckle.ncsl.nist.gov/~lorax/gallery/trip/white_sands.html

---

Albuquerque Unfortunately, this commercial site is stingy in providing accommodation, dining, and shopping info as yet. But it does have a good section on things to do for free in this birthplace of great minds and great meals. Visit the Petroglyph National Monument and see the graffiti of ancient juvenile delinquents, or wander around the streets of Old Town, where the Pueblo Indians vend their wares and the scent of chili and piñon is

DETOURS

Laguna Pueblo

"Ka-waikah mean 'Lake People.' It is the largest Keresan speaking pueblo, with around eight thousand members and a heritage of Shoshone, Tanoan, Keresan and Zuni cultures. They prize thinking above all human attributes, consequently they value intellectual activity and education.

"Laguna Pueblo comprises six major villages scattered over many acres, with the political center at Old Laguna.

"Livestock grazing was a traditional occupation, but because one of the world's richest uranium fields is located on the reservation, many men became miners.

"In the nineteen-seventies, the traditional craft of pottery making was reestablished. Fine work in red, yellow and orange in geometric designs, similar to Acoma work, was created by a number of craftsmen."

—from **Pueblo Cultural Center**

in the air. ✓**INTERNET**→*url* http://www.neosoft.com/citylink/albuquer/default.html

New Mexico Museum of Natural History and Science Kids will love this museum, chock-full of dinosaurs dug up from the New Mexican desert and other delights. Visit the exhibits online, or get info on how to find the Museum in Albuquerque. ✓**INTERNET**→*url* http://www.aps.edu/htmlpages/nmmnh.html

Pueblo Cultural Center, Albuquerque In New Mexico, Native Americans (other than Navajo) do not reside on reservations; instead they still live in the self-governing towns they have inhabited for hundreds of years. Learn more about their unique culture with a virtual, or actual, visit to this Cultural Center. Each of the pueblos, like Taos, continuously occupied since 1200 A.D., or Acoma, resting alone atop a mesa without even a road until the 1960s, is described here. Pueblo feast days open to the public are listed, but be sure to contact the tribal council first at the number provided. ✓**INTERNET**→*url* http://hanksville.phast.umass.edu/defs/independent/PCC/PCC.html

Santa Fe Accommodations An indispensable resource for potential Santa Fe travelers that lists all kinds of local lodgings, from luxury megaliths (El Dorado) to B&Bs (Galisteo Inn). ✓**INTERNET**→*url* http://www.bolack.com/santafe.htm

Santa Fe Convention and Visitors Bureau Santa Fe has been one of the state's most popular destinations for years, so this site is well prepared for the tourist. Find out how to reach the Oldest House in America, where to find the Inn at the End of the Santa Fe Trail (La Posada), and how to get to the International Museum of Folk Art. Several hotel reservation services are listed here too. The events calendar will even tell you if Tucker Binkley is still playing lounge music at Vanessie. As the locals say, "See ya at the Pink" (the Pink Adobe, that is). ✓**INTERNET**→*url* http://www.nets.com/santafe.html

Santa Fe Online This site claims to offer all the trappings of Santa Fe without the hassles of airfare or parking. Wander through the art galleries that made Canyon Road famous, or shop for books and exemplars of Santa Fe style (like those damn pastel howling coyotes). Other Santa Fe staples—coffee joints and alternative medicine—are covered here, too. ✓**INTERNET**→*url* http://www.sfol.com/sfol.html

A Santa Fe street corner—http://www.cs.kuleuven.ac.be/~swa/route66/new-mexico/

La Plaza de Taos Telecommunity Walk the streets that Kit Carson and Mabel Dodge Luhan once roamed in this cybertour of Taos. Illustrated pages are devoted to the nearby Taos Pueblo, the oldest city in the U.S., and the famed ski area. A list of restaurants and hotels makes planning a trip to the real thing easy. So head right up the Rio Grande Road! ✓**INTERNET**→*url* http://laplaza.taos.nm.us/index.html

NEW YORK

For New York City sites, see page 282.

Destination Guide—New York Geostats, business resources, sightseeing suggestions, tourist listings, and hotel and nightlife recommendations for the entire state are found here. Also, don't forget to read the dos and don'ts: do travel New York State's 524 miles of canal—you can even rent a boat for a week; don't pronounce Houston Street in New York City like the Texas city—(it's pronounced howse-ton here). ✓**E-WORLD**→*go* travelers→Destination Guide→U.S./Canada Profiles→States L-Q→New York

Niagara Region Bed & Breakfast Information Lodging information, complete with online brochures, and registration at some establishments are avail-

(cont'd pg. 285) →

New York City

If the only thing that's stopping you from taking Times Square is figuring out how to get to New York City, turn to **Fodor's Worldview** and they'll help you plan a trip. Then the **New York Subway Navigator** and the **Paperless Guide to New York City** will make sure you don't end up on a Bronx-bound express when you want to visit Chelsea. Ignore all that nonsense about dangerous streets—New York is a lovely place to visit, as **Explore New York** is at great pains to show. There are **NYC Museums** filled with fine art, folk art, photography, history, and dinosaurs. Then there's the food—dim sum, pizza, bagels, and curry—in **Zagat's Guide** and **nyc.food**. Thus sustained, you're ready to hit the clubs with the **Village Voice Guide to NY at Night**—remember it's a city that never sleeps, so there's lots to do after all good Bostonians are tucked in.

The Manhattan skyline—downloaded from Compuserve's Corner Forum

On the Net

Across the board

Explore New York A tourist-oriented guide to the city (actually, just Manhattan) that explores most of the big attractions and also includes uptown sights such as Harlem, The Cloisters, and El Museo del Barrio. The site is all hypertext, so you'll have to use the directions here to see the attractions listed here. ✓**INTERNET**→*url* http://emall.com/ExploreNY/NY1.html

Fodor's Worldview—New York City Fodor's gives you its reviews of hotels—from budget to luxury—restaurants, nightlife spots, and all the other Big Apple tourist attractions, along with practical advice for getting around, staying safe, and finding bargains. ✓**AMERICA ONLINE**→*keyword* worldview→usa→new york

New York Forum Get the lowdown on travel scams, debate public works proposals, discuss current issues in the local news, ask questions about upcoming events, or find out if the subway fare is going to go up again during your visit (it won't affect your wallet too much, but it will affect your mood). No New York topic is too mundane or silly to be discussed at this site. ✓**COMPUSERVE**→*go* travel forums→New York→Newslink Forums→Messages *and* Libraries→visiting/living NY

Paperless Guide to New York City Visitors would do well to check out this online survival guide before taking the J train to Williamsburg. Plan your trip using the guide—it describes the city's neighborhoods, from the Theater District to Tribeca. A street navigator even lets Netters plug in a street address and get a cross-street. ✓**INTERNET**→*url* http://www.mediabridge.com/nyc/

Museums

Museum of the City of New York One of New York's great historical museums, but not one of the better known ones. Here you can view excerpts of current exhibits and enjoy thumbnails and JPEGs of pieces from the permanent collection, which includes a stunning collection of Tiffany lamps. ✓**INTERNET**→*url* http://www.netresource.com/mcny/home.html

NYC Museums You can visit the Metropolitan, the Guggenheim, the Cooper Hewitt, the Jewish Museum, the Brooklyn Museum, and even the Children's Museum online. Get information about educational programs, see highlights from the permanent collections, and view special exhibitions without pesky tourists blocking your view! ✓**INTERNET**→*url* http://astor.mediabridge.com/nyc/museums

Whitney Museum of American Art Selected works from seasonal exhibitions are displayed, along with paintings from the permanent collection, which focuses on twentieth-century American art (Andy Warhol, Jean-Michel Basquiat, and Edward Hopper are among the major artists represented). Like the museum, this site sustains heavy traffic. ✓**INTERNET**→*url* http://mosaic.echonyc.com/cgi-bin/whitney/welcwhit.pl

Nightlife

Village Voice Guide to NY at Night The quintessential guide to all there is to do at night in the City that Never Sleeps. The site is simple to use: Choose from self-explanatory sections like Eat, Drink, or Clubbing. Then select your nightspots by area. You'll get listings of the hippest places (gay / lesbian and hetero) to visit. You might want to take a cab to your destination—by the time you write down the address, the scene might be fading away. ✓**INTERNET**→*url* http://mosaic.echonyc.com/~voice/nighttit.htm

Restaurants & cafés

@Cafe Mosey over to the East Village for a drink and a bite to eat at this large yet intimate restaurant; while waiting for the appetizer, why not ask Glenn to help design your home page, read your email, or check out some sites on the Net. At @'s site, scan the restaurant's menu or visit the cool NYC links, including one to *LGNY* (a gay weekly) online. ✓**INTERNET** ...→*url* http://www.fly.net/ ...→*email* spider@fly.net ✍ *Email with general correspondence*

nyc.food (ng) Forget Zagat's! If you want to know the best place for roti, a good egg cream, or fresh pasta, you've got to talk to a native. New Yorkers put their two cents in with recommendations on local favorites and information on hip new places to go—which are no longer hip once everyone else finds out! If you're a bargain traveler, you'll appreciate the supermarket reviews here; everyone seems to agree that Fairway tops them all. ✓**USENET**→nyc.food

Take a walk on the Brooklyn Bridge—http://www.netresource.com/mcny/s6.jpg

Fodor's Choice...

Views to Remember

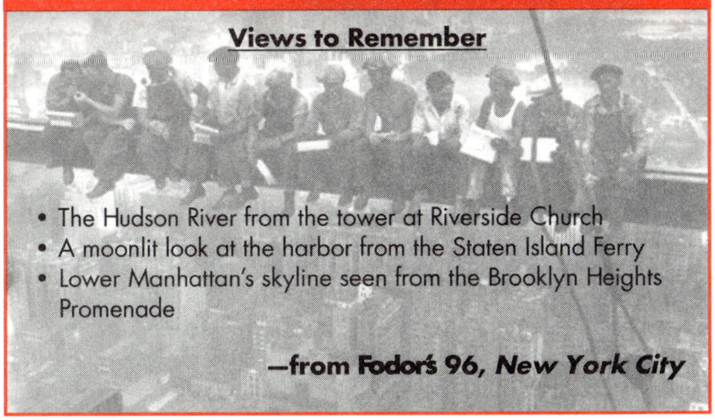

- The Hudson River from the tower at Riverside Church
- A moonlit look at the harbor from the Staten Island Ferry
- Lower Manhattan's skyline seen from the Brooklyn Heights Promenade

—from Fodor's 96, *New York City*

Zagat's Guide The well-regarded guide gives you the skinny on hundreds of New York restaurants of every type—it even cross references them by price, neighborhood, cuisine, and criteria, such as late night, casual, gay, fireplaces, and views. A good source to ensure that you don't inadvertently take your matronly Aunt Delores to Lucky Cheng's. ✓**COMPUSERVE**→*go* zagat→access restaurants→new york city

The outer limits

Coney Island Mermaid Parade The annual parade draws some very unlikely mermaids, as the photo archive here illustrates, but the event is still a big hit at the old amusement park. Register here to enter, get some costume ideas, and learn the Mermaid Song. ✓**INTERNET**→*url* http://dockmaster

The Chrysler Building at night—downloaded from Compuserve's Photoforum

.phantom.com/mermaid.html

Staten Island Info-Web For those who dare to step off that ferry, here is what awaits you. If you plan to stay, check the hotel listings; there is also a clickable map, so you can visit Tottenville—the southernmost point in New York State—Snug Harbor, the Richmondtown Restoration, and the Staten Island Zoo (and we don't mean the ferry). ✓**INTERNET**→*url* http://www.SI-Web.com/NYCinfo.html

The Bronx Home Page (ml) Let's have a great big Bronx cheer! The Website's most interesting feature is its photo archive, which profiles the history of the only mainland borough in New York. You'll also get the specifics on how to visit the Edgar Allan Poe Cottage, the famous zoo, and local theaters and Latin music clubs. ✓**INTERNET** ...→*email* majordomo @lists.best.com ✍ *Type in message body:* subscribe BRONX-L <your email address> ...→*url* http://www.videostore.com/aventura_travel/bronx/

The Long Island City Homepage Long Island City, Queens (pronounced "Queents" in New Yorkese) is a stone's throw from Manhattan. In addition to Eagle Electric's dreary factories and the towering Citicorp Building, you'll find there the borough's first historic district, an artist's community, and film studios in operation. Here, get an overview of the neighborhood, visit some local artists and see their works, and link to other community resources. ✓**INTERNET**→*url* http://www.licweb.com/

Transportation

New York Subway Finder This goes one step beyond the navigator site—select any address in Manhattan, and you're given subway directions in seconds. For the outer boroughs, sorry; you'll just have to rely on the extremely knowledgeable taxi drivers you've heard so much about. ✓**INTERNET**→*url* http://www.automatrix.com/~bak/nysf.html

New York-Subway Navigator Decipher the labyrinth of subway lines (you certainly can't understand the maps) and commuter rail systems that keep New York connected. Fortunately the graffiti, the crime, and the pleasant subway aromas don't come with this site. ✓**INTERNET**→*url* http://metro.jussieu.fr:10001/bin/select/english/usa/new-york

nyc.transit (ng) The subways are the hot topic because of the recent fare increase, the new tokens, and the introduction of the long overdue farecard. Here New Yorkers gripe about their neighborhood stations and the quality of service, and debate whether trains should be carpeted like the Washington D.C. Metro cars. ✓**USENET**→nyc.transit

DETOURS

"I just wanted to put in my two cents (actually an extra twenty-five cents) about the subway fare hike...I really don't mind paying the extra quarter for the transit hike. It won't kill me, but then again, I don't live and die by the subway.

"The thing is...I haven't seen it mentioned that the subway hikes are coming very close to the large-scale adoption of the new Metrocard system! I know it's been around for a long time, but it hasn't gotten to every station (at least not to my local station), and I assume that there will be a big celebration when it does!

"From what I have heard about Metrocard so far, it has been an absolute BUST! Apparently it is losing money fast! Now, the machines and cards didn't come free, and the transit authority was ready to face big repercussions if the idea didn't catch on very quickly!"

—from **nyc.transit**

able for inns on the U.S. and Canadian sides of the Falls. ✓INTERNET→*url* http://vaxxine.com/bb

Online Travel Guide for Upstate New York Where shall you go first—the Finger Lakes or the Thousand Islands? Is there skiing in the Catskills? Here, the rest of New York north of The Big Apple is separated into different regions, each providing you with listings of area attractions. You can get a B&B listing for the Adirondack Mountain area, visit the town of Tonawanda online, and find the best places for viewing the fabulous foliage. Virtually all the information here is hypertext; you'll have to actually make the trip to appreciate the visual aspects of it all. ✓INTERNET→*url* http://www.roundthebend.com/

Dune Resort Hotels An advertisement for this chain, with hotels located throughout the Hamptons on the South Fork of Long Island. ✓INTERNET→*url* http://www.webscope.com/hotels/dune/

The Hamptons Web Thanks to this page, anyone with Web access can visit the exclusive area known as The Hamptons. The listings here (hotels, beaches, cafés, wineries, shopping, nightlife, etc.) include many images of beautiful places and people. ✓INTERNET→*url* http://www.peconic.net/hamptonsweb/

Saratoga Performing Arts Center To celebrate its 30th season, the Center has assembled its Web page and posted monthly concerts featuring acts as diverse as Bonnie Raitt and the New York City Opera. ✓INTERNET→*url* http://www.albany.globalone.net/spac/

Saratoga Travel Guide If you're planning a trip to Saratoga Springs for the horse races this year, find your hotel and dining spots here, then head over to the Saratoga Performing Arts Center to see if you can catch a performance after the race. Or read the events calendar for area activities, drop in at Skidmore College, or connect to a page on nearby Lake George. ✓INTERNET→*url* http://www.infovantage.com/NY/saratoga/

NORTH CAROLINA

Carolina Oink Express A promotional page for the infamous King's Restaurant in Kinston that's been serving up its secret barbecue recipe for more than 60 years. From the Website you can order pounds of the pig stuff to be delivered to your own home, along with serving instructions and suggestions for complementary dishes. ✓INTERNET→*url* http://www.eastnc.coastalnet.com/business/food/kings/kings.htm

NCNetWorks A virtual tour guide to the buffet of North Carolina attractions, this site offers links to pages on the modern cash crops of the Tar Heel State—professional sports, film producing, and furniture. (Nicotiana tabacum is conspicuously overlooked.) You'll also want to cruise this site's virtual Interstate 95 when planning any road trip through central North Carolina, especially if Cracker Barrel isn't your idea of authentic cuisine. ✓INTERNET→*url* http://www2.interpath.net:80/ncnetworks/

North Carolina's Outer Banks Elongated shores and scrub forests, sour-gum baskets and saltwater taffy, sunsets and moonrises—these things coalesce amid sunshine and friendly people in the Outer Banks. Read short essays on lighthouses, and gather coastal lore from this site. One section of the site is devoted to the Lost Colony at Roanoke. ✓INTERNET→*url* http://www.outer-banks.com/default.htm

Pinehurst Area Golf The town's prestigious Pinehurst Resort recently sponsored the Tour Championship and the U.S. Senior Open. In 1996, Pine Needles Resort will host the U.S. Women's Open (see, even the South accepts women putters). The page offers helpful information on local golf

Fodor's Choice...

Museums

MID-ATLANTIC
The Phillips Collection (Washington, DC)

MIDWEST
The Art Institute of Chicago (IL)

SOUTHWEST
Kimball Art Museum (Fort Worth, TX)

GREAT PLAINS
Nelson-Atkins Museum of Art (Kansas City, MO)

—from Fodor's 96, *USA*

schools, courses, and golf vacations for the resident or the tourist. ✓**INTERNET**→*url* http://www.sandhills.org/golf/golf.htm

Asheville and Surrounding Area Flanked by the Blue Ridge Mountains and blanketed with rhododendrons, Asheville has been ranked among the top ten tourist cities in the U.S. for the past five years and has earned the nickname, "The Paris of the South." Close to skiing, hiking, and fishing areas, Asheville also has much to offer those more interested in open skies than in the majestic Biltmore Mansion. Gather information on local hotels and eateries, and consult a yearly calendar of events around Asheville. ✓**INTERNET**→*url* http://www.unca.edu/asheville/asheville.html

Charlotte Online Hive of the Hornets, den of the Panthers—Charlotte is home to many cultural species, and yet hasn't been the same since the World Wrestling Federation moved away. Charlotte is also the home of a burgeoning arts scene. The Mint Museum, the Afro-American Cultural Center, and Lupie's Cafe are a sociologist's trinity for studying Charlotteans in action (not to mention cool places to visit). This site posts a calendar of events, maps, and lodging information for the Queen City. ✓**INTERNET**→*url* http://www2.interpath.net:80/ncnetworks/clt-intr.html

NORTH DAKOTA

Hillsboro, ND In the dried bottom of an ancient lake surrounded by fertile farmland, is Hillsboro, population 2,000. What's special about Hillsboro? It's just about the nicest place you'll ever go—they've even got their own home page! Well, travel over, take a walk through snow here during the winter (or is it the summer?), and say hello to the folks in town. ✓**INTERNET**→*url* http://134.129.18.248/

Route 66 in Tulsa—http://www.cs.kuleuven.ac.be/~swa/route66/oklahoma/photo.html

Volden Farm Bed & Breakfast If you'd really like to get away from it all, come to the eastern prairie of North Dakota and the Volden Farm. On 300 acres of wide open space, enjoy the seclusion of this farmhouse. Each morning, a breakfast of Swedish pancakes, Norwegian cheeses, and other Scandinavian delights is served. Outdoor activities are plentiful, including berry picking, snowshoeing, cross-country skiing, and golf. Contact information is provided for reservations. ✓**INTERNET**→*url* http://www.virtualcities.com/~virtual/ons/nd/s/nd65s01.htm

OHIO

Ohio Travel Forum Travelers and residents discuss issues having to do with Ohio—the Lake Erie Islands, intrastate travel, RV camping, Ohio's cities and attractions, historic sites, and accommodations. If you've got a dining or shopping favorite, want information about hotels, or are visiting King's Island because the Brady Bunch did—post your message here. ✓**COMPUSERVE**→*go* ohio→Messages *and* Libraries

The Akron Art Museum Works from the permanent collection (Frank Stella's *Diepholz* and Chuck Close's *Linda*) are displayed online with high-quality images. The Museum's vital statistics are also here—where to find it, when it's open, and how much it costs to get in. ✓**INTERNET**→*url* http://www.winc.com/~aam/

Cincinnati The self-proclaimed "Queen City" was once called Porkopolis, because of the slaughterhouses that lined Cincinnati's streets. Take this quick virtual tour and see the magnificent skyline, Fountain Square, the Museum Center, King's Island Amusement Park, and other attractions. Also included more detailed information about tourist attractions, nightlife, and upcoming events. ✓**INTERNET**→*url* http://www.iac.net/~davissd/cincinnati.html

Cleveland The fire on the Cuyahoga River has been extinguished, and from the ashes a hot tourist destination is emerging. Billing itself as the premier destination on the North Coast (Lake Erie), Cleveland is increasingly less a place to drive through and more a place to stay. The city now sports the recently opened Rock-and-Roll Hall of Fame; Playhouse Square offers Broadway shows and excellent repertory companies. Let this site be your guide to entertainment hot spots (The Flats and the Warehouse District along the river), lodging, cultural offerings (don't miss the Cleveland Museum of Art), and fine dining options in the city along the Lake. ✓**INTERNET**→*url* http://www.cleveland.net/cleveland/

Cleveland Museum of Art Contact information, but no images from the collection of this museum that features a wide variety of art. ✓**INTERNET** ...→*url* http://www.cwru.edu/CWRU/buildings/cultural/art_museum.html ...→*url* http://www.gatech.edu/CARLOS/AAMDO/CLEVint.htm

---

Rock and Roll Hall of Fame This splashy new museum has a splashy Website to match. Cool icons lead you to the "500 Songs That Shaped Rock-and-Roll" (see if your favorites are here) and Web pages for individual artists. You'll be able to walk through the hall and preview the award-winning architecture of I. M. Pei. The site tells who's been spotted there recently incognito. As if that weren't enough, you'll also get a link to local hotel, transportation, restaurant, and entertainment listings to help you arrange a trip to Cleveland. ✓**INTERNET**→*url* http://www.rockhall.com/

Columbus Ohio's capital is celebrated for its German Village, its status as an insurance center, the newly restored Ohio Theater, the huge Ohio State University (60,000 students on one campus), and one of the nation's largest gay and lesbian populations (who'd have thought?). Columbus citizen Mark Gunderson offers information about hip bars and restaurants that you won't find in the average tourist guide. ✓**INTERNET**→*url* http://www.infinet.com/~markg/columbus.html

---

Culture in Toledo While vacationing in Toledo, you may want to watch a Toledo Mudhen's baseball game, visit the acclaimed museum, kick up your heels at the Polkathon, or attend the symphony. Perhaps you'll have time to do them all—get the facts here about these and other local attractions. You also get a peek at the sparkling new skyline rising over the river. ✓**INTERNET**→*url* http://www.toledolink.com/~matgerke/toledo/toledo.html

OKLAHOMA

Route 66 Old Route 66 has a longer stretch in Oklahoma (318 miles) than in any of the other seven states it crosses. No longer in use (and not appearing on any maps), it still manages to be popular enough to have songs, fan clubs, books, and magazines dedicated to it. You'll find here a photo gallery of places of interest, travel tales, and advice for those attempting to trace the route, with a section especially for Belgians (huh?). Keep an eye on the upcoming events section for news of the forthcoming Route 66 Museum in Oklahoma. ✓**INTERNET**→*url* http://www.cs.kuleuven.ac.be/~swa/route66/main.html

---

Virtual Oklahoma An entire state packed into one Website! You'll visit Oklahoma's cities and towns; look for hotels, restaurants, and nightclubs; browse the museums without battling the crowds; and get information on festivals, rodeos, and other interesting day trips. ✓**INTERNET**→*url* http://commercial/commerce/index.html

---

Oklahoma City This is one of the nation's geographically largest cities—it's almost twice the size of New York City. The large map here will be useful in planning your stay, and clicking on the names of the various districts take you on virtual tours of those areas. Visit historic Bricktown, with its antique stores, restaurants, comedy clubs, and other entertainment venues. Or tour East Central OC, where you'll find the State Capitol (with oil rigs on its grounds), the Kirkpatrick Center (a complex of seven different art and heritage museums), the Cowboy Hall of Fame, and the City Zoo. Besides the tours you'll find links to many local sports teams—sports are a major pastime here. ✓**INTERNET**→*url* http://www.keytech.com/okc/okchome.shtml

---

Oklahoma City Zoo One of the oldest zoos in the Southwest, the Oklahoma City Zoo now has over 2,500 animals in captivity. Click on the map to read about some of them—the cheetahs, dolphins, and sea lions are currently featured. Don't forget your camera! ✓**INTERNET**→*url* http://www.cpb.uokhsc.edu/okc/okczoo/zoomap.html

---

Tulsa Home Page Hypertext information (and a few audio clips) about points of interest in Tulsa—visit the zoo, see the huge Praying Hands sculpture on the ultramodern Oral Roberts University campus, or attend the city's many rodeos, state fairs, and festivals (such as Oktoberfest). ✓**INTERNET**→*url* http://www.wiltel.com/tulsa/tulsa.html

---

Tulsa Philharmonic A site that carries the Philharmonic's current schedule. ✓**INTERNET**→*url* http://www.webtek.com/tulsaphil/

OREGON

Oregon Coast Driving Guide A perfect guide for the serious road-tripper. Excellent graphics make this site the most user-friendly compass for exploring Oregon by car. The page outlines highways and secondary roads in the state and, with a simple click, provides a calendar, brief history, and list of the local attractions—the annual Teddy Bear Show or Cranberry Festival might be of interest. The site also highlights some of Oregon's cultural offerings in its online magazine, including the state's numerous folk art cafés. ✓**INTERNET**→*url* http://www.oregon-coast.com/

Oregon Reserve Owned and operated by Explorer Travel Service, Oregon Reserve acts as a middle party for booking a vacation in the Pacific Northwest. Though unable to finalize reservations online, their Web page provides descriptions and photos of several hand-picked hotels in a broad price range. Contact the company with the info listed here. ✓**INTERNET**→*url* http://www.opendoor.com/OregonReserve/OregonReserve.html

Metro Washington Park Zoo Station (Portland) Take a cybersafari to the Metro Zoo. Begin by choosing the Zooliner or a Steamer Train (cute titles for JPEG or .GIF options) to browse the zoo, and you're off. Stop by the Baby Animals page for a photo of the baby giraffe and the musk ox. If you're interested in actually going to the zoo, this Website will tell you how to get there. ✓**INTERNET**→*url* http://www.teleport.com/~sbower/wpz.html

Portland Art Museum The Portland Museum home page gives general information and outlines the museum's history. Sadly, there are no pretty pictures. ✓**INTERNET**→*url* http://www.pam.org/~pam/

PENNSYLVANIA

For Philadelphia sites, see page 289.

The Pennsylvania Dutch Country Information Center Dutch country means rolling green countryside, antique markets, horse-and-buggy rides, covered bridges, biking and hiking, and an inside glance at Amish culture. Whether you want to camp out with the family or spend a romantic weekend at a B&B, you'll find here everything you need to plan your trip to the land of apple butter—maps, information about the Amish (picture taking must be approached with delicacy), a list of 25 things to do for free in the area, and links to pages advertising lodging, shopping, dining, and tour services. ✓**INTERNET**→*url* http://padutch.welcome.com/

Travel.org-Pennsylvania An extensive index for those visiting Pennsylvania, offering links to reviews and listings for lodging, transportation options, entertainment, and the great outdoors in the Pennsylvania area. A good starting place for exploring the Keystone State. ✓**INTERNET**→*url* http://travel.org/pennsyl.html

Chocolate Town U.S.A. Ever see the Simpsons episode in which Homer dreams of romping in the Land of Chocolate? Hershey, Pennsylvania, would fulfill Homer's every fantasy! This site tells you everything you ever wanted to know about chocolate—it includes a history of chocolate, nutrition information, fun facts, and a biography of candyman Milton S. Hershey. The site also gives a tour of the Hershey factory

An interesting juxtaposition—http://www.cmp.ucr.edu/exhibitions/netex_history_intro.html

(cont'd pg. 291) →

Philadelphia

Do you want a pop to go with that cheesesteak? Traveling virtually to Philly might not get you a nice hot lunch, but it will give you a taste of the charms of the birthplace of the United States. Start by wandering the same streets that Ben Franklin did with a **Virtual Tour of Historic Philadelphia** (the rumours about Ben and Betsy Ross have never been substantiated). Once sufficiently charmed by the remnants of history, head to **Get A Life** (it is the City of Brotherly Love right?) or **Liberty Net** for the update on clubs, museums, and baseball. Fill your culture quotient with a trip to the **Philadelphia Museum of Art**, and your stomach at **Eats**. So pack up—the Liberty Bell and Phil's Cheesesteaks are waiting.

The Philadelphia skyline—from http://www.realtime.net/~jozef3/philphot.html

On the Net

Across the board

Get a Life Not sure where to go for great underground theater? Planning a biking tour but aren't sure about your route? Want to make sure the Eagles are playing on home turf when you visit? This guide has done all the footwork for you. Browse through picks and pans, articles, and general info about dining, cinema, theater, museums, galleries, family fun, clubbing, sports teams, outdoors activities, out-of-town weekends, weather, and more. The site is well produced and stuffed to the gills, so if you can't find anything to do after clicking through here, then you really do need to get a life. ✓**INTERNET**→*url* http://www.phillynews.com/life/index.htm

LibertyNet The most comprehensive site for the Philadelphia region, the Web page provides extensive information on restaurants, from the famous Le Bec Fin to Geno's Steaks (where you can get amazing cheesesteaks!), cultural attractions, such as the Shofuso and the Painted Bride Theater, and accommodations to fit every budget, from youth hostels to the Four Seasons Hotel. ✓**INTERNET**→*url* http://libertynet.org/

NetStreet Going on a business trip to Philly? Looking for places to shop, eat, or rub elbows with Philadelphia's finest? Then allow NetStreet to show you a few things about the city. Composed of advertisements for local businesses (from dry cleaners to an Indian restaurant) and links to personal home pages, this site is not exactly an objective, unbiased guide, but it will outline some of your options for vacationing and doing business in Philadelphia. ✓**INTERNET**→*url* http://www.netstreet.com/

Philadelphia Guide Philly's Prodigy subscribers post their cheers and jeers for local sightseeing spots, restaurants, lodging, shopping, outdoors and kids activities, and entertainment. Some of the attractions offer links to their own Prodigy pages. ✓**PRODIGY**→*jump* travel→City Guides→Philadelphia

Philadelphia Information Resource Center A guide to Philly compiled by a native, with reviews and basic info about apartments, businesses, restaurants, shopping, sightseeing, transportation, and upcoming events. The reviews are often amusing (if at times a bit rough)—e.g., the nightlife section features the author's personal stories of bar fights and rude coat checks more prominently than his actual assessment of the clubs—and the entries are usually text only. If you're looking for a very personal perspective on the City of Brotherly Love, you'll probably enjoy this page. ✓**INTERNET**→*url* http://icg.stwing.upenn.edu/~konrad/philly.html

Virtual Tour of Historic Philadelphia An enjoyable walk through the historical sights of Philadelphia, this page offers detailed information on dozens of landmarks and locales, with history, trivia, tourist info, and images of places like the Betsy Ross House, the Liberty Bell, Chinatown, South Street, and Penn's Landing. ✓**INTERNET**→*url* http://www.libertynet.org/iha/virtual.html

Culture

Natural History Museum From dinosaurs to yaks, African geology to Chinese archeology, the Natural History Museum showcases a multi-cultural, multi-epoch collection of natural science exhibits and archives that rank with the best in the world. Their home page isn't as cybersaavy as many museum sites on the Net, but you can get a lot of text-only information about special shows and a few images of the museum and its libraries. ✓**INTERNET**→*url* http://www.acnatsci.org/museum/

Philadelphia Museum of Art One of the most prestigious museums in the country offers this hypertext guide to several of its galleries, such as East Asian Art, European Painting before 1900, and Twentieth Century Art. Within each gallery, two or three of the more important works are showcased—Vincent Van Gogh's *Sunflowers*, Marcel Duchamp's *The Large Glass (The Bride Stripped Bare by Her Bachelors, Even)*—with background information and small images. Abstracts of current and upcoming exhibitions, as well as general information and a short history of the museum, are also provided at the site. ✓**INTERNET** ...→*url* http://libertynet.org/~pma/pmahome.html ...→*url* http://www.libertynet.org/~pma/

The Franklin Institute Science Museum Get struck by lightning, tour a human heart, travel to a future earth, ride in one of the first steam engines ever built, lift 500 pounds with your bare hands, see a movie 60 feet high, and visit the stars. No it's not a dream sequence in a Salvador Dali film—it's the Franklin Institute, one of the coolest places on earth or in space! This site is almost as much fun as the real thing. You'll get exhibit summaries featuring informative movies and links to special kiddie projects and online experiments. On top of that, there are science-oriented news briefs and articles. A visit to the page will prove that the Franklin Institute is not just for kids. ✓**INTERNET**→*url* http://sln.fi.edu/

Restaurants & cafés

Central Philadelphia Café List Descriptions, reviews, addresses, and phone numbers of the hottest places to drink your double-shot mochachino decaf gelato float with a twist of lemon. ✓**INTERNET**→*url* http://homepage.seas.upenn.edu/~cpage/coffee.html

Eats Part of the Get a Life site, this fabulously comprehensive guide to food in Philly and beyond is by far the best resource on the Net for the famished in Philly. Search the enormous Restaurant Rover database by type of cuisine or location, or read local food critics' reviews for some recommendations. ✓**INTERNET**→*url* http://www.phillynews.com/life/eats/eats.htm

Where to Eat in Historic Philadelphia This site provides a list of addresses and phone numbers for restaurants in the Philadelphia metropolitan area and surrounding regions. You'll find an alphabetical list of addresses and phone numbers for each restaurant. ✓**INTERNET**→*url* http://www.libertynet.org/iha/philfood.html

Fodor's Choice...

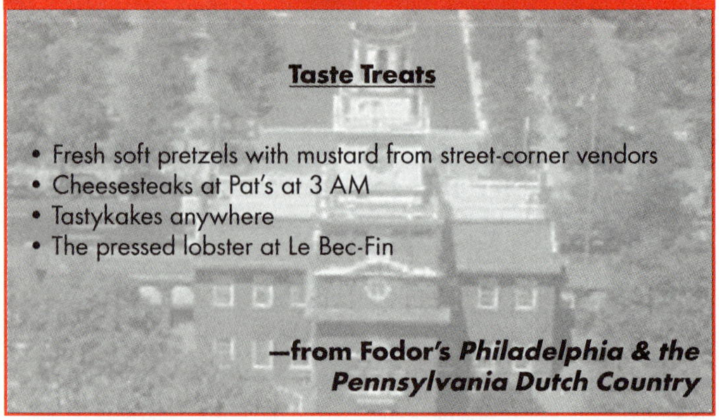

Taste Treats

- Fresh soft pretzels with mustard from street-corner vendors
- Cheesesteaks at Pat's at 3 AM
- Tastykakes anywhere
- The pressed lobster at Le Bec-Fin

—from Fodor's *Philadelphia & the Pennsylvania Dutch Country*

online and lists information on offline tours. ✓INTERNET→*url* http://www.microserve.com/~hershey/welcome.html

PittsburghNet A great resource for anyone planning a trip to Pittsburgh, the page offers links to city maps, sightseeing highlights (from aviaries to amusement parks), and listings of hotels, inns, and B&Bs. A special section called, Doing What Pittsburghers Do, puts you on the inside track for local cultural events. ✓INTERNET→*url* http://www.pittsburgh.net/pghnet/lifestyle/visiting/visiting.html

The Andy Warhol Museum Home Page If you're in Pittsburgh, and want to explore the work of the most influential pop artist of all time, take a gander at this site, which features a virtual tour of the museum. Learn about Andy's life, from his humble beginnings, through his more-than-fifteen minutes of fame, up to his tragic death. The site also provides images of Warhol's more important works, screening and exhibit schedules, general info and catalog listings, as well as a FAQ for the museum ("How do I get there? What restaurants are available in the Museum?"). ✓INTERNET→*url* http://www.warhol.org/warhol/

RHODE ISLAND

Rhode Island Tourist Information There's a lot to do in Rhode Island even though it is the smallest state in America (at 1,214 square miles, it's less than twice the size of Oklahoma City). Discover the depth of offerings in the Ocean State with the calendar of events, hotel and restaurant listings, and guides to camping, boating, golfing, biking, and swimming opportunities. ✓INTERNET→*url* http://www.brown.edu/Student_Services/Rhode_Island/welcome.html

Rhode Island's Best Bed and Breakfasts, Inns, and Small Hotels From the heart of Providence down to Block Island, Little Rhody is dotted with B&Bs, some of which are profiled in great detail at this Web page, with lovely photographs and illustrations. Call the individual inns for additional information or to make reservations. ✓INTERNET→*url* http://www.virtualcities.com/~virtual/ons/ri/rionsdex.htm

Welcome to Newport This home page takes you on a guided tour of Newport's famous mansions: Rosecliff, Hammersmith Farm (where Jacqueline Onassis lived during her youth), Chateau-Sur-Mer, and The Breakers. After visiting Newport's homes of the rich and famous, get info on Newport's annual Jazz Festival and scores of restaurants, shops, and accommodations. If you're planning to visit during the summer, which is likely, check out the weather report at this page before you head out. ✓INTERNET→*url* http://www.aqua.net:80/newport_test.html

Providence CityLink Following CityLink's usual format, text listings of what to see and do, and where to eat and stay, are provided for Providence. Of particular note are the Museum of Art at Rhode Island School of Design, John Brown House, and, of course, Brown University. You might also trek over to The Arcade, built in 1828, which bills itself as America's first shopping mall. Roger Williams Park and Zoo are great for the kids. The Archive Museum of Johnson and Wales University's Culinary Institute will help you build up an appetite. ✓INTERNET→*url* http://www.neosoft.com/citylink/providen/default.html

SOUTH CAROLINA

Appalachian Web of South Carolina Mountains in South Carolina? Of course there are. The Appalachians stretch down into the sandhills, offering topographical diversity for those touring the area. The Website provides impressive photos and helpful information on accommodations, attractions, and regional history. ✓INTERNET→*url* http://www.acog.greenville.sc.us/

Golf Courses in South Carolina If you have ever once thought about playing golf in South Carolina, this is a Website not to be missed. A color-coded map shows the location of every course in the state. Click on the course name and get phone numbers, addresses, and prices, along with specifics like slope, course length, and the course's architect. ✓INTERNET→*url* http://www.gdol.com/course/sc/

Hilton Head Short lists of tourist resources on South Carolina's island paradise are the focus of this page. The information is divided into two parts—What to Do and Where to Stay. Not surprisingly, the What to Do info is overwhelmingly dominated by the list of golf courses; get the names, locations, and phone numbers of 20 courses. The Where to Stay section offers similarly brief listings for almost 20 hotels. ✓INTERNET→*url* http://scenic.ricommunity.com/scenic/tourism/hiltonhd.htm

South Carolina Botanical Garden The South Carolina Botanical Garden strives "to serve as an interdisciplinary public garden whose focus is research and education in the areas of botanical and cultural conservation and the

The Badlands of South Dakota—http://anansi.panix.com:80/~wizjd/cgi-bin/getphoto.cgi/

environment." Wow. It's open 365 days a year from sunrise to sunset and is within a stone's throw of the Clemson University campus. Get directions at the Website and go. ✓**INTERNET**→*url* http://agweb.clemson.edu/hort/scbg/intro.html

The South Carolina Directory Spotlighting Charleston, this page offers useful information for navigating around the quintessential Southern city. Gather info on the eclectic Spoleto Festival, or map out a day tour of the city's gardens. Search the travel directory for a service of your choice (pick from Abott & Hill, Charleston Travel, or TAI Cruise Desk, among others), and definitely check the site's restaurant directory for an alphabetized list of addresses and phone numbers for Charleston's restaurants. ✓**INTERNET**→*url* http://www.awod.com/gallery/cac/

The South Carolina Official Tour Guide A complete and extensive tour of the golden beaches, championship golf courses, historic plantations, scenic foothills, outlet shopping, and events happening in the Palmetto State. A clickable map lets you visit tourist areas all over the state—so whether you're in the mood for shagging on the sand at Myrtle Beach or golfing in the Pee Dee country, the info here helps you plan. ✓**INTERNET**→*url* http://www.sccsi.com:80/sc/

The Ultimate Carolina Vacation Planner A jackpot of resources for the Carolina explorer. This page spotlights the top five tourist sites of the two Carolinas—the Outer Banks, Charleston, Myrtle Beach, Kiawah Island, and Hilton Head. Under each locale are useful links, such as Current Weather, Calendar of Events, Just for Kids, Trivia, Golf, User Forums, and a Plan Your Vacation section. ✓**INTERNET**→*url* http://www.aesir.com/Welcome.html

SOUTH DAKOTA

Black Hills Tourist Attractions The Black Hills, so named because of the wealth of coal mines located within them, are among South Dakota's most compelling attractions. Within the range is Mount Rushmore, where you can see the four biggest people in rock and a new, emerging memorial, this one dedicated to Crazy Horse. Find information here on both memorials and on nearby Rapid City, as well as local weather reports. ✓**INTERNET**→*url* http://www.sdsmt.edu/regional/regional.html

State Department of Tourism Click on the map for tourist information on every part of the state. Since South Dakota's greatest resource is its natural beauty, essays abound here on state parks and outdoor recreation options. Maps are provided to guide you throughout the region, along with a calendar describing upcoming events in the area, Native American points of interest, and city attractions. Be sure to visit the Black Hills, the Badlands, and Mount Rushmore. ✓**INTERNET**→*url* http://www.state.sd.us./state/executive/tourism/tourism.html

The Great Sioux Nation Discover within these pages the history of the Sioux. Learn about their lives on the reservations; witness the construction of the mammoth memorial to Crazy Horse, Lakota leader; and find out what happened at Wounded Knee. Check the schedule of powwows held around the state—great opportunities to learn about Sioux culture thorugh ethnic cuisine, such as "fry bread" and *wojapi*, a fruit pudding. Links to tribal home pages are also available. ✓**INTERNET**→*url* http://www.state.sd.us/state/executive/tourism/sioux/sioux.htm

TENNESSEE

For Graceland sites, see page 312.

The Official Tennessee Vacation Guide Delta Country, the Heartland, the Plateaus and Valleys, Mountainous East, First

Frontier—explore Tennessee country at this site, organized by region and city. You'll find here descriptions of all the big sights, including the Grand Ole Opry, the Country Music Hall of Fame, Beale Street, Graceland, Dollyland, and dozens of delights you never knew existed. ✓**INTERNET**→*url* http://www.state.tn.us/other/vacguide/mainpage.htm

Dixon Gallery and Gardens, Memphis, Tennessee Whether you are visiting the museum, with its focus on eighteenth- and nineteenth-century fine and decorative arts, or the 17-acre English park garden, with woodlands, greenhouses, and sculpture ranging from eighteenth century to contemporary, the Dixon Gallery and Gardens can be enjoyed year-round. This site provides exhibition abstracts, as well as a history, general information, and images so lovely you can practically smell the magnolias. ✓**INTERNET**→*url* http://gray.music.rhodes.edu/Dixon.html

Institute of Egyptian Art and Archeology, Memphis, TN This site features links to museum history and general information, images and text about the exhibits, and a virtual tour of Egypt. The Institute, under the auspices of Department of Art of the University of Memphis, showcases over 150 artifacts ranging in importance from the sublime—the mummy of Iret-iruw—to the ridiculous—a 4,000-year-old slice of bread. ✓**INTERNET**→*url* http://www.memst.edu/egypt/main.html

Mud Island, Memphis, TN Mud Island is home to the Mississippi River Museum, a tribute to the Mighty Mississippi, with its five-block-long replica of the river, as well as a monorail and a display of the most famous bomber of WWII—the Memphis Belle. At this site you'll find links to images of all the attractions, as well as dining and admission info, an events calendar, and even a trivia contest. ✓**INTERNET**→*url* http://www.magibox.net/~mud/

National Civil Rights Museum, Memphis, Tennessee The National Civil Rights Museum, built at the Lorraine Motel where Martin Luther King was assassinated, is a testament to the movement's formative and ongoing struggle against racism. This site offers links to membership and general info, a virtual tour of the galleries, a museum history, and other civil / human rights pages, as well as special focus links on the 1995 Conference on Freedom and on the late, great Duke Ellington. ✓**INTERNET**→*url* http://www.magibox.net/~ncrm/

Nashville at the Ultimate World Links to text and home pages for the best cultural attractions, lodging, food, events, sports, and entertainment in Tennessee. From the Belle Meade Plantation to the Grand Old Golf Amusement Center, from the Calypso Cafe to Motel 6, from the Tennessee Dance Theater to the Museum of Tobacco Art, Nashville has everything—it isn't just for music anymore. ✓**INTERNET**→*url* http://www.ultimatew.com/tn/nashvill/docs/home.html

Nashville, Music City Vacation Guide A fantastic resource featuring a hypertext guide to the sights and sounds of Nashville. A visit here will yield info on attractions, festivals, recreation, tours, lodging, transportation, shopping, camping, dining, resorts, conventions, nightlife, and fun facts! The largest indoor statue in the world is located in Nashville—a 42-foot likeness of Athena looms over Centennial Park. ✓**INTERNET**→*url* http://nashville.musiccityusa.com/tour/

Nashville Scene This online magazine offers views and reviews on everything that's going on in Music City. Links here can take you to a photo gallery; forums covering the best of regional and Nashville talk; a movie schedule; an events guide; back issues of the magazine; and a fabulous, searchable dining index offering contact info and abstracts for every kind of fare, from ribs to pheasant under glass. ✓**INTERNET**→*url* http://www.nashscene.com/cgi-bin/pagegen.pl

TEXAS

The Travelers Edge—Texas City Files Information about Dallas / Fort Worth, Houston, and San Antonio may be found here. Resources include the top sightseeing attractions, nightlife options, transportation into and around the cities, and business services: office equipment rental, secretarial services, telecommunications, and translators. You can also find listings of visitor services like currency exchange and emergency care as well as of visitor's bureaus and local periodicals. ✓**EWORLD**→*go* travelers→city files→u.s. cities

Travelers Corner—Texas Here you'll find a general overview of the state, plus listings of what to do in various cities and regions. As Texas is a large state, the list is plentiful. The dos and don'ts page here is especially long, with many things to do, but lots of don'ts (don't pick wildflowers, don't tell Texans how you do things better at home, don't swim alone in the Gulf, don't assume Spanish-speaking people immigrated from Mexico—there are families whose forebears arrived in Texas before it was a state). ✓**AMERICA ONLINE**→*keyword* Traveler's Corner→U.S. Profiles→R-Z→Texas

Austin Visitor's Guide Austin boasts a burgeoning music scene and the sophistication that comes from being a college town. Generally held to be more liberal than the average Texas town, it's becoming an increasingly popular tourist destination. This comprehensive guide to the best music clubs, visitor attractions, hotels, restaurants, and shopping options is all hypertext, though thoroughly informative. ✓**INTERNET**→*url* http://visit.ci.austin.tx.us/

Dallas Cityview Entering this site is like walking into an immense shopping mall, which is appropriate since Dallas's North Park Center was the first indoor mall built in the U.S. Pick up a shopping bag and collect info on the city's movie theaters, hotels, restaurants, nightclubs, shops, real estate, concerts, and museums. Or take a virtual tour of Dallas, which takes you to noted districts such as Deep Ellum, the city's first black neighborhood, and an avant-garde center of art galleries, clubs, and restaurants, and the West End, a revitalized brick-warehouse district. This is the Web's most comprehensive guide to Dallas. ✓**INTERNET**→*url* http://www.cityview.com/dallas/

Dallas Museum of Art Online See what the Dallas Museum of Art has to offer with this online gallery of over 200 digital images that feature every room in the museum, the sculpture garden, and even the Dallas skyline. The .GIFs are all quite large (visiting online could take more time than walking through in person). Information is also provided about the museum's comprehensive programs and resources. ✓**INTERNET**→*url* http://www.unt.edu/dfw/dma/www/dma.htm

Fort Worth Dallas's sister city, 30 miles to the west, demonstrates that it isn't the "Cowtown" people think it is. Among the attractions listed here are Sundance Square downtown, the Stockyards, Noble Planetarium, Six Flags over Texas, and of course, the Texas Rangers. Much more graceful than glitzy Dallas, it's well worth a visit or stay. The site provides hotel listings and dining options throughout the city; emphasis is on activities for the family and outdoor recreation. ✓**INTERNET**→*url* http://www.cityview.com/cgi-bin/imagemap/cityview?358,192

Galveston Island Located at the mouth of the Houston Ship Canal, Galveston is a resort spot and a great excursion from the city. The visitor's guide (which includes hotels and local restaurants) is online; take the Treasure Train Island Tour to best see Galveston. Discover here such local attractions such as Moody Gardens (a ten-story rain forest pyramid), the Texas Seaport Museum, and the Historic Homes District. ✓**INTERNET**→*url* http://www.phoenix.net/~afactory/galveston/welcome.html

Houston Here in Houston, there is trenchant opposition to a proposal to build a subway—even if the city does comprise over 500 square miles. People in Houston love their trucks and cars, and you'll need a vehicle yourself to get around in this large city. (It's fitting that Mobil sponsors this travel site.) Also find here guides to entertainment, sightseeing options (take a Gray Line bus tour or visit

DETOURS

Moody Gardens

"Discover a ten-story Rainforest Pyramid with over 2,000 species of exotic plants, animals, and butterflies from Asia, Africa and the Americas. Images in 3-D IMAX that leap off the screen to the awesome sensation of IMAX digital sound. Gourmet meals with spectacular nightly Dancing Waters fountain displays at our waterfront Garden Restaurant. Nature-inspired gifts from around the world. Acres of gardens and jogging trails to explore. Daily cruises aboard the luxurious Colonel Paddlewheel. And, the soft white sands, waterfalls and fresh-water lagoons of Palm Beach, with its Yellow Submarine for the little ones, plus regulation volleyball courts, paddleboats, Texas-sized spas.

Texans of all shapes and sizes come to the Galveston area to relax after a long day drilling for oil, breaking broncos, or running for political office."

—from **Galveston Island**

AstroWorld), the Museum of Fine Arts, and Hermann Park. Find also information about nearby Galveston. Although you may be here on the new Prodigy software, don't expect any images. ✓**PRODIGY**→*jump* travel→Mobil Travel Guide→U.S.States→Texas→Houston

San Antonio San Antonio has a Spanish flavor that's rooted in its Mexican heritage. The King William Historic District; the Alamo; the lush, canal-like Riverwalk filled with bistros and hotels; the acclaimed zoo; and music spots—they all await you in San Antonio. Take a virtual tour of the Riverwalk here aboard a gondola that will remind you of old Venice, and also check hotel listings, including amenities and prices (you can even reserve rooms online). Also find here info on restaurants and city transportation (by riverboat, streetcar, and bus), and links to the 1203 Artspace gallery, the Hill Country, and Fredericksburg—a German village. ✓**INTERNET**→*url* http://www.cains.com/

UTAH

Utah Shakespeare Festival When you think of The Bard you think of Stratford-on-Avon, West End London, Midtown Manhattan, Central Park, and...Utah? Believe it or not, Utah is home to one of the country's largest Shakespeare festivals, and you can get the details on the yearly event at this Website. A visitor's guide links you to accommodations, dining, transportation, and reservation info, and the site provides images and abstracts for all the plays showcased—not just Shakespeare's, but also contemporary works by George S. Kaufman and Stephen Sondheim. ✓**INTERNET**→*url* http://www.infowest.com/shakefest/index.html

Utah Travel Guide Utah will be host to the 2002 Winter Olympic Games, but if you can't wait till then to visit, you may want to take a look at this page, which features some truly breathtaking images and links to pages on activities and sights in Utah (links are categorized by location and activity). Most of the sections for cultural attractions and lodging contain lists of names without so much as a contact number or address, but the outdoor recreation sections are more comprehensive and include a searchable campground database that links you with the facility that best suits your needs. Definitely a hit-or-miss resource. ✓**INTERNET**→*url* http://www.netpub.com/utah/w

Salt Lake Convention and Visitors Bureau A very well-produced site, with lovely images and links to basic information on all the city has to offer—cultural attractions, dining, lodging, and more. In addition to contact information for services and activities, the page offers links to a ski and weather report, an events calendar, local news, the 2002 Winter Olympics, trivia, and myths about Salt Lake City. ✓**INTERNET**→*url* http://www.intele.net/slcvb/

VERMONT

Ben & Jerry's Homemade, Inc. Can you name the 31 Ben & Jerry's flavors? If not, then it's time for an ice-cream factory tour. Located in Waterbury, Ben & Jerry's offers half-hour tours demonstrating how the famous dessert is made. The tour ends in the scoop shop, where you can taste free samples, or purchase as much as you like for the road. The online tour isn't quite as tasty, but you can satisfy your craving by checking the scoop shop locator to see if there is a shop near you. (There are over 120 scoop shops in the U.S. and abroad.) While you're here, have your fortune told by Habeeni Ben Coheeni—the Ben & Jerry genie. ✓**INTERNET**→*url* http://www.benjerry.com/

Utah's Brigham Young monument—http://www.netpub.com/utah/regions/saltlake/

Brattleboro A small city on the Connecticut River in the east, Brattleboro has long held a reputation as a progressive community. Take a look at photos of the town, and read about its illustrious history. A calendar of events describes craft fairs, hayrides, and music festivals; the excellent health-food restaurant, Common Ground, still upstairs at 25 Elliot Street, is a must. ✓**INTERNET**→*url* http://www.sover.net/~bratchmb/

Couture's Maple Shop There is no shortage of places in Vermont to purchase maple syrup (or fudge and teddy bears). This shop, however, is online, and syrup, maple cream, and gift packages may be ordered via email or toll-free number. The shop is in Westfield, in the heart of the Northeast Kingdom. ✓**INTERNET**→*url* http://www.pbpub.com/vermont/couture.htm

Grafton, Vermont A picture-perfect village, as the photos here will illustrate, with all the antique shops, sugar houses, and B&Bs you would expect. There is also a large creative community here; meet the artists and view their works in the Covered Bridge Collection. Artists Bradford Voight and Jean Winston present watercolor paintings of local scenes; George V. H. Moseley has authored poetry and books concerning minorities in South China. The site includes a guide to other local talent, along with a calendar of events. ✓**INTERNET**→*url* http://www.sover.net:80/~grafton/

Scenes From Vermont Vermont, especially during the fall, is one of the most scenic places you'll ever visit. The Green Mountain State is dotted with charming villages, each centered around a common green; hilltop farms; crowded ski resorts, and the occasional ice creamery—you can see them all here. First select a B&B—choose by location, cost, and/or amenities, or select the one that looks the most appealing. Then visit a general store, such as the one in Taftsville, or Sugarbush Farm, where you can purchase delicious smoked cheddar cheese (in real life and online). View the scenery throughout Vermont by region; of particular interest is the Northeast Kingdom—it's near the Canadian border and has an independent spirit analogous to that of Québec. ✓**INTERNET**→*url* http://www.pbpub.com/vermont/

Stratton Arts Festival This annual fall show features over 200 Vermont painters, sculptors, photographers, ceramists, and other artisans. Held for the past 32 years in a 10,000-square-foot gallery at the base lodge at Stratton Mountain, it now includes demonstrations of the crafts. Very few works are presented here, so take a trip to the mountain and check it out with the info listed here. ✓**INTERNET**→*url* http://www.sover.net/~artsfest/

Sugarbush Farm An authentic working dairy farm where Vermont cheddar cheese is produced, Sugarbush Farm, located near Woodstock, features demonstrations of the cheese-making process, as well as a shop where you can make your purchases. Bring a printed copy of the Web page with you for a 10% discount on your order. ✓**INTERNET**→*url* http://www.pbpub.com/vermont/sugrbsh.htm

Snow geese at Vermont's Dead Creek—http://www.cit.state.vt.us/vtlife/fall95/dedcrek.htm

Vermont Bed & Breakfasts For images and detailed descriptions of some of Vermont's best inns, this is your guide. Visit the Hugging Bear Inn in Chester or the Maplewood at Fair Haven; see which hotels have fireplaces in the guest rooms, or if there are swimming pools for relief from the scorching Vermont summer sun. Explore more than 30 inns. ✓**INTERNET**→*url* http://www.virtualcities.com/~virtual/ons/vt/vtonsdex.htm

VIRGINIA

Virginia Tourism Basic Facts about the state that claims the American Dogwood as its state flower. Learn where to go, where to eat, and what to see (Colonial Williamburg makes a big appearance). ✓**INTERNET**→*url* http://www.nomius.com/~va/virginia.htm

WASHINGTON

Cambots at UW You've heard the myths about Seattle weather. Now you can experience the reality with this site, which offers a video image that is updated at regular intervals, usually about every five minutes, 24 hours a day. Travelers will appreciate the preview of the day's weather. ✓**INTERNET**→*url* http://www.cac.washington.edu:1180/home/cambot.html

Mount St. Helens For those who really like to get a lot of bang for their vacation buck, there is no better vacation spot. The Website holds interesting profiles of the mountain before and after the 1980 explosion, as well as a page on the city of Longview, which is using this site to promote the joys of living there again—the mountain even has a visitor center and coffee shop. So head here to find out how you can trek up to the crater and haul some ashes. Since an estimated 500 million tons were released, there's no shortage of them. ✓**INTERNET**→*url* http://www.teleport.com/~longview/msh.html

San Juan Web Sail away to these favorite getaways for Pacific Northwest natives. This site profiles the major islands, complete with contact info for local hotels and restaurants. How does a kayak tour, followed by dinner at the Hungry Clam and a night in a four-poster at Olde Roses Manor sound? And remember, any visit to the San Juans is incomplete without a trip to the Whale Museum in Friday Harbor. Ferry schedules are included. ✓**INTERNET**→*url* http://www.sanjuan.com/

The Emerald Web The Emerald Web contains absolutely everything even remotely connected to Washington State and Seattle, and a great deal more besides. No, really. Jump from here to the Recreation and Entertainment section, and you'll be bowled over with links to the outdoor adventure of Olympic National Park or the indoor adventure of Seattle's alternative music scene. Travelers will especially enjoy the tourism links, which offer up festivals, B&Bs, deep-water fishing charters, and hometown pages, each packed with useful info. And that's not even mentioning the restaurants, coffeehouses, clubs, and guides to bicycle and foot tours. For those traveling to Seattle or through Washington State, this should be the first stop. ✓**INTERNET**→*url* http://www.cyberspace.com/bobk/

Washington Profile What a surprise—in the dos and don'ts section here, the pundits suggest bringing an umbrella! But there are also suggestions for treats for all types. Buy some fresh salmon at Pike Place Market or catch fish for yourself on a fishing tour off Illuaco. ✓**EWORLD**→*go* travelers→U.S. files→Washington

Washington Resource Listing Lots of people think of mountains and evergreens when they think of Washington State, and rightly so, but did you know the state also has also dry hills, deep blue lakes, majestic river gorges, and the U.S.'s only certified rain forest? Discover all about the natural attributes of Washington with a quick visit to this site, which profiles the state's National Parks, Forests, and Wilderness areas. Also find links to pages advertising outdoor tour agencies, cycling clubs, and even places to get crampons for your ascent from Camp Muir to the summit of Mt. Rainier. ✓**INTERNET**→*url* http://www.gorp.com/gorp/location/wa/wa.htm#attraction

Washington State Ferries Make sure the ferry from Port Angeles to Seattle doesn't leave you standing on the dock looking chagrined. Visit this site, which posts the schedules for the notoriously timely ferry service. ✓**INTERNET**→*url* http://www.marinenetwork.com/~marinent/news/

Washington Wine Tour Washington State wines are becoming common on the liquor store shelf. The state's top ten wineries are profiled here, with addresses, hours of operation, and even consumer evaluations of the final product. ✓**INTERNET**→*url* http://agustus.csscr.washington.edu/personal/bigstar-mosaic/wwtour.html

Bed and Breakfast Inns of Seattle This small selection of inns offers the gracious charms of the Colonial Manor and the down-home comfort of B. D. Williams's house. Get profiles and contacts for each B&B at the page. ✓**INTERNET**→*url* http://sensemedia.net/1247

Seattle, The Emerald City There's no yellow brick road to guide you to this Emerald City, but there is this site online to guide you once you get there. The Info Center section here helps you get around town on public transport, and oddly enough, links you to crime-location maps (New Yorkers will then know which neighborhood to visit if they're feeling homesick). Check the section's Entertainment District to find out if the Mariners are playing, or if there's yet another Kurt Cobain memorial going on somewhere in the city. ✓**INTERNET**→*url* http://www.seattle.net/SeattleHome.html

WEST VIRGINIA

Tour West Virginia Click on the name of a county to find out what places to visit or what resources are available in that area. If you know that Charleston is located in Kanahwa County, for example, it's simple to access Charleston pages. Otherwise, you'll find your way around the state with some trial and error, but you'll be an expert on the local geography when you're done. ✓**INTERNET**→*url* http://198.77.4.68/lynx_dev/wv_form.html

Upshur County A range of activities await you in the county. In Buckhannon, visit Wesleyan College, or attend the West Virginia

Strawberry Festival. Take an excursion to the zoo or to the county parks, or take to the ski slopes (this isn't called the Mountain State for nothing). What will you find here? Large JPEGs of the scenic mountains, along with road maps and hotel listings to make your trip easier. ✓**INTERNET**→*url* http://wvlink.mpl.com/upshur

Charles Town Not to be confused with West Virginia's capital, Charleston, this historic town was named after George Washington's half-brother Charles. Thumbnails at this site provide a glimpse of the colonial architecture that distinguishes the town. highlighting events such as the annual Charles Town Races (the event is over 200 years old) and local attractions like the Jefferson County Museum. If you decide to stay for a spell, check the list of local accommodations. ✓**INTERNET**→*url* http://www.intrepid.net/~jsantos/~ctown.html

Charleston Did you know that Charleston is home to the largest state capitol dome in the United States? If not, then you may not know about the multitude of museums, historic houses, and festivals here, either. A detailed calendar of what's going on in Charleston is provided, with listings of recreational resources and sporting events. ✓**INTERNET**→*url* http://www.citynet.net/charlstn.html

Virtual Morgantown Take a tour of High Street in this bustling college town nestled in the Appalachians. A clickable map of the downtown area allows you to get a glimpse of what life is like here if you're considering a few years at West Virginia University, or just settling down. Also find here an index with town and county resource information and public transportation schedules. Another map at the site points the way to area hotels within the city and has links to the university and the local Convention and Visitor's Bureau. ✓**INTERNET**→*url* http://www.dmssoft.com/mrgntwn/

WISCONSIN

Frank Lloyd Wright in Wisconsin Travel online to the Badger State, and visit homes designed by the renowned modern architect. A virtual walking tour of Taliesin (which is one of Wright's most prominent designs) is available, as well as brief video clips of a number of his speeches on architecture. ✓**INTERNET**→*url* http://flw.badgernet.com:2080/flw.htm

Hayward, Wisconsin Lakes Area The Hayward area is noted for the best freshwater fishing this side of...Hayward. The site provides a guide to the best fishing holes, as well as a list of local historical sites, such as Al Capone's Place, the Logging History Museum, and the National Freshwater Fishing Hall of Fame. Listings of lodges in the area will aid you in planning a trip to Hayward. ✓**INTERNET**→*url* http://www.netjunkies.com/~timg/hayindx1.html

The Travelers' Edge—Wisconsin What is there to do in Wisconsin anyway? Well, with hundreds of lakes, there are all sorts of water-sports opportunities. If water sport for you is tossing back the suds, try the Miller or Pabst breweries in Milwaukee. Or perhaps you'd enjoy a visit to a cheese factory (there are several all over the state) or a concert (of any sort) in Madison. Information on all these activities, and more, can be found here. ✓**EWORLD**→*go* travelers→Destination Guide→U.S./Canada Profiles→States R-Z→ Wisconsin

Greater Madison Wisconsin's seat of government is located between Lakes Mendota and Monona (don't confuse them). Home to the main campus of the University of Wisconsin, Madison offers much for both students and visitors to do. Check this Web page for up-to-date events calendars, lodging and dining listings, and outdoor-activity suggestions for water enthusiasts (Wisconsin is the original Land o' Lakes). ✓**INTERNET**→*url* http://www.inmarket

Fodor's Choice...

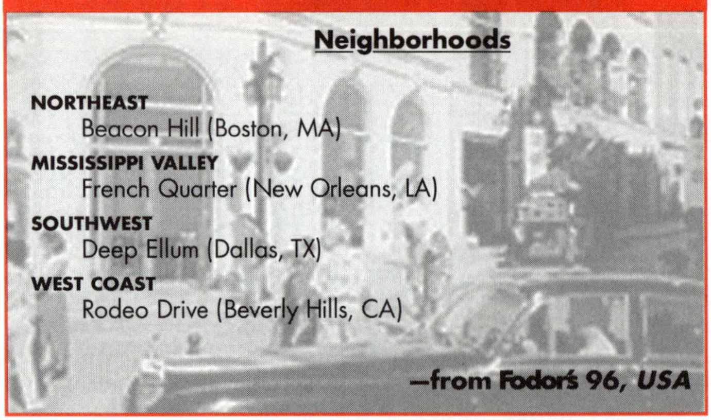

Neighborhoods

NORTHEAST
Beacon Hill (Boston, MA)

MISSISSIPPI VALLEY
French Quarter (New Orleans, LA)

SOUTHWEST
Deep Ellum (Dallas, TX)

WEST COAST
Rodeo Drive (Beverly Hills, CA)

—from Fodor's 96, *USA*

.com/madison

Milwaukee—A Great Place on a Great Lake A concise but comprehensive guide to what's going on in Milwaukee—all in hypertext format. Listings cover bars and nightlife, outdoor activities (especially boating on Lake Michigan), museums (the Milwaukee Art Museum and the Wisconsin Black Historical Society), the arts, and other attractions (mostly breweries and microbreweries, but also the First Wisconsin Center's Observation Deck). The site offers no photos, but the comprehensive listings more than make up for that shortcoming. Link here to a page of Milwaukee restaurant recommendations in newsgroup format, contributed by residents and visitors alike. ✓**INTERNET**→*url* http://www.solutions.net/rec-travel/north_america/usa/wisconsin/milwaukee.html

Unofficial Bars of Milwaukee A virtual tour of watering holes favored by the natives in the Beer Capital of the U.S. Included are bars with a real German feel (Gasthaus Zur Krone on South 2nd and Von Trier on North Farwell) and artsy-style bar / coffeehouses (The Nomad World Pub). The site welcomes you to add your favorites to the list as well. ✓**INTERNET**→*url* http://www.uwm.edu/~brooklyn/bar.html

WYOMING

Amerisource Travel Wyoming What's in Wyoming for the eager traveler? Jackson Hole ski resort, Old West towns like Cody, and dozens of parks. Link to reports on Wyoming travel resources—ranches, hotels, cabins, campgrounds, restaurants, and shops are profiled—and watch Wyoming's Net presence grow. ✓**INTERNET**→*url* http://amerisource.com/travel/wyoming/wymenu1.htm

Big Horn Safari Tour historic Wyoming by snowmobile with Big Horn Safari, which offers an online rate sheet and facts about the Big Horn mountains. ✓**INTERNET**→*url* http://wave.sheridan.wy.us/~z_travel/bhsafari.html

Bike the Big Horns, Wyoming The title of this Website refers not to the horns on your bicycle, but rather to the Big Horn Mountains, the northern Wyoming range that is heaven for mountain bikers. This page describes the range and then links to other Wyoming outdoor-activity pages. ✓**INTERNET**→*url* http://wave.sheridan.wy.us/~btech/bikepage.html

Cheyenne, Wyoming A wonderfully concise guide to Wyoming's capital, with brief descriptions of upcoming events, museums (including the Cheyenne Frontier Days Old West Museum, which includes the largest covered-wagon collection in the country), and historic sites (like the French Merci Train, sent by French citizens in 1948). And remember if Utah's puritanism is getting you down, there's always Cheyenne. ✓**INTERNET**→*url* http://jackalope.lcc.whecn.edu/cheyenne.html

Cody County The home of Buffalo Bill and the gateway to Yellowstone National Park, (But remember, never annoy an elk, walk too close to a geyser or feed the bears or rangers.) Cody County is one of the most spectacular regions in the entire nation. Link to local businesses, learn about the Shoshone National Forest, and download a weather report. ✓**INTERNET**→*url* http://wave.park.wy.us/cody.html

Jackson Hole Watched over by an image of Olympian Tommy Moe, ski ambassador to Jackson Hole, this page contains more information about Jackson Hole ski resort than you could possibly want—unless, of course, you're actually planning on traveling there. Download weather reports and trail maps, get lodging recommendations, and then learn about shopping, dining, and entertainment opportunities. And if you mention the Internet when you book your vacation, you'll receive a free Jackson Hole poster. ✓**INTERNET**→*url* http://www.jacksonhole.com/ski/

Windy Wyoming Web Wyoming's mountains illustrate this site, which includes a virtual map of the state and links to resources on art, business, education, entertainment, recreation, geography, and weather. Events listings are generous, including everything from theater listings for the University of Wyoming to parades in Casper, so you'll never feel like you've accidentally traveled to a Wild West wasteland. ✓**INTERNET**→*url* http://math.uwyo.edu/State_Links.html

Wyoming Hunting Page When you book a hunt in Wyoming, be sure to use a licensed outfitter, or you may find yourself lining up a five-point in the company of a rank incompetent. And don't forget to obtain a hunting license and to respect hunting seasons. How do you get the info you need to make these important things happen? Come to this page, which offers a hunting FAQ, along with a link to the Sheridan Chamber of Commerce. ✓**INTERNET**→*url* http://wave.sheridan.wy.us:80/~noutfit/huntpage.html

Canada

It's not just a second string United States. Canada is a fantastic travel destination in its own right, filled coast to coast with interesting culture, clean cities, beautiful landscapes, and friendly Canadians. **The Canada Resource Page** is a great introduction to Canadian society, and **The Heritage Project** promotes all that is Canadian with pride. Discover a multi-cultural metropolis at the **Vancouver Home Page** or learn how to pan for gold at **Yukon Web Services**. **The Calgary Web** takes you to the famous stampede, while **The Newfoundland Home Page** takes you as far downeast as it's possible to go. Imbibe in French Canadian culture at **Web Québec** or read **The Saskatoon Star Phoenix**, and that's just the beginning.

Modern-day Vancouver—http://www.aurora.net/pie/htm/vaninfo.html

On the Net

Across the board

Canada Board Phil writes to the message board: "My wife and I are visiting Toronto early in November. Any suggestions for 'don't miss' restaurants, museums, walks, shows, etc., would be much appreciated. We have Toronto Symphony tickets for Saturday night. And I've printed some of Zagat's comments regarding restaurants, but of course, personal comments count for a lot." And in response, Katherine comments, "I ate at Brasserie Zola in the Bloor Street area of Toronto and thought it was wonderful. It had been recommended by a local, and we were very pleased." These are the kind of first-hand recommendations and hints that make this an ideal place to pick up travel tips for your next trip to the Great White North. ✓**PRODIGY**→*jump* travel→travel bb→Canada

Canada Resource Page A comprehensive collection of links about Canada and Canadian resources. Use this page to jump to pages on current Canadian news events (Québec and the new $2 coin are currently making headlines), vital statistics about the country (currency exchange info, a page on Canadian Province flags, etc.), and tourist sites (the Canadian Passport Office, the Official Via Rail Canada site, and Air Canada, among others). To research a trip up north, you couldn't begin with a better site than this one. ✓**INTERNET**→*url* http://www.cs.cmu.edu/Web/Unofficial/Canadiana/README.htmlN

Culture

Native Language Speakers: Canada Every single member of the Atikamekw tribe of northern Québec (3,225 people strong) speaks the tribal tongue. Get a brief description of the languages and culture of all Canadian tribes here. ✓**INTERNET**→*url* http://www-ala.doc.ic.ac.uk/~rap/Ethnologue/eth.cgi/Canada/

soc.culture.canada (ng) While U.S. citizens can't resist posting their border-crossing experiences, Canadians dominate the group with discussions of domestic politics, the environment, the country's bilingualism, trade relation-

Royal Canadian Mounted Police—http://www.scs.carleton.ca/ottawa/ottawa.html

ships, and the highly charged debate over Québec's sovereignty. Too often for most members' tastes, boorish Americans jump in with anti-Canadian comments. But for every Maple enemy, there are many more enthusiastic posts about our Great Northern Neighbor, often from Americans looking for travel tips. ✓**USENET**→soc.culture.canada

The Heritage Project What makes you think of Canada? A moose? A maple leaf? A mountain? This online magazine is devoted to the preservation and promotion of Canadian national identity. Available in both English and French, the magazine offers readers a discussion of things that symbolize Canada, listings of heritage fairs, and features on Canadian culture. ✓**INTERNET**→*url* http://heritage.excite.sfu.ca/hpost.html

Alberta

Access Alberta Short profiles and tourism information on guest ranches, whitewater rafting, and fishing camps in the Alberta area. Tour operators are also online here. ✓**INTERNET**→*url* gopher://freenet.edmonton.ab.ca/11/i/access

Banff You'll think you somehow ended up in Switzerland when you visit this Canadian Rockies resort. The page holds some of the breathtaking views visitors have in store, as well as a link to the Banff National Park page, full of wildlife and trail maps. ✓**INTERNET**→*url* http://www.cuug.ab.ca:8001/VT/banff-town.html

Calgary Web Calgary's come a long way from its start as a Mountie fort in 1875. But it still prides itself on being Canada's own Wild West, full of oil-boom profits and home to the famous Calgary Stampede. Browse through the online directory for info on everything you need to visit Calgary—from hotel listings to honky-tonk bar recommendations. ✓**INTERNET**→*url* http://lexicom.lexicom.ab.ca/

British Columbia

BC Ferries Great news—there's a new dock at Bella Bella! Check time schedules, routes, and fares for one of the province's most important modes of transportation. ✓**INTERNET**→*url* http://bcferries.bc.ca/ferries/

British Columbia A lot is packed into this small guide full of great suggestions for what to do in this beautiful province. A cruise through the spectacular landscape of the Inside Passage sounds unsurpassable. Or opt for the cosmopolitan attractions of Vancouver; its vibrant ethnic communities are described in detail—Chinatown, Germantown, the Punjabi Market, and Scottish tea shops. Head to the dos and don'ts section for advice on avoiding bears and for the number to report forest fires (Zenith 5555). ✓**AMERICA ONLINE**→*keyword* Traveler's Corner→International Profiles→Canada→British Columbia

British Columbia Regional Information At this site you can take hypertours of the varied landscape of B.C., from the mountains of Kootenay Country to the vineyards of Okanagan Similkameen. Each tour features profiles of B.C. parks and sample itineraries. Links at the page lead to ferry information and to special sections on skiing, sport fishing, gold hunting, and adventure and marine travel. ✓**INTERNET**→*url* http://www.tbc.gov.bc.ca/tourism/regions/regions.html

Getaways of British Columbia This listing of more than 1,000 B&Bs and lodges in British Columbia puts you in touch with a place to stay way up in the Cariboo Chilcotin or in the more-traveled climes of Victoria and Vancouver. ✓**INTERNET**→*url* http://interchange.idc.uvic.ca/~getaways/

Royal British Columbia Museum The Royal British Columbia Museum in Victoria is quite simply one of the best museums in the world, and its Website is no slouch either. Get a preview of the museum's natural history, oceans, native peoples, and modern history exhibits here. ✓**INTERNET**→*url* http://rbcm1.rbcm.gov.bc.ca/

The Butchart Gardens-Victoria You can almost smell the roses at this virtual garden. Find out how to reach this famous Vancouver Island attraction, and even make group reservations or buy a flower-filled calendar online. ✓**INTERNET**→*url* http://butchartgardens.bc.ca/butchart/

Vancouver Home Page Vancouver's resources offer something to every traveler—from the city lover to the nature fan. You can ski and sail on the same day, or just wander in the 1,000 acres of Stanley Park. Or enjoy the history of Gastown, the nightclubs, or an excellent dinner at Noodlemaker's in Chinatown. This admirably complete guide tells you how to enjoy it all, from the Museum of Anthropology's wonderful mask collections to the gaming tables of the Great Canadian Casino. Information on accommodations, transportation, and dining is just a click away from this page, too. ✓**INTERNET**→*url* http://www.pie.vancouver.bc.ca/pie/htm/first.html

Victoria's Virtual Tourist Office As soon as you watch the movie housed here, you'll be convinced of the charms of British Columbia's capital. Lavishly illustrated profiles of local attractions provide further incentive to visit—preview cobbled streets, the museum, and the fabulous gardens. Great accommodations and dining recommendations round out the site. ✓**INTERNET**→*url* http://vvv.com/vtourist/toffice.html

Manitoba

Explore Manitoba According to the Website, friendly Manitobans from across the beautiful province are waiting to welcome you into their community. But even if you get mobbed the moment you arrive by adoring locals bearing gifts and goodwill, that doesn't guarantee that they know where to find Sarah the Camel—a 24-foot high symbol of the Spirit of the Sands. You might also need some help finding the best things to do at the Oak Hammock Marsh and Interpretive Centre, or what time of year you can head down to the Beef and Barley Festival. Iselndingadagurinn—the official Icelandic Festival of Manitoba—might forever remain a mystery to you. Your best bet is to go to this page, where you'll find links to images, essays, and home pages for Manitoba's attractions, ecotours, special events, accommodations, and more. ✓**INTERNET**→*url* http://www.eitc.mb.ca/manitoba/itt/travel/explore/index.html

Search of Winnipeg Restaurants An alphabetical listing of hundreds of restaurants in the Winnipeg area, from Aalto's Family Dining to Zorba's Pizza, is here. ✓**INTERNET**→*url* http://www.wpg.ramp.net/~offramp/business/restaurants/restsearchwpg.html

Welcome to Winnipeg This site links you to text and images reflecting a rich and diverse community. Search the index by keyword, or browse by activity or location to find info on special events such as the International Children's Festival, and on cultural attractions such as Canada's oldest and most acclaimed dance troupe—the Royal Winnipeg Ballet Company. ✓**INTERNET**→*url* http://WWW.Solutions.Net/tourismw/

Winnipeg Art Gallery—Upcoming Events A simple site with links to schedules of concerts, art exhibitions, art-discussion forums, tours, lectures, and poetry readings in Winnipeg. ✓**INTERNET**→*url* http://pooh.freenet.mb.ca/BSFN/iphome/w/wag/index.html

Winnipeg Symphony Orchestra Links to images and information on the maestro, the musicians, and the music of the renowned Winnipeg Symphony Orchestra. Festival listings and performance schedules are available, as is information on the orchestra's many albums. ✓**INTERNET**→*url* http://www.ee.umanitoba.ca/wpg/WSO.html

Maritime Provinces

New Brunswick Be sure to bring a sweater to New Brunswick, but leave your pearl-handled .38 at home—firearms are a no-no in Canada. This little profile explores the charms of this maritime gem, from Caraquet, the oldest French settlement and home to Evangeline, to the flora and fauna

Fodor's Choice...

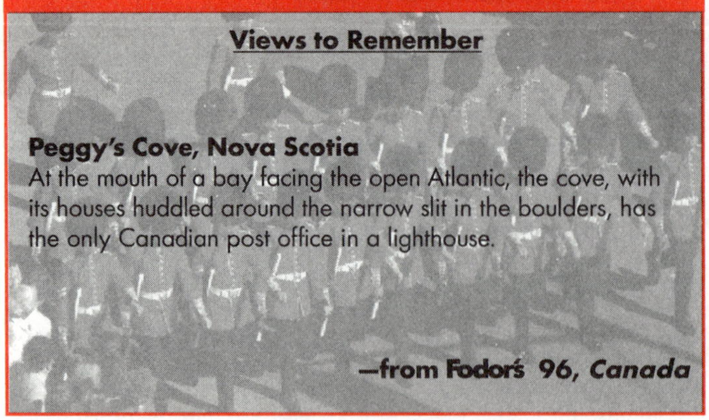

Views to Remember

Peggy's Cove, Nova Scotia
At the mouth of a bay facing the open Atlantic, the cove, with its houses huddled around the narrow slit in the boulders, has the only Canadian post office in a lighthouse.

—from Fodor's 96, *Canada*

of Fundy National Park, which runs along the famous bay of the same name. If nature and history aren't your cup of tea, you can always try Moncton Magic Mountain Water Park for splashing fun. ✓**AMERICA ONLINE**→*keyword* Traveler's Corner→International Profiles→Canada→New Brunswick

New Brunswick Official Touring Guide Among New Brunswick's claims to fame is its status as the second-largest exporter of peat moss in the world (Don't miss the Peat Moss Festival in July). The inventor of the ice cream cone hailed from Sussex Corner, and Nackawic has the largest ax in the world (15 meters). In addition to providing these fun facts about New Brunswick, this online guide also explores nature's power—the Bay of Fundy has the "highest and wildest" tides in the world, each rush equals the volume of the 24-hour flow of all the rivers in the world! You'll also find general travel information (including lodging) and four excellent scenic hypertours here. ✓**INTERNET**→*url* http://www.cuslm.ca/tourist/welcome.htm

New Brunswick Outdoor Adventures An advertisement for a company that organizes whale-watching, scuba, sailing, and kayaking trips. Get details here or fill out the email form for more info. ✓**INTERNET**→*url* http://www.csi.nb.ca/tourism/

Labrador Sportfish Limited Vince and Jim Burton want to help you land Atlantic salmon, speckled trout, and Arctic char. (Indeed this promotional page does show a guy holding a really big fish.) Find out about the company's tours at this Website. ✓**INTERNET**→*url* http://www.nfld.com/nfld/clients/jburton/index.html

Newfoundland Home Page Come here to discover the world of fishermen, cod balls, and rocky coast so vividly portrayed in Annie Prioux's *The Shipping News*. The Lure of Newfoundland section entices visitors northward, while information gathered from the rec.travel Library offers suggestions on B&Bs and the challenges of crossing the Trans-Labrador Highway (Many believe that no such road even exists.) An interactive map illuminates the history of the region; just click to visit Viking settlements or the relatively cosmopolitan joys of St. John's. ✓**INTERNET**→*url* http://www.compusult.nf.ca/nfld/tourism/tourism.html

Newfoundland Tourist Information This site offers all sorts of intriguing travel advice, including how best to avoid unpleasant encounters with fairies. ("Either never go in the woods alone, or if you do, wear odd socks and turn your sweaters inside out, and carry bread or silver coins in your pockets.") A glossary of Newfie terms lets you know to be perturbed if someone calls you an *angishore* (a weak, miserable person) and not to order *doter* if it appears on the menu (an old seal). There's a history lesson here too, as well as excellent hypertours through the lands wandered by Thorvald Eriksson early in the millennium. Regional information helps you book a room at any one of the hotels listed here. ✓**INTERNET**→*url* http://www.wordplay.com/tourism.html

Cape Breton Showcase Journey to this rockbound coast, home to hardy French and Scottish settlers for generations. This site exhibits local arts and handicrafts, but it also provides a list of local attractions and accommodations for interested visitors. ✓**INTERNET**→*url* http://www.webcom.com/~morandan/

Fortress of Louisberg Home Page Take a step back into the 18th century with a visit to this virtual version of a French fort on the east coast of Canada. Excerpted from a CD-ROM, this page presents QuickTime movies and pictorial histories of the Fortress of Louisberg and a tour of Cape Breton Island. Especially interesting are the sections detailing the intricate reconstruction of the fort and glimpses of 18th-century life and battles. ✓**INTERNET**→*url* http://eagle.uccb.ns.ca/~jhussey/owenfitz/home.html

MacPherson House, Nova Scotia A promotional page for a B&B that offers homemade jam to complement the toast mandated by the second "B." ✓**INTERNET**→*url* http://www.eucanect.com/tourism/mac-hous.html

The Greater Halifax Visitor Guide Just hop on the *Bluenose* in Bar Harbor, Maine, and head off for the attractions in Halifax. This site is packed with info for a night on the town—find out what's playing at the movies and the local clubs and how to book a pleasant B&B with ease. Several hypertext articles describe the city's culture and history. (If you arrive in July or August, be sure to stop by the City Hall for tea with the mayor.) ✓**INTERNET**→*url* http://ttg.sba.dal.ca/nstour/halifax/

Prince Edward Island Electronic Visitor's Guide A great hypertext tour, this site lets prospective visitors know where to hike, cycle, camp, and even eat in Canada's smallest province. Check out the new series of trails along old rail lines. ✓**INTERNET**→*url* http://www.gov.pe.ca/info/vg/

Northwest Territories

Fishing and Wilderness Adventures in Canada, Virtual North A promotional page for a company that helps you act on your fantasies of living like Grizzly Adams. Get previews of its tours and contact info here. ✓**INTERNET**→*url* http://pcs.mb.ca/~vnorth/vnorth.html

Northwest Territories Only the adventurous should head for the far north of Baffin Island suggests this guide. Those who do will certainly never forget the stunning landscape of Auyuittuq (the land that never melts) National Park, north of the Arctic Circle. Replete with tips to help you enjoy the area, the guide recommends caribou hunting, the hot springs at Nahanni National Park, and bringing lots of bug spray. ✓**AMERICA ONLINE**→*keyword* Traveler's Corner→International Profiles→Canada→Northwest Territories

Ontario

Ontario Traveler Get descriptions of Ontario's cities, including Toronto, Ottawa, Kingston, and Thunder Bay; each listing features sights you must visit and travel resources—especially for the business traveler. Helpful lists of dos and don'ts tell you to take proof of custody if divorced and traveling with your children, and not to be surprised if Ontario is quite hot in the summer. ✓**AMERICA ONLINE**→*keyword* Traveler's Corner→International Profiles→Canada→Ontario ✓**EWORLD**→*go* Travelers→U.S./Canada Profiles→Canada→Ontario

Cyberperk Pick up an address and description of services for this cybercafé located at 347 Dalhousie St. in Ottawa. ✓**INTERNET**...→*email* cyberperk@cyberperk.com ✍ *Email with general correspondence*...→*url* http://www.cyberperk.com/cyberper/home.htm

Ottawa Travel Guide Rumor has it that Queen Victoria selected Ottawa as the nation's capital by closing her eyes and pointing at a map. You might want slightly more guidance if you are planning a trip to Ottawa, so a visit to this site with information on Ottawa's hotels, restaurants, events, and transportation might be in order. ✓**INTERNET**→*url* http://www.solutions.net/rec-travel/north_america/canada/ontario/ottawa.html

Ottawa X Press Ottawa has the reputation of being one of the most boring capital cites worldwide. This online entertainment weekly endeavors to change that reputation with weekly listings of events and reviews of film festivals and concerts, picks of promising nightspots, and steamy personals (Capital Connections) for your reading pleasure. ✓**INTERNET**→*url* http://resudox.net/paper/xpress.html

Ottawa-Canada's Capital Get online, take a virtual tour of Ottawa, and see Rideau Canal (during winter it freezes and becomes a seven-mile skating rink), the House of Commons and Parliament buildings, Royal Mounted Police, and the famous Tulip Festival—one of the most-acclaimed tulip festivals outside the Netherlands. Very little information, however, accompanies the images. ✓**INTERNET**→*url* http://www.scs.carleton.ca/ottawa/ottawa.html

eye.Net An online publication about Toronto's art and nightlife scenes. If you want to know about gallery openings, hot local bands, the club of the moment, or where you can see Crispin Glover (think *Back to the Future*), check here first. ✓**INTERNET**→*url* http://www.interlog.com/eye/

Road Trips from Toronto As pleasant as Toronto is to visit, it's always nice to take an excursion into the countryside. Maps and directions will guide you to the Niagara Falls region (also known as the source of those wonderful Canadian wines), Sand Banks, Warsaw Caves, and Algonquin Park. Descriptions of longer trips

Ontario's Hog's Back Falls—http://www.scs.carleton.ca/ottawa/ottawa.html

tell you how to journey to Québec, the Maritime Provinces, and Boston. ✓INTERNET→*url* http://www.io.org/~acbatek/roadtrip.htm

Subway Navigator TV scenes that depict New York City's subway are often filmed in the Toronto system—the trash, grime, and crime are added for effect. Find your way through the tubes with the info listed here in English and French. ✓INTERNET→*url* http://metro.jussieu.fr:10001/bin/select/english/canada/toronto

Toronto Web Learn all about Toronto here, from its early history to its modern incarnation. When done with your studies, take a virtual tour, available in thumbnail or JPEG format, and ride to the top of the CN Tower (the world's tallest structure—1,835 feet!), explore City Hall, roam through Eaton Centre, or slam into the Hockey Hall of Fame. You can also find listings of hotels, restaurants, and nightspots, and a list of attractions for the kids. ✓INTERNET→*url* http://torweb.com/overview/overview.htm

Québec

Bonjour Québec In addition to hotel and lodging information, you'll find maps, photos, and descriptions of sightseeing attractions in Québec listed here. Plan your Québec vacation with the site's info on the cities of Montréal and Québec, the Gaspé Peninsula, and hiking in the Laurentians, among other highlights. ✓INTERNET→*url* http://www.roblyn.com/tourque/quehome.htm

CyberHotel In English or en Français, select your criteria for accommodations within the province (including the Laurentians and the Gaspé), such as price (in Canadian $), city, amenities (such as view, fireplace, or TV), and activities offered. The database then provides you with the names of hotels that match your wishes. The database is bilingual, so be prepared for the information to go back and forth between English and French. ✓INTERNET→*url* http://www.cyberhotel.com/hotelsqc/

The Montreal skyline at dusk—http://www.roblyn.com/tourque/montreal.htm

soc.culture.québec (ng) Discussion here is primarily in French (preserving French culture is a big issue in Québec). Debates rage on about the recent referendum to determine if Québec should secede from Canada. Zeljko votes yes (for distinct status), as Québec can then determine its future as it pleases; Susan votes against secession, fearing violence in the aftermath. Denis responds to her (English) posting in French, taking a different stance. If politics isn't for you, the opportunities to practice your French are excellent. ✓USENET→soc.culture.québec

Café Electronique Check into this cybercafé and get online with any of its 70 terminals. The café's menu and address are at the Website. ✓INTERNET ...→*email* café@infobahnos.com ✍ *Email with general correspondence* ...→*url* http://www.infobahnos.com/~café/

Montréal Metro A site featuring a beautiful map of the island city's subway. While you have the option of English or French maps, the station names on both are in French. ✓INTERNET→*url* http://www.cityvu.com/HTM/MTLMETRO.HTM

Montréal Museum of Fine Arts The museum's permanent collection, which emphasizes modern Canadian and European art, is online here; images shown here are cross-referenced with an index of artists. ✓INTERNET→*url* http://www.interax.net/tcenter/tour/mba.html

The Story of Montréal Did you know that Montréal is the largest French-speaking city in the world after Paris? This is among the many facts you can discover here. The history and architecture of the city are featured; enjoy a virtual tour with wonderful JPEGs—especially of Vieux Montréal (the old city). Tourist information is offered on sightseeing tours and sights, such as Ile Ste-Hélène, the Place des Arts, Museum of Fine Arts, and the Chateau de Ramezay. ✓INTERNET→*url* http://www.cam.org/~fishon1/montrea.html

Québec Sur Scène *Practiquons ton Français mes amis*—the text here is all in French. If you can read it, you'll be presented with a daily schedule of Québec City's entertainment events, which might be rock or jazz concerts, theater performances, variety shows, or film festivals on any given day. ✓**INTERNET**→*url* http://www.clic.net/surscene/

Web Québec The opening page of this site shows the famous Le Chateau Frontenac, Québec City's landmark hotel built in 1893. After selecting to proceed in English or French, you have the electronic magazine's menu to guide you. If you haven't made hotel reservations for your trip yet, do that here. Many wonderful cafés are previewed, and the site also takes you on a tour of the old walled city, museums, the Citadel, and the old port. Information on the above, as well as on nightlife, gay spots, and day trips, is available. ✓**INTERNET**→*url* http://www.megatoon.com/web-Québec/

Saskatchewan

Saskatchewan Photo Gallery Photos of people, cities, and wildlife in this prairie province are here; see if you can identify the animals, meet young people at the university in Saskatoon, and see why Regina is nicknamed Queen City. ✓**INTERNET** ...→*url* http://www.cs.usask.ca/tourist/saskatchewan.html ...→*url* http://www.uskX.ca/~lowey/saskatoon/about_saskatoon/pictures.html ...→*url* http://calypso.cs.uregina.ca/Regina/AboutRegina/photogall.html

Saskatchewan Towns and Cities See the province from the eyes of the locals who maintain these Web pages. Here is where you will find inside info on events, lodgings, and restaurants in Regina (originally named Pile of Bones), Saskatoon, and other local towns. ✓**INTERNET**→*url* http://duke.usask.ca/~lowey/Saskatchewan/cities/index.html

Saskatoon Star Phoenix The daily paper for Saskatoon, Saskatchewan (Say that three times fast). Learn what's going on in the City of Bridges, hear about regional issues, and ponder whether Québec's possible secession will make this the new Canadian hot spot. ✓**INTERNET**→*url* http://www.wbm.ca/users/sphoenix/index.html

Scotty Don't look for the Starship *Enterprise*'s engineer here. This virtual page is devoted to Saskatchewan's beloved Tyrannasaurus Rex, Scotty, who was unearthed near Eastend in the Valley of Hidden Secrets. If you've become disenchanted with Barney, get to know a real dinosaur for a change. ✓**INTERNET**→*url* http://herald.usask.ca/~scottp/scotty/scotty.html

Yukon

Yukon Board The first road all the way through this territory was built during World War II to forestall a Japanese invasion. The area is so expansive, no road had conquered it before then, and so you shouldn't feel bad if you need a little help making your way through the Yukon! Read this useful guide, which suggests stopping en route to the north at the Native American town of Burwash Landing. Or relive *The Call of the Wild* in the almost-ghost gold rush town of Dawson City, where the area's gold-panning championship is held every four years. Pay special attention to the dos and don'ts of the Yukon—make sure to take lots of cash, try some reindeer sausage, but don't feed the bears. ✓**AMERICA ONLINE**→*keyword* Traveler's Corner→International Profiles→Canada→Yukon

Yukon Web Services According to this Website, the Yukon sports "six caribou per person and a grizzly bear for every family of five." If you're not dropping everything to head up there right now, come to the page and read more about the adventures that await you in the Yukon. If you decide to make the trip, the site suggests 12 different itineraries for everything from ski expeditions to RV trips, each with a list of great trail or roadside attractions and the numbers and names to set them in motion. ✓**INTERNET**→*url* http://www.wimsey.com/yukon

Ottawa's tulips—http://www.scs.carleton.ca/ottawa/ottawa.html

Part 8

Theme Travel

Amusement parks

Everyone knows Disney World, that paradise of theme park fun. Decades after Walt Disney's decease, his dream lives on, in Orlando, in Anaheim, and on the Net—where domestic sites like the **Walt Disney World Home Page** and the **Disneyland FAQ** help parents answer questions about that upcoming trip to the Magic Kingdom, and international sites like **Tokyo Disneyland** prove that kids the world over can get a little Goofy if they're given the opportunity. And if you fear Walt's corporate megalith, there are plenty of other theme park sites online, from **Valley Fair** to **Sea World/ Busch Gardens**.

Nixon & Disney at the Monorail opening—from http://www.ni-inc.com/~dsmith/

On the Net

Across the board

Coaster Cover This site is dedicated to those souls for whom a stomach-jolting drop, and several minutes of sheer terror are the nearest thing to Nirvana they will ever reach. Here you can search for a particular coaster by name, park, state, type, or designer (fan of Ron Toomer or Anton Schwarzkopf?). Check out the coaster chat on rec.roller-coaster or find out from the FAQ where the local coaster fan club meets. ✓**INTERNET**→*url* http://sunsite.unc.edu/darlene/coaster/coaster.html

rec.roller-coaster (ng) Turn here to find out which coaster is the steepest (the Ultra Twister at Astroworld in Houston) and which is the fastest (Steel Phantom at Kennywood in Pennsylvania). Foreign coasters offering other significant thrills include Canada's Mindbender, which has the highest G-force, and the Port Aventura in Spain, which has the most inversions. Contact information for coaster societies worldwide is also provided. ✓**USENET**→rec.roller-coaster ***FAQ:*** ✓**INTERNET**→*url* http://www.cis.ohio-state.edu/hypertext/faq/bngusenet/rec/roller-coaster/top.html

Theme Park Board Do you get dizzy with excitement when you think about Disney World? Are you just counting the minutes until your next ride on the water slide at Valleyfair in Minnesota? Or are you still fretting about the fate of the freak show at Coney Island? You'll find ample company with whom to discuss any theme park in the world at this page. ✓**PRODIGY**→*jump* travel bb→theme parks

Disney

Disney Board Erin wonders if the $1,650+ trip to the Magic Kingdom with her two children is worth the money. Unfortunately responses shout "yes!" and suggest hitting Epcot too. Come here to find out which seasons have the shortest lines and to gather other useful tips. Since a trip to Disney World seems to be a must for every American family (at least once), there are always plenty of people here willing to give advice about visiting the American mecca. ✓**AMERICA ONLINE**→*keyword* travel forum→travel boards→U.S.traveler →disney world

Disney World Disney's official site contains profiles of all the attractions of the Magic Kingdom,

Epcot Center, and Disney-MGM Studios. But the real bonus here is the Vacation Planner, which helps you decide between the luxury of the Grand Floridian Resort and the rustic charms of camping at Fort Wilderness. You can even book online. Everything you need to manage your visit, including maps, tips on handicapped access at Disney, and lists of dining and shopping opportunities, is at your fingertips. With a visit to the message boards, you can even get the lowdown from fellow travelers on the restaurant at the Polynesian Resort and the Disney golf course. ✓**AMERICA ONLINE**→*keyword* disney

Disneyland FAQ Don't head into Tomorrowland unprepared! This FAQ provides the current year's prices, opening hours, and a brief synopsis of the major attractions. This site also notes ride maintenance schedules and new additions. ✓**INTERNET**→*url* http://www.cis.ohio-state.edu/hypertext/faq/usenet/disney-faq/disneyland/faq.html

Disneyland Paris Forget that boring old Louvre and head to Space Mountain instead. Everything anyone ever wanted to know about the park is here—hours, ticket prices, and even what types of souvenirs are for sale. The Web page's FAQ answers the really important questions—what does Disneyland Paris have that its counterparts don't? (Answer: Le Taniere du Dragon, for one.) And do the ghosts at Phantom Manor speak English? (No.) The only thing you can't find out here is where to buy EuroDisney stock, but that might be a blessing in disguise. ✓**INTERNET**→*url* http://www.informatik.tu-muenchen.de/cgi-bin/nph-gateway/hphalle1/~schaffnr/etc/disney/

Disneyland Park, Anaheim, California Many will come to this excellent site to plan their assault (it may feel like an assault with two ten-year-olds and a toddler in tow) on America's oldest wonderland. Many will visit the site for excellent suggestions here from Disneyland pros—including what times of day are best for avoiding lines. Still others will stop at the Web page for maps of the park's shops, rides, other attractions, and—most important—its rest rooms. But all will discover that this page is an unparalleled source on all things Disney, even offering the unexpected delight of a recipe for Walt's Chili in the Disneyland Recipe Collection. ✓**INTERNET**→*url* http://www.best.com/~dijon/disney/parks/disneyland/

Disneyland Pictures No grown-ups will block your view of the Lion King Parade at this site! With the excellent photos at this page, you'll get a clear shot at the really big shows and new attractions. Currently the centerpiece of the site is a presentation on the new Indiana Jones Temple of the Forbidden Eye ride. Besides pictures of the ride, you'll get an Indy FAQ that tells you what happens on the ride from beginning to end and hands out spoilers for those who don't want to be unpleasantly surprised. ✓**INTERNET**→*url* http://sdcc13.ucsd.edu/~jakeller/DLpics.html

Disneymania Look in the libraries here for maps and all the Mickey .GIFs you can stand. Additional articles in the library profile each Disney resort for discriminating Disneygoers. After reading up in the library, head over to the Disneymania topic on the message boards where the debate rages over the relative merits of MGM Studios and Universal Studios. Or just meet like-minded people whose fondest wish is to spend Christmas with their cartoon pals. (The Liberty Tree Tavern

Fodor's Choice...

The Magic Kingdom

With the steepest drop of any flume ride in existence, Splash Mountain makes you feel like Wile E. Coyote as you head over that final hang-onto-your-hat moment.

—from Fodor's *Walt Disney World, Universal Studios and Orlando*

offers a delicious turkey dinner!) ✓**COMPUSERVE**→*go* florida→Messages *and* Libraries→Disneymania

Indiana Jones Adventure, Temple of the Forbidden Eye Grab your handy archeologist's felt hat and your bullwhip (doesn't everyone have one?) and head for Disney's much touted new thrill-ride. Discover a full preview of what the site's creator calls a cross between Star Tours, Pirates of the Caribbean, and Mr. Toad's Wild Ride. ✓**INTERNET**→*url* http://www.perry.com/disney/indy/indy.html

Tokyo Disneyland Tokyo Disneyland's attractions, as well as schedules and travel information, are all outlined here. If you're not planning a trip to the Japanese park, you might still enjoy the online visit to an American Small Town or the Wild West. ✓**INTERNET**→*url* http://www.toyo-eng.co.jp/NewHome/Messe/UsefulInfo/Play/TDL/index-e.html

Walt Disney World Home Page Welcome to Walt Disney World's official Web home. View the joys of Splash Mountain or the World of Energy here in full-color glory. Not only the Magic Kingdom and Epcot Center, but also Typhoon Lagoon and Disney-MGM Studios await all, full of fun. Make reservations for a dream vacation right online—you can book a week at the Polynesian Resort and order Magic Kingdom passports from the comfort of your own home. ✓**INTERNET**→*url* http://www.travelweb.com/thisco/wdw/wdwhome/wdw.html

Yesterland Does Disneyland seem different from the way it was when Aunt Ida took you there in 1969? That could be because it is. Now the only way you can ride the Mine Train and Rocket to the Moon or visit the Indian Village is online. Wax nostalgic with this illustrated homage to thrills gone by. ✓**INTERNET**→*url* http://www.mcs.net/~werner/yester.html

U.S. parks

Bellmont Park "Free Park Admission," proclaims the home page of this venerable beach park in San Diego. Find out here how to celebrate its 75th anniversary through a brief list of attractions and several alluring photos of fireworks and crashing waves. ✓**INTERNET**→*url* http://www.well.com/user/niche/belmont.htm

Cedar Point, Sandusky, Ohio Does flying down a twisty track at death-defying speeds while standing upright in a tiny train car sound fun to you? Then you'll enjoy the info here about Cedar Point's newest attraction—the stand-up roller coaster. Although this page isn't an "official" site, it has its finger on the pulse of Ohio's favorite fun-spot. Here you'll find rumors about park expansion, plucked from the loose lips of employees. (A 300-foot tall Super Mega Coaster and offsite parking in Sandusky are in the works. WOW.) Full travel and accommodations info is also included. ✓**INTERNET**→*url* http://shipofools.lit.cwru.edu/cpintro.htm

Coney Island Circus Sideshow Even though a McDonald's now occupies this show's former home, the "freaks, wonders and human curiosities" are still available to inquiring minds. Visit this promotional site for the last 10 in 1 (ten acts for one price) circus in the world and learn more about Electra, The High Voltage Lady, Kiva, The Fire Eater and Human Volcano, and Indestructible Indio, The Escape Artist and Pain-Proof Man. Come one, come all...get price and location info here. There's even an email address for the barker. ✓**INTERNET**→*url* http://dockmaster.phantom.com/coney/pages/sideshow.html

Idlewild Park Overview, Ligonier, PA Heading down to Route 30 near Ligonier, Pennsylvania looking for a good time? Why not take a ride on the Wild Mouse at Idlewild Amusement Park? Get a sneak preview of the steel tubular roller coaster and of other park attractions like the Black Widow Spider, Fairy Tale Land, and the Extreme Elements Sports Challenge. Operating hours and contact information are also provided. ✓**INTERNET**→*url* http://

www.pitt.edu/~trmst11/idlewild.html

Marine World Africa USA Come face to face with the creatures of the deep at Marine World Africa USA's home page. Snapshots of the sea stars are here—dolphins, killer whales, and sea lions. There are also brief descriptions of underwater tours that boast a tropical reef and "feared predators." The Africa portion of the park features Bengal tigers and elephant rides (just like Kenya). Contact information and schedules for this Vallejo, California attraction are provided. ✓**INTERNET**→*url* http://www.freerun.com/napaval ley/outdoor/marinewo/marinewo .html

Schlitterbahn Waterpark & Resorts, Texas Deep in the desert heart of Texas lies a massive waterpark (65 acres of slides, chutes, and soggy Texans). Find out more about the special attractions of Schlitterbahn—including the only uphill water coaster in the world—at this site. ✓**INTERNET**→*url* http://www.schlitterbahn.com/

Sea World/Busch Gardens Sea World's site is truly impressive—it's packed with information about the animals and their watery world. Kids can head here to write a report for school and parents will enjoy knowing that their theme park choice has real educational value. Shamu's even available to answer aquatic questions online. In terms of practical travel information, you'll have to make do with addresses and phone numbers. ✓**INTERNET**→*url* http://www.bev.net/education/SeaWorld/homepage.html

Valleyfair Shakopee, Minnesota has more than cows to brag about. It's got the Hydroblaster—a super-duper water coaster. (Perhaps a winter visit is unwise.) Find out about Valleyfair's other rides and park admission prices. ✓**INTERNET**→*url* http://www.tgimaps.com/MPLS/VALLEYFAIR/valley fair.html

International

Huis ten Bosch, Japan *Goedenmiddag!* Welcome to *Huis ten Bosch*, a picture-perfect Dutch village complete with canals, windmills, and even a *Breukelen*. This village is nowhere near The Hague—it's in Nagasaki. Find out all about this popular attraction at the Website, which can even help you book a room at the Hotel Amsterdam in Japan. ✓**INTERNET**→*url* http://www.bekkoame.or.jp/~suga/htbe1.html

Paramount Canada's Wonderland Paramount offers a greater variety of roller coaster experiences than any amusement park anywhere. Choose from the 33 described here, complete with manufacturer, track type, length, time, and the year of construction (very important). Find out all about the other thrills that can be experienced (and how much they cost) at this park north of Toronto. Email for more information. ✓**INTERNET**→*url* http://www.canada.ibm.net:80/wonderland/w

Thundering Sierra Tired of just hanging around on some beach along the Adriatic? (Most people wouldn't feel to sorry for you.). Then try Mirabilandia, home of Thundering Sierra, the tallest wooden roller coaster in Europe. (It makes the Cyclone at Coney Island look like a bike with training wheels!) The park also has some exciting water rides for those hot Italian summer afternoons. Get more information on the park and its laser and fireworks shows at this site, which also carries great pictures of people on coasters with their mouths hanging open!) ✓**INTERNET**→ *url* http://www.linknet.it/mi rabilandia/

Bizarre tours

There's a lot more available to travelers than Club Med. In fact, there's a whole great big wacky world out there, some of it pleasantly tasteless. Tired of rubbing elbows with the rich and famous at Biarritz? Why not try the **White Trash Tour of the United States**? Threaten the kids with a trip to **Alcatraz** or a kiss from a toothsome reptile at the **Everglades Alligator Farm**. The romantic (or deep) will enjoy pondering the immensity of the universe at the **Centro de Observacão Astrónomica no Algarve** in Spain, and contemplating the end of the universe at a few of the stops recommended by **The Bureau of Atomic Tourism**. You'll be proud to show off the t-shirt proving you've been to a really exotic destination—**Wall Drug**, the **Haunted Verdun Manor**, or **Graceland**.

The foreboding Alcatraz Island— from http://www.csulb.edu/gc/libarts/am-indian/

On the Net

United States

A Tourist Trap on the Info Highway If you can't afford a vacation this year, the Tacky Tourist Club of America's Seattle Chapter has assembled a virtual tour of a petting zoo (where you can pet a pygmy goat). For a souvenir of your virtual trip, order a "We Visited the Internet Petting Zoo" bumper sticker online! ✓**INTERNET**→*url* http://www.halcyon.com/robin/ttca/welcome .html

Alcatraz A sound file of Leon "Whitey" Thompson, prisoner number AZ1465, welcomes you to his former humble home—commonly known as "the Rock," "Hellcatraz," or "Uncle Sam's Devil's Island." An excellent illustrated tour walks visitors through all aspects of Alcatraz's history—from its time as a fort to its occupation by the American Indian Movement from 1969 to 1971. Surprises make the online Alcatraz experience seem real—a QuickTime movie runs you along a famous escape route to the sound of sirens. If all this whets your appetite for the real thing, contact information from the National Park Service (which maintains the island) is included. ✓**INTERNET**→*url* http://www.nps.gov/alcatraz/

Everglades Alligator Farm Did you know that the sex of baby alligators can be influenced by the temperature at which the eggs are kept? Learn even more about our ominous gator friends at this Homestead, Florida, farm, where they let the unwary hold and kiss the inhabitants. The farm also sponsors airboat tours through the critters' natural swampy home—the Florida Everglades. For tour descriptions, directions, and an email address for the farm, stop here. ✓**INTERNET**→*url* http://florida.com/gatorfarmer/

Graceland We're going to Graceland, Graceland, Memphis, Tennessee. If the home of the King is part of your travel plans, get a preview here. Net travel guru Philip Greenspun provides photos and commentary—on the Jungle Room, the various portraits of Elvis in the house, and other highlights. ✓**INTERNET**→*url* http://www-swiss.ai.mit.edu/summer94/grace

land.html

Haunted Verdun Manor Every town has one, and in Forney, Texas, the haunted house is Verdun Manor. Get a tour of the house from the mummies of Michael Verdun and his cyanotic wife, Cassandra, and see the pleasures of the house, including reenactments of "painful experiments performed on human beings abducted from the surrounding countryside." (Uh-huh.) Verdun's home page gives directions to Forney. ✓**INTERNET**→*url* http://www.webcom.com/~verdun/verdun.html

Hidden Mickeys at Walt Disney World They're slipping people Mickeys all over Disney World! Join Tim Shaw and his family in their relentless search for hidden Mickey motifs all over Disney World. Read the Mickey-hunting FAQ, see examples of hidden Mickeys—the bridles of the horses on Main Street USA, shadows from the railing of Cinderella's Castle at mid-morning, in a mural at the Chinese Pavilion in Epcot—and think about hunting for mice yourself. (Additions to the list are welcome and confirmed by other Disneyphiles.) ✓**INTERNET**→*url* http://bb.iu.net/tshaw/trs/HiddenMickey.html

Minin' Gold: The Recreational Gold Prospecting and Mining Page You won't find any secret treasure maps at this site, but you will get a list of locations in California that have been known to produce some of the shiny stuff. The site offers information on the American River, Alpha's Diggins, and other spots in Northern California where all that glitters is actually gold. ✓**INTERNET**→*url* http://www.dnai.com:80/gold/

Route 66 Get your kicks along the most famous of American roadways. This informational site was put together by a European fan of pop culture who could find almost no information on the route (recently designated a National Historic Trail). If you don't have the time or the convertible to drive the whole route, there is an excellent interactive map, which supplies photos, "must-sees," and connections for further information. Help preserve our national highway history by joining one of the Route 66 Associations listed here, or buy a 66 video in the online gift shop. Editor's Recommendation: the TeePee Motel in Gallup, New Mexico. ✓**INTERNET**→*url* http://www.cs.kuleuven.ac.be/~swa/route66/main.html

The White Trash Tour A tour for those who love to eat pork rinds, marry their cousins, and watch monster-truck rallies—or those who aspire to do those things. Suggested stops include San Clemente (Tricky Dick's Hometown), the Circle K all-night store in Globe, Arizona, The KC East Truck Stop in Kansas City, Missouri, the Coors Brewery in Golden, Colorado, and the Happy Time Pub in Savonlinna, Finland (for those globe-trotting white trash). Unfortunately, there are no addresses or phone numbers listed for any of the attractions. ✓**INTERNET**→*url* http://marigold.colorado.edu/~arbetter/whitetrash.html

Wall Drug, South Dakota Anyone who has ever driven I-90 through South Dakota probably remembers what seemed like thousands of signs announcing the glories of Wall Drug—rumor has it there are now Wall Drug signs in Shanghai and Paris. The Website tells you exactly how to get to Wall Drug. ✓**INTERNET**→*url* http://www.state.sd.us/state/executive/tourism/20reason/wall.htm

International

A Tourist Expedition to Antarctica Amateur explorer Lee Liming boarded the Marco Polo on January 26, 1994, bound for the coldest adventure of his life—a month-long cruise to Antarctica. A detailed journal of his trip is at this site

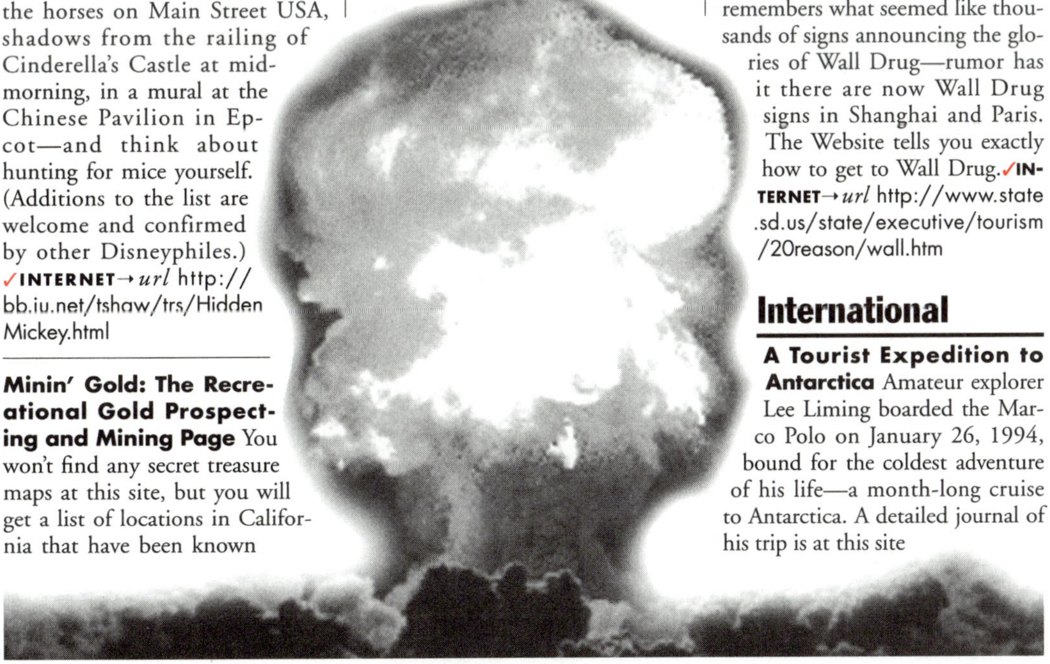

along with a host of pictures (many of them are almost entirely white). There are schematics of the ship and quotes from a Marco Polo promotional brochure, but no info on how to contact Orient, its mother line. ✓**INTERNET**→*url* http://http2.sils.umich.edu/Antarctica/Story.html

Calendar of Pyrotechnic Events OOOOOOOH! Love a good fireworks show? Look no further than this worldwide calendar of noisy and scenic events and plan accordingly. December brings the Natchitoches Festival, Louisiana's annual fancy-fireworks display; in February pyrotechnic clubs gather in Lake Havasu City, Arizona; the spectacle on the last Saturday of July in Gifu City, Japan, is not to be missed. A link to the Pyro Page is provided for those with more than a passing interest in things that burn. ✓**INTERNET**→*url* http://tad1.cit.cornell.edu/Tom/Pyro/PyroCalendar.html

Centro de Observação Astronómica no Algarve The perfect place to wish upon a star—billed as an "astronomy holiday center," the observatory in the Algarve region of Portugal offers an unobstructed view of Omega Centauri in the spring, all of Scorpio in the fall, and an excellent library. Choose from full- or part-time room and board packages, and fill the days with golfing, bird-watching, and beach-bumming. A hypertext essay elaborates on the highlights of this unique vacation opportunity, and the site offers booking by email. ✓**INTERNET**→*url* http://www.emoticon.com/astro/coaa.html

Fly With Us! This company lets you fly at 9gs over Moscow in a *MiG-29UB*. After a physical, you and your pilot climb into your g-suits and away you go. You may even take the controls and perform aerial tricks according to "your comfort." Read all about this service at the Website. ✓**INTERNET**→*url* http://www.intnet.net/mig29/brochure.html

One of Verdun Manor's werewolves—http://www.webcom.com/~verdun/verdun.html

The Bureau of Atomic Tourism In the recent words of the French foreign minister—"Don't think of it as a bomb, think of it as a device that explodes." The Bureau of Atomic Tourism is dedicated to preserving the history of the "more bang for the buck," "missile gap" mentality. Here you'll find a list of museums dedicated to the likes of the Titan missile and the creation of plutonium-239. You can even visit a breeder reactor! Of course, what would atomic tourism be without the sites—Nagasaki, Hiroshima, and Trinity Flats. Full travel information is included at the Website—rest assured there are hot dogs for sale at Trinity Flats. And helpful warnings are posted like "Don't take pieces of glass created by the heat of the explosion home as souvenirs." ✓**INTERNET**→*url* http://www.oz.net/~chrisp/atomic.html

The Kolding Submarine Center Some unemployed Dutch youth got together and asked Gorbachev for a used Whiskey-class Russian submarine in 1992—and he gave it to them. Now the U-359 is a tourist attraction and a symbol of peace floating in Kolding harbor. Take a virtual tour of the sub and learn how to contact the Center at this site. ✓**INTERNET**→*url* http://man-ray.mit.edu/www/Kolding/U359.html

Whale Watching Web This collection of links takes whale watchers to the home pages of whale-watching tour operators worldwide. You'll have a whale of a time watching off the coast of Alaska, Japan, or Antarctica. ✓**INTERNET**→*url* http://www.physics.helsinki.fi/whale/

Outdoors

On your last few family vacations, things haven't gone all that well. The kids got claustrophobic sitting in the car, the motel beds were lumpy, and your husband ate his way through Colonial Williamsburg. You feel like fighting that inertia is an uphill climb. Turn that frustration into a battle plan—go outdoors and climb uphill. The Net is full of exciting resources for the active at heart, from general sites like **Worldwide Trekking Adventures** to local climbing pages, both national (**Grand Canyon River Running**) and international (**Victoria Ranges Rock Climbing Centre**). And when you're turning mountains into molehills, pack up those pitons and head over to the **Kilimanjaro Climb**. Or just relax in the nation's own backyard—the **National Park Service Home Page** opens the door to the 300-plus areas set aside for America's outdoor enjoyment.

A view of Chaco Canyon, New Mexico—from http://www.chaco.com/park/index.html

On the Net

Across the board

Backcountry Home Page Spend a lot of time here, and you might end up scratching virtual chigger bites. Updated frequently, the site has a good news section: everything from heater recalls to Bigfoot sightings is duly noted. Anyone for whitewater rafting or ice climbing? Link to Gear Reviews and Recommendations to find information on which mittens will help you keep your grip. And then there are the FAQs, which offer advice on several difficult situations that arise when bonding with nature. How, for instance, do you deal with acute mountain sickness, giardiasis, and bears? Find out here. For real beginners the Learning It link has perhaps the most important backcountry advice—how not to get lost and what to do if you do. Looking for trudging companions? Check out the list of hiking clubs. Thinking of hiking on an exotic trail? Traverse trip reports and explore the Places of Interest link. The site also carries a backpacking checklist, a survey of camping food, and a wilderness test. Which is slowest? A grizzly, Carl Lewis, or a pronghorn antelope? If you spend a lot of time in the woods, you may need to know. ✓**INTERNET**→*url* http://io.datasys.swri.edu/Overview.html

Colin E. Johnson's Backcountry Page "Don't Fence Me In," proclaims nature aficionado Colin E. Johnson. His site certainly doesn't, providing numerous links to related Websites like the National Park Service, backwoods schooling, and outdoor FAQs. It's a great starting point for outdoor adventuring. ✓**INTERNET**→*url* http://www.css.itd.umich.edu/users/colinj/backcountry.html

GORP—Great Outdoor Recreation Pages Thinking of a trip that doesn't include a Hilton and a hairdryer? GORP undoubtedly is the best source of outdoor information on the Web. These intertwined pages of Net links provide tons of information for trip planning and some useful outdoor advice. Use the club and organization pages to find adventures close to home. GORP pages are wide-ranging—physically as well as topically—covering even Antarctica. If you want to stay within our borders, there are plenty of descriptions of everything our great nation has preserved for us—wildlife refuges, battlefields, parks, forests, and monuments, too. Links connect to hiking, biking, climbing, fishing, skiing, paddle sports, and bird watching sites! Gear Information helps adventurers get outfitted and helps simplify foreign travel with articles like "Alternative Fuel Names" (is essence C the same as kerosene?). GORP is also home to the Adventurous Travel Bookstore, a searchable database of 1,200-plus books and maps, with an online ordering facility. This outdoors site is so complete that, along with health advice on how to handle poison oak, snake bites, and tainted water, it provides connections to the World Health Organization's traveler's advisories and the Medical College of Wisconsin. ✓**INTERNET** →*url* http://www.gorp.com/

Great Outdoors Forum Are llamas the hiking wave of the future? Are guns a constitutional right? Will it really dissuade a bear from making you his lunch if you spray him with pepper spray as if he's some big backwoods mugger? Talk about where to catch the cacti in bloom or what the best bargains are in outdoor gear and freeze-dried foods in this forum dedicated to the great outdoors. ✓**COMPUSERVE**→*go* outdoorforum

---

Outdoor Activities Forum On the message board at this forum, listen in as a sea scout from Scotland chats with an Eagle Scout from Florida about canoeing. Or join in a discussion with motorboat owners about the relative merits of single vs. twin engines. And, on a different message topic, a traveling salesman proclaims his love of birdwatching. As long as it takes place somewhere beyond the range of formica and wall-to-wall carpeting, it's fair game for this forum. ✓**COMPUSERVE**→*go* climbing

---

Outdoor Adventure Online Every day is the same. You take the 8:10 a.m. from Rye into your job in Midtown...but, wait. It doesn't have to be that way. A whole world of adventure is waiting at Outdoor Adventure Online. Start planning your outdoor getaway by browsing the site's top-20 favorite adventure tours. Backcountry dogsledding in Wyoming? Kayak touring in Thailand? Ballooning in Burgundy, France? All sound great, but don't miss the page's calendar, which may hold the perfect once-in-a-lifetime event for you—an ostrich race, a killer triathalon, or the wild woman Snowboard Camp. Meet up with others of your ilk through the list of clubs and groups. Topics from trekking to polar bear safaris are covered and include safety advice and reviews of guide services. Once you've settled on an adventure, peruse the site's news for updates on wilderness medicine and travel restrictions. Outfit yourself with a new tent only after reading the great gear reviews in the library. And when you've settled on a Wild West dude ranch experience, simply head to the Destinations section and retrieve the number for Frying Pan River Ranch. You're on your way to saddle sores. ✓**AMERICA ONLINE**→*key word* outdoor adventure online

---

Outside Online A mammoth Website with slick graphics devoted to outdoors activities. Come here to commune with nature-related magazines, event calendars, stores, and links. Created by the same people who brought you the Satchel Sports pages. ✓**INTERNET**→ *url* http://web2.starwave.com:80/outside/

Adventure travel

Adventure Travel Directory This site is for the seriously hardy. Rugged outdoors people find links to scuba, fishing, and biking info—all sports and fixations are served here. Search for adventure by location, too—how about ice

Fodor's Choice...

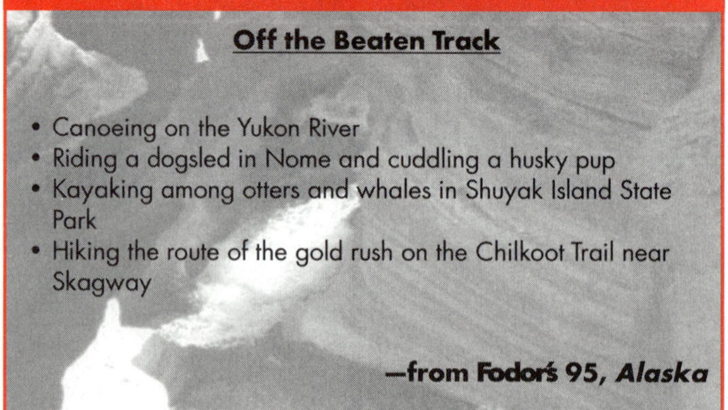

Off the Beaten Track

- Canoeing on the Yukon River
- Riding a dogsled in Nome and cuddling a husky pup
- Kayaking among otters and whales in Shuyak Island State Park
- Hiking the route of the gold rush on the Chilkoot Trail near Skagway

—from Fodor's 95, *Alaska*

climbing in Norway or an Amazon canoe trip? If nature's your game, there's a wealth of links to environmental and educational associations and ecotour operators. Plus you can get outfitted online through links to stores that sell ice picks and insect repellant. Start any cyberadventure here. ✓**INTERNET**→*url* http://ecotravel.com/

Adventurous Traveler Bookstore Map List Order maps of trails up Kilimanjaro, through the Mayan ruins of the Yucatán Peninsula, or to many other places. ✓**INTERNET**→*url* http://www.gorp.com/atb/maps.htm

The Avid Explorer The guide to cruising is the highlight of this travel agency's page. Who could refuse a 13-day adventure on the tall ship *Mandalay* in the Windward Isles? The site also has details about the kinds of vacations taken by the rich and famous. How does breakfast delivered by canoe in Moorea sound? ✓**INTERNET**→*url* http://www.explore.com/

The Polar Regions Home Page Find out here about the hottest new vacation destinations. First get acquainted with the local residents—bears, seals, penguins (and scientists). Get serious by linking to scientific explorations of the regions—block of ice in the north, great white fields in the south. There are even live links to research stations. Once you're fully acclimatized, you can get travel information for the beginner's polar regions in Alaska, Norway, and Canada, or head right to the links leading to travel services promising Antarctic expeditions and circumpolar navigation around the North Pole. ✓**INTERNET**→*url* http://www.stud.unit.no/~sveinw/arctic/

Travelogue The green and the adventurous can link to the Sierra Club Home Page, the Great Outdoor Recreation Pages, Route 66, and nearly vertical routes in Nepal. Bay Area information includes a guide to local attractions, a hotel reservation service, a winery listing, and a 12,000-entry restaurant guide. Links to national travel services are also included. ✓**INTERNET**→*url* http://www.belgasoft.com/travel.html

Worldwide Trekking Adventures Detailed, illustrated travel itineraries from a company specializing in safaris and treks. ✓**INTERNET**→*url* http://www.travelsource.com/trekking/

Clubs

Sierra Club Homepage The home page for these passionate defenders of the wilderness (the group's slogan reads, "One Earth, One Chance") contains a history of the organization, current action alerts, essays on major ecological issues, and profiles of the earth's major eco-zones. The site includes descriptions of Sierra Club Outings for 1995—everything from snowshoeing and dogsledding to bicycling and backpacking. You can visit the shores of Baikal in southern Siberia or pick your way through Cottonwood Basin on a burro. Of course, you'll have to leave your home to do these things, but the online Sierra Club lets you order brochures, join the national club, and find out more about local clubs, student organizations, and other environmental groups. ✓**INTERNET**→*url* http://www.sierraclub.org/index.html

Hiking

Backpacker Magazine *Backpacker* magazine is online with current and back issues, consumer

Climb every mountain—http://www.dtek.chalmers.se/Climbing/Giflkatz.html

information, and message boards for woodsy chat. In the area of the forum known as Trailhead Register, hikers share trip reports, try to find hiking partners, and even do a little gear swapping. Backpacker Chat hosts live discussions on the outdoors, even sponsoring panel discussions on controversial topics like the wisdom of fighting fires and Newt and the New Environmentalism. Avid sportspersons will love the online buyers' guide, which rates outdoor gear of all types, from mittens to camp stoves. ✓**AMERICA ONLINE**→*keyword* backpacker

Hiking and Backpacking Campers and hikers can link from here to National Park, Forest, and Wilderness area servers, Web pages for hiking clubs throughout the world, and other backcountry sites. The extensive range of resources makes it fairly easy to find a hiking group in your area or to look into campgrounds for upcoming trips. Contact names and numbers are listed for all major U.S. trail associations. ✓**INTERNET**→*url* http://www.gorp.com/gorp/activity/hiking.htm

OTES: Over The Edge Sports Want to live dangerously—or just want to think about it? Learn how to enhance your adventure résumé with rock ice climbing, ocean kayaking, or cave diving with this site. This bulletin board, though just getting off the ground, is already filled with hardy souls sharing favorite challenges and biographies. This forum is for the kind of crowd that views scars and moments of abject terror as badges of honor. The site also offers gear exchange, a few informational documents, and promises a calendar of death-defying events in the near future. ✓**EWORLD**→*go* otes

Sam's Hiking Page Sam is one pumped outdoorsy dude. (Check out Sam's Climbing, Skiing, and Mountain Biking pages.) Get inspired by the photos of Sam's outdoor adventures, or jump to other outdoor sites and newgroups with the links he's collected. ✓**INTERNET**→*url* http://pool.ee.engr.uky.edu/fineberg/hike.html

United States

Alaska Alpine Club Need to earn some extra credit in "Prusik, Rappel, Z-pulley, and Anchors" or "Glacier Travel, Crevasse Rescue"? Sign right up. The site offers information on mountaineering classes in Alaska, including schedules and prices. ✓**INTERNET**→*url* http://info.alaska.edu:70/1s/Alaska/rec/aac

Bay Area Orienteering Club Being lost can be fun. In fact, it can be quite an adventure, and when a person chooses to lose himself in the outdoors with only a compass and map to help him find his way, it has a name—orienteering. The Bay Area Orienteering Club announces weekly events on this site. Detailed directions for the locations of all events are posted here. ✓**INTERNET**→*url* http://www-leland.stanford.edu/~wriley/baoc.html

Cal Hiking And Outdoor Society CHAOS, an outdoors club consisting primarily of UC Berkeley students, sponsors outdoor activities. Check here for a list of weekly trips, California Rangers stations, and local snow conditions. The FAQ at the site offers an amusing overview of CHAOS and its history (so why is everyone called Dave?), and the mailing list provides a forum for members of CHAOS to discuss events. ✓**INTERNET**→*url* ftp.csua.berkeley.edu/pub/hiking-club/README.html

A precarious position—http://www.dtek.chalmers.se/Climbing/Gifkatz.html:

Climbing in New Mexico As the Partridge Family says, "Point me in the direction of Albuquerque." It's the central reference point for this handy guide to the red rock sites in the Land of Enchantment. Difficulty ratings, routes, best approaches, and best seasons for the most popular climbing sites are provided here, along with local editorializing in the form of helpful hints: "Two things can ruin your day in Socorro—cactus and the New Mexico Tech Climbing Club." ✓**INTERNET**→*url* http://icomp.com/sriver/map.html

Explore Mount Timpanogos Take a virtual trip through Mount Timpanogos near Sundance, Utah. The site showcases pictures of the area, a map, and popular trail details for those planning to pay a visit to Robert Redford's hometown. ✓**INTERNET**→*url* http://lal.cs.byu.edu/people/jones/ketav/timp/timp.html

Guide to Hidden Climbing Areas The climbing material comes from the HST Underground Climber's Guide and is somewhat colloquial. You won't find "Nixon's Nose" on any topo map, but it's a great challenge. This site tells you which cracks to follow, which to avoid, and how to get something new out of an already surmounted face. The guide offers regional information on Sugarloaf, White Rock, Annapolis, Great Falls, Catoctin Mountain, and Rocks State Park. ✓**INTERNET**→*url* http://welcomehome.org/climbing/in-house.guide

Maryland Heights Guide-

Bright Angel Canyon, Grand Canyon National Park—http://www.kbt.com/gc/img0061.html

book Need camping information and native climbing rules for the Maryland Heights area? Check out this Website. Climb descriptions here are very detailed, covering almost every hold from top to bottom. Some are titled by their difficulty level ("A5"), while others are more imaginatively named ("Bacon and Eggs, Good Guess, Wasted"). ✓**INTERNET**→*url* http://darkstar.cygnus.com/climbing/mdheights.html

Outdoor Recreation at Georgia Tech The Outdoor Clubs at Georgia Tech offer instruction and equipment rental for most skill levels and outdoor sports. Check here regularly for news about upcoming trips that are sponsored by the clubs. How does two weeks paddling in the Grand Canyon or a week traversing the John Muir trail sound? ✓**INTERNET**→*url* http://www.mindspring.com/users/craig/orgt.html

Simple Annapolis, MD Rock Guide This brief guide provides directions to popular climbs, as well as a map that notes climbing areas. ✓**INTERNET**→*url* http://welcomehome.org/climbing/ann.rocks.guide

Square Top Mountain, CO Detailed trip report on a day-long Colorado climb. ✓**INTERNET**→*url* http://io.datasys.swri.edu/trips/Square_top.html

The Deep South Climber's Companion Order a guide to climbing sites in Alabama, Georgia, and Tennessee. ✓**INTERNET**→*url* http://east.isx.com/~lrumanes/climbing/deepsouth.html

White Mountains Server Absolutely everything a hardy hiker needs for fun in New Hampshire's White Mountains. Start with the interactive map, choose a peak like Mt. Moosilauke, check out hut accommodations online, compare altitudes, and take a hypertext trail tour past the wreckage of the B-18 down to the crystal clear lake. ✓**INTERNET**→*url* http://www.cs.dartmouth.edu:80/whites/

Wisconsin Hoofers Outdoor enthusiasts in the University of Madison area can check here for information on Hoofer-sponsored outdoor adventures, training, and courses. Horseback riding, anyone? ✓**INTERNET**→*url* http://rso.union.wisc.edu/hoofers/hoofhome.html

National Parks

A Trip Through the Grand Canyon Feel the rush of the river beneath the raft and the spray on your face. You will if you visit this site documenting every rapid and rock encountered in a trip through the Grand Canyon. It's well worth the trip—wear your life jacket. ✓**INTERNET**→*url* http://river.ihs.gov/GrandCanyon/GCrt.html

Backcountry Campsites in Rocky Mountain National Park Not only does backcountry camping not include RVs, it doesn't include a little hibachi at a nice, clean, numbered site either. At this site a brief text guide to backcountry protocol is available for those new to roughing it. Sites are listed by distinguishing features (cleft rock, grove of aspen) and closest trail marker. Be sure to check with rangers about fire danger before you consider toasting marshmallows in the wild. ✓**INTERNET**→*url* http://io.datasys.swri.edu/CO_parks/RMNP_site.html

Chaco Canyon This site has an overview of the park and extensive material pertaining to the history of the Anasazi, who built the vast complex some thousand years ago. After getting a flavor of this awe-inspiring site (one of the home points for the Harmonic Convergence), check the online National Park Service brochure for contact information, maps, and camping regulations. ✓**INTERNET**→*url* http://www.chaco.com/park/

Glacier National Park A frequent visitor gives basic information, including contact numbers, for this spectacular park in big sky country. Be inspired by the pictures of his recent Grinnel Glacier climb. ✓**INTERNET**→*url* http://www.cs.montana.edu/cs/local/glacier.html

GORP's U.S. National Parks and Preserves Resource List The Great Outdoor Recreation Pages (GORP) National Park information is the most complete on the Web, even better than the National Park Service's own site. Not all parks are covered evenly here, but 52 hotspots from the Katmai National Park and Preserve in Alaska to Everglades National Park in Florida are carefully described. In the GORP pages you'll find basic information on outdoor activities—like hiking, fishing, and boating—accommodations, backcountry permits, etc. Great attention is paid to what makes each park special—climate, flora and fauna—and special attractions like the bat flight at Carlsbad Caverns National Park in New Mexico. It's a great source for outdoor vacation planning. ✓**INTERNET**→*url* http://www.gorp.com/gorp/resource/US_National_Park/main.htm

Grand Canyon National Park Homepage Although not affiliated with the National Park Service, this site has a lot of useful information for prospective visitors, including weather reports and reviews of local food and lodging services. Take the hypertext guided tour of the south rim and get a sense of the majesty of the canyon. The trail information is especially good. It includes maps, mileage, difficulty ratings, equipment requirements, and full-page descriptions of the sights to be seen. ✓**INTERNET**→*url* http://www.kbt.com/gc/

Grand Canyon River Running Did that Meryl Streep rafting movie, *The River Wild*, put you in the mood for adventure? Trips through the Grand Canyon tend less toward confrontation with hoodlums than communion with nature. Feel the spray in your face with this site's fantastic river trip of movies, text, and maps. Review the permit guidelines for private trips, or find out how to contact commercial operators. Browse the selected reading list—you'll have plenty of time to prepare, since the waiting list for some trips can be years long. ✓**INTERNET**→*url* http://www.tucson.ihs.gov:3001/

Grand Canyon Travel Guide Detailed text guide to the Canyon and surrounding sights, complete with transportation and weather information. Keep in mind that Bright Angel Trail is used by mules and may not be the best choice for hikers in the hot summer sun. ✓**INTERNET**→*url* http://www.digimark.net/rec-travel/north_america/usa/arizona/grand_canyon_rafting.henden

Great Smoky Mountains National Park Mainly descriptive, this site attempts to convey the ambience of the Smokies through tall tales, a vernacular glossary, and native voices in large sound files. Enter the world of the Cherokees and mountain people via computer, and you'll probably end up wanting to make the trip in person. ✓**INTERNET**→*url* http://www.nando.net/smokies/smokies.html

National Park Service WWW Server They're all over the country, they're beautiful, they're intriguing, and best of all, they're yours—hundreds of national parks, historic sites, monuments, and recreation areas. At this wonderful site, you can make a virtual visit to areas as diverse as the green grasses of Gettysburg National Battlefield, the rugged peaks of Grand Teton National Park, the sands of Cape Hatteras National Seashore, or the silent ruins at Chaco Canyon. Each area is featured online with an illustrated brochure, complete with hours and contact numbers, and many have a great deal more—virtual tours, maps, and historical essays. ✓**INTERNET**→*url* http://www.nps.gov/

Olympic National Forest Basic information about the park's history, its animal and plant life, and its climate, as well as a slide show of park images. ✓**INTERNET**→*url* http://www.sequim.com/park/park.html

Park Search In addition to providing the nation with polar-tex sweaters, L.L. Bean is offering another invaluable service—from their full-color home page, you can search to find the great outdoors nearest you. Choose a locale, activity, or specific name and search—you'll get the name of the nearest park that suits your criteria. A search for an area in the Pacific Northwest offering historic

Scenic Yellowstone Falls—http://www.forestry.umt.edu/yellowstone/

sites, canoeing, and nearby lodging turned up 12 options—from the little-known Jessie M. Honeyman State Park in Florence, Oregon, to the Lake Chelan National Recreation Area adjacent to North Cascades National Park in Washington, to others in California and Alaska. But the service doesn't end there. Click on a choice and get a visual preview of the natural wonders in store for you, as well as contact information and a full checklist of the location's outdoor attributes. ✓**INTERNET**→*url* http://www.llbean.com/parksearch/

Rocky Mountain National Park This visitor created site provides the park's brochure, maps, weather, and highway information. Read the trip reports to discover the best fields for huckleberries in July, or gaze at the pictures and imagine replacing traffic noise with a rushing stream. ✓**INTERNET**→*url* http://www.cs.colostate.edu/~dallin/rmnp.html

Smoky Mountain Field School Lectures and field excursions are offered year-round by the staff of Great Smoky Mountain National Park and the University of Tennessee. This site provides descriptions of the offerings, a schedule, and registration information. Topics range from nature sketching to bat biology to "Incredible Edibles and Traditional Medicinals." The adventuresome can try their hands at orienteering or sign up for week-long excursions in the Smokies or on the Appalachian Trail. ✓**INTERNET**→*url* http://web.ce.utk.edu/departments/noncredit/smoky/smoky.html

Smoky Mountain On-Line Directory A directory of important telephone numbers, addresses, and contacts for one of the most visited parks in the nation—Great Smoky Mountain National Park. Annotated with reviews and descriptions of recreational outlets ranging from horse rentals to locksmiths to restaurants, this guide is filled with an impressive amount of detail (e.g., the vegetable soup is famous at the Brass Lantern restaurant). The most popular park trails are evaluated for difficulty and scenic properties. ✓**INTERNET**→*url* gopher://www.lib.utk.edu:70/00/Information-by-Subject/G%3a/smoky1.txt

Old Faithful, blowing off steam—http://www.forestry.umt.edu/yellowstone/

US National Parks, Forests, and Monuments Done Disneyworld? Fed up with Europe? Try this collection of links to explore America's wonderlands. It can point traveling outdoorspeople to specific parks, the National Park Service's own Web pages, and other large link collections like the Great Outdoor Recreation Pages. Pick a park, any park, say the Grand Canyon, and experience a virtual river trip or a hike along the south rim. Not sure which direction to head the stationwagon? Browse specific park sites or the NPS WWW page. ✓**INTERNET**→*url* http://akebono.stanford.edu/yahoo/Environment_and_Nature/Parks/US_National_Parks__Forests__and_Monuments

Utah National Parks Descriptions and contact numbers for parks, monuments, historic sites, and recreation areas in Utah. Try the hypertext tours of the bigger parks like Canyonlands and Bryce, which provide trail information and enticing images. ✓**INTERNET**→*url* http://sci.dixie.edu/NationalParks/nationalpark.html

Trails

Appalachian Mountain Club The Appalachian Mountain Club of the White Mountains is a gracious host, providing an interactive map on its home page. Choose a mountain that looks appealing, and receive a picture and description of nearby AMC cabins, some of which accommodate up to 90 hikers. Use their trail maps to plan your trip and connect to other local high points, like the trail home page and the Appalachian Adventure trip chronicle. ✓**INTERNET**→*url* http://www.lehigh.edu/ludas/public/www-data/amc.html

Appalachian Trail Home Page The Appalachian Trail wanders 2,140 miles from Mt. Katadhin to Springer Mountain, GA. This home page has descriptions of the segments passing through each state, including hiking highlights and practical information about day trips and accommodations. Each section is also loaded with hypertext connections to attractions along the way, from museums to ski areas. The Appalachian Trail Conference posts its FAQ here, along with lists of local trail clubs. ✓**INTERNET**→*url* http://www.fred.net/kathy/at.html

Potomac Appalachian Trail Club This very active club hosts weekly hikes and longer treks, not to mention sponsoring a mountain rescue team. Use this site to get information about reserving space in one of their many cabins, to arrange a ski tour, or to order maps and guidebooks. ✓**INTERNET**→*url* http://io.datasys.swri.edu/PATC/patc.html

International

aus.bushwalking (ng) An Australian newsgroup where avid practitioners of the craft exchange information on favored trails and commiserate over leaking Gortex jackets. ✓**USENET**→aus.bushwalking

Australian Bushwalker's Page Head out and see where your feet take you—the large open land of the Outback is calling. Go walk about this list of Australian bushwalking clubs, equipment reviews, shops, trip reports, weather reports, and maps. This Website also contains an archive of interesting aus.bushwalking threads, conveniently indexed by thread. ✓**INTERNET**→*url* http://www.anatomy.su.oz.au/danny/bushwalking/index.html

Climbing Guide to Norway Become as tough as a Viking—climb Norway. Full of hypertext maps, this site introduces prospective visitors to the magic of Norwegian hot spots like L'Rdal, Stavadalen, and Fagernes. General information includes climbing ethics (pitons are frowned upon), a description of climbing grades, a list of outfitters, and an extensive bibliography. Choose an area on the map for more specific climb descriptions and listings of whom to contact for assistance. ✓**INTERNET**→*url* http://www.stud.unit.no/~kristian/climb_guide_norway.html

Fontainebleau FAQ The insider's guide to one of France's premier climbing sites, complete with information on accommodations, maps, and detailed descriptions of the different climbing routes. The site also offers tips for first-time climbers: bring a piece of carpet to stand on while changing into climbing shoes to avoid sand between the toes. ✓**INTERNET**→*url* http://www.eeb.ele.tue.nl/climbing/areas/france/bleau.html

Irish Climbing Page For the best climbing stores in Dublin, head north over the Ha' penny Bridge. This site combines gear description and route information with the lyrical sensibility of the Emerald Isle—don't punch pitons into the "dark, brooding cliffs" of Dalkey. ✓**INTERNET**→*url* http://www.maths.tcd.ie/hyplan/hawk/climb.html

Kilimanjaro Climb A veteran of a Serengeti safari and a Kilimanjaro climb shares his insights. And what does he tell us? Well, keep an eye out for thieves on trains, be careful of complaining about the food while on safari, and don't use the outfitter who left him tentless on Kilimanjaro. Information on transportation and currency exchange is also available. ✓**INTERNET**→*url* http://everest.cs.ucdavis.edu/~wee/east-africa.html-Kenya and Tanzania Trip Report

New Brunswick, Canada, Outdoor Adventures Come climb Mount Sagamook, the Maritimes' highest peak. This electronic brochure features a description of regional trails and a list of tour operators. ✓**INTERNET**→*url* http://www.csi.nb.ca/tourism/page6.html

Rock Climbing in Europe This multi-lingual site is packed with useful tidbits, including a list of rock-climbing gyms and outfitters. Click on a country to explore that nation's rock offerings. The grading and geology of each prime area is described in detail—and each

A view of Arches National Park in Utah—http://www2.ari.net:80/home/npca/

description is accompanied by transportation and accommodation guides. The information is personalized by experienced European climbers, who add stories and comments. Juan advises all to keep a lookout for falcons around Clavijo in Spain. And if you have some climbing expertise of your own, you can add your favorite climb to the collection using the on-site template. ✓**INTERNET**→*url* http://www.eeb.ele.tue.nl/climbing/

Scottish Climbing Home Page Do Scots climb in kilts? The question remains unanswered. But everything else you need to know about scaling the crags of the highlands can be found here at the home page of the Edinburgh University Mountaineering Club. This site is as user friendly as they come, with icons linking visitors to a map, the climbing archive, and a hypertext index of many other features, like gear shops, guidebooks, and climber commentary. The most popular Scottish climbs are reviewed by the climbing pros. Climbers can check the weather conditions to make sure that mist, fog, or snow doesn't interfere with the generally sunny climbing climate. ✓**INTERNET**→*url* http://www.ucs.ed.ac.uk/~p91152/climbing/

The Alpine Club of Canada WWW Pages Want to get away to where Mounties roam free? This Website features information on adventuring in the vast Northland and a list of local chapter contacts for the Alpine Club of Canada. You'll also find here a list of Canadian climbing gyms to help you get into shape, recommended reading, and maps to help you plan your wilderness trip. In the Backcountry Facilities Directory, a clickable map shows the location of the Alpine Club's huts, and links to reservation information and advice on camping etiquette (no loud music, quiet by 10, don't chop wood indoors). ✓**INTERNET**→*url* http://www.cimtegration.com/sport/climbing/acc/acc.htm

---

Tramping in New Zealand FAQ What others may call bushwalking the Kiwis of New Zealand term tramping. And trampers bring new meaning to the phrase "back to nature." Many don't even bring a tent on their trips. Would-be trampers are advised to check out this FAQ for safety hints and advice on finding good guides and huts. Detailed trip reports are included to give prospective trampers a feel for the most popular tracks. ✓**INTERNET**→*url* http://io.datasys.swri.edu/NewZ.html

---

Tuan's Mountaineering Page Tuan is a French mountaineer who proudly proclaims, "I have in fact no ethics other than reaching the summit by myself and staying alive." Fair enough. In addition to good links to other Web climbing sites, Tuan's page has loads of insider tips about climbing in France. Treat yourself to Tuan's musings about the spiritual quest of the solo climber. ✓**INTERNET**→*url* http://robotics.eecs.berkeley.edu/~qtluong/mountain.html

---

Western Climber The official magazine of the Climbers Association of Western Australia sponsors lots of interesting discussion for climbers worldwide—most recently a vigorous panel discussion on the ethics of bolting. With frequent technical commentaries by world-renowned climbers, this page is an excellent site whether you're in Western Australia or not. ✓**INTERNET**→*url* http://www.cage.curtin.edu.au/~climbing/Magazines/WC3/western1.html

DETOURS

"A poisonous snake bite is a serious accident. It can lead to severe pain or other problems, occasionally even death. However in North America it is not nearly as dangerous as most believe. These snakes seldom bite humans and even when they do such bites are seldom fatal. There is no need to allow fear of snakes to ruin your enjoyment of the outdoors.

"Snakes will usually avoid you if you give them a chance. Try to be sure they know you are coming, don't reach into places they might hide, be careful turning over rocks, boards etc. Leave snakes alone unless you are sure they are safe. This also applies to dead snakes and detached heads—reflex bites are just as dangerous as bites by a live snake.

"If someone is bitten, *DO NOT* cut into the wound area. You will probably do more damage than the snake did."

—from **Backcountry Home Page**

Cruises

Cruise ships are like floating cities—although they're cities with no homeless problem, a large population of idle rich, and a stunning amount of conspicuous consumption. And cruise ships are also one of the most popular travel options in the world, a good way to get from Point A to Point B in cushy surroundings. See movies. See shows. Sightsee in colorful international ports. And eat like you've never eaten before—like Welles, like Brando, like Farley. Online, cruise enthusiasts can learn the ins and outs of ice sculptures and captains' tables at **Cruise Connection** and compare notes on past voyages at **rec.travel.cruises**. And in case you think cruises are deadly dull, learn from history at **The Titanic Home Page**.

M.V. CostaClassica—*from http://mmink.com/mmink/kiosks/costa/costatravel.html*

On the Net

Across the seas

Cruise Connection Cruise Connections presents myriad cruising options, from Delta Queen paddle steamer trips on the Mississippi River to grand worldwide voyages on Holland America's *S.S. Rotterdam* to theme cruises. Several cruise lines at this site provide itineraries, cabin layouts, prices, and photos of their ships and destinations. Stop by and decide which voyage is best for you. ✓**INTERNET**→*url* http://www.premier.net/~accent/

Cruise Forum A wide range of issues are discussed among novice and veteran cruisers—ask where to book a cabin to avoid seasickness, and an old salt will respond that midship staterooms on lower decks are recommended for those without their "sea legs." Caribbean cruisers are asking about the damage in ports of call after hurricanes have swept through: "Will anything on St. Bart's be open when the ship docks there?" A big cruisers' concern surprisingly, is parking—not for the ship, for their cars at the port of embarkation. Hints on what to wear and what to tip are always sought, but most importantly, there are questions about your expectations which will help you find the cruise most suited to your interests. If you are an older person used to white-glove service and dressing formally, sailing the *Star/Ship Oceanic* and being served by Goofy in the dining room might not be your cup of tea. But then again... ✓**COMPUSERVE**→*go* Travel Forums→Messages→Cruises

Cruise Review Library Afraid the *QE2* will be populated solely by elderly widows drinking Gin Slings in tea gowns? Assuage your fears by cruising this selection of ship reviews excerpted from the newsgroup rec.travel.cruises. The library also includes a FAQ and links to two cruise industry newsletters. If you're planning your next cruise, then check out the rave review of a trip up the Volga on a boat named the *Fyodor Dostoyevsky*. ✓**INTERNET**→*url* http://www.digimark.net/rec-travel/cruises/rtc.html

Cruise Reviews If you're taking no chances on your cruise, especially on a brand new ship (look at how the *Titanic* turned out), browse through these reviews before making your travel arrangements. Some reviews are excerpted from cruise travel publications, most are written by passengers. The reviews not only give you impressions of new ships, but also describe particular cruises; how they may have differed from past cruises, how sister ships compare (sailing on flagships such as Norwegian Cruise Line's *S.S. Norway* provides a more elegant experience than a comparable cruise on the aging *S.S. Starward*). By the way, once a ship reaches the ripe old age of 15, it's usually considered a has-been unless it's a treasured favorite and undergoes several refits (such as the *QE2*'s and *S.S. Rotterdam*'s $35 million+ renovations). Passengers here will tell you what problems they've encountered and how the crew handled them, provide money saving tips, and even display photos of themselves aboard their favorite liners. ✓**COMPUSERVE**→*go* Travel Forums→Libraries→Cruises

Cruisin Some people are obsessed with trains, others with planes, and still others with cruise ships. And while this Website caters to the cruise ship hobbyist by featuring the dimensions of several cruisers, it also meets the needs of tourists. Cruisin outlines shore excursions, the latest liners to hit the oceans, and weekly specials for different lines. Book a voyage yourself by filling out Cruisin's online survey. The company will make a tentative booking for you, which you later confirm with your credit card. ✓**INTERNET**→*url* http://www.crocker.com/cruisin

K.L. Smith's CruiseLetter The CruiseLetter is filled with articles of interest to veteran and virgin cruisers alike. Editor K. L. Smith stuffs every issue with reviews of recent launches, tips on dress codes, stories about gastronomic delights on the high seas, notes on trouble-free air connections to different ports of embarkation, and highlights from various shore excursions. ✓**INTERNET**→*url* http://www.lane.on.ca/pubs/C-letter/index.html

rec.travel.cruises (ng) Some people on this active newsgroup are planning a cruise and looking for feedback about the ships they're considering; others are seeking companions who may be traveling on the same cruise. And with all the cruise line mergers (they're like banks these days), many people are trying to keep track of their favorite ships: The *Royal Viking Queen* is now Cunard's *Queen Odyssey*; the *Enchanted Seas* (originally the *S.S. Brasil*, and formerly *Volendam*, *Monarch Sun*, and *Bermuda Star*) is no longer a floating hotel in Russia—it's Commodore Cruise's *Enchanted Seas* again. Although the newsgroup tends to be very information oriented (cruise recommendations, ticket sales, and travel-agent advertisements are typical fare), it is also a comfortable forum for sharing cruise experiences. Ron speaks of surviving the maiden voyage of Carnival's *Sensation*, whose passengers included Kathie Lee and Frank Gifford (with Cody). Aggie raves about her cruise aboard the *Tropicale*, while Shaun laments that modern cruise ships look like floating apartment buildings. Another post describes a stormy trans-Atlantic crossing. If the topic is cuises, you can climb aboard this newsgroup to discuss it. ✓**USENET**→rec.travel.cruises

The Cruise Board Many cruise related categories are available for browsing: there are the usual categories segregated by cruise line, as well as travel tips, FAQs and shore excursions. Then there are the online "personals" in Going My Way? Here, people tell you when and what ship they're on, describe themselves, and ask if you'd like to "hook up." Most are probably looking for alternatives in the event that the couple(s) assigned to their dining room table turns out to be boring. Veteran cruisers may find nostalgia in Whatever Happened To...? Many are asking about the *S.S. United States*. Once America's pride, it was built to rival the Cunard Line's *Queen Mary* and *Queen Elizabeth* in transatlantic service and speed. It was the last liner to hold the Blue Riband award for speed across the Atlantic (3 days, 10 hours at an average 35.5 knots; its actual speed—a U.S. military secret—exceeded 50 knots!). There are also categories for disabled cruise travelers; most new ships and some of the older ones have extra-wide cabins and have removed barriers throughout the ship (such as door lips, and steps). Virtually any issue, from family

M.V. Seabourne Spirit—*from http://mmink.com/mmink/carnival/seabourn.html*

cruising, theme cruising, to cruising other passengers on the sun deck can be discussed here. ✓**AMERICA ONLINE**→*keyword* travel→Travel Forum→Travel Boards→List Categories→The Cruise Board

The Titanic Home Page One of the most famous ships in history, the *Titanic* even has a worldwide fan club. It also has a Web page, complete with .GIFs and information on the passengers and events that transpired on the famous ship. There is also information on the White Star Line and the *Titanic*'s sister ships, the *R.M.S. Olympic* and *Britannic*. ✓**INTERNET**→*url* http://gil.ipswichcity.qld.gov.au/~dalgarry/

Cruise lines

A Cruise on the Song of Flower Picture sailing to Europe or Russia on an intimate luxury liner with only 172 wealthy passengers. And if thoughts of visiting northern capitals—such as Amsterdam, Stockholm, and Helsinki—in first class accommodations have you excited, then come to this site to read the travelogues of former passengers and to get contact information for booking your cruise. ✓**INTERNET**→*url* http://dockmaster.phantom.com/ceo5/song.html

Anytime Cruises Charter your own private motoryacht and sail through Alaskan waters and the Inside Passage. Trips depart from Juneau, and prices include bait and fishing gear (if you'd like to arrange your own supper). The Website has pictures of Anytime's ships and crews as well as reservation information. ✓**INTERNET**→*url* http://www.gsn.com/bin/welcome_enter.exe/Anytime_Cruises/Yahoo/sports/fishing/travel/alaska/anytime/anytime.htm?mode=graphics&customer_id=

Barging Around Europe—Canal Bliss Thinking about a barge cruise of Europe? This Website describes the experiences of travelers cruising from Amsterdam to Denmark. Itineraries and prices (in Australian dollars) are included. ✓**INTERNET**→*url* http://www.peg.apc.org/~firehorse/barge/barge.html

Carnival Cruise Line Imagine sailing aboard one of Carnival's Fun Ships, and then use the links here to reach information about Windstar Cruises, Holland America Line, and Seabourn Cruise Line—all of which were recently acquired by parent company Carnival. ✓**INTERNET**→*url* http://mmink.com/mmink/carnival/carnival.html

Clipper Cruise Line The Clipper Cruise Line's adventure-travel ships explore the inland waterways of the Americas that larger ships cannot access. Clipper cruises are ideal for those who want to learn more about the environment of their destinations by attending educational lectures, snorkeling, and swimming in virgin waters. Mention this Web page when booking your trip and receive $50 off your fare. ✓**INTERNET**→*url* http://ecotravel.com/clipper/

CopaCasino CopaCasino is the only ocean liner casino on the Gulf Coast. Use the information at this site to book your CopaCasino cruise, board your ship at Gulfport, Mississippi, and look forward to around-the-clock madcap mayhem. ✓**INTERNET**→*url* http://www.gulf-coast.com/info/casinos/copa.htm

Cunard Cruise Line This page advertises "Internet specials" for transatlantic crossings on the *Queen Elizabeth 2* and the newly acquired *Royal Viking Sun*. ✓**INTERNET**→*url* http://mmink.com/mmink/kiosks/costa/cunard/cunard.html

Dolphin Cruise Lines Dolphin combines value with the luxury of classic liners—you'll enjoy an affordable cruise on a ship with graceful lines, teak decks, and real portholes that open! However, as the "official cruise line of Hanna Barbera," your waiter in the *S.S. Seabreeze*'s elegant dining room is likely to be dressed as Fred Flintstone or Yogi the Bear. Upcoming cruise itineraries and fares are available along with lovely .GIFs of the small fleet. ✓**INTERNET**→*url* http://mmink.com/dolphincl/dolphinhome.html

Flotilla Holidays Sailing on a private yacht is still an exclusive luxury, but Flotilla Holidays organizes trips on which several passengers can share the expenses. This site describes how to charter or sail with a small group in the Mediterranean on 27-foot vessels. ✓**INTERNET**→*url* http://www.vossnet.co.uk/yacht/brokers/sovereign/flotilla.html

Freighter World Cruises Around the world in 80 days? What if it took a little longer? If you have plenty of time on you hands, freighter cruises could be for you. While foregoing the niceties of casinos, Vegas-style revues, and formal dining, freighter cruises offer unconventional, and sometimes spontaneous, itineraries in return. A freighter can carry up to 12 passengers (with more than 12, U.S. law requires a full-time ship's doctor). Several lines are represented here with schedules and prices. ✓**INTERNET**→*url* http://www.gus.com/travel/fwc/fwc.html

GalaxSea Cruises This online cruise agent advertises weekly specials on trips with all the major cruise lines, including Norwegian Cruise Line, Royal Caribbean, Holland America,

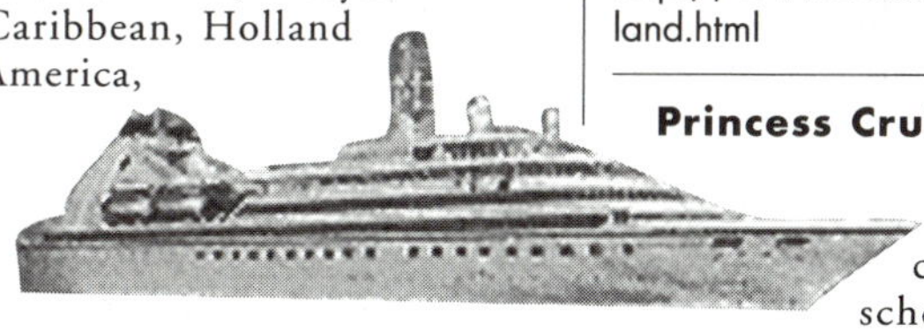

Princess, Carnival, and others. GalaxSea also offers corporate cruise programs (which include seminars to initiate first-time sailors). And you might even win a free cruise—visit the site to find out how! ✓**INTERNET**→*url* http://www.best.com/~galaxsea/

Holland America Line To promote the elegant ocean lines' renowned Alaskan cruises, Holland America Line sponsors this Website with cruise schedules, descriptions of the ships, including the line's grande dame *S.S. Rotterdam*, and reservation info for cruises and any hotels, flights, or car rentals needed to get you to the ship. ✓**INTERNET**→*url* http://alaskan.com/promos/holland.html

North Atlantic Cruises The *QE2* isn't the only boat afloat on the North Atlantic—you can sail those icy waters like a Viking off the coast of Greenland on the *Leifur Eriksson*, an adventure cruiser. On board you'll enjoy full Internet access; you can give your friends up-to-the-minute reports. The Website has more info on North Atlantic Cruises. ✓**INTERNET**→*url* http://www.centrum.is/com/vinland.html

Princess Cruise Lines See thumbnails of the Princess fleet and schedules for the line's Alaskan cruises, which take seven days to travel from Vancover to Anchorage. ✓**INTERNET**→*url* http://alaskan.com/promos/princess.html

Royal Caribbean Cruise Line Most of the info here promotes the Royal Caribbean Cruise Line to travel agents and meeting planners. For the average traveler, there is also an extensive FAQ that answers some basic questions, such as, "Will there be enough to eat?" and "Do I have to participate in the activities?" ✓**INTERNET**→*url* http://mmink.com/rccl.html

Windjammer Barefoot Cruises Are shoes really optional on Windjammer Cruises? Do passengers have to hoist the sails? The answers to these questions and more are at this site, along with pictures of the entire fleet (sailing and steamships), price information, and special theme cruise schedules. Singles anyone? ✓**INTERNET**→*url* http://wheat.symgrp.com/symgrp/windjammer/

Travel agents

Compu-Cruise by Rosenbluth With hundreds of itineraries and online reservation capability, Rosenbluth is one of the most sophisticated online cruise brokers. Download cruise graphics and learn all about why people like to spend days and nights in big boats drinking, eating, and dancing. Or if you already know why they do it, visit the site just to dream a little. ✓**COMPUSERVE**→*go* ros-35 ✓**PRODIGY**→*jump* cruise scan

Fishing

What's the most relaxing vacation you can imagine? Sitting on a Cote D'Azur beach while your new French "friend" rubs coconut butter into your feet? Holing up in a cabin in the Vermont woods to read, drink, and sleep late? Well, a good fishing trip shames these travel options. As any angler knows, there's nothing like the feeling of holding the pole, listening to the line cut the water gently, waiting for the first nibble, the fateful bite. Online, you can cast your Net at **alt.fishing**, **Fishing Library**, and **Alaska Fish Cruise**.

Small girl, big catch—from http://www.peak.org/~robertr/photos.html

On the Net

Across the board

alt.fishing (ng) Vincent has business in Houston later in the month; on his one free afternoon, he wants to cast a line, and he asks for local fishermen to tell him where the fish are jumping. (According to Bob, Lake Fork is the place to go.) Nick wants to fish in Key West next week, and he's requesting recommendations for good bait shops in the area. And Marie is looking for a fishing partner to test the waters in Hawaii with her. Like these Netters, you can get advice and tips at this newsgroup to help you plan your next fishing expedition. ✓**USENET**→ alt.fishing

Fishing Library The regional fishing reports housed at this site give tips on where to angle near Los Angeles and the best place to bait your hook in Boca Raton. In addition to the reviews of local fishing holes, this site also offers many fishy resources, including fishing images, fish reading lists, newsletters about fishing, and even a software program that teaches how to tie flies. ✓**COMPUSERVE**→*go* outdoorforum→Libraries→Fishing

U.S. info

Colorado Fishing A small but growing collection of information about fishing in Colorado, including phone numbers of local organizations, Colorado regulations, and fish pictures. ✓**INTERNET**→*url* http://www.ofps.ucar.edu/~john/ff/co_ff.html

Denbigh Starkey's Bozeman, MT Fishing Page This Website gives an overview of the big fishing rivers in the Bozeman, Montana region and advice on which flies to use when fishing there. ✓**INTERNET**→*url* http://www.cs.montana.edu/people/starkey/fishing.html

Fishing in Montana Cast your bait at this site for info on fishing in Montana—you'll get descriptions of the state's rivers and their fish species and lists of local fishing facilities. In addition, the Website offers information about maps, licenses, and the duration of the fishing season. ✓**INTERNET**→*url* http://www.mt.gov/commerce/travel/fishing.htm

Fishing Stuff from Oregon Links to resources on the Web related to fishing in Oregon, including fishing reports, weather reports, and daily updates on the water levels of several Oregon rivers. ✓**INTERNET**→*url* http://zebu.uoregon.edu/~dmason/Mckenzie/weather.html

Fly Fishing in Arizona Everything you ever wanted to know about fly-fishing in Arizona, including official news and regulations from the state, a list of popular destinations with brief descriptions, names and addresses of fly-fishing organizations in Arizona, addresses of local fly shops, descriptions of local fly patterns, fishing images, and a huge set of links to other fly-fishing sites on the Net. ✓**INTERNET**→*url* http://www.indirect.com/user/jshannon

Joe's Connecticut Fishing Page Joe's page extols the great fishing waters to be found in Connecticut. Joe offers descriptions of bass and trout management areas, a list of trophy-trout lakes, and virtual tours of the Housatonic and the Miramichi Rivers. ✓**INTERNET**→*url* http://www-bprc.mps.ohio-state.edu/cgi-bin/hpp/flyfish.html

Miramichi River Route The fish literally fly in New Brunswick's Miramichi River—they have been seen jumping as a high as a meter out of the water. Use the map at this Web page to follow the route swum by Atlantic salmon as they make their way down the Miramichi. The site also offers descriptions of and information about towns along the route. ✓**INTERNET**→*url* http://www.cuslm.ca/tourist/michi1.htm

Missouri Flyfishing Page A quick reference to fly fishing in Missouri which provides license information, news on local organizations and today's weather, suggested flies for fishing in Missouri, knot-tying techniques, reports on several Missouri fishing destinations, overviews of rivers and parks, and links to dozens of other fishing sites on the Web. ✓**INTERNET**→*url* http://www.agron.missouri.edu:edu/flyfishing/

New Mexico Fly Fishing Besides an overview of fly-fishing in New Mexico and a library of fly-fishing stores, the site also offers descriptions of knots and fly tying and links to several other fishing sites. ✓**INTERNET**→*url* http://www.unm.edu/~datkins/flyfish/flyfish.html

Northern California Fly Fishing Northern California, the Eastern Sierras, and Oregon are explored at this site, which provides maps for and fishing-oriented reviews of several bodies of water in these areas, including Lake Almanor, Deer Creek, and Pleasant Valley Creek. ✓**INTERNET**→*url* http://www2.ecst.csuchico.edu:80/~jschlich/Flyfish/flyfish.html

Southern California Waters Fishing Report A page of fishing reports written by locals about angling areas in southern California, including Los Angeles, San Diego, and Ventura. ✓**INTERNET**→*url* http://www.rain.org/~marlin/report.html

The Illinois Fishing Page Before casting a line in Illinois, stop by The Illinois Fishing Page (updated every few weeks) to pick up a weekly fishing tip and to read feature articles on fishing. Local fishing shows are also announced at this site. ✓**INTERNET**→*url* http://www.cba.uiuc.edu/~rtaylor/fish/fish.htm

The Oregon Department of Fish & Wildlife Official fishing-related reports from the department. ✓**INTERNET**→*url* http://eagle.dfw.or.gov/

Wisconsin Fly Fishing Page According to this Web page, more than 2,500 Wisconsin streams and rivers are classified as trout waters. The page showcases the fish-filled Wisconsin waters and the organizations created to oversee them. In addition, this site has a gallery of fishing graphics and dozens of links to additional fishing sites, like the Virtual Fly Box and the Fly Fishing Bulletin Boards. ✓**INTERNET**→*url* http://heather.wis.com/cgi/index1.cgi

Yellowstone Fishing Reports & Lodges Henry's Fork is closed. The fishing conditions at Yellowstone Lake are fair, but Yellowstone River's condition is excellent. Check out the status of your favorite fishing spots before buying your can of worms. Several Yellowstone lodges have joined the site with information about their services. ✓**INTERNET**→*url* http://www.srv.net:8001/yellowstone/outdoors.html

U.S. tours

Alaska Fish Cruise This Web page describes the company's various fishing tours (including prices), lists terms and conditions for reservations, and provides a telephone number and email address to contact the company. ✓**INTERNET**→*url* http://www.gsn.com/bin/welcome_enter.exe/Alaska_Fish_Cruise/Yahoo/sports/fishing/travel/alaska/juneau/juneau.htm

Capt. Mike Duclon Captain Mike has been a professional tour guide for fishing expeditions since 1984. Read about his services and contact him using the telephone number and email address at this site. ✓**INTERNET**→*url* http://www.cftnet.com/members/duclon/capt2.htm

Catchum Sportfishing The home page of Catchum Sportfishing describes fishing opportunities off the coast of Kona, Hawaii. For tour schedules and prices, click the reservations button and send the company an email requesting additional information. ✓**INTERNET**→*url* http://www.ilhawaii.net/~fish/

Dana Wharf Sportfishing A promotional page for a California-based company that offers deep sea fishing, whale watching, and sportfishing boat tours. Come here to learn seasonal tour schedules, discount offers, and contact information. ✓**INTERNET**→*url* http://www.ernestallen.com/tr/ca/DanaWharfSportfishing/

Saint-James Fishing Adventures Saint-James arranges trips departing from Sunnyvale, California. The Website shows pictures of the boat and its captain and lists prices and descriptions of daily excursions. ✓**INTERNET**→*url* http://www.boatnet.com/boatnet/charter/Saint-James/STJames.html

Taylor Made Charters See pictures of some really big fish and get itineraries, prices, and contact information for Taylor Made fishing tours. ✓**INTERNET**→*url* http://www.alaskan.com/vendors/taylor.html

Treasure State Outfittin' This Website promotes the company's fishing expeditions to the waters of Libby, Montana, where the site promises "some of the best blue-ribbon fishin' around." ✓**INTERNET**→*url* http://www.libby.org/TSO/montana.html

International info

Angling Club Lax-Á Imagine going to Iceland to salmon fish in the summer, trout fish in the fall, shoot geese in the winter, or attend fly-fishing school year-round. The Angling Club has put up a Website to encourage anglers to consider making the trip. Detailed descriptions and a photo album of the rivers and the tours are provided. ✓**INTERNET**→*url* http://www.ismennt.is/fyr_stofn/lax-a/uk/anclub_uk.html

Salmon River & Lake Ontario Fishing Reports You can fish for King Salmon on Lake Ontario from late June through September. (The state record is 47 lbs 13 oz.) On the Salmon River, the heaviest runs are from September through December. Details about when to fish for different species, the average size of the fish, and current catch records are available here as well as several articles and reports on local fishing. ✓**INTERNET**→*url* http://gray.maine.com/fish-ny/

The River Tweed Considering a trip to Scotland for some salmon fishing? Catch Scottish fishing statistics, lodging information, and price indexes at this page. ✓**INTERNET**→*url* http://www.scotborders.co.uk/fishing/index.html

International tours

Charlotte Fishing Expeditions Thinking about fishing off the Queen Charlotte Islands, British Columbia during your next vacation? You might want to check out the prices and tour itineraries here. ✓**INTERNET**→*url* http://www.terranet.ab.ca/~comm/fishing/homepage.html

Cutting Loose Expeditions A promotional page that lists phone and fax numbers for a company that features fishing tours to Florida, the Bahamas, Mexico, Nicaragua, Panama, Venezuela, Canada, and Florida, among other locations. ✓**INTERNET**→*url* http://www.gorp.com/cutloose.htm

Equinoxe Angling Adventures Western Canada offers fishing opportunities all year round. Equinoxe organizes trips throughout the year to numerous locations in the western Great White North, and the company tells you all about their services at the site. In addition, the page offers a map of Canada, a gallery of fish pictures, daily reports on weather in Canada, and even a link to the Amazing Fish Cam. ✓**INTERNET**→*url* http://infomatch.com/~equinoxe/

Northwest Voyagers Organizing fishing trips is the specialty of Northwest Voyagers. Read about its various tours, which even go to rivers and streams in Costa Rica and India, and get a toll-free reservations phone number at this site. ✓**INTERNET**→*url* http://nwlink.com/~spazspar/nw_voyag/nw_voya1.html

Playing Hooky Charters This Florida based company wants you to skip school (or work) and go fishing. It lays out your escape plan at this site, which lists prices and availability of its expeditions in the Gulf of Mexico. If you're lured in, call, write, or email Playing Hooky with the info given here. ✓**INTERNET**→*url* http://intrism.hcsys.com/phc/

Sooke Salmon Charters Ltd An advertisement for a company featuring tours off Vancouver Island, Victoria, British Columbia. ✓**INTERNET**→*url* http://dataflux.bc.ca/celuszak/c001/Salmon.html

The Anglers Connection An advertisement for a company that takes fishermen to lakes and rivers in Alaska, Wyoming, Canada, and Belize. If you're interested, contact Anglers with the telephone number or email address listed here. ✓**INTERNET**→*url* http://wave.park.wy.us/~anglers/anglers.html

Gay & lesbian travel

In some ways, gay travel is like any other travel. Gay men and lesbians like taking cruises, going to museums, discovering great restaurants off the beaten path, and oohing and aahing at monuments of architecture. And in other ways, gay travel is unlike any other travel. From Fire Island to Provincetown, from San Francisco to Key West, gay vacation spots have their own attractions, events, accomodations, day tours, and nightlife. From the **Gay and Lesbian Travel Web**, which offers wise counsel and helpful hints, to **The Pink Pages**, which collects gay resources in Amsterdam, the Net is full of sites catering to homosexual journeyers. And if you've forsworn the *Swinging on a Star* revival for the Indy 500, visit **Gay and Lesbian Indianapolis**.

A detail from Amsterdam's Pink Pages—http://www.euro.net/5thworld/pink/pink.html

On the Net

Across the board

Anton Forget the number of the Gay and Lesbian Switchboard at your destination? Don't worry, you can find listings, and possibly that number you need, in this online guide. Search by continent and country for places of interest; you're provided with contact information and sometimes a short description of the establishments. ✓**INTERNET**→*url* http://204.137.145.254/anton/

Gay and Lesbian Travel Web Plan your trip with pride from this site, which accesses RSVP cruise tours, travel magazines, B&B services, and special event information (Mardi Gras in New Orleans or Sydney for example). Request brochures or contact gay-friendly travel agents from here. ✓**INTERNET**→*url* http://www.gayweb.com/travel.html

The Gay Traveler America Online's complete gay-and-lesbian traveler resource features listings of queer tour operators, events calendars, and IGTA (International Gay Travel Association) member listings, including hotels, airlines, and cruise lines, as well as links to gay travel World Wide Web pages. For recommendations, helpful hints, and warnings about destinations from other travelers, head to the message board here. You'll get insider information from the best sources and possibly make new friends online. ✓**AMERICA ONLINE**→*keyword* gay→The Gay Traveler

United States

Bay Area CyberDykes (ml) Discussion for lesbians in the Bay Area. Pick up tips on where to go the next time you're in town. ✓**INTERNET**→*email* majordomo@queernet.org ✍ *Type in message body:* subscribe ba-cyberdykes <your email address>

Boston Queer in Beantown with no place to go? Don't want to go to Chaps again? Look here for schedules of events in the Boston area, such as productions of *Angels in America*, book readings, and the next meeting of the New England Bears. ✓**INTERNET**→*url* http://ftp.std.com/NE/bosgay.html

Boston sappho-list (ml) For Boston-area members. ✓**INTERNET**→*email* boston-sappho-request@mc.lcs.mit.edu ✍ *Write a request*

Colorado and Rocky Mountain Community Directories

Although the Rocky Mountains haven't changed since the days when Steven Carrington had to take flak from his father—the recent Amendment 2 debate is a perfect illustration—the area still boasts an extraordinary number of gay-friendly businesses willing to go on record. This site carries a list of them with contact information—find B&Bs, ice cream parlors, plumbers, and many other businesses where you can spend your gay dollars. ✓**INTERNET**→*url* http://www.tde.com/directories/

Gay and Lesbian Chicago Centered mostly near Lincoln Park on North Halsted Street, gay Chicago offers plenty of fun. Info on gay cafés, bars and clubs, publications, and organizations can be accessed from here; learn how to dine and dance at Roscoe's or gyrate at Vortex, among other places. ✓**INTERNET**→*url* http://www.tezcat.com:80/~alan/

Gay and Lesbian Indianapolis Perhaps it's time for dinner and you need a guide to the gay bar and restaurant scene in Indy. Look no further. Directions and brief descriptions are available for almost a dozen bars and restaurants. Also find here info about gay related publications, supportive businesses, and events in Hoosier country. ✓**INTERNET**→*url* http://www.inetdirect.net/gli/

Lesbian and Gay Community Center, New York In the Big Apple, if you are a Republican Indian lesbian architect with children who mountain bikes, there is an organization that suits your needs. Over 400 groups meet at the Center; it's extensive monthly calender is listed with contact information for the groups. Also, find here links to *LGNY*, a news and entertainment weekly, and listings of more clubs, bars, and parties than even Michael Musto could attend. So if you want to attend a 12-step meeting, visit the Clit Club, or see what's happening at the Roxy, stop here. ✓**INTERNET**→*url* http://www.panix.com/~dhuppert/gay/center/

Maine Gay Network Contact information and schedules for several gay, bi, and lesbian organizations in Maine, and an index of news stories about gay rights in Maine. ✓**INTERNET**→*url* http://www.qrd.org/QRD/www/usa/maine/gaynet.html

---

Pittsburgh Lesbian, Gay, and Bi Resources A directory of events, bars, bookstores and video stores, organizations, restaurants, and travel services for gays, lesbians, and bisexuals in the Pittsburgh area. The site also links to home pages for Pittsburghers who've come out on the Web. ✓**INTERNET**→*url* http://www.city-net.com/~gayboy/pghlgb/index.html

---

West Hollywood Home Page In representing Los Angeles's gayest enclave, West Hollywood's Web page breaks down the Boystown scene for you. Start off with an ASCII-art map of Santa Monica Boulevard, where you can click on anything from the Axxis to the Backlot to Rage for brief reviews, addresses, and closing times. If you're looking for a specific type of scene, click on your favorite category: cruisy clubs, neighborhood bars, young guys' clubs, and dance clubs. While information for women isn't as plentiful, you can still choose from Revolver or Girl Bar for advice on your upcoming WeHo travails. ✓**INTERNET**→*url* ftp://ftp.netcom.com/pub/jc/jclark/web/wehoweb.html

---

Wyoming Pride Page If you're gay and traveling to Wyoming, your friends may think that your choice of vacation destination is, well, a little queer. But this page proves that sexual orientation is not monolithic in the Badlands, with links to lesbian, gay, bi, and transgender resources statewide. United Gay and Lesbians of Wyoming even sponsors social events, so remember to check in before you visit. ✓**INTERNET**→*url* http://plains.uwyo.edu/~lasaga/lgb.html

Fodor's Choice...

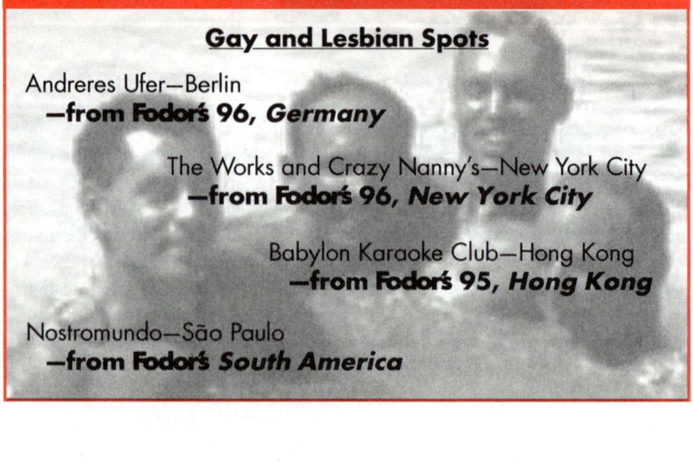

Gay and Lesbian Spots

Andreres Ufer—Berlin
—from Fodor's 96, *Germany*

The Works and Crazy Nanny's—New York City
—from Fodor's 96, *New York City*

Babylon Karaoke Club—Hong Kong
—from Fodor's 95, *Hong Kong*

Nostromundo—São Paulo
—from Fodor's *South America*

International

Austrian Lesbian and Gay Home Page Lesbisch? Schwul? Lesbian or gay, this homo page has information on queer happenings in Austria. Find a date on the Linz Queery-Box mailbox, or get contact info for gay organizations throughout the country, from Vienna's Schwung to Queer Klagenfurt. The site requires proficiency in German. ✓**INTERNET**→*url* http://www.oeh.uni-linz.ac.at:8001/homo/

Dutch Queer Resources So you've fallen in love with a Dutch guy or girl, want to move in with him / her, and live legally and happily ever after in Europe's gayest city? At this site you can research the ins and outs of becoming a concubine in Holland. You'll also find information on local, gay-related media coverage, culture, sports clubs, counseling, and health issues, as well as excerpts from the Dutch constitution's provisions for the rights of gays and lesbians. ✓**INTERNET**→*url* http://www.xs4all.nl/~heinv/dqrd/index.html

---

France Queer Resources Directory A guide to having a good ol' time in gay Paree, from descriptions of Gai Pied's Bastille Day Ball to the 6th annual Salon de l'Homosocialité. Use the directory to decide whether you'd rather hang out with Father Jacques Pérotti at the Centre Lesbienne et Gai's weekly homosexualité et spiritualité event or camp it up on the dance floor at Le Queen. In addition to listing queer symposiums, rallies, support groups, and parties, this site includes profiles of queer organizations' events in Paris and the provinces. ✓**INTERNET**→*url* http://acacia.ens.fr:8080/home/delmas/fqrd/fqrd-e.html

---

Gay Abandon A membership organization for gay and lesbian travelers to Australia and New Zealand; offers online registration and information. ✓**INTERNET**→*url* http://www.net-quest.OntheNet.com.au/webbin/gayaban.html

---

Gay Québec A user-friendly guide to lesbian and gay resources in the province. Hotels, B&Bs, restaurants, bars and clubs, organizations, publications, and even personals can be found here. Links connect to other sites, including Montréal's Lesbian and Gay Center (located in the Gay Village there). The site is bilingual and primarily covers Montréal, Québec City, and Hull. ✓**INTERNET**→*url* http://www.gaibec.com/

Gerdes (Queer CyberSpace) On your way to Stockholm? Don't leave home without checking Sweden's RFSL address and telephone list. This Swedish site has contact information for many important gay businesses and services in Sweden, everything from pubs and clubs to counseling organizations to local gay radio broadcasts. ✓**INTERNET**→*url* http://www.big.hfb.se/~gerdes/queer.html

---

Lesbian, Gay, Bisexual Guide to Great Britain Resources for queens throughout the Kingdom can be found here—select the region and see what's on in your area. Of course, there are tons of London listings, from the Switchboard to gay night at the Fridge, but you'll be surprised at where the community pops up—we are everywhere. Other information is here as well, such as women's resources, people coming out, gays, lesbians, and bisexuals of color, and a humorous page on "how to spot a gay man." ✓**INTERNET**→*url* http://phymat.bham.ac.uk/LGB/

New Zealand Resources List While New Zealand's reputation as a great place for lesbians and gays doesn't compare to that of neighboring Australia, the country recently passed a national bill forbidding discrimination on the basis of sexual orientation or AIDS. Find out about the bill's specifics, and gather travel tips for visiting Auckland, Wellington, or Christchurch at this Website. ✓**INTERNET**→*url* http://www.geko.com.au/users/QRD/NZ/nzintro.html

---

Outrageous Tokyo Tokyo isn't exactly a mecca for gay rights activists. Only 1,200 people showed up at the annual Gay Pride Parade in one of the world's largest cities. But underneath the woodwork, and with a little help from *Outrageous Tokyo*, an English-language gay quarterly, you'll find a few outlets for the non-political majority. Shinjuku 2-chome, gay-lesbian central in Tokyo, boasts approximately 20 gay bars (but only three for lesbians). If you have Adobe Acrobat, you can download a map of the district and take a virtual walk through the streets yourself. ✓**INTERNET**→*url* http://shrine.cyber.ad.jp/~darrell/outr/home/outr-home.html

---

Queer in Israel A small collection of information about gay life in Israel. ✓**INTERNET**→*url* http://qrd.tau.ac.il/

SchWeb—Schwul im Web Schwul means "faggot" in German, and the word seems to have been reclaimed. Most of this page is for events in Germany, but you'll find information on pride celebrations throughout Europe. And even if you haven't planned on a trip abroad to alleviate boy trouble, the "Dear Boy" advice column might still make this site worth a visit. ✓INTERNET→*url* http://www.casti.com/GQRD/svsk/svsk.html

The Amsterdam Pink Pages Headed to Amsterdam for a dirty weekend? The Pink's Pages serve as a guide to fun in the capital of euro-gaydom. There's advice on where to find a naked male maid (see Erotic Cleaning Services), links to the People Male Escort page, and a downloadable movie explaining how to put on a condom. The online version of Amsterdam's free, gay listings magazine, *Rainbow*, provides a schedule of gay-related parties and events, plus classified ads. And if you're scared of getting lost in the Red Light District's medieval alleyways at 5:00 a.m., a downloadable map of the city will lead you back to your room at the Stable Master. You can also take a virtual tour of Mr. B's leather store (among other shops), post a message on the boards for the Kinky Pink dating club, or explore the links to other gay sites online, such as the 1998 Gay Games Page. ✓INTERNET→*url* http://www.euro.net/5thworld/pink/pink.html

The Gay, Lesbian & Bisexual Resource Directory for Canada Whether you're looking for the lowdown on Church Street clubbing in Toronto or lunching at Teddy Bear's Picnic in Vancouver, this site covers the gamut of queer-related happenings in the Great White North. Students shopping for a gay-friendly collegiate environment should check out the list of gay and lesbian groups at Canadian universities. Professionals can use the resources here to research corporations offering same-sex benefits to their employees. There's even a list of links to gay Canadians with their own home pages. ✓INTERNET→*url* http://pmax.dymaxion.ns.ca/~kc/iglbrd/canada/Welcome.html

The Philippines Queer Pages The extensive resources here are listed in English, Spanish, and Tagalog. You'll find a history of gays, lesbians, and bisexuals in the Philippines, for background, then listings of bars, clubs, and social and political organizations in Manila, Quezon City, and other towns, with detailed descriptions—you'll know which nights are the most popular at Miss Piggy's. Links to other Pacific Island gaylebi resources are here also. ✓INTERNET→*url* http://www.geko.com.au/users/QRD/NZ/nzintro.html

Travel Web—Hong Kong The boys and girls in Hong Kong are living it up; the British Crown colony reverts to Chinese rule in 1997—which will likely end the freedoms currently enjoyed there. Find here your basic gay tourist guide that includes lists of places to eat, drink, and be merry: cruising areas, saunas, and nightclubs. Gay-friendly accommodations and English-language gay bookshops are included in the listings. ✓INTERNET→*url* http://www.cts.com/~drcarr/gay_travel/hkin.html

Wild Fruit! Queen Apparent of London nightlife, Yvette sponsors a monthly gay dance known as Wild Fruit! in Brighton, an hour south of London. Even if you can't make it for "the delicious Miss Tasty Tim's" mix of house, garage, and commercial dance music, download pictures of the daisies in their platinum blond coiffures, plus information on Wild Fruit's Alternative Miss pageants in Brighton and Manchester. ✓INTERNET→*url* http://www.pavilion.co.uk/UniversalFlavour/WildFruit

DETOURS

"How do you spot a gay man? It's not always practically possible to follow him home and see if his house is stylishly furnished by Ikea. It's not always possible to examine his CD collection for the subtle but telling signs of his sexuality—Kylie Minogue, high energy, and seventies Disco, with a liberal sprinkling of Judy Garland and Shirley Bassey.

"Perhaps our quest for knowledge should begin with a look at the more readily accessible signs—his clothing. Does every gay man wear his sexuality on his sleeve? Where leather and latex are a dominant feature, all questions seem futile. After all, one would have to be seriously out of touch with one's fellow Homo sapiens to enquire as to whether the Village People were gay! Similarly, high heels, sequins and side-splits provide us with a fairly unambiguous 'YES!' in response to our enquiries. But what about the lumberjack shirt?"

—from **Lesbian, Gay, Bisexual Guide to Great Britain**

Casinos & gambling

Vacationing is always a gamble. But then there are those vacations that are real gam- bles—weekend getaways in casino Edens like Reno, Monte Carlo, and Atlantic City. If you've ever wanted to squander your life's savings playing games of chance, go right ahead. And go ahead with the blessing of the Net, which is full of sites that will help you locate the nearest baccarat game or share tips with other Perfect Blackjack players. And after you've worked up the necessary confidence, preview your trip by checking out casino sites online, from **The Lake Tahoe Gaming Page** to the somewhat less famous **Wisconsin Casinos**.

Fremont Street, Las Vegas, Nevada—http://www.teleport.com/~mbn/gambling.html

On the Net

Across the board

Casino Guide Sponsored by *The Detroit News*, this page is a cornucopia of casino and gambling information. The Gambling Advice section addresses gambling money management (Tip: "Don't take checkbooks, ATM cards, or credit cards to a casino.") and provides a glossary of terms to use at the tables—"double down," "hole card," and a "red-black bet" are all explained. The Where to Play section lists casinos in Detroit and surrounding areas. And the Casino Guide doesn't lack for playing tips—its How to Play the Games section spells out the basics of craps, baccarat, and poker in such straightforward terms, that even a child could play (but not legally). ✓**INTERNET**→*url* http://www.detnews.com/CASINO/CASINO.html

Casinos Worldwide The best feature of this Website is its Casino Finder, a clickable world map that accesses names, phone numbers, addresses, and brief reviews of gambling establishments worldwide. Use the map to find the house of your dreams, and then head to one of the seven casino chat rooms here to talk about casino gambling with other enthusiasts. ✓**INTERNET**→*url* http://www.acmeweb.com/casino/index.html

Gamer's Card Games To practice your gambling strategies, download any one of the hundreds of shareware programs housed at this library. Virtual gamblers can choose Canasta, Real Video Poker, the Wilstar Slot Machine, and the Pot O'Gold Slot Machine shareware, among others. ✓**COMPUSERVE**→*go* gamers→Libraries→card games

rec.gambling (ng) Do you have a burning desire to beat the machine at video poker? Has the game of baccarat always seemed too complex to master? Were you surprised to learn that Red Dog is more than just a type of beer? Then this newsgroup might be of interest to you—it's a meeting place for gamblers worldwide where they exchange betting and gambling tips and advice on all types of casino games—from Caribbean Stud Poker to Drivel. The FAQ stores the collected knowledge of the newsgroup and answers questions like "Where can I get discounts on gambling books and software?" ✓**USENET**→rec.gambling *FAQ:* ✓**INTERNET**→*url* ftp://rtfm.mit.edu/pub/usenet-by-group/rec.gambling/

Sterling & Thaller You've booked your trip to Las Vegas without realizing you don't know a straight from a flush. Never fear—each week this site offers two new tips on betting methods for roulette, craps, blackjack, keno, and other casino games. Sterling & Thaller also advertises its offline gambling guide, *Gambling, Gambling, Gambling*; just click the ordering button for purchasing information. ✓**INTERNET**→*url* http://www. littlebit.de/gambling/

Casino guides

Atlantic City Casinos An alphabetical listing of addresses and contact information for a number of casinos on the Boardwalk, including Bally's Park Place, Showboat Casino and Hotel, and The Taj. ✓**INTERNET**→*url* http://www.ezweb.com/casinos.html

Carl's Casino Guide More than just a guide to casinos nationwide, Carl's page also offers industry news of casino closings, buyouts, and special discounts and offers. Carl's reviews list house statistics (Circus Circus has 1,468 slot machines) and casino telephone numbers as well as short descriptions of their services ("Harrah's pitches its casino as a friendly atmosphere to gamble, and they are right. You'll like the fact that there are three floors to roam around along non-smoking areas. Overall the slot action is good and the table games have decent games. The food is good, but they tend to be stingy with the comps. I like Harrah's. All around good fun."). ✓**INTERNET**→*url* http://www.cris.com/~Carlr/

Casino Locations Ante up to this excellent casino guide offering phone numbers for every Las Vegas casino, plus a map pinpointing the locations of Reno casinos. The site also addresses questions like "Where are some cheap places to stay in Vegas?"; "Where are some good places to play in Reno?"; and "Where is Foxwoods?" ✓**INTERNET**→*url* http://www.conjelco.com/faq/casino.html

Casinos in the Netherlands Zandvoort. Groningen. Scheveningen. They sound like words you mutter under your breath after losing at roulette, but they're really the names of Dutch towns that offer casinos and gambling. This compact site lets you check out the houses in ten Dutch cities—just click on the name and get a list of casinos, games, and telephone numbers. ✓**INTERNET**→*url* http://www.nbt.nl/holland/casinos/cs-name.htm

Lake Tahoe Gaming Page A list of telephone numbers for casinos in the Lake Tahoe area, including Caesar's Tahoe, the Cal-Neva Resort Hotel Spa Casino, the Horizon Casino Resort, and the Lakeside Inn and Casino. ✓**INTERNET**→*url* http://dol.meer.net/locns/tahoe/gaming/index.html

Las Vegas Casinos A site with links to the pages of some of Vegas's largest houses, including Stardust, the Fremont, and Sam's Town Hotel & Casino. This site covers services (dining, rooms, gambling) offered at each establishment and a few links to casinos outside the area, such as the Treasure Chest Hotel & Casino in Louisiana and Philadelphia's Silver Star Hotel & Casino. ✓**INTERNET**→*url* http://www.vegas.com/vegas com/castour/castour .html

Las Vegas Casinos Guide Every casino in Las Vegas and the surrounding towns is cataloged here. The list is long, but information in scanty—you'll find no more than the casino's name, address, telephone number, and room rates. ✓**INTERNET**→*url* http://www.pcap.com /hotel.htm

Minnesota Casinos There's more to do in Minnesota than watch the grain grow! This listing of casinos offers addresses, phone numbers, and pictures, and it shows that gambling is alive and well in the heart of the Bible Belt. ✓**INTERNET**→*url* http://www.primenet.com/~trix/casino.htm

Mississippi Beach Casinos Collect some clams on the 26-mile Mississippi Beach by heading to one of the many casinos in Biloxi and Gulfport, including the Copa, the Lady Luck, the Isle of Capri, and Treasure Bay. The Website features telephone numbers for each casino listed. Click on the casino's name for more detailed information—a description of available services, room rates, and event schedules. ✓**INTERNET**→*url* http://www.gulf-coast.com/info/casinos.htm

Reno Casinos Listing There are over 50 Reno casinos, and this site lists information on them all—from Circus Circus to the Riverboat to the Silver Club. Since the list is not alphabetized, you'll need to scan the entire list if you're looking for information on a specific casino. ✓**INTERNET**→*url* http://www.reno.nv.us/reno/casino.html

Wisconsin Casinos Read all about casinos in the Badger State at this page. The alphabetical guide lists the casinos and their addresses, telephone numbers, hours of operation, and the number of tables and machines available. ✓**INTERNET**→*url* http://www.primenet.com/~wrc/wiscon/wicas.html

Golf

Bill, who has been your traveling companion for almost 20 years, has had it with your temperamental behavior on vacations. "It's my way or the fairway," he says. Fairway? Probably he means "highway"—extreme anger will fritz the circuits like that—but Bill's frustrated outburst gives you an idea for a different kind of driving trip. Greens. Sand traps. Pants so plaid they overpower the unplaid world surrounding them. That's right—golf! From **The Golf Home Page** to the **Golf Course Database**, valuable golf resources are par for the course on the Net. Visit the home of golf—the United Kingdom—by browsing the **AA Golf Courses**. Polish your game by talking hook, slices, and more at AOL's **On the Green/Golf**. And then check out the dozens of sites devoted to individual golf courses.

Merion Golf Club, Ardmore, Pennsylvania—from http://dunkin.princeton.edu/.golf/

On the Net

Across the board

Golf Archive Course descriptions, golf images, information on clubmaking, and an explanation of handicaps, along with a summary of the archive's contents. ✓**INTERNET**→*url* http://dunkin.princeton.edu/.golf/

Golf Information Service Linked to the gigantic golf course database, this is one of the best online services for golfers seeking to plan a trip or to locate a golf course near their home. Search the database to find a course that suits your needs, get a list of all golf resorts in your area, order merchandise, or scan lists of golf schools, publications, organizations, and tournaments. ✓**AMERICA ONLINE**→*keyword* golfis

On the Green/Golf What does AOL's golf area have to offer online golf fans? News and notes, a chat area, a simulation game, and a library that includes golf digests and a number of fantasy courses for downloading. ✓**AMERICA ONLINE**→*keyword* gs→golf

The Golf Home Page Everything you've always wanted in a cybercaddy but were afraid to ask for, including links to other important golf sites, tips on golf-club customization, scorecards from local golf courses across the country, and a golf FAQ—as well as a few golf cartoons. ✓**INTERNET**→*url* http://voyager.whoi.edu/~pete/golf/

United States

Chardonnay Golf Course Go golfing in the heart of California wine country with the help of this site, which contains course and resort info for the Chardonnay Golf Course in Nappa. But remember—friends don't let friends golf drunk. ✓**INTERNET**→*url* http://www.freerun.com/napavalley/outdoor/chargolf/chargolf.html

Golf Course Database Still fuming over that first hole at the Scarlet Oaks course in Nitro, West Virginia? Interested in learning more about the Sung Nam Golf Club in Yongsan, South Korea? Live your golf dreams and relive your golf nightmares with this database of hundreds and hundreds of golf courses (353 in California alone). While this site is connected to the large scorecard database, courses listed on this page include additional information on course architects, as well as contact information. ✓**INTERNET**→*url* http://www.traveller.com/golf

Golf Course Database Hundreds of golf courses listed by state and maintained by GolfAmerica. Entries include address and phone information, a summary of all course holes, and information on the surrounding area. Can you walk the course? Are there homes around the course? Does the clubhouse have a restaurant? ✓**AMERICA ONLINE**→*keyword* golfis

Golf Courses in South Carolina Click on any course name on this map of South Carolina (which should be renamed the Golf State), and get information on courses all over the state (not just in Hilton Head)—phone numbers, addresses, and prices, along with specifics like slope, course length, and the course's architect. ✓**INTERNET**→*url* http://www.gdol.com/course/sc/

GolfData Web On-Line Home Page One of the most comprehensive golf sites on the Web, with a database of 15,000 American courses, discount coupons for those courses, online subscription information for a variety of golfing publications (*Northeast Golfer*, *Par Excellence*), playing tips from a PGA player (Jeff Maggert), an electronic golf shop, an electronic travel service, and a listing of more than 300 golf schools. While this site is a pay service ($4.95/month), it also has a selection of materials available for free, including essays on famous courses such as Turnberry and a program guide to The Golf Channel. ✓**INTERNET**→*url* http://www.gdol.com

New Hampshire/Vermont Course Cards A guide to a handful of courses in the New Hampshire / Vermont area, including the Dartmouth golf course and the Hanover Country Club. ✓**INTERNET**→*url* http://ausg.dartmouth.edu/~pete/golf/local-courses.html

Pinehurst Area Golf This famous course in North Carolina offers a Web page with helpful information on local golf schools, courses, and golf vacations for the resident or the tourist. ✓**INTERNET**→*url* http://www.sandhills.org/golf/golf.htm

Southern Utah Golf Courses A guide to a dozen courses in southern Utah, also known as Color Country. ✓**INTERNET**→*url* http://sci.dixie.edu/StGeorge/Golf/golf.html

Stanford Golf Course A single page devoted to the Stanford University golf course, with a map, tee distances, pars, and other illustrations. ✓**INTERNET**→*url* http://akebono.stanford.edu/~jerry/golf.html

International

AA Golf Courses A database of courses and resorts in England and Ireland—green fees! refreshment facilities! funny accents!—along with links to other services offered by the U.K. Automobile Association. ✓**COMPUSERVE**→*go* ukgolf

Golfing Alberta, Canada An extensive guide to golfing Alberta, with course listings and equipment tips for the northern (Rockies golf), central, and southern sections of the province, as well as extensive listings for the Edmonton metropolitan area. Information includes club membership, costs, hours, and contact phone numbers. ✓**INTERNET**→*url* http://bear.ras.ucalgary.ca/brads_home_page/CUUG/golf.html

Swing that club!—http://zodiac.tr-riscs.panam.edu/golf/19thhole.html

Lanier's Golf Database One of the premier search services for online golf courses, with thousands of golf courses listed, described, and sorted by name and location. Lanier's golf database also contains a number of basic golf articles, including "A Good Golf Course—What is it?" ✓**COMPUSERVE**→*go* golf

The Bermuda Golf Home Page Bermuda's chock-full of golf—eight full courses give it the most golf courses per square mile of any country on earth, and they are all covered in exhaustive detail here. Get info on all the courses at the Website. ✓**INTERNET**→*url* http://coos.dartmouth.edu/~aer/GOLF/

Honeymoon

Ralph and Alice Kramden didn't get away all that often, but other honeymooners do, going straight from the wedding to an Edenic vacation where they can soak up sun (or sea-spray), stare soulfully into one another's eyes, and fantasize about the blissful years to come. Online, the newly wed (or affianced) travel planner can investigate the possibilities with the help of **Island Weddings & Honeymoons**, **Weddings By the Sea**, **Instant Travel Honeymoons**, and more.

Honeymooning in Fiji—http://www.netilus.com/Matagi-VacTypes.html

On the Net

Across the board

Honeymoon Travel Info *Honeymoon* magazine sponsors this site, which features reviews of exotic, unique, and private honeymoon resorts worldwide. Check back each week for a new set of resort reviews. ✓**INTERNET**→*url* http://www.honeymoon.com/

soc.couples.wedding (ng) Cynthia asked for suggestions for good honeymoon locations, and she received enough responses to keep her and her groom traveling for the rest of their lives. And not everyone suggested Niagara Falls or a cruise to Bermuda. Suggestions ranged from a stay at the Cliff House Lodge Country Inn in Denver to a Windjammer Barefoot honeymoon cruise to a roughing-it honeymoon at the Drake Bay Wilderness Camp in Costa Rica. ✓**USENET**→soc.couples.wedding

Destinations

A Wedding Made in Paradise A marriage and honeymoon in Maui? If that sounds ideal to you, then head to this page, which describes the many services available there, including rentals of marriage officiators (religious or non-religious), scads of outdoor churches, music, limos, and even wedding stationery services. This site provides basic descriptions and contact information. ✓**INTERNET**→*url* http://www.maui.net/~wedmaui/page2.html

Caesars Nestled in the Pocono Mountains of Pennsylvania is Caesars, a full-service spot for brides and grooms. Besides offering special five-day honeymoon packages, Caesars boasts a full range of activities, including skiing, indoor swimming, tennis, and golf. In addition to a description of Caesars services and rates, this site features an irresistible photo of a couple bathing in a champagne glass-shaped bathtub. ✓**INTERNET**→*url* http://www.hardiman.com/malls/rmcm/travel/caesars/index.html

Caribmoon Bermuda does not require a blood test or health certificate to be married there, but you do have to publish a "Notice of Intended Marriage" in a local paper two weeks beforehand. Visit this site to learn the rules and regulations of marrying in the Caribbean locales of the British Virgin Islands, Anguilla, Antigua, Bermuda, the Bahamas, Barbados, the Cayman Islands, Grenada, Jamaica, St. Lucia, St. Vincent, the U.S. Virgin Islands, and St. Kitts and Nevis. You'll also find contact info for a variety of hotels on those islands. ✓**INTERNET**→*url* http://www.caribweb.com/caribweb/caribmoon/

Catalina Weddings Get married and honeymoon on Catalina Island with the help of this service.

Packages include a non-denominational service, a certified wedding certificate, sparkling champagne (or cider), and rooms at the Victorian-style Seacrest Hotel. ✓**INTERNET**→*url* http://www.catalina-island.com/guide/catwed.html

Couples Jamaica You don't have to be married before you get there (or even at all), but Couples Jamaica encourages taking (or renewing) your vows at the resort by offering complimentary weddings! It's included in the price of the resort's package, which also includes unlimited access to scuba and windsurfing equipment, water-tricycles, and glass-bottom boat rides, plus all meals and snacks! Read about this resort and get pricing info here. ✓**INTERNET**→*url* http://www.webcom.com/~travel/couples.html

Honeymoon City Motel, Niagara Falls Contact information for this motel, which stands within spray-shot of the famous Falls. ✓**INTERNET**→*url* http://www.niagara.com/falls/

Instant Travel Honeymoons Just tell this service when and where you want to honeymoon, and Instant Travel will take care of all the details. Whether you wish to recover from the wedding on the beaches of Jamaica or on the slopes of the Swiss Alps, Instant Travel will arrange your honeymoon trip and stay. German brides and grooms are welcome also: Sie sprechen Deutsch bei Instant Travel! ✓**INTERNET**→*url* http://www.cgl.com/~it/honeymoo.html

Island Weddings & Honeymoons For a list of travel agents that specialize in weddings and honeymoons in the Caribbean, turn to this site. You'll get the names, telephone numbers, and email addresses of companies such as All-Inclusive Vacations and Unforgettable Island Weddings. ✓**INTERNET**→*url* http://www.webcom.com/~travel/wedding.html

Lake Tahoe Telephone numbers for every service you may need for your wedding and honeymoon on Lake Tahoe—from churches and chapels to heavenly honeymoon hideaways. ✓**INTERNET**→*url* http://www.virtualtahoe.com/VLT2/WeddingsHoneymoons/Weddings.html

Las Vegas Wedding Chapels From drive-through quickstops to traditional churches, Las Vegas has a wedding chapel to fit every taste. (Elvis would have loved tying the knot at the Graceland Wedding Chapel.) This site holds service descriptions and telephone numbers for nearly 30 chapels. ✓**INTERNET**→*url* http://www.vegas.com/wedding/wedhome.html

Las Vegas Weddings & Honeymoons You don't need to get married to enjoy a chocolate truffle extravaganza with a bottle of champagne, but if you book a honeymoon and wedding through this service, the vittles will be thrown in. Concise descriptions of its various honeymoon packages plus pricing and contact information are given here. ✓**INTERNET**→*url* http://www.pcap.com/cw_wed.htm

Wedding with Makana The Hawaiian island of Kauai offers a multitude of services for weddings, including musicians, photographers, limos, tuxedo rentals, and witness services. Descriptions of the island, weddings, and honeymoons are online here. ✓**INTERNET**→*url* http://www.hotspots.hawaii.com/wed.html

Weddings by the Sea If you want a small wedding (it must be six people or fewer) at Half Moon Bay, 40 miles south of San Francisco, Weddings by the Sea will arrange everything for the event, including two nights at a B&B for the new bride and groom, a professional photographer, a wedding bouquet and boutonniere, and an ordained officiant. Read service, pricing, and contact info at this site. ✓**INTERNET**→*url* http://coastside.net/WhistlerE/weddings.html

Travelogues

Honeymoon in Australia If you're thinking about consummating your union in the Outback, this essay will convince you it's the right place to do it. Franz Aubrey Metcalf and his wife, Nina, describe many of Australia's attractions for lovers. ✓**INTERNET**→*url* http://Alpha.Solutions.Net/rec-travel/pacific/australia/qld-honeymoon.metcalf.html

Ian and Lisa's Honeymoon After flipping through a large collection of Ian and Lisa's wedding pictures, read a description of their trip to Thudufusi in the Maldives. If you don't know exactly where the Maldives are (let alone Thudfusi), don't worry. Ian and Lisa provide a detailed map of the island (which is in the Ari Atoll), as well as hotel and dining suggestions for the island. ✓**INTERNET**→*url* http://www.kfs.org:80/~ian/wedding/honeymoon/

Scuba

You don skintight black rubber, cover your eyes with a mask, and pull on some really funky shoes. No, you're not on your way to a rather risqué evening at a "private" club. You're a scuba diver in search of an underwater challenge. Start your hunt at **Eric's Scuba Page** or **Aquanaut**, where you'll find everything from dive site reviews to technical information on Nitrox and rebreathers (that might just ensure that you return to the surface unbent). Converse with other mouth-breathers on AOL's **Scuba Forum** or the **Scuba Mailing List**, where divers exchange fish stories ("so this really, really big barracuda was heading my way") and their favorite undiscovered sites. If you don't have any friends willing to head underwater several hundred feet with you, **SoloBuddy** can help you plan a trip anyway.

Exploring the briny deep—from http://www.batnet.com:80/shicho/see%26sea/

On the Net

Across the board

Aquanaut A huge hubsite for diving Websites, Aquanet offers links to every kind of online scuba resource, from a product marketplace to commercial home pages, dive site info—general and regional) to underwater image collections, information services such as Global Sea Surface Temperature Maps and the Marine Organisms Database and many other online archives. Breathe naturally, fall back in, and explore. ✓**INTERNET**→ *url* http://bighorn.terra.net/aquanaut/

Eric's Scuba Page Eric, the systems manager of the School of Oceanography at Washington State, insists that no government-funded time was spent creating this extraordinary site. If that is true, he must spend most of his free time diving and Website designing. Eric's site is both user-friendly and informative, providing lots of links to other scuba sites, technical information on Nitrox and rebreathers, TDI and NAUI dive agency pages, and local (Seattle-area) dive-site reviews. The entire site is indexed and searchable by keyword. ✓**INTERNET**→ *url* http://diver.ocean.washington.edu/

Internet Scuba and Snorkeling Resources Get ready to head into the murky deep with this scuba Website. It offers links to scuba sites like Diving Destinations, Eric's Scuba Page, and Jake's Dive Locker. When you're not off linking to other Net resources, explore the on-site Adventure Bookstore, which sells diving guides. Reviews and synopses of the guides are also available. ✓**INTERNET**→ *url* http://www.gorp.com/gorp/activity/Scuba.htm

The Scuba Forum Put on your wet suit and dive into the amazing resources at the Scuba Forum. If you're trying to decide between Jamaica and the Mediterranean for your next diving trip, turn to the Scuba Board here for recommendations throughout the world. (Hundreds of posts on the board show that Hawaii, the Bahamas, and Cozumel are very popular dive spots.) The Scuba Board is also an excellent place to read about diving regulations and licenses for different destinations. After choosing a location for your next scuba trip, you can read up on the best equipment to take by checking into the Dive Equipment section. If you're a first-time diver and need to be certified before your scuba vacation, see the list of certification agencies available at this forum. ✓**AMERICA ONLINE**→ *keyword* sports→scuba forum

UK Diving Resources Divers worldwide rejoice in this Website—it's admirably complete. A learned site, it has book reviews and computer programs that will interest aqua nuts. Divers can also keep up to date with announcements of events, conferences, and diving news The *Lusitania* was recently made a restricted diving site. U.K. divers submit enthusiastic trip reports (such as John's recent exploration of WWII ships off Normandy) and there are local site reports (watch out for strong tides off Perch Rock near Caernarfon). UK Diving Resources also offers links to other scuba pages and a whole section on scuba diving in the Red Sea—the promised land for divers. ✓**INTERNET**→*url* http://www.cru.uea.ac.uk/ukdiving/

International sites

British Sub-Aqua Club Can't they just say "scuba" like everyone else? From its location in South Wirral, Cheshire, the British Sub-Aqua Club reigns over certification and training in the U.K. Certification requirements for legal diving in the British Isles are available at this site, as are syllabi and descriptions of courses, such as the ever-popular Decompression Workshop or Boat and Engine Maintenance. ✓**INTERNET**→ *url* http://www.cru.uea.ac.uk/ukdiving/bsac/

Diving in Australia Submerge yourself in information about diving off Australia. This Website features a clickable map that accesses descriptions of over 90 sites off Queensland, New South Wales, Victoria, and Tasmania, just to mention four. (One diver's review of Tinderbox in Tasmania: "Tinderbox is a shallow shore dive, following a rock wall. A divers' trail has been set up to follow with descriptions on guideposts. Visibility can be limited, and the diving area can get crowded, as many diving schools use it as a training ground.") You can also use this site to link to diving clubs and services all over the continent, like the Monash University Underwater Club in Victoria and the Cullen Bay Dive Centre in the Northern Territory. ✓**INTERNET**→*url* http://leja.cs.utas.edu.au/Diving/Diving.html

Diving in Malaysia FAQ According to this site, the best time to dive off the eastern coast of Malaysia (Perherntian, Redand, Lang Tengah) is between March and October. The best time to see giant leatherback turtles in Malaysian waters is during August and September. This FAQ provides site descriptions, as well as contact information for Malaysian tour operators. ✓**INTERNET**→*url* http://galaxy.cz3.nus.sg:8100/~leews4/scuba/dim.faq

Jake's Dive Locker Yo ho ho and a bottle of rum, a collection of dive reports and maps, and an online magazine about diving off the Philippines. ✓**INTERNET**→*url* http://www.jake.com/DIVE/locker.html

Scuba in Singapore Check out the clickable map for those few diving spots that still exist around one of the busiest ports in the world. The University of Singapore also lists its scuba courses, gear-rental options, and upcoming trips to the more appealing shores of Malaysia. ✓**INTERNET**→*url* http://galaxy.cz3.nus.sg:8100/~leews4/scuba/scuba.html

Site guides

rec.scuba (ng) Planning a scuba trip to Belize? Steven advises strongly against one local operator, whose instructors don't know which way is up, whose boats tend to sink, and whose food is less than appetizing. Jerry warns about customs regulations and recommends that taxis be taken after dark in Belize City. Or maybe you'd prefer the Caymans? Or Fiji? Or Greece? Read about hundreds of diving destinations worldwide at this newsgroup. ✓**USENET**→rec.scuba

Scuba Diving Kathy requests info on treasure dives in Florida, hoping to help finance her vacation, and Barney suggests she try Sebastian Inlet. Rob and Laura, novice divers from Kansas, get help locating easy dives and the best outfitters along the Great Barrier Reef. Several professional dive operators also frequent the board and offer insights on what to look for in a charter dive. Though lacking technical talk, this board, for dive recommendations and fish stories, is fun. ✓**PRODIGY**→*jump* sports play bb→scuba diving

Scuba Forum Where's the best spot to dive in the Caribbean in November? Are there any places to cave dive in California? Is it possible to do day-trip dives in Cozumel if your hotel is in Cancun? For the answers to these and other scuba-site questions, this forum's message board is the place to go. Libraries here house site reviews, as well as general scuba information. ✓**COMPUSERVE**→*go* diving

Scuba Mailing List (ml) Discuss the unusual feeling of breathing underwater with others who enjoy scuba diving. ✓**INTERNET** ...*email* scuba@cc.itu.edu.tr ✍ *Email with general correspondence* ...→listserv@cc.itu.edu.tr ✍ *Type in message body:* subscribe <your full name>

Wreck Database Don't get your hopes up—most wrecks aren't filled with Spanish doubloons awaiting your plundering hands. But check this database for where to find large wrecks like the *Titanic* or small ones like the *Rusty Nail*. ✓**INTERNET**→*url* http://www.opal.com/aquanaut/wreckdbw

Tour agents

Blue Mesa Travel An advertisement with tour price information and telephone numbers for a company specializing in diving off-Cozumel. ✓**INTERNET**→*url* http://www.travelbase.com/activities/scuba/blue-mesa/

Florida Down Under Get a description of the company's services, and learn how to reach them for further information about diving tours to sites worldwide. ✓**INTERNET**→*url* http://www.opennet.com/fdu/

Go Diving Diving trip information from a company that goes to Belize, Bonaire, the Cayman Islands, Costa Rica, Roatan, and St. Lucia, among other places. ✓**INTERNET**→*url* http://www.travelsource.com/scuba/godiving.html

Rocky Mountain Diving Center Tours Descriptions (including prices) of scuba diving tours off Australia, Fiji, Honduras, and other locations. The Website also offers contact information for interested parties. ✓**INTERNET**→*url* http://www.csn.net/rmdc/

See & Sea Travel An email address as well as phone and fax numbers for See & Sea Travel are available at this Website, along with a full price list for their tours. ✓**INTERNET**→*url* http://www.batnet.com:80/shicho/see%26sea/

SoloBuddy Although this company is called SoloBuddy, it offers tours for singles and families alike. Learn about their various tours, and find telephone and fax numbers, as well as an email address for the company, at this Website. ✓**INTERNET**→*url* http://www.solobuddy.com/tours/scuba/scuba.html

Sporting Life Travel This Indiana-based company organizes scuba trips to destinations worldwide. Download a fax form or get a telephone number at the Website for

Fodor's Choice...

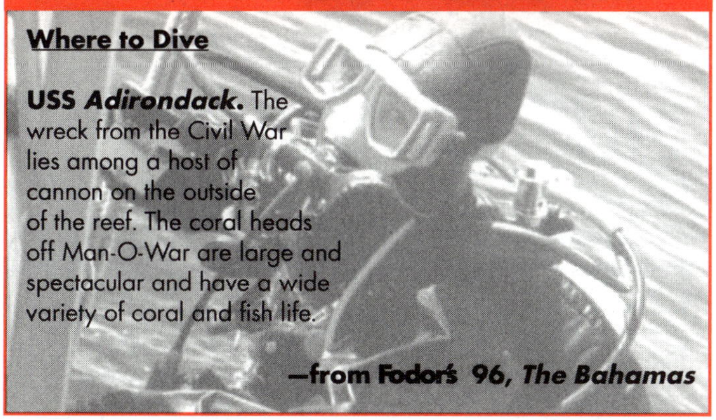

Where to Dive

USS *Adirondack*. The wreck from the Civil War lies among a host of cannon on the outside of the reef. The coral heads off Man-O-War are large and spectacular and have a wide variety of coral and fish life.

—from Fodor's 96, *The Bahamas*

further information. ✓INTERNET→*url* http://underground.net/New musicians/mmttpt.html

Tierra Mar Travel The site offers diving tour descriptions and contact information for Tierra Mar Tours, as well as links to travel-related sites like Kobla's Currency Converter and the Library of Congress Map Collection. ✓INTERNET→*url* http://www.geopages.com/thetropics/1660/

Tropical Penguins Scuba Travel A promotional page for a travel company specializing in scuba trips. ✓INTERNET→*url* http://underground.net/Newmusicians/mmttpt.html

U.S. sites

Monterey Dive Guide This guide to diving in Monterey has it all, including listings for diving destinations, stores, and food and lodging, as well as no-holds-barred evaluations of favorite places. The author loved his night dive at Del Monte Beach and the chowder with garlic and cheese at Vivolo's. He recommends avoiding Lover's Cove during the day because of an excessive number of surfers. And, as for McAbee2: "Oh, how I hate McAbee2. If my attitude toward it changes, I'll let you know, and I'll write more." ✓INTERNET→*url* http://www.halcyon.com/jong/scuba/monterey.html

Ohio Diver's WWW Page Scuba is probably not the first thing that comes to mind when one thinks of Toledo, but Ohio does not lack for diving opportunities. Check here for lists of clubs, upcoming dives, and site reports. The Instructor's Corner provides equipment comparisons and articles on the bends and diving computers, among other things. ✓INTERNET→*url* http://www.infinet.com/~gmcmanus/diver/ohdiver.html

Pacific Offshore Divers Do you know the way to San Jose? If so, and you like to dive, head to this local diving organization's page. Find out about course offerings like Introduction to Wreck and Navigation and club outings that often seem to be accompanied by beach barbecues. Maybe life really is better in Southern California. ✓INTERNET→*url* http://www.thesphere.com/PODI/

Puget Sound and Pacific NW Dive Site Reviews Eric, the Pacific Northwest's Web diving guru, has evaluated 56 local sites for difficulty and underwater panorama. His "way cool" clickable map lets you pick a site, say Mukilteo State Park, and hands you thumbnail descriptions along with travel and safety information. ✓INTERNET→*url* http://diver.ocean.washington.edu/pnwdivereviews.html

Scuba Diving at Boynton Beach Often referred to as "Florida's best-kept secret," Boynton Beach may not remain so for long after the Web-wandering millions see its charms described at this attractive site. The page provides up-to-the-minute diving-condition reports; water temperature forecasts; locale descriptions, accompanied by pictures of sea turtles, anemones and even an occasional man-o-war; and Ray McAllister's column on tips for marking great dive spots. ✓INTERNET→*url* http://www.emi.net/~bdenton/scuba.html

Seattle Dive Spots Jon has graciously shared his favorite daytime dives in the Seattle area in this hypertext guide. Choose from the likes of Salter Park, Titlow Beach, and Edmonds Underwater Park. Each description contains depth, visibility, difficulty, current, time, and directions from Seattle. Flora and fauna also are lovingly described. Ever seen a geoduck or a Turkish Towel? ✓INTERNET→*url* http://www.halcyon.com/jong/scuba/seattle/seattle.html

Southern Nevada Diver's Association What do denizens of Las Vegas do when they're not dealing blackjack? According to this club's informational Web page, they sail away on the Bottom Scratcher or the Sand Dollar to local dive sites. Don't miss the club raffles or the discounts offered by local scuba shops. ✓INTERNET→*url* http://www.unlv.edu/SCUBA/SNDA/

Skiing

The sensual pleasures of skiing are undeniable—the white snow, the clear air, the slow burn of the hot buttered rum in the lodge after a long day of letting the moguls pound your legs into submission. If you've ever skiied, you know that it's one of the best ways to combine exercise and sightseeing; if you've never skiied, you should. Netschussers can start their quest for mountain knowledge at **The Snow Page** and **Ski America**; preview runs by visiting the **Ski Map Server**; and then check out the pages devoted to individual resorts, whether Canadian (**Blackcomb Mountain**), American (**Aspen Snowmass Online, Looon Mountain Ski Area**), or international (**Ski Touring in Scotland for Non-Residents**).

Deep, fresh powder—from http://www.adfa.oz.au/aais/Pictures/Pictures00.html

On the Net

Across the board

GORP Internet Skiing Resources There are certainly other Websites with more comprehensive ski coverage, but GORP's numerous links are well organized and annotated. Select World Ski Reports to see where the powder is best and then head to the local resort pages for prices and pictures of Bozeman, Montana, or Sunday River, Maine. If you're looking for ski buddies try GORP's list of ski clubs. Cross-country advocates will find links to several good Nordic pages. ✓**INTERNET**→*url* http://www.gorp.com/gorp/activity/skiing.htm

Ski America Ski America has provided information on ski resorts for almost 30 years, and many of their resort reviews are online here. Although not a complete listing (only one of the many resorts in New Mexico is reviewed), it is a good place to comparison shop. You can also obtain information on cut-rate lift tickets for many ski areas. ✓**INTERNET**→*url* http://www.skiamerica.com/biz/skiamerica/

Ski Map Server Maps, yes, but so very much more. This massive site has everything a Net-skier could possibly need. There are links to other ski sites worldwide here. Try the Snow Page's European ski collection or jump to Ski Colorado. There are also gopher and FTP links for the truly slope obsessed. Finally, there are the maps, more than 70 to date, collected by the site's creator. What's a ski map? It shows the basic layout of a slope, specific trails, and mountain and slope elevations. Important stops, like the ski lodge, are also noted. If you want to relive your last trip to Sundance, there is a map here for you. Have recurrent James Bond superskier fantasies? Take a look at the map of Murren in Switzerland, the site of the Bond film *On Her Majesty's Secret Service*. Missing Aspen? There always Beau Jo's pizza menu to bring back the Colorado experience. ✓**INTERNET**→*url* http://www.cs.umd.edu/~regli/ski.html

Ski Tips When you go skiing, you may need to improve your technique, and this site will help you—with help on everything from displacing your weight to conquering steep slopes. ✓INTERNET→*url* http://vanbc.wimsey.com/~waddell/skitip5.html

Skiing the Internet A small Website with a collection of ski links and slope reports. Hundreds of documents on every conceivable skiing topic (the result of a gopher search) are linked to this site. So if you want to access the Austrian Alpine Information Service, the Apache Sunrise Ski Report, and the newsgroup rec.skiing all from one place, go to this site. ✓INTERNET→ *url* http://fire.clarkson.edu/edu/tc/tc94/kingkd/kdk.ski.html

Ski-Web Bored and boiling in Biloxi, Brenda headed to this huge Website to plan a much-needed ski vacation. She spent several contented hours consulting the vast number of regional information links, weighing the advantages of Telluride in Colorado against Sugarloaf in Maine. But wait, what about Chile or Australia? Once she settled on Colorado, Brenda took advantage of SkiWeb's links to discount air fares and to hot ski spots. After saving on her plane ticket, she decided to buy new bindings, so she linked to the Ski Industry Association's Web page. Did Brenda enjoy her time on the slopes? She sure did—and so did the doctor from Memphis she met on the chairlift. ✓INTERNET→*url* http://diamond.sierra.net/SkiWeb/

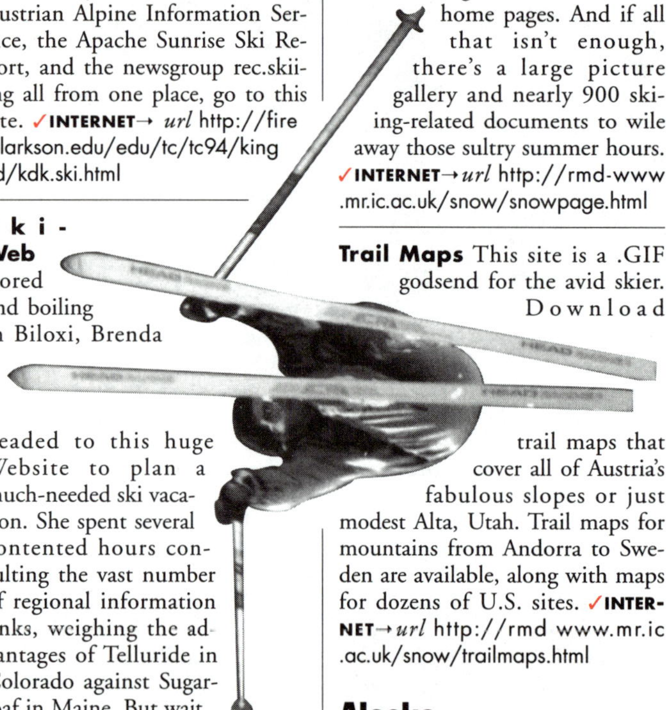

The Snow Page This is the best skiing site going—a massive collection of links to resorts, newsgroups, archives, and home pages worldwide. There are also maps, conditions reports, travel services, and online ski shops to assist in every aspect of a cyber ski bum's life. You can jump to several online 'zines or find out about the "snow people" on the Net by linking from here to their home pages. And if all that isn't enough, there's a large picture gallery and nearly 900 skiing-related documents to wile away those sultry summer hours. ✓INTERNET→*url* http://rmd-www.mr.ic.ac.uk/snow/snowpage.html

Trail Maps This site is a .GIF godsend for the avid skier. Download trail maps that cover all of Austria's fabulous slopes or just modest Alta, Utah. Trail maps for mountains from Andorra to Sweden are available, along with maps for dozens of U.S. sites. ✓INTERNET→*url* http://rmd www.mr.ic.ac.uk/snow/trailmaps.html

Alaska

Alaska Alpine Club Information for the skier and mountaineer. Check out the daylong seminar on avalanche safety and the class on skis, boots, and tents. ✓INTERNET→*url* http://info.alaska.edu:70/0/Alaska/rec/aac/class1

Arizona

Arizona Snowbowl Ski Area Report Daily conditions report. ✓INTERNET→*url* http://www.ksu.edu/unicorn/phxflg.weather

Sunrise Park Ski Resort Gamble with your limbs on these slopes and then with your loot at the casino. This illustrated hypertext page describes this Arizona resort, which is run by the White Mountain Apache Tribe. ✓INTERNET→*url* http://www.primenet.com/~azskis/skipage.html

California

Far West Ski Report Daily ski conditions reports for California areas. ✓INTERNET→*url* http://garnet.msen.com:70/0/vendor/aminews/ski-reports/farwest.rep

Lake Tahoe Highway Conditions Check here for snow condition announcements before driving on mountain roads in the Lake Tahoe area. State Route 89 and the Monitor Pass may look fine on the map, but they might be closed due to heavy snowfall. ✓INTERNET→*url* http://www.sierra.net/roads.html

Mammoth Mountain Chair 16 has been replaced by a high-speed detachable quad chairlift, and there is also a new paint scheme of earth tones and greens in the Main Lodge. Take a peep at this resort, which boasts 150 trails and 70 percent sunny days. ✓INTERNET→*url* http://www.cccd.edu/~markb/ski/mj/mammoth/

Southland Ski Server It may never rain in Southern California, but it does snow in the San Gabriel Mountains. You can get resort info, trail maps, and rates at this site, plus "real-time freeway information" and much-needed snow driving tips (chains are still your best friend in bad weather) from the CHiPs. ✓INTERNET→*url* http://www.cccd.edu/ski.html

Colorado

Aspen Snowmass Online This virtual chamber of commerce provides details on skiing and other things to do at this enchanting Colorado locale. ✓**INTERNET**→*url* http://www.aspenonline.com/aspenonline/

Aspen/Snowmass Resorts This lovely guide describes all the best runs (from Northstar to Little Nell), slope conditions, and transport schedules. There's a local events calendar for aprés ski enjoyments, like Mozart concerts and church festivals. ✓**INTERNET**→*url* http://www.infosphere.com/ski aspen/index.html

Colorado Avalanche Warnings Check here for potentially lifesaving bulletins from the National Weather Service in Denver. ✓**INTERNET**→*url* gopher://gopher.Colorado.Edu:861

Colorado Cross-Country Skiing Sick of the crowds and lift lines? Then explore Colorado cross country skiing with the trail descriptions and contact numbers provided here. ✓**INTERNET**→*url* http://www.aescon.com/ski/xcountry.htm

Colorado Snow Report Daily ski conditions report for the Colorado area. ✓**INTERNET**→*url* http://www.ksu.edu/unicorn/denrec.weather

Rocky Mountain Ski Report Daily conditions reports. ✓**INTERNET**→*url* http://garnet.msen.com:70/0/vendor/aminews/ski-reports/rockies.rep

Ski Areas in Colorado Info on many Colorado areas, including run lengths, lift capacities, prices for ski lessons, snow report numbers, slope elevations, and much more. Some of the areas have home pages, and this site links to them. ✓**INTERNET**→*url* http://www.boco.co.gov/~aemlu/skiing.html

Ski Colorado This Website is a complete ski resource for the fabulous Rockies. Start with the numerous ski resort briefings. Select Purgatory and learn about trails, lifts, ski lessons, and children's programs there. But there's more to do than ski, and each locale is lovingly described—read up on Durango's Wild West past, high mountain geology, restaurants, and accommodations. After you've chosen a slope, look for a bargain ski tour package. Comparison shop for equipment rental from three online purveyors or shop through online stores. If Nordic is your snow passion, there is a list of the best cross-country areas statewide, too. When the trip is imminent, don't forget to check weather and road conditions here. ✓**INTERNET**→*url* http://www.aescon.com/ski/index.html

Summit County, Colorado For slope statistics, click on the appropriate skier on this handsome map and get info on Copper Mountain, Frisco, and Breckinridge, among others. Click on the nearest town for history and accommodation information. ✓**INTERNET**→*url* http://www.colo.com/summit/home

Fodor's Choice...

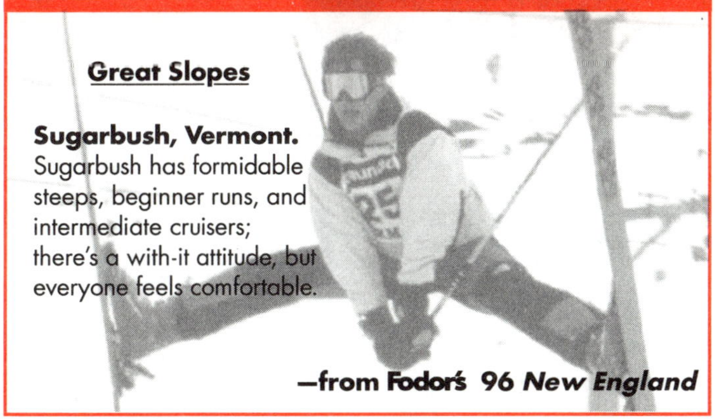

Great Slopes

Sugarbush, Vermont. Sugarbush has formidable steeps, beginner runs, and intermediate cruisers; there's a with-it attitude, but everyone feels comfortable.

—from **Fodor's 96 *New England***

Iowa

Sundown Iowa's all flat with cornfields, right? Not at Sundown, as this page full of facts, history, prices, and pictures attests. But don't jettison all your notions of farmland—the ski-jump run does end at the John Deere factory, right in front of the tractor lot. ✓**INTERNET**→*url* http://twister.ResGen.Com:80/~bpollock/sundown/sundown.html

Maine

Sugarloaf Mountain Don't miss this page's Internet deals of the week with money off on everything from lift tickets to meals. In addition to slope stats, this page also offers a cyberlodge for chat and technical talk from mountain pros. ✓**INTERNET**→*url* http://www.ultranet.com/biz/sugarloaf/

Sunday River Get conditions, cross-country trail maps, and nightlife suggestions for this resort in Bethel, Maine. ✓**INTERNET**→*url* http://www.uml.edu/~koverber/Sunday.html

Michigan

Boyne Mountain Guaranteed skiing! Yes, this resort's page lists rates, fast facts, conditions, and an online guarantee: snow or your money back. ✓**INTERNET**→*url* http://www.iquest.com:80/michweb/boyne/

Michigan Ski Page Head to this site for listings of northern Michigan's cross-country ski trails and resort descriptions, rates, and conditions. Get the inside scoop on the best in Alpine and Nordic skiing by reading articles from *Great Lakes Skier Magazine.* ✓**INTERNET**→*url* http://www.iquest.com/michweb/ski/

Northern Michigan Cross-Country Ski Trails Cross-country skiing is not just for breakfast any more—try the Grinder, a three-mile lighted trail for night skiing. This online guide reviews the trails in Sand Lakes Quiet Area, Boyne Nordican, and Crystal Mountain. ✓**INTERNET**→*url* http://www.iquest.com:80/michweb/ski/terrell/

Skiing in the Gaylord Area Look for descriptions, contact numbers, and accommodations and dining information for skiing in the Gaylord area of Michigan. Cross-country fans won't want to miss the excitement and beauty of the Whoopay Loop on the Pine Baron Pathway. ✓**INTERNET**→*url* http://www.iquest.com/michweb/gaylord/gskiing.html

Montana

Denbigh Starkey's Bozeman, Montana, Skiing Page According to skiing know-it-alls, Big Sky Mountain has the shortest lift lines in the nation. Get slope, cross-country, and travel info for this lesser-known paradise. ✓**INTERNET**→*url* http://www.cs.montana.edu/~starkey/skiing.html

Nevada

Tahoe Ski Information Ski and road conditions (see if poles and chains are required), lift prices, and a link to the Tahoe Sheriff are all online here. If you are enamored of Tahoe, don't miss the real estate deal of the week in this page's classified ads section. ✓**INTERNET**→*url* http://diamond.sierra.net/SkiWeb/sierras/cond01.html #squaw

New England

New England Alpine Ski Report Don't let your ski trip be ruined by lack of snow. Check these daily reports on New England ski areas, with downhill, cross-country, and snowboard information. ✓**INTERNET**→*url* http://www.ksu.edu/unicorn/abrec .weather

Northeast Ski Reports Reports on ski conditions for Vermont, Massachusetts, Maine, and the region. ✓**INTERNET**→*url* http://garnet.msen.com:70/0/vendor/aminews/ski-reports/ne.rep

New Hampshire

Loon Mountain Ski Area Smart loons will visit this page for ski discounts and a daily ski report. Cross country enthusiasts will enjoy the trail maps and technical tips. ✓**INTERNET**→*url* http://www.Mainstream.com:80/~loon/

Ski Resorts: New Hampshire This Website for skiing in the live-free-or-die state features up-to-the-minute weather reports, trail conditions, and mid-week promotions to save skiers big bucks. You can also jump from here to Web pages for resorts like Bretton Woods and King Pine. ✓**INTERNET**→*url* http://www.mainstream.com/~loon/

New Mexico

New Mexico Ski Report From Taos to Sipapu, this daily updated document reports snow depths, forecasts, and trail conditions for New Mexico. ✓**INTERNET**→*url* http://www.ksu.edu/unicorn/abqrec.weather

Ski New Mexico Use the interactive map to experience the lift to the steepest trail in the state, Al's Run at Taos. The New Mexico Tourist Authority runs this site, which provides information on Alpine, Nordic, and snowboarding statewide. ✓**INTERNET**→*url* http://www.nets.com/skinm

New York

Ski Areas of New York Did you know that there were 1,073,330 ski poles sold in New York in 1993? Keeping track of ski pole sales is not the only feature of the Website. It also provides vital weather reports, camping availability information, and phone numbers for all of New York's ski slopes. ✓INTERNET→*url* http://www.microserve.net:80/SkiNewYork/index.html

Oregon

Oregon Ski Report Information Check for daily slope reports for the Portland area. ✓INTERNET→*url* http://www.teleport .com/~mikec/orresorts .html

Pacific Northwest

Cascade Ski Report A professional meteorologist and avid Cascade skier posts reports about the weather and road conditions. Take a look at the infrared weather maps for long-term planning. ✓INTERNET→*url* http://www.net-serve.com/ski-report.html

---

Crystal Mountain Descriptions of the terrain, ski school courses, and snowboard park at Crystal. ✓INTERNET→*url* http://www.theworld.com/recreati/ski/slopes/places/northwes/crystalm/resort.htm

---

Northwest Ski Report If you're wary of trusting resort-generated conditions reports, turn to the skier-generated reports at this page. Just off the slope, skiers warn of corn snow or flash the news of five new inches on Snoqualimie. Submit your own report on any Oregon, Washington, or Idaho run. The site also offers links to resort pages, weather reports, and other ski Websites. ✓INTERNET→ *url* http://www.fhcrc.org/dwaring/skipage.html

---

Timberline Lodge Click on this page's bookcase icon for area maps, current snow conditions, ski school information, hotel information, and a calendar of local events. After you get the pertinent ski data, take a virtual stroll around this gorgeous lodge. ✓INTERNET→*url* http://www.westlinn.com/timberline/

Southeast

Southeastern Ski Report Daily conditions reports for North Carolina, Virginia, West Virginia, Tennessee, and Georgia ski areas. ✓INTERNET→*url* http://www.ksu.edu/unicorn/rdurec.weather

Utah

Powderhound Ski Report High above the plains and the Great Salt Lake lies the Wasatch ski area. Visit this site for area snow forecasts and slope reports. ✓INTERNET→*url* http://www.icw.com/skireport.html

---

Ski Utah This site changes every day, listing new ski bargains and up-to-the-minute ski conditions for both Alpine and Nordic resorts. There are also hypertext guides for several Utah ski areas. Submit your own slope review with the handy online form here. ✓INTERNET→*url* http://www.imall.com/ski-utah/ski-utah.html

Vermont

Jay Peak This "honest assessment" by a Jay Peak regular offers trail evaluations, cross-country guides, and maps. But that's not all. It also has advice on how to save money on your trip—for example, if you spend your evenings in Québec, you may benefit from the exchange rate. ✓INTERNET→*url* http://www.rpi.edu/~guidom/jaypeak.html

---

Killington Is Killington still making snow? Read the online commentary and look for special prices at this attractive page. ✓INTERNET→*url* http://www.cybermalls.com/cymont/killingt/index.htm

---

Killington Vermont The vertical drop at this New England resort puts the "kill" in Killington. If you're still interested, visit this Website for more information. ✓INTERNET→*url* http://www.netimpact.com/biz/killington/

Mad River Glen, Ski It If You Can Shop this resort's cybermall or just check trail conditions and lift rates. ✓INTERNET→*url* http://www.cybermalls.com/cymont/madriver/madriver.html

---

Northern Vermont Cross-Country, Backcountry and Telemark Skiing This site is a New England cross-country skier's survival package. It offers descriptions of ski areas, information on local ski clubs, and lists of Telemark ski instructors. Skiers can also get up-to-date weather information, advice on equipment and safety issues from the experts, and links to other Nordic sites worldwide. ✓INTERNET→*url* http://salus.uvm.edu/VTXCSki.html

---

Ski Info: Vermont Visit the skiing photo gallery here or take a guided tour of Jay Peak. Ratings of eastern ski areas written by Net skiers are also available. ✓INTERNET→*url* http://mole.uvm.edu/skivt-l/

Vermont Ski Areas Associa-

tion Don't miss the popular television show Vermont Skiing Today—consult the broadcast schedule at this site. Vermont ski resort reviews are also online here. ✓INTERNET→*url* http://www.cybermalls.com/cymont/vtski/vtski.htm

Vermont Skiing Today—Conditions Report More than just another conditions report site, Skiing Today also offers discounts for Internet skiers and lists of contact information for Vermont resorts. ✓INTERNET→*url* http://www.cybermalls.com/cymont/vtski/crtoday.htm

Vermont Winter Sports Forecast Daily updates listing temperatures, snow conditions, and forecasts for the Vermont area. ✓INTERNET→*url* http://www.ksu.edu/unicorn/albrecbt.weather

Wunderski's Ski Tent This home page has phone numbers and lift prices for several Vermont mountains, in addition to links to World Cup results and selected ski articles. ✓INTERNET→*url* http://www.uvm.edu:80/~mswartz/matt.html

Virginia

Skiing Basic contact information for the Massanutten and Wintergreen resorts. ✓INTERNET→*url* http://www.elpress.com/staunton/SKI.HTML

Washington

Washington State X/C Skiing Head to this site for phone numbers, a bibliography, and weather reports for Washington ski slopes, as well as detailed trail reviews that mention the "entertaining dips" on particular runs. ✓INTERNET→*url* http://www.eskimo.com/nordic/wa.html

Wisconsin

Ski Info: Wisconsin Hypertext reports from Nordic skiing literati and the scoop on slope difficulty, trails, and prices for various Wisconsin resorts. ✓INTERNET→*url* http://www.gcg.com/misc/xc/madxc.html

Wyoming

Jackson Hole Lots of ski, travel, and tourism info here. Don't miss the picture of thousands of elk hanging out at a Wyoming refuge. ✓INTERNET→*url* http://www.wis.com/cgi/jackson.cgi

Canada

Blackcomb Mountain Make your reservations for this British Columbia resort online. ✓INTERNET→ *url* http://www.whistler.net/blackcomb/index.html

Ottawa Cross Country Skiing Information Yes, one can obtain information on trail conditions in Ottawa here, but the site also tracks the World Loppet Nordic races. Use the contact numbers to register for the 90-km Engadin Skimarathon in Switzerland. Really feeling rugged? Read up on the 170-km Canadian Ski Marathon, billed as a family event. The creator is adding links to other Nordic sites worldwide. ✓INTERNET→*url* http://www.physics.carleton.ca/Ottawa/X-C/

Ski Canada The names Jasper, Lake Louse, and Banff are music to a skier's ear. Find out about these and other, lesser-known Canadian slopes (like Alberta's Marmot Basin) at this site. Look for slope and resort descriptions, maps, and contact numbers. Send in your own trip report once you've slipped down the slope. ✓INTERNET→*url* http://gpu2.srv.ualberta.ca/~bbolt/skican.html

Ski Info—British Columbia This site promises to be "Western Canada's most comprehensive online ski kiosk." Still under heavy construction, it currently features sections on Whistler and Blackcomb. ✓INTERNET→*url* http://www.wimsey.com/bcski.html

Western Canada Ski Guide Simply click on the map of British Columbia and Alberta for phone numbers, facility info, rates, and directions to ski highspots like Canmore (which was home to many 1988 Olympic events). ✓INTERNET→*url* http://skiing.geo.ucalgary.ca/WCSGuide/Guide.html

Whistler Mountain Whistler Mountain, home of the Warsteiner World Downhill, has its own weekly online newsletter called *Pique*, which is filled with articles on both skiing and cybersurfing. Check here for the newsletter, mountain conditions, and local tourist information. ✓INTERNET→ *url* http://www.whistler.net/whistler/index.html

International

aus.snow (ng) The land of surfers also has avid skiers. Can you belive how much a used snowboard is going for in Australia these days? John from New South Wales can't, but then Evan from Victoria comes to the rescue with a generous offer of a 1992 model. Antipodal skiers meet here to pass on reviews and advice, sell and trade equipment, and, frequently, to pray for snow. Check the archives for info on slopes, accommodations, lift tickets, and technique. Don't miss the skiing stories and the inspired prose of Aussie powderhounds. ✓**USENET**→ aus.snow

Australian Alpine Information Server Down Under and longing for downhill? This server has daily conditions for all Australian slopes, along with a useful guide to snow types to help the uninitiated interpret reports. The bottom half of Thredbo is grass. Pretty clear, eh? ✓**INTERNET**→*url* http://www.adfa.oz.au/aais/

Chilean Ski Guide What do you do once the cruel spring has come? Try Chile, where the skiing season spans from May to November. This attractive site lists restaurants, hotels, and resorts for various Chilean spots, such as Farellones-El Colorado, which lies 50 km west of Santiago. ✓**INTERNET**→*url* http://clubmidd.middlebury.edu/Courses/internet/students/passikof/final.html

Craigieburn Ski Club An illustrated description of this advanced terrain ski slope. ✓**INTERNET**→*url* http://info.alaska.edu:70/0/Alaska/rec/aac/class1

High Tatra Mountains General tourism information about this range in Slovakia. This site is loaded with rhapsodic descriptions, pictures, and contact information. ✓**INTERNET**→ *url* http://www.eunet.sk/slovakia/tatra-mountains.html

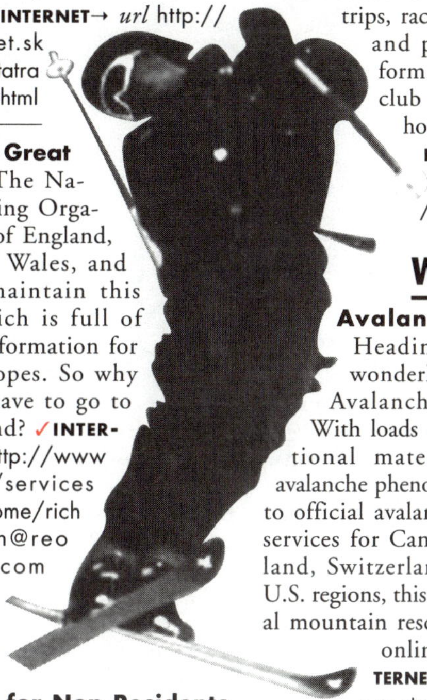

Ski Info: Great Britain The National Skiing Organizations of England, Scotland, Wales, and Ireland maintain this page, which is full of contact information for British slopes. So why does Di have to go to Switzerland? ✓**INTERNET**→*url* http://www.hal.com/services/juggle/home/richarjohnson@reo.mts.dec.com/ski.html

Ski Touring in Scotland for Non-Residents The author of this document warns that "the snows on Scotland aren't so much deposited as blasted onto the mountains." That notwithstanding, this document gives all the pertinent information needed to plan a Highland snow holiday. ✓**INTERNET**→*url* http://rmd-www.mr.ic.ac.uk/snow/ski-tour-scotland.html

Slovenia South of the Austrian Alps lies the new republic of Slovenia and its many spectacular ski areas—Kanin, Kobla, Vogel, Zatrnik, and Aelenica/Ljubeji. Even if pronounciation is a problem, you can learn about the ski attractions of this World Cup site, which offers 17 adult lifts and runs for all levels. ✓**INTERNET**→*url* http://www.ijs.si/slo-map.html

University of York Ski Club Instead of wandering moodily about the moor, University of York students are planning ski trips, racing down slopes, and perfecting their form. Find out about club activites on this home page. ✓**INTERNET**→*url* http://www.york.ac.uk/~socs190/

Weather

Avalanche Gopher Heading for a winter wonderland? Check the Avalanche gopher first. With loads of general educational material about the avalanche phenomenon and links to official avalanche monitoring services for Canada, Italy, Scotland, Switzerland, and various U.S. regions, this is the professional mountain rescue community's online network ✓**INTERNET**→*url* gopher://u.cc.utah.edu→uafc

National Snow and Ice Data Center According to the National Snow and Ice Data Center, its mission is "to broaden understanding of snow and ice, of their properties, characteristics and contexts, and of their significance for human activity." Become one with our frigid friends by perusing this collection of monographs on avalanches, paleoglaciology, and extra-terrestrial ices (alien snow cones?). ✓**INTERNET**→*url* http://floeberg.colorado.edu:1733/

rec.skiing.announce (ng) News flash...there will be powder at Steamboat tomorrow! A daily check-in will keep you abreast of everything going on in the ski world, from announcements of applications for races to final results of competitions to up-to-the-

Burnin' up the slopes—http://www.adfa.oz.au/aais/Pictures/Pictures00.html

minute AMI ski condition reports. A frequently posted guide points skiers in the direction of other Web resources. ✓**USENET**→rec.skiing.announce

Regional Ski Reports Take a peek at the snow-outlook map to see if the frozen rain gods have answered your prayers. Read daily condition reports for areas nationwide—from wet granular to hard-packed powder. If you can ski it, they can find it. ✓**AMERICA ONLINE**→*keyword* skireports

Ski Areas Get the slope skinny with this document. Be sure to master the codes at the beginning of the page so you can interpret the listings for worldwide ski areas from Achenkirk in Austria to Mount Weigele in Alberta, Canada. These reports list the vital statistics for each area: slopes and lifts, skiable acres, average snowfall, vertical drop (eek), and snowboarding access. Resort contact numbers are listed. ✓**INTERNET**→*url* http://www.explore .com/E_areas .html

Ski Conditions and Ski Resort Guide The Santa Fe ski basin still has a 77-inch base and 38 open trails (at least when we checked here). Conditions of 100 other areas were also available. If you haven't yet chosen where to get your lift ticket punched, try the resort guide here. You can search by locale or by feature. And what kinds of features are important? Excessively romantic resorts, cross country, child care, or spas? Each review gives price and attraction information, and lets you jump to other resorts in the state, too. ✓**PRODIGY**→*jump* skiing

U.S. Ski Reports Everyone knows how frustrating it is to pack up the car, drive to the mountain, and unpack the car, only to remember that it's the middle of August, and that the snow has turned to water. Avoid this unpleasant situation by checking in on ski reports—in this case, lots of them. The largest distributor of ski reports in the world runs this site, which offers ski conditions reports for the major U.S. ski areas. Base snow amounts, recent cover, open trails, and weather forecasts are all noted. ✓**INTERNET**→*url* http://garnet.msen.com:70/1/vendor/aminews/ski-reporrts

DETOURS

"After you have some experience, you find yourself longing to try those slopes you've heard all your friends rave about--you know them, the guys who would be right at home in a Warren Miller film? The only two obstacles between you and being able to ski the really steep stuff is technique and fear. Fear is the worst obstacle. It can make you freeze up. Once you've freaked out, you will find yourself stiffening up and leaning backwards. Your skis will immediately shoot out ahead of you and you'll wipe out. Keeping your weight forwards is paramount. In fact, the steeper the terrain, the more aggressive you need to be with your stance. You can't afford to let fear get in the way. On really steep terrain, head for the moguls. Moguls are your friends. Use the tops of them to bleed off your speed. Remember to let your legs bend when you begin skiing up the mogul and to extend your legs when skiing off the back side."

—from **Ski Tips**

Appendices

Internet Providers

by region and state

National

America OnLine
800-827-6364 (vox)

CompuServe
800-848-8199 (vox)

Delphi
800-695-4005 (vox)

GEnie
800-638-9636 (vox)

Internet Express
800-592-1240 (vox)

NETCOM On-Line Communications Services
800-501-8649/408-554-8649 (vox)

Prodigy
800-776-3449 (vox)

Southern States

Interpath
800-849-6305 (vox)

Alabama

Community Internet Connect, Inc.
205-722-0199 (vox)

db Technology
205-556-9020 (vox)

interQuest
205-464-8280 (vox)

WSNetwork Communications Services, Inc.
800-463-8750/334-263-5505 (vox)

Arkansas

Cloverleaf Technologies
800-830-9677/903-832-1367 (vox)

IntelliNet
800-290-7677 (vox)

Arizona

Crossroads Communications
602-813-9040 (vox)

Internet Direct of Utah, Inc.
602-274-0100 (vox)

Opus One
602-324-0494 (vox)

Primenet
800-463-8386/602-870-1010 (vox)

RTD Systems & Networking, Inc.
520-318-0696 (vox)

Systems Solutions Inc.
602-955-5566 (vox)

California

Access InfoSystems
707-422-1034 (vox)

Aimnet Information Services
408-567-3800(vox)

CC NET
800-CC-NET4U/510-988-0680 (vox)

QuickNet
714-895-3075 (vox)

CONNECTnet Internet Network Services
619-450-0254 (vox)

CRL
415-837-5300 (vox)

CTS Network Services
619-637-3637 (vox)

Cybergate Information Services
209-486-4283 (vox)

Delta Internet Services
714-778-0370 (vox)

DigiLink Network Services
310-542-7421 (vox)

Direct Net Access Inc.
510-649-6110 (vox)

Directnet
213-383-3144 (vox)

EarthLink Network, Inc.
213-644-9500 (vox)

Electriciti
619-338-9000 (vox)

HoloNet Information Access
510-704-0160 (vox)

Infoserv Connections
408-335-5600 (vox)

INTERNEX
408-496-5466 (vox)

ISP Networks
408-653-0100 (vox)

KAIWAN Internet
714-638-2139 (vox)

LanMinds, Inc.
510-843-6389 (vox)

Lightside, Inc.
818-858-9261 (vox)

LineX Communications
415-455-1650 (vox)

NetGate Communications
408-565-9601 (vox)

Northcoast Internet
707-443-8696 (vox)

Primenet
800-463-8386/602-395-1010 (vox)

QuakeNet
415-655-6607 (vox)

Scruz-Net
800-319-5555/408-457-5050 (vox)

Sierra-Net
702-832-6911 (vox)

South Valley Internet
408-683-4533 (vox)

ViaNet Communications
415-903-2242 (vox)

The WELL
415-332-4335 (vox)

West Coast Online
707-586-3060 (vox)

WombatNet
415-462-8800 (vox)

zNET
619-755-7772 (vox)

Colorado

Colorado SuperNet, Inc.
303-296-8202 (vox)

Community News Service, Inc.
719-592-1240 (vox)

CSDC, Inc.
303-665-8053 (vox)

ENVISIONET, Inc.
303-770-2408 (vox)

Indra's Net, Inc.
303-546-9151 (vox)

Old Colorado City Communications
719-528-5849 (vox)

Rocky Mountain Internet
800-900-7644 (vox)

Stonehenge Internet Communications
800-786-4638 (vox)

Connecticut

CONNIX
203-349-7059 (vox)

Futuris Networks, Inc.
203-359-8868 (vox)

I-2000, Inc.
516-867-6379 (vox)

Paradigm Communications
203-250-7397 (vox)

District of Columbia

CAPCON Library Network
202-331-5771 (vox)

CharmNet
410-558-3900 (vox)

Genuine Computing Resources
703-878-4680 (vox)

Internet Online, Inc.
301-652-4468 (vox)

usNet, Inc.
301-572-5926 (vox)

Delaware

SSNet, Inc.
302-378-1386 (vox)

Florida

CocoNet Corporation
813-540-2626 (vox)

CyberGate, Inc.
305-428-4283 (vox)

IDS
401-885-6855/800-IDS-1680 (vox)

The EmiNet Domain
407-731-0222 (vox)

Florida Online
407-635-8888/800-676-2599 (vox)

InternetU
407-952-8487 (vox)

MagicNet, Inc.
407-657-2202 (vox)

MetroLink Internet Services
407-726-6707 (vox)

PacketWorks, Inc.
813-446-8826 (vox)

Polaris Network, Inc.
904-878-9745 (vox)

PSS InterNet Services
904-253-7100/800-463-8499 (vox)

SymNet
904-222-8555 (vox)

Georgia

Internet Atlanta
404-410-9000 (vox)

MindSpring
404-888-0725 (vox)

Prometheus Information Network Group, Inc. (PING)
800-746-4835 (vox)

Hawaii

Hawaii OnLine
808-533-6981/800-291-5951 (vox)

LavaNet, Inc.
808-545-5282 (vox)

Pacific Information Exchange, Inc.
808-596-7494 (vox)

Sense Networking
408-335-9400 (vox)

Idaho

Micron Internet Services
208-368-5400 (vox)

Primenet
800-463-8386/602-870-1010 (vox)

Illinois

American Information Systems
708-413-8400/312-255-8500 (vox)

Allied Access, Inc.
800-463-8366 (vox)

InterAccess Co.
800-967-1580 (vox)

Open Business Systems, Inc.
708-250-0260 (vox)

Ripco Communications, Inc.
312-477-6210 (vox)

Tezcatlipoca, Inc.
312-850-0181 (vox)

WorldWide Access
708-367-1870 (vox)

Indiana

Evansville Online
812-479-1700 (vox)

HolliCom Internet Services
317-883-4500 (vox)

IgLou Internet ServiceS
800-436-4456 (vox)

IQuest Network Services
317-259-5050 (vox)

Metropolitan Data Networks Limited
317-449-0539 (vox)

Net Direct
317-251-5252 (vox)

World Connection Services
812-479-1700 (vox)

Kansas

DATABANK, Inc.
800-200-8985/913-842-6699 (vox)

Interstate Networking Corporation
816-472-4949 (vox)

Primenet
800-463-8386/602-870-1010 (vox)

SouthWind Internet Access, Inc.
316-263-7963 (vox)

Kentucky

IgLou Internet ServiceS
800-436-4456 (vox)

Louisiana

Communique Inc.
504-527-6200 (vox)

I-Link Ltd
800-454-6599 (vox)

NEOSOFT
800-438-6367/713-968-5800 (vox)

Maine

Agate Internet
207-947-8248 (vox)

Maryland

CAPCON Library Network
202-331-5771 (vox)

CharmNet
410-558-3900 (vox)

FredNet
301-631-5300 (vox)

Genuine Computing Resources
703-878-4680 (vox)

Internet Interstate
301-652-4468 (vox)

jaguNET Access Services
410-931-3157 (vox)

Softaid Internet Services Inc.
410-290-7763 (vox)

usNet, Inc.
301-572-5926 (vox)

Massachusetts

CENTnet, Inc.
508-454-5688/617-492-6079 (vox)

FOURnet Information Network
508-291-2900 (vox)

The Internet Access Company
617-276-7200 (vox)

intuitive information, inc.
508-342-1100 (vox)

Mallard Electronics, Inc.
413-732-0214 (vox)

North Shore Access
617-593-3110 (vox)

Pioneer Global
617-375-0200 (vox)

ShaysNet.COM
413-772-2923 (vox)

StarNet Internet Access (Advanced Communication Systems, Inc.)
508-922-8238 (vox)

TerraNet, Inc.
617-450-9000 (vox)

UltraNet Communications, Inc.
800-763-8111/508-229-8400 (vox)

Wilder Systems, Inc.
617-933-8810 (vox)

The World
617-739-0202 (vox)

Michigan

Branch Information Services
313-741-4442 (vox)

ICNET / Innovative Concepts
313-998-0090 (vox)

Isthmus Corporation
313-973-2100 (vox)

Msen, Inc.
313-998-4562 (vox)

RustNet, Inc.
810-650-6812 (vox)

Minnesota

InforMNs
612-638-8786 (vox)

Internet Connections, Inc.
507-625-7320 (vox)

Intrnet.Net
800-254-2818 EXT. 100 (vox)

Red River Net
701-232-2227 (vox)

StarNet Communications, Inc.
612-941-9177 (vox)

Missouri

Allied Access, Inc.
800-463-8366 (vox)

THOUGHTPORT
314-474-6870 (vox)

Montana

Montana Online
406-721-4952 (vox)

North Carolina

Red Barn Data Center
910-750-9809 (vox)

SunBelt.Net
803-328-1500 (vox)

Vnet Internet Access
800-377-3282/704-334-3282 (vox)

North Dakota

Red River Net
701-232-2227 (vox)

Nebraska

Internet Nebraska
402-434-8680 (vox)

New Conclusions, Inc.
800-345-9669 (vox)

New Hampshire

Destek
603-635-7263 (vox)

info@millcomm.com
603-635-3857 (vox)

MV Communications, Inc.
603-429-2223 (vox)

NETIS Public Access Internet
603-437-1811 (vox)

New Jersey

Carroll-Net
201-488-1332 (vox)

Castle Network, Inc.
800-577-9449/908-548-8881 (vox)

The Connection
201-435-4414 (vox)

I-2000, Inc.
516-867-6379 (vox)

INTAC Access Corporation
800-504-6822 (vox)

InterCom Online
212-714-7183 (vox)

Internet For 'U'
800-638-9291 (vox)

Internet Online Services
201-928-1000 EXT.226 (vox)

K2NE Software
609-893-0673 (vox)

New Jersey Computer Connection
609-896-2799 (vox)

New York Net
718-776-6811 (vox)

NIC - Neighborhood Internet Connection
201-934-1445 (vox)

Planet Access Networks
201-691-4704 (vox)

Internet Providers

New Mexico

Southwest Cyberport
505-293-5967/505-271-0009 (VOX)

ZyNet SouthWest
505-343-8846 (VOX)

Nevada

Great Basin Internet Services
702-348-7299 (VOX)

InterMind
702-878-6111 (VOX)

NevadaNet
702-784-4827 (VOX)

Sierra-Net
702-831-3353 (VOX)

wizard.com
702-871-4461 (VOX)

New York

Computer Solutions by Hawkinson
914-473-0844 (VOX)

Creative Data Consultants (SILLY.COM)
718-229-0489 EXT.23 (VOX)

E-Znet, Inc.
716-262-2485 (VOX)

East Greenwich, Rhode Island
401-885-6855 (VOX)

Echo Communications Group
212-255-3839 (VOX)

escape.com - Kazan Corp
212-888-8780 (VOX)

I-2000, Inc.
516-867-6379 (VOX)

Ingress Communications Inc.
212-268-1100 EXT. 105 (VOX)

INTAC Access Corporation
800-504-6822 (VOX)

InterCom Online
212-714-7183 (VOX)

The Internet Channel
212-243-5200 (VOX)

Internet For 'U'
800-638-9291 (VOX)

Internet Online Services
201-928-1000 EXT.226 (VOX)

Interport Communications Corp.
212-989-1128 (VOX)

LI Net, Inc.
516-265-0997 (VOX)

Maestro
212-240-9600 (VOX)

Mnematics, Incorporated
914-359-4546 (VOX)

Moran Communications
716-639-1254 (VOX)

Network Internet Services
516 543 0234 (VOX)

New York Net
718-776-6811 (VOX)

NY WEBB, Inc.
800-458-4660 (VOX)

NYSERNet
315-453-2912 EXT.294/286 (VOX)

Panix
212-741-4400 (VOX)

PHANTOM (MindVox)
212-989-2418 (VOX)

The Pipeline Network
212-267-3636 (VOX)

ServiceTech
716-546-6908 (VOX)

TZ-Link
914-353-5443 (VOX)

Wizvax Communications
518-273-4325 (VOX)

Ohio

APK Net, Ltd
216-241-7166

The Dayton Network Access Company
513-237-6868 (VOX)

EriNet
513-436-1700 (VOX)

Exchange Network Services, Inc.
216-615-9400 (VOX)

IgLou Internet ServiceS
800-436-4456 (VOX)

Infinite Systems
614-268-9941 (VOX)

Internet Access Cincinnati
513-887-8877 (VOX)

New Age Consulting Service
216-524-8414 (VOX)

Oarnet
800-627-8101 EXT.217/614-728-8100 (VOX)

Oklahoma

Questar Network Services
405-848-3228 (VOX)

Oregon

Data Research Group, Inc.
503-465-3282 (VOX)

Europa
503-222-9508 (vox)

Hevanet Communications
503-228-3520 (vox)

Open Door Networks, Inc.
503-488-4127 (vox)

Structured Network Systems, Inc.
800-881-0962/503-656-3530 (vox)

Teleport, Inc.
503-223-4245 (vox)

Transport Logic
503-243-1940 (vox)

Pennsylvania

City-Net
412-481-5406 (vox)

King of Prussia, PA 19406
610-337-9994 (vox)

Microserve Information Systems
800-380-4638/717-821-5964 (vox)

OASIS
610-439-8560 (vox)

PREPnet
412-268-7870 (vox)

PSCNET
412-268-4960 (vox)

SSNet, Inc.
302-378-1386 (vox)

Telerama Public Access Internet
412-481-3505 (vox)

YOU TOOLS Corporation
610-954-5910 (vox)

Rhode Island

IDS World Network
401-885-6855 (vox)

South Carolina

A World of Difference, Inc.
803-769-4488 (vox)

Global Vision Inc.
803-241-0901 (vox)

SIMS, Inc.
803-762-4956 (vox)

South Carolina SuperNet
803-748-1207 (vox)

SunBelt.Net
803-328-1500 (vox)

Tennessee

The Edge
615-726-8700 (vox)

GoldSword Systems
615-691-6498 (vox)

ISDN-Net Inc.
615-377-7672 (vox)

Magibox Incorporated
901-452-7555 (vox)

Preferred Internet Services
615-323-1142 (vox)

The Telalink Corporation
615-321-9100 (vox)

The Tri-Cities Connection
615-378-5355 (vox)

Texas

The Black Box
713-480-2684 (vox)

Cloverleaf Technologies
903-832-1367 (vox)

Electrotex,Inc.
800-460-1801/713-526-3456 (vox)

I-Link Ltd
800-454-6599 (vox)

Illuminati Online
512-462-0999 (vox)

Internet Access of El Paso
915-533-1525 (vox)

Internet Connect Services
512-572-9987 (vox)

NEOSOFT
800-438-6367 (vox)

Real/Time Communications
512-451-0046 (vox)

Sesquinet
713-527-4988 (vox)

@sig.net
512-306-0700 (vox)

Texas Metronet, Inc.
214-705-2900 (vox)

USiS
713-682-1666 (vox)

Zilker Internet Park, Inc.
512-206-3850 (vox)

Utah

DATABANK, Inc.
913-842-6699 (vox)

XMission
801-539-0852 (vox)

Virginia

CAPCON Library Network
202-331-5771 (vox)

CharmNet
410-558-3900 (vox)

CLARK
410-254-3900 (vox)

DATABANK, Inc.
913-842-6699 (vox)

Genine Computing Resources
703-878-4680 (vox)

Internet Interstate
301-652-4468 (vox)

usNet, Inc.
301-572-5926 (vox)

Widomaker Communication Service
804-253-7621 (vox)

Washington

Eskimo North
206-361-1161 (vox)

Halcyon
800-539-3505/206-455-3505 (vox)

Internetworks, Inc.
206-576-7147 (vox)

Network Access Services
206-733-9279 (vox)

Northwest NEXUS
206-455-3505 (vox)

Olympus Net
360-385-0464 (vox)

Pacific Rim Network, Inc.
360-650-0442 (vox)

Pacifier Computers
206-254-3886 (vox)

Seanet Online Services
206-343-7828 (vox)

SenseMedia
408-335-9400 (vox)

Skagit On-Line Services
360-755-0190 (vox)

Structured Network Systems, Inc.
800-881-0962/503-656-3530 (vox)

Teleport, Inc.
503-223-4245 (vox)

Transport Logic
503-243-1940 (vox)

WLN
800-342-5956/360-923-4000 (vox)

Wisconsin

Exec-PC, Inc.
800-393-2721/414-789-4200 (vox)

FullFeed Communications
608-246-4239 (vox)

MIX Communications
414-351-1868 (vox)

NetNet, Inc.
414-499-1339 (vox)

WiscNet
608-265-7661 (vox)

West Virginia

WVNET
304-293-5192 (vox)

Wyoming

wyoming.com
800-996-4638/307-332-3030 (vox)

Canada

CCI Networks
403-450-6787 (vox)

Communication Accessibles Montreal
514-288-2581 (vox)

Debug Computer Services
403-248-5798 (vox)

Information Gateway Services
613-592-5619 (vox)

Island Net
604-383-0096 (vox)

HookUp Communications
905-847-8000 (vox)

Okanagan Internet Junction
604-549-1036 (vox)

Sunshine Net, Inc.
604-886-4120 (vox)

netspeak™

@	Separates the **userid** and **domain name** of an Internet address. Pronounced "at."
anonymous FTP	Method of logging in to public file archives over the **Internet**. Enter "anonymous" when prompted for a **userid**. See **FTP**.
Archie	A program that lets you search **Internet FTP** archives worldwide by file name. One variant is called **Veronica**.
ASCII	A basic text format readable by most computers. The acronym stands for American Standard Code for Information Interchange.
bandwidth	The data transmission capacity of a network. Used colloquially to refer to the "size" of the Net; some information transmittals (e.g., multitudes of graphic files) are considered to be a "waste of bandwidth."
baud	The speed at which signals are sent by a **modem**, measured by the number of changes per second in the signals during transmission. A baud rate of 1,200, for example, would indicate 1,200 signal changes in one second. Baud rate is often confused with **bits per second (bps)**.
BBS	"Bulletin-board system." Once referred to stand-alone desktop computers with a single modem that answered the phone, but can now be as complicated and interconnected as a commercial service.
binary transfer	A file transfer between two computers that preserves binary data—used for all non-text files.
bits per second (bps)	The data-transfer rate between two **modems**. The higher the bps, the higher the speed of the transfer.
bounced message	An **email** message "returned to sender," usually because of an address error.
bye	A log-off command, like "quit" and "exit."
carrier signal	The squeaking noise that modems use to maintain a connection. See also **handshake**.
cd	"Change directory." A command used, for example, at an **FTP** site to move from a directory to a subdirectory.
cdup	"Change directory up." Can be used at an **FTP** site to move from a subdirectory to its parent directory. Also **chdirup**.
chdirup	See **cdup**.
client	A computer that connects to a more powerful computer (see **server**) for complex tasks.
commercial service	General term for large online services (e.g., America Online, CompuServe, Prodigy, GEnie).
compression	Shrinkage of computer files to conserve storage space and reduce transfer times. Special utility programs, available for most platforms (including DOS, Mac, and

	Amiga), perform the compression and decompression.
cracker	A person who maliciously breaks into a computer system in order to steal files or disrupt system activities.
dial-up access	Computer connection made over standard telephone lines.
dir	"Directory." A command used to display the contents of the current directory.
domain name	The worded address of an **IP number** on the **Internet**, in the form of domain subsets separated by periods. The full address of an **Internet** user is **userid@domain name**.
email	"Electronic mail."
emoticon	See **smiley**.
FAQ	"Frequently asked questions." A file of questions and answers compiled for **Usenet newsgroups**, **mailing lists**, and games to reduce repeated posts about commonplace subjects.
file transfer	Transfer of a file from one computer to another over a network.
finger	A program that provides information about a user who is logged into your local system or on a remote computer on the Internet. Generally invoked by typing "finger" and the person's **userid**.
flame	A violent and usually *ad hominem* attack against another person in a **newsgroup** or message area.
flame war	A back-and-forth series of **flames**.
Free-Net	A community-based network that provides free access to the **Internet**, usually to local residents, and often includes its own forums and news.
freeware	Free software. Not to be confused with **shareware**.
FTP	"File transfer protocol." The standard used to transfer files between computers.
get	An **FTP** command that transfers single files from the **FTP** site to your local directory. The command is followed by a file name; typing "get file.name" would transfer only that file. Also see **mget**.
GIF	Common file format for pictures first popularized by CompuServe, standing for "graphics interchange format." Pronounced with a hard *g*.
gopher	A menu-based guide to directories on the **Internet**, usually organized by subject.
GUI	"Graphical user interface" with windows and point-and-click capability, as opposed to a command-line interface with typed-out instructions.
hacker	A computer enthusiast who enjoys exploring computer systems and programs, sometimes to the point of obsession. Not to be confused with **cracker**.
handle	The name a user wishes to be known by; a user's handle may differ significantly from his or her real name or **userid**.
handshake	The squawking noise at the beginning of a computer connection when two modems settle on a protocol for exchanging information.
Home Page	The main **World Wide Web** site for a particular group or organization.
hqx	File suffix for a BinHex file, a common format for transmitting Macintosh binary files over the **Internet**.
hypertext	An easy method of retrieving information by choosing highlighted words in a text on the screen. The words link to documents with related subject matter.
IC	"In character." A game player who is IC is acting as his or her **character**'s persona.
Internet	The largest network of computer networks in the world, easily recognizable by the format of Internet **email** addresses: **userid**@host.

Internet provider	Wholesale or retail reseller of access to the **Internet**. YPN is one example.
IP connection	Full-fledged link to the **Internet**. See **SLIP**, **PPP**, and **TCP/IP**.
IP number	The unique number that determines the ultimate **Internet** identity of an **IP connection**.
IRC	"**Internet** relay chat." A service that allows **real-time** conversations between multiple users on a variety of subject-oriented channels.
jpeg	Common compressed format for picture files. Pronounced "jay-peg."
ls	"List." A command that provides simplified directory information at **FTP** sites and other directories. It lists only file names for the directory, not file sizes or dates.
lurkers	Regular readers of messages online who never post.
lynx	A popular text-based **Web browser**.
mailing list	Group discussion distributed through **email**. Many mailing lists are administered through listserv.
mget	An **FTP** command that transfers multiple files from the **FTP** site to your local directory. The command is followed by a list of file names separated by spaces, sometimes in combination with an asterisk used as a wild card. Typing "mget b*" would transfer all files in the directory beginning with the letter *b*. Also see **get**.
Net, the	A colloquial term that is often used to refer to the entirety of Cyberspace: the **Internet**, the **commercial services**, **BBSs**, etc.
netiquette	The rules of Cyberspace civility. Usually applied to the **Internet**, where manners are enforced exclusively by fellow users.
newbie	A newcomer to the **Net**, to a game, or to a discussion. Also called **fluxer**.
newsgroups	The **Usenet** message areas, organized by subject.
newsreader	Software program for reading **Usenet newsgroups** on the **Internet**.
port number	A number that follows a **telnet** address. The number connects a user to a particular application on the telnet site. LambdaMOO, for example, is at port 8888 of lambda.parc.xerox.com (lambda.parc.xerox.com 8888).
posting	The sending of a message to a **newsgroup**, bulletin board, or other public message area. The message itself is called a **post**.
pwd	A command used at an **FTP** site to display the name of the current directory on your screen.
real-time	The **Net** term for "live," as in "live broadcast." Real-time connections include **IRC** and **MUD**s.
remote machine	Any computer on the **Internet** reached with a program such as **FTP** or **telnet**. The machine making the connection is called the home, or local, machine.
RL	"Real life."
server	A software program, or the computer running the program, that allows other computers, called **clients**, to share its resources.
shareware	Free software, distributed over the **Net** with a request from the programmer for voluntary payment.
sig	Short for **signature**.
signature	A file added to the end of **email** messages or **Usenet** posts that contains personal information—usually your name, email address, postal address, and telephone number. **Netiquette** dictates that signatures, or **sigs**, should be no longer than four or five lines.
SLIP and PPP	"Serial line **Internet** protocol" and "point-to-point protocol." Connecting by

	SLIP or PPP actually puts a computer on the Internet, which offers a number of advantages over regular **dial-up**. A SLIP or PPP connection can support a graphical **Web browser** (such as Mosaic), and allows for multiple connections at the same time. Requires special software and a SLIP or PPP service provider.
smiley	Text used to indicate emotion, humor, or irony in electronic messages—best understood if viewed sideways. Also called an **emoticon**. The most common smileys are :-) and :-(
snail mail	The paper mail the U.S. Postal Service delivers. The forerunner of **email**.
spam	The posting of the same article to multiple **newsgroups** (usually every possible one) regardless of the appropriateness of the topic (e.g., "Make Money Fast").
sysop	"System operator." The person who owns and/or manages a **BBS** or other **Net** site.
TCP/IP	The "transmission control protocol" and the "**Internet** protocol." The basis of a full-fledged Internet connection. See **IP Connection**, **PPP**, and **SLIP**. Pronounced "T-C-P-I-P."
telnet	An **Internet** program that allows you to log into other Internet-connected computers.
terminal emulator	A program or utility that allows a computer to communicate in a foreign or nonstandard **terminal mode**.
terminal mode	The software standard a computer uses for text communication—for example, ANSI for PCs and **VT-100** for UNIX.
thread	Posted **newsgroup** message with a series of replies. Threaded **newsreaders** organize replies under the original subject.
timeout	The break in communication that occurs when two computers are talking and one takes so long to respond that the other gives up.
URL	"Uniform resource locator." The **World Wide Web** address of a resource on the **Internet**.
Usenet	A collection of networks and computer systems that exchange messages, organized by subject in **newsgroups**.
userid	The unique name (often eight characters or less) given to a user on a system for his or her account. The complete address, which can be used for **email** or **fingering**, is a userid followed by the **@** sign and the **domain name** (e.g., Bill Clinton's address is president@whitehouse.gov).
Veronica	See **Archie**.
VT-100 emulation	Widely used terminal protocol for formatting full screens of text over computer connections.
WAIS	"Wide area information server." A system that searches through database indexes around the **Internet**, using keywords.
Web browser	A **client** program designed to interact with **World Wide Web servers** on the **Internet** for the purpose of viewing **Web pages**.
Web page	A **hypertext** document that is part of the **World Wide Web** and that can incorporate graphics, sounds, and links to other **Web pages**, **FTP** sites, **gophers**, and a variety of other **Internet** resources.
World Wide Web	A **hypertext**-based navigation system that lets you browse through a variety of linked **Net** resources, including **Usenet newsgroups** and **FTP**, **telnet**, and **gopher** sites, without typing commands. Also known as WWW and the Web.
zip	File-compression standard in the DOS and Windows worlds.

Index

A

Index

Index

F

Index

J

K

L

Index

M

N

Index

Index

X

Y

Z

Michael Wolff & Company, Inc.

Michael Wolff & Company, Inc. is one of the leading providers of information about the Net and the emerging Net culture. The company's Net Books Series, presently at ten titles—*NetGuide, NetGames, NetChat, NetMoney, NetTrek, NetSports, NetTech, NetMusic, NetTaxes, and NetTravel*—will expand to more than 25 titles in 1996. This will include *NetJobs, NetVote,* and *NetMarketing, NetDoctor, NetOut, NetSpy, and NetSciFi.* The entire Net Books Series (to date) is now available on the company's Website YPN—Your Personal Network (http://www.ypn.com). And *Net Guide*—"the *TV Guide*™ to Cyberspace," according to *Wired* magazine editor Louis Rossetto—is now a monthly magazine published by CMP Publications.

Michael Wolff & Company was founded in 1988 by journalist Michael Wolff to bring together writers, editors, and graphic designers to create editorially and visually compelling information products in books, magazines, and new media. Among the company's other recent projects are *Where We Stand—Can America Make It in the Global Race for Wealth, Health, and Happiness?* (Bantam Books), one of the most graphically complex information books ever to be wholly created and produced by means of desktop-publishing technology, and *Made in America?*, a four-part PBS series on global competitiveness, hosted by Labor Secretary Robert B. Reich.

The company frequently acts as a consultant to other information companies, including WGBH, Boston's educational television station; CMP Publication; and Time Warner, which it has advised on the development of Time's online business and the launch of its Website, Pathfinder.

Mary Goodwin, who directed the *Fodor's NetTravel* project, is a senior editor at Michael Wolff & Co. Kristin Miller, senior writer at Michael Wolff & Co., has taught in the history department at Columbia University and has contributed to many books, including *Where We Stand, NetChat, NetGames,* and *NetMoney.* Assistant editor Shaun Witten has been active in the travel industry and is an avid traveler.

Uncaptioned Images

California East Brother Light Station, Inc., p. 34, http://www.traveldata.com/biz/inns/; Old Drovers Inn, p. 38, http://www.calvacom.fr/relais/accueil.html; Cathay Pacific Airways vintage Betsy, p. 44, http//www.cathay-usa.com/; NYC subway token, p.50, http://www.mediabridge.com/nyc/transportation/subways/; Man on camel, p. 71, http://www.mordor.com:80/hany/egypt/eg_pics1.html; Pyramid, p. 71, http://www.mordor.com:80/hany/egypt/eg_pics1.html; The Great Sphinx, p. 72, http://www.mordor.com:80/hany/egypt/eg_pics1.html; Man with sunglasses and turban, p. 74, http://geogweb.berkeley.edu/GeoImages/Miller/millerone.html; Zebras, p. 78, http://gaia.ecs.csus.edu/; Bas-relief of soldiers with staffs, p. 81, http://tehran.stanford.edu/Images/Ancient/ancient.html; Anjargarrison, p. 82, http://www.hiof.no/ludvigsen/webdoc/elies_pictures.html; Temple of Bacchus in Baaba, p. 84, http://www.hiof.no/ludvigsen/webdoc/elies_pictures.html; Buddha, p. 91, http://www.webart.com/asianart/eskenazi/eskenazi.html; Vajradara sculpture, p. 92, http://www.webart.com/asianart/eskenazi/eskenazi.html; Asian art, p. 92, http://www.jnw.com/mw/index.html; Pagoda, p. 93, http://www.jnw.com/mw/index.html; Buddha sculpture, p. 98, http://www.hk.super.net/~webzone/hongkong.html; Mt. Fuji, p. 100, http://www.cs.uidaho.edu/~marc9442/fuji.html; Sushi, p. 101, http://www.early.com/spotlight/kikohouse/home.html; Sumo wrestlers, p. 102, http://akebono.stanford.edu/~jerry/sumo/pics.html; Calimaki, p. 102, http://www.early.com/spotlight/kikohouse/home.html; Panning for gold on Negros, p. 107, http://www.lonelyplanet.com.au/dest/sea/graphics/phil12.htm; Dog statue, p. 110, http://www.cs.ait.ac.th/~wutt/wutt.html; Guardstone, p. 114, http://IndiaOnline.com/travel.html; At the Taj Mahal, p. 115, http://philae.sas.upenn.edu/Hindi/taj.jpg; Mask, p. 121, http://insane.apana.org.au/~samoc/nepal.htm; Dubar Square, Patan, p. 122, http://insane.apana.org.au/~samoc/nepal.htm; Mount Annapurna, p. 126, http://www/aleph0.clarku.edu/rajs/Shangri_La.html; Native with instrument, p. 133, http://www.usyd.edu.au/su/emu/OZ/face62.html; Koala bear, p. 135, http://www.usyd.edu.au/su/emu/OZ/face62.html; Kangaroo crossing sign, p. 137, http://www.usyd.edu.au/su/emu/OZ/touristsydney.html; Sydney Opera House, p. 138, http://www.usyd.edu.au/su/emu/OZoz.html; New Zealand waterfall, p. 142, http://www.akiko.lm.com/tour/; Map of Europe, p. 149, http://grafton.dartmouth.edu:8001/Irc/culture/europe/; Czech symbol, p. 155, http://www.cesnet.cz/html/cz/basic-information.html; BCS graffiti, p. 156, http://www.gatech.edu/graf/prague/Prague_2.html; Hammer of Thor, p. 157, http://www.commerce.wca95.org/eriksbergshallen/preview.html; Eiffel Tower, p. 161, http://meteora.ucsd.edu/~norman/paris/Monuments/Eiffel/; Paris Metro entrance, p. 161, http://meteora.ucsd.edu/~norman/paris/; Brandenburg Gate, Berlin, p. 169, http://www.chemie.fu-berlin.de/bilder/brb_tor.gif; Coin, p. 170, http://www.perseus.tufts.edu/; Coat of Arms, p. 172, http://www.fsz.bme.hu/hungary/budapest.html; Barman, p. 174, http://www.misty.com/ulysses/vip/a_vip.htm; *The Creation of Adam*, p. 176, http://www.christusrex.org/www1/sistine/0-Tour.html; Statue of Dio Nilo, p. 176, CompuServe's Graphics Corner Forum; Leaning Tower of Pisa, p. 177, http://www.tulane.edu/lester/text/Western.Architect/Rome/Rome.html; Silhouette of Kremlin Church, p. 186, http://nearnet.gnn.com/gnn/wic/photo.14.html; Barcelona Cathedral, p. 191, http://www.gol.com/spain/barcelon.htm; Loch an Eilein, p. 196, http://www.cs.ucl.ac.uk/misc/intro.html; Big Ben, p. 201, http://www.bayscenes.com/sp/bigben/bigben.htm; Bagpipes, p. 203, http://pipes.tico.com/pipes/Makers/MikeMacHarg.html; Tour group, p. 205, http://www.tcs.co.at/guide/e_activ/texte/wandern.htm; Ruins, p. 206, http://force.stwing.upenn.edu:8001/~durduran/cyprus.html; Statue, p. 212, http://mayaquest.mecc.com/Uxmal.html; Mayan bas-relief at Cobá, p. 213, http://www.wotw.com/wow/mexico/cancun/coba.html; Sitting Mayan sculpture, p. 217, http://www.fdl.cc.mn.us/~isk/maya.html; Sloth iguana, p. 218, http://webtravel.org/cr/tortuguero.html; Frog, p. 222, http://webtravel.org/cr/tortuguero.html; Sun, p. 223, http://www.greenbuilder.com/mader/ecotravel/ecotravel.html; Man on horse, p. 224, http://larch-www.lcs.mit.edu:8001/~evs/bolivia/bolivia.html; Clouds, p. 225, http://www.lonelyplanet.com/dest/sam/argie.htm; Head sculpture, p. 227, http://informns.k12.mn.us/~grant/images/mayasites/html; Coffee beans, p. 228, http://www.primenet.com/bid/coffeeworld/colombia.html; Mayan art, p. 229, http://www.realtime.net/maya/meso.html; Mayan art, p. 230, http://www.realtime.net/maya/meso.html; Snorkeler, p. 234, http://www.cntraveler.com/; Statue of Roger Conant, p. 244, http://www.star.net/salem/; The Hollywood Bowl, p. 248, http://www.cmp.ucr.edu/exhibitions/netex_history_intro.html; Peach logo, p. 256, http://www.webguide.com/; Yellowstone National Park, p. 259, http://tempest.ecn.purdue.edu:8001/~taylor/images/summer94/indexb.html; Lake Shore Drive, p. 261, CompuServe's Gallery Forum; St. Charles streetcar, p. 267, http://www.yatcom.com/neworl/naborhud/uptown/stcar6.jpg; Bryce Canyon National Park, p. 273, http://www.netpub.com/utah/playgrnd/natlprk/random/npbcrd1g.htm; Empire State Building, p. 282, http://turnpike.net/emporium/C/CAPNET/worldlm.htm; Chrysler construction crew at lunch, p. 283, CompuServe's

Bettmann Archive; Boston monument, p. 285, http://www.cs.virginia.edu/~rdc8a/photos/boston_monument.html; Independence Hall, p. 290, http://www.realtime.net/~jozef3/philphot.html; Rodeo Drive, Beverly Hills, p. 298, http://www.kcbs2.com/005/004/index.htm; Maple leaf, p. 300, http://www.cesi.it/flags/ca.html; Mounted police, p. 302, http://www.scs.carleton.ca/ottawa.ottawa.html; Carousel horse, p. 308, http://www.access.digex.net/~rburgess/photo/glen_echo_04.jpg; Matterhorn and Sleeping Beauty's castle, p. 309, http://www.lido.com/disney/art/castle-matterhorn.jpg; Coney Island's Cyclone, p. 310, ftp://gboro.rowan.edu/pub/Coasters/Images/Coney_Island/cyclone; Girl wrestles gator, p. 312, http://florida.com/gatorfarmer/; Nuclear explosion, p. 313, http://www.webcom.com/~gwalker/HEW/nuke.html; Deer creek, p. 315, http://www.sierraclub.org/outings/; *M.V. Regal Princess*, p. 324, http://alaskan.com/promos/princess.html; *M.V. Silver Cloud*, p. 325, http://pc-78-120.udac.se:8001/WWW/Nautica/Ships/Silver_Cloud.html; *M.S. Estonia*, p. 325, http://pc-78-120.udac.se:8001/WWW/Nautica/Ships/Viking_Sally.html; *M.S. Holiday*, p. 327, http://mmink.com/mmink/carnival/carnival.html; *S.S. Seabreeze*, p. 327, http://mmink.com/dolphincl/dcl/shipsnav.cgi?109,38; *M.V. Seabourne Spirit*, p. 327, http://mmink.com/mmink/carnival/seabourn.html; Fisherman, p. 328, http://www.inetmkt.com/fishpage/pics.html; Trout, p. 329, http://www.geo.mtu.edu:80/~jsuchosk/fish/fishpage; Fisherman with elbow extended, p. 330, http://www.inetmkt.com/fishpage/pics.html; Four men in pool, p. 331, http://www.gayweb.com/408/408a.html; Dice, p. 335, http://www.ntexas.com/people/sportbet/casino.htm; Golf ball, p. 337, http://www.catalog.com/shop/golf/golfball.htm; Newlyweds, p. 339, http://www.sonic.net/baltarphoto/photo.html; Hammerhead shark, p. 342, http://www.batnet.com:80/shicho/see%26sea/photos.html; Diver holding shark, p. 342, http://www.batnet.com:80/shicho/see%26sea/photos.html; Diver, p. 343, http://www.panix.com/~tab/other/album.shtml; Diver wearing apparatus, p. 343, http://www.panix.com/~tab/other/album.shtml; Divers with manta ray, p. 344, http://www.batnet.com:80/shicho/see%26sea/photos.html; Dolphins, p. 344, http://www.cs.fsu.edu:80/projects/fall94ug/group8/pics.html; Shark, p. 344,http://dorothy.as.arizona.edu:8008/uw-photo/images/all.html; Ski jumper, p. 345, http://www/adfa.oz.au/aais/Pictures/Pictures00.html; Underview of skier, p. 346, http://www/adfa.oz.au/aais/Pictures/Pictures00.html; Sugarbush skier, p. 347, http://www/adfa.oz.au/aais/Pictures/Pictures00.html; Skier # 17, p. 348, http://www/adfa.oz.au/aais/Pictures/Pictures00.html; Skier with striped clothing, p. 349, http://www/adfa.oz.au/aais/Pictures/Pictures00.html; Skiboarding, p. 350, http://www/adfa.oz.au/aais/Pictures/Pictures00.html; Skier wearing goggles, p. 351, http://www/adfa.oz.au/aais/Pictures/Pictures00.html

Notes

Notes

Notes

Notes

BARTERING WITH A BEACH HOUSE IN BRAZIL

You could take a plane, a boat or even a Volkswagen bus to Brazil. But only the Web can put you or your client's products and services in front of millions around the world in a blink of an eye.

Simply put, at **Accelerated Media** we create, host and market web sites for businesses. If you want to sell plastic pink flamingos to doctors in Iceland, we can create a web site to fit your needs. Custom concepts, writing and design. Just call **1.800.WEB-4950**

Host your Web Site

$25. /month

info@accelerated.com 1.800.WEB.4950 http://www.accelerated.com